PRAISE FOR GERALD ASTOR'S
BATTLING BUZZARDS

"ABSORBING, INFORMATIVE . . . TELLINGLY DETAILED." —*Kirkus Reviews*

"Superior as an example of oral history." —*Booklist*

"QUICK AND WELL-PACED, this will please even the most jaded of readers." —*Army* Magazine

THE MIGHTY EIGHTH

"No one does oral history better than Gerald Astor. . . . Here the men of the mightiest air force ever built tell their story in their own words—of trials, tribulations, triumphs, terror, and tedium." —Stephen Ambrose

"FASCINATING . . . invaluable in terms of understanding both the process of protracted war and its effect on the human spirit. Excellent in weaving these stories into a broader analysis of the Eighth's role in the air war with Germany, Astor demonstrates once again that he's one of the most accomplished oral historians at work today."
—*Publishers Weekly*

"Revealing and vivid . . . His many interviews of American airmen turn up some fascinating anecdotes, catching the grim realities of air combat in a way that more conventional histories cannot." —*Kirkus Reviews*

Please turn the page for more extraordinary acclaim. . . .

A BLOOD-DIMMED TIDE

"ORIGINAL . . . EVOCATIVE . . . BRILLIANT . . ."
—*Publishers Weekly*

"Consistently gripping . . . a vivid vision of warfare from the foxhole." —*Daily Press* (Newport News, Va.)

"A GRIPPING STORY . . . will no doubt take its place as a classic." —*The Record* (Troy, NY)

"The immediacy and clarity of enlisted men's accounts form the core reality here, giving a palpable sense of infantry and tank warfare. Strong narrative, sound history, and a good read." —*Kirkus Reviews*

"AN ABSORBING BOOK, fascinating for its first-person detail." —*Richmond Times-Dispatch*

"A compelling, effective contribution to World War II history." —*Booklist*

OPERATION ICEBERG

"THIS IS ORAL HISTORY AT ITS FINEST."
—*The Washington Post Book World*

"There probably will never be a book that does a better job of capturing the experience of the people who were there."
—*The Flint Journal*

"UNFORGETTABLE." —Gannett Suburban Newspapers

"A FINE WORK . . . both historically accurate and compelling." —*Newport News Daily*

"A MOVING COLLECTION . . . a fitting tribute to all those who served so honorably." —*Kirkus Reviews*

GERALD ASTOR

CRISIS IN THE PACIFIC

THE BATTLES FOR THE PHILIPPINE ISLANDS BY THE MEN WHO FOUGHT THEM

MARINES' MEMORIAL CLUB
609 Sutter Street
San Francisco, Ca. 94102

A DELL BOOK

Published by
Dell Publishing
a division of
Random House, Inc.
1540 Broadway
New York, New York 10036

Dell® is a registered trademark of Random House, Inc., and the colophon is a trademark of Random House, Inc.

Dell books may be purchased for business or promotional use or for special sales. For information please write to: Special Markets Department, Random House, Inc., 1540 Broadway, New York, N.Y. 10036.

Library of Congress Catalog Card Number: 95-50032

ISBN: 0-440-23695-9

Manufactured in the United States of America

Published simultaneously in Canada

Reprinted by arrangement with Donald I. Fine Books

January 2002

10 9 8 7 6 5 4 3 2 1
OPM

For those who endured.
For the boys, Ted, Larry and Andy,
and for the women in my life,
Sonia, Karen, Stacy and Lindsay.

CONTENTS

CONTENTS

ACKNOWLEDGMENTS

FIRST AND FOREMOST I thank the many people listed under Roll Call for their generosity in sharing with me their memories and their private papers and for their patience in answering my questions.

I am also indebted to a number of institutions that are repositories for documents and publications that were vital in my research. In this connection, I am grateful to Dr. Richard J. Sommers and the U.S. Military History Institute, Carlisle Barracks, Pennsylvania; Maj. Connie Moore and the U.S. Army Center for Military History, Washington, D.C.; the U.S. Naval Historical Center, Washington, D.C.; Paul Stillwell and the U.S. Naval Institute at Annapolis, Maryland; Alan Aimone and the U.S. Military Academy Library at West Point; Dr. Walton S. Moody, historian of the U.S. Air Force; Dr. Benis M. Frank and the U.S. Marine Corps Historical Center, Washington, D.C.

Other individuals who contributed to this book include: Mark Hunter of the 44th Tank Battalion Association; Col. John Olson (USA Ret.), who not only provided a wealth of information in his books but also provided leads for additional sources; Dr. Bob Muehrcke, who was not in the Philippines but knew some from his Americal Division who were; Ed Hudson with the USS *Cabot* Association; Capt. Charles Smith (USN Ret.), Executive Director of the

American Society of Naval Engineers; Frank Schultz, Secretary of the 32nd Division Veterans Association; Dr. Hargis Westerfield, an authority on military history; Sinclair Browning, who was kind enough to share with me factual research on the period that is the basis of her novel *America's Best*; and Russ Catardi for furnishing leads.

PREFACE

AT THE TIME of the fiftieth anniversary of the invasion of Normandy on June 6, 1944, the outpouring of books on the subject occasioned an essay by Samuel Hynes, a Navy pilot during World War II and a professor of English at Princeton. He had written his own memoir, and he remarked that personal narratives of war generally "aren't about emotions: they have to do with physical particulars, equipment, terrain and weather, sights, sounds and smells, the punishment the body takes from wounds, illness, hunger, heat, cold." Hynes indicated that if the authors intended to provide a feeling of how it was, then they would seem to have failed.

Having immersed myself in such individual accounts—this is my fifth book that tells of WW II through the words and memories of those who participated—I can vouch for the accuracy of Hynes's reading but not necessarily his conclusion. The details, the sights, sounds, smells, the physical sensations described by those involved do have a capacity to evoke in a reader at least a semblance of the feeling of how it must have been, a shudder of horror, a flush of exaltation, a mournful shiver. In some instances, the author does speak of emotions. But in my experience, words that focus on feelings create no more of an emotional response than descriptions of what happened.

Frequently, the effort to recall sensations becomes an intel-
lectual exercise, like attempts to capture in language the
feelings generated by a piece of music or a painting.

The most common literary weakness of individual memoirs lies in an inability to separate out the details that have
only a personal significance from matters that resonate with
readers. This is the nature of the beast, war. An individual
soldier, even a MacArthur, however heroic or brilliant,
doesn't determine the course of modern war any more than
a single person builds a cathedral. War is a group enterprise.
The campaigns in the Philippines consisted of millions of
acts by hundreds of thousands of people. A solitary human
was submerged in the multitudes and buried under the
weight of machines and technology. The man with the gun,
even an artillery piece, was but a tiny spark in a long night
rent by thunderous lightning. Although desperately concerned with preservation of the small self, a combatant's
potential to build his story to a peak is destroyed by the
absence of a crowning event. And for even the massive
armies there was no last battle. The climax of WW II lay in
the explosions of the A-bombs, but for the troops, the
fighting just petered out. There was no decisive battle
marked by some heroic act and that is certainly true of both
the defense and liberation of the Philippines.

That being said, within the protracted struggle some did
perform with extraordinary valor and only the monstrously
oversized convulsions of the war renders their deeds puny
in terms of the final outcome. To those on the scene these
people still stand as giants, although as people of character,
as someone to live next door to, they may fall well short of
the desirable. As is always the case, amid the horror and
obscenity of war, glory occasionally flames bright, albeit at
an exorbitant price. And to those of us not present, all
who, however terrified, stood firm in the face of the onslaught of death and destruction deserve the label of hero.

Was there something different about the crisis in the
Pacific? To cite WW II campaigns with which I am familiar,
the Battle of the Bulge in the European Ardennes was a

six-week-long period in which command and control broke down and men survived in small groups and on their own initiative. D-Day, on the drafting boards for two years, the largest and most carefully scripted operation in its time, saw the best laid plans go astray. Okinawa was a cautionary tale, the price paid when a defeated army refuses to quit. The Philippines, from the fall to the liberation, spreads the impact of war over a large canvas, one that involves civilians and in which political forces and egos played significant roles.

As with my other books on WW II, I ask questions about schooling, the respondents' attitudes about world affairs, their evaluation of the people around them. Those who served in World War II went through the Great Depression. They were raised in a period when racial segregation was the law and discrimination the custom of the land. They were the children of the first half of the twentieth century with its prejudices and values.

I do not pretend to offer a linear, encyclopedic history but a mosaic within the context of the times. Like all eyewitness accounts, what was seen or heard may differ. Memory lapses or ego may distort who did what unto whom. I am fully aware that some units, some people who were close to the center of what happened are not covered. Some perspectives, some events may seem repetitious but generalizations from a single experience or anecdote are risky. Issues like the handling of prisoners or the death and destruction wrought by modern weapons demand the weight of more than an individual perception.

Personal accounts can be self-serving or may take credit for the work of others, but this is not an effort to provide a record. Instead, the anecdotes, the memories of the physical details and, occasionally, even the feelings recollected offer senses of from where people came, a waft of what they brought to the scene and most of all their own perspectives on what happened. In lieu of psychological debriefings, this may best serve to inform what it was like.

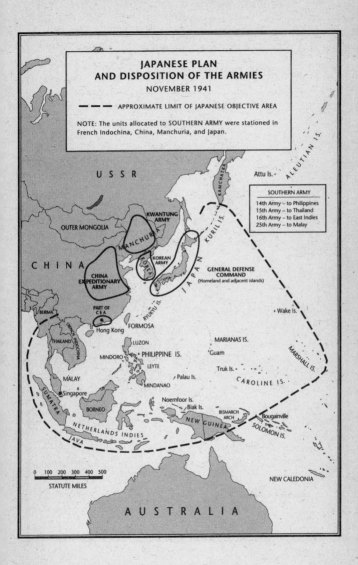

**JAPANESE PLAN
AND DISPOSITION OF THE ARMIES**

NOVEMBER 1941

— — — APPROXIMATE LIMIT OF JAPANESE OBJECTIVE AREA

NOTE: The units allocated to SOUTHERN ARMY were stationed in
French Indochina, China, Manchuria, and Japan.

SOUTHERN ARMY

14th Army – to Philippines
15th Army – to Thailand
16th Army – to East Indies
25th Army – to Malay

U S S R

Attu Is.

ALEUTIAN IS.

OUTER MONGOLIA

KWANTUNG
ARMY

MANCHURIA

KAMCHATKA

KURILS IS.

CHINA

KOREAN
ARMY

KOREA

JAPAN

GENERAL DEFENSE
COMMAND
(Homeland and adjacent islands)

CHINA
EXPEDITIONARY
ARMY

PART OF
C E A

RYUKYU IS.

Wake Is.

BURMA

Hong Kong

FORMOSA

THAILAND

INDOCHINA

LUZON

MINDORO

PHILIPPINE IS.

LEYTE

MARIANAS IS.

Guam

Truk Is.

MARSHALL IS.

MALAY

Palau Is.

MINDANAO

CAROLINE IS.

SUMATRA

Singapore

BORNEO

Noemfoor Is.

Biak Is.

BISMARCH
ARCH.

Bougainville

NETHERLANDS INDIES

JAVA

NEW GUINEA

SOLOMON IS.

0 100 200 300 400 500

STATUTE MILES

NEW CALEDONIA

A U S T R A L I A

THE PHILIPPINE ISLANDS

Aparri

Vigan

LUZON

Lingayen Gulf

Baguio

Dagupan

San Jose

Tarlac

Cabanatuan

☐ *Clark Air Base*

Manila

Olongapo

Mariveles

Corregidor I.

Cavite

PHILIPPINE

SEA

SOUTH

CHINA

SEA

MINDORO

MASBATE

ROMBLON

SAMAR

Tacloban

LEYTE

Dulad

Leyte Gulf

PANAY

Iloilo

NEGROS

CEBU

Ormoc

BOHOL

DINAGAT IS.

PALAWAN

SULU

SEA

MINDANAO

Davao

Zamboanga

Moro Gulf

Davao Gulf

0   50   100   150
STATUTE MILES

CELEBES SEA

BATAAN, CORREGIDOR, MANILA BAY, AND THE LINGAYEN GULF

JAPANESE INVASION JANUARY-FEBRUARY 1942
Japanese Penetration — — — U.S. Positions

LINGAYEN ASSAULT JANUARY 1945
U.S. Forces — — — U.S. Beachhead

Lingayen Gulf

- Baguio

Agoo
Santo Tomas
- Rosario
- San Fabian
- Pozorrubio

AMERICAN
LANDINGS
JAN 1945

Jan 11
Jan 10
Jan 9

Sual
- Dagupan
Lingayen
- Calasiao
Bugallon
- San Carlos
Aguilar
- Malasiqui

- Binalonan
- Urdaneta

ARMY BEACHHEAD LINE

- San Jose

L U Z O N

- Cabanatuan

Tarlac -

CLARK AIR BASE
- Angeles

Dingalan
Bay

JAPANESE
INVASION OF
BATAAN
JAN-FEB 1942

Olongapo
Main Battle
Position
Moron
Mabatong
Subic Bay
Guitol
Mauban
Bagac
Orion
Rear Battle
Position

Manila
Bay

Manila

NIGHTS
26-27 JAN
1-2 FEB
Catbolo Pt.
Anyasan Pt.
BATAAN
Mariveles

NIGHT 22-23 JAN
Quinouan Pt.
Longoskawayan Pt.

Cavite

0 10 20 30 40 50
STATUTE MILES

CORREGIDOR I.

CHAPTER I

FIRST STRIKES

ON SUNDAY NIGHT, December 7, 1941, in the Philippine Islands—because of the international date line, five thousand miles away it was Saturday, December 6, 1941, in Hawaii and Washington, D.C.—the 27th Bombardment Group tossed a bash at the Manila Hotel in honor of their Army Air Force commander, Gen. Lewis Brereton. Amid a raunchy affair that featured the "best entertainment this side of Minsky's" (a reference to a chain of burlesque houses in the States), General Brereton chatted with Rear Adm. William R. Purnell, chief of staff for the top Navy officer in the Far East, Adm. Thomas C. Hart, and Brig. Gen. Richard K. Sutherland, his opposite number for the supreme commander of all the American and Philippine military, Gen. Douglas MacArthur.

According to Brereton, Admiral Purnell remarked that it was only a question of days or perhaps hours until the shooting started. Sutherland agreed, adding that the War and Navy Departments in Washington expected hostilities might erupt at any moment. Brereton immediately instructed his chief of staff to place all air units on "combat alert" as of Monday morning, December 8.

The party at the Manila Hotel wound down sometime after midnight. The airmen straggled back to their quarters in the darkest hours of the morning. They had only themselves for company; months before, as relations between Japan and the United States deteriorated and Nazi Germany overran much of Europe, wives and children had been ordered to the United States as a precaution.

Shortly before eight that morning, the first gales of Japanese planes swept down from the north to blast Hawaii's huge naval base at Pearl Harbor. Within two hours phalanxes of aircraft methodically blasted a flotilla of battleships, cruisers, destroyers and lesser vessels. The typhoon of torpedoes, bombs and bullets also wreaked havoc upon the Army Air Force at Hickham and Wheeler Fields. Nor were American installations the only victims as heavy strikes rocked Malaya, Thailand, Singapore, Hong Kong and Shanghai.

Ten minutes after the first explosives rained down upon the hapless Pearl Harbor anchorage, at 2:30 A.M. his time, a startled radio operator at Asiatic Fleet headquarters in Manila intercepted a stunning, unencrypted Morse code message, issued under the aegis of Adm. Husband E. Kimmel, the Honolulu-based Pacific Fleet Commander: "Air Raid on Pearl Harbor. This is no drill." Because he knew the unique technical style of the Hawaii sender, the Manila sailor realized the communique was genuine and alerted his duty officer, Marine Lt. Col. William T. Clement, who in turn contacted Admiral Hart.

A youthful naval officer then, Charles Adair remembered, "He [Clement] then called the various staff officers. I was in the apartment house where I was living when I got a call about 3:15, maybe a little earlier. All he said was, 'Charlie, come on down to the office.' I didn't even ask him what had happened because I knew what had happened. I was sure of it. I didn't keep him on the phone. I got dressed as quickly as I could and walked rapidly or ran part of the way through the park and over to where Headquarters was located [in the Marsman Building, at Pier 7 in Manila].

"Once I got into the office, the communicators handed me a tape about six feet long or so, and I started pulling it through my fingers. 'This ship sunk. That ship sunk,' et cetera, with the details of some of the things that had gone on."

Comdr. S.S. Murray, the recently arrived boss of a submarine division operating out of Manila, had finished a familiarization cruise in the local waters and was celebrating with a round of golf on Saturday, December 7. "I also paid my initiation fee to the Army-Navy Club in Manila— about a hundred dollars. I got my receipt, went back to the *Holland* [a submarine tender on which underseaboat crews stashed extra gear and slept during brief stopovers in port] that night to get under way the next day for some exercises. A few minutes before 2:00 A.M., I was awakened by Comdr. James Fife, chief staff officer, Commander of Submarines, Asiatic, saying that Pearl Harbor had been attacked.

" 'Get up and get the submarines started going on patrol.' After Fife awakened me and we had talked to the squadron commander, in the meantime sending for all the submarine skippers . . . we started getting them ready."

As a junior officer on the sub *Seadragon*, Norvell Ward shared an apartment with three colleagues in Manila, and missed any official alarm. "We were having breakfast at the Army-Navy Club in Manila, picked up the Manila *Herald*—'Japanese attack Pearl Harbor!' We caught the ferry over [to the Cavite Naval Yard where his sub was undergoing an overhaul] and there we were at war."

Destroyer skipper Edward Parker rejoined his division at Tarakan, a port in Borneo, after a voyage to the Philippines to collect mail flown in from the States. "It was a Saturday when we got in. While we were alongside the dock, I thought maybe I'd go over and get some beer for the boys. 'No liberty will be granted' [ordered the destroyer group commander, Arthur Robinson]. So we anchored, sat quietly and had the movies. I went over on Sunday morning to see the division commander . . . They didn't have any information.

"Early Monday morning, about 3:15, the voice over the

tube said, 'Captain, important message coming in from the *Marblehead* [flagship for the destroyer division].' I put on my bathrobe and ran up. 'The Japanese had attacked Pearl Harbor, or something like that. Govern yourself accordingly.' [I thought] What the hell does 'govern yourself accordingly' mean?"

Within half an hour, Admiral Hart as head of the U.S. fleet in the area was digesting the news and broadcasting it to his fleet.

Not until perhaps an hour after the first report was received at Manila Navy headquarters did General Sutherland learn of the blow at Pearl Harbor and then only from a commercial newscast. An enlisted army signalman happened to have tuned in to a California radio station. He immediately reported to his duty officer and the word passed up to Sutherland, who telephoned the MacArthur penthouse atop the Manila Hotel.

"Pearl Harbor!" the astounded MacArthur supposedly exclaimed. "It should be our strongest point." Within ten minutes, at 3:40 A.M., a call from Washington, D.C. to MacArthur confirmed the news bulletin. According to MacArthur, he asked his wife Jean to fetch his Bible and he read for a while before rushing off to confer with his staff.

Ten years later, Hart explained the failure to inform the Army of Kimmel's urgent message. He insisted Clement had tried to get through to someone at headquarters for the U.S. Army Forces, Far East, but could not get a response. He allegedly passed the word to a staff officer at his home.

But while the news slowly percolated into other military services, it instantly boiled over in naval circles.

Lt. John D. Bulkeley, USNA '30, head of the six-boat Motor Torpoedo Boat Squadron 3, says, "The night of December 8 we were all asleep in the officers' quarters at Cavite when my telephone rang about three in the morning and I first learned the Japs had struck at Pearl Harbor. I was told, 'We are at war' and that Rear Admiral [Francis] Rockwell wanted to see me immediately."

Mary Rose Harrington, a Navy nurse at the hospital compound beside the Cavite navy base, remembers, "I was on night duty. It was a beautiful moonlit night and after I'd made rounds of the sick officers building I thought I'd walk outdoors. But the assistant master of arms came dashing in to say that Honolulu had been bombed. Then I saw a captain and with another officer whom I knew was the war plan officer, talking loudly and we started to wake people up in the middle of the night."

Nor did the Air Force's Brereton hear of the war's opening salvo from the Navy. Fliers from the Army's 3rd Pursuit Squadron stationed at the Iba airfield had nearly confronted Japanese intruders just about the same hour as the bombs and torpedoes ravaged the fleet at Pearl but the planes from Formosa had veered off.

At the main Philippine airbase, Clark Field, sixty miles north of Manila, someone heard a radio news flash about the Japanese bombardment of Pearl Harbor. In the absence of verification from any official sources, however, during a period in which rumor rampaged through military circles, the only action taken was to notify the base commander.

Meanwhile, MacArthur's staff contacted Brereton and told him what they knew—which was limited. There had been no official declaration of war by the Japanese and the information on what had happened at Honolulu remained sketchy. At 5:00 A.M. the Air Force chief checked in at headquarters.

For most of the military personnel in the Philippines the news reached them haphazardly. Some units received word fairly quickly to mobilize and report to their assignments before dawn. Others became aware almost by pure happenstance.

West Pointer Harold K. Johnson, a captain serving as operations officer for 57th Infantry, a Philippine Scouts regiment, said, "We had heard rumors all over Manila on Sunday, December 7, that an attack had been made on Hawaii but the rumors were not given very much credence because it appeared to be such an illogical action to those of us of relatively junior rank and in subordinate positions in the Philippines. We figured we were the prime target and we had mixed viewpoints.

"There was an element of complacency . . . because we listened to and believed the Navy and the boasts that they would drive the Japanese fleet from the sea within a matter of a week or ten days. At the same time we knew we were a long way from the West Coast and if the Navy didn't drive the Japanese fleet from the sea, why, we were in trouble.

"It was Monday morning on December 8 before our regiment finally got the word. I was having breakfast in my robe about 6:30 when I got a call from a friend of mine. He said, 'Colonel Clarke wants you to alert the regiment to move out of the barracks.' [My friend] was a company commander from a sister regiment, serving in Bataan at the time, doing some survey work and cleaning up trails."

Johnson quickly asked for a confirmation of the order from Clarke and with that instantly set to his tasks. "I could see, all during [my time on] Bataan and during prison camp days, those two fried eggs sitting there staring up at me from the breakfast plate that were never consumed."

Col. Clifford Bluemel, USMA '09, assigned as commander of the 31st Philippine Division, also swallowed the preliminary hard facts at breakfast. "On the morning of December 8 I ate in the mess with Colonel [John] Irwin, Captain Bauer and one other officer.

"Bauer came into the mess and said, 'Did you hear the radio?'

"I said, 'I don't have any radio. What is it?'

"He said, 'Pearl Harbor, Wheeler Field and Hickham Field were all bombed! The planes were destroyed on the ground, and a lot of the fleet was damaged!'

"I said, 'Oh my God! Who did it?'

"He said, 'The Japs did it.'

"I said, 'Well, we are at war now.' "

Quartermaster Lt. Col. Irvin Alexander, a mustang (former enlisted man and now an officer) who matriculated at West Point via the University of Indiana and a stint as a machine gun corporal with a federalized national guard during World War I, was at Fort Stotsenburg, some fifty miles north of Manila. "At breakfast on the morning, our radio told us that Pearl Harbor had been attacked with considerable naval damage. The announcement brought our breakfast to a mournful end, for we knew war was inevitable, and that we were on the hottest of war's seats."

Philip Fry, an infantry officer who had arrived in the islands less than three weeks before, recalled being at Ft. William McKinley in the 45th Infantry Regiment barracks hard by the first golf green and close to the officers club and the tennis courts. He had spent his first nineteen days on the links, enjoying the comforts of the club, shopping for silks and other presents for his wife, betting on jai alai and visiting a Manila nightspot where he tipped a musician to play "Intermezzo," a song he and his wife had savored during his previous tour there.

"On the morning of December 8, just around dawn, I was awakened by some officer rushing in and announcing that we were at war. He told of the attack on Pearl Harbor as, dressed in our pajamas, we eagerly crowded around him for the news.

"I dressed quickly and walked to the club, found the place in an uproar, everyone seeking news. I managed to get a cup of coffee, left the club and started walking to division headquarters. On the way I saw the 57th and 45th Infantry forming in full field equipment preparatory to taking the field. Decided then to cast my lot with one of these fine old regiments. I had no desire to enter a first-class shooting war with untrained troops. I asked for immediate assignment to the 57th Infantry and got it just like that."

Unlike Mary Rose Harrington, Army nurse Madeline Ullom, stationed at Sternberg General Hospital in Manila a few miles from Cavite, greeted the morning of December

8 blissfully unaware of what had happened. "A generous slice of luscious papaya with a squeeze of tangy lime was ever a good way to begin breakfast. The lithe Filipino lad with the big armful of newspapers wended his barefoot way among the tables. His big brown eyes were solemn. His wide cheery grin was absent. His soft murmur was barely audible as he handed each, 'Your paper, mom.' Big black headlines across the front page blared the attack on Pearl Harbor."

At the northern tip of Luzon, the closest point to the Japanese forces stationed on Formosa, the Philippine Army's 11th Division guarded the beach approaches centered around the town of Aparri, a site once loosely controlled by the Japanese during the fifteenth century. Like all Philippine military units, Americans either commanded or "advised" the indigenous soldiers.

Information reached some units in the islands even later. Col. Glen R. Townsend served as the commanding officer of the 11th Regiment. "About ten o'clock on the morning of December 8," recalled Townsend, "one of the Filipino officers came to tell me he had heard over his car radio that Japanese planes had bombed Hawaii. I thought of Orson Welles and the men from Mars.

"But Captain Pilar insisted, so I walked with him to his car nearby. When he turned the radio on, the announcer was just telling about the bombing of Baguio [the summer capital of the Philippines and site of some military installations]. That convinced me there was a war on, but if more was needed it came an hour or so later. Eighty-four Japanese bombers passed directly over the camp. We later learned that these struck Clark Field."

Sgt. Tom Gage, Jr., having reached the Philippines less than three weeks earlier as chief clerk of the Army Air Corps 34th Pursuit Squadron, occupied a tent on a low bare hilltop beside sugarcane fields that were being cleared for runways of the new Del Carmen Airfield. "A little before noon, one of the cooks, Shorty Batson, came running down to tell me they had heard on the Manila radio that

Pearl Harbor had been bombed. Shortly after, I heard what sounded like distant reports of firecrackers exploding. I stepped out and took a look around the sky and over towards the direction of Clark Field [fourteen miles to the north]—the sky was covered by black dots. My first thought was 'My God! Look at the enemy planes—there's thousands of them.' It took a few minutes for me to sort out the antiaircraft bursts and barely visible were two lines of very small black dots, flying in formation, above and beyond the shell smoke.

"I immediately hotfooted across the area and found Lt. Jack Jennings, the squadron adjutant, in his tent, reading a book! I told him Clark Field was being bombed. His reply was, 'Is that official, Sergeant?' I replied, 'Hell, Lieutenant, look out the back of your tent! Clark Field is going up in smoke!' "

The war that began at Pearl Harbor now menaced the Philippines, the closest U.S. stronghold to Japan and an obvious prize if the Imperial Empire expected to seize control of the Western Pacific and Southeast Asia.

CHAPTER II

BACKDROP

TO MOST FOREIGNERS posted there, the Philippines and particularly the Manila environs offered an attractive place for military duty or work. Strategically located in what has been called the "geographic heart of the Far East," the Philippines also straddled the major commercial routes to Japan, China and Southeast Asia. Its site and the trade policies of the United States as the parent country encouraged investment of Western capital, particularly by American companies. As a result, Manila and the larger cities of the archipelago housed a substantial foreign population: employees of firms doing business in the area, professionals in engineering, manufacturing and finance, retirees from the companies who found the islands congenial for life on a pension or savings. Western-owned enterprises paid salaries that, particularly during the Great Depression, enabled them to flourish on a scale not possible in their homelands where materials and labor ran far higher. The low wages for natives likewise favored members of the military and their families, who even on their more meagre pay could afford houseboys, cooks, *lavenderas,* caretakers for kids, bespoke tailors, housing, fine handcrafted furniture and textiles, all beyond their means at a Stateside post.

The scents, scenery, sounds, weather, people, cus-

toms—the exotic ambience of the Philippines—were unlike anything in the homelands of the Occidentals. Within
the islands themselves blazed vivid contrasts, especially
when measured by the gage of their greatest city, Manila.
Not more than a few hundred miles from cosmopolitan
Manila lived tribes stripped to the bare essentials of the
Stone Age. Inside the city, large pockets of the impover-
ished occupied homes made of bamboo and *nipa,* a broad-
leaf thatching, while some blocks distant loomed massive
stone edifices, government buildings whose pillars and
concrete replicated the federal structures of downtown
Washington, D.C.

Between Manila and the other cities, only a handful of
paved roads and a limited amount of railroad track snaked
through the countryside. But from the outskirts of Manila
toward the metropolis's center, the alleys and narrow
streets widened into tributaries that eventually flowed into
broad, spacious, towering, palm-bordered avenues like
Dewey Boulevard. Along these thoroughfares lay the sky-
scrapers of commerce and industry, high-rises and homes
of the affluent, and the establishment's posh Manila Hotel.
By and large, the Filipinos worked for the Westerners,
rather than the other way around. The colonials, as they
did elsewhere, restricted opportunities for the locals to
mingle socially. The armed forces carried their segregation
a step further with their Army-Navy Officers Club, which
not only kept out the natives but also walled off the commissioned ranks from their inferiors.

The pleasures of the Philippines were recalled by William Mack, a 1937 graduate of the U.S. Naval Academy:
"Life as a young officer in the Philippines and in China was
very nice. I think my total pay was $143 a month and we
lived in a small apartment that first year in a place called the
'goldfish bowl,' which was sort of like a motel with all the
rooms facing each other. You'd hear somebody call down
in the morning, 'Hey, Joe, it's time to go—our boat leaves
at 7:10' and it was relayed down the way by people eating
breakfast or in bed.

"The girls loved it—they could go down to the market in a taxi for fifteen cents and buy very expensive Japanese china for their house and fine linens very inexpensively and go to the movies for ten cents in downtown Manila. We were members of the Army-Navy country club, which was a very nice place for a minimum fee, and there was a polo club out on the outskirts of Manila. This was the only time I ever had a maid until I became an admiral. We paid her five dollars a month and she'd wash and cook a little and make limeade. We lived better while I was an ensign than we ever did before or since.

"Most of the petty officers had been there for some-times twenty or twenty-five years. They were allowed to ship over and stay. Most of them had Philippine girlfriends ashore." For those who had no steady liaison, Manila offered the usual vices of prostitution, boozing and gambling favored by men away from home. "They were hard drinking, big and hairy tough guys who had been out there a long time," recalled Mack of the enlisted men. And the Navy demanded that its officers present a spit and polish formality: "You wore your sword and white services when you went ashore [on official duties with outsiders]."

Army nurse Lt. Madeline Ullom volunteered to serve in the Philippines because of stories related by those who had already completed a four-year tour there. "There were the treasures they displayed, from the hand-carved teak and camphor wood chests, and my desire to experience life in the Orient."

Her arrival in Manila brought pomp, circumstance and a whiff of romance. "The band played. The crowd waited on the pier. Cars driven by chauffeurs quickly transported us the short distance to the Army and Navy Club. Friends and personnel greeted us. A party atmosphere prevailed. Hours sped away to the late afternoon as the vibrant sunset hues began to filter across the sky above the bay and Dewey Boulevard.

"The first of four unusual rides began through the streets of Manila. Each ride was different and under various circumstances. Calesas and carromatas [carriages], drawn by horses with jingling bells, streaming tassels and nodding plumes, competed with shining limousines, many automobiles, unusual trucks, noisy streetcars and buses and leisurely strolling pedestrians for right-of-way. Horns blew. Sirens screeched. Everyone appeared placid and fearless on the profusely tree-lined streets and boulevards. Many near collisions [occurred] in this cosmopolitan city of many races and different nationalities.

"The chauffeur stopped at the diagnonal walk with two lions at each end of the wall. The nurses' quarters are located in the hospital compound [Sternberg General Hospital]. Hibiscus, acacia, palms, tropical foliage with orchids anchored to the trees mostly hid the two-story building. A screened porch extended across the front of the first and second stories. A huge spacious living room looked inviting with reed rug, light bamboo furniture with bright colored cushions nestling in the sofas, chairs and on ottomans.

"Windowpanes were shell filled to emit a soft light. Huge ceiling fans slowly revolved. Our rooms were located down the rear corridor from the dining room. The walls between rooms ended about three feet from the ceiling and curtain entrances between two rooms provided more ventilation. Community bath facilities were at the end of the hall."

The nurses, like Ensign Mack, relied upon the cheap native labor. "A *lavendera* would do one's laundry on the patio, providing at least a couple of changes of clothes daily, for two-and-a-half dollars a week. Our houseboy, dressed in white trousers and loose-fitting shirts, would take the laundry and return it to the closet or atop the dresser. Shoes were placed outside the door each morning to be cleaned for a charge of fifty cents a week.

"Chinese tailors in the Walled City—Intramuros—made shirts, slacks, white towel coats with colored monograms on the pockets to our specific measurements. The towel coat was very absorbent and useful after tennis and bowling at the Army-Navy Club. Chinese merchants came to the quarters after payday with huge packs of beautiful linens and silks. They were displayed all day on the living room rug. The more experienced nurses taught us to look, to examine and to bargain until our guidelines were established.

"Rosie's Dress Shoppe was a focal point to select clothing for that special occasion. An afternoon of shopping at Rosie's was pleasant. The diminutive lady in slacks and high platform sandals was most solicitous that each visitor would sit in the most comfortable chair, sip the coolest drink and view from a most favorable angle the latest styles via clippings from Philadelphia."

Undoubtedly there were many of these "special occasions" as Ullom spun through a social whirl that included polo matches, jai alai games, golf, swimming, tennis, tea dances, evenings at the Manila Hotel, the Army-Navy Club and the hangout, Tom Dixie's Kitchen. She took trips to local tobacco, hat and hemp factories, toured plantations and agricultural stations, prowled the native markets and stores, drank in extraordinary sights like the bat flights at the Montalbam Caves, the numerous active volcanos and the Chinese cemetery on "the night of recollection." She shot through whitewater in a *banca,* a native craft, and inspected villages where life had gone unchanged for hundreds of years.

One of the more impressive experiences came after a "smooth glide over the sparklingly placid waters of Manila Bay. Corregidor appeared like a giant, green tadpole stretched out against the deep blue of the South China Sea. The profuse vegetation gave the impression of a mammoth flower garden on the tadpole's back. The [other] fortified islands, Fort Drum, Fort Frank and Fort Hughes were guardians. The Mariveles Mountains on the verdant Bataan Peninsula were two miles away."

During her visit to the three-and-a-half-mile-long, one-and-a-half-mile at its widest Corregidor, Ullom stood on the porch of the medical officers' quarters at night and saw the lights of Manila. She rode a car around the fortress isle and gazed at "steep green cliffs and down into deep and dark blue-green ravines," part of the natural defenses. She marveled at the supposedly impregnable Malinta Tunnel, a 912-foot-long, 24-foot-wide cave bored into the side of the rock that formed Malinta Hill. Inside the Tunnel, she saw the areas assigned to various military units in the laterals, 160-foot-long offshoots, 15 feet wide.

Maj. Albert Svihra, USMA '22 and a law school graduate, brought his family along when assigned as a legal officer in the Philippines in 1940. His personal automobile arrived three months later and he wrote to his parents, "We were certainly stranded here without it, particularly as the first two weeks we stayed in some temporary quarters and had to go about a mile to the Officers Club for our meals. After we got settled in, it wasn't so bad as deliveries of groceries, etc. are made right to your door. A bus drawn by mules comes by for the children to take them to school and my office is but a few minutes from our quarters.

"Our Christmas was somewhat different from former ones. We had a tree for the children but it did not seem the same, even to them—not when they could run around in play suits and go swimming at the pool Xmas morning." His personal responsibilities and his duty did not allow Svihra the same opportunities as those of Madeline Ullom. He noted he had seen little more than "rice paddies, small native villages called barrios. . . . It is like a different world altogether."

Foreign civilians, particularly those with important jobs, lived on an even grander scale. Betsy McCreary lived in Iloilo, capital city of Panay Island, while her father, a former government official, worked for a railroad company operating on Panay and nearby Cebu. The McCreary clan had an Iloilo home on a large parcel of railroad company property. In 1941, fifteen-year-old McCreary was a member of a small American-European community that centered much of its social life around the Iloilo Club with its tennis courts, indoor badminton court marked out on the ballroom floor, and the inevitable men's bar. "It also had a library where we would come in the evenings and read *Life, Saturday Evening Post, Tatler* and *London Illustrated News* in which I followed the lives of the Princesses Elizabeth and Margaret Rose.

"It was an idyllic life," she recalled, "being a white colonial, living in the Philippines. We had two maids and a seamstress. There were four gardeners, the chauffeur, the *lavendera* with her assistants, the cook who probably had her own assistants—family members in the outbuildings which was their domain. It was very hot; there was no air-conditioning except in movie houses. After running around you might take three showers a day. I would take one, leave my clothes on the bathroom floor along with the wet towel. Before the night was out, all my changes of clothes had been washed and ironed and put back in place."

The family followed local custom. Says McCreary, "I was never allowed downtown to the fabric store or the dressmaker's unless I had a brother, the chauffeur or one of the maids with me. I remember seeing American movies showing carefree young kids sauntering to the corner drugstore to meet their friends for an ice cream soda. And not an adult in sight. To me they seemed to have such freedom."

Like almost all of the colonials, McCreary attended private schools. In 1941 she was enrolled in the Brent School, an Episcopal institution located in the mountains of northern Luzon. "Only Americans and Europeans could attend," remembers McCreary. "We had a lot of Navy juniors from Shanghai and Hong Kong. They came to Brent because in Hong Kong they would have to go to a British school where American history would certainly not be part of the curriculum. And if these Navy boys wanted to follow their fathers to Annapolis, they would have to know American history. The last year we lost the Army and Navy kids. [Dependents of U.S. service personnel had been ordered home en masse.]

"The 'day hops' were children of miners [there were gold and copper operations around Baguio] and then there were the boarders, the Army and Navy kids, children from Manila or like myself from one of the southern islands or from one of the sugar centrals [large cane processing installations] on Luzon where there wouldn't be a school except for the Filipino children." One of her fellow students at Brent was John Eisenhower, the son of Dwight D., then a major serving on MacArthur's Philippine staff.

While the Americans prospered and enjoyed their lives in the Philippines, their rivals for Pacific hegemony had been building themselves into a world power. Although the Japanese struck without a formal declaration of war and at an unexpected site, a confrontation between the West and the Imperial Empire had been brewing since the turn of the century. Following the first explorations by intrepid sailors in the early eighteenth century, the British, Dutch and French had already established themselves in the Far East via colonization of southeast Asian territory when the United States first raised its flag in the region. Commodore Perry in the middle of the nineteenth century opened trade with Japan through shotgun diplomacy and then the United States acquired the Philippines as one of the spoils of war from the defeat of Spain in 1898.

Japan became a player in the imperial game with its shift from an isolated, feudal agrarian society to a modern industrial nation, signaled initially by success in the war with Czarist Russia in 1904–05. In the role of an ally of the West during World War I, Japan participated minimally, but cashed in with some gains from the former possessions of Germany's empire. These included trusteeship over the Carolina, Marshall and Marianas Island groups, east of the Philippines.

As early as 1907, the United States had engendered resentment in Japan with the first significant laws to ban Asiatic immigrants. By the early 1920s, friction between competing East and West interests heightened amid efforts to devise a formula for control of military outlays.

Ultimately, the Washington Conference specified a ratio for capital ships and armament that left Japan forty percent below both Great Britain and the United States. However, the restrictions also influenced the design of American heavy cruisers. Limited to ten thousand tons displacement, these vessels were forced to sacrifice speed, armor and armament in order to have available the fuel necessary to operate in the Western Pacific from existing U.S. bases.

The treaty, to the dismay of American naval strategists, also forbade further fortifications in the Pacific islands controlled by the United States as well as those under the British, French and Japan. Efforts to revise the agreement at London in 1930 brought some compromises that satisfied none of the parties.

By the mid-1930s, the more aggressive elements of the Japanese military-industrial complex, responding both to an Imperial tradition and the ravages of a worldwide depression, dominated their country's affairs. In 1931, a bogus incident in the Chinese province of Manchuria provoked a full-scale attack. Japan conquered the unorganized defending army and created a puppet, "independent" state called Manchuko.

During the 1930s, a series of attempted coups and assassinations shook Japan. Ultimately, the proponents of a greater Japan as the only means to preserve the Empire triumphed. Expansion became the goal. The policy dictated a substantially larger army and navy. That meant circumventing the international treaties by surreptitiously building a pair of huge battleships, the *Yamato* and the *Musashi*, which were so much bigger than anything that existed that if the United States had attempted to match them, the American vessels could not have passed through the Panama Canal.

To Western diplomats and military strategists, the Sino-Japanese War of 1937 and the bellicose statements issued from Tokyo ordained a collision course with the forces of Nippon. Achievement of Japanese aims could not be satisfied with indigenous resources and the only way to sustain the Empire lay in a southern advance. That meant bumping heads with the British, Dutch, French and Americans rather the Soviet Union, a northern military threat but not a tempting reservoir of raw materials.

Americans sympathized with the Chinese as newsreels showed the ravages of war inflicted upon civilians. When Japanese bombers sank the American gunboat *Panay* on the Yangtze River in 1937 hostility rose sharply, even after an apology and indemnity payment. American civilians and service personnel in China perceived a growing arrogance that bordered on contempt among those Japanese military whom they encountered.

Western powers sought to curb the ambitions of their rival through diplomacy and when thwarted there resorted to an embargo that denied Japan raw materials, particularly oil. The Japanese denounced the A,B,C,D countries (America, Britain, China and the Dutch) as intent on destroying their way of life and their culture. They sought to rally support by claiming they would liberate all of Asia from Western imperialism.

For the United States, the Philippines—which blocked access to the Dutch East Indies, the British South Pacific possessions (including Australia) and our own outposts at Guam and Wake—were an obvious target for any military moves. The archipelago's northernmost reaches lie less than 350 miles from mainland Asia. Flight distance from Formosa (Taiwan), the big island wrested away from China by Japan, is perhaps 700 miles to the Philippines' largest city, Manila.

Triangular in shape, numbering 7,100 separate islands—little more than one-third even have names—the Philippines stretch more than 1,100 miles from north to south and nearly 700 miles east to west. The biggest of the landmasses, Luzon, equals Denmark, Belgium and Holland combined. Mindanao, the second largest, is slightly greater in size than Indiana.

Tropical in climate, much of the archipelago was covered with thick jungle and contained vast swamps and rice paddies that swelled and shrank with rainy and dry seasons. Swift-flowing streams and deep arid gullies created during the dry months crisscrossed the land. Rugged ridges of hills and steep ranges of mountains further divided the countryside. Hot humid days on the plains and in cities like Manila during the long summers sent inhabitants who could afford it to the cool, dry climes of mountain resort towns like Baguio, the summer capital.

The 1935 census listed a population of thirteen million with a variety of ethnic and tribal bodies. The most common background was described as Filipino-Malay, descendants of voyagers from Southeast Asia. Another strain had an Indonesian heritage. The most indigenous people, shrinking in numbers, were the *Negritos,* genuine pygmies whose average height fell short of five feet. A substantial number of Chinese, Europeans, Americans and Japanese added to the mix.

Most Filipinos followed Christianity, with Roman Catholicism dominant, but Moros or Moslems in large numbers worshipped on Mindanao and a chain of smaller islands to the southwest. Buddhists and pagans also practiced their particular beliefs.

The severe terrain and the often treacherous waters between the islands separated people. A Babel of languages and dialects limited communication between the inhabitants and baffled Americans. All of these natural elements would influence events during both the defense and subsequent liberation of the Philippines.

Although the United States had decisively defeated the Spanish fleet in the Battle of Manila Bay in 1898 and routed the occupying army, some citizens did not immediately accept American control after a peace treaty in which Spain ceded the territory to the United States. A Filipino doctor, Emilio Aguinaldo, who had led a revolt against the previous occupiers, fighting alongside the Americans, now battled the new masters. Captured by U.S. troops, Aguinaldo signed an oath of allegiance to Uncle Sam in 1901 and the Philippines became a U.S. possession.

As comfortable as it was for the white colonials, America by the 1930s had lost its appetite for territory so far from the mainland and for rule so inimical to the tradition of freedom. That these colonial holdings no longer seemed profitable also weighed upon the minds of government officials, particularly as the Great Depression blighted the economy. Responding to needs at home and the agitation within the islands, an agreement between the United States and local leaders specified that the Commonwealth of the Philippines, established in 1935, would receive complete independence in 1946. Until that time, the United States would control only matters of foreign affairs and defense with participation in these activities by the local government. The citizens elected Manuel Luis Quezon as the first president of the Commonwealth.

Eager as the islands were to escape from American rule, the political powers recognized the threat from Japan. In this matter, the desires of both the Philippine authorities and the United States were the same. Aware of the potential for a conflict with Japan, Quezon hired an old friend, Gen. Douglas MacArthur, then chief of staff for the U.S. Army, as military advisor.

The Philippines was familiar turf to Douglas MacArthur. His father, Gen. Arthur MacArthur, a Civil War veteran, had participated in the campaign to oust the Spanish from the Philippines and then subdue a rebellion against American rule. Immediately after graduation from the U.S. Military Academy at West Point as top man in his Class of 1903, Douglas MacArthur worked as an engineer in the Philippines to help map the territory. "The Philippines charmed me. The delightful hospitality, the respect and affection expressed for my father, the amazingly attractive result of a mixture of Spanish culture and American industry, the languorous laze that seemed to glamorize even the most routine chores of life, the fun-loving men, the moonbeam delicacy of its lovely women, fastened me with a grip that has never relaxed."

It was not all lush, tropical romance, for on one

occasion MacArthur shot it out with a pair of "desperadoes," killing both with his pistol. He reported that his sergeant rushed up, surveyed the damage and in an Irish brogue remembered by MacArthur said, "Begging thu Loo'tenant's paddon, but all the rest of the Loo'tenant's life is pure velvet."

A few years later MacArthur found himself on a mission in Mexico as part of an effort by Washington to curb what it considered excesses by that country against U.S. citizens. Again he wound up in the midst of a shootout and his exploits brought a recommendation for a Medal of Honor, but the War Department squelched the proposal.

By World War I, MacArthur had advanced to the rank of colonel, serving as chief of staff for the U.S. 42nd Division, sometimes known as the Rainbow Division, part of the American Expeditionary Force that fought in France. "I had long felt it was imperative to know by personal observation what the division had to face . . . I went to see General de Bazelaire [a French commander] but he was reluctant to authorize me to join a French raiding party out to capture Boche prisoners. I told him frankly, 'I cannot fight them if I cannot see them.' "

The patrol proved every bit as dangerous as General Bazelaire feared, with a crawl through barbed wire, artillery, small arms fire and grenades. "The fight was savage and merciless," recalled MacArthur. "When we returned with our prisoners these veteran Frenchmen crowded around me, shaking my hand, slapping me on the back and offering me cognac and absinthe." The Allies pinned a Croix de Guerre on MacArthur to which his own commanders added a Silver Star.

MacArthur continually led his men out of the trenches, and his personal bravery plus his adept strategy and tactics as a brigade commander added four more Silver Stars and a pair of Distinguished Service Crosses. A brigadier general by the Armistice and commander of the Rainbow Division, MacArthur achieved a reputation for personal courage under fire and irregular military dress. "I wore no iron helmet because it hurt my head. I carried no gas mask because it hampered my movements. I went unarmed because it was not my purpose to engage in personal combat, but to direct others. I used a riding crop out of long habit on the plains. I fought from the front as I could not effectively manipulate my troops from the rear."

Always dapper, younger than most senior officers, MacArthur developed a rapport with the doughboys of that era. His successes and his style also generated a hearty disdain in some colleagues and superiors.

During the early 1920s, MacArthur returned to the Philippines for a three-year stint and became friendly with the former rebel and now political leader, Manuel Quezon. In succeeding years he did a tour as commandant at West Point and ascended to the post of Army chief of staff. For a time he adroitly managed to avoid political bear traps during an era of turmoil, ranging from the court-martial of Gen. Billy Mitchell (the early exponent of air power), the pressure of disarmament forces and the ever thinner budgets for the military.

He railed against the opposition: "Pacifism and its bedfellow Communism are all about us. . . . For the sentimentalism and emotionalism which has infected our country we should substitute hard common sense." His views generated denunciations that included voices in Congress. "I was harassed ceaselessly in the effort to force me into acceptance of their appeasement . . ."

In his role as chief of staff MacArthur focused on the profession of war and its future. He studied the past and thought of the future. He foresaw maneuver and movement as decisive, recognizing that planes, tanks and mechanization meant the end of WW I–style trench combat with its massive, immobile armies confronting one another. He argued in favor of stockpiling the strategic materials that would become so critical for WW II and he reestablished the Order of the Purple Heart, a medal issued to those wounded or killed due to enemy action.

But in 1932 he stumbled. Some twenty-five thousand

WW I veterans, accompanied often by their families, had encamped in Washington, D.C., while they sought federal payment for their service during the war. They dubbed themselves the Bonus Expeditionary Force (BEF) and MacArthur, always hostile to any group that seemed to lack respect for the forces of law and order—the habits of a lifetime in a military environment—scoffed at what he perceived as a rabble of malcontents. "In the end," said MacArthur, "their frustration combined with careful needling by the Communists, turned them into a sullen, riotous mob."

According to *American Caesar,* William Manchester's admired biography of MacArthur, he considered ninety percent of the bonus marchers fakes although a Veterans Administration survey found ninety-four percent had Army or Navy service records, with more than two-thirds having served overseas.

MacArthur mobilized troops to deal with the squatters. After members of the BEF scuffled with soldiers near the Capitol, the General defied orders from President Herbert Hoover and directed his forces to evict the main body of supplicants from a campground across the Anacostia River. In the ensuing melee, tents, shacks and makeshift shelters were put to the torch, and tear gas and bayonets were used to rout the civilians, leaving two babies dead and a child lacerated by a bayonet. (In his book, *Reminiscences,* MacArthur insisted no one was killed.)

Backed up by Secretary of War Patrick Hurley, MacArthur gracefully attributed his victory over the BEF to his commander-in-chief, thereby robbing Hoover of any chance to disassociate himself from the actions. But it was truly a Pyrrhic victory. President Franklin D. Roosevelt, inaugurated little more than six months later, bent on curing the Depression and suspicious of MacArthur's ambitions, kept him and his army on a short leash and starved for funds. Tarred by a personal scandal involving a mistress, described as a "Eurasian beauty," buffeted by cliques in the military establishment whose animosity dated back to WW I and resented by veterans for his treatment of the BEF, MacArthur, after Roosevelt refused to extend his tour as chief of staff for more than a matter of months, expected to retire.

At that moment Manuel Quezon, who as a youthful guerrilla major had surrendered his sword to Gen. Arthur MacArthur, arrived in Washington, D.C., to confer about defense of the Commonwealth until full independence a decade later. In a typical piece of political wizardry that removed a person whom he considered a threat and at the same time strengthened the U.S. position in the Far East, Franklin Roosevelt arranged for Congress to fund a U.S. military mission in the Philippines. Quezon found MacArthur delighted to accept the post of military advisor, with $33,000 a year added to his salary as a U.S. major general, a considerable stipend for the 1930s. To serve as MacArthur's chief of staff, the War Department assigned Maj. Dwight David Eisenhower, an aide to MacArthur when he commanded the U.S. Army. (The experience led Eisenhower to respond later to a question of whether he knew MacArthur: "I studied dramatics under him for four years in Washington and five in the Philippines.")

MacArthur sailed to the Philippines on the steamship *President Harding,* taking along with him his ailing mother, Pinky MacArthur. At sea, the general courted an attractive, diminutive thirty-seven-year-old, Jean Marie Faircloth, a native of Murfreesboro, Tennessee. The two continued to spend increasing amounts of time together in Manila, and in 1937 they were married. A son, Arthur MacArthur IV, was born in 1938.

The general had taken up residence in a six-room penthouse atop the Manila Hotel and immersed himself in building the Philippines into a defensive stronghold, "a Pacific Switzerland." Under the strategy created by his predecessors in the War and Navy Departments, MacArthur was expected to operate in accord with War Plan Orange (WPO), modified slightly over the years and coded as WPO-1, WPO-2 and finally WPO-3.

The War Plan Orange scenario envisioned meeting a thrust by the Japanese at the Philippines with a retreat of the defenders into the narrow, junglelike peninsula of Bataan, which lay along the western edge of Manila Bay and was backed up by several fortified islands, including the redoubt at Corregidor whose big guns could deny any enemy the use of the Manila anchorage. The resistance would be expected to contain the Japanese until the military might of the United States, convoyed by the Navy, would cross the Pacific and blast the invaders from the archipelago.

Interviewed by Clare Boothe Luce on a visit by her to the Philippines, MacArthur had responded to her question of a formula for defensive warfare with the terse response "Defeat." He had also informed Luce of his notions for offensive warfare: "Did you ever hear the baseball expression, 'Hit 'em where they ain't'?" WPO in any shape hardly fitted MacArthur's vision for waging war. While not openly disavowing WPO, he determined to design an organization that need not retreat to Bataan.

Instead of a small, elite military capable of holding off a much larger opposition by dint of carefully prepared, well-stocked positions that employed terrain and vegetation for its own advantage, MacArthur sought to develop enough ground, air and sea strength to make any strike at the Philippines too costly for the Japanese, even after independence in 1946. He envisioned an army which, with its active duty and reserve elements, added up to forty Filipino divisions, four hundred thousand soldiers, trained, equipped and led by a cadre of officers schooled at a local replica of West Point. His navy would be fifty speedy, torpedo-armed boats that would ply the surrounding waters with such swiftness and stealth that they could disrupt the approach of any large ships. For control of the sky he considered 250 aircraft necessary. To go from blueprints to reality, MacArthur estimated a period of ten years and an expenditure of a quarter billion dollars by the Commonwealth along with subsidies from the United States to meet its responsibilities.

For all of the years he had spent in the Philippines previously and his experiences as chief of staff during the first years of the Great Depression, MacArthur's schemes lacked a sense of reality. The belief that American officers and noncoms along with those Filipino graduates of West Point could transform the conscripts into fully qualified soldiers after five-and-a-half months of training was a fantasy. The men, however willing, were not reared in the kind of industrial society that marked the West. They did not have either the experience or the education to adapt quickly to the demands upon modern troops. When they started to arrive at the training camps in 1937, those charged with transforming the draftees into soldiers discovered their recruits spoke eight distinct languages and eighty-seven different dialects. More than one-fifth, including some designated as first sergeants or company clerks, were illiterate in any tongue. The sharp divisions and deficiencies in language skills and customs seriously hampered instruction and communication.

Equally defeating, the Commonwealth was no more prepared to provide the kinds of appropriations necessary to field the requisite number of men and equipment each year than was the United States with its own armed forces. The original local budget of $25 million annually was almost instantly pared to less than one-third that figure and, in the year preceding Pearl Harbor, appropriations came to a measly $1 million.

General MacArthur, however, continued to argue that he could and would make the Philippines impregnable. Both his case and his achievements were hampered by his alienation from Washington, D.C. Pacifist elements regarded MacArthur as a warmonger. Few in Congress cared to expend great sums on fortifications or armaments for a place that would soon be free of U.S. control. MacArthur's influence in the States waned further as he was forced to retire from active duty as an American officer when he refused to relinquish his appointment as the Philippine commander with the rank of field marshal.

MacArthur's inability to procure military hardware and money for the defenses of the Commonwealth stirred doubts in Quezon. The Japanese conquests in China persuaded Quezon that a declaration of neutrality might be the one way to avoid turning his country into a battleground. He even contemplated dismissal of MacArthur and shocked his field marshal with a public statement, "It's good to hear men say that the Philippines can repel an invasion, but it's not true and the people should know it isn't." Newspapers in the Philippines published the conflicting views of the president and his military advisor, causing considerable anxiety among the reading public. (Again, MacArthur's memoirs do not indicate any difference of opinion with Quezon.)

While MacArthur initially could not persuade either the government in Washington or the one in Manila to open the public purse for defense—indeed, the stinginess of the Commonwealth legislators forced a cutback in even the meagre effort to create a local army; morale fell and time in training shrank—events on the world stage obligated those responsible to rethink their positions.

The bombs and bullets that shattered the peace of Europe in September 1939 emphatically declared that neither negotiations nor appeasement could prevent war. The *blitzkrieg* juggernaut of Nazi Germany that rolled over Poland, Denmark, Norway, Holland, Belgium and finally France, the bare escape of British troops from Dunkirk, the siege of London by Adolf Hitler's *Luftwaffe*, cast doubt over the ability of Great Britain to defend its Far East empire.

The Japanese seized the opportunity to take over French Indochina and pressured Dutch and French colonies to accept Tokyo's concept of a "Greater East Asia Co-Prosperity Sphere," in which there was little doubt who would be the senior partner and chief beneficiary. The top

U.S. Army officer in the Philippines, Maj. General George Grunert, agreed with MacArthur that appeasement of the Japanese would only encourage further aggression. Whereas MacArthur's shouts of alarm may have been regarded as aimed at self-aggrandizement, Grunert, an insider, could influence Washington.

No slouch at exploiting an opportunity himself, MacArthur wrote to the current occupant of the Army chief of staff slot, Gen. George C. Marshall, and noted that since the Philippine Army soon would be absorbed into that of the United States—a leap of MacArthur's imagination since the War Department had not yet come to that decision—he expected to shut down his office as military advisor. He suggested to Marshall the establishment of a Far East command covering all U.S. Army activities and nominated himself to be in charge.

After dithering over the idea for several months, worsening conditions convinced the policymakers to adopt MacArthur's idea. Along with extra appropriations designed to strengthen the indigenous forces, a cable from Marshall on July 27, 1941, announced creation of the United States Army Forces in the Far East (USAFFE) and recalled MacArthur to active duty, designating him the commanding officer. In his memoirs, MacArthur remarked, "I was given the rank of lieutenant general, although my retired rank was that of a full general."

MacArthur now had the role he coveted and a platform from which to importune ears no longer deaf to the sounds of Japan's marching feet. But America was close to ten thousand miles away, its defense factories only slowly gearing up and their main customers, Great Britain and the Soviet Union, already in a shooting war with the Axis Powers of Germany and Italy, also demanding the tools to fight.

CHAPTER III

OPENING ROUNDS

MACARTHUR ASSUMED THAT his mission, which had begun in 1935, was to prepare the archipelago for an inevitable clash with the Japanese. During the first few years of his tenure, even as he futilely strove to impress the politicians and brass hats half a world away as well as those a stone's throw off from his Manila headquarters, the Philippines, as Mack, Svihra, McCreary and others testified, remained a kind of paradise for those Americans posted there. But the general understood that paradise to be on the verge of calamity and grappled with his circumstances.

Short on money, equipment and trained fighting men in 1941, MacArthur's USAFFE could nevertheless boast of some assets and, with President Roosevelt convinced that confrontation with Japan appeared inevitable, the promise of a substantial enhancement of resources as quickly as possible. On hand the general could count upon a cadre of 297 graduates of West Point. The most senior were MacArthur and a former football all-American, coast artilleryman Col. Paul Bunker, Class of '03. The most junior included several from the Class of '41—infantry lieutenants like Alexander "Sandy" Nininger and Hector Polla, who arrived only ten days before the attack on Pearl Harbor. Mixed in were officers from almost every class between—former cavalryman Gen. Jonathan Wainwright

'06, infantry specialist Gen. Clifford Bluemel '09, engineer Col. Hugh J. Casey '18, the military law expert Albert Svihra '22, Italian-born infantry leader Floyd Forte '34 and bomber pilot Colin P. Kelly '37. The practice of admitting a few men from the Philippines to West Point resulted in nineteen well-schooled Filipino officers like Vicente Lim '14 and Fidel V. Segundo '17, both of whom commanded Philippine Army divisions.

In the delicate minuet to prevent trodding on the sensitive toes of the host people, forty-five of the American West Pointers along with a number of non-Academy, regular army officers and noncoms were attached to the existing—largely on paper in some instances—twelve Philippine Army divisions. Although they technically served as advisors to the Filipino officers, the latter almost always deferred to the Americans.

To achieve his goals MacArthur, on September 1, 1941, began to mobilize the Philippine Army. Elements of the ten reserve divisions, who theoretically had already undergone some training, were to be called up gradually until a total of seventy-five thousand would be on active duty by December 15.

MacArthur, who received his fourth star as a full general shortly after he assumed his new post, while hectoring Washington to satisfy his dire needs, voiced optimism for the future. In October 1941 MacArthur became privy to a plan known as Rainbow Five, the overall Allied strategy for war with Japan and with the other Axis powers (the British, the Dutch and the free French were already at war with Germany and Italy). He conceded the loss of the U.S. possessions of Wake, Guam and the Philippines. The scenario assumed that in a two-ocean, worldwide conflict the Philippines could not be held. In that respect, Rainbow superseded Orange.

MacArthur, while not opposing Rainbow Five, argued that it was a mistake to write off the Philippines. Instead he persuaded Marshall and Adm. Thomas Hart, the area naval commander, that he could stop the Japanese at the water's edge. He believed the enemy would not make its move before April 1942 and by then MacArthur insisted he would field more than one hundred thousand well-trained and equipped troops backed up by a strong air corps while Hart's fleet would deal with the Japanese Navy.

The decision to scrap the defensive bastion philosophy of WPO and then revise Rainbow Five to include preservation of the Philippine Islands dictated significant changes in operations by the Philippine military commander. Guarding the potential landing sites among the roughly 250 miles of Luzon beaches demanded a considerably larger army than would have been required to retain only Bataan and the fortified positions at the mouth of Manila Bay. MacArthur thus discarded the plan to augment the highly professional Philippine Scouts with a limited number of well-equipped soldiers, and instead pursued quantity rather than quality. The change of arena also meant a major shift in logistics, deployment of food, ammunition, fuel and other supplies in order that these items could be retrieved by the defenders of Luzon's approaches rather than by those who were to retreat to Bataan. MacArthur's choice of strategy and its fulfillment would have a critical effect on the struggle to defend the Philippines.

As the portents of war gathered in ever darker clouds, the highest American civilian official on the scene was Francis Sayre, the U.S. High Commissioner. After being warned of the crisis with Japan, Sayre met in his State Department capacity with Hart and MacArthur on November 27. Both Sayre and Hart feared an imminent thrust by the Japanese. However, recalled Sayre, "Back and forth paced General MacArthur, smoking a black cigar and assuring Admiral Hart and myself in reassuring terms that the existing alignment and movement of Japanese troops convinced him that there would be no Japanese attack before spring."

Although the public perception, aided and abetted by the strength of his personality and oratory, regarded MacArthur as the man in charge of the Far East, in reality he commanded only the U.S. Army. His opposite number for the Navy, Rear Adm. Thomas Hart, three years older, an 1897 graduate of the U.S. Naval Academy, was stiff-necked, irascible, the epitome of the martinet. He zealously guarded his prerogatives and it was inevitable that relations between the two military leaders would be frosty.

Like MacArthur, Hart had received little in the way of reinforcements as 1941 ebbed. The major additions amounted to a dozen submarines and six PT boats as well as the understrength 4th Marine Regiment transferred from duty in China. The U.S. Asiatic fleet consisted of Hart's flagship, the heavy cruiser *Houston,* a single light cruiser, thirteen WW I four-stack destroyers, the subs and the PT boats, plus a handful of miscellaneous craft including tenders, gunboats, minesweepers and tankers. Conspicuous by their absence were any battleships or aircraft carriers. Two dozen PBYs, the notoriously slow moving amphibious patrol planes, made up the fleet air arm.

William Mack said that when he came to the Asiatic Fleet in 1939 there was an underlying feeling of trouble ahead. "It was totally a peacetime system. But I think we all knew, in our hearts, that war was just around the corner —the corner being one or two years. About six months later, the ship was given sonar, which meant the ships in the Asiatic Fleet were considered the front line. We suddenly realized that they were being serious back in the States—they were giving us something we were going to have to have. Before that time, we had depth charges in the destroyers and that was it. The doctrine for finding a submarine [before sonar] was simply to sight its periscope, take a bearing on it, estimate the range and run down toward him to drop some depth charges."

The installation of sonar aboard the destroyers was a tangible sign of the approach of war. In November 1940, said Mack, all dependents began to be evacuated. "The fleet tempo changed considerably. We no longer went to China—we stayed around the Philippines. For the last year before the war started we were roughly on a war footing;

we still had awnings [for shade against midday sun] and
movie machines but we were expecting something to happen." At the same time Mack continued to wear his formal
whites and carry a sword when going ashore, until just
about a month before the start of the war.

For Capt. Floyd Forte, a West Pointer born in Viesti
Foggia, Italy, in 1910, the pace quickened slightly ten
months before war broke out. To a classmate he wrote,
"I've had a very interesting time in the Philippines. Service
at Ft. McKinley was a lot of fun, weather good, lots of golf,
lots of nice people. Last February [1941] we started to
increase the tempo a little. Our Scouts [the career Filipino
military outfit] were increased in number and there was
golf on weekends only."

Madeline Ullom also noted a change of ambience. "In
May 1941, social activities greatly decreased. Curfews were
routine. Alerts were frequent. Field exercises were longer
and more intensive. The Army-Navy Game, the event of
the year, when reservations at the club were made months
in advance, was all but canceled."

Still, she says, "An American flag moved gently in the
breeze above the central entrance to Sternberg. A feeling
of security filled the atmosphere. The military corpsmen
and Filipinos were skilled and efficient. A high quality of
duty performance was required and obtained. Supervision
was meagre. Professional dedication at all times was para-
mount. Inspection days brought no apprehension."

Whether he merely wished to reassure his kin or was
genuinely ingenuous, Maj. Al Svihra expressed little concern about a possible crisis. "We have some fairly decent
local English newspapers and four radio broadcasting stations in Manila so that we keep pretty well posted with the
news. I never hear any more foreign broadcasts of the war
and I am just as happy, because it was mostly all bunk
anyhow. I expect that people here are much less concerned
with the war and war talk than people in the States."

Maj. Philip Fry, who already had one tour in the Philippines on his record, had returned there in November. Al-

most immediately upon his arrival he noticed a project at the Ft. McKinley officers club. "I started over there with Ted Lilly [an officer acquaintance from a previous tour]. Just outside of the front of the club I saw the entrance to an immense dugout, the shaft down was within twenty feet of the steps of the club. It led down for fifty or more feet. This dugout was beneath the area of the officers club, the tennis courts and the command general's quarters. It had a series of corridors and compartments and was designed as a divisional command post but it was never completed." The swift passage of events would prevent further work or use.

Another recent arrival, Sam Grashio, wore the gold bars of a second lieutenant and the wings of silver as a P-40 pilot assigned to the 21st Pursuit Squadron. After two years at Gonzaga University and a couple of years in the Washington Air National Guard Grashio began training in the Air Corps.

"I thought of flying only in the narrow sense; taking to the air in the best World War I movie tradition, embellished with goggles and helmet, scarf waving in the breeze. I thought little about *why* I was training and flying so much. Of course I knew that war had been going on in Europe ever since September 1939, but in flying school I thought of it mostly when a fellow cadet of Greek lineage would needle me about what his countrymen were doing to the Italian troops Benito Mussolini had so injudiciously sent to invade Greece.

"My mistaken perception of the world deepened soon after the 21st Pursuit Squadron sailed from San Francisco on November 1, 1941. Our ship was the *President Coolidge,* a former luxury liner then being used as a troop transport. Life was lovely; there were no duties, the food was magnificent and we did not even know where we were going." Not until the vessel reached Hawaii did Grashio and his colleagues figure they were bound for Manila.

"Nothing happened that might have suggested, even remotely, that a real war was not far off," said Grashio.

"On board the *Coolidge,* there were a number of senior officers who had just graduated from the National War College. Having little to do, I listened to them extensively. To a man they were convinced that there would be no war with Japan because the Japanese would not be so stupid as to start a war they would be certain to lose within a few weeks."

A cold dose of reality should have struck Grashio on December 6 when he heard a speech from Col. Harold George, a senior airman. George warned war was imminent, that the Japanese had three thousand planes in Formosa only six hundred miles away and already they had been seen doing aerial reconnaissance over the Philippines. George concluded with remarks that indicated he believed Grashio and his fellow fliers were members of a "suicide squadron."

Grashio, unconvinced, offered to bet the squadron commander, Lt. Ed Dyess, five pesos there would be no war with Japan. "Ed took the bet at once and laid another five it would begin within a week."

On that timetable, the members of the 21st had painfully little time to prepare. Their machines were as fresh as the pilots; only eighteen of the twenty-four allotted had been removed from their shipping crates and assembled by December 8. Four had never even been flown and the others were not yet adjusted for maximum performance.

Non-Filipino civilians in the Philippines tried to decipher mixed signals. Jean George [no kin to the airman], whose mother had emigrated from Vancouver, Washington, and whose father was an Australian executive who had worked for American firms in Manila before Jean and her sister were born—1919 and 1918 respectively—recalls discussions among her parents and other adults. "I knew there was unrest in the United States about the Japanese. During our trip to the States in 1940, Mother's relatives begged us not to return to the Philippines—as 'there's going to be a war.'"

However, the family returned to their lives in the Philippines—her sister was already married and Jean, employed by the Associated Steamship Lines as a stenographer, was engaged to a U.S. Army officer assigned to the 31st Infantry Regiment.

She was aware that U.S. military dependents, including classmates of Betsy McCreary's, had been sent home but she had no knowledge of any concern for those with her status. She quotes from *Interrupted Lives*, a book of accounts by four women interned during WW II in the Philippines: "Quite a few months before Pearl Harbor, we learned that the military dependents had been evacuated from the Philippines. Of course, this was a clue that something was going to happen.

"American and European businessmen went to the High Commissioner's office and asked what was going on and should they plan to evacuate too. They were told there was no threat, but there was an elaborate evacuation plan in place should we need it—there was nothing to worry about."

The George family went about its routine, as did thousands of others with a similar status. But by November 1941, Navy officer William Mack had been in the Philippines for almost twenty-five months. Ordinarily, a tour in peacetime lasted a year. "In a sense the morale was good because you were ready to go to war. On the other hand morale was very bad because we'd been there for more than a year and Admiral Hart had given no sign of shortening our tours. You might as well be dead. That's the way people felt. If war started, the ships were very inadequate against modern Japanese ships. Many of the destroyers had been written off as probably never being able to make it."

At the Navy Department in Washington the experts doubted MacArthur's forces could hold off an onslaught on the beaches and not be forced to retreat along the lines of War Plan Orange. Although Hart wanted to fight it out with the Imperial Navy in Philippine waters, he was instructed to safeguard his vessels by deploying them southward. Furthermore, since his fleet was considered to be part of the overall Rainbow strategy he had to be prepared to sail to the Dutch East Indies and join with the Allied ships there.

As a young naval officer, Robert Lee Dennison received an assignment from Hart to be a contact with the commander of USAFFE. "MacArthur had a very elementary understanding of the use of a navy. He, like a good many Army officers of his time, looked on a navy as a seaward extension of the Army's flank and that's all. There was no personal contact between Hart's staff, MacArthur's staff or MacArthur or Hart. MacArthur didn't know what we were up to in terms of ship movements or what our war plans were, nor did we know what his plans were. That was the purpose of my being in this particular capacity."

Glen Townsend, as a U.S. Army colonel, assumed command of the 11th Regiment, a component of the Philippine Army's 11th Infantry Division, in September 1941. "I found that the regiment was composed of Ilocanos and Igorrots in about equal numbers. I found that they spoke eleven different dialects and that Christian and Pagan had little liking for each other. All of the enlisted personnel had taken the prescribed five-and-one-half-months training. They were proficient only in close order drill and saluting. The officers, being mainly political appointees, had less training than the men they were supposed to lead." To "advise" the regiment, the American aides to Townsend added up to ten other officers and seven enlisted men.

Townsend was appalled the most, however, by the minimal personal gear possessed by his men and the unit's lack of adequate equipment. His Filipino soldiers had no blankets, raincoats, mosquito bars, entrenching tools or steel helmets. On their feet they wore rubber soled shoes and for headgear they used pith helmets. The standard uniform was one pair of khaki shorts and one shirt. They also owned one set of blue denim fatigues. The antitank company supposed to field 37 mm guns had none. The entire regiment depended upon four trucks and eight field telephones. There were 81 mm mortars, but no ammunition other than that designed for target practice would be available until three months after the Japanese had invaded.

For the basic infantryman's weapon, the U.S. Army sold the Commonwealth its surplus Lee Enfield rifles. Unfortunately, the stock of these pieces was too long for the short-statured Filipinos and could not be aimed by them with the butt in the crotch of the shoulder where the recoil could be comfortably absorbed. Instead, soldiers were forced to brace their Lee Enfields against their upper arms ahead of the shoulder and they incurred nasty bruises, lowering their ability to effectively fire the rifles.

On the plus side, Townsend says the would-be soldiers struck him as physically fit, eager to learn and presenting no disciplinary problems.

It seems obvious that MacArthur miscalculated what it would take to create an effective local army. Clifford Bluemel, who as a young lieutenant in 1914 had served a tour in the Philippines, was among those who had returned there as the war clouds darkened. "I got there in June 1940 to command the 45th Infantry, Philippine Scouts. It was a good regiment, about sixty men to a company. [In August 1941] I was told that three colonels, Brougher, Jones and Bluemel, would run a school to train staff officers for ten Philippine Army divisions. They were all Filipinos, some of them graduates of West Point.

"I ran the school from 8:00 in the morning until 11:30 and from 1:00 to 4:30 in the afternoon. Then we all went out and walked for fifty minutes—everybody. I also ran the school from 7:00 to 9:00 at night. They thought that was terrible and that I was a rough SOB. But I had only six weeks to train them. I even ran it all day Saturday sometimes, and they didn't like that. Sunday they had off. When I threatened to run it on Sunday, I almost had a riot one time."

MacArthur and his chief of staff, Richard Sutherland, visited Bluemel at his school. "We had drinks and talked about different things. MacArthur talked about the Tojo Cabinet which had been formed in Japan. He said, 'The

Tojo Cabinet is not the war cabinet. The Tojo Cabinet will fall, and there will be another cabinet which will be the war cabinet.' This was his opinion around the first of November." It proved dead wrong.

MacArthur's conviction that the political process in Japan had not yet reached the war kindling point indicates his confidence that he still had time to prepare. Bluemel had no intelligence that could contradict his chief but other remarks by MacArthur took him aback. "Before I went to the Philippines, an officer who had been the military attaché in Germany gave a talk on the handling of the three-regiment divisions by the German Army. It was to me an ideal system. We had that four-regiment division, and it took six hours to get an order down to get the division moving. The former attaché said a German general could get a three-regiment division moving in no time with an oral order. He just gave an infantry colonel his mission and boundaries, attached a battalion of light artillery to him and so on.

"I asked MacArthur what he thought about it. He talked for half an hour. The man, I think, had never read and found that the Germans had a three-regiment division. It began to shake my confidence in him a little. I thought 'That man doesn't even know anything about handling a three-regiment division. Yet the Philippine Army has three-regiment divisions.' "

With the school course completed by mid-November, Bluemel was assigned to command the 31st Division of the Philippine Army, organized and mobilized in Zambales Province. Recalled Bluemel, "I went to see this great Philippine Army that MacArthur had trained. The enlisted men of my command were all Filipinos. Most of them spoke Tagalog and some English. Several spoke other dialects.

"They [the 31st Division] were supposed to have had five months training prior to induction in the service. The basic training given them during that five months period was poor. Most of them had fired five rounds or less with the World War I Enfield. Very few had fired the .30 or .50 caliber machine gun. Apparently the artillerymen had never fired the 75 mm gun and in some cases had never seen one fired.

"There was a Colonel Irwin, who had the 31st Infantry Regiment. Irwin had been a major in the 45th, and I had utmost respect for him. He was a fine officer—a man who would do things. He had the regiment organized."

However, to Bluemel's shock, Irwin informed him the regiment had never been on the target range. Bluemel instructed Irwin, "The principal thing the infantry must know is how to shoot and how to march. That's basic infantry training, because they've got to be able to march and when they get to their destination, they've got to be able to get fire superiority quickly and beat the enemy." He arranged for the troops to use the target range at the Olongapo Naval Base at Subic Bay.

At the range, one battalion from the 31st Infantry managed to expend some fifty rounds per man and a second battalion fired half that amount. The arrival of the 4th Marine Regiment from China at Olongapo closed the range to the Army and a third battalion from the 31st never got to squeeze off a single bullet. The troops would not have a further opportunity to use their weapons before they met the enemy in actual combat.

The 4th Marines who took over the area at the Olongapo range included a twenty-five-year-old bandsman, Elmer Long, Jr. A Maryland farmer's son, Long had starred in baseball while at high school but he was restless. "In 1934, at seventeen years of age, I wanted to get in the Marines, to go some place and do things. I could not get in the line units but my father signed for me to enter the United States Marine Band. I really had no combat training; in those days Marines in boot camp did none except for one week firing the rifle and pistol. At the time there were seventeen thousand Marines in the Corps and eighteen thousand cops in New York City."

Long played his horn for the Marines and eventually

was sent to Shanghai as a member of the 4th Marine Regiment. Together with seven hundred other leathernecks he stepped off the ocean liner *President Harrison* at Olangapo, December 2, 1941.

Towards the end of November, according to Bluemel, "the Army-Navy game was to be played. I got a table reserved at the Army-Navy Club. Some people were going to sit there with me, and we were going to have some drinks and listen to the game." Ordinarily the broadcast of the football game was an excuse for a gala, a highlight of the Manila social season with partisans of the two services enthusiastically partying. However, in deference to the Far East crisis, the celebration had been canceled.

Still Bluemel figured he could at least quietly enjoy the game at the club and he dropped by MacArthur's headquarters to obtain a pass for the day. To his astonishment, the G-3 [plans and operations officer] told him no passes were to be granted for the weekend. And he was advised to see Sutherland and ask to see a secret report.

"I went in and told him the G-3 sent me and that there's a document I should see. It went something like this: 'The conference with the Nomura delegation [special envoys from Japan to Washington] has been terminated and will not be renewed.' I said, 'My God! That's war! When the Japanese are ready to attack, they don't declare war; they attack, and then declare war.'" As a student of history, Bluemel was remembering how the Japanese opened their assault on Russia in 1904, and subsequent conflicts in Manchuria and China.

As commander of the 31st Division, Bluemel quickly reported to Jonathan Wainwright, in charge of the northern Luzon defenses. Wainwright knew of the radiogram about the breakdown in negotiations. In fact, he had been looking for Bluemel and now directed him to start organizing beach defenses.

The strongest defensive unit was the Philippine Division. It included the U.S.-manned 31st Infantry Regiment, which with only eighteen hundred GIs added up to little more than half of the normal contingent. However, the remainder of the outfit came from the Philippine Scouts, the one local fighting force that from an effectiveness standpoint matched the best from the States. Although the Philippine Army was almost literally a paper tiger, the Scouts, formed into the 45th and 57th Infantry Regiments, were professional soldiers. The Scouts dated back to 1901 when the U.S. Congress authorized recruitment of a force of Filipinos for service in the U.S. Army. Its appropriations came directly from the U.S. Army rather than from moneys designated for the territory. Equipped and armed on par with the 31st Infantry Regiment, the Scouts brought pride and élan to their job. Although certain tribal customs like a fealty to kinsmen and elders occasionally annoyed their American compatriots, the Scouts also displayed a sense of discipline that earned admiration even from those U.S. officers who ordinarily considered Filipinos inferior.

As the war approached, most of the officers continued to be drawn from the U.S. Army—West Pointers, regulars and reservists called to the colors. Majors Floyd Forte and Dudley G. Stickler led elements of the 45th while Cap. John Olson, Maj. Philip Fry and Lt. Alexander Nininger all fought with the 57th. Some Filipino graduates of West Point also occupied command positions. Many of the Scouts achieved the status of non-commissioned officers.

As an elite organization, the Scouts could be selective about admission and in the quality of personnel the outfit matched the soldiers from the States. The Scouts also equalled the GIs in equipment; the infantrymen carried the latest weapon, the M-1 Garand rifle. Some of the Scouts at first disdained the M-1, which featured faster firepower rather than the accuracy of the Springfield in which a soldier carefully squeezed off each shot.

Although MacArthur bombarded Washington with requisitions for the new M-1 Garand rifles, the other troops labored with either Springfield '03s or the highly unreliable Lee Enfield. Neither weapon could unleash the number of bullets in a given time as an M-1. Ancient machine guns, dud mortar shells, a lack of adequate or big enough artillery, a shortage of vehicles—whatever a modern army needed the USAFFE could only order and hope it would arrive in time. Indeed, early in December MacArthur received word of a convoy of cargo and troop ships steaming towards the Philippines under the guidance of the cruiser *Pensacola*. The holds and decks of the vessels carried the mortar and artillery shells so desperately needed and bore the crated aircraft of the 27th Light Bombardment Group whose pilots had already taken up residence in the Philippines.

The defenders had already welcomed the American-crewed 192nd and 194th Tank Battalions, with 108 light tanks as well as some additional coast artillery.

In his original prescription for a successful defense, MacArthur spoke of a fleet of fifty or sixty torpedo boats. Attached to the Asiatic Fleet at the time of Pearl Harbor were only the six 77-foot craft of Motor Torpedo Boat Squadron 3, commanded by Lt. John D. Bulkeley, a 1933 USNA graduate and already a man of some reputation.

Son of a New York stockbroker, Bulkeley says he still wonders why he chose a naval career. He was not a good student and graduated in the lower echelons of his class. With appropriations on a starvation level, the Navy handed out diplomas to everyone but awarded a commission only to those in the top half of the class.

Mustered out to civilian status, Bulkeley now tried to become a pilot in the U.S. Army, but he washed out. He was rescued when Franklin Roosevelt, a former Secretary of the Navy who was anxious to improve the strength of that branch, decreed that all who completed the course at the Academy should be granted commissions.

As a young officer Bulkeley demonstrated a verve and impetuosity that carried him to the brink of serious trouble. Well before the outbreak of hostilities, he became suspicious of the attention paid to fleet maneuvers by some visiting Japanese. Bulkeley managed to steal the briefcase of these alleged spies. Assigned to the Asiatic fleet, Bulkeley met and successfully wooed a British subject from Hong Kong. That affection, however, did not dissuade him from almost creating an international scene during an argument with some of her countrymen's naval officers. The upshot was his rude removal from a British man-of-war. And when summoned to appear before Adm. Ernest J. King in regard to some non-regulation behavior, Bulkeley took advantage of his anonymity on the occasion and slipped away in his boat before dawn.

In 1941 Bulkeley received command of Squadron 3. Although he had still hankered for a career in the air, he remarks, "When a four-star admiral says, 'You're the man,' you follow the orders." By the time he came to the Philippines, the easy life described by William Mack was gone. He also had little doubt of what lay ahead, having been in China when the Japanese sank the *Panay* and witnessing the belligerent attitude of the Imperial forces. Bulkeley and his fellow torpedo boat crewmen spent their time investigating the waters around the archipelago and prudently located caches of fuel and supplies for future emergencies. "I was damned if I knew what I would be expected to do in the Philippines. I figured my missions would be determined by the theater commander."

The addition of the six torpedo boats hardly added up to the seagoing power that MacArthur envisioned as necessary. The third leg of his planned buildup, however, more closely approached his blueprint. With eighty-one hundred Air Corps men—flight crews, mechanics and other ground service experts—stationed in the Philippines by December 7, 1941, these troops constituted the single largest complement of Americans.

What is remarkable about the Army Air Corps presence in December 1941 is how much had been accomplished in a short period. The first true effort to build a Philippines-based air wing began in May 1941, a bare six months before the first bombs dropped. The War Department dispatched a conservative, old-school officer plagued by poor health, Gen. Henry Clagett, to survey the needs. Fortunately, Clagett's chief of staff, a dedicated aviator who flew during WW I, Col. Harold George, compensated for his superior's lack of imagination with vision and energy. His success or failure, however, rested upon forces beyond the scope of either his wisdom or his industry.

The tasks ahead seemed insurmountable. The men from Washington learned that only four airfields with military capacity existed on Luzon, whose major city of Manila lay a mere five hundred miles from Japanese bomber bases on Formosa. Furthermore, only Clark Field could be considered a first-class base. Both Nielsen Field, the fighter strip near Manila, and Iba, the base along the western coast, lacked facilities for service of planes. Ground access to Nichols, the principal field for fighter planes, six miles south of Manila, depended upon a single narrow road that crossed a river bridge. One well-placed bomb could isolate Nichols from any entry or exit except by air. Furthermore, although it had hard-surfaced runways, improper drainage rendered one section useless during the rainy season.

A visiting expert, Group Captain C. Darval from the Royal Air Force, politely informed his hosts and subsequently Washington in a written report of the vulnerability of the Luzon air establishment. He pointed out the absence of camouflage, dummy strips or protection against a parachute assault. He criticized the placement of fields so close to beaches where they could quickly come under attack from the ground and sea. He noted that flimsy, flammable structures held supplies and maintenance shops. And he warned of the dire consquences of too many planes concentrated in a few places. He called this lack of dispersal the single greatest weakness. Few planes were camouflaged; pilots said they could see the shimmering silver of aircraft from twenty-five miles away. There were no protective revetments dug for planes nor were there air raid shelters for ground servicemen and off-duty flight crews.

This report meandered through the bureaucracy for months and did not come to the attention of the Army chief of staff until November 1941, by which time it was far too late to implement the recommendations. Under prodding from George, a handful of aviation engineers had started the laborious process of carving out additional strips throughout the islands but the pace was so slow none was completely finished before the enemy struck.

At the time Captain Darval described the desperate state of airbase affairs, however, the problem of dispersal was more a matter of imagination than reality, for the USAFFE had pitifully few planes and even these were ancient, obsolescent types that, even if they got off the ground, would have been no more effective than fleas trying to deflect a herd of rampaging elephants.

With George sounding the Klaxon, however, and with the backing of MacArthur, authorities recognized that genuine airpower might be enough to halt a Japanese advance at least long enough for a Philippine rescue operation. The best and latest America could provide began to arrive in the islands. Some of the first pilots shipped to the Philippines in 1940 had been taken aback to discover that in combat they were expected to fly the same outmoded P-26 in which they had trained. But as the sense of urgency heightened, P-35s arrived and then the latest, the P-40 Warhawk.

To bolster the thin ranks of the Air Corps, the 34th Pursuit Squadron, equipped with P-40s, was hastily dispatched overseas. It reached Manila on November 20, 1941. The outfit's chief clerk, Sgt. Thomas Gage, Jr., a 1940 enlistee from Tulsa, was among those aboard the *Coolidge* when it docked after the twenty-day voyage from Hawaii. At that last port of call Gage, filling in as a supply sergeant, desperately scrounged for the necessities of military life. He was able to obtain things like brooms, mops, shovels; even two pairs of long-john underwear for the men were issued, but the port quartermaster refused to include barrels of anti-freeze, claiming it was not needed in the tropics. The 34th's water-cooled P-40s thus landed in the Philippines lacking a basic fluid for proper operation.

"We arrived," says Gage, "on November 20, Franklin D's [President Roosevelt] Thanksgiving Day [moved up a week in hopes of boosting Depression-sluggish retail sales with extra shopping days before Christmas]. Mess Sergeant Timothy Hardy set up his field kitchens on the docks and served hot dogs and sauerkraut. He apologized for not having the turkey and dressing other outfits were getting but said he couldn't handle it under the circumstances."

A week later, on the traditional feast day, the 34th again dined on franks because the unit was in the process of shifting from Nichols Field to the raw new Del Carmen airstrip, designed to handle both fighters and big bombers but at the time a mere dusty, hot strip hacked out of sugar cane fields.

The 34th could hardly have been a happy group. "When we arrived at Nichols and after we got our P-40s put together," says Gage, "we were ordered to exchange our P-40s for the worn-out P-35s the 24th Group had been flying. One thing, when you are a stepchild you'll get the dirty end of the stick.

"The P-35s' engines were completely worn out when we got them. They had [ten months earlier] been on a ship bound for some Swedish colony and when the ship was in Manila they had been commandeered. The instruments were in Swedish." The details of diversion of these Seversky-manufactured aircraft from their original destination to the U.S. Air Corps differ slightly in official accounts but the condition of the planes was as Gage describes it.

Construction at Del Carmen had hardly started before the 34th moved in. They were supposed to be only the first of several units to be stationed at what was expected to be a field capable of handling B-17s. Even as the 34th moved in, ordnance people scattered five hundred and one thousand pound bombs in the brush for eventual use by the oversized tenants.

There was no running water, no latrine and only a small river available for the basic amenities. The nearest town lay three miles off but the biggest problem was the strip itself.

Dust as much as six inches deep layered the bare ground. Airfield engineers had used molasses to cover the surface as they graded the runways, hoping that would solve the dust problem, but to little avail. Sometimes after one pilot took off, the next man in line could see nothing for three to five minutes. The grit fouled the tired engines of the P-35s beyond the aid of primitive maintenance.

"We were issued," says Gage, "twelve Springfield rifles and six drum Lewis machine guns for aerodrome defense. The Lewis guns had no sights and the drums were loaded with no tracers. We dug six pits, six feet deep and about four in diameter. In the center of each was placed a steel pole on which a Lewis was mounted. Each pit had a drum, reserve drums were in a central supply and a runner was to fetch them when needed." Such was the extent of the anti-aircraft preparations at Del Carmen.

By the first week of December 1941, the statistical count for 24th Pursuit Group showed seventy-two P-40s and eighteen P-35s available for combat. However, as Sam Grashio had seen, some planes had just been assembled and delivered; their machinery was untested and needed tune-ups. Additional P-40s were still in crates awaiting assembly. None of the pursuit planes were outfitted with adequate oxygen equipment, therefore the fliers could not handle enemy aircraft at the higher altitudes. The slower P-35s, lightly armored, with worn out engines and .30 caliber machine guns, were hardly suitable for 1941 aerial warfare.

The state of readiness of some front-line Air Corps units is exemplified by a memory of Tom Gage. On the night of December 7–8 [before Pearl Harbor] he heard the familiar sound of shotgun shells exploding as the whistle of Squadron Commander Samuel Marrett alerted the pilots. "It was a disaster as they tried to take off in the darkness, running into one another. I saw lights, planes taxiing and roaring, swirling dust everywhere. A fire started and so did the yelling and hollering. We could dimly see the silhouette of a P-40 on fire. The pilot was burned in his cockpit. Several ships were completely washed out. In my opinion, our pilots could not fly the underpowered P-35s properly—the engines were shot—and the pilots that had our P-40s didn't have the know-how to fly those nose-heavy boogers off dirt runways. That's one reason so many of the PI fighter planes washed out the first days."

The fighter aircraft—the nomenclature of early WW II described them as pursuit planes—had never been the first priority of George and MacArthur. Both of them considered the prime requisite for a defense lay in the bomber and particularly the newest version, the B-17 Flying Fortress, which seemed an extremely effective weapon.

An impressive start in dispatch of the four-engine bombers had landed a total of thirty-five in the Philippines, which was almost triple the number stationed in Hawaii. Backing up the Fortresses, the Philippine command could call on some aging and obsolete B-18s and B-10s, useful at best for reconnaissance and ferrying supplies. Aware of the danger of keeping all thirty-five Fortresses in one target basket and expecting reinforcements, the Air Force had begun to construct a field on a former pineapple plantation on Mindanao, well out of range of the Formosa threat. On the eve of the Japanese attack, sixteen of the B-17s had been flown to Del Monte Field, Mindanao. The remainder were to follow and make that their base until suitably protected places could be created on Luzon.

The presence of the B-17s appeared to provide a devastating potential weapon against any invasion fleet. But even these bombers, which were among the earlier models of the B-17, lacked essential features that later became standard equipment. The first B-17s entered battle without the power turrets, heavy armor and tail guns that would carry the fight deep into Germany and blast Pacific sites late in the war.

On paper the Philippine Air Force bolstered the Americans. But its sixty aircraft included forty-two P-13s, primary trainers. The planes listed for combat were obsolete, a dozen P-26s and three B-10s.

Perhaps the worst deficiency in the defense system for airfields and other installations was the absence of a functioning early warning system. The latest radar systems, ones that could detect both heading and altitude of aircraft, key to the summer, 1940, Royal Air Force success against the might of German bombers in the Battle of Britain, were almost totally absent from the Philippines. To supplement the inadequate electronic systems, inexperienced watchers, still being schooled in aircraft recognition and equipped with binoculars, were expected to spot incoming traffic—through clouds or at extreme altitudes—and then relay the information over an antiquated telephone network. Even if the information arrived in timely fashion, effective antiaircraft batteries were practically nonexistent.

The pace of preparedness increased dramatically in the last month or two before December, but the assembled military might was still insufficient to stop a better organized and better armed Japan. Whether the forces under MacArthur and Hart would have been ready by April, the general's anticipated date for an attack, is conjecture. The Japanese, well supplied with intelligence from countrymen living in the Philippines and aided by dissident Filipinos hostile to the existing government and the American presence, were aware of the growing defense efforts. The move to war on December 7, 1941, reflected the desire of the expansionist elements in Japan not to gamble on MacArthur's chances of achieving his goal by springtime.

MacArthur, like others in his command, expressed astonishment over the attack on Pearl Harbor, believing the Philippines would always be the first objective. But the Japanese may well have been aware of War Plan Orange, predicated upon the ability of the U.S. Navy to bring relief to the Americans and Philippines holding out on Bataan.

Now, having successfully ravaged the American fleet at Pearl Harbor, Imperial Japan focused on the first line of defense in the Philippines, American air power.

CHAPTER IV

THE HAMMER FALLS

TO GLEN TOWNSEND, commander of the 11th Infantry Regiment in the Philippine Army, eighty-four Japanese bombers heading south over his encampment around 11:00 A.M. had confirmed the earlier radio news reports of war. Actually, planes from Formosa sortied well before that time.

As early as three in the morning, while the last revelers of the Air Corps party at the Manila Hotel straggled home, the primitive radar screen at the Iba airbase on the western coast picked up the telltale blips of incoming aircraft, heading from Formosa over the China Sea. Because all U.S. planes were grounded that evening, those at the radar screen had no doubts of the identity of the intruders.

The 3rd Pursuit Squadron stationed at Iba scrambled its P-40s. The would-be interceptors, with orders to fire at any alien aircraft within twenty miles of the shoreline, knew from the radar the heading of their quarry. However, because the system then in use could not advise altitude, the P-40s arranged themselves at staggered levels above the ground. Unfortunately, the Americans could go no higher than fifteen thousand feet without the proper oxygen equipment. Those back at Iba watching the radar saw the two groups of blips converge, but the U.S. pilots never saw the enemy who were probably five thousand feet above them.

Inexplicably, the Japanese, who could have continued right on over the oblivious 3rd Pursuit Squadron, reversed course and returned to their base. Failing to find the incoming flight, the P-40s landed at their base where the command remained on alert. At 6:30 they too learned from a news bulletin of the Pearl Harbor strike.

Sam Grashio, stationed at Nichols Field, recalled, "About 2:30 A.M. on December 8, Lt. L. A. Coleman, the officer of the day, banged on the door of the officers living quarters and yelled to us to report at once to the operations tent. We dressed in a rush, jumped into a waiting vehicle and sped away. Dyess announced enigmatically that there was an emergency, but ten minutes later he told us to go back to our quarters. It seemed to me I had just fallen asleep when Coleman began banging on doors again. This time he shouted at us to get dressed, that Pearl Harbor had been attacked! It was about 4:45 A.M. We dashed back to Nichols. Dyess confirmed that Pearl Harbor had indeed been bombed by the Japanese. He ordered us into our new P-40E pursuit planes and directed us to start our engines and stand by on the radio."

Other U.S. airfields also sounded alerts as word of the Iba radar find was relayed; then a series of official and unofficial statements brought word of the attack upon the installations in Hawaii. There was a brief lull for the major Air Corps units while the Japanese opened the assault on the Philippines by first attacking the radio station at Aparri on the northermost tip of Luzon. Then Japanese fighter planes operating from a carrier destroyed two Navy PBYs in Davao Gulf near Mindanao but missed their tender. Shortly after, the enemy hit at the airfield located near Baguio.

"That first morning," recalled Betsy McCreary, "we knew about Pearl Harbor from the radio. Just as we got out of chapel some planes in beautiful formation flew over the school. We waved and cheered. Our mighty Air Corps. It was so exhilarating. Then about an hour later, we learned we had cheered the planes that bombed Camp John Hay, about a mile from Brent.

"Classes were canceled for the day and local families came and got their children. The rest of us, the boarders, just stood around and waited and speculated on how long the war might last. A week? A month? No, ten days at the most and we would repulse them."

The Japanese air strikes provoked a host of defensive missions. The P-40s started patrols to cover the vital installation of Clark Field. As a precaution, the duty officer at Clark ordered B-17s stationed there into the air. Pilots at airbases not involved in these operations remained by their planes, ready on signal to meet the invaders.

Missing from these efforts was any sort of offensive blow on the Americans' part. Behind the failure to initiate any such action lies a murky tale involving confusions of command and decision. When General Brereton, who had replaced General Clagett in November as air commander for USAFFE, learned of the raid on Pearl Harbor he immediately hurried to MacArthur's headquarters, instructing his subordinates to ready the B-17s for a raid, with Formosa the obvious target. But instead of being able to confer with MacArthur, Brereton could not get beyond the chief of staff, Brig. Gen. Richard Sutherland, an imperious, zealous officer whose arrogant manner made him the most unpopular man on MacArthur's staff.

Sutherland brusquely informed Brereton that his boss was too busy with Admiral Hart to discuss the immediate role for the Air Corps. That MacArthur and Brereton did not confer is the one undisputable fact about what occurred in the early hours of December 8, Manila time. According to Sutherland's recollections, the airman announced that he would attack Formosa with his B-17s. The chief of staff claims that after Brereton declared his intentions, Sutherland inquired, " 'What is the target? Where are the fields?' He did not know. He had no target data. There were twenty fields on Formosa. General Brereton had no notion of what he would attack and he would almost certainly lose his planes." Brereton later insisted he had proposed hitting the Japanese troop ships crowded into Takao Harbor on Formosa.

Accounts from various sources indicate that at the hour Brereton attempted to see his commander-in-chief and obtain permission for the bombing raid on Formosa, MacArthur was unwilling to make any move against the Japanese. Absent a declaration of war from any party, he spoke of warnings from Washington that he not take any action the Japanese might seize upon as provocative. He later explained to a historian, Louis Morton: "My orders were explicit not to initiate hostilities against the Japanese." Indeed, Brereton on returning from his meeting with Sutherland and learning his staff had already worked out a mission to bomb Formosa said, "No, we can't attack till we're fired on." He further explained that while he was told to prepare the bombers for operations they could not begin until approval from MacArthur's headquarters.

In his memoirs MacArthur remarked that upon word of a force of enemy bombers over the Lingayen Gulf on course for Manila at 9:30 A.M. he was still "under the impression that the Japanese had suffered a setback at Pearl Harbor, and their failure to close in on me supported that belief. I therefore contemplated an air reconnaissance to the north, using bombers with fighter protection, to ascertain a true estimate of the situation and to exploit any possible weaknesses that might develop on the enemy's front." Subsequently, he says, he changed his mind, having learned that the Japanese had succeeded in their Hawaiian venture.

Although the attack on Pearl Harbor had been confirmed by Washington and clearly signaled an act of war, MacArthur, in an altogether uncharacteristic fashion, dithered for five hours. Finally, at 10:10 A.M., through Sutherland, he agreed to photo-reconnaissance flights, the first steps necessary for an attack by the B-17s.

MacArthur, in the course of denying that he ever consulted with Brereton or knew of any interview the airman had with Sutherland, added, "As a matter of fact, an attack on Formosa, with its heavy air concentrations by our small bomber force without fighter cover, which because of the great distance involved and the limited range of the fighters was impossible, would have been suicidal. In contrast, the enemy's bombers from Formosa had fighter protection from their air carriers, an entirely different condition from our own."

He was probably correct in his estimate of the outcome of a B-17 raid on Formosa, but his reasoning smacks of hindsight and is incomplete. The American bombers would have been easy prey because of their own deficiencies: thin, unarmored fuselages; cumbersome, manually operated turrets; and absence of tail guns. However, the range of the P-40s in the Philippines did fall well short of the requirements to escort the bombers to Formosa and return. And the lack of oxygen equipment for high altitude flight meant the fighters could not stay with their flock.

Few if any U.S. strategists possessed accurate intelligence on the quality of the Japanese air force. MacArthur speaks of the bombers from Formosa as being convoyed by carrier-based fighters, but in fact the Japanese Zero had been modified and its pilots trained in ways that added hundreds of miles to its range. The sorties against Luzon, including those which would strike the vital American installations early in the war, employed land-based Zeros.

As an intelligence officer for the Air Corps in the Philippines, Capt. Allison Ind enthusiastically supported an immediate retaliation on Formosa by the B-17s. "We had no illusions," said Ind. "These folders [descriptions of objectives on Formosa] were not comparable with the exact and elaborate sheets of the RAF and the *Luftwaffe,* prepared as they had been over a dozen, a score and more years. We had none of their beautifully calibrated bomb-target maps indicating best approaches and even bomb release lines for given speeds and altitudes. But we had something complete enough to make this bombing mission a very far cry from the blind stab it would have had to be otherwise. Maybe we could deliver a real hurt, if not a staggering blow, to the enemy at his very point of departure for an invasion action against the Philippines."

Others, however, thought quite differently and the Air Corps finally settled for a three-bomber photo-reconnaissance mission set for takeoff around noon. The mission was delayed while technicians located the proper cameras and arranged for them to be flown to Clark Field from Del Monte.

Whatever the discussions at USAFFE Headquarters during the morning of December 8, the airmen throughout the area responded to a pair of warnings. Brereton's Washington boss, Gen. Henry "Hap" Arnold, telephoned the Philippines to caution against a repeat of the Hawaiian experience where the American planes were caught by the attackers on the ground, neatly lined up and primed for destruction. Even without the advice from half a world away, when the radar at Iba had indicated incoming hostile traffic, the duty officer at Clark Field ordered sixteen of the B-17s (one was grounded for mechanical problems) to get out of harm's way. The bombers placidly cruised the skies in great circles for two hours, staying in radio contact with the nearby communications tower.

By 11:00 A.M., with no imminent attack by Japanese planes in the area, most of the aircraft, P-40s and B-17s, were back on the ground. While ground crews hastily refueled the ships and stocked the prescribed ordnance for the bombers, air crews snatched a few moments of rest or a quick snack. The latest instruction for the bomber command was to initiate a photo-reconnaissance mission over Formosa, and at twilight the main body of Flying Fortresses, acting on the intelligence gathered, would strike the enemy.

About 11:30, Iba alerted all Air Corps bases of a large formation of planes coming in from the China Sea, apparently vectored on Manila but the heading also meant the enemy would approach Clark Field. Unfortunately, mis-communications, failure of the telephone and telegraph system coupled with the coordinated, multi-targetted approach of the Japanese overwhelmed the Americans.

The warning of approaching planes over the China Sea scrambled flights of fighters. The 3rd Squadron at Iba saw nothing in the vicinity of their home field and neither could they spot anything amiss at either Manila or Clark Field. Running low on gas, the members of the 3rd returned to Iba. Just as planes formed up for an orderly landing, Iba literally went up in flash and smoke. Japanese bombers, cruising at twenty-eight thousand feet, out of sight and well out of range of the P-40s, had unloaded devastating strings of explosives across the base. The place was completely destroyed, the radar station and its operators wiped out, every building reduced to rubble, anyone not in a foxhole dead. Five P-40s were lost and the surviving flights scattered to emergency sites, with several crashing from lack of fuel or damage from dogfights.

At Nichols Field, P-40 pilot Grashio said, "After the initial alert, we cut our engines, got out of the cockpits and sat under the wings, and waited as seemingly endless hours dragged by. Suddenly about 11:30 A.M. we received an urgent call to prepare for action, though just what action was unspecified. Soon, Dyess divided our eighteen P-40s into three groups and led two of them, A and B, into the air. I was to lead the remaining six, Flight C, and follow him, but a couple of our planes developed minor engine difficulties that delayed us just long enough that we lost contact with A and B flights. Only about 11:50 did my flight actually get into the air. We flew to Laguna del Bay, a huge lake just south of Nichols Field, and for the first time tested our .50 caliber machine guns by firing short bursts into the water. More of the fruits of unreadiness appeared only minutes later. Two pilots in my flight reported that their engines were throwing so much oil on the windshields that they couldn't see. They could only go back to

Nichols. This left four of us [Lts. Joe Cole, Johnny Mc-Gown and Gus Williams].

"By now Flights A and B were not only out of sight but for reasons unknown out of radio contact as well. Since I had received no orders other than to get into the air and follow the other flights, our isolation was complete. Since I had to do something, I radioed [the others] that we should fly towards Clark Field, sixty miles north. It seemed a logical target for Japanese planes flying in from the north."

The fighter squadrons, alerted by Iba, prowled the skies, searching sectors over the China Sea, Bataan and Corregidor. One report claims slow communications and excessive clouds of dust prevented the P-40s at the Del Carmen field from getting off the ground promptly. Another account says that the 34th Pursuit Squadron stationed there never received orders to cover Clark Field. Since the unit flew the antiquated P-35, how effective they could have been is dubious. Whatever the reason, Clark Field, during the period when its own planes from the 20th Pursuit Squadron required refueling, lay naked. The gaps in the arrangements to protect the big base with planes from other stations meant Clark's only means to keep its precious assets from destruction required warnings that allowed time to disperse the aircraft. But the notification system rested upon a chain of weak links.

The bombs that smashed the radar installation at Iba eliminated the most definitive source of information. The native observers, trained to report approaching flights, relayed their information over the lines of the notoriously unreliable Philippine telephone system to air headquarters at Nielson Field. In turn, the word passed over the teletype or by radio to the different squadrons. But by midday of December 8, the wires that normally carried the messages were dead, victims either of sabotage or the frequent technical problems. Furthermore, heavy interference plagued the radio transmissions—subsequently, Japanese sets that could have jammed the airwaves were discovered in the vicinity of the U.S. bases.

"We arrived over Clark Field about 12:20 P.M.," remembered Grashio. "It was a gorgeous day. The sky was blue and the air smooth as glass. Observing the idyllic look of the whole area I still could not feel that I might become personally involved in a shooting war at any moment. It may seem incredible that anyone could have been in such an abstracted condition eight hours after Pearl Harbor but I accepted the fact of war only when it hit me in the face, and there were many like me.

"Observing nothing unusual at Clark, C Flight flew westward towards the China Sea. Suddenly I spotted planes at about our altitude (ten thousand feet) moving south. We closed in, pulses racing. No sweat! They were only some other P-40s. Before we could get close enough to tell which squadron they belonged to, however, our earphones were suddenly filled with hysterical shouts from the tower operator far below, 'All P-40s return to Clark Field. Enemy bombers overhead.' These ominous words were almost immediately intermixed with the terrifying *whoomp* of bombs exploding. To my utter astonishment, the formation of P-40s continued serenely on a southerly course, climbing gradually. Obviously they had not heard the frantic order to return to Clark. What had happened to their radios? It was the second snafu on a day that was to be filled with them."

At 12:30 P.M., about the moment that Grashio recognized a friendly group of P-40s and while the 19th Bombardment Group staff continued to plot the assault upon Formosa, Clark Field's 20th Pursuit Squadron P-40s taxied to the runway, ready for the signal to take off. Already, bombs had been loaded into several B-17s and the aircraft scheduled to collect photo-intelligence on Formosan bases rumbled into position for the start of their mission.

Lt. Fred T. Crimmins, Jr., commander of one plane, started to walk across the field toting a machine gun that required a minor fix. His crew, grabbing lunch, was astonished to hear an unconfirmed radio report that at this very moment Japanese bombers were over Clark Field. Crimmins reached a hangar and passed the weapon to a sergeant for repair when the base Klaxon sounded its urgent alarm.

The pilot and the mechanic rushed outside and peered into the sky. In the clear blue above, from over the mountains to the northwest, they saw two precision Vees, one behind the other. Serenely droning towards them at eighteen thousand feet, the pair heard the engines even as the first of the P-40s roared down the runway, now frantic to get off before the hammer fell.

There had been no warning at all, according to those on the scene, and it was a matter of seconds or perhaps a few minutes between the sight of the Japanese flights and the fall of the bombs. And when these plummeted to the target the devastation was horrendous.

The pattern of the two bomber waves spewed explosives across the field, shattering the officers' quarters, the parked P-40s, the headquarters building, the maintenance shops and hangar areas. Almost every structure took a hit, and many blazed flames without restraint because the apparatus to control fires had been destroyed. No means to summon help existed; the blasts obliterated the communications center. The 200th Coast Artillery, responsible for antiaircraft, coped with ammunition manufactured a minimum of nine years earlier. Most fuses were badly corroded and an expert guess reported that only one of every six of the three-inch rounds actually fired.

Tracers and flaming debris ignited nearby trees and the long grass, which to one observer went "roaring and crackling like an evil beast." A giant pall of dust and a thick black cloud from a burning oil dump rose so high in the air that a pilot near Iba saw the sinister cloud. At ground zero, the fumes reduced visibility to well below a hundred feet.

Flight C from the 21st Pursuit Squadron, with Sam Grashio in command, started to respond to the control tower appeal for help. "Right at this critical juncture," said Grashio, "Joe Cole radioed that his engine was throwing oil so badly that he could not see out of his windshield. Like the two others with the same trouble, he had to return to Nichols Field. This left McGown, Williams and myself. We turned back towards Clark. In the distance I got my first glimpse of the spectacular destructiveness of war. It was astounding! Where the airfield should have been the whole area was boiling with smoke, dust and flames. In the middle was a huge column of greasy black smoke from the top of which ugly red flames billowed intermittently. Momentarily, I thought how utterly, abysmally wrong the senior officers on the *Coolidge* had been, a reflection almost immediately replaced by pity for those on the ground who must be going through hell. I said a quick prayer, asking God to help them and thanking Him for sparing me, at least for the moment, from being on the receiving end of Japanese bombs.

"About 12:50 P.M., directly over the field, I noticed several enemy dive bombers perhaps eight hundred feet below us and two thousand feet above the ground bombing and strafing. All our flight training had been directed towards moments and opportunities like this. I signaled my wingmen to attack. Just then, an enemy dive bomber shot out of the smoke maybe five hundred feet below. I looked at once for McGown. He was nowhere in sight. Gus had disappeared too.

"Instead, about a hundred yards behind and above me were two Zeros, closing in. They opened fire. I veered sharply to the left. My plane shuddered as a cannon burst hit the left wing and blew a hole big enough to throw a hat through. For the first time that day I had the hell scared out of me. Momentarily, I was sure I was going to die on the first day of the war. Instinctively, I began to pray again, this time with greater fervor than before.

"I also remembered what Ed had told me many times; never try to outmaneuver a Zero; go into a steep dive and try to outrace it. I pushed the throttle wide open and roared for the ground. The wind shrieked past me and the earth flashed upward at horrifying speed. According to the book I was courting suicide. Technical manuals specifically warned against a power dive in an untested plane, and I was in a P-40 that had been in the air a grand total of two hours. But with two Zeros on your tail, the admonitions in technical manuals are not the first things you think about.

"My luck held. When I tried to pull out of the dive at treetop level just west of Clark the plane responded magnificently. Glancing back, I was overjoyed to see the two Zeros falling steadily behind. The superior diving capability of the P-40 had saved my hindquarters."

Grashio said he saw enemy tracers pass increasingly wide of the mark and eventually the pair of Zeros turned away. "I breathed a prayer of thanks only to break out anew in a cold sweat. Would I be able to land with the gaping hole in the wing? I radioed Nichols tower for advice. I was told to climb to eight thousand feet above an uninhabited area and simulate a landing. Wheels and flaps down, I did so. The hole in the wing presented no problems. Nevertheless, many curious and doubtless apprehensive people stood along the runway when I came down about 1:30, the first pilot to make it back to Nichols from combat."

On the ground at Clark Field, airmen and ground crews struggled to recover, dispensing what medical aid they could to the injured and seeking to arrange transport for them to the Fort Stotsenburg Hospital. But the respite from onslaught was pitilessly short as dozens of Japanese fighters roared through the smoke. Machine guns and 20 mm cannons hammered away at the parked Flying Fortresses, totally exposed to the strafing runs. Only a few had been ruined by the high altitude attack of a few minutes earlier, but the fighter runs completely wrecked all but two or three and these absorbed some damage. The three planes scheduled to survey Formosa lay in smoldering ruins, having never left the earth.

Most of the personnel could only hunker down in their foxholes as the assault ravaged the base. Some B-17 gunners rushed to their planes, seemingly oblivious to the danger, and sought to train the machine guns in the grounded planes against the invaders. Amidst the gunfire, explosions, flames and smoke, medics aided by other officers and enlisted men succored the hurt and continued to evacuate them by any vehicle that could move—ambulances, trucks, reconnaissance cars.

Four of the P-40s at Clark managed to get airborne before the bombs rendered the field useless. Five others in the process of taking off and five more lined up to await their turn were turned into junk by the detonations. The quartet that escaped the carnage registered three downed Zeros. A handful of other interceptors that rushed to the scene claimed several other kills. But the costs to the enemy were negligible. Furthermore, these first dogfights revealed how superior the Japanese Zero was to the American fighters, in speed, maneuverability and ability to travel longer distances. And the Japanese pilots demonstrated a proficiency that their adversaries quickly came to respect.

Maj. Alva Fitch, commander of a battery for the 23rd Field Artillery Regiment, a Philippine Scouts outfit, was at his Fort Stotsenburg post near Clark Field on the morning of December 8. Although aware of the news, Fitch and his battery had received no orders and were busying themselves with digging in for protection against air raids.

"We were just sitting down to luncheon when Johnny, hearing a suspicious noise, went outside. I looked at my watch. It was 12:48. Johnny called to us from the yard. We saw a flight of fifty-three bombers [most accounts say fifty-four] very high. We speculated as to their identity for a very few seconds and took to the ditch. About one minute later, Clark Field exploded. The entire Clark Field area erupted in a column of smoke and dust and with an awful and impressive roar.

"I ran for the barracks where I found the Battery engaged in antiaircraft operations with Springfield rifles, with far more danger to themselves than to the airplanes. The rifles had been recently issued and only a few of the men had ever fired them before. I stopped the rifle fire, and put the men in the trenches we had dug earlier.

"By this time, attack planes were strafing the airplanes on the ground, and the AA installations in the vicinity. I remember seeing one P-40 come out of the smoke with a Jap on his tail. They passed low over the Battery and turned back into the smoke. This started the troops firing again. I am still surprised that none of them were killed by their own barrage."

Irvin Alexander, who was in charge of supply matters at Fort Stotsenburg learned by radio of the war's opening blast. He recalled, "As we went about our duties that morning we had little more information but heard a rumor that Baguio had been bombed. At lunch I turned on the radio at 12:30 P.M. to hear the news from Don Bell, our favorite Manila announcer. He reported Baguio had been bombed that morning and there was an unconfirmed rumor that Clark Field had also been initiated. Clark Field being less than a mile from where we were sitting, I laughed, as I started to say, 'Another example of the accuracy of the news.'

"In the middle of the sentence my face froze, for I became aware of the whistling approach of hundreds of bombs. This shrieking was followed by terrific explosions which made our house shake and groan like it was in the midst of a violent earthquake. We rushed out to the parade ground to see columns of smoke and dust rising from the airfield. Searching the sky, I discovered the attackers, a Vee-shaped formation of fifty-four bombers, high up, perhaps twenty thousand feet, heading for home. The war had begun for us."

Word of the Pearl Harbor attack and reports of incoming aircraft reached the operational elements of the 34th Pursuit Squadron at Del Carmen and pilots took off because of the alerts. But the support staff like Tom Gage, working in the squadron offices away from the line, remained ignorant, until learning the news from a short-wave radio news flash, because the generator in their area broke down. As a result, Gage, flabbergasted by the report from one of the cooks, almost simultaneously saw the enemy bombers over Clark Field.

The action at Clark Field lasted only about forty-five minutes but when the Japanese withdrew, nothing useable remained of the best of the American air stations in the Philippines. Not a single plane that had been on the ground could fly. Bomb craters pockmarked the strips. Fires raged in the gutted hangars and buildings. Casualties numbered fifty-five dead and more than a hundred men wounded. (One estimate of losses doubles these statistics.) MacArthur and his people now faced a defense of the Philippines with half of their B-17 arsenal gone, and a similar situation with available fighters. Furthermore, the damage to Clark meant the remainder of the Fortresses would have to operate from Del Monte in Mindanao, nearly a thousand miles south. Longer flying distances meant additional stress on engines and crews, and loss of time for carrying out missions.

What happened at Clark Field was a miniature replica of the disaster at Pearl Harbor. The destruction of Clark Field, however, and the severe loss of lives and first-line aircraft, like the question of who said what to whom when Brereton reported to MacArthur's headquarters in the early hours of the day, generated only a muted controversy. Nothing of the magnitude that convulsed the commanders responsible for the welfare of the Hawaiian military establishment occurred.

Within hours of the disaster, an outraged General Arnold, as chief of the Army Air Forces and Brereton's boss, chewed out the commander of the Far Eastern Air Force, demanding "how in hell" he could have been caught with his bombers down a full nine hours after hearing of what happened at Pearl Harbor. Gen. George C. Marshall, as MacArthur's superior, failed to personally scold his subordinate but soon afterwards remarked to a correspondent,

"I just don't know how MacArthur happened to let his planes get caught on the ground."

The apportionment of blame became confused with other issues. Sutherland swore that word of an impending strike had been sent by the air warning office at Nielson Field to Clark from fifteen to thirty minutes before the blows rained down and that receipt of the message was confirmed. The bomber commander at Clark just as stubbornly insisted he had no inkling of the oncoming enemy.

MacArthur, Sutherland and Brereton participated in a confused, inconclusive roundelay about the presence of the shattered B-17 fleet at Clark. In November MacArthur, says one account, had professed uneasiness about the Fortresses being located within range of marauders from Formosa bases and directed that they be dispersed to the Del Monte field. Brereton, however, said the idea to shift the bombers to Mindanao was his idea. Sutherland insisted that Brereton was ordered to move the B-17s. An incontrovertible fact is that only half the planes were at Del Monte, with the rest scheduled to follow soon. One explanation is that more B-17s were due in the islands and there would not be room to accommodate all at the still-under-construction base. Also, the housing of all Flying Fortresses in the south was never contemplated; even those consigned there were expected to return to Luzon shortly.

The U.S. Air Force in the Philippines fell victim to a variety of ailments, ranging from insufficient money, poor planning, lack of proper equipment and bad judgment, and had no chance against a carefully plotted and executed raid by the enemy.

Early in December, Adm. Thomas Hart had taken advantage of the tens of thousands of square miles of ocean available for dispersal of his fleet and prudently dispatched much of it out of immediate reach of any attack. Only five destroyers—two of which were under repair—and the bulk of his submarines were left in the waters of the Manila Bay area. The remainder of Hart's forces were well south, and once the news of Pearl Harbor reached Hart, he ordered his vessels even further out of Philippine waters, to the neighborhood of the Dutch possession of Borneo.

The first and second days of the war thus passed with no significant consequences to the U.S. Asiatic Fleet. Japanese planes further pummeled air installations on Luzon while mechanical problems aborted two reconnaissance flights by B-17s seeking the requisite intelligence on Formosa.

Maj. Albert Svihra remembered the first attack on the organization's headquarters at Fort McKinley on Tuesday, December 9, at 1:30 A.M. "Colonel Stowell of the Signal Corps, with whom I lived, and I were awakened by the then familiar sound of the air raid siren. This was followed shortly by the sound of droning airplane motors. Although it was moonlight, we could see nothing when we stepped, or I should say rushed, from our quarters. It was difficult to know what to do under such circumstances and about all we could decide on was not to remain in our quarters. So, slipping on our dressing gowns and a pair of slippers, we hurried to try to find shelter in some hole or depression in the ground—for we had heard that this was one method of protection against bursting bombs.

"We had scarcely passed out of the house when we heard several loud explosions, seemingly quite near, if not actually on the Post. Then followed several more, and still later more and more, but at a greater distance. I had slid down the side of a draw just in the rear of the quarters and lay there quietly until I could hear no more explosions. Colonel Stowell had taken cover in a small deep ravine about fifty yards down the road. I knew I was plenty scared and I believe Colonel S. would admit he was also."

Innocence and ignorance had thus persisted even into the first days of the war—men continuing the pajama-robe dress of peace and still untutored in the basic notions of protection against aerial attack.

On December 10 the Japanese savaged the airfields again, but fifty-four bombers focused their attention on the single most important naval station in the Philippines,

Cavite on the south shore of Manila Bay. Unhampered by
U.S. interceptors frantically trying to fend off the assaults
on their airfields, the Japanese planes flew over Cavite at
twenty thousand feet, beyond the range of the puny antiaircraft battery of the installation, and dumped their ordnance.

With deadly accuracy, bombs burst in the navy yards,
blasting the power plant, dispensary, repair shops, warehouses, barracks and radio station. What did not succumb
to high explosives erupted in fires that overwhelmed
the men and damaged apparatus struggling to extinguish
them.

Even before December 8, Admiral Hart had assigned
most of his ships to more southern seas, points well away
from the base in Manila Bay. However, on the day of decision, two destroyers were in the navy yard undergoing repairs and the *John D. Ford*, the four-stacker with William
Mack aboard, hovered nearby, awaiting its annual overhaul. "[When] we received a message from Pearl Harbor,
we immediately activated our explosives systems and
ripped down the awnings and we were all ready. We knew
we weren't going into the yard but we didn't know
what to do until somebody told us, so we were lying off
Cavite."

The ship remained on station and on the morning of
December 10, the crew saw a few Zeros fly by but nothing
happened until noon, Mack recalled. "Then, fifty-four
high-level bombers came over at about ten thousand feet
and made practice runs on the waterfront of the Philippines and the ships in the harbor and on the Cavite naval
yard. They made three dry runs; they were actually unopposed; there were no P-40s anywhere in sight.

"We were sitting there thinking that was going to be a
great show when all our P-40 pilots got away from the
country club and went up there and showed them a thing
or two. But not one P-40 showed anywhere.

"These fifty-four aircraft were bombing first the Philippine waterfront and then Manila and they devastated that.

Then they went around in a sort of triangular circle and devastated the shipyard where the *Pillsbury* and *Perry* were frantically trying to get themselves back together and get out. They [the planes] came across where the *John D. Ford* was [amid merchant ships] and dropped bombs on all of us but we were not hit."

Also undergoing overhaul at Cavite was a pair of submarines, *Sealion* and *Seadragon,* skippered by Comdrs. Dick Voge and Pete Ferrall, respectively, with Norvell Ward as one of Ferrall's junior officers. With their ships tied up alongside one another, the two captains, and some of the crew like Ward, scanned the skies. Ward remembered, "We watched the Jap bomber formation go over at about twenty-two thousand to twenty-five thousand feet, watched them make a practice run from west to east, then turn around and come back and make their first bombing run from east to west. We saw the bombs drop on the pier and other buildings up in the shipyard. We saw them release, we saw them coming down, but we knew on that run that they were going to miss us, just a little bit, and they did." The absence of fighters to interfere or effective ground fire gave the Japanese the leisure to make dry runs before the actual attacks, thereby enabling them to enhance their effectiveness.

"We manned our .50 caliber guns. We manned our three-inch gun, as did the *Sealion,*" said Ward. "Dick Voge turned to Pete Ferrall and said, 'I think we're damn fools staying up here on the bridge.'

"Pete said, 'I agree with you.' Dick cleared his people off the topside and we cleared ours. Voge had all of his go down below into the control room, whereas on the *Seadragon* some of us stayed up in the conning tower. I stayed there and so did Sam Hunter. Diaz, our chief pharmacist's mate, remained up in the conning tower among two or three others. Pete Ferrall went down to the control room.

"On the next run the *Sealion* received two bomb hits, one right on their conning tower and the other in the after engine room. If anyone had been in the conning tower of the *Sealion* they would have been wiped out. The *Sealion* lost three men, I believe, who were in the after engine room when the bomb hit.

"Shrapnel from the *Sealion*'s conning tower went through ours. It took off the back of Sam Hunter's head and shattered Diaz's arm. I was standing there with my hand on Sam's shoulder, and I was fortunate in that I got scraped across the belly by some shrapnel. Sam was killed instantly; Diaz was able to walk to the hospital and I had a superficial wound. There were no other injuries." Although the explosions on the *Sealion* damaged the *Seadragon*, the tender *Canopus* pulled it away from the dock for subsequent repairs.

Lt. John Bulkeley's Torpedo Boat Squadron 3 responded to the air raid warning signal as the enemy approached Cavite and sped out into the comparative safety of Manila Bay. "The admiral sent us a two-hour warning that they were coming—from Formosa and headed on down in our direction across northern Luzon. So we hauled our boats out into the bay. They kept beautiful formations . . . and they came in at about twenty thousand, with their fighters on up above to protect them from ours—only ours didn't show! I kept thinking," says Bulkeley, "wait until those Army pilots leave the officers' club and go after them. We knew we couldn't get appropriations for the Navy; all the money was going into those P-40s. I hadn't heard anything about the destruction of Clark Field and the other air fields."

Bulkeley and the rest of the squadron quickly discovered they were among the targets. "They swung over Manila and began to paste the harbor shipping. It was a beautiful clear day, and I remember the sun made rainbows on the waterspouts of their bombs. They were 150 to 200 feet high and it made a mist screen so dense you could hardly tell what was happening to the ships.

"But then that beautiful Vee pivoted slowly and moved over Cavite—began circling it like a flock of well-disciplined buzzards. They were too high to see the bomb bay doors open, but we could see the stuff drop slowly, picking up speed; only as we watched we found we had troubles of our own. Because five little dive bombers peeled off that formation, one by one, and started straight down for us. When they were down to about fifteen hundred feet, they leveled off and began unloading.

"Of course, we gave our boats full throttle and began circling and twisting, both to dodge the bombs and get a shot at them. Our gunners loved it—it was their first crack at the Japs . . . They'd picked out one plane and were pouring it up into the sky, when we saw the plane wobble, and pretty soon she took off down the bay, weaving unsteadily, smoking, and all at once, two or three miles away, she just wobbled down into the drink with a big splash."

Another PT claimed two more kills. In a brief moment of levity, Bulkeley later received a message from a superior: "Dear Buck: I really think your gang is getting too tough. The latest report is that 'Three dive bombers were seen being chased over the Mariveles Mountains by an MTB.' Don't you think this is carrying the war a bit too far?"

That flicker of humor may have lifted the PT skipper's emotions, but he expressed his dismay at the sight of Cavite after the enemy finally ended its two-hour rampage. "They'd flattened it—there isn't any other word. Here was the only American naval base in the Orient beyond Pearl Harbor pounded into bloody rubbish . . . We began loading in the wounded to take them to Canacao Hospital . . . There was half an inch of blood on the landing platform at Canacao—we could hardly keep on our feet, for blood is as slippery as crude oil—and the aprons of the hospital attendants were so blood-spattered they looked like butchers."

Bulkeley and his crews returned to Cavite prepared to transport more of the injured but Adm. F. W. Rockwell, Hart's deputy, told them to leave before the ammunition magazine blew, taking anything nearby with them. "So we picked up from the gutters and streets a lot of cans of food we knew we would need—they were from the bombed warehouses—stacked them in the boat, and set out."

The scavenging by Bulkeley typified his talent for improvisation and preparation for the unexpected. Although the losses at the Cavite yard included spare parts for his squadron, Bulkeley had squirreled away extra engines in local garages.

After confirmation of the start of hostilities, Lt. Madeline Ullom at Sternberg Hospital says a red-bordered form labeled "Immediate Action" directed the staff to "discharge all patients who can possibly go. A very few helpless patients remained on the wards."

Fox holes were dug on the lawns of the hospital for protection. When air raid sirens wailed several times that first day, the cries of "Hit the dirt!" showed the disadvantages of white uniforms. A warehouse issued fatigues ordinarily worn by men but quickly tailored to appropriate sizes. Ullom and the others received gas masks and helmets.

"Filipino troops and the constabulary were armed and patrolled the streets," says the onetime nurse. "Manila was in blackout. Heavy curtains hung over the windows. Blue paper covered flashlights. Rumors were abundant. Rumors were believed because we could not comprehend that Americans were not capable of almost the impossible."

The impact of war closed in upon the nurses. "Casualties flowed into Sternberg. Huge abdominal gashes, an arm or a leg almost severed, a hunk of buried or protruded shrapnel were common sights. The dead and dying were interspersed among the wounded. Facilities were taxed beyond capacity to adequately and immediately operate and treat the multitude. The waiting section extended to the lawn between the wards and surgery. Patients were lined up side by side, on stretchers and blankets. Big bloody dressings reflected the hues of magnificent poinsettias.

"Hypodermics were injected to take the edge from severe pain. A colored mark on the forehead provided quick reference to determine time of medication. The

Emergency Medical Tag fastened to the top pajama button kept records. Considerate men often implored us to care for a fellow soldier he felt was more critically injured, although he was next in line.

"Chaplains Oliver and Tiffany along with others moved among the casualties to administer the Last Rites, to console the injured. With religious duties completed, they carried litters, acted as messengers. Many former Army nurses, stationed at Sternberg before marriage, hastened to volunteer their services.

"Everyone was on duty, time meant nothing. Many took turns sleeping on the operating tables, on the floor between raids. When the first bombs fell near Sternberg I was so scared I felt petrified. A patient's abdomen had just been opened when an air raid alarm sounded. We continued to operate. Bombs fell on the nearby Pasig River. The thin galvanized roof above surgery rattled. We were so busy that outside sounds seemed far away. After that session, my fears left me."

Admiral Hart, with an eagle-eyed view of the destruction of Cavite, his prime base, from atop the Marsman Building, naval headquarters, lost only one docked submarine but the raid cost the Navy a major source of maintenance and supply, including more than two hundred torpedoes stored at Cavite. Without adequate facilities, with no protection against a Japanese thrust from the air and badly undergunned in any surface encounters, the Navy wrote off the Philippines. Except for the submarines, the six-boat PT squadron and a few PBYs, the Asiatic Fleet abandoned the local waters. Within three days, MacArthur had lost not only two potential offensive weapons; he was bereft of the vital means for any defense of the beaches.

CHAPTER V

THE JAPANESE INVADE

ON THE AFTERNOON of December 8, the badly rattled members of Sam Grashio's 21st Pursuit Squadron regrouped at Nichols Field, minus a number of their planes and pilots, early casualties. Under orders, Dyess gathered the remnants of his flock and led them back to Clark Field where, according to Grashio, he guided them safely down to a field pitted with craters and covered with several inches of dust as fine as flour.

"That night we survivors," recalled Grashio, "still half-dazed, slept in the jungle. When we awoke at dawn, somewhat recovered from the shock of the previous day's disaster, it occurred to someone that we might be caught napping again so we were ordered to take our P-40s up to fifteen thousand feet and get into position ready to attack. When a plane taxied to take-off position, the cloud of dust that rose exceeded in size and density anything I had ever seen prior to the clouds caused by the bombing of the day before. Moreover, the field was full of bomb craters. Thus three-minute intervals were prescribed between takeoffs.

"Even so, there were several accidents. One pilot lost his engine, careened madly into the jungle and was killed. I got airborne without mishap but Bob Clark who followed me, did not allow enough time for the dust to settle, lost his way and crashed blindly into a parked B-17 bomber.

There was a sudden flash of light, a violent explosion and hail of bullets all over the area as flaming gasoline from the plane's ruptured tanks set off the six loaded .50 caliber machine guns it carried. Bob was killed instantly.

"My own promising start was short-lived. At about nine thousand feet, my engine started cutting out and losing power. Down I came, trying desperately to identify the problem and to restrain my panic. Soon the engine cut in again, then went out, then cut in once more. Gradually I gained control of the plane in the sense that I felt reasonably sure I could land, though it was clear I could not maintain flying speed. The sticking point was that there was a certain identification procedure for landing which specified entry corridors. This I would have to ignore if I was to get the plane down at all. So I came in from an unexpected direction. Our antiaircraft batteries, understandably trigger happy after the events of the day before, promptly opened fire on me. Fortunately, their marksmanship had not improved overnight. I got down unscathed."

Mechanics went to work on Grashio's P-40 and that afternoon another pilot took the plane up. The engine quit again, but on this occasion the power failed during takeoff, causing a fatal crash. The earlier flight had landed at an auxiliary field, then moved to a new airdrome on Bataan, leaving Grashio behind. In the chaos of the first weeks of the war, he would not find his squadron for a full month.

For Alva Fitch with a battery of 2.95-inch mountain guns sometimes described as pack artillery, the commotion caused among his troops by the raid at nearby Clark Field on December 8 remained his only glimpse of the war as nearly two uneventful days passed. Having established a bivouac in the jungle a short distance from Stotsensburg, Fitch had posted sentries. Their major problem was panicky survivors from Clark Field who sought refuge.

However, a rumored parachute assault brought a summons for Fitch and his men to protect Stotsenburg. "The Battery looked ridiculous with the guns dug in in front of Post Headquarters, astride the flagpole, shooting towards the hospital. On the morning of the tenth, a flight of twenty-seven bombers raided Stotsenburg without much damage. They bombed the stable line and the utilities. Several cavalry horses were killed or wounded. The ice plant was put out of order. My stables were damaged. Then they flew up the China Sea Trail where my animals were being exercised and strafed them. None of my animals were hit, but my ex-orderly, Macan, was shot in the head. The bullet tore a hole in his helmet and bounced off his skull. He was vastly annoyed as his horses escaped. Macan was taken to the hospital, but returned to the Battery that afternoon in spite of the efforts of the medicos to retain him.

"The parachute alarm was caused by some Americans and some Japs bailing out over near Mt. Arryat. Two of the Japs were brought to Stotsenburg that afternoon. Private Macan tried to kill one of them by way of revenge for his discomfiture of the morning. He was frustrated by Colonel Maher, chief of staff. Macan was somewhat offended by Colonel Maher's treatment of him. He asked me a few minutes later who was going to kill them and when."

Fitch and his pack artillery battery remained in the vicinity of Stotsenburg, protecting headquarters against nonexistent threats to the central Luzon site that for the moment lay well outside any danger of ground attack.

Maj. Philip Fry, reluctant to become an advisor to one of the newly formed, untrained Philippine Army organizations, had seized an opportunity to volunteer his services to the 57th Infantry, the well-established Philippine Scouts regiment that was preparing to move out on December 8. "This decision cost me an immediate promotion to lieutenant colonel but was well worth it. Frank Brokaw was with me and was assigned to the same outfit.

"I spent the first few hours stripping my equipment to the bare essentials. My carrying space was limited to my musette bag and a bedding roll. The CO of the 57th, Col. George Clarke, was visibly pleased to have a few senior officers assigned. The 57th had been badly depleted of senior people by the organization of the Philippine Army.

All they had left were a bunch of youngsters. My rank entitled me to Ted Lilly's job as executive officer but I wanted my own command of combat troops and asked for a battalion. I was assigned the 3rd, Frank Brokaw the 2nd Battalion. We were given guides and staff cars and off we went to locate our new commands.

"The 3rd Battalion position was located in a draw between officers row [housing designed for commanders] and Guadaloupe. The units were badly congested and a beautiful target for the bombing attack I expected in a few minutes. I assembled the officers and informed them of my assumption of command. They were all so young, and a bit dazed by the speed of events.

"We started preparations for a move that night. We had sufficient weapons carriers but needed busses to move the men. I was given thirty-three civilian busses and two Ford sedans for me and my staff. At dusk we started out and it was a terrible nightmare. My orders were changed so many times they had me dizzy. Our convoy of about sixty vehicles was turned around. The roads were jammed; every mile there'd be a traffic jam. On both sides the rice paddies were flooded. There was absolutely no cover of any kind. All officers were on foot, trying to make our way through. We were in a helluva fix and the Philippine defense could have been given a mortal blow that night, but the Nips were busy working our airfields.

"We broke through and headed for San Fernando. Our position was regimental reserve near Florida Blanca. We were the first battalion to arrive and were completely under cover by daylight. Poor George Clarke was there and frantic about the remainder of the regiment. He kept bothering me about them until I suggested he go look for them because we were busy. Not a nice gesture but I was provoked beyond endurance.

"Early on the morning of December 12 I was handed a message that said about a thousand enemy paratroopers had landed behind our lines near Abucay Hacienda. My battalion was ordered to proceed to that place at once. The mission was to destroy or capture the enemy. My admiration of the Scout as a soldier and a fighting man mounted. They were not only ready for battle but eager to show their American officers they could and would beat the best that Japan had to offer."

Fry's command, however, was denied an opportunity to demonstrate its worth, for as Alva Fitch had also discovered, reports of enemy paratroopers were unfounded.

On a map the island of Luzon has the rough shape of a mitten, with the thumb at the left as it narrows towards its southern end. Running down from the northern tip, perhaps 275 miles from the principal city of Manila, extend several rugged mountain ranges that peter out into the central plains just above Manila. An invasion force striking at the fingertips would have a long, difficult line of march toward Manila, particularly in the face of a well-orchestrated defense. However, the space between the thumb and the rest of the glove approximates the Lingayen Gulf, an indentation from which a network of highways and roads leading to Manila provides a much more attractive route for conquest.

Gen. Jonathan Wainwright commanded the forces assigned to wall off all of northern Luzon. Under him served three Philippine Army divisions, a Philippine Scout cavalry regiment and infantry battalion, a single battery of field artillery—Alva Fitch's outfit—and a supply unit. On paper it was a formidable number of soldiers but the territory stretched over thousands of square miles including mile upon mile of beach. The steep mountains, thick vegetation and lack of many suitable roads restricted communication and movement.

Far more devastating, Wainwright's army was little more than a paper organization. The Filipino divisions expected to halt any enemy incursions were all of the ilk described by Glen Townsend and Clifford Bluemel: reservists who had been summoned to duty in September, most of whom had little instruction or learning in the art of war. With War Plan Orange supplanted by Rainbow Five, the ammunition, foodstuffs and other necessities for combat had to be moved to sites accessible to the defenders spread around Luzon. With a paucity of transportation facilities, the problems of supply storage loomed ever greater.

Glen Townsend as a commander in the 11th Division had begun work on his beach defenses immediately after he received word of war. "We had no materials but we chopped down the coconut trees and the Mayor of Dagupan sent a thousand civilians into the surrounding countryside to strip barbed wire from the fences. Within two or three days we had commandered fifty trucks and motor vehicles with civilian drivers."

After grabbing a pair of inconsequential tufts of land in the ocean, the Babuyan Islands north of Luzon, the Japanese came ashore in quest of two ports: Aparri, located at the tip of what would be a ring finger in the Luzon mitten; and Vigan, along the western shore.

So thin were Wainwright's forces that he had only a single company of infantry in the vicinity of Aparri and not a man at Vigan. The initial enemy troops splashing ashore at Aparri probably numbered about two thousand. To the shocked eye of the U.S. officer in charge, however, the invaders seemed five times as great. In any event, since he had less than two hundred untrained and ill-equipped defenders he ordered a retreat without the exchange of a single shot.

From Del Carmen, Lieutenant Marrett led the 34th Squadron on a mission. "After takeoff," recalls Gage, "there were conflicting orders to change the destination." Marrett chose to intercept at Vigan rather than Aparri. Deteriorated engines forced nine of the original sixteen P-35s scrambled to turn back. P-40s, which had preceded the 34th to the area, had been able to work over the landing forces with fragmentation bombs and strafing runs and any Japanese air cover had left the area.

With only pairs of .30 and .50 caliber machine guns, the remnants of the 34th dove on the beachhead, the barges and some larger vessels near the shore. Marrett led the attack, picking out for himself a ten-thousand-ton vessel. He made several passes at it and then bore in at almost masthead height while surrounding cruisers and destroyers threw shells at him. Just as the squadron commander began to pull out of his dive, his target blew up; he apparently had ignited an ammunition cache. The blast ripped away the wing of Marrett's plane. Other pilots saw his plane crash into the sea even as debris from his victim started to splash down into the water.

"The squadron came back to Del Carmen just before noon," says Gage. "I remember one of the pilots remarking how machine gunning the troops landing on the beach made him sick to his stomach because of the slaughter."

But there was neither time to mourn Marrett nor listen to war stories at Del Carmen. "We had some P-40s there fueling up. As the P-35s came in and landed, some Zeros came right in with them. They proceeded to beat up the base camp and shoot up the line. Myself, my two clerks Robert Reynolds and Dermott Toycen, along with Lieutenant Jennings and several pilot officers ran over the hill away from the line into the edge of the woods and lay down flat. We couldn't see but we could sure hear. Spent bullets buzzed around. One even clanged off the edge of Reynolds's tin helmet.

"The attack only lasted a few minutes but it seemed like hours. After the enemy left, it was real quiet—then we could hear the flames crackling. We could see a P-40 hooked to a gasoline truck, both on fire. One of our men had been caught in the open and took cover under the gasoline tank truck. After tracers set that on fire, he slipped under the P-40. When the fire traveled down the hose and set the plane on fire, he just got up and strolled away, ignoring the strafing completely.

"T. Sgt. John H. Miller reportedly took one of the Lewis guns and cradling it in his arms walked out on the runway and fired it up until it jammed. Four of the Lewis guns jammed on their first burst. The sixth gun, the one

Arthur Campbell had, gave a very good account. Arthur fired all three of his drums. [Campbell, ordinarily a supply clerk, had taken the precaution to clean each bullet in his drums.] He evidently irritated one of the Zero pilots enough to cause him to stand his plane on end in attempting to silence the Lewis. When Campbell ran out of ammo, the line armorer Sgt. Raymond Mullins, ran to Campbell's pit with a couple of drums of ammo. The Lewis finally quit firing because the barrel was too hot.

"T. Sgt. Bill Cott and his crew were on duty in the radio shack. It was partly underground and they were calling May Day to anyone who could hear and come. I understand there were one or two P-40s in the melee. Someone knocked down one Zero that day. We don't know who for sure. But on this day all the propaganda rubbish about the inferior Japanese material went down the drain. Those fuel wing tanks dropped by the Zeros were far better than ours."

With the Filipino infantry hastily backing off, the one blow aimed at the incoming troops near Aparri came from the sky, as remnants of the Air Corps in the shape of a pair of B-17s attacked the landing fleet. Capt. Colin Kelly of the 14th Bombardment Group piloted one of the two planes. Kelly had been expected to serve as one of the cheerleaders during the Army-Navy Game celebration at the officers club but with the shindig canceled, he had spent the first days of the war at the Del Monte field on Mindanao, having hurriedly fled Clark Field for dispersal purposes on December 6.

With Clark patched up enough to service B-17s, Kelly and several others arrived on the morning of December 10 to carry out missions against an aircraft carrier reported in the neighborhood. In the air heading north, Kelly, toting three six-hundred-pound bombs in his racks, became separated from the others.

From almost four miles up, the crew gazed down on the enemy ships, some of which were blasting away at the coastline while others were ferrying in men and supplies. Kelly ignored these targets for the moment and searched for the aircraft carrier but although the hunt went almost to Formosa, the target was never spotted. Returning towards Luzon, the airmen picked out the biggest vessel off the coast, what they believed was a battleship.

Bombardier Meyer Levin, a corporal in an Air Corps era when the job did not carry a commission, tracked the ship and at the appropriate moment released the bombs. To the men in the Flying Fortress, it appeared as if they scored two near misses and one direct hit. Kelly headed for home but not before his navigator, Lt. Joe Bean noticed a half dozen Japanese fighter planes take off from far below at the Aparri airfield, which the enemy now possessed.

Kelly's B-17 was coming down through the clouds, preparing for touchdown at Clark now in sight, when suddenly the navigator's dome exploded into pieces and the instrument panel shattered. A burst of fire beheaded the radio operator stationed at the left waist gun and wounded another gunner. The fighters observed by Bean had tracked them more than a hundred miles and now closed in for the kill. Bullets ripped into the left wing and flames enveloped the plane; the fuel tanks of the earliest operational B-17s were not self-sealing.

Kelly consulted the crew on the damage, then ordered them to bail out. Levin and Bean frantically worked to pry open the bottom escape hatch whose pins were corroded. Levin went first and then Bean, who saw co-pilot Lt. Donald Robins moving towards the top escape hatch. Then the aircraft disintegrated with a mighty blast. Dangling from his parachute, Bean saw four others swinging in the air. Still not finished, the enemy fighters swept by to strafe the men floating down. A bullet chipped Bean's ankle but the others escaped unscathed.

Search teams from Clark found the badly burned co-pilot who had been blasted free of the ship when it exploded. Somehow he managed to yank his ripcord and reached the ground alive. But Kelly's body was discovered amid the wreckage. He was the first graduate of the USMA to die in the defense of the Philippines.

Irvin Alexander said, "The saddest duty we had at Stotsenburg was to bury our friend Colin Kelly. He was a wonderful youngster who would have been a top-notch combat commander in the Air Corps if he had lived a little longer. Everyone who knew him had great faith in him and affection for him."

Alexander claimed to have spoken with co-pilot Robins, who explained that the oxygen tank exploded, blowing Kelly out of the escape hatch. With the ship in a tight spin, Robins said he was held fast by centrifugal force until a sudden, unexpected lurch allowed him to escape.

With only defeats to announce, the authorities quickly proclaimed Kelly a hero, awarded him a posthumous Distinguished Service Cross for allegedly sinking the battleship *Haruna*. Post–WW II research revealed that no battleship ever was in the area nor did the attack sink any Japanese ship. Samuel Marrett, who probably struck a more effective blow for the cause and with greater disregard for his own survival, received a Distinguished Service Cross but none of the fame and glory accorded Kelly. Marrett, as a mustang or former enlisted man elevated to the ranks of the commissioned, struck his chief clerk, Tom Gage, as a "bitter" man. For reasons of personality, background or misperception of the events, the publicity focused on the West Pointer.

The Air Corps had succeeded in disrupting the beachhead at Vigan with the early morning raid by five B-17s accompanied by P-40s and then the 34th's P-35s. The attack damaged and beached a pair of transports, sank a minesweeper, inflicted some damage to a pair of warships and chewed up a number of soldiers. But it was the last well-choreographed effort by the FEAF as successive waves of enemy planes reduced U.S. air operations in the Philippines to spasms of little import. The run at Del Carmen had destroyed twelve P-35s and damaged the remaining six so badly that the 34th to all intents and purposes was grounded. Conditions were almost as bad with other squadrons. When night fell on December 10, the defenders could count on only thirty airworthy fighter planes.

Americans in Manila began to appreciate the situation. On duty at Sternberg General Hospital, Madeline Ullom recalled, "A large formation of silver planes were silhouetted against the blue sky. The rumor must surely be true. We smiled. Reinforcements had arrived. Bombs suddenly began to drop on the nearby Pasig River. Shell windows fell from the eye-ear-nose-throat clinic. Crystal chandeliers in the officers' ward dining room swayed from the ceiling. The heavy lead crystal was never expected to move. The sound of the bombs hurt our eardrums. The feeling pierced our hearts. The truth was apparent. We were soon to remark, 'If you see one plane flying in formation, you know it is ours.'"

Despite what amounted to a pinprick for the Japanese off Vigan, enemy fighters from the former U.S. airfield at Aparri demonstrated the success of the invasion force. The defenders were confused and already back on their heels. One American officer with the 21st Philippine Division said that after some dark shapes hovered near the mouth of the Agno River, a field artillery unit opened up. "It was like dropping a match in a warehouse of Fourth of July fireworks," he remarked. "Instantly Lingayen Gulf was ablaze. As far as the eye could see the flashes of artillery, shell-bursts, tracer machine gun bullets and small arms . . . Thousands of shadows were killed that night." Townsend recalled, "On the night of December 10, I heard a fusillade of rifle and machine gun fire on a nearby river."

In the morning, the only evidence of anything amiss was a single life preserver, which may not even have been Japanese. Neither sunken vessels nor corpses of blasted bodies were found. "Later," Townsend, "we read in the Manila papers that the Japs had landed at Lingayen but after a terrific battle they had been annihilated." The erroneous report of the victory stemmed from a Filipino commander who insisted his forces repulsed an enemy landing. Interrogations and documents after the war indicated a single enemy motor boat had ventured into the area on a reconnaissance mission.

Alva Fitch noted, "In general, things were fairly quiet. A tremendous amount of false information continued to come by telegraph. This kept the staff in turmoil. Apparently there were a lot of Fifth Columnists in the telegraph system. It was so bad that all information and even orders received by telegraph were suspect and had to be verified.

"A few days after the landing at Vigan, we received a telegram from a 'Colonel Jones' of the Constabulary saying that a column of forty thousand Japs with some mechanized equipment was marching south from Vigan to Dameras. It was fairly routine to hear of fictitious landings in force, of parachute landings and of large Jap convoys. The telegraph service became so unreliable that eventually motor or airplane couriers were used for delivery of most important orders."

The confusion created by poor communications, misinformation and unwillingness to digest bad news affected MacArthur's judgment. Even after the war was over he would write in his *Reminiscences:* "On December 10 . . . twelve transports with naval escorts landed troops at Aparri in the north and Vigan on the west coast. Our air force attacked these transports, sinking four and damaging three others. [Actually, the foe lost only three of its troop and cargo carriers.] . . . At the end of the first week of war there had been many widely scattered actions, but the all-out attack had not yet come. The enemy had carried out fourteen major air raids, but paid dearly in the loss of transports, planes and troops, and at least two major warships damaged. He had attempted a landing in the Lingayen area, but was repulsed with severe loss by a Philippine Army division. At Aparri, Vigan and Legaspi there had been only local activity."

In fact, the Japanese at Clark Field lost only seven fight-

ers compared with the horrendous damage done to American planes, personnel and installations. Americans were
credited with four kills at Del Carmen but lost an entire
squadron plus several P-40s. Japanese casualties at other
airfields and at Cavite and other Navy bases were similarly
negligible when weighed against the damage inflicted. The
Lingayen defeat was sheer fantasy and the "local activity"
at the three Luzon sites amounted to a firm foothold on
the island. As General Wainwright put it, "The rat was in
the house."

What was true was that the main body of MacArthur's
army had yet to engage the enemy. The Japanese units,
under Lt. Gen. Masaharu Homma, 14th Army commander, rapidly trekked south in a strategy designed to
pinch off northern Luzon. The objective of the invaders
from the west was control of Lingayen Gulf. With that site
in their hands, the invaders could land large numbers of
troops and supplies for a swift dash to Manila. Meanwhile,
another unopposed landing on the southeastern coast at
Legaspi on December 12 confronted the American-led
forces with an enemy knocking on the back door.

The booty for the Japanese included an air strip near
Legaspi. Three B-17s operating from the Del Monte base
attempted to attack the occupants only to discover themselves overmatched against the now resident Japanese
fighter planes. Only one Flying Fortress managed to escape
unscathed to its home base; the two others crash landed.
Further operations by the big bombers from Del Monte
were in jeopardy. MacArthur agreed with Brereton's decision to move the remainder of the B-17s to Darwin, Australia. They flew off on December 15, four days before the
opening round of a series of heavy assaults from the air
upon Del Monte.

Whether or not MacArthur at the time of the first Japanese landings truly believed he still had a shot at denying
the enemy the Philippines, he realized early on the shaki-
ness of such an ambitious strategy. On December 12 he
sent word to Philippine president Quezon to ready himself

for movement to Corregidor on four hours' notice. "Startled" by the ominous import of this message, Quezon conferred with the military leader that night. MacArthur advised the Filipino official there was no immediate concern but only that he was "preparing for the worst in case the Japanese should land in great force at different places." Under these circumstances, explained MacArthur, effective strategy would require a concentration of Filipino-American units and the site would be Bataan.

And to the horror of Quezon, MacArthur continued that the plan would require the shift of his headquarters, the High Commissioner's office and the Commonwealth government to the rocky fastness of Corregidor. In such event he would declare Manila an open city.

An incredulous Quezon asked, "Do you mean, General, that tomorrow you will declare Manila an open city and that some time during the day we shall have to go to Corregidor?" MacArthur emphatically reassured him that this was only a contingency strategy and he merely wanted the president to be aware of the possibility.

At the start of hostilities, Wainwright assigned Clifford Bluemel and the 31st Philippine Army Division responsibility for defending the South China Sea coastline near Zambales, perhaps sixty miles south of the Lingayen Gulf landing zones. Bluemel, a choleric type, tried to cope with the almost total unreadiness of his men. "I remembered that when the Germans started a war, the first things that they bombed were airfields and barracks. I realized I had to get that Philippine division out of the barracks because if they started bombing them, I would never get the darned division together again since it was untrained rabble. I sent them all out, spread them all along the beach."

Nearly a week of war had passed when Bluemel discovered that his latest additions, the artillerymen, who had undergone their basic training, had never fired their 75 mm guns. Under his instructions, each battery expended two rounds per gun because that was all he felt he could spare.

Bluemel, outraged by the responsibilities thrust upon an "untrained rabble," was equally vehement in his disparagement of the revised Rainbow Five plan that expected units such as his to repulse the Japanese. "MacArthur and Sutherland were trying to draw up a plan in a few days after discarding the one that had been worked on for twenty-five years, which to me, shows inability to command." He criticized his commander for adopting a strategy that ignored the peculiarities of terrain and roads. "MacArthur practically had no transportation for us. He was too busy thinking about meeting them at the beaches. The artillery was old wooden-wheeled artillery and I had nothing to tow it. We had to portage it. I sent a young officer to a mine and he confiscated some fifty trucks and brought them to me. We pushed the guns up on the trucks to portage them. We couldn't tow them because the wooden wheels would fall off if we went at truck speed. We could not even have run three or four miles an hour with them, the way we moved horse-drawn artillery. It's something MacArthur should have known."

The 31st Division area included the now destroyed airfield at Iba. According to Bluemel, some of the American enlisted men "took to the hills" after the air raids blasted their base. "A Filipino came to me with a note from them, 'We won't come in unless we get a note that it's all right.' They thought the Japs had landed." A hand-written message from Bluemel convinced the fugitives that Americans still controlled the territory and they returned.

Bluemel had the habit of riding his horse up and down his zone during the night. He said, "I came in from reconnaissance on the morning of December 24. I had a Filipino officer, Pastor Martelino, who was a graduate of West Point and a very intelligent man, who said, 'There's a message in code.' But I had no code; we had no code book. I got on the phone and found somebody who had a code book. He sent it out to me, and I translated it: 'You will move your division to Bataan immediately.' I started the movement with buses of the Trytran Bus Company which I confiscated. A fellow named [Raymón] Magsaysay was the manager; he later became president of the Philippines. Magsaysay went with me in charge of the buses."

As early as December 19, signs of a reversion to War Plan Orange—retreat to Bataan in hopes of preserving a presence until relief could arrive—showed up in the deployment of the Filipino-American forces. The 26th Cavalry, a Philippine Scout regiment, had traveled north to meet the invaders and Fitch's guns accompanied them. But while in bivouac Fitch received word directing his battery to Bataan. The artillerymen marched south for three nights where Fitch heard the disquieting news to continue their retreat.

"The Philippine Army was withdrawing into Bataan. General Bluemel's division from Zambales was coming in the night. Time was of the essence. The only road would be no place for mules [which pulled the pack artillery pieces] with a division of the Philippine Army using it.

"There was no other course but to go on to Balanga in the daylight. This was no pleasant prospect. To move my mules down a narrow road, entirely flanked by impassable fish ponds, in daylight through heavy traffic, and with Jap planes swarming overhead would not be pleasant.

"The Battery had marched all night with full war loads and the men and animals were dead tired. We began arriving about dusk. The animals were strung out at long intervals. I rode my horse off the road onto a grass plot in the public square to watch them pass. A couple of policemen came rushing out of the Municipio to tell me of my outrage and to save their lawn. I hadn't the heart to tell them their damned town would be blown off the map in a few hours. We made bivouac that night in a semi-exhausted state. We had marched from Tarlac in three days, and more than thirty-five miles in twenty-four hours.

"We had no hay but commandeered a stack of palay

[local fodder] to feed the animals. Early the next morning, the Governor of Bataan and the owner of the palay paid me a call. After due formalities, His Excellency explained he was concerned for the financial interest of his constituent. I wrote them a receipt for twenty dollars' worth of palay. When they saw the amount, they wanted it in two receipts of ten dollars each. I tore it in two, gave each of them half."

Fitch said that several nights after he reached Bataan a commotion that included artillery fire awakened him to a possible surprise assault. With an associate he embarked on a reconnaissance and to his relief discovered his fears were groundless. But en route to his bivouac area he stalled in a traffic jam. "While we were waiting," reported Fitch, "a man stuck his pistol against my ear and told us to get moving or he would kill us. It was General Bluemel. He had been reduced to a state of semi-insanity by the task of moving his division from Zambales to Bataan, and was trying to clear the traffic jam before daylight. We helped him and got home before morning."

Philip Fry of the 3rd Battalion, the 57th Infantry, also initially moved to block the Japanese advance. "On December 19, because of probable landings at Subic Bay near Olongapo, orders came to move there and defend the Zig Zag Trail in that sector. This being a daylight move, I instructed all units to maintain thirty seconds between any vehicles to avoid any tendencies to close up on straight stretches."

The troops reached their designated spot and started to dig in and prepare defenses covering the trails. But as Fry and the others in the outfit readied themselves for battle, they received new instructions and once again shifted their location. By the end of December, the 57th had withdrawn to Bataan, to occupy the right flank of defenses from Matabang on the shore of Manila Bay and behind the Balantay River extending westward for about three-quarters of a mile.

When Fitch finally bedded down on Bataan it was

Christmas Eve and for Fry it was several days later but the
enemy pressure had begun to build up just as they started
to travel south. The main elements for the offensive, carefully shepherded by strong navy forces, debarked at points
along the Lingayen Gulf on December 22 and at Lamon
Bay, two hundred miles southeast of the Lingayen incursions, on December 24.

There were no significant Air Corps resources available
to ravage the Japanese fleet in the Lingayen Gulf, but the
U.S. Navy still had one seemingly powerful weapon, its
flotilla of submarines. Admiral Hart, responding to a plea
for naval assistance, sent three subs to strike the enemy
ships.

The *Stingray,* the *Saury* and the *Salmon* all slipped in
among the covey of Japanese troop ships, freighters, landing craft and warships engaged in debarking men. The invasion force was already in the shoal waters near the shore
by the time the three subs got into position to make their
forays. But they sank only two vessels.

Charles Adair, a member of Admiral Hart's staff, remarked, "These people would fire. They could see the torpedoes and knew where they were going. They could hear
them hit, bounce off, and nothing happened. Then they
would get a terrific depth-charging, for the Japanese
destroyers would chase them, drive them under and depth-
charge them. The Lingayen Gulf is not very deep anyway—in some places about 120 feet or even less.

"When they came back and Admiral Hart wanted to
know what happened they'd tell him they hadn't sunk anything. He would want to know why and they were unable
to tell him. General MacArthur would want to know why
the submarines hadn't been able to sink any ships with the
torpedoes and I'm sure Admiral Hart had no answers to
give him. He couldn't believe that such well-trained submarine officers could be so ineffective. That went on until
morale was very low so far as the submariners were concerned."

How many of the invaders at Lingayen and elsewhere

were framed in the periscopes and had torpedoes fired at them is unknown. But the consistently disappointing results underscored a miserable failure in Navy weaponry caused by an effort to conserve funds. The standard Mark-14 torpedo, costing ten thousand dollars each, was considered so expensive that it had never been tested with a live warhead. Instead, during peacetime, submarines and destroyers fired missiles armed with water-filled warheads. Once the war began the Mark-14, more often than not, failed to hit the target or to explode when it managed to home in. Not until 1943 would Bureau of Ordnance experts finally correct problems with the depth mechanism and exploders.

The ill-prepared pair of Philippine Army divisions assigned to block entry at Lingayen folded quickly, although an occasional unit fought bravely and inflicted casualties before being overrun. The Filipino soldiers streamed backward in an ever-deepening rout. The chief resistance to the enemy advance came from Fitch's former associates, the 26th Cavalry, Philippine Scouts, mounted on horses, "a true cavalry delaying action, fit to make a man's heart sing," commented their overall commander and ex-cavalryman, Jonathan Wainwright.

But within two days of the Japanese landing, as Christmas Eve approached, the 14th Army under Homma grasped the best roads in the islands, daggers pointed at Manila. Although Homma had about 43,000 men come ashore at the Lingayen sites, MacArthur informed his boss General Marshall that the invaders numbered from 80,000 to 100,000 and he could only field about 40,000, "in units partially equipped." In fact, MacArthur actually had probably double the number of men in uniform commanded by Homma. The general himself traveled by Packard automobile into Luzon to confer with Wainwright, who now asked permission to retreat. A message from Gen. George Parker, the Southern Luzon commander, reported 10,000 Japanese from the Lamon Bay landings were advancing on Manila. When all this had been translated onto a map, MacArthur read its import: his Luzon forces were in imminent danger of being trapped in a standard pincers strategy.

Quezon's worst fears took tangible shape. On December 23, the USAFFE commander advised all his subordinates that "WPO is in effect." On the afternoon before Christmas he drafted an announcement: "In order to spare Manila from any possible air or ground attacks, consideration is being given by military authorities to declaring Manila an open city, as was done in the case of Paris, Brussels and Rome during this war."

CHAPTER VI

RETREAT

ON DECEMBER 23, the day MacArthur informed his subordinates of his decision to yield Manila, Betsy McCreary and the others at the Brent School also accepted the harsh truth of their situation. "All the teachers and students were summoned to the Pines Hotel in town. There we learned that whatever army we'd had in Baguio had pulled out. The city was undefended and the Japanese were in the foothills. I knew it was a possibility, but I didn't know it in the sense of *accepting* it until it actually occurred. My thinking was this war can end without my ever having seen either an American or Japanese soldier. We're up in this little Shangri-La and the war may just swirl around the lowlands.

"The radio kept assuring us that despite being outnumbered, our boys were on their way. Almost to the last day we heard reinforcements were coming. Among the adults, the count on how long the war might last had gone up to six weeks.

"At the gathering of Baguio's American and Allied civilians grew the idea of self-internment. Rather than having individuals rousted from their homes at gunpoint, we would meet with a commanding officer as a group. Baguio had about five hundred European and American civilians and with our dormitories practically empty, a group of them moved into the boys, girls and toddlers dorms.

"I was bored, restless and I said to a schoolmate, Margaret Morris, 'Let's go for a walk.' We went down the hill from the school office near the playing field and just as we got there, coming up the road was a yellow taxicab with a Filipino driver and it roared past us to the school. We raced behind it.

"Then the four or five soldiers who were jammed into the cab got out. They were small and wore these dirty, baggy uniforms and they looked bewildered. We were incredulous. These were the conquerors? The victors? We just couldn't believe it.

"There were two Japanese civilians and one of them asked for cars. He asked if they could *borrow* cars that would be returned. Some of the townsmen gave their car keys and the Japanese who could drive took them. Of course the owners never saw them again."

Ignorance of the true state of affairs might be expected among schoolgirls like McCreary but information was frequently as difficult to obtain in high military circles. Until the very last days of the crisis before the shooting war commenced, contact between the Army and the Navy had been tenuous. Robert Lee Dennison, whom Admiral Hart deputized as his liaison with MacArthur, recalled, "There was no personal contact between Hart's staff, MacArthur's staff or MacArthur and Hart. MacArthur didn't know what we were up to in terms of ship movements or what our war plans were, nor did we know what his were. That was the purpose of my being in this particular capacity. It wasn't much use until the war did break out."

According to Dennison, the lack of coordination and communication was not because MacArthur was unwilling to share information. "MacArthur was completely open with me. When I first reported to him he called his staff in and instructed them in my presence that they were to show me all the dispatches that were exchanged between themselves and Washington and he intended to do the same.

And this was whether I asked for [the material] or not, because how could I ask for something I didn't know existed. I was appalled to find Willougby [Col. Charles], the G-2, telling the G-2 in the War Department things that were completely different from what MacArthur was telling the chief of staff of the Army. There was no communications intra-staff worth a damn."

Apart from the contribution internal disarray made to confusion and ignorance, Dennison said that MacArthur suffered from an "elementary understanding of the use of a navy. He, like a good many Army officers of his time, looked on the Navy as a seaward extension of the Army's flank and that's all." As a consequence, MacArthur never seemed to feel it necessary to consult with his opposite numbers about a strategy or policy decision but acted as if the Navy, although independently commanded, should simply follow his lead.

According to Dennison, he went to MacArthur's headquarters one morning around nine. "He said, 'Before I talk with you, I want you to hear what I'm going to tell my staff.' He called them in and he said, 'Gentlemen, I'm going to declare Manila an open city as of midnight tonight.' "

Dennison claimed, "This was the first anybody had ever heard of it. After he [finished] I said, 'May I go back and talk to Admiral Hart?'—which I did. Hart didn't usually show much emotion but he said, 'What!' Then he got up out of his chair and said, 'Sit down and write that down!' I wrote a simple sentence, 'At 9:10 this morning, General MacArthur told me,' and so on.

"Hart read it and still couldn't believe it, because he'd been making preparations to operate out of Manila. They'd moved the submarine tender *Canopus* alongside the sea wall in the port district. We'd taken off warheads, torpedo exploders and distributed them all over that general area so they wouldn't be concentrated in one place and put camouflage over the tender. She was in shoal water so that if hit she wouldn't submerge. We were planning on

continuing submarine operations. We had barges of fuel oil
all around the Manila area and all kinds of supplies which
we couldn't possibly get out. We needed more than a few
hours, which meant we couldn't back up this concept of an
open city because we had to have those supplies . . . It
was an example of complete lack of consultation or accord
between two senior commanders—MacArthur didn't comprehend what this would mean to us."

Hart now polled his staff—or what was left since a considerable number had sailed with much of the fleet to the
temporarily safer area near Java. His question was whether
he should remain in the Philippines. Dennison remarked,
"We all knew damned well that what we said didn't make
any difference. We told him he wasn't serving any useful
purpose there. He'd sent his flagship down and he was
based ashore. We didn't have any ships except three destroyers I think and some submarines."

Indeed, without Manila and its facilities there was no
place from which the Navy could effectively operate in the
Philippines. Hart left aboard the submarine *Shark*, turning
over command of those Asiatic Fleet forces still in the Philippines to Adm. Francis Rockwell.

The miasma of disorder that afflicted MacArthur's staff
and its relationships with other organizations marked the
Navy as well. Dennison, on instructions from Hart, traveled to Corregidor, the new headquarters for the American
defense, to meet with Rockwell. "Hart, typically, hadn't
briefed Rockwell on what his war plans were, what his
thoughts were. When I put Hart aboard the *Shark* he told
me the gates to the south were closed, the Japanese fleet is
there; we can't get any more ships out. This was just stupid. The destroyers didn't have any torpedoes, they were
running short of fuel oil and they had to get out, or sit
there and have everybody killed. I told Rockwell I didn't
agree with Hart and why. And we did get the ships out."

Near chaos developed with the designation of Manila as
an open city—the concept of an open city meaning that
the defenders would not use Manila for military purposes

and therefore the enemy should not bomb or attack it. Thousands of soldiers with their weapons in "retrograde maneuvers" or retreating to Bataan could only reach there by passage through Manila over a number of days after MacArthur's proclamation.

Submariner S.S. Murray, after receipt of the word on Manila's status, recalled returning to the Army-Navy Club where he spent his few off-duty hours. "I went down in the bar of the Club and met the Army officers coming in from the east coast of Luzon. Their troops were just arriving in the outskirts of Manila and they had until midnight that night to start moving by foot to Bataan. They were supposed to be there the next night [a distance of perhaps sixty miles].

"They had been on a forced march ever since the Japanese had landed on the east coast and I've never seen such a bitter, frustrated crowd in my life. Most of them were weeping because they said, 'They wouldn't even let us shoot once at the Japs and we had twice as many troops as they had.'" The laments notwithstanding, MacArthur's strategy recognized that the Southern Luzon Force could not have remained viable once the Northern Army was overwhelmed, even though the terrain may have favored the defense.

"The next day, being Christmas," said Murray, "we were getting our plans ready for leaving and thought we would celebrate and have Christmas dinner. The YMCA said they would give us all Christmas dinner, turkey with all the trimmings and cream of celery soup. We said we'd like it at ten o'clock. The Japs have a way of coming over at eleven.

"We had just started in on our soup when the air raid warnings came. The Japs were already almost on us. We made a dive for any shelter, taking along our soup, since the turkey was already in some platters that we hurriedly covered up with some garbage cans and other things.

"One bomb landed at the front door, one at the back door and one on each side. We were under about four inches of concrete flooring and it blew dust all over us. We knew they were heading for that building because Tokyo Rose had already announced where our headquarters were. Our soup was just filled with concrete, cement and dirt. Our turkey was completely embedded, so we got no Christmas dinner.

"We finished packing up and about 4:30 a Filipino PT boat took us to Corregidor. We moved into the place that Submarines Asiatic and Commander Wilkes had arranged several months before to be a good, final standout for the submarines and where we had spare parts and quite a bit of dried food stored."

For many in Manila there was neither an opportunity nor a real choice of evacuation. Mary Rose Harrington, the Navy nurse posted to the medical facility near Cavite, had left that area. "It was too vulnerable out there. They made arrangements for us to work at several places in Manila. They set up a main operating center at the Jai Alai palace and took over several schools. Mary Chapman and I set up at one of the schools where we had a few patients. On December 23, the Army doctors and nurses told us they had orders to move to Bataan. We were told we could do whatever we wanted. We had no orders.

"The saddest of days was when the Army left and Manila was declared an open city. We got bombed but they hit mostly bodegas and ships on the waterfront. The Red Cross offered to send our wounded by boat to the southern islands. Someone screwed up; the corpsmen and ambulances moved only Army patients." Without the means or direction to flee, the Navy nurses awaited the conquering army.

Nurse Madeline Ullom, as a lieutenant in the U.S. Army, saw a number of her sorority receive orders to join the defenders on Bataan. The first contingent of twenty-four Army, one Navy and twenty-five Filipino nurses left in a twelve-bus motor caravan to set up shop at Hospital Number One at Limay.

"The drivers waited about ten minutes between every

departure to provide a greater safety factor and to try to dispel the convoy idea. Many stops were necessary to seek roadside shelter from the planes which bombed and strafed most of the day."

A second batch of twenty-five nurses embarked on Christmas night to sail for Corregidor and another group boarded a boat that evening for a trip to Mariveles on the southwestern tip of Bataan. Successive shipments ferried the remainder of the Army and Filipino medics to Corregidor and Bataan. The water voyage was as perilous as that by land, with enemy bombers overhead and through minefields laid by the Navy.

The authorities, however, ordered Ullom and some colleagues to stay in the city to treat wounded. "Manila was declared an Open City," she remembered. "The American flag was not hoisted to the pole above Sternberg General Hospital's entrance. A desolate, helpless and unrealistic sensation gripped me. So many of my close friends departed. Officers no longer carried arms. Japanese prisoners were released. Lights of the city shone at night, although not as extensively as before the first week in December."

But on December 29, she received word that she and the others were to prepare for evacuation. "Surgery was quiet. I packed some instruments which I knew were the only ones in the department. I went to bed early. After midnight, Josie Nesbit [one of the senior staff] awakened me. She whispered to come quietly. I slipped into the fatigues, gave a parting glance to the mementos on the dresser, to the dresses hanging in the closet, slung the gas mask and helmet with the musette bag on my shoulder to tiptoe down the stairs.

"Some tanks rolled by the quarters. We moved to the door to better see them. Hope continued to exist. Josie cautioned us to keep back from the porch in the darkness. We were not certain whose tanks were rolling along Arrocerras Street."

Ullom got into a field ambulance for a vastly different ride than the one she so happily described as part of her arrival pleasures. The driver skirted huge bomb craters as the vehicle, without headlights, bumped along the pitted roadway to the port area. "Ships were blazing in the Bay. Buildings were burning along the waterfront. Structures of jagged concrete still were visible. Heaps of wreckage and crumbled ruins were everywhere. The sky was more vivid towards Cavite than the spectacular and vivid sunsets we often watched from Dewey Boulevard. Loud blasts punctured the quiet. A stretching flame, an exploding substance colored and streaked the horizon."

As the inter-island steamer *Don Esteban* left the pier, Japanese planes hovered in the sky before bombing and shooting up the port area. Ullom saw the pier on which she had stood only shortly before now a blazing mass. With dawn, the *Don Esteban* increased its speed and lessened the danger of blindly colliding with a mine. After a "big, delicious breakfast," the steamer docked at Corregidor.

Ullom felt secure again. She remarks, "The Rock, the Eternal Rock, were the terms for the fortification. Phrases of conversation mysteriously linked its features to an unconquerable entity."

On Christmas Eve, the *Don Esteban*'s passenger list was substantially more imposing than a collection of medical personnel. When MacArthur abandoned Rainbow Five and reverted to War Plan Orange he moved his headquarters to the Rock and the office opened for business on Christmas Day. "Manila," said MacArthur, "because of the previous evacuation of our forces, no longer had any practical military value. The entrance to Manila Bay was completely covered by Corregidor and Bataan and, as long as we held them, its use would be denied the enemy. He might have the bottle, but I had the cork."

Actually, the evacuation of MacArthur's army was very much in progress and its success still in doubt when the general announced his new location. It was not a single but a double retrograde operation if the bulk of both the northern and southern Luzon forces were to withdraw into Bataan. Wainwright, confronted with a steady erosion of his army from casualties inflicted by the enemy and desertion by the untrained, undisciplined troops, withdrew behind the Agno River, a natural barrier for anyone seeking access to Manila from the north. With this temporary respite, Wainwright actually talked of a counterattack—if his boss would order up the most effective fighting forces in the entire defense, the Philippine Division with its Philippine Scouts and the U.S. 31st Regiment.

However, MacArthur did not accede to the request for the Philippine Division and he now informed Wainwright that War Plan Orange was in effect and the soldiers under Wainwright must fight delaying actions that would allow the bulk of his army to escape to Bataan. Although supported by the 192nd and 194th Tank Battalions, a pair of U.S. National Guard units, Wainwright's army continued to fall back under pressure from Japanese infantry supported from the air.

One of the strong points for a Bataan defense lay in the limited access to the peninsula. But while the choke points favored the forces established there, it posed a threat to retrograde moves by Wainwright's North Luzon Force (NLF) and the South Luzon Force (SLF) under Brig. Gen. Albert Jones. The route to Bataan for both required passage across the Pampanga River over the Calumpit bridges, one of which handled highway traffic and the other served the railroad.

Military vehicles, soldiers on the march and a thick stream of Filipinos with wagons, animal-drawn carts, a few cars somehow not commandeered by the military, and civilians on foot packed the route to the bridges. In the sky, flights of Japanese planes continued to bomb and machine gun military targets and portions of Manila. They ignored the long column snaking towards Bataan but resolutely attacked designated targets. Unlike the Germans in Europe who understood that disruption of road traffic often prevented an effective retreat, the Japanese hewed to the prescribed plans and, as they would demonstrate throughout

the war, lacked an inclination to improvise and exploit unexpected opportunities. Indeed, General Homma, had he
elected to concentrate his army upon the elements bound
for Bataan, might well have destroyed the forces of Wainwright and Jones. But he too stuck to the script, which
made the capture of Manila top priority.

With some desperate defensive efforts delaying those
Japanese units that were approaching the Pampanga,
Wainwright himself crossed the bridge. At 1:00 A.M. on
New Year's Day, 1942, he heard a rumbling that signaled
the approach of tanks. The anxiety eased as the armor from
the 192nd and 194th Tank Battalions rattled through the
darkness and across the river. The main remnants of both
the NLF and SLF continued to make their way towards
Bataan. At about 6:15 A.M., twin four-ton dynamite
charges dropped both spans into the deep, unfordable current of the Pampanga. For the moment, the Filipino-
American Army was intact and secure.

Much worse than the shrinkage of the turf controlled by
the United States and the loss of forty percent of the
troops because of casualties and desertion was the lack of
vital supplies. As part of MacArthur's strategy, the troops
evacuated Fort Stotsenburg; up in smoke went as much as
three hundred thousand gallons of gasoline and large
amounts of high-octane aviation fuel. Tons of food, clothing and other military gear were left behind.

John Olson, a West Pointer and adjutant for the 57th
Regiment of the Philippine Scouts, learned of Stotsenburg's abandonment while completing a message mission. Olson, who reported the news to his superior, recalls
that "Major Johnson directed Captain Anders to investi-
gate. He did so and returned laden with soap, toothpaste,
candy, film, cigarettes and a number of other items from
the post exchange. Col. George Clarke [the regimental
commander, a veteran of WWI but described as a highly
emotional and ineffective officer] denied Major Fisher permission to send men and vehicles into the post on the
grounds that they 'might be hit by fragments of Japanese

or American bombs.' [Aviation engineers at Clark Field detonated ordnance they could not take away.]

"Major [Royal] Reynolds, whose patrols had ventured into the post, sent all the vehicles he could get his hands on to salvage whatever they could. From this trip they got large quantities of clothing and food. Among the clothing were winter overcoats that members of the 31st Infantry had worn when the regiment was sent to Siberia in 1919. Though of interest, they were left for the Japanese in favor of more useable items. The salvage party did bring back thirty-six Smith & Wesson .45 caliber revolvers. The most valuable acquisition was enough Class C rations to fill two buses. They were to be worth the equivalent of gold later in the campaign when food became scarce. In spite of the haul, there was much more that could have been saved. But the timidity of the regimental commander prevented any further exploitation of the abandoned supplies."

The items written off at Stotsenburg can be attributed to panic, but a much more basic logistical difficulty arose from the substitution of Rainbow Five for War Plan Orange late in the game. To feed the army that would deprive the invaders of a foothold in the Philippines, quartermasters deposited huge stocks of food in the central Luzon plains where they would be accessible to Wainwright's forces. According to Bluemel, a Filipino captain told him that one million pounds of rice had been left at the Cabanatuan storage area.

From the commander of the depot at Tarlac, Bluemel heard that two thousand cases of canned food and clothing could not be taken by the retreating army because it belonged to Japanese companies. The refusal, allegedly from MacArthur's headquarters, to allow confiscation of items owned by citizens of the invading nation would seem to carry the rights of private property to an extreme. To further complicate supply problems, commanders of many units refused to return the precious vehicles that brought materials to them, hanging on to the trucks and cars for their own use or in the event of an emergency. The law of the jungle infected some units, which hijacked and commandeered transportation, wrecking any systematic efforts by the quartermaster organizations.

No one stepped forward to halt this anarchy. Richard Sutherland, MacArthur's chief of staff, commented that his boss never had any interest or understanding of logistics and that this flaw would be crippling. The theory for WPO's premise of resistance to conquest by an army defending in the Bataan redoubt rested on some critical logistical assumptions. The strategists expected a force of perhaps forty thousand troops with appropriate equipment and other necessities to be able to withstand the estimated Japanese army for six months.

MacArthur's plan to prevent the Japanese from overrunning Luzon had upset the schedule for stockpiling the munitions, food and other vital items on Bataan. When he reinstituted the concept of a defense centered there, the supply system like some great ocean liner forging in one direction could not instantly reverse course but shuddered as it sought to halt its momentum before becoming dead in the water, useless. The confusion and absence of a disciplined system might have been overcome by a forceful attention to the problem, but a monumental miscalculation overrode whatever anyone did.

Instead of the compact, well commanded, skillful body of forty thousand troops envisioned, tens of thousands more men reached Bataan. Some arrived as members of the intact but unreliable Philippine Army divisions; others from shattered units that seeped through the jungle. Along with the Filipinos came a horde of Air Corps and Navy men, their primary mission in the Philippines now vanished with the disappearance of the planes and ships. They now became ground forces. Under the authority of WPO, the military expected to evacuate civilians on the peninsula. With the Japanese rushing forward and the Filipino-American forces in retreat, no one attempted to reduce the local population. Furthermore, refugees who feared Japanese occupation of their home areas swelled the numbers of noncombatants on Bataan. With as many as eighty thousand uniformed men on Bataan and an extra ten thousand civilians added to the residents, the food and medical supplies on Bataan were pitifully inadequate from the beginning.

CHAPTER VII

THE SIEGE OF BATAAN BEGINS

THE COMING OF THE NEW YEAR brought more woe to men of the 34th Pursuit Squadron who had bedded down at the Orani field. "The school blackboard in our room at Orani," says Gage, "had penmanship specimens in both English and Tagalog—'There is much fine talk but little work'—'*Sabis salita sulang su gawa.*' I looked out the window at three quarreling orphans who helped the mess crew and yelled, '*Sabis salita sulang su gawa.*' Immediate silence and withdrawal from me and afterwards they skirted away, distrusting my knowledge of their language."

He hardly had time to savor his linguistic triumph. "About noon of that day, we had the hell bombed out of us. The strike came just at lunch time. I remember getting into one of the slit trenches with my mess kit in my hand. To the best of my knowledge I finished the meal. General opinion was they were trying to hit the highway bridge over the river at Orani which they missed completely. However, they did get two direct hits on the gasoline tanker trucks that were parked in the village. The drivers, not from the 34th, were killed and the town was set afire.

"In the adjoining trench were some of our officers and one local man down on his knees, his rosary beads clicking at a rapid rate. Before the bombing was over, Arthur Campbell came raging into the area, yelling for all of us to get off our fannies and down towards the fire to try and prevent a complete burnout.

"Our front porch at the school house was swamped with women bringing their wounded children and babies in for treatment. Some of the locals hotfooted it by us at that time—some with pigs slung on poles and some with chickens in baskets. In a few hours, the village of Orani was deserted. The bombers caught another outfit on their chow line up the road from us. Their casualties were rather heavy.

"We continued at Orani until January 7. During this time I went back in the direction we had come from with a small truck convoy to scavenge anything we could get in the way of supplies. We moved at a snail's pace, bumper to bumper with trucks and overhead, flight after flight of Japanese bombers. Luckily for us they had no bombs to spare and also equally lucky no fighters were interested in us. We had no place to hide in the rice fields."

While Americans and Filipinos alike had struggled and straggled towards Bataan, General Homma enjoyed a triumphant entrance into Manila. The occupying soldiers moved into public buildings, hotels, university and school buildings. Japanese officers, prepared with occupation pesos, bought up souvenirs wherever they found an open store. Governmental offices, banks, newspapers and other establishments came under Japanese control. All British and American citizens, including Navy nurse Mary Rose Nelson and stenographer Jean George, were herded together on the campus of Santo Tomas University for internment.

With control of the big city established, General Homma unleashed his armies on the last line of American and Filipino troops blocking access to Bataan. The available defenders considerably outnumbered the fighting men fielded by the Japanese commander, although the American top brass continued to insist the enemy had far more troops. For their part, Japanese intelligence undercounted the defenders, figuring MacArthur could call upon roughly forty thousand or so underfed, poorly trained and dispirited soldiers.

When the attackers pressed forward, the Philippine Army regiments continued to yield ground. Only the support of artillery and heavy fire from the two American tank battalions prevented swift progress by the enemy. But the longer-range Japanese artillery blasted holes in the defensive lines and the last of the Luzon armies fell back to the positions from which Bataan was to be retained. Officially, the defense of Bataan began on January 7, 1942, as Wainwright assumed command of the west sector while Gen. George M. Parker received responsibility for the east sector.

The new command situation for the remaining one thousand square miles of Luzon still in possession of USAFFE radically transformed the 34th Pursuit Squadron. "On January 7," says Gage, "we abandoned Orani and moved to Little Baguio. We were in the jungle, under tall trees. Very hot, very muggy. We were told we were now infantry. The men were organized in groups and were taking superficial infantry training from the two or three old hands in our outfit that had been in WW I. I thought T. Sgt. Michael H. Bruaw, an ex-line chief, was a little too old and a little too heavy to be racing up and down through the jungle scrub trying to teach a line of skirmish. No one was very happy with this phase."

The relatively easy success against the armies arrayed for the defense of the island persuaded the Japanese High Command that conquest of the remnants on Bataan would not require as much force as originally planned. To consolidate and expand their control of Southeast Asia, the Japanese, already swiftly advancing through Malaya towards Singapore, snatched away some of Homma's best ground and air troops for the invasion of Java.

In place of these experienced and effective soldiers, the 65th Independent Brigade, with sixty-five hundred men, landed on January 2, to enter the field. The enlisted personnel, all conscripts, had only a month of training and the commander, Lt. Gen. Akira Nara, a graduate of the U.S. Army Infantry School, class of '27, described his organization as "absolutely unfit for combat."

The consequences of hurling men with little more knowledge than how to march into the maw of battle showed immediately. On January 8 the invaders began a drive south on the eastern side of the peninsula. Advancing on the defenders' line anchored at Mabatang near Manila Bay, elements of the 65th Brigade tramped along a road in a column of fours with their horse-drawn artillery trailing along. Observation posts on the slopes of nearby mountains spotted them and called in the 155 mm artillery, already registered for targets on the highway. A torrent of shells burst among the Japanese soldiers, killing and maiming many. Whenever the barrage slackened, the troops dutifully re-formed into their columns and renewed their trudge towards death and destruction, for what the defenders could only describe as a "turkey shoot." First blood in the battle for Bataan was drawn mainly from the invading Japanese forces.

Considerably heavier casualties than anticipated did not, for the moment, lessen the pressure exerted by the Japanese. The 57th Regiment of the Philippine Scouts, with Philip Fry having been recently promoted from major to lieutenant colonel and CO of the 3rd Battalion, opposed the thrust. "On the afternoon of January 10 our patrols reported contact with a strong Japanese combat patrol. Companies were notified to be on the alert and increase their local security. About 2:00 P.M. rifle and machine gun fire commenced in the I Company sector. We had these flare-ups before where stray carabao wander into minefields, set off one. The men, on edge, would immediately fire a few shots into the darkness. As soon as the firing started I called Captain [Herman] Gerth, I Company CO, and was informed he was on the front line. I managed to get Captain Haas of Company K on the phone, who said his sector was quiet. I told Haas to send a patrol to look over the I Company sector and find out what was going on. Not being satisfied with the information available, I left Pete in charge of the command post and started out for the observation post.

"On my way up the firing became more severe. One of the runners was shot through the arm. In spite of his pleading and tears, I ordered him back to the first aid station, as our first casualty. By the time we arrived at the OP the firing had become even more severe and the machine guns had joined in. In fact, the entire left sector was violently active.

"Gerth was on the OP phone waiting for me. He told me that his entire company was engaged and the Japs were advancing through our minefield. I could see and hear the flash of the mines going off. They were supposed to withstand six hundred pounds pressure but lots of them were homemade and would go off at the slightest provocation. I told Gerth to pour it on them and help would be forthcoming if needed.

"A great shout of *'Banzai!'* came from the front and the Japs started an old Civil War charge. I got Haas on the phone and told him to sweep Company I's front with his machine guns. It was slaughter. All of our guns had been carefully sighted for mutual support and the Japs were caught by terrific fire both frontal and flanking. Even now I can't understand why the Japs launched an attack of this kind against modern weapons. My only explanation is they had not faced trained troops before and thought that if enough noise were made the opposition would simply fade away. The attack was smashed before it got under way. The Scouts were jubilant. I made a hurried trip to the front lines and warned them to expect another more serious attack soon. Our casualties were only five wounded, including my runner.

"The second attack began about 1:00 A.M. It was preceded by considerable small arms and mortar fire. Our lines were smothered and the OP came in for its full share. The entire battalion front came into action. This time the enemy brought up his tanks and hit us hard. Once again the main effort was against Company I. We were forced to put our fire back along the final protective line. A few of the enemy started filtering through and circling behind the Company I sector. As soon as Gerth sensed this he very properly asked for help. I just couldn't afford to commit my reserves so early in the game.

"Captain Coe, the artillery liaison officer, was with me. He designated the cane field [to the front of the defenders] and asked for immediate fire. Captain Grimes, the heavy weapons company commander, was nearby and directed to concentrate all mortars in the same place. The concentrated fire of these mortars alone would have been terrific. But we had World War I ammunition and averaged about six duds out of every ten rounds fired.

"We abandoned the new light mortar guns at Ft. Mc-Kinley because the ammunition for them had never arrived. We were badly handicapped without our own protective weapons and forced to rely heavily on the artillery. Captain Coe had Colonel Luback on the phone and asked me to talk to him. Luback said the regiment had taken control of all artillery support out of the hands of battalion commanders. This was incredible. I believed some mistake had been made. My only reaction at the time was irritation.

"I asked Luback to keep his line open while I contacted the regiment and got Major Johnson, regimental S-3. I explained the situation and asked him to authorize a barrage. Johnson was evasive so I asked him to put George Clarke [the 57th's commander] on the phone. Once again I went over the situation with Clarke. He had the same line of conversation as Johnson and we ended in a furious exchange of words but no artillery!" The supposed excuse for Clarke's behavior was his fear that any use of artillery would bring retaliatory fire upon his headquarters. Harold Johnson, who also served under Clarke, described him as "phobic" about air attacks.

Outraged and frustrated, Fry rallied his forces. "Company K as well as Company I was now heavily engaged, with more and more snipers armed with Tommy guns filtering through the lines. They were coming mostly through the 41st Infantry [Philippine Army unit manning the left flank] and circling behind us. Both Gerth and Haas were asking for supporting fire and they were badly worried. They didn't have a thing on me. The Scouts were willing fighters but after all it was their first combat experience. They were bound to be affected by fire into their backs."

The men under Fry pulled back under the onslaught and reestablished their lines, a little deeper into Bataan. But the enemy seemed relentless in purpose and heedless of losses.

Fry recalled: "January 11 about 10:00 P.M. there were signs of formation for a coming mechanized attack from the Nip side. The sounds of tanks couldn't be mistaken. We took preparatory countermeasures. Our mortars and artillery went into action at once. The antitank weapons, 37 mm cannons, .50 caliber machine guns and a battery of 75 mms were silent. They had strict orders not to fire a single shot unless tanks were seen approaching. Otherwise they would give their positions away.

"The attack was broken up before the tanks could be used. The Japanese opened up with heavy and light mortar fire against our front lines. Not much damage was done thanks to excellent foxholes. Soon everything we had was in action. The firepower of a battalion armed with modern weapons is something. The Garand rifle is beyond my descriptive powers. It is a mystery to me how anyone can come through it [the battalion firepower] alive. But they do. And they came with the now familiar cry of 'Banzai!' The fight was on. Once again the filtering tactics, but on a much larger scale. We had men stationed in commanding positions waiting for them. Here, at least, there was plenty of individual combat. The Nips poured men into the battle. They had face and prestige in the East at stake. This battalion of Scouts, though badly outnumbered, were desperately eager to place the number of a new American-Filipino regiment among the war great."

Fry mentioned a method to deal with the infiltration of enemy soldiers, the creation of anti-sniper parties consisting of riflemen, demolition engineers and some volunteers like Lt. Alexander "Sandy" Nininger. A Georgia-born youth, he had spent a portion of his childhood living near West Point where the sight of hiking cadets inspired him to matriculate at the Academy. Nininger, fresh out of the infantry school at Fort Benning, had only come to the Philippines and the 57th Regiment in November 1941, his furlough prior to overseas shipment cut short by the growing crisis.

Three weeks before the 57th Regiment confronted the enemy on Bataan, Nininger, assigned to Company A of the 1st Battalion, received a promotion to first lieutenant. His area was for the moment dormant, except for the murderous snipers. According to his superiors, Nininger volunteered to accompany one party of Scouts bent on rooting out the infiltrators. His company commander, Cap. Frederick Yeager, gave Nininger the names of six or eight of the best marksman in the outfit but specified they must all be volunteers. Everyone elected to participate, and the heavily armed patrol set out. Those behind them heard heavy exchanges of gunfire and explosions. The party returned intact with their ammunition expended. Nininger insisted on another expedition but this time he selected only three Scouts for the mission.

"After some time," writes John Olson, "they came running back. Shouting to his men to remain, the lieutenant grabbed some more grenades and a bandolier of ammunition and raced back into the trees. He was never seen alive again. His body was found later leaning against a tree. Lying around him were three dead Japanese, one of whom was reported to have been an officer. Nininger's pistol and a Browning automatic rifle that he borrowed from another member of K Company had been taken by the enemy, even though they made no attempt to recover their own dead."

Subsequently, Nininger was posthumously awarded the nation's highest military decoration, the Congressional Medal of Honor. He was the first American to receive this honor during World War II.

Nininger seems to have demonstrated genuine valor although the eyewitness testimony that is a prerequisite for a Medal of Honor is murky. His regimental commander Colonel Clarke wrote more than two years later: "Sandy received permission to go forward in the 3rd Battalion sector. He was loaded down with grenades and with a Garand rifle slung over his shoulder. He carried under his arm a Japanese 'tommy gun.' Sandy shot his first Jap out of a tree and as the body fell at his feet he was so excited he stood up in the face of terrific rifle fire and yelled like a schoolboy. He threw grenade after grenade. Men of Company K counted twenty Japs killed by his grenades.

"Many reports of further action by Sandy were made by the second in command of the 2nd Battalion in the counterattack to regain Company K's position. Sandy had apparently used up all his ammunition and was now using his bayonet. His final action, as described by this same officer, was when he saw Sandy, wounded again, and when he seemed to be staggering from loss of blood, three Japs charged towards him with bayonets. He killed all three of them and apparently fell of exhaustion . . . Suffice it to say his action acted like a tonic on the men around him, and added greatly to the success of our counterattack."

Nininger's heroics drew similarly high praise in purple prose from others who could not possibly have witnessed the events. But the encomiums, like that of Clarke, in the form of letters to the dead man's family seem inspired more by desires for reflected glory than for drafting a factual record.

While Nininger and the embattled Scouts of the 3rd Battalion sought to repulse the onrushing Japanese, a renewed appeal for artillery support was approved. Major

Johnson, instead of consulting Colonel Clarke, arranged for barrages in the cane fields directly in front of the Scouts.

The defenders momentarily halted the offense. Said Fry, "From Haas I learned of the destruction of one tank, and two others withdrawing, caught by our antitank guns and didn't like it. The .50 caliber machine guns which turned them back were too light to destroy them. Company K was doing all right but Company I was taking the brunt of the attack."

Gerth personally went among the front line platoons, leaving Lt. Arthur Green in his command bunker. A bullet struck the company commander in the groin at 0330. Carried to the command post, Gerth tried to carry on, reporting the situation. The battalion supply officer, Capt. John Compton, hearing about Gerth, received permission to go forward and aid Gerth.

According to Fry, "A portion of the line was penetrated. Green was telling me this over the telephone when all of a sudden he exclaimed, 'They got Johnny! [Compton]. There he goes down.' I told Green to hold on and I would send help to him right then. I turned to Brown who was standing right beside me and ordered an immediate counterattack in the I Company sector.

"I had one more call from Green, his last one, stating his company was being forced back; casualties were heavy but the remainder was fighting hard. I told him of Company L's entry." While Gerth continued to pass on details to Fry, Lieutenant Green, leaving the safety of the dugout, headed for the forward positions of the I Company troops. As he consulted and advised, he incurred a fatal wound to the head.

"Haas reported his left flank exposed, Company I shot to pieces and his company being outflanked. I told him about Company L's entry and for him to give all possible assistance. I believed the enemy had shot the works and I was hoping for a breakthrough with Brown's Company L being timed correctly.

"I called regiment and informed them of the situation and that my reserve had been committed. I asked that at least one company of the regimental reserve be placed at my disposal. Company E was assigned to me and ordered to report to my battalion support line and there await orders.

"This action on the part of Regiment was a very generous one and paid big dividends. Company L under Captain Brown hit the hole in the I Company sector hard. He established contact with Haas, relieving the strain there, but failed to contact the 41st Infantry. Things quieted a bit."

Although a lull fell over the front, Fry remained aware of threats to his sector's positions because of an exposed flank. He organized a counterattack, believing in homage to Nathan Bedford Forrest, a hero of the Confederacy during the Civil War: "The stage was set and it was a question of who would get there fustest with the mostest." Company E, which Fry borrowed from the regimental reserve, plus a handful of men from other units, would carry out the mission. Other companies set up machine guns to hammer the foe if he tried to pull back.

"The attack was a beautiful one," wrote Fry, "an inspiring sight to see. The Scouts had been trained for years in the company in attack and it was a model of precision and played for keeps. The reward of perfection was retention of one's life. If this attack had been staged at Fort Benning to show visiting firemen the mechanics it would not have been improved upon. I knew the outcome at once. With such leadership as Childers [Captain Don, E Company commander] was showing and such trained fighters as these Scouts, it couldn't fail. The Japanese were trapped. They fought bravely and tried to withdraw in orderly fashion but they were caught by the machine guns positioned for the purpose."

The fight spread to the rest of the opposing forces in the area. When the shooting ended, the 57th had regained its original line. Fry believed an entire Japanese regiment had been involved and for the first time an invading force had been beaten.

John Olson, as the adjutant at Regiment, described the scene at daylight: "The picture that greeted the sleepless eyes of the surviving Scouts as the sun rose was one of utter chaos and devastation. Broken and bloody bodies were sprawled all over the foxholes and open ground throughout the I and left of K Company sectors. Forward of the front lines, mangled Japanese corpses were strung on the barbed wire like bags of dirty laundry. Abandoned weapons were strewn everywhere. The occasional bursts of fire from enemy-occupied holes, while sometimes provoking retaliatory fire from the Scout strong points, served to keep down any friendly movement . . . Everyone, even the enemy, seemed content to desist temporarily."

The losses to the Scouts added up to more than a hundred. Although Fry claimed the bodies of both Green and Compton were never recovered, he was wrong about the latter. Indeed, another young officer, Lt. Kenneth Wilson, a close friend of Compton, obtained permission to retrieve the body. Unfortunately, the enemy noticed him while he tried to drag the corpse through the wire defenses and a hail of bullets ended his life.

Harold Johnson, as executive officer of the 57th, coped with Fry's requests for aid and the need for replacements caused by the high number of casualties among the American officers and Scout noncoms. At the same time he strove desperately to provide additional ammunition and supply, but his by-the-book superiors flatly refused on the grounds that all allocations of artillery shells would be based upon a calendar basis. The schedule restricted batteries to less than one hour of fodder per day.

Johnson went over the heads of the commanders to reach MacArthur's deputy, Richard Sutherland. The chief of staff, having visited the 57th two days before the opening of the attack, agreed with Johnson and forthwith directed ordnance to replace each day's expenditure of ammunition as it was consumed rather than hewing to a calendar. Furthermore, Sutherland recognized the failings of George Clarke and started a hunt for a new regimental leader.

Replacement of company and platoon leaders became a top priority. Fry directed Haas to dispatch Lt. David Maynard, the sole remaining officer in Company I, to Company K as a successor to the wounded Gerth and KIA Green. Hardly had Maynard assumed his new position than he was killed while on a mission to eradicate some persistent snipers.

The pool of potential replacements continued to drain away. An urgent request for additional commissioned help brought an American quartermaster captain on the scene. He arrived, reconnoitered the scene and, in the words of John Olson, "concluded this was no place for a quartermaster officer, so he disappeared after dark and was never seen again by anyone in the 57th."

At dawn on January 10, the same day that Fry and his outfit met the Japanese attack, a PT boat carried MacArthur and Sutherland from Corregidor to Bataan for an inspection of the terrain and defenses. In his *Reminiscences*, MacArthur said, "I had to see the enemy or I could not fight him effectively. Reports, no matter how penetrating, have never been able to replace the picture shown to my eyes." This visit would be the only one made by the general to the peninsula during its three-month siege.

The survey by MacArthur covered an area south of where Fry's embattled forces, in the II Corps, repulsed the initial assaults on the eastern edge of the front lines. Driven west, MacArthur conferred with the I Corps commander, Wainwright, who offered to show his boss where his 155 mm guns awaited the enemy. MacArthur supposedly replied, "I don't want to *see* them. I want to *hear* them."

According to Clifford Bluemel, the CO of the 31st Division, then part of the I Corps, Wainwright summoned all of the generals to meet with their supreme leader. "We spoke to him and shook hands," recalled Bluemel. "He said, 'Help is definitely on the way. We must hold out until it arrives. It can arrive at any time. Parker [Maj. Gen. George, II Corps commander] is fighting the enemy on the Manila Bay side [site of the 57th Regiment battle involving Fry] and he'll hold them. He'll throw them back. We've just got to hold out until help arrives.' "

Bluemel took no issue with the general's optimism then nor did he criticize him for misleading his subordinates. To have talked in terms of defeat could only have led to a quick collapse of resistance.

In fact, rather than search for any substance to the bravado, Bluemel said that when MacArthur asked if there were any questions, he thought of a conversation with one of his captains who had questioned whether they would lose their money deposited in the Philippine Trust Company. Bluemel remembered he had several hundred dollars there as well.

To MacArthur, Bluemel said, "There's some of these young officers who have money in the Philippine Trust Company. They are afraid they'll lose it. One fellow has nineteen hundred pesos. That's a little over nine hundred dollars."

MacArthur responded, "You tell these young officers not to worry. When this is over, I will get a bill through Congress to reimburse them for every cent they lose." MacArthur was undoubtedly relieved that no one pressed him for evidence that the enemy would be stopped and reinforcement was imminent. [Contrary to his reassurances, Bluemel said that when the war ended and the survivors had indeed lost their assets, MacArthur never sought any compensation from Congress.]

IT WAS ALSO on January 10 that General Homma sent the following message to MacArthur:

"You are well aware that you are doomed. The end is near. The question is how long you will be able to resist. You have already cut rations by half. I appreciate the fighting spirit of yourself and your troops who have been fighting with courage. Your prestige and honor have been upheld.

"However, in order to avoid needless bloodshed and to save the remnants of your divisions and your auxiliary troops, you are advised to surrender.

"In the meantime, we shall continue our offensive as I do not wish to give you time for defense . . . Our offensive will be continued with inexorable force and will bring upon you only disaster . . ."

MacArthur ignored the demand and the Japanese showered the Filipino-American positions with leaflets of dubious grammar and syntax:

"The outcome of the present combat has been already decided and you are cornered to the doom. But, however, being unable to realize the present situation, blinded General MacArthur has stupidly refused our proposal and continues futile struggle at the cost of your precious lives.

"Dear Filipino Soldiers!

"There are still one way left for you. That is to give up all your weapons at once and surrender to the Japanese force before it is too late, then we shall fully protect you.

"We repeat for the last!

"Surrender at once and build your new Philippines for and by Filipinos."

The week before the 57th engaged in its fierce series of battles with the enemy and MacArthur toured part of Bataan, he became aware of the meagre food stocks available for both civilians and troops. An inventory indicated only enough to feed one hundred thousand men for thirty days. On January 5 MacArthur approved a recommendation of his quartermaster that placed all troops and civilians on Bataan and Corregidor on half-rations, as Homma's surrender message stated. The diet amounted to roughly two thousand calories daily, almost adequate perhaps for sedentary individuals but far below the needs of troops working or fighting for twenty hours a day. Furthermore, vital nutritional elements were missing from the reduced fare.

Some units temporarily supplemented the short rations with items scrounged from depots during the retreat.

The troops in the field also hunted for their meals. Irvin Alexander remarked, "Any carabao which was encountered in the jungle was classed as wild and neither his ancestry nor his ownership was investigated."

The Bataan defenders tightened their belts and awaited renewal of the assault. Although the 57th and other units inflicted heavy casualties on the Japanese initially, they had continued to press forward, shrinking the II Corps foothold on the eastern portion of Bataan. The enemy forces threatened to break through along the left flank of Parker's corps and push down the middle of the peninsula. Parker had asked for reinforcements to help stave off Homma's armies.

"I got a call one night to come up to Wainwright's headquarters," said Clifford Bluemel whose 31st Division protected an as yet unchallenged section of the west coast of Bataan. "He said, 'Your division's going to be moved over to the Manila Bay sector.'

"I said, 'My God! I haven't reconnoitered anything over there. All my reconnaissance has been on the China Sea side and out in Zambales.'" Poor mapping, few roads and spotty trails through thick vegetation fomented Bluemel's anxiety. Any shift of men and equipment entailed the possibility of literally becoming lost.

"There was to be a guide to show me how I was to get to Guitol [a hamlet four or five miles behind the front lines]. I was to be in reserve. General Parker told me on the telephone, 'You follow the road. There is a wire that leads up there. All you have to do is follow the wire.' But there were dozens of wires. I was in a car and I followed this wire and that wire. I ran into an artillery battery and finally someone showed me where Guitol was. I got the troops up there, but we were bombed on the way up. That was the first time the division had been under fire."

While the bulk of his soldiers remained in reserve,

Bluemel dispatched one regiment to support the Philippine Army's 41st Division, commanded by Gen. Vincente Lim, another Filipino alumnus of the Academy. "I went up to see how they were getting along," said Bluemel. "On the way back I ran into a Japanese patrol behind the lines. There was a truck trail through a sugarcane field. I wanted to go up through the trail to get back to my command but was cut off by the Jap patrol.

"There was a Philippine Scout engineer detachment with one machine gun and a lieutenant. I said, 'You form up a point of an advance guard here, and we'll go up that trail.' But by God, he wouldn't move.

"About this time I saw a captain with thirty Filipino Army men. He said, 'General, I think the Japs are there. I'll tell you what we'd better do. Comb that tree and all that area with a machine gun. Then I'll go into the sugar cane and you can go up the trail.' He made a remark to those Filipinos. 'Go on in there. What the hell's the matter with you! Goddamn you, you can't live forever!'

"They went in and drove out the Japanese patrol. I started up but those engineer Scouts wouldn't move. There was a little Filipino soldier there and after that he became my bodyguard. Nobody would go up the trail but he said, 'General, I'll go.'

"I said, 'All right, we'll go. You go ahead and I'll go with you.' Then I turned to these Philippine Scouts and said, 'I'm a brigadier general. I'm going up this trail, all of you goddamn yellow sons of bitches that are cowards stay there.' They came. From then on I found I could get them to obey orders by cursing."

Even though the enemy was apparently driven off, Bluemel soon found himself under attack. "Some of my own troops opened fire on me. I got off the trail into the sugarcane field. I lay down on my stomach and I could hear the bullets cutting through that sugarcane over my head. Finally they stopped. I went to the trail and waved my hat. There were some Filipino soldiers who belonged to my division. I said, 'What the hell do you mean by shooting up your own division commander!' "

The flow of battle in the west replicated the grudging retreat of Parker's people and the same erratic performance by the defensive units. In mid-January, a Japanese column, consisting of a regimental combat team with the 122nd Infantry at its core, traveled by foot and native boats down the western coast, the turf defended by the I Corps under Jonathan Wainwright. Apprised of the threat, Wainwright dispatched the 1st Philippine Division, led by Gen. Fidel Segundo, a Filipino West Point graduate, abetted by two troops from the already bloodied 26th Cavalry.

Alva Fitch, assigned to provide artillery support for Bluemel's organization in the beginning of January, received an order from Wainwright that attached him to the 1st Division of the Philippine Army. Fitch, a man with little respect for the indigenous people of the islands, referring to them frequently as "Gooks," said of Segundo, "He swore very well in several languages and passed much of his time swearing at his troops and staff for their stupidity. I very much fear, however, that he had a very limited grasp of the duties of a general officer in combat.

"During a reconnaissance of mine for trails and routes of communication, I found that the troops were not where they should be, and that our flank was dangerously exposed. I quickly reported this to Segundo. He poohpoohed me, and proved me wrong by showing me on his map where the troops were. I then reported to Colonel Vanture [1st Division artillery chief] in hopes he would be able to catch the general in a more receptive mood and convince him. Nothing was ever done."

Fitch observed refugees from other outfits drifting into his positions. "The 23rd [Field Artillery] had been badly shot up. They lost their guns and no little prestige. They were badly outgunned by the Japs, and the infantry broke in front of them, a routine practice with the Philippine Army but very surprising in the U.S. 31st Infantry [a regiment of Americans not to be confused with Bluemel's 31st Division made up of Filipinos]."

The artilleryman decided to try a stint as a forward observer, locating targets. "As I went up a sunken trail, I heard voices. I stopped to listen but couldn't tell if they were Gooks or Nippies, so I continued on. As I rounded a turn in the trail, I found myself facing a Jap machine gunner. I went back around the corner quickly, in fact so quickly I lost the two hand grenades that were clipped to my belt. I landed on my face, with machine gun bullets buzzing past my ears like a flight of angry bees."

Fitch escaped, realizing that without his grenades it would be imprudent to attack a machine gun with only a pistol. He organized a squad of six or eight Filipino riflemen to go after the machine gun but discovered the foe had vanished. As he returned to his original base, a dismayed Fitch said he saw not a single soldier, except those who had accompanied him. "They had all gone home for their supper, a regrettable but characteristic action."

On January 16 he saw a frustrated American colonel try to extend the flank of the defensive positions. But the soldiers, after tentatively moving out, would retreat without any sign of the enemy. Fitch noticed a battalion repairing a bridge. "A single sniper opened long-range fire on them. They stampeded." After their commander unloosed a volley in the direction of the lone adversary the foe ceased shooting. The bridge was completed but orders now called for a pullback of more than a mile, leaving an intact span for use by the Japanese.

After a day of inactivity, Fitch said, "Lieutenant King, who was in the OP, called to report a Company of Nippies on the open beach in the immediate vicinity of the registration point. We immediately put all available fire on it. The Nippies who escaped took shelter in a nearby swamp. We shelled the swamp for a while, just to worry them.

"Later in the morning, while at the OP, I saw a banca [small Filipino boat] sail down the beach. The Filipinos all rushed down to the beach to meet the refugees. The refugees were three Jap soldiers. All parties saw their mistakes about the same time. The Japs jumped back in their boat, and the Gooks ran like hell. Unfortunately for the Nippies, a heavy machine gun opened up on them. They were quickly joined by everyone in the vicinity. The Japs and the banca were riddled. The whole thing sounded like a small war.

"About five hundred yards north was Nag Balayan barrio, the left flank of the outpost position, held by one Company commanded by a Filipino lieutenant. When he heard the firing, he set fire to the barrio and withdrew his Company, to assist his companions.

"It took two or three hours to get them back in position. We fired a barrage through the barrio for them, then Semmens [an American officer and advisor] took the troops up and put them back in position. He returned, found the lieutenant, convinced him it was safe and took him up."

The comedy of errors, marked by moments of disaster, continued. When an enemy mortar dropped a pair of rounds to the rear and front of the observation post, Fitch managed to get his battery to knock the position out with a single shell. But the exploding mortars set off confused small arms fire from behind and in front of Fitch. The bullets from the edgy Filipino recruits whizzed past his head from both directions and escalated until the entire battalion in the area was discharging weapons, mostly in the air. With darkness the outburst ceased but one jittery Filipino mortar crew blasted the barrio of Nag Balayan, killing a handful of friendlies.

According to Fitch, about a hundred enemy soldiers attempted to get through wire entanglements but none of the 1st Division soldiers fired at them. Semmens, on duty at the observation post, chased or killed them with several artillery rounds. Fitch reported that the defenders broke and ran when the Japanese rattled their positions with an artillery barrage. "They tried to run past me but I stopped them and sent them back. After a few minutes, Platt [another American officer] shot the Jap battery out with his 75 mm battery."

Still the foe probed the defensive positions, sometimes with a frightening intensity. "As we had no air protection, the Jap planes and boats came and went very much at will. During the afternoon a cruiser shelled our positions for a while with very heavy guns, but with absolutely no effect."

To Fitch the process started to resemble a cat and mouse game with no question about who played which role. "This day, January 19, was very quiet, too quiet. It seemed to me that the Nippies were either preparing for a big attack, or trying to find some way around our position. My knowledge of the weakness of our flank gave me considerable worry."

CHAPTER VIII

THE ROCK

WHILE THE BODY of the Filipino-American defense sought to contain the enemy on Bataan, the brain directed movements from the 2.74 square miles of Corregidor, the Gibraltar of the Pacific. Tadpole shaped, the island's head lies two miles south of Bataan while the tail points towards Manila Bay. The bulbous end of Corregidor thrusts six hundred feet above sea level and on Topside, as it was known, stood the basics of an army post—headquarters, barracks, officers quarters—all grouped around a parade ground. A small golf course adjoined the parade grounds. The cliffs of Topside, cut by a pair of ravines, dropped precipitously to the water.

Adjacent to Topside, on a small plateau called Middleside, were more quarters for officers and noncoms, a hospital, service club and schools for children. East of this area the land fell away to almost sea level and was only six hundred yards in width. Known as Bottomside, the low area contained docks, warehouses, a small barrio, San Jose, and the vital power plant. Life upon Corregidor depended heavily on the energy generated on Bottomside to pump fresh water from wells, refrigerate perishable foods and move the electric railroad that supplied military installations. The topography changed radically as one continued from Bottomside towards the tail end. Another hump,

Malinta Hill, almost four hundred feet high, rose above the water. Beyond this outcropping, on the extreme eastern edge, lay a small air strip and a Navy radio station.

It was from Malinta Hill that MacArthur and his staff directed the struggle to preserve the American presence in the Philippines. To protect the nerve center for a War Plan Orange strategy, engineers had burrowed deep into the side of Malinta Hill to construct a fourteen-hundred-foot-long, thirty-foot-wide tunnel. From the main shaft with its railroad track running through it extended twenty-five laterals, narrower four-hundred-foot-long branches. A separate network of tunnels with a connection to the main passageway served as an underground hospital. The Navy dug its own system opposite the hospital and also had access to the main branch through a quartermaster area.

Blue mercury vapor lights pierced the gloom of Malinta Tunnel, reflecting off the six-foot-high, endless line of packing crates containing supplies. Signs that denoted organizations identified the province of the laterals. Within the confines of stale, hot air, insects including bedbugs tormented the residents. People intent on their business constantly jostled against others; solitude was impossible. The claustrophobic ambience drove some to stay outside even though exposed to enemy shells. Others developed "tunnelitis," unable to leave the seeming security of underground.

From within this labyrinth of caves USAFFE issued orders, communicated with the States, administered its military and civilian responsibilities, kept a hospital and provided living quarters for many of the principals including the MacArthur family, the Quezons and others. The ventilation of the entire underground city relied upon Bottomside's power plant.

To maintain fortress Corregidor against a naval attack a seemingly formidable array of heavy guns, principally coast artillery housed in concrete bunkers, menaced anyone who approached by sea. But there were acute deficiencies. The big sticks were all of World War I vintage. They were geared for action against ships, not in support of ground troops. The antiaircraft weapons lacked the best ammunition for use against planes. And although emergency generators could operate the big guns, long-term efficiency required the services that only Bottomside could provide.

Three smaller islands bolstered Corregidor's control of Manila Bay. Tiny Caballo (Fort Hughes), only a quarter-mile square in area, lay due south. It bristled with eleven batteries of artillery including antiaircraft. Also blocking access through the south channel to the Bay were Carabao (Fort Frank) and El Fraile (Fort Drum), a pair that contributed another thirty-two heavy pieces to the arsenal. Engineers had transformed Fort Drum into a unique phenomenon. They lopped off the top of El Fraile down to the waterline. With the ground as a foundation, they poured in concrete to create a stationary battleship whose superstructure, with twenty-foot-thick walls, stuck up forty feet from the channel. With fourteen-inch guns, standard for seagoing dreadnaughts, seated in armored turrets, and other artillery, Fort Drum seemed impregnable.

Farther east sat Carabao (Fort Frank) with its own heavy weapons and beach defenses. Most of its shoreline consisted of one-hundred-foot-high cliffs, making it an uninviting target for invasion.

The four Manila Bay installations, plus Fort Wint at Subic Bay, formed an organization known as the Harbor Defenses under Maj. Gen. George F. Moore, commander over Corregidor. As the Japanese forced the retreat into Bataan, Fort Wint became untenable. The artillerymen there transferred to Wainwright's I Corps while those guns that could not be redeployed were destroyed.

Life on Corregidor during the first few weeks after the evacuation of Manila was subdued, broken only by the start of air raids. Madeline Ullom counted twenty-one Army nurses like herself plus a dietician and physical therapist on duty at the medical station along with the doctors. Food rations were more of an inconvenience than a severe hardship as boats from the southern islands ran the tightening blockade by the Japanese Navy. The vessels that reached the Rock brought fresh fruit, vegetables and even candy along with other supplies.

"The mess hall lateral," says Ullom, "was also used as a chapel with different denominational services. Personnel and patients attended. The whiz of a shell on the head of a bomb without your name on it was a cause for reflection. 'Call the chaplain' was never necessary. As quickly as patients arrived, the chaplains mingled among them to perform ecclesiastical duties. The chaplains also pitched in to help lift and transport patients.

"A quiet evening was conducive to a few hands of bridge in the mess hall. Newsmen, the Jacobys, the Mydans, Clark Lee and others stopped by to chat. The reporters also visited patients in the wards. The Voice of Freedom broadcast at 0630, 1230 and 1930 each day. These were times to congregate and listen. The programs contained news from USAFFE headquarters. Broadcasts ended with 'Corregidor still stands.' "

Some of the Rock's residents, noted Ullom, stared into the skies of the clear nights, looking at the brilliant stars and picking out constellations like the Southern Cross. Others broke into community sings. "Those from Texas invariably began with 'The Eyes of Texas Are Upon You,' followed by 'The Yellow Rose of Texas.' Other favorites included 'Home on the Range,' before the songfest would end."

The population of Corregidor continued to grow as the advance of the enemy shifted the Marine garrison stationed first at Olongapo and then Mariveles, the port on the southern tip of Bataan. On December 26 the roughly one thousand leathernecks of the 4th Regiment, including erstwhile bandsman Elmer Long, boarded vessels that ferried them out to the Rock.

According to one of their officers, "There was much talk among the men about its big guns and underground system of defense. Inspired by the memory of photographs of the Maginot Line, they conjured up pictures of underground barracks and supply lines direct to gun positions. Ever since the 1st Battalion had moved from Olongapo to Mariveles Harbor the very day the war had started, we had often gazed out over the water with curious eyes at the 'Rock.' We watched Jap bombers steer clear of the antiaircraft barrages. It was pointed out that Corregidor's antiaircraft was so good that the Japs had not even dared to bomb it yet."

The first Marines to arrive moved into barracks at Middleside. Posted to guard the entrances of MacArthur's offices, a sergeant remarked, "We had darn good duty. We ate with the staff and had plenty of butter and eggs."

On December 29 the air raid sirens sounded on Corregidor, as they had so often in the past without incident. Convinced this was one more false alarm, the denizens of the Rock paid little attention to the planes. But then bombs rained down upon portions of the island, with several striking at Middleside. Most of the Marine 4th Regiment dropped to the floors of their buildings as the explosions testified to limits of Japanese fear of Corregidor's defenses.

"An army officer came in the room in which we [A Company, 1st Battalion] were," said one leatherneck, "and informed us that there was no need to worry because the barracks roof was bomb proof. A few minutes later, a Jap bomb had penetrated the roof on the other end of the barracks." The Marines soon moved outdoors to tents set up near the beach areas they would be expected to hold if an invasion began.

With the Marines now in residence, the number of people on Corregidor added up to fifty-five hundred men plus assorted civilian refugees connected with the uppermost echelons of command—the families of MacArthur, Quezon and Sayre, along with some Filipinos acting as houseboys. The abundant portions of butter and eggs disappeared.

On the December 29 raid the twin-engined bombers maintained an incautious level of only eighteen thousand feet. The 60th Coast Artillery, throwing up three-inch shells and some .50 caliber machine gun lead, made the fliers pay for their insouciance. Several planes began smoking and the enemy formations, recognizing the error in judgment, climbed to a safer height. The bombardment scored heavily against barracks, warehouses and other unshielded surface installations, killed twenty-two and wounded another eighty, but did little damage to the essential defensive armament of the Rock.

Further aerial punches over the next week shattered more buildings, gouged ugly craters in the once lush greenery but left the fortress intact. The residents, now aware of the deadly consequences if caught in the open, learned to either dig in or take shelter in places like the Malinta Tunnel. For their part, the Japanese approached Corregidor with respect for its gunners, a distinct hindrance to their attempts to blast the redoubt into submission.

According to Sam Grashio, the Americans grievously underestimated the Japanese aircraft and the professionalism of the enemy fliers. "Though the pilots were not particularly imaginative or adaptable, many of them were veterans of campaigns in China where they had become experts at set pieces. I once saw the leader of a flight of four Japanese dive bombers drop out of formation and attack one of our antiaircraft batteries. He immediately drew fire from all four guns of the battery who thereby revealed their positions. At once the other Japanese pilots peeled off, one by one, in perfect order, each picking out a different AA gun. In one graceful synchronized dive they silenced the whole battery and sped away."

General Moore had named Col. Paul D. Bunker, nominally in charge of the 59th Coast Artillery manned by Americans, to run the seaward defenses of the Rock. At the start of the war, Paul Bunker had already worn an army uniform for thirty-eight years. He was, in fact, a classmate of Douglas MacArthur at the Academy and an athletic star. "Bunker had been twice selected by Walter Camp for the

All-American team," remembered MacArthur. "I could shut my eyes and see again that blond head racing, tearing, plunging—210 pounds of irresistible power." Indeed, Camp chose Bunker as a tackle in 1901 and as a halfback the following year, one of only two players ever named for two different positions.

Bunker first set foot on Corregidor with the 59th in 1915 and, after tours in various areas, returned to the Rock and the same coast artillery regiment in 1940. An opinionated man freely given to criticism tinted with the prejudices of his era, Bunker exuded spit and polish. "He appeared to walk at attention as he made his daily inspection of various batteries under his command," said one account.

In his diary, Bunker jotted down his record of life on Corregidor. A January 3 entry noted: "Awoke early and went down to relieve the watch officer. Breakfast and then bath and shave as usual . . . They sprang the usual air alarm on us which usually occurs when that lone Jap observation plane comes over every morning, thus wasting an hour." After an all-clear and a visit to his headquarters, he continued, "Bought toothpaste and shaving cream in the heap of ruins which was once our Post Exchange. Drove to my quarters for Kleenex and bookcase. Lunch at Wheeler [a battery] on Topside . . . As all was quiet went to my dugout to arrange its contents when Wham-o! She started. This was our second dose of Jap bombing, composed of four courses across the Rock, said to be by two flights of six and eight planes, some of them the largest of the Jap bombers.

"Got into my car for a tour of inspection. Arrived at barracks at 2:35 and what a scene of devastation met the eye! Huge patches of corrugated roofing missing and scattered in painfully distorted shapes all over front and rear parades [grounds]. Captain Julian [Harry] met me and smilingly reported, 'Colonel, I have no office now.' A huge bomb had landed just across the car track in the rear of his place and blew out a crater twenty-five feet deep and forty feet across, cutting rails and trolley wires and shattering every window on the rear face of barracks. A smaller direct hit on [the] Mechanic shop where the Mech had practically finished making me a filing cabinet! Our regimental workshop [was] burning fiercely and of course, no water at Topside.

"One could see, from the direction of wind, that it would also burn the other buildings, including the 'Spiff Bar.' I went up into my library and found utter chaos. Glass case containing my shell collection blown to smithereens and thousands of books littering the floor everywhere and even some outside. Going downstairs I found soldiers already looting the PX like ghouls . . . Stationed a sergeant as guard temporarily."

Accompanied by several staff officers, Bunker toured the area, made photographs of the damage and "then to the Club where we waxed sentimental over the ruins of the place of happy memories for all of us."

Bunker and others on Corregidor now observed a respite from aerial bombardment. "We began to wonder what the cessation meant. One explanation lay in the USAFFE News that Formosa had been so severely bombed yesterday that the Jap bombers could not take off! Would that it were true, but my hunch is that they were too busy attacking our Bataan forces." Another theory claimed the Japanese found the responses from the antiaircraft units overwhelming. Actually, the real reason for a temporary respite was a need for Japanese combat aircraft to deal with Gen. Claire Chennault's "Flying Tigers," Americans putting up stiff resistance in the skies over Burma.

Although everyone was supposed to be on short rations, Bunker reported sitting down to a breakfast of hotcakes and coffee disturbed only by slow service. With no foe to dodge or shoot at, Bunker and his associates groused about the lack of initiative of the Navy, complained about a burning barge whose smoke obscured the field of fire, chafed over the performance of Filipino troops, played poker into the late evening and topped off their days with shots of Scotch whiskey. He remarked without rancor that he had probably lost the money banked at the Philippine Trust.

On January 21 he headed his diary, "Seventh day of No Bombs." He continued a description of his day: "It certainly is beautiful weather, now. There is a little orchid, just outside my dugout, which is just completing its blooming and the last two tiny blossoms fell off yesterday. They were almost of the same color as the hot-house specimens sold in the States. After breakfast, I sat on Wheeler 'parade' and enjoyed the weather, until the men started sweeping.

"Drove to [a building site], kicked a Navy gang out of the PX where they were stealing chairs for their tunnel. Inspected beer kegs at Spiff Bar but we agreed they're no good for water. Several of the men from my headquarters battery have had bad diarrhea and vomiting. We are getting the fly pest under better control but there are still too many.

"Drove to my quarters to view the ruins, as I usually do daily. Straightened up a few things around but had no heart to do much. Showed Welch [his orderly] the table linen and contents of chiffonier to pack in powder can this afternoon. Then went to my dugout and passed away the time making the detailed dimension drawing of a leg of our divan table, repairing the table when I get the chance.

"It was quiet and peaceful outside my dugout. The swish of waves down on the South Shore, a gentle rustle of leaves overhead, birds twittering and chirping—and a wild rooster with his tenor challenging crow, much higher in pitch than that of a tame rooster. Captain McCarthy came around and I told him to get busy with more camouflage over my dugout.

"With [staff members] I took dinner at the usual hour of 4:00 P.M. with Captain Steiger at Battery Cheney and it was excellent. For one thing the rice was well cooked and not a soggy mess; the quantities also were good and the apple cobbler for dessert might well have been made from fresh apples."

Bunker then returned to his dugout and watched a squad trying to string a camouflage net. "For a joke, had them dump it into the entrance to Colonel Foster's tent. Everything was quiet so adjourned to the 'Club' and played poker until 11:00 P.M." He lost a dollar, then finished the evening by offering the hospitality of drinks at his tent to associates before retiring.

In his diary, the coast artillery officer, still relatively comfortable on Corregidor, disparaged the Filipino soldiers. "The infantry, catching sight of a few Japs, ran back through the artillery positions, laughing and shouting and, holding up their two first fingers to form a 'Vee' for 'Victory,' continued their flight to the rear. When they retreated from Lingayen they abandoned so many of their 75 mm field guns that now they have none and so the 155 mm (manned by our coast artillerymen) have to do their own work *plus* that of the missing 75s.

"It is an obvious fact that the Philippine Army is worthless because the Filipino will *not* fight under Filipino officers. And there are practically no Filipino officers who are worth a damn. The graduates of the 'Philippine West Point' at Baguio are sometimes pretty fair but others are political appointees whose only idea is to line their pockets. They have no control over their men."

On January 23 Bunker added, "Mellnik [Steve, an artillery officer] at Headquarters told me today that things look black for our Bataan forces because the 'heroic' Philippine Army is deserting en masse, leaving their positions at night, sifting through the Jap lines and working their way around to Manila! And these are the scum for whom we are fighting and whom President Quezon calls 'Our Heroes' and praises their bravery. The Scouts hold them in utter contempt—evidently correctly!"

The one resident of Corregidor who seemed totally unconcerned about the air raids was MacArthur, who refused to seek shelter. As the siren sounded, his four-year-old son

Arthur would howl, "Air Raid!" Antiaircraft crewmen yelled "Meatball!" or "Scrambled Eggs," referring to the enemy wing insignia, and everyone headed for the safety of the tunnels. But MacArthur insisted on leaving his office and walking outside to watch the attack without even a helmet to protect him from debris or shrapnel.

In his role as the Navy liaison with the Army, Robert Lee Dennison visited MacArthur on several occasions. "I was in his office one day in this ramshackle wooden building atop a wall when the air raid alarm went off. We couldn't reach these bombers at the altitude they were flying so they could just bomb at will. Their practice was to make dummy runs to test out the wind and then they'd make a firing run. In this particular raid, we were the target. MacArthur's staff always beat it to a tunnel with their files and their gas masks and what all. I eased forward to the edge of my chair to leave, thinking of course that MacArthur would be going to the bomb shelter. When he saw what I was doing, he said, 'I'm enjoying our conversation and I'd like to continue it, if you care to stay here with me.' I thought, if he can take it, I can. How ridiculous! He's the one that ought to have been in a bomb shelter. So we sat and continued our conversation with all these bombs going off all around us. That was MacArthur. He was fatalistic."

High Commissioner Francis Sayre, Manuel Quezon and the staff, from company grade through the uppermost echelons, were in awe of their leader's lack of fear while the Japanese launched their thunderbolts from above. Sayre recalled an incident where he was among a group outside the shelters with MacArthur when a sudden bombardment exploded. Everyone except the Supreme Commander dropped to the dirt. "Anyone who saw us," remarked Sayre, "must have had a good laugh—at the General erect and at ease while the High Commissioner lay prone in the dust. I have often wondered whether he was as amused as I. In any event, his expression never changed." Sayre also remembered that MacArthur once remarked that "he

believed death would take him only at the ordained time."
The nickname of "Dugout Doug," bestowed at a later
period when MacArthur escaped from the Philippines and
capture, was singularly inappropriate to describe his behavior on the Rock, or for that matter in other instances when
he came under fire.

Seemingly oblivious to danger, MacArthur also ex-
horted his flagging troops. He issued a statement on January 15: "Help is on the way from the United States.
Thousands of troops and hundreds of planes are being dispatched. The exact time of arrival of reinforcements is
unknown as they will have to fight their way through Japanese attempts against them. It is imperative that our troops
hold until these reinforcements arrive.

"No further retreat is possible. We have more troops in
Bataan than the Japanese have thrown against us; our supplies are ample; a determined defense will defeat the enemy's attack.

"It is a question now of courage and determination.
Men who run will merely be destroyed, but men who fight
will save themselves and their country.

"I call upon every soldier in Bataan to fight in his assigned position, resisting every attack. This is the only road
to salvation. If we fight we will win; if we retreat, we will
be destroyed."

The message adds further mystery about the workings
of MacArthur's mind. This was the only occasion on which
he indicated numerical superiority for his own army; his
reports to Washington and his memoirs constantly spoke
of the greater strength of the foe. The statement, "thousands of troops and hundreds of planes are being dispatched," was deceptive if not deliberately ambiguous.
Any men and equipment moving to the Pacific were
bound for Australia, not the Philippines. In his *Reminiscences,* MacArthur identified the source of his error: "A
broadcast from President Roosevelt was incorrectly interpreted because of poor reception in the Philippines, as an
announcement of impending reinforcements. This was

published to the troops and aroused great enthusiasm, but when later corrected, the depression was but intensified." It is hard to believe a radio broadcast would be the means to inform the Pacific War's top commander that vital reinforcements were on the way.

Paul Bunker greeted the exhortation with reserve. Of the expected additions of men and machines he noted, "If the Navy is responsible they'll never get here. Rumors are persistent that instead of six months' reserve of food, we have only three months. Brass hats in Malinta Tunnel have a rotten mess and are complaining that our enlisted men are too well fed—even though they are on half-rations. Perhaps that is one reason for the stink they are raising because we salvaged the food from those grounded and sunken barges."

Army nurse Madeline Ullom says she initially took Mac-Arthur's statement at face value. "Every morning before breakfast I walked to the top of Malinta Hill to see if the promised convoy was arriving." A month would pass before she realized help would not come from over the horizon.

CHAPTER IX

BATAAN BEGINS TO CRUMPLE

WITH THE REST of the Philippine Division, Al Svihra had taken up residence on Bataan. Like almost every other U.S. ground forces officer in the Philippines, Svihra received a promotion, becoming a lieutenant colonel. He wrote marginally reassuring letters to his family. In one to his parents he said, "The days are warm and breezy, the nights clear and cool. While this operates to the comfort of the troops, it is equally advantageous to the enemy who can keep up relentless aerial attacks. Planes are droning over us from early morning, when they carry out reconnaissance flights, to about midafternoon. Most of the bombing and strafing is conducted from about 11:00 A.M. to about 3:00 P.M. Owing to the frequency of activity during the middle of the day, we have only two meals a day. So far we have been getting enough to eat, have plenty of streams in which to bathe and can get sufficient sleep in the hours of military inactivity."

To his wife Ila he expressed his love and his affection for their children. He sent detailed instructions on their financial affairs and gave little indication of the deteriorating state of the defenses. "Air bombing and artillery fire continues to be the order of the day, the enemy doing most of the former, and our troops most of the latter. Short periods of intense activity are interspersed with longer periods of inactivity which are getting rather boring."

Even as the enemy intensified its attacks, Svihra focused on those evacuated to the safety of the States. "I just noticed a statement made by Secretary of War Stimson, warning that the United States must expect sporadic coastal attacks . . . If there is any real danger of such, Long Beach [where his wife and children were living] would certainly be one of the places attacked on account of the oil wells and airplane industry located near it. I believe it would be well to keep in mind the possibility of moving inland . . . You can't always be sure that the enemy's bombing is going to be accurately aimed at the objective."

In a letter to his brother he noted, "From our position we have witnessed a great deal of bombing of our artillery positions and could also see the enemy planes dive bombing and strafing our front lines. But do their damndest, the Japs have been unable to do any great damage. We have also viewed several aerial combats between our fighters and the Jap fighters. You have only to read the communiques to know how these have resulted in plenty of losses to the enemy in spite of their numbers." In fact, with so few U.S. planes still operational, the Air Corps was almost entirely restricted to reconnaissance patrols.

Referring to his assignment as the division's judge advocate, Svihra confided, "I brought out an armful of work when I left [Fort McKinley], but as there have been very few court-martial cases since taking the field, I have had plenty of time to catch up with the back work. I had it all caught up by the middle of January in spite of many camp duties. Legal work is not very heavy in time of war, so I have some spare time. I have filed service regulations, read up on *Rules of Land Warfare,* a manual on the Japanese Army, and Winthrop's *Military Law and Precedents,* a classic old work on the history and development of military law.

"In their spare time, the Philippine Scout soldiers in our camp have been making bamboo furniture, bamboo fly traps and rat traps, fly swatters, and all sort of things, including pipes and cigarette holders. They have even given American soldiers demonstrations on the use of bamboo for making benches, stands and beds. In the evenings we either go to bed at 8:00 o'clock or sit up and talk. Lights of course are taboo, so that leaves long, uninteresting evenings."

Svihra was a division headquarters officer and his experience of the war hardly replicated that of men much closer to the invaders. At the start of the third week in January, Alva Fitch and his artillery battalion feared an imminent and dangerous thrust from the enemy. His anxiety deepened as the expected morning meal did not arrive. Fitch's direst expectations proved well founded. Elements from a Japanese battalion had either infiltrated through the thick underbrush or else slipped through a gap between two units. The Japs set up a roadblock behind the 1st Division and shut down the only major road suitable for moving heavy equipment and supplies.

The command post at the rear informed Fitch that his superior, Col. Halstead Fowler, commander of the 71st Field Artillery Regiment [Philippine Army], had been wounded and Fitch was now in charge of the 71st Artillery and units attached to it.

Fitch recalls that when he reached headquarters "the CP was in a stew. The gooks were chattering like so many monkeys. A force of Japanese had gone around our right flank and cut our communications exactly at the rear echelon of the Pack Battery, five kilometers back. All forms of communication were cut. Fowler, when he heard about it, had gone back and tried to drive them out with an automatic rifle. He had been hit twice in the back and lungs, but had escaped and returned to the regimental aid station.

"General Segundo had spent the night in Colonel [Kearie] Berry's CP [Berry directed the 3rd Regiment of Segundo's division]. On the morning of the twentieth,

Segundo promptly took command of the situation and tied hell out of it. He took our reserve battalion of infantry, deployed them across the road and started beating the jungle back towards the rear echelon. In this manner, the Japs had until 5:00 P.M. to organize their position before we ever made contact with them. They used their time well." Not only did the enemy set up antitank obstacles and lay mines that repulsed relief from U.S. armor, but also more of their comrades somehow managed to pick their way through the defenders' forward positions and add their strength to the original infiltrators.

Fitch commented in disgust: "When Captain Laird who was commanding the reserve battalion hit them, he made almost no impression. He was forced by darkness to halt after having gained only a few yards."

The best efforts of Fitch and associates to turn their artillery on the enemy behind them proved ineffective. Snipers picked at the defensive positions; mortars inflicted casualties and the artillerymen with supporting infantry remained cut off.

"About 4:00 P.M.," said Fitch, "a gook lieutenant, unknown to me, told me the road was open. I relayed the information to Colonel Berry. He sent an ambulance loaded with wounded to the rear. The road was not open. The Japs shot up the ambulance. Colonel Fowler and one other man who could walk escaped. The Filipinos decided the Japs were using the ambulance as a machine gun and literally tore it apart with rifle fire. Of course the wounded were still in it.

"I found myself with seven hundred men who had not eaten for twenty-four hours. I got a sack of rice from the Philippine Army Infantry, and found a carabao during the night; each man got a little to eat."

When Berry suggested they try to blast their way through, using the self-propelled guns, Fitch declined and in retrospect admitted he was wrong. But at the time he recalled a similar effort in which those involved suffered heavy losses from snipers. "We were well aware of the Japanese filling the trees with snipers under such circumstances. It seemed to me that the probability of loss outweighed the probability of success."

Meanwhile, said Fitch, when General Segundo realized his attack failed, he and an aide followed an obscure trail back to the safety of the defensive lines. Fitch and his companions could not escape by that route for it would require abandonment of their field pieces.

"On the twenty-second," said Fitch, "the Japs began closing in on us from all sides. We had no reserves after we had committed Laird's battalion in the rear and it was rapidly tiring. During the afternoon I called a conference of all of my battalion commanders and gave instructions for the destruction of guns and other material when the position should fall.

"We had received no word from General Wainwright and had no communications whatsoever. Our position was extremely precarious. The troops had received only one meal since the interruption of communications and the capture of our rear echelon. Our ammunition was about gone, and we knew that a heavy battle was under way on the other side of Bataan. The principal reserve of General Wainwright's corps [Bluemel's 31st Division] had been moved to support the other battle before our communications had been cut. We could expect very little help and our force was exhausted."

Indeed, as Fitch said, the resolute resistance of the men of the 57th Regiment (Philippine Scouts) on the east end of the line stopped the Japanese cold, but the Filipino positions were jeopardized by a collapse of the defense on their left flank. Unless the interlopers could be pushed back, the II Corps would need to fall back.

General Parker ordered the U.S. 31st Infantry and the 45th Infantry, the other Philippine Scout regiment, to counterattack. The troops moved out with less than precision coordination. The Americans jumped off well before their Filipino comrades reached the scene. The GIs achieved some good gains but then the attack stalled against a stiffening and increasingly numerous enemy.

With the arrival of the 45th on the scene, the II Corps brass plotted a joint operation. But although the Filipino-American forces hit the Japanese hard, they could not dislodge them from a salient that compromised the defensive line. Furthermore, both enemy artillery and dive bombers pounded the 45th and 31st Regiments. The embattled forces pleaded for tank support but the commander of the two American-staffed tank battalions refused, claiming that the terrain was unsuitable for armor. Infantry officers believed the timidity unwarranted, arguing that the foot soldiers only needed the tanks for cover and that the ground was flat enough for the armor to maneuver.

With no significant gains and some potential threats to the attacking units, strategists directed the 57th to pull back and assume responsibility for the extreme left flank of the Corps. What looked good on a map proved extremely difficult to achieve. Access to the designated position depended upon a trail that deteriorated into an impassable path for vehicles. "As in many situations during the early days of the war," said John Olson who was there, "no one on the higher staffs had taken the trouble to verify all of the facets of WPO-3. So no provision had been made to ensure that supply and evacuation could be effective for the organization given this portion of the line to defend." Logistical ignorance continued to exact a toll.

For engineers to hack a road through the thick growth would require five days, an unacceptable delay. Regimental supply organized mule trains to pick up supplies dropped by vehicles at the point where the trail became inaccessible for trucks. Harassed by Japanese planes, the troops still managed to transport enough to sustain the infantrymen for several days. The planners worked out an intricate choreography: trucks or buses to haul soldiers as far as possible; night marches to avoid the threat of air attacks; and a schedule of which unit stepped out first. Military police patrolled the roads and trails but only partially prevented traffic jams. Periodic salvos of Japanese artillery rained down upon critical sites under enemy observation during daylight hours and added to the difficulties.

Despite all of the problems, the 57th managed to reach its objective and started to dig in. Only then did higher headquarters opt for a new strategy and direct a withdrawal. Luck spared disaster during a bumper-to-bumper pullback along a narrow road as a Japanese plane dropped a flare illuminating the entire column in gridlock. For some inexplicable reason, an artillery, mortar or aerial barrage did not strike the hapless mass of troops. They reverted to reserve status.

Colonel Berry advised Fitch they would marshal their forces during the night and then try to fight their way back to the defensive lines. But even as Berry started to issue orders to his battalion commanders, a runner brought a message from Wainwright, directing the surrounded units to "Hold your positions. Plenty of help on the way. Food will reach you tomorrow."

The besieged troops hunkered down, employing what means they could to consolidate their position. A Japanese cavalry unit slipped into the area and triggered a firefight. Far worse, the battalion under Captain Laird, which had been committed to an attack against the enemy in the rear, slipped away. They made good their escape but left the men with Fitch and Berry vulnerable.

"Laird did not notify Colonel Berry. In fact, we discovered his defection the next morning when Japs began arriving in the vicinity of our CP in buses from our ex-rear echelon. By 9:00 A.M. on the twenty-third our position had become untenable. All wire communication was broken. I lost all but one of my OPs. Rifle fire was coming through my CP from the front and the inland flank."

By radio, Fitch relayed a message from Berry to Wainwright through the Field Artillery Brigade headquarters. Wainwright responded but used 26th Cavalry code, which Fitch and his people could not decipher. The unread communique told Fitch not to fire on barges approaching his area since they would be carrying food. Actually, the Navy would not send any because of the danger.

"About ten o'clock, I gave the order to destroy all guns, except the 2.95″ pack guns which were to be carried, and ordered all battalions and batteries to assemble at a point about a kilometer to the rear of my CP. I told Colonel Berry I was going to try and get my artillerymen back along the coast to Bagac. When I arrived at the assembly area, I found that Lieutenant Platt had been wounded. He had received bullets through one foot, thigh and his testicles, and couldn't possibly walk. Colonel Fowler was also there.

"I found myself with seven hundred men, of which eighty were Scouts from the Pack Battery, the remainder untrained and undisciplined PA artillery. I had four unwounded American officers. Three were good men, one worse than useless." Fitch split his force into several groups and arranged for litters to carry the wounded officers, Platt and Fowler. Then, about noon, the move toward safety began.

"I stayed as near the shore as the trails and cliffs would allow. It was extremely difficult going. No mule could possibly have made it. Progress was slow but we did not encounter any Japanese in force, except a patrol of about a squad which quickly withdrew. About the middle of the afternoon Colonel Fowler caught up. He had thrown away his litter and actually walked fifteen kilometers over that trail, only three days after receiving two bullets in his lungs.

"Just at dark I reached the main road about four kilometers above Bagac. I confiscated a car from some PA staff officer and went to division headquarters to get food for my men. The Filipinos wished to give it to me tomorrow but Colonel Vanture got me a bus, some corned beef hash, bread, tomatoes and water. By midnight, we were fairly well assembled and fed."

Still, the band of artillerymen remained a target for aerial attack or a thrust by ground forces. Although the dispirited soldiers teetered on the brink of exhaustion they embarked on another march that settled most of them under jungle cover before daylight.

While Fitch had successfully guided his group out of the enemy trap, some from the other parties had run into trouble. The two officers, Semmens and Stillman, as part of the bunch accompanying the wounded Platt, found themselves on a trail too steep to climb with a man on a stretcher. "They had gone back to the beach," said Fitch, "and built a raft to get Platt past the place. Neither Platt nor Stillman could swim. The water was a little rough and Platt . . . had become frightened and overturned the raft. All three had gotten ashore on a small island, about fifty yards from the shore. Semmens had then come down on the shore looking for a banca and reached Bagac without finding one. When he arrived at my CP, he was looking for corps headquarters to get help."

Subsequently, reported Fitch, Stillman, Platt and a Filipino orderly stranded with them, put together their own raft and floated to the mainland. Using his pistol to persuade, Stillman convinced several itinerant PA soldiers to act as bearers for the wounded Platt. But after a brief trek overland during which they added a bayonetted Filipino to their crew, the porters deserted. They discovered a leaky banca and Stillman then guided the craft to Bagac.

Fitch took a quick inventory and could list almost nothing on hand except defenseless soldiers. "I was unable to get any additional equipment for my men," said Fitch. "All except the Scouts had thrown away nearly everything. Nearly all had canteens, about twenty percent had mess gear and very few had blankets. We had no unit equipment whatsoever. It was decided to divide up and distribute these men as replacements to infantry units in the division. Colonel Vanture and I decided to withhold the Scouts and a few selected officers."

He then admittedly ignored orders from higher-ups in an attempt to retain officers and enlisted men whom he believed could staff a reconstituted artillery battalion under his command. Threats of court-martials, couched in oblique or blunt terms, snapped back and forth. But eventually Fitch worked out a compromise that put him in charge of a Philippine Army outfit, buttressed by a number of Scouts and some American officers. With his housekeeping once more in order, Fitch again faced off against the enemy.

Not only were Fitch and his companions in dire circumstances but the entire Bataan defense was threatened by a clever maneuver instigated by General Homma. The Japanese loaded a battalion of infantrymen aboard barges at the recently captured port of Moron and set out for Caibobo Point, one of a series of almost finger-like protrusions along the western shore of Bataan and behind the bulk of Wainwright's I Corps.

Hastily mounted, the amphibious operation miscarried during a series of misfortunes. A lack of proper maps prevented the navigators from distinguishing Caibobo from the many similar headlands and coves leading to the objective. Treacherous tides and a cranky sea sickened soldiers and added to the woes of those directing the landing barges.

But the worst to befall the ill-fated troops was their discovery by PT-34, skippered by Lt. John Kelly with squadron commander John Bulkeley also on board. "We were returning to our base on Bataan early in the morning," said Bulkeley, "from a patrol off Subic Bay. We saw these barges and charged in among them, strafing them with .50 calibers and raising general hell but without very decisive results." In the darkness, a dim light had appeared low in the water. When PT-34 came within twenty-five yards of what was now perceived as a boat, Bulkeley hailed it with a megaphone to determine friend or foe. A burst of machine gun fire and a stream of tracers established the relationship. Bulkeley himself took up an automatic rifle while the four machine guns on PT-34 pumped bullets at the craft now headed for the shore. With armor plate at the bow and stern, the Japanese boat sought to keep the steel

plates between it and the attackers who in turn maneuvered for a side angle.

An enemy bullet ripped into the ankles of Ens. Barron
Chandler, Kelly's second in command. But the enemy
barge had taken too many hits and soon sank. According
to the stripped-down narrative of Bulkeley, "We concentrated, after a general dispersion, on two barges that appeared to be crippled and sank them. The last one was
boarded before sinking by myself, and two live prisoners
were taken with a lot of papers which were delivered to
Corregidor. That first gave the news of the strength and
force of the attempted landing. The Japanese barge sank
with me and I was in the water hanging on to the two Nips
till Bob Kelly rescued me. It was a good thing that I had
been a water polo player."

The intervention by PT-34 completed the disarray of
the small flotilla. Not a single man reached the target,
Caibobo Point. Instead, a third of the men came ashore at
Longoskawayan Point ten miles southeast of the objective
and the rest of the battalion landed about three miles from
Caibobo.

Guarding the beaches where the latter group came
ashore were the Air Corps comrades of Tom Gage in the
34th Pursuit Squadron. The official U.S. Army history,
The Fall of the Philippines, states that "the airmen failed to
make proper provision for security, for there was no warning of the presence of the enemy. The gun crews, awakened by the sound of the Japanese coming ashore in pitch
blackness and unable to fire their .50 caliber machine guns,
put up no resistance. After giving the alarm, they, in the
words of an officer 'crept back to their CP.' "

Tom Gage offers a somewhat different version. "For
several days," remembered Gage, "we could see mast tops
just over the sea's horizon, coming down from the north
to even with our position and then patrolling back and
forth. Rumors said it was a battleship, minesweeper, cruisers, tug boats pulling barges. No matter, during the night

of the twenty-second barges did land in a ravine or gully that ran down to the seashore. Our furthest northern point was a machine gun (.50 caliber) placed inside a rock barricade. In the early morning of the twenty-third, Japanese soldiers climbed out on top and approached the gun position. Some men thought they were Filipino soldiers, even called a greeting to them which was answered with rifle fire. Pfc. John W. Morrell from Ohio was killed. The remaining men of the gun crew withdrew.

"Lt. Jack Jennings took a patrol later in the day into this area and came under heavy fire. He was wounded in the knee and Sgt. Paul Duncan was hit in the thigh by something of a large caliber. Paul died during the night in the squadron aid station. Several others from the 34th also incurred wounds from tangles with the invaders."

Nevertheless, the Japanese achieved total tactical surprise and no significant resistance. With the delivery of the documents by Bulkeley to Corregidor (erroneous only in that it named Caibobo Point as the landing site), the alarm sounded by the 34th Pursuit Squadron ground troops and a visual sighting of the enemy force by a lookout, the defenders now sought to eliminate the enemy threat. The sector most endangered by the Japanese presence included the vital Bataan port of Mariveles. As the base for the Navy, defense of Mariveles depended upon one of the many improvised units, the Naval Battalion, with men drawn from the PBY Patrol Wing, the *Canopus* crew, shore personnel from Cavite Naval Base, and Battery A and Battery C of the 4th Marines. It was a collection of former shore-based torpedomen, storekeepers, yeomen, a motley of naval rates and some Marines under the leadership of Comdr. Francis J. Bridget.

Frank Bridget—"Fidgety Francis" to some of his men because of his relentless insistence that they "get war conscious"—seemingly was not the stuff of a land-battle tactician. An Annapolis graduate, Bridget flew PBYs and had served as squadron commander in the Philippines. But after a series of air raids destroyed all nine planes, Bridget had volunteered to form a security force that would defend the naval station at Mariveles.

During the week or so after the unit's creation, the new foot soldiers began courses under supervision of Marines in such unfamiliar subjects as marksmanship, squad tactics and the use of the bayonet. Aware that their ordinary Navy whites made the men easier targets, the novice foot soldiers desperately attempted to dye their uniforms khaki but instead produced rather bright, mustard-colored garb.

It was some time after eight on the morning of January 23 that Bridget listened to a frightened call from the lookout. "Longoskawayan, Lapiay and Naiklec Points are crawling with Japs," supposedly shouted the observer. "We're getting the hell out of here, right now!" After those few words and despite requests for further information, Bridget heard only the ominous sounds of rifles.

In his excitement, Bridget briefed and then dispatched two separate outfits, one from Battery A and one from Battery C, to deal with the enemy until he could round up more men. Compounding his mistake, he failed to advise either battery that a second friendly force would be active in the vicinity. The two units marched off into the wilds leading up to Mt. Pucet.

One platoon blundered into a small group of enemy and a firefight ensued. The Navy ensign in charge and his senior Marine noncom both incurred wounds, but the invaders retreated. The untrained Navy troops kept firing long after the foe vanished into the jungle. Another platoon routed a handful of Japanese with more bursts from their rifles. The sounds from these encounters reached the ears of other Americans with twitchy fingers on the triggers. Inexplicably, with all of the untrained, quick-shooting men thrashing about the underbrush, a pitched battle between Americans did not occur.

The first effort of the novice infantrymen wiped their sectors clean, but the main element of the enemy amphibious force was still on the scene. Still, by nightfall on January 24, Bridget's ersatz infantry had control of Mt. Pucet. A dead Japanese soldier's diary reported the presence of a "new type of suicide squad" dressed in brightly colored uniforms, a reference to the dyed navy whites. He marveled at their tactics. "Whenever these apparitions reached an open space, they would attempt to draw Japanese fire by sitting down, talking loudly and lighting cigarettes."

The presence of an enemy force in their backyard galvanized some defenders intent on glory. "We had a visit from a one-star general," said Gage, "an old cavalry man with campaign hat, boots and jodpurs. I was nearby when he talked to Capt. Robert Wray, now the CO of the 34th. He suggested a 'turkey shoot'—Wray should take a patrol down to sea level around the north point and 'flush' the enemy out. He and no one else knew how many enemy were jammed up that gulley."

Wray apparently did take some men into the ravine and returned with one dead, several wounded and, Gage believes, then created a self-serving, glowing account of the affair, sufficient enough to earn him a Silver Star. Other than the captain's statement, there is no indication of any serious damage to the enemy nor any useful intelligence gathered.

Frank Bridget felt the major responsibility for dealing with the interlopers belonged to him. With only six hundred men in his outfit, most of whom were bluejackets who still knew little about infantry tactics, Bridget requested help in dealing with the approximately three hundred Japanese soldiers gathering on Mt. Pucet. He knew that from this position the enemy could cut the essential West Road between the upper peninsula and Mariveles. The 71st Division of the Philippine Army supplied some men, including a pack howitzer with crew; others came from the provisional infantry unit cobbled together out of members of the Air Corps' 3rd Pursuit Squadron; and the American 301st Chemical Company donated some of its complement.

Bridget's makeshift army sought to displace the

Japanese from Mt. Pucet and the Longoskawayan peninsula but the bulk of the seaborne force had moved into
Quinauan Point after passing the thin beach positions of
the 34th Pursuit Squadron. Brig. Gen. Clyde Selleck, required to defend the ten miles of the entire southwestern
Bataan coast between Caibobo Point and Mariveles, ordered Lt. Col. Irvin Alexander and his regiment to drive
the invaders into the sea. After his initial mission of survey-
ing the territory to be manned by the 71st Infantry Division, Alexander now led the 1st Philippine Constabulary
Regiment.

Inducted into the Army only in December, the Constabulary ordinarily served as an indigenous police force.
Their background did not include infantry training. Irvin
hurriedly mobilized his 3rd Battalion and with them set
out for a confrontation with the enemy. Rugged terrain,
overgrown trails and a single passable road delayed movement long enough for the Japanese to dig in.

Alexander ordered an attack. "The noise of the firing
remained stationary," said Alexander. "It was clear that we
were making no progress. I ran through the jungle towards the sound of the firing. That I arrived safely at my
destination was due to the good fortune that there were no
Nips along the way. Upon my arrival at the position of the
battalion I was informed it had been halted by heavy rifle
and machine gun fire. The size of the enemy force was
undetermined but it might have been as much as a battalion, judging from the sound of the firing.

"The battalion commander explained that he had attacked frontally without making any attempt to explore
either flank. When I tried to get a company to make an
envelopment of the right flank of the Nip position I got
nowhere, because the Filipinos did not want to leave the
vicinity of the road. After I had moved to try to start the
envelopment myself, the Nips must have spotted me for
they opened up with a heavy machine gun which snipped
off many leaves uncomfortably close to my head. I lost no
time hitting the dirt, but before my head got there, a bul-

let struck the ground in the same spot where my head hit an instant later. Wiping the dirt out of my eyes, I realized I was badly scared, so much so that my brain seemed to be paralyzed."

An officer from the engineers with no business on the scene but drawn by the fighting drawled, "That guy was sort of shooting at you, wasn't he?" The comment, said Alexander, broke his physical and mental stupor.

"I explained to the battalion commander the necessity for a flanking attack and assured him I would go with it. A Filipino corporal who saw the logic, jumped up shouting and kicking at his men to get them moving. It was difficult to get the men started, but we had to get results. The Nip machine gun opened up again, killing the corporal and several men, thereby putting a stop to our flanking attack. That corporal was a gallant man who deserved recognition, but later, when I tried to find out his name, I was unable to locate anyone who even remembered the incident."

Unable to generate any advance, Alexander decided to advise Selleck he needed help. The nearest telephone for communicating with headquarters lay two miles away by trail. Alexander tried to take a shortcut through the jungle, fell and belly-whopped down a thirty-foot hill but managed to talk Selleck into dispatching a pair of British-made Bren gun carriers armed with a .50 caliber to knock out the Japanese automatic weapons.

"The carriers, which had engines and tracks like tanks," said Alexander, "made a great deal of noise, advertising to the Nips that we were being reinforced by heavier equipment. The mission assigned to a carrier was to move rapidly towards the enemy gun position, engaging it with fire from its .50 caliber machine gun. The vehicle made its run as planned, turned around the curve in the road and opened fire, to be greeted immediately by fire from a small cannon. The first cannon shot bounced harmlessly off the steel bumping bar in front. The second shot went through the light armor, exploding near the machine gunner, wounding him severely. The driver, seeing he was outclassed in firepower, backed into the jungle far enough to turn around, then came out at full speed."

The erosion of manpower continued. "Walking wounded coming back along the road acquired Filipino soldiers far in excess of the numbers required to help them. One man had a leg wound, but could still walk. Five riflemen friends were with him, half carrying him, his pack and his rifle. I stopped them all, calling for a first aid man to take the wounded soldier. I took the others back to the firing line. Several repeated, 'We have not had our chow. We are too weak to fight.' "

MacArthur's chief of intelligence, Col. Charles Willougby, accompanied by a member of his staff, showed up for a firsthand look at the problem. They and the dismayed Alexander kept meeting soldiers straggling away from the front. The trio of Americans sent them back to their posts. But, noted Alexander, "Finding a number of officers standing behind trees, we tried to get them to take some tactical action; we had no success."

Alexander said he made another determined effort to launch an attack. "There were no Filipino officers present, and the men were not going to be pushed, so I saw I had to lead them. I crawled ahead of the line about ten feet. By shouting and waving my arms, I managed to get the line to crawl up to me.

"We moved a couple of times more, while Ted [an American officer, last name unknown] kept shouting a description of what he could see from the flank. He said we were very close to the Nip line which was made up of individual foxholes, except for a machine gun position which had two or three men in it. He announced that he could see a Nip sticking his head up, to which I answered, 'Shoot the son of a bitch!'

"His voice suddenly sounded very excited as he yelled, 'Look out! They are turning the machine gun in your direction!' I could not see a thing as I raised up on one knee, holding my rifle in front of me with both hands. Something struck the rifle with a metallic sound, jarring my hands pretty severely. Feeling an additional jolt on my right thumb, I turned it up to see a phosphorus core of a trace bullet burning into my flesh. Before I became aware of any pain in my right hand, I had started jerking it violently. At last the phosphorus came off, leaving the top half of the thumb almost as dark as a piece of charcoal. Not until the pain eased up did I notice that one finger of my left hand had been shot away, and another one had been considerably mangled.

"After I recovered my wits, I ran a little to the left rear of where I was hit so that my location would not be the same when the Nips fired again, and then I was sick. For thirty-six hours, with the exception of four hours sleep, I had been going at top speed."

Willoughby came to Alexander's aid, bandaging his hand and then leading him to a first aid station. "Ted" remained with the battalion until a substitute officer could replace him. Back at the aid station, the surgeon examining Alexander discovered a sliver of metal in his breastbone. It had pierced fifty-four folds in the map Alexander carried in his shirt front. Driven from the aid station to the Bataan hospital, Alexander admitted, "I had that same feeling of relief I had noticed and deplored in Hugh [last name unknown] when he left us. That feeling was a mixture of thankfulness for being practically still in one piece and of pleasure at the opportunity to go to a place of comparative safety and comfort. On the other hand, I had a small guilty feeling that I was running away from the boys."

Indeed, as Fitch said, the resolute resistance of the men of the 57th Regiment (Philippine Scouts) on the east end of the line stopped the Japanese cold, but the Filipino positions were jeopardized by a collapse of the defense on their left flank. Unless the interlopers could be pushed back, the II Corps would need to retreat.

It was then that General Parker ordered the U.S. 31st Infantry and the 45th Infantry, the other Philippine Scout regiment, to counterattack, without success. The Japanese held their line. Once again, the defenders all along the line received word for an orderly pullback from what had been designated as the Abucay-Moron line to a new east-west belt along the Pilar-Bagac road.

But even as the strategists rearranged their front, the hazard of the Japanese presence in the Points between Mariveles and Bagac required quick action. Not only had USAFFE strategists thrown General Selleck's forces into the fray alongside Bridget but also after Col. Paul Bunker pleaded the case, Battery Geary, crewed by Philippine Scouts on Corregidor, blasted the enemy positions with huge shells from its guns. It was the first use of U.S. Coast Artillery against an enemy since the Civil War.

"We could not see where the big shells or bombs were falling from, they seemed to be falling from the sky," said a Japanese prisoner. "Some of my companions jumped off the cliff to escape the terrible fire."

The psychological effect of the big guns may indeed have shattered the spirit of some of the inexperienced enemy, but the interdiction capacity of the U.S. Coast Artillery emplacements on the Rock was severely limited. Most of the huge weapons on Corregidor fired flat trajectory missiles, almost useless against an enemy hugging the reverse slope of a ridge.

In support of the Filipino-American soldiers attempting to root out the opponents on the Points, fourteen thousand yards from Corregidor, the big guns at Geary lobbed shells at their most extreme range. Early in the month, a hit from an airplane had collapsed a half-completed air raid shelter, suffocating most of Geary's top noncoms. Their replacements were still learning their jobs when Bunker finally received permission to open fire. Although a forward observer did accompany the men on Bataan to pinpoint targets, the ragged performance of guncrews led to inaccuracy and, worse, several short rounds that inflicted casualties upon about a dozen sailors serving as riflemen.

The efforts by Bridget and Alexander with the Constabulary failed to oust the Japanese. Disgusted by the performance and what he perceived as a timid approach, Wainwright sacked Selleck and replaced him with Brig. Gen. Clinton Pierce whose immediate task became the elimination of the enemy on the Points.

CHAPTER X

THE SECOND LINE

TO DEAL WITH the interlopers, Pierce called upon the Philippine Scouts from both the 45th and 57th Regiments. An excruciatingly slow convoy of trucks, buses and cars inched along dense jungle roads that twisted up and down razor-backed ridges, cut through deep gorges and crossed swift rushing streams.

After reviewing the accounts of the action of the 57th while it fought the Japanese near Abucay, USAFFE headquarters had relieved the ineffective George Clarke as the commander of these Scouts and replaced him with Phil Fry, the senior officer with the regiment. Fry's tenure proved short. Afflicted with high blood pressure, he collapsed and woke up in the hospital where doctors diagnosed a small stroke. Although he recovered within a few days he clearly was not physically fit for the job of regimental leader. His old pal Lt. Col. Ted Lilly assumed the post, and under his supervision the 57th attacked the Japanese dug in on the slopes of Longoskawayan.

An infantryman well schooled in the theories of fire and movement, jungle tactics and coordination with artillery, Lt. Col. Hal Granberry, together with his executive officer Maj. Robert Scholes, expertly directed the 460 men of the 57th Regiment's 2nd Battalion in their engagement. The Japanese resisted fiercely—some men fought hand-to-hand—but the Scouts relentlessly swept the enemy from their positions. Pushed to the edge of a precipice, some threw away their weapons and then hurled themselves from the cliffs into the water where they either drowned or fell victim to marksmen.

The corpses of the invaders lay exposed for several days, putrefying in the sun while the Scouts cleaned out the caves along the shoreline where some Japanese soldiers sought to hide. Not until the mopping-up ended could a burial detail dig holes large enough for a mass grave to accommodate more than a hundred bodies. Another two hundred men were estimated to have been either blown up by the artillery, drowned or interred by their comrades. Casualties for the Scouts numbered eleven dead and about forty wounded.

Even as the Scouts, the Naval Battalion and other units savored victory at Longoskawayan Point, the battle for Quinauan Point, seven miles north, raged. The effort by the Constabulary troops directed by Irvin Alexander had become a cropper, and the irregulars thrown into the fight, including ground and aircrews from the 21st and 34th Pursuit Squadrons, could not dislodge about six hundred Japanese.

The five hundred men of the 3rd Battalion, 45th Infantry, Philippine Scouts, drew the mission to dislodge the stubborn enemy and push them into the sea. After two days of intense skirmishes in the dense jungle, gains could only be measured in terms of a few yards. A company from the 57th Scouts entered the fray to reinforce the attackers.

According to Capt. John Olson, the enemy demonstrated great skill in exploiting the terrain, digging in deeply, camouflaging positions and hiding deadly snipers in the canopy of trees overhead. "The trick was to dig a deep bell-shaped hole. The diameter at the surface was just wide enough to permit one man to expose his head and just enough of his shoulders to hold and fire his rifle. Without presenting much of a target, he was also able to lob a grenade the short distance that usually separated him from the attacking Filipinos. Mortar rounds [many of which were duds anyway because they were so old] seldom did damage unless they landed in close proximity to the holes. The Japanese propensity for utilizing freshly cut foliage made them almost invisible in the thick vegetation of the jungle. In fact, they were detectable only from the flash or smoke of their firing. It was then that the long hours of training in marksmanship that the Scouts had undergone in the prewar days paid off. Only experts such as they could have eliminated these fleeting targets. But this was a double-edged threat they faced. At its bottom, the hole was enlarged to hold a second soldier. Once the first man was hit, his companion pulled him down into the hole and took his place. So the hot, dangerous frustrating exercise had to be repeated."

The 3rd Battalion commander launched an ill-advised head-on assault against the entrenched foe and he himself was killed when he blundered into the enemy lines. His replacement, Capt. Clifton Croom, could count on only half of the original force, and those still on their feet described his soldiers as "bone-tired from loss of sleep and exposure." Croom asked General Pierce for tanks.

Aware of the erosion of their initial landing force, the Japanese tried to reinforce them by sea. In the first of these efforts, on January 27, a group of about two hundred routed members of the Constabulary were posted for beach defense. The invaders then vanished into the interior. The combined efforts of Constabulary troops and provisionals formed from the personnel of the 17th Pursuit Squadron did little damage to the newcomers. Prompt deployment of available soldiers from various Scout units, however, bottled up the Japanese and eventually they were rooted out.

A stroke of good luck aided the Filipino-American forces and prevented a possible disaster from the second reinforcement attempt. A document found on the body of a slain Japanese officer spoke of a plan to reinforce the beachheads and drive towards Mariveles. Alerted to a possible attempt to land additional troops, observers spotted a fleet of barges heading towards the contested area.

Sam Grashio, limited to flying reconnaissance missions from the field near Cabcaben, recalled, "Somehow our Intelligence got some remarkably accurate information: on February 1 at about 10:30 P.M., a Japanese ship would tow thirteen landing barges crowded with a thousand troops into nearby Aglaloma Bay.

"At the appointed hour, our shore batteries abruptly shone their searchlights onto the barges, turning them into sharp, silvery silhouettes against the black waters of the South China Sea. As targets they were perfect. The other pilots and I, singly and in two-ship formations, flew back and forth over them, no higher than two hundred feet, strafing every barge repeatedly, from end to end with .50 caliber machine gun bullets until we ran out of ammunition. Most of the barges sank.

"It seemed to me at the time that every last enemy soldier must have died either from gunfire or from drowning, though many years afterward I read an account that stated that about four hundred Japanese troops did manage to get ashore, where all but three were killed by our troops.

"When it was all over, around 2:30 A.M., General George was ecstatic. He grabbed each of us in a Russian-style bear hug and recommended all of us for Silver Stars." Along with the blows struck by the four P-40s in Grashio's flight, the unfortunate Japanese reinforcements reeled from a bevy of shells fired by field artillery outfits and small arms fire from Scouts on the shore. Among the participants in the ground fighting was Ed Dyess, Grashio's former squadron commander. He led a group of former Air Corps men, some of whom, according to Grashio, could be heard inquiring how to fire their weapons even as they moved into combat.

Dyess and some of his men boarded two armored launches and a pair of whaleboats conned by Lt. Comdr. H.W. Goodall, Bridget's exec, for an expedition against survivors holed up in the beachfront caves. The small craft peppered the openings with 37 mm cannon and machine guns before the airmen waded ashore to toss grenades into any visible aperture. Scouts and other airmen with rifles on the cliffs above covered the seaborne attackers.

Satisfied they had eliminated any holdouts, the party reboarded their boats, only to find themselves besieged by a quartet of Japanese dive bombers. Fragmentation bombs and machine gun strafing sank all four craft, killed three and wounded Goodall and four others. One airplane was shot down.

Increasingly, few or no prisoners were taken. Reports of mutilated Filipino-American wounded and civilians circulated. Grashio spoke of one pilot who bailed out only to have enemy fighters shoot him and his parachute to pieces, causing the airmen to adopt a policy of no prisoners.

While reinforcements were denied to the enemy, hundreds of the original invasion force continued to present a problem. Poor coordination marked the first experience of the Scouts with tanks dispatched to their aid. The foot soldiers, instructed to keep 100 to 150 yards behind the armor, could not protect the hapless tanks from mine and grenade attacks. Individual Japanese soldiers dashed from the thick cover beside the trails, plastered a magnetic mine against a tank and then scurried into the jungle before the device exploded. On other occasions, they simply detonated a contact mine by pulling a string that had been placed across the path of the tank. The Scouts, however, learned quickly. Instructed to stick close to the tanks, the riflemen picked off would-be mine layers before they had a chance to place the explosives. The determined troops contained the drive designed to conquer the western half of Bataan, but maintenance of the Filipino-American lines required a pullback beyond a stretch of major east-west road from Pilar to Bagac. However, the new positions gave excellent positions for fire on anyone who tried to use the highway.

The Japanese strategists sought to rescue the seaborne

troops that had tried to outflank the defensive positions. Several motorboats and twenty-one collapsible craft crept down the coast from Moron while aircraft dropped instructions to the beleaguered Japanese. Unfortunately for them, the message also dropped inside the territory controlled by the Scouts. All units readied themselves, and a proposed midnight rendezvous of the hapless invaders met instead volleys of small arms and artillery. A pair of P-40s gunned the small flotilla. In the melee some of the rescue fleet was sunk and the remainder turned back to the safety of the open water. Soldiers who sought to swim to safety either drowned or were pinned down by sharpshooters. The remnants of the small craft returned the following night and managed to remove thirty-four men, but that ended efforts to save the stranded.

To the east, in the area defended by the II Corps, the Japanese were applying pressure at a point centered around Trail 2, which plunged into the heart of the peninsula. Responsibility for the area, known as Sector C, belonged to Clifford Bluemel, who understood he would have at his disposal his entire 31st Division composed of the 31st, 32nd and 33rd Regiments.

Bluemel recalled that he assigned his three regimental commanders to designated positions and they supposedly moved their units into place during the night. "There was no communications open," said Bluemel. "The next morning I got an early breakfast, picked up all my staff and headed for the front line. I made it a rule to visit the front line before the fighting started. When I got reports, then I knew what was here, what was there and what the situation was when the conglomerate reports came in.

"Trail 2 was the main entrance, so I went down it. The 33rd Infantry was not there. The 32nd was in position. I met an American officer who had a battalion of the 31st Regiment. He said, 'Where's Colonel Irwin [the regimental commander]? He sent a message to join him.'

"I blew my top then. I said, 'Listen, I'm the commanding general of this division and no one else can give you an order. You put that battalion back in the line where I told you, and you keep it there till I tell you you can move. I don't care if Jesus Christ tells you to move it. You keep it there until I tell you to move it.' He went back into the line and there he stayed.

"Irwin [later] told me that the night before he was ordered to take out two battalions but the order didn't come through me. The orders went directly to Irwin to take his regiment, less a battalion, and go over to the Manila Bay side, and he did it."

Bluemel said he continued his inspection of the division's deployment. He searched for his 33rd Regiment, also missing. "Finally a Filipino told me, 'I saw the assistant regimental supply officer and he says the 33rd won't be with us.' It was taken away from me and I wasn't told about it. There was a big hole there on Trail 2. Who took those regiments away from me, I don't know—whether it was done by MacArthur's headquarters or Parker's [Gen. George, II Corps commander].

"I had a hole in the line which you could walk through. I had a battalion headquarters company from the artillery, fifty or sixty men, armed as infantry." They were available because a few days before about two thousand recruits had reported and, when asked how many he would accept, Bluemel grabbed them all. The newcomers filled such units as the artillery battalion, but since they had no field pieces they served as riflemen, equipped with obsolete Lee Enfields.

Bluemel assigned this skimpy band of soldiers to plug the gap. "The engineers had dug foxholes and done some good work preparing the line. But in our front was a sugarcane field. I said, 'Clear this field!' They asked, 'What'll we clear it with?' I told them, 'You've got bayonets. Use them.' They cleared a nice field of fire."

The handful of artillerymen armed with rifles could hardly have been expected to do more than delay an attack by even a company of Japanese soldiers at Trail 2. Bluemel decided to commit a chunk of the reserves. "I had a G-2 [intelligence officer], a very bright young Filipino named Villa. The 32nd had two battalions on the line and they had one in reserve. I'd learned you never send oral messages in combat and I wrote out one and gave it to Villa to take to the colonel of the 32nd. I told him a battalion was to be put in the line opposite Trail 2.

"I told Villa, 'You see all these foxholes? I want you to see a soldier in each foxhole before you get back to my headquarters, even if you're there until the day after tomorrow.' When he got back about 7:00 that night, he said, 'The battalion is in.'

"A little later the Japs attacked us. Right in that place they made their main effort. I hollered murder to Parker. We had quite an argument. I never liked Parker and he didn't like me. He said, 'We're sending you up another regiment from the 41st Division.'

"Of all the conglomerations, taking a regiment out of my division and sending it over towards the China Sea side, and taking a regiment from another division and sending it over to me!" Bluemel immediately moved the reinforcements from the 41st Infantry into the line athwart Trail 2 with the intent of relieving the defenders from the 32nd Regiment.

An American captain who knew Bluemel from a tour in Panama and was serving as an advisor to the 41st, confided to him, "You know Lim [General Vincente, the Filipino 41st Division commander]. He took away our machine guns." Astounded, Bluemel contacted Lim and shouted at him. "I gave him hell. 'What do you mean by taking away the machine guns!' He answered, 'They said the regiment was going to be in reserve and wouldn't need them.'" Bluemel scornfully demanded Lim's source but had only one recourse. "I left the machine gun company of the 32nd Infantry [instead of relieving it] in the line with their machine guns.

"The next night they attacked again and poured it on. They bombed hell out of us and shelled us with artillery all the way back to my command post. But we held." Indeed, the enemy report on its operations described itself as beset by "a fierce bombardment" from artillery and "a tornado of machine gun fire."

Bluemel rightfully boasted, "If I hadn't gone out to the front line, assuming it was there, the Japs would have walked right up Trail 2 and Bataan would have fallen. If I had stayed back in my command post, it would have been a bad state of affairs." Not only was the planned advance through Trail 2 halted, but Bluemel organized a counterattack that eventually pushed the Japanese back across the Pilar River.

During the first week of February, the campaign to conquer Bataan penetrated the defenders' lines to the west of Bluemel. The large-scale enemy forces plunged into a dense jungle of cane, bamboo and hardwood trees. Creepers and vines formed an intricate lattice that cut visibility to ten or fifteen yards. Creeks and rivers coursed at sharp angles, merged and split until men could not decide which stream led where. The network of narrow trails meandered seemingly at random. Reliable maps did not exist; attempts to sketch the terrain ended with contradictory outlines. As a result, both sides moved blindly and contact between the warring parties occurred almost by accident.

At first, the Japanese benefited from the disorganization and weakened state of its adversaries. The 1st Division of the Philippine Army, commanded by Gen. Fidel Segundo, had taken such a beating and abandoned so much of its equipment during its earlier encounters with the invaders that men who had lost their entrenching tools dug holes and trenches with mess kits and cleared fields of fire with bayonets.

The Japanese secured positions behind the Filipino-American lines that became known as "the Pockets." They dug in using the skilled camouflage techniques they would consistently demonstrate throughout the war. Artillery proved almost useless against the Pockets. Forward observers could not pinpoint targets and gunners were hampered by the absence of maps to indicate ranges and topography. The prevalent high trajectory weapons only shattered treetops, and the plethora of dud mortar shells limited the effectiveness of this basic piece of weaponry for close support.

Wainwright personally directed the overall defensive operations against the incursion in the Points and at the Pockets as much as possible. During an inspection trip his car rounded a curve and was suddenly visible to enemy gunners. Incoming shells pounded the area and the occupants leaped out in search of cover or foxholes. Wainwright, however, noticed a captain from his cavalry days in Virginia, called him over and then calmly sat atop a heap of sandbags chatting with his old comrade. For the eighteen minutes of the barrage, Wainwright, his back exposed to the flying shrapnel, quietly reminisced.

Navy lieutenant Malcolm Champlin, that branch's liaison to Wainwright, who had accompanied Wainwright, said he asked the general why he took such a risk. Recalled the Navy officer, "He said, 'Champ, think it over for a minute. What have we to offer these troops? Can we give them more food? No, we haven't any more food. Can we give them supplies or equipment or tanks or medicine? No. Everything is running low. But we *can* give them morale, and that is one of my primary duties. That is why I go to the front every day. Now do you understand why it is important for me to sit on sandbags in the line of fire while the rest of you seek shelter?' "

Sutherland, MacArthur's chief of staff, while recognizing Wainwright as a man "utterly without fear," considered him weak as a strategist and tactician. At the start of the Bataan campaign, claimed Sutherland, Wainwright proposed immediate withdrawal to the tip of the peninsula. The USAFFE chief of staff said his boss sent Wainwright "one of the most blistering letters I have ever seen MacArthur write."

Be that as it may, the defenders, guided by Wainwright and his local commanders, gradually marshalled their superior manpower, brought up tanks—notwithstanding his remark to Champlin—and squeezed the foe. As usual, the efforts of the Scouts—the 45th Regiment—met with success. Platoon leader Willibald C. Bianchi earned a Congressional Medal of Honor, knocking out a pair of machine guns while suffering three wounds, including a pair of bullets that struck him in the chest. Tough fighting at a significant cost in casualties annihilated the substantial number of enemy invested in the Pockets. The entire Japanese campaign to conquer Bataan ground to a standstill.

While the defenders had begun to feel the effects of short rations, fatigue and disease, the enemy had also succumbed to the brutal conditions of combat in Bataan, where the temperature averaged ninety-five degrees and the terrain was inhospitable to an attacking army. Instead of the customary sixty-two ounces of food daily, the Japanese soldiers nearly starved on only twenty-three ounces. Malaria and dysentery ravaged the Nipponese and medical supplies ran desperately short. Most of all, the jumble of Filipino-American forces, slowly but with deadly effect, battered the Japanese. General Homma, who had expected to declare victory by the end of January, now saw his 16th Division of 14,000 soldiers reduced to only 700 combat-ready troops. The 65th Brigade, nominally 6,500 strong, could muster only 1,000.

A temporary respite settled over the war zone during mid-February. Although this breather enabled the Japanese to replace and resupply its forces, no such relief reached the defenders. Col. Glen Townsend, commanding the 11th Regiment, which played a principal role in reducing the Pockets, noted, "The 26th Cavalry had eaten its horses. Rations were reduced from sixteen ounces a day to eight and then to four. Twice a week we got small amounts of carabao, mule or horse meat. There was no flour, vegetables or sugar. The quinine was exhausted, malaria rampant. Almost everyone had dysentery. The hospitals and aid stations were jammed with sick and wounded [there were as many as seven thousand patients in Hospitals Number One and Two].

"The Japanese dropped propaganda leaflets telling of Filipino families eating big meals and there were pornographic shots included. The Filipino soldiers were urged to kill U.S. officers and join the Japanese. The effort to turn the men was unsuccessful."

Maj. Harold K. Johnson, a member of the 57th Regiment, offered similar observations. "I saw soldiers squatting beside trails, boiling a piece of mule hide or carabao hide in a tomato can and chewing away at the hide, trying to get some nourishment. The soldiers never really complained but all the time you could just see the question in their eyes, 'What in the world have you done to us.' "

Johnson recalled making a reconnaissance and coming upon a former bakery in his sector. "I remember picking a loaf from a stack, ripping the crust off, reaching in and getting the dough out of the inside, a delicious meal." He reported one surprise in performance. "When we got into Bataan, people that had been earmarked for transfer because of age to a relatively sedentary activity with a post or station complement turned out to be some of the best soldiers and small unit leaders we had. They were best in physical staying power, best in terms of native cunning, best in demonstrating initiative and in just plain courage. [This was] in contrast to many of the younger soldiers who just didn't seem to have a heart for tough going."

Along with the troops on Bataan, those on Corregidor endured half rations, but food recovered from barges and sunken vessels around the island shores supplemented supplies. Even as the troops on Bataan sucked on boiled hide, Paul Bunker on Corregidor recorded eating a dinner topped off with a piece of pie. "Probably the last," he noted in his diary, "because of the flour shortage. We are now on a ration that allows only one ounce of flour and seven ounces of bread per day." Meagre as it sounds, any amount surpassed that available to the soldiers on the Bataan peninsula.

Alva Fitch confirmed the already desperate condition of his artillerymen. "The ration was very low, one to two ounces of rice, one quarter ounce of milk and one quarter ounce of sugar with an occasional issue of spoiled carabao or mule. Later [I learned] that for two weeks we were being fed on 3.9 cents a day. I am sure that by the time these supplies passed through various elements of American and Filipino quartermaster distribution agencies, we were fortunate if we received two cents' worth and that's not a figure of speech. About once every week or ten days, a small amount of canned goods would be issued to the Americans to supplement the Philippine Army ration. This was badly cut as it came down through channels and by the time it reached Regiment, it was very small indeed. Colonel Hunter regularly sent a part of it as a gift to the Division CO as a present. The amount that was sent on to me varied, depending on how much Hunter wanted to keep for himself.

"Many had malaria or dysentery. We ran out of quinine and nearly all other medicines. I ran a forty-bed hospital in my battalion. It was always full. Actually, when a man became strong enough to walk, he was returned to duty to make room for another who couldn't walk. I had a good Filipino doctor in charge, the only doctor in the regiment who knew enough to dress a minor wound. This soon became apparent to Dick Hunter, who took him for his personal doctor and gave me one of his bums. Never have I felt so completely outraged and frustrated. I insulted the old man [Hunter] in every way I could think of, short of slapping his face, but it did no good."

Blockade runners from the southern islands and those who undertook a few daring forays from Australia increasingly ran afoul of Japanese warships. Submarines operated with greater impunity, but their limited cargo capacity was used to bring in munitions, remove items like gold bullion and shift personnel like code experts, pilots and naval specialists who were deemed essential for prosecution of the war. Inevitably, some of those evacuated owed their rescue to whom they knew rather than what they knew, and that engendered some resentment. In a rare offensive mode, the *Seadragon* scored one of the few successes at sea, sinking a fully loaded 6,441-ton transport outside Lingayen Gulf.

The lull from mid-February to the end of the month did not fool the defenders into believing they had staved off defeat. The ring around the archipelago remained as tight as ever. No friendly fleet appeared over the horizon; the well publicized *Pensacola* convoy had long ago docked in Australia to disgorge its cargo and soldiers. No flights of American bombers roared overhead and the orders of the day tightened everyone's belt.

The quiet period benefited Irvin Alexander, who had been driven to Hospital Number Two for treatment of his wounds. "After filling out a number of papers the receiving clerk took me to the operating tent where there were already two wounded soldiers waiting. It was almost a half hour before my turn came to climb on the operating table. I found myself among friends, for a large part of the operating staff on duty at that time had been at Fort Stotsenburg prior to the war.

"They certainly did a fine repair job on me in the minimum of time and with no pain. I should qualify that slightly, for Jim came over to look at the piece of metal in my chest while my left hand was being sewed up. Casually picking up a pair of tweezers, he got a good hold on the metal and pulled straight out until my skin was as tight as a drum head, before I had time to call him more than a few uncomplimentary words. He gave the tweezers a twist, like turning a corkscrew, and extracted the slug."

Because the officers ward was already full, one of the surgeons invited Alexander to share his tent with two other men, an artilleryman and "a swaggering, loud-talking young cavalryman." Groggy from his long day and injuries, Alexander fell asleep while the others gabbed well into the night.

When Alexander awakened the next morning he was bewildered by the vision presented by his hospital. "Instead of confining clean white walls around me, I was still hemmed in by the jungle. There were towering trees which appeared to reach the sky and almost concealed it except for occasional small patches. The underbrush had been cleared from the area occupied by the ward, and the beds, which had been placed in rows as neatly as the trunks of the trees would permit, extended as far as I could see. Two wall tents on one side for the offices of the doctor, nurses and corpsmen, two water faucets for the water needs of the patients, and two latrines in the trees near the far corner constituted all of the facilities for that ward of more than two hundred patients."

Inmates and staff dined on two sparse meals a day. The fare consisted of two heaping tablespoons of corned beef hash and one small slice of field bread. Once a week the kitchens splurged, serving up a "medium-size portion of delicious fruit pie."

With both hands bandaged, Alexander relished a bath and alcohol rubdown from a Filipina nurse. "I came to know her as an extremely competent, intelligent and faithful woman who was devoting twelve hours every day to the patients of our ward. No one would have called her beautiful, but her personality and devotion were so outstanding that it was always a pleasure to all patients to see her trim little figure approaching."

Alexander was pleasantly surprised by the results in this crude setting. "In that primitive ward there was only one death during my two weeks in the hospital, and he was a man who had developed gangrene before he arrived."

One afternoon several enemy planes flew an apparent reconnaissance mission in the vicinity of the hospital. At the sound of their engines, the cavalry officer who shared quarters with Alexander sought shelter in a nearby slit trench, a few of which had been dug for use by the staff in case of raids. It was not practical to prepare places for the patients since most were bedridden.

Another resident advised Alexander that the young man had developed stomach pains after several narrow escapes with his cavalry unit. "He was," said Alexander, "what his own people call 'windy,' describing an individual who could not take it. Later that afternoon, one of the surgeons reported they could find no condition in his abdomen that should cause pain. The young man's face had terror written all over it as the surgeon departed. When next Sunday came, the cavalryman had a long talk with his priest and then [said] he was ready for duty. He left us Monday morning. On his way back to his outfit a bomber, working over the highway he was on, dropped a bomb, blowing off both his legs. When news of his death came back to us, I could not help pondering the accuracy of his premonition of his death.''

Although the Japanese had lost far more men in combat than had the Filipino-American forces, suffered as severe deprivation in food and been hit equally hard with disease, they still possessed overwhelming advantages, owning both the sky and the sea, with the power to reinforce and resupply without interference. Soon fresh, well-equipped enemy troops landed to execute the final siege. The air power, temporarily diverted to the campaigns against the Dutch East Indies, returned to savagely punish Bataan and Corregidor.

The Administration in Washington, D.C., had already written off the Philippines. Always a long shot, War Plan Orange required for success a fleet capable of carrying massive numbers of troops and gear five thousand miles. Shattered hulks at Pearl Harbor and the imperatives of a two-ocean war, factors never factored into the original planning, reduced WPO to irrelevance. Gloomily contemplating month after month of defeat, the policymakers desperately seized upon MacArthur both as an irreplaceable strategist and a rallying figure. He had earned this stature more through his skills in diplomacy and public relations than for any smashing victories.

A disheartened, sick Quezon had proposed acceptance of a Japanese offer that would grant the Philippines independence. He dictated a cable to President Roosevelt in which he complained that the United States had abandoned the Commonwealth and it was "my duty as well as my right to cease fighting." MacArthur persuaded Quezon not to transmit the message.

However, as Quezon continued to grumble about the ineffective American defense of his land, Washington politicos offered only encouragement, but no material aid. MacArthur, as middleman, skillfully navigated a tricky course. Surrendering before exhausting all possible resources would be a terrible blow to U.S. morale. At the same time MacArthur endeavored to convince the Filipino leaders that their citizens were not being sacrificed to salve American pride and provide breathing space for mobilization of resources in the United States. Sergio Osmena, Quezon's vice-president, buttressed MacArthur's argument, suggesting to his president that history would perceive him as a traitor if he capitulated. For the wheelchair-bound, tubercular Quezon's protection and perhaps to remove him from a stage where his cries of desertion might still echo, the submarine *Swordfish* evacuated the Quezon family to the southern Philippines. Ultimately, the Commonwealth leader flew to safety in Australia. High Commissioner Francis Sayre and his family accompanied Quezon.

MacArthur's orders stipulated resistance as long as humanly possible, and he expected to die with his boots on. To his aide, Sidney Huff, he confided, "They'll never take me alive." Wife Jean, offered the opportunity to accompany the Quezons on the escaping sub, refused. "We have drunk from the same cup, we three [including their son Arthur] shall stay together." Instead of the MacArthur dependents, the *Swordfish* carried away a footlocker with the general's medals, the couple's wills, some investment securities, their son's birth certificate and first baby shoes, a bundle of personal photos and a few similar personal items.

The doughty spirit MacArthur presented to the world was not lost on his superiors half a world away. Correspondents filed stories of his fearlessness during air raids, detailed his almost daily visits to the cots of the wounded, painted portraits of his constant sessions with his commanders to plot moves that could thwart the enemy. After a Japanese sub tossed a few harmless shells at Santa Barbara on the U.S. west coast, MacArthur needled Washington, "I think I'll send a wire to the California commander and tell him if he can hold out for ten more days I'll be able to send him help."

Winston Churchill, having only melancholy news to issue about his own nation's predicament, addressed the House of Commons: "I should like to express . . . my admiration of the splendid courage and quality with which the small American army, under General MacArthur, has resisted brilliantly for so long, at desperate odds, the hordes of Japanese who have been hurled against it . . ."

American soldiers on Bataan had begun to look at MacArthur differently, however, expressing resentment at a commander seemingly safely ensconced in an impervious fortress. The GIs, increasingly cognizant that no help was on the way, referred to him as "Dugout Doug" and composed the ballad "Battling Bastards of Bataan." They chanted:

> "No mama, no papa, no Uncle Sam,
>   No aunts, no uncles, no nephews, no nieces,
>   No rifles, no planes, or artillery pieces,
>   And nobody gives a damn
>   We're the battling bastards of Bataan."

In marked contrast, the Filipino soldiers seemed to maintain their faith in MacArthur. More importantly, the stories printed in newspapers and magazines played him up to the American public as an authentic hero.

Military and political leaders at home and abroad urged that MacArthur be extricated from Corregidor because he was an essential weapon needed for continuance of the war. He seemed a heroic figure, and his capture or death would give the Japanese a propaganda coup. A February 23 directive from MacArthur's superior, General Marshall, instructed MacArthur to spend a few days lining up defenses on Mindanao and from there proceed to Melbourne for command of all U.S. troops in the Pacific Theater.

To MacArthur, according to people on the scene like newsman Clark Lee of the Associated Press, the orders meant desertion of the men to whom he had pledged "to fight to his destruction on Bataan and then do the same on Corregidor." In his memoirs MacArthur wrote, "My first reaction was to try and avoid the latter part of the order, even to the extent of resigning my commission and joining the Bataan force as a simple volunteer [an improbable fantasy]."

The assembled officers, according to MacArthur, vociferously protested the idea. "Dick Sutherland and my entire staff would have none of it. They felt that the concentration of men, arms and transport which they believed were being massed in Australia would enable me almost at once to return at the head of an effective rescue operation." The general agreed to reconsider. A day later, MacArthur allowed himself to be convinced by the wishful thinking of his subordinates, based on rumors and interpretation of vague messages about shipments of men and machines. He agreed to leave, but on his own timetable.

Over the next few weeks MacArthur recalled, "I began seriously to weigh the feasibility of trying to break through from Bataan into the Zambales Mountains to carry on intensified guerrilla operations against the enemy." Obviously, the general was once more intoxicated by dreams of ventures far beyond the capacity of his ragtag army. In light of the condition of the Filipino-American forces, piercing the Japanese lines was preposterous. More urgings from Washington persuaded MacArthur to schedule his departure before the foe foreclosed any escape.

CHAPTER XI

BATAAN FALLS

ORIGINALLY, MACARTHUR AND a party that included his family, a Cantonese nurse named Ah Cheu who was their son's *amah,* plus a bevy of Army and Navy personnel, expected to travel on a submarine that was due to pick them up at Corregidor on March 14. But news broadcasts that MacArthur would soon command all Allied forces in Australia alerted the Japanese to his imminent departure. The Imperial Navy tightened its watch, dispatching additional minelayers, destroyers and other patrol vessels. MacArthur felt he could not wait for the sub. "I had decided to try and pierce the blockade with PT boats," wrote MacArthur. The revised arrangements called for the MacArthurs, Ah Cheu and Dick Sutherland to leave on the night of March 11, on board PT-41, commanded by John Bulkeley. The other "essential" passengers, on board PT boats 32, 34 and 35, would rendezvous with Bulkeley near the entrance to Manila Bay and start the voyage south. In fact, the War Department had authorized only Dick Sutherland to leave with MacArthur, expecting the rest of the USAFFE staff to remain behind with the general's successor for further defensive efforts.

In Washington, Marshall was surprised to learn of the coterie that accompanied MacArthur, but the slot given Ah Cheu generated enough criticism for MacArthur to defend her inclusion. He insisted, "Few people outside the Orient know how completely a member of the family an *amah* can become. Because of her relationship to my family, her death would have been certain had she been left behind."

On the eve of his departure, MacArthur summoned Wainwright, to whom he would turn over command of Luzon. At that moment Wainwright's forces controlled at most a couple of hundred square miles since the enemy now occupied almost the entire island. A separate CO, Gen. William F. Sharp, was named for other portions of the archipelago—Mindanao with twenty-five thousand men and the Visayan grouping garrisoned by twenty thousand. There was also a commander for the fortified islands in Manila Bay. Strategic and tactical command of the Philippines remained vested in MacArthur, residing in Melbourne, four thousand miles away.

MacArthur recalled his final meeting with Wainwright: " 'Jim,' I told him, 'hold on till I come back for you.' " Wainwright in his memoirs offered a much lengthier version of MacArthur's remarks. In his account, MacArthur addressed him as "Jonathan" and vowed he was leaving only under repeated orders of the President. "I want you to make it known throughout all elements of your command that I am leaving over my repeated protests." He did reassure his subordinate that if he got through to Australia he would come back.

Along with the words of support and confidence Wainwright, in addition to the command of a badly depleted army in wretched physical condition, received a box of cigars and two jars of shaving cream from the departing chief.

In dramatic terms, MacArthur recalled the scene at the dock on the night of March 11. "I could see the men staring at me. I had lost twenty-five pounds living on the same diet as the soldiers, and I must have looked gaunt and ghastly standing there in my old war-stained clothes— no bemedaled commander of inspiring presence. What a change had taken place in that once-beautiful spot! My eyes roamed that warped and twisted face of scorched rock. Gone were the vivid green foliage, with its trees, shrubs and flowers. Gone were the buildings, the sheds, every growing thing. The hail of relentless bombardment had devastated, buried and blasted. Ugly dark scars marked smouldering paths where the fire had raged from one end of the island to another. Great gaps and forbidding crevices still belched their tongues of flame."

He said he thought of those who would stay, like his classmate Paul Bunker. "He and many others up there were old, old friends, bound by ties of deepest comradeship. Darkness had now fallen, and the waters were beginning to ripple from the faint night breeze. The enemy firing had ceased and a muttering silence had fallen. It was as though the dead were passing by the stench of destruction. The smell of filth thickened the night air. I raised my cap in farewell salute, and I could feel my face go white, feel a sudden convulsive twitch in the muscles of my face. I heard someone ask, 'What's his chance, Sarge, of getting through?' and the gruff reply, 'Dunno. He's lucky. Maybe one in five.'

"I stepped aboard PT-41. 'You may cast off, Buck,' I said, 'when you are ready.' "

Bulkeley later said he had full confidence that his boats could deliver their human cargo to safety. Although he had no sophisticated instruments to help him navigate through the thousands of islands in the darkness, Bulkeley said, "I had been in the Philippines for a long enough time and gone through the islands many times. I never doubted success and I was damn glad to get out of Corregidor."

Racing through a stiff wind that sent water lashing the faces of all aboard, forced to stop periodically to clean gasoline strainers, changing course to make a time-consuming swing away from land after signal lights from shore seemed to inform the enemy navy, only three of the PTs reached the first stop after nearly twelve hours afloat.

With PT-32 unable to continue for the moment, its

passengers transferred to PTs 34 and 41. In tandem they set out for Cagayan on Mindanao. On the morning of March 13, the boats docked precisely on schedule, having traveled 560 miles through Japanese-patrolled waters.

B-17s from Australia were due to pick up the entire party for the final leg of the trip. But inter-service strife muddled operations. The big planes, rather than being under the command of the Air Corps, fell under the jurisdiction of the Navy, which was then engaged in preserving naval assets in the Dutch East Indies. Adm. Herbert Leary refused to lend air-worthy bombers to rescue MacArthur. In desperation the Air Corps sent off a Flying Fortress deemed unuseable for tactical missions. After it coughed and smoked during a wobbly landing, MacArthur examined it and declared he would not fly in it nor permit any of his associates to risk themselves in such a rickety crate. The pilot took off, wobbling even more than when the ship arrived. (In MacArthur's *Reminiscences*, he claims General Sharp rejected that plane even before the refugees from Corregidor reached the Del Monte airfield, but his memory betrayed him here.)

Blistering cables from MacArthur to Australia and to Washington persuaded Admiral Leary to provide a trio of B-17s. One turned back because of engine trouble, but the other two flew almost twenty-three hundred miles to Del Monte Field where ground crews trundled away the portable trees that camouflaged the strip. Crammed into the aircraft, leaving behind their limited baggage of one suitcase per person, the passengers endured a bumpy, cold, five-hour trip of more than fifteen hundred miles before arriving at Batchelor Field, fifty miles from Darwin. The landing spot was a last-minute choice after word came of a dive bomber raid in progress at Darwin, perhaps another sign of enemy patrols stalking MacArthur.

The general said it was at Batchelor that he issued the most famous pronunciamento of World War II, "I shall return." Manchester's biography of MacArthur reports that the statement was made to the press which met him at the Adelaide railroad station while he was en route to Melbourne. In light of the details supplied by Manchester, his account appears more likely.

The use of the first person singular provoked considerable argument, with detractors citing it as damning evidence of MacArthur's egomania. However, according to Manchester, the suggestion to use "I" instead of "We" originated with Carlos P. Romulo, then a lieutenant colonel and formerly a newspaper editor and publisher, who had been charged by MacArthur with handling news for USAFFE. Sutherland, while on Corregidor, had suggested "We shall return," but Romulo argued that while Filipinos believed the United States had let them down they maintained their faith in MacArthur. "If *he* says *he* is coming back, he will be believed."

Whatever the source, MacArthur gloried in its use. "I spoke casually enough, but the phrase, 'I shall return,' seemed a promise of magic to the Filipinos. It lit a flame that became a symbol which focused the nation's indomitable will and at whose shrine it finally attained victory and, once again, found freedom. It was scraped in the sands of the beaches, it was daubed on the walls of the *barrios,* it was stamped on the mail, it was whispered in the cloisters of the church. It became the battle cry of a great underground swell that no Japanese bayonet could still."

The American propaganda machines trumpeted the slogan. Only a few days after MacArthur left, Sam Grashio and several other pilots flew over Manila and other sites to drop leaflets in which MacArthur sought to explain why he had left. "He also called upon them to be courageous, and promised that U.S. forces would return soon to rescue them," noted Grashio. Later, submarines handed out cartons of supplies bearing the three-word quotation.

The looming defeat of the MacArthur defense of the Philippines notwithstanding, the general was awarded the Medal of Honor "for conspicuous leadership in preparing the Philippine Islands to resist conquest, for gallantry and intrepidity above and beyond the call of duty . . . He mobilized, trained and led an army which has received world acclaim for its gallant defense against tremendous superiority of enemy forces in men and arms. His utter disregard of personal danger and under heavy fire and aerial bombardment, his calm judgment in each crisis, inspired his troops, galvanized the spirit of resistance of the Filipino people and confirmed the faith of the American people in their armed forces."

For the moment, regardless of how it originated and how much the phrase "I shall return" was sounded or inscribed, MacArthur as a figure in the defense of the Philippines was now off stage. The problem was he did not know it.

To the confusion of the War Department in Washington, MacArthur apparently did not make clear the legacy of his command arrangements. It was assumed that he had endowed Wainwright with power over the entire archipelago forces. Made aware that such was not the case, the interested parties exchanged a flurry of messages. MacArthur told his boss, General Marshall, that he still expected to control operations in the Philippines. Marshall declared the MacArthur plan unsatisfactory, advising President Roosevelt of the difficulties in managing four separate commands in the Philippines from a base four thousand miles away. Roosevelt promptly elevated Wainwright to lieutenant general and officially notified him he now headed the U.S. Forces in the Philippines (USFIP). The decision was carefully explained to MacArthur who, for the moment, accepted the new arrangements without objection.

The reactions to MacArthur's exit by the Americans who stayed varied. Irvin Alexander said, "We were electrified by the news that General MacArthur and a part of his staff had gone to Australia. Of course, there was a great deal of resentment among those left behind, and the expression 'Ran out on us' was on many tongues, but if there was a single officer who would not have given his right arm to have gone with him, at least he would have settled for his left. I can never forget my elation when Ted came to my headquarters to tell me that General MacArthur intended to send for the remainder of his staff, and alerted me to be ready to go to Corregidor at an hour's notice, for he and two others were scheduled to go with the next group of staff officers. It was our great misfortune that our call never came."

MacArthur's former West Point classmate Paul Bunker initially expressed his continued faith in the general. "We have been at war almost four months now and so far as we can see, no slightest effort has been made to help us. From the first, knowing the Naval War College 'solution' [reference to both WPO and Rainbow Five] to the Philippine Problem, I have secretly felt that we are slated to play the part of another Alamo. However, if anybody can help us it is MacArthur. He is our only chance. It is disturbing, however, to read that our President has appointed a 'Board' of all nations to control the 'strategy of the War in the Pacific'—why hamper MacArthur. He says he once told Roosevelt, 'If you once lose the Philippines, you'll never get them back.' Now let's see what he will do! This blockade is throttling us."

Capt. Alvin C. Poweleit, a doctor, noted in his diary, "This morning we learned that General MacArthur had left Corregidor via PT boat. Several men were upset by this. However, most of them felt he could do a better job in another area like Australia."

Sam Grashio, still flying one of the paltry stock of airworthy planes, said, "His departure occasioned some bitter remarks about 'Dugout Doug' from men who had long envied the Corregidor garrison for what they presumed was the easier life of the latter or who blamed MacArthur for the inadequate defenses of the Philippines. There were also gripes that the general had taken along the family's Chinese maid and, according to 'latrine rumors' even a refrigerator [false, as was one that said the family took out a mattress stuffed with money]. I never shared that discontent. Like most GIs at all levels, I felt somewhat let down to learn that the chief was no longer with us, but it seemed to me mere common sense to save him for the rest of the war rather than let him fall into the hands of the enemy."

To John Olson, fighting with the 57th Infantry, Philippine Scouts, however, the news was depressing. He noted that a rumor had circulated of General Homma's suicide, a reaction allegedly for the disgrace in not having overrun Bataan. "Perhaps this was to counter the dishearteningly accurate report that Gen. Douglas MacArthur had transferred to Australia. While this was explained as making it possible for him to command the reinforcements that had been promised since late December, it encouraged very few who heard it. Promises and predictions were not chasing the enemy from the Philippine archipelago."

To Madeline Ullom, it was a military decision. "General MacArthur was ordered to depart. He must obey orders. Perhaps in Australia, he could accomplish more."

Clifford Bluemel spoke of MacArthur as a magic talisman. "There are always soldiers who say it's nice to fight under a lucky commander. I figured MacArthur had been a lucky commander and I said to some of the American officers, 'We've lost our luck' and I think we did.

"I think it hurt morale all the way down to the frontline people. I had to tell them, because if I didn't, the Japs had loudspeakers. They were talking to the men, telling and begging them to desert. I told them, 'Help is going to come. He's going to bring it back.' I had to lie a little bit. I didn't believe it."

Among the harshest comments were those recorded by Gen. William E. Brougher, commander of the Philippine Army's 11th Division, in his diary. Insisting that the top ranks knew the Philippines could not be defended, he called the concept "a foul trick of deception . . . played on a large group of Americans by a commander-in-chief and a small staff who are now eating steak and eggs in Australia. God damn them!"

Meanwhile, USFIP commander Wainwright coped with his meagre resources in men and supplies. It was clear that all efforts to break the blockade had failed, that the Luzon defenders could count on only insignificant amounts of food or medicine to reach them. Already puny food rations continued to dip in February and March. The Bataan soldier, American or Filipino, lived by late March on less than twenty ounces of food a day. Rice in barely palatable, soggy portions replaced wheat products like bread or potatoes. One officer's Bataan account gave a gourmand's appraisal of the tiny amounts of meat. "I can recommend mule. It is tasty, succulent and tender—all being phrases of comparison, of course. There is little to choose between calesa pony and carabao. The pony is tougher but better flavor than carabao. Iguana is fair. Monkey I do not recommend. I never had snake."

Those on Corregidor ate better than the troops fighting on Bataan. Rear echelon troops managed to siphon off some items destined for the front lines. Commanders took to inflating their roster numbers in order to draw extra rations—a division that normally counted sixty-five hundred men, dispatched two-thirds of its men for service elsewhere, then claimed it was feeding eleven thousand. Squabbling over the apportionment of food stocks wracked relations with headquarters, quartermasters and those engaged in distribution. Cigarette-hungry soldiers, down to an average of one smoke a day, created a black market that pushed the price of a pack to as much as five dollars.

The low-calorie diet wasted muscle and depleted fat reserves. Men acted listless after any spurt of exertion. Serious vitamin deficiencies inevitably produced scurvy and beriberi. Malaria, dengue fever and amoebic dysentery thrived in the weakened bodies. Barefoot Filipino fighters developed hookworm.

Nurse Madeline Ullom had moved from Corregidor to Hospital Number One on Bataan. In the beginning conditions had been tolerable, despite fifteen-hour shifts. "Fresh carabao meat sometimes supplemented the diet. Fresh fruits and vegetables were occasionally obtained from markets. The time eventually arrived when the usefulness of the cavalry horses passed. Juanita, who was an ardent horse fan, found it difficult to choke down the mouthfuls.

"Cards and jigsaw puzzles were made from pictures and cardboard for the rehabilitation of bed patients. Filipinos carved cigarette holders, pipes and vases from bamboo. A volleyball and badminton field were marked. Duty personnel exercised while bed patients watched the competition. Soldiers constructed two chapels; each had a seating capacity of about fifty.

"A radio was the center of communication, to listen to the Voice of Freedom broadcast from Corregidor. Mimeograph news dispatches were distributed. A trophy table displayed souvenirs from the Japanese—a camouflage suit, sword, money, guns.

"The *Canopus* was spoken of almost reverently. The submarine tender was equipped with foundries, machine shops, store rooms and living quarters. A standing invitation to dinner was issued to the nurses. Delicious dinners on white linen table clothes with silver seemed like another world."

Apparently not even a second bombing attack upon the vessel could end its hospitality or that of other fortunate units. "The crew manned guns, helped the Army, continued repairs and hosted dinners. Personnel at the motor pool had good contacts with the barrio. They invited us for the treat of a good meal."

But the progress of the war eroded even simple pleasures. "The supply of plasma and for blood transfusion was soon exhausted. Doctors and enlisted men donated blood. The influx of many orthopedic cases used up the supply of traction ropes. Jungle vines were substituted. Backs ached from long dawn-to-dusk hours of changing dressings of patients on beds about one foot from the ground. Amputees without hope of prosthesis tried to learn balance and movement in their weakened condition. Gauze was washed, sterilized and reused. Amputees spent long hours stretching and folding gauze. The transfer of patients from

Hospital Number One to Number Two could not compete with the increase in admission rates."

As Wainwright assumed command, he still could list just under eighty thousand soldiers in his two-hundred-square-mile fief. But a large proportion could not be described as fighting troops and among those who could, doctors diagnosed a combat efficiency below forty-five percent. In outfits like the Scouts, the best ones that Wainwright could field, company strength dropped considerably and not even recruitment of the most capable from the Constabulary nor the promotion of men of proven worth to upper-echelon noncoms or even the ranks of officers could compensate for the losses.

Wainwright and his staff learned that reports of General Homma's suicide had been in error, and that he had received more than twenty-five thousand fresh soldiers, more and heavier artillery and, equally important, a massive influx of air elements with a mission to pulverize the Bataan defenders.

Alva Fitch noted, "In early March the Japs resumed the bombing of Corregidor. By the middle of March they began reinforcing the artillery in Bataan. Every day or so a new battery would appear in my area. We would heckle them for two or three days, and they would leave us and appear in the Pantingan River area over towards the east side of Bataan. Observers reported heavy movement of supplies into Bataan from the north. It was obvious that the Japs were planning a major attack.

"Throughout the siege we were showered with propaganda leaflets. They included restaurant menus, lascivious pictures, fictitious letters from happy Filipinos who had escaped, tickets to be given the Japanese, showing they had authorized your surrender, etc. In March, this became more bitter and contained instructions for the Filipinos to shoot their American officers and cooperate with the Japanese." There is no record that any of the indigenous people turned upon their American officers.

At Hospital Number One, Madeline Ullom recalled,

"On March 29, a bomb dropped at the hospital entrance. The Japanese apologized for the accident." Hardly had the expression of regret been made, however, when she reported, "The hospital was bombed at 10:17 on March 30. A direct hit landed on the ward which Hattie Brantly had left [for duty at a new outdoor section]. Traction ropes and jungle vines were slashed to permit patients to slide under beds. The force of concussion threw Juanita to the floor. A second wave of bombardment hit. Devastation was everywhere. Trees were uprooted. Fragments of clothing and parts of bodies were in the tree branches. Roofs were pulverized. Sides of buildings were splintered. Beds were twisted, dead and wounded were partially buried in debris. Many died of shock.

"Blood streamed from Rosemary Hogan's face and shoulders. A corpsman helped her to surgery. Rita Palmer's face and arms were gashed. Her shirt and skirt were severed with the forces of the blasts."

"On April 3," noted John Olson, "the sun when it rose looked down upon a peninsula torn by incessant and devastating bombardment from virtually every tube of the available Japanese artillery pieces. The artillery fires were reinforced periodically by the heavy thumps of bombs which shrieked in clusters from dive bombers which flew with almost complete impunity back and forth across the lines."

According to Olson, an uninterrupted, five-hour deluge of bombs and shells literally blew a hole in the sector of the jungle defended by the Philippine Army 41st Division. The enemy plunged forward while an ongoing barrage prevented reserves from moving up to seal the hole. "Except in the western portion, the defenders had been reduced to a dazed, disorganized, fleeing mob. Nothing that the American and Scout advisors tried succeeded in stopping the bewildered and terrified Philippine Army personnel. A major rupture of the line had been achieved."

Exploding missiles interrupted Easter Services at Hospital Number One. The steady flow of casualties to the battered medical units became a torrent. "By five in the evening on the next day," said Ullom, "shells were raining. Word was that the Japanese had landed at Cabcaben which was only two kilometers away." Nurses like Ullom could not handle the volume. "Beds were assigned before those who occupied them were discharged prematurely to return to combat. Front lines seemed to vanish. Most of the patients suffered from gunshot and Hospital Number Two sent buses, trucks and ambulances to transfer patients."

Fitch witnessed the same overture to the final assault. "Our own news agencies kept reassuring the troops that everything was under control. By the sixth, all of our reserves had been committed and the Japs were advancing even more rapidly. At noon of the eighth, I was told to move my battalion about fifteen miles to my rear, about ten miles from Mariveles. I started my ammunition back during the afternoon. About dusk, I was told to remain in my present position, that Mariveles would be abandoned and we would make our final stand on the west side of Bataan. There was considerable confusion and no one seemed to know what was going on."

Deploying tanks and piercing the Filipino-American lines in a number of places, the Japanese surrounded some defenders and swept others to the rear in a rout accelerated by their air arm which blasted the trails or roads packed with men and the few vehicles and field pieces not abandoned or shoved into ravines and ditches when passage became obstructed.

Paul Bunker on Corregidor began to wonder whether his former West Point classmate could or would do anything. "Our air force in Australia seems more concerned with attacking the Japs in India for the benefit of the sprinting Englishmen [showing his scorn for the defeated British] than in paving the way to helping us. MacArthur's radio to the CIO [labor union] in the USA indicates to me that he is again hearing the Presidential Bee buzzing about his head. If so, and he succumbs (in addition) to the blandishments of British propaganda, then there is but very little that we can hope for here in the Islands. We'll all be sold down the river." The Coast Artillery commander quoted some doggerel on that theme and concluded, "The worst of it is that we are being 'betrayed' by the 'land that bore us.' " [a chorus phrase].

On the following day, Bunker vigorously exercised his choler. "The USFIP daily bulletin tonight was more nauseating than usual: MacArthur asking blessing of the Minister who baptized him—and Wainwright broadcasting a sycophantic speech to the USA, lauding Roosevelt and telling how 'heroic' the poltroon Philippine Army is and how brotherly the Filipinos are! Faugh!"

On April 7, Bunker recorded dismal news. "It appears that our Philippine Army Bataan forces have crumpled and run, letting the Japs penetrate our center and roll up our right." His big guns on Corregidor were ordered to fire in support of the defenders but the attackers were unfazed by the cannonade.

With the enemy about to overrun the hospitals, the authorities forestalled the capture of the women. "Around eight on the evening of April 8," said Ullom, "nurses at Hospital Number One and Number Two were ordered to take a small bag and be ready to depart immediately. It evoked mixed feelings from the nurses. Many were reluctant to go. They felt an obligation to nurse the seriously and critically ill patients. But they knew orders must be obeyed. The doctors came to see them leave. Goodbyes were hasty with promises to see each other again.

"The emotions of three nurses can readily be imagined. Dorothea Daly and Capt. Emanual Engel, Jr., were married in February 1942 in the hospital chapel while bombing could be heard in the distance instead of music. The bride wore khaki trousers with a borrowed khaki skirt over them. Lucy Wilson intended to marry Lt. Dan Jopling of the Coast Artillery the next day but now wouldn't be there. Helen Summer planned to marry Lt. Arnold Benjamin. A chaplain handed her a gold watch, key chain and

ring when he told her Lieutenant Benjamin had requested
this. He heroically led his men as he lost his life on Mount
Samat.

"About midnight, the nurses from Hospital Number
One were in a small open boat. It tossed about in the water
as blasts hit nearby. Guns on Corregidor were hitting the
Japanese on Bataan. Shells whizzed overhead repeatedly.
Men on all sides were attempting to swim to Corregidor.
At 3:30 the pier was reached finally, amidst flashes of gun-
fire and blast of bombs."

Later, the evacuees from Hospital Number Two endured an even more harrowing trip than their colleagues.
They had gathered at the Mariveles dock in the early
morning hours while defenders demolished stores of TNT,
warehouses, munition dumps and storage tanks rather than
allow them to fall into enemy hands. For as long as seven
hours, the nurses and personnel accompanying them huddled in ditches, under trucks, in an engineers tunnel or in a
culvert. Meanwhile, the orgy of destruction continued to
streak the sky with streams of colored fire and smoke.
Sailors scuttled the few ships and the faithful *Canopus*
backed out into fifteen fathoms of water and then slowly
settled to the bottom as water flooded the torpedo warhead locker and forward magazine.

Even Mother Nature ripped into the hapless of Bataan.
An earthquake shivered the ground, sent men sprawling,
bounced the beds in Hospital Number Two, shook the
walls of Malinta Tunnel on Corregidor, swayed the trees,
panicked screaming monkeys.

The II Corps on the eastern side of the peninsula began
to run out of room to back up as the enemy advanced from
the north and on the western flank, driving troops under
Bluemel towards Manila Bay. Bluemel supposedly had
three regiments and a battalion of his own tied in with two
more regiments under Col. John Irwin. In fact, surrenders,
desertions, killed and wounded had depleted what would
have added up to well over ten thousand combat troops to
twenty-five hundred who, said one officer, "were all so

tired that the only way to stay awake was to remain standing. As soon as a man sat or laid down he would go to sleep."

In point of fact, as communications broke down and the defenders broke ranks to retreat, Bluemel could personally exercise command over only a small portion of the men. He spoke for many of the embittered at the front as he exploded to a handful around him: "Those god damned bastards back there have been sitting on their damned fat asses for months, eating three squares a day before retiring to their comfy beds for a good night's sleep. They've had their heads in the sand like a covey of ostriches. They haven't known what is going on, what has happened and they haven't listened. And now it's all down the drain. I can't pull their dead asses out of the fire, and I don't know of anyone else who can except the Good Lord, but I don't see Him taking the trouble." While Bluemel overstated the living conditions to the rear, the orders he received indicated at best wishful desperation and at worst woeful ignorance.

On April 8, the troops led by Bluemel yielded along the Alagan River, the final natural barrier to the enemy advance. The haggard general, who had suffered the same extreme physical deprivations as his soldiers, had halted at night by a stream of water, waded out to a rock, removed his shoes and socks to bathe his sore, swollen feet. When his II Corps commander and nemesis Gen. George Parker reached him by field telephone and told Bluemel to form yet another line of defense, Bluemel scolded his superior: "You sit back there on your dead tails in your comfortable, well-lighted CP and draw a line on a map with a grease pencil and tell me to hold it. I am lying here in pitch black dark, with no map and only a vague idea of where I am. I have been fighting and falling back on foot for the last seventy-two hours. I have no staff, no transportation, no communications except the phone I hold in my hand. My force consists of remnants of the only units that have fought the enemy, not run from them. The men are barely able to stagger from fatigue and lack of food which we have not had for over twenty-four hours. Yet you cannot send me one of your many fat, overworked staff officers to show me where I am to deploy the handful of men I have. Where is the food we need to revive our starving bodies? Where is the ammunition we need to fire at the enemy? Where are the vehicles and medics to treat and evacuate our wounded and disabled?

"I'll form a line, but don't expect it to hold much past daylight. OUT!" As Bluemel and his staff tried to organize a cogent defense they too felt the earth tremble beneath them. They first thought that hunger and fatigue had induced hallucinations but then realized it was a quake.

The battle reports caused Wainwright to advise MacArthur, "I am forced to report that the troops on Bataan are fast folding up." He named three divisions of the Philippine Army as "disintegrated," and concluded, "The troops are so weak from malnutrition that they have no power of resistance."

Even as MacArthur digested the news of the collapse of the Luzon defense, Wainwright telephoned Gen. Edward King, commander of the armies on Luzon. Wainwright suggested that the I Corps, under Gen. Albert Jones, which remained intact because the enemy chose to make its push down the eastern side of Bataan, launch an attack against the enemy's flank as it tried to overrun the II Corps.

Jones flatly rejected the strategy. He argued his men lacked the stamina or strength to cope with the demands of the maneuver. Nor did they have the resources to move heavy equipment and artillery, prerequisites to any chance of success. Furthermore, Jones said the troops designated to spearhead the attack would need eighteen hours before they could be deployed. Although King's chief of staff, Gen. Arnold Funk, did not specifically utter any words about a surrender, the probability of such an act was implied. Wainwright, obedient to orders from MacArthur, continued to insist that the Bataan force must not yield.

In Australia, MacArthur said, "Rumors reached me of an impending surrender. I at once radioed General Marshall, informing him that under any circumstances or conditions I was utterly opposed to the ultimate capitulation of the Bataan command. If Bataan was to be destroyed, it should have been on the field of battle in order to exact full toll from the enemy. To this end, I had long ago prepared a comprehensive plan for cutting a way out if food or ammunition failed. This plan contemplated an ostentatious artillery preparation on the left by the I Corps as a feint, a sudden surprise attack on the right by the II Corps, taking the enemy's Subic Bay positions in reverse, then a frontal attack by the I Corps. If successful, the supplies seized at this base might well rectify the situation. If the movement was unsuccessful, and our forces defeated, many increments thereof, after inflicting important losses upon the enemy, could escape through the Zambales Mountains and continue guerrilla warfare in conjunction with forces now operating in the north. I told him I would be very glad to rejoin the command temporarily and take charge of this movement.

"But Washington failed to approve. Had it done so, the dreadful 'Death March' that followed the surrender, with its estimated twenty-five thousand casualties, would never have taken place."

Nothing better than this statement demonstrates the fantasies that had swathed MacArthur's thinking for the defense of the Philippines. From his first decision to meet an invasion with an untrained, ill-equipped army through the final moments when he proposed that the starving, sick [eighty percent with either malaria or dysentery], ammunition-poor, artillery-weak, rag-tag aggregation, an army largely in name, carry out an attack against a well-led, fully equipped foe supported by an abundance of big guns and aerial supremacy, he seemed to believe he could control reality by means of his will.

MacArthur voiced his faith in this "sudden surprise attack" even after the war when the need to deny defeat no longer existed. Wainwright, who had dutifully echoed his superior, years later said of General King, "[He] was on the ground and confronted by a situation in which he had either to surrender or have his people killed piecemeal. This would most certainly have happened to him within two or three days."

Irvin Alexander attended the conference at King's command post while the strategists wrestled with Wainwright's notion of an attack by I Corps. Remembered Alexander, "Calling General Wainwright's headquarters again, [King] demanded to know what the decision was with reference to I Corps in view of the fact that General Jones had reported to General Wainwright exactly as he had to General King, that he could not launch an attack . . . There was a considerable pause, during which I assumed that a discussion was going on at the other end of the line. Two or three minutes later, General King said, 'Thank you very much' and hung up. Turning to his staff, he reported that General Wainwright could not agree to a surrender of Bataan as General MacArthur had ordered him to hold on, but that if General King did surrender on his own authority, there would be no interference with any element of his command." Wainwright later would categorically deny he held any discussion with King about the option of surrender.

Said Alexander, "The general went on to say that if he survived to return home he fully expected to be court-martialed, and he was certain that history could not deal kindly with the commander who would be remembered for having surrendered the largest force the United States had ever lost."

After further review of the situation with his staff officers late during the night of April 8, King concluded he had no alternative but to submit to the enemy. He made the decision on his own, knowing full well it directly disobeyed the orders emanating from both Australia and Corregidor.

King dispatched a pair of emissaries to the front lines

where a platoon of Japanese soldiers, flashing bayonets, charged the two-man truce party. The Americans frantically waved a white bedsheet and convinced an officer through sign language that they wished to see the commanding officer. Subsequently, an interpreter translated a message from King, and the enemy commander, Maj. Kameichiro Nagano, dictated a time and place for a meeting with King.

The first hours of the session went badly. General Homma had expected the U.S. envoy would be a representative of Wainwright and prepared to speak for all Filipino-American forces in the islands. King could speak only for the Luzon army. King bargained an immediate armistice for assurances that all prisoners would be treated in accord with the Geneva Convention and that the sick, wounded and weary ride in trucks with gasoline expressly saved for this contingency. The Japanese dismissed the plea for an immediate halt to the shelling, saying that their pilots, already in the air for missions, could not be recalled before noon and raids would continue until that hour. Apparently also irate because King could not give up the defense of the entire archipelago, the victors demanded unconditional surrender of those under King's command. The discussion dragged on for ninety minutes before King, desperate to spare useless bloodshed, assented. Even then, his conquerors demanded every individual and unit accept the uncompromising terms.

The chaos continued even with the cessation of hostilities. Alva Fitch recalled, "A messenger told me to report to General Stevens's CP as Colonel Hunter's representative." [Luther Stevens commanded the 91st Division which Fitch's artillery supported.] "When I arrived, the staff was sitting around with long faces, drinking coffee. I was given a cup of coffee and a chair. General Stevens blew his nose a couple of times, and said: 'Major, General King has gone to Japanese headquarters to surrender the Bataan forces. The terms are not yet known. Be prepared to complete the destruction of your guns and materiel before 6:00 A.M.

[There is a discrepancy between Fitch's timetable and the official record but there is no reason to doubt his memory of the experience.]

"I reported this to Colonel Hunter and assembled my battalion commanders and staff. I gave them the news and instructions as to what to do to their guns and equipment. About 4:00 A.M. I received a call from General Stevens. He said the Japs had refused to accept the surrender. And that we were to fight it out on our own. My Filipinos didn't like this much, nor for that matter did I. About half an hour later, he called again and said that the surrender had been accepted. To carry out previous instructions except that we would not destroy transportation as the Japs had agreed to use that to get us out of Bataan.

"The next few hours were very noisy. The sound of demolitions and of burning ammunition dumps gave the impression of a fair sized battle . . . We had a good meal, posted guards for local security and I went to sleep.

"By the time I awakened on the tenth, most of the sounds of fighting had stopped. We received orders to stack arms and display white flags. All day we heard stories of how the Japs were treating prisoners. Generally, they indicated that we could expect fair treatment. My lieutenants were in favor of taking to the hills. All had malaria, some had dysentery and we had no medicine. I feared that it would be a year or eighteen months before the Philippines were retaken. I didn't believe we could live that long among the Filipinos without being captured or betrayed by them. Eventually they [his subordinates] all took my advice and stayed with me."

When Col. Irvin Alexander returned to the 71st Division Headquarters he reported to Brig. Gen. Clinton Pierce, who succeeded Clyde Sellect as the outfit's commander. "I informed the division commander that most of my American officers and a number of the best Filipinos had spoken of going to the hills instead of surrendering. I suggested the possibility of the general leading a picket detail through the Nip lines. He answered, 'If the commanding general had wished that I take a patrol to the mountains, he would have told me. I have received orders from my commander to surrender myself and my command and I am a soldier who carries out orders.' I asked him if he would authorize the immediate departure of a patrol if someone else led it. He answered, 'No!' "

The upper-echelon officers waited for official word of acceptance of a cease-fire. Word came that the enemy had started an attack and Alexander received orders to block the Japanese using a battalion of Scouts already on hand and another battalion that would join them subsequently. "The men had been informed before noon that the war was over, and they had thrown their arms away, substituting white flags for their guns. I tried to get them off the road into the jungle but I was not successful. The story of surrender spread like wildfire, so that the newly arrived men started to throw their arms away. I appealed to the battalion commander who did get his companies into position but I knew there was no fight left in the men.

"General King had surrendered us, yet I had command of a defensive force which was practically useless, under orders to allow no Nips to pass our position. The American officer with me tried to reassure me by telling me there would be at least one man to back me up when I started shooting."

To Alexander's enormous relief, he received instructions to withdraw into a bivouac at their permanent camp. "I assembled all of the Americans at supper to repeat my conversation relative to taking to the hills. I told them I was not in good enough physical condition to try to pass through the Nip lines. I [explained] I saw it my duty to stay and accept surrender but I would order out a patrol consisting of all those who felt their chances were better in the hills. Moreover, I would take full responsibility for their absence in the event they did not come back. After a brief discussion among themselves, every man decided he would stay."

General Funk delivered the news of a truce to Bluemel

by field telephone. Bluemel was to withdraw his people to an isolated position where they could escape contact with the enemy while rations would be sent to them. The general with men from his 31st Division, Philippine Scouts of the 57th Regiment and the 26th Cavalry and some troops from the 14th Engineers formed into a column trudging towards a safe area.

At this moment, Harold Johnson, commander of the 3rd Battalion, 57th Infantry, arranged for his people to retreat after the 31st withdrew without informing him. "We had two days where they debated taking to the hills. While we trusted $97^1/_2$ percent of the Filipinos, we knew there was about 2 percent you couldn't trust and they would sell you for a penny to the Japanese."

Although the surrender negotiations had been under way for several hours, Japanese infantrymen continued to push forward rapidly. Bluemel recalled, "While moving on [a] trail, [I] was leading the column with a patrol of two men and came under rifle and machine gun fire in the open at a distance of about a hundred yards. The troops of the 26th Cavalry were deployed and an engagement commenced. At this time the attention of the 31st Division's commanding general [Bluemel] was called to the fact that Headquarters Luzon Force surrendered at daylight and directed firing to cease at that time, that it was now almost noon and a fight was commencing. If the command fought its way out of this situation, it would be to surrender at Mariveles or some other place as there was no place to go or other troops which could be reached and that many casualties would be incurred for no useful purpose. It was decided to stop the fight and surrender."

This may well have been the final firefight involving organized defenders on Bataan.

CHAPTER XII

THE DEATH MARCH

IN THE HANDFUL of hours that remained before the Japanese overran all of Bataan, Wainwright endeavored to send as many as seventy-five hundred men to Corregidor. He hoped to reinforce his garrison with proven units like the 45th Infantry Philippine Scouts, a field artillery battalion with its weapons, and other soldiers. He agreed to take to the fortress all Navy personnel, mostly Americans, with their precious stores of food, fuel and boats.

Transportation specialists rummaged about to float a shuttle service employing a minelayer, inter-island steamer, launches and barges towed by powered vessels. The entire operation fell apart as gridlock on trails and roads as well as interdicting fire from the enemy prevented the 45th from ever getting to the docks. Only a couple of artillery pieces with a battery made the trip.

Through binoculars, a horrified Wainwright and staff watched a motley group of servicemen and civilians improvise their own craft, sometimes as flimsy as a few bamboo poles lashed together. Others even plunged into the oily, shark-infested water and stroked towards the Rock while Japanese artillery lobbed shells among them and snipers picked off the bobbing heads. A mixed bag of about two thousand eventually joined the eight thousand already on Corregidor; had everyone whom the command authorized reached the island, the limited food supplies would have run out within ten days.

On Bataan, the Japanese had bagged as many as seventy-eight thousand men. As King feared, he had surrendered the most men ever by an American commander. The volume staggered the victors, who had anticipated only about forty thousand troops opposing them. Not only were there nearly double the amount of captives but also the speed of victory far exceeded the Japanese timetable. In little more than one week they had achieved what they believed would require at least one month of operations.

Under these circumstances the absence of a plan to handle prisoners is understandable. There had been no preparations to provide the food, water or transportation needed for the tens of thousands who surrendered. Adding to the potential for disaster was the attitude of the victors. Resentment towards those whose bullets, grenades and shells had killed friends was understandable and expectable. But racism also influenced behavior. The Japanese considered themselves a superior ethnic strain and treated the subjugated Filipinos, along with the Chinese, Polynesians, Koreans and other Asians, as inferior. Their knowledge of the United States, much of it drawn from Hollywood's gangster movies or Westerns and coupled with propaganda, persuaded them Americans were crude, thuggish people bent on the destruction of the Japanese way of life. Perhaps most responsible for the low esteem in which the Japanese held their American captives was *Bushido*, the inculcated warrior code that taught the Japanese soldier to prefer death to surrender. For a foe to yield while still able to fight generated contempt, particularly among the officers. Conditions and attitudes combined to create what would be a two-week-long ordeal infamously known as "the Death March."

The horror developed slowly; the men caught up in it had no inkling of what lay ahead. On the Luzon peninsula, those who could not flee awaited their fate as prisoners. The confusion generated by the rapid rout continued, as neither their officers nor their captors provided direction. Tom Gage, whose chores as a clerk had continued to keep him out of the front lines even as those in his squadron formed one of the many provisional rifle units, remembered, "When we got the news that Bataan had been surrendered—something like jungle telegraph spreads by osmosis—everyone started gathering in the headquarters-supply area. We built a fire in the central area and began throwing the .45s into the fire, less clips of course. Rifle bolts went into the fire too. Campbell came over and suggested we drift towards the supply trailer and see if we couldn't get ourselves some new clothes. I put on everything new and picked out several pairs of socks. I also put on a brand-new pair of brown army shoes, size 7 EEE. Before we left I went to the safe to get some money I had there for safekeeping. The safe was pretty well cleaned out but I found my envelope and two or three others. I remember giving Batson his.

"On April 9, we were told to move out. About this time, Captain Wray and the officers took the cars that would run and struck off. I think they were aiming for Mariveles to get to Corregidor. I don't think a single officer stayed with the enlisted men. We were trucked in relays to area headquarters."

Some in Gage's area had been approached by Filipinos offering to sell food. After agreeing to a deal, the Americans followed the natives. Reports the former sergeant, "They found a mountainous food dump, and we had been starving for the past two months. Everyone could get all the milk [condensed], chocolate, corned beef [canned] they wanted. There were a lot of K rations too.

"We had to load up on a truck and I was empty in the canteen. [He was denied coffee from a community pot because of resentment towards headquarters personnel.] Our truck wouldn't run so it was towed to Mariveles by another loaded truck. We were packed in standing. On the way down we saw our first Japanese troops. They were stringing telephone wire up the road. When we got to

Mariveles we were not allowed off the trucks. In the morning, they would let a few off the back but we could not wander. I filled my canteen with ditch water and dosed it liberally with either chlorine tablets someone gave me or iodine. (Everyone didn't dislike me.) I've never understood why I didn't get dysentery or typhoid from this water—maybe I overdosed it with chlorine. But never, never again would I be caught short of water.

"We were put through our first shakedown, they were looking mainly for weapons. I retained my field bag and food, tin helmet and a book—*For Whom the Bell Tolls.* We were in this place the tenth, eleventh and twelfth. Most of the 34th [Pursuit Squadron] searched each other out and gathered in one general area. We were all approached on turning in our chow to Mess Sgt. Hardy and having him make as many meals as he could. Sergeant Hardy did a good, fair job; I recall we had something to eat every day. Captain Wray and his officers came straggling in, barehanded. They didn't get too far down the Mariveles road before the Japanese pulled them out of their cars.

"The road to our pen came downgrade quite a ways. I happened to be standing right at the bottom on the eleventh when I heard a noise like nothing I'd ever heard before. I sensed something wrong because I moved well off the road and about that time the leaders of the Filipinos came pouring down—just like a flash flood. It was panic. I figured the Japanese guards at the head of the grade had killed some and started the stampede.

"Campbell and I 'volunteered' to help gather up loose and extra equipment. The guards were forcing everyone to divest themselves of any equipment, belts, canteens, packs, etc. We helped for a little bit at the main dump under the eyes of a couple of guards. After a bit, we picked out for each of us a belt and two canteens and a full infantry pack. The guards grinned and nodded. After a while when we left, they offered no objections.

"April 12, 3:00 P.M. they threw us out on the main road and we started the march out of Bataan."

P-40 pilot Sam Grashio had passed up two opportunities to escape from the Philippines. "When it became obvious to all that the end was near on Bataan, Ed Dyess [the squadron commander] received a phone call from Lieutenant Colonel Gregg, senior air officer left on the peninsula. He told Ed to get on board an incoming plane and fly south to Mindanao for eventual evacuation to Australia. I was with Ed at the time and heard his reply, 'We haven't surrendered yet. I can't leave my men.'

"He knew I was married and had two daughters (my wife had a child by a previous marriage). He asked me if I wanted to leave and I asked what he intended to do. He repeated what he had told Gregg. I replied I would stay too. Later Ed made the same offer to Leo Golden, who was also married, and who had a son. He got the same response.

"I would like to claim that Leo and I acted out of some profound sense of military duty but whatever our dispositions, our military duty was not clear. Would it not have been more truly our 'duty' to save our skins and hope to come back to fight the Japanese another day? I chose to stay for the most direct of reasons, my deep respect for Ed Dyess, the man who had already taught me so much about loyalty, unselfishness and courage. If remaining on Bataan was good enough for Ed, it was good enough for me. His conduct contrasted sharply with that of some others. I was amazed to see colonels pull rank on each other ruthlessly in order to get on board anything leaving Bataan in its last days."

A second opportunity to get away had presented itself when on April 8, the day before the men on Bataan put down their weapons, Dyess nominated Grashio to fly reconnaissance far to the south. With a belly tank to extend his range, Grashio could have kept going to one of the more distant islands from which escape to Australia might be possible. He spent a restless night weighing the alternatives, wondering about his wife and a child born after he left the States whom he had never seen. He says it was thinking about what Dyess would do in a similar situation that determined he would return to Bataan.

Indeed, on the following day the final mission provided a perfect opportunity for Dyess, himself, to flee. Instead, he assigned the plane to Jack Donaldson with orders to drop bombs on Japanese lines and then fly south to Ilo. Donaldson thus avoided capture.

Once King surrendered the Bataan forces, Dyess loaded a group from the squadron in a command car and drove to Mariveles on the strength of a rumor that a submarine or even a B-17 might be available. Discovering the rescue craft were phantoms, Dyess on April 9 organized a search for a boat and enough fuel to reach Corregidor. Neither item turned up.

"Nothing was left now but to try to rejoin our outfit," remembered Grashio. "Cold reality enveloped us within a few minutes. We met a Japanese tank and staff car. We stopped at once, threw up our hands and waved white handkerchiefs. A Japanese soldier standing in front of the tank motioned us to drive closer. We did and again alighted with our hands up. A Filipino interpreter who was with the soldier complained that we were violating surrender instructions because we still wore side arms. The Japanese without a word proceeded to club Dyess mercilessly. For good measure, he then stole two rings of mine, a crash bracelet and a pen and pencil set. Then he motioned for us to get back into the car and resume driving towards our outfit. As we proceeded, our captor pulled close to our vehicle, smiled inexplicably and threw my jewelry back into our car. But as soon as we stopped, other Japanese lined us up in groups of a hundred, and stole my possessions all over again, save only my flying ring which I managed to tie inside my underwear."

According to Alva Fitch, "About noon of the eleventh [a full day after King accepted the Japanese terms] a Jap force occupied the area of the creek from which we were getting our water. I went to pay a call on the commander thereof. He was quite civil and told me to send my

Filipinos to Bagac and that he would give me a pass to take my Americans to Mariveles. I sent the Filipinos to Bagac at once and with one car and one truck we started for the Jap CP. We were no sooner on the road than trouble began. A party of Japs took our truck and car and began taking watches, money, etc.

"I walked the three hundred yards to the CP and protested. The officer was 'so sorry' but 'you should bring all of your men to my CP.' After about two hours of argument and waiting, he gave me another car and a pass to Mariveles. He cautioned us not to drive after dark.

"We started for Mariveles, driving fast so as to get as far as possible before something happened. We went about five kilometers before we were stopped by a Jap whose car was broken down. After about an hour of arguing in a wide mixture of tongues, he took our car and told us to wait, that he would bring it back. It was just getting dark. We knew from experience that the road was no place to wait, so we crawled off into the jungle and holed up for the night.

"The next morning, we split our last can of beans and started walking. It was a hot day, a dusty mountain road with considerable traffic. Every time we encountered any Japs we were searched and robbed of a few more of our possessions.

"About 10:00 A.M. we arrived at a motor pool where we located the car taken from us the night before. We showed our pass and opened negotiations for the recovery of 'our' transportation. After thirty minutes we got [an] answer: 'Very sorry but I have no car to give you.' We resumed our walk.

"The west side of Bataan is quite devoid of rivers. The few streams were so contaminated that we didn't dare drink from them. We were unaccustomed to the sun, so it didn't take long to become thirsty. Our loads were light. All they had left me was one pair of extra socks and my empty canteen. In the early afternoon we were able to thumb a ride in an empty truck and rode for about ten kilometers.

"We arrived in Mariveles about 3:00 P.M. and expected to find food and transportation to wherever we were going. We found nothing except several hundred Americans, as bewildered, hungry and poverty stricken as ourselves. We were herded into what had been the public square and thoroughly searched. While this was going on, Corregidor started firing on Mariveles with what appeared to be twelve-inch mortars. They must have been using armor piercing shells as all rounds buried themselves in the mud without exploding. I don't believe anyone was injured.

"After about an hour of milling around, a Jap climbed up on a truck and made a speech. 'You take a little walk to Balanga. Maybe you get food there.' Balanga was about forty kilometers away. I didn't think we could make it but I was no longer in a position to dispute with the Imperial Japanese Armed Forces."

As Fitch's report indicated, one immediate policy of the Japanese was to separate the indigenous people from the U.S. soldiers. What also soon became clear was that the occupiers of the Philippines made no distinction between rank and file. The diary of Clifford Bluemel indicated the attitude from the first day of his incarceration:

"April 9, 1942. Captured in company with Col. Lee Vance [CO 26th Cavalry], Col. Edmund J. Lilly [CO 57th Scouts] . . . Questioned by G-2 [Intelligence], 21st Jap Division. Hit in head by Jap lieutenant colonel. Believe name is Kusiamato. No food since breakfast. Slept on ground, during night moved to tent [with others] that was closed and the odor was terrible. I laid on the ground with my head near the door so I could get air.

"April 10, 1942. Shortly after daylight I was again taken to Kusiamato, who again questioned me. He gave me a handful of cold rice, some tea for breakfast. We marched towards Mariveles with the division. After about an hour a truck was obtained. Stopped in abandoned army camp.

Here we were permitted to scavenge and I found a pair of trousers, three pair of socks, shaving brush, shirt and mess kit. No dinner or supper. A Jap soldier gave us some sugar and water during the night. Slept on ground, no blankets.

"April 11, 1942. Shredded coconut and sugar for breakfast. The five of us were put in a truck to go to Orani. Truck also contained Philippine Scouts and Philippine Army enlisted men. Truck reached Balanga, the five officers were put on a truck returning south from where we came. We were taken off about ten kilometers south of Cabcaben, turned over to a Jap detachment, told we would remain in zone of Corregidor shell fire until Corregidor fell. We were given some American canned food. Each of us was given a cot. We were permitted to go to a nearby stream and bathe."

On the following day, Bluemel's diary describes a move to another site nearby, where the general met several quartermaster officers and enlisted men. A detail was dispatched in search of rations. On April 13, a large body started towards Cabcaben. Riding in a former U.S. Army truck under guard, Bluemel and fifteen officers and enlisted men passed columns of Japanese troops on their way to Mariveles. Shells whistled in from Corregidor and both the Nipponese and their prisoners clambered out of the vehicle and took cover.

A Japanese soldier confronted the Americans as they scurried into the brush. He brandished a hand grenade. "We had with us a quartermaster civilian employee who spoke excellent Japanese. He talked with the soldier who appeared as if he intended to throw the grenade at us. The quartermaster worker told us the Jap had said, "If you are afraid, why did you start this war?""

The truck brought them back to Balanga where Bluemel downed a plate of rice and endured another grilling about the fortifications on Corregidor. He convinced the interrogators he knew nothing of value. They lodged him in a guard house with Brig. Gen. Luther Stevens, an

American officer with the Constabulary, and Maj. William J. Priestly from the 57th Infantry.

Released from the confines of the guardhouse on April 15, Bluemel along with Stevens and Priestly joined an American column of fours and started to walk towards Orani. "At night," said Bluemel, "we sat down in the same formation, and leaned against the drawn up legs of the man behind us." The terse April 16 entry of the diary noted: "Left Orani A.M., no breakfast. Stevens hit by Jap on passing truck. Jap sentry made me leave him, threatened to shoot me if I did not move."

After the war, Bluemel amplified his description of the incident. "A Jap riding in a passing truck struck Stevens on the forehead with a bamboo pole. Stevens staggered and his glasses fell off. I held him with my right hand and caught his glasses with my left. We fell out of the column and sat down. He said, 'That was hard to take.' The column passed. At the end, a Jap with a rifle on his left shoulder and a .45 caliber revolver (U.S.) in his right hand stopped, pointed the revolver at me, grunted and motioned for me to get up. I tried to tell him in English that a general was hit and hurt. He pulled back the hammer and again grunted and motioned for me to get up. I did. He then pointed the revolver at Stevens and did the same. I helped Stevens up. I still tried to argue with the Jap. He motioned Stevens off the road and into the dry rice paddies. He went about fifteen yards. I thought the Jap was going to shoot Stevens. The Jap then pointed the revolver at me and motioned me up the road to join the column. He left Stevens in the rice paddies and then ran past me to the column. I rejoined the column."

On the road again, Bluemel said he heard shots to the rear. He feared Stevens had been executed as his diary noted, "Saw Filipinos who had been shot a few minutes before. A grueling march, no food, little water, many who fell out shot."

The group stumbled into Lubao after dark and

Bluemel, who managed to buy some rice and sugar en route, gulped it down when they halted for the night. At Lubao, Bluemel discovered a Japanese officer who spoke English. "I told him I was a general and asked for a ride, as I understood all generals were given them. While talking with him, a squad of American officers marched in, halted and reported. [They were late, having fallen behind the main body of the column.] The Jap immediately accused them of trying to escape and said they would be shot. I told him if they planned to escape they would not have marched in a squad formation. It showed they had no intention of escaping. They had become tired and dropped behind. They had marched in the required formation to join the column. The Japanese officer sent them to the other prisoners near us. He gave me a large meal at his mess."

Alva Fitch, having conceded he was no longer in a position to argue with the enemy, had started the forty-kilometer hike towards Balanga. Near little Baguio the prisoners managed to fill their canteens and then the Japanese separated the Filipinos from the Americans who spent a hungry night without bedding but with hordes of insects. "A few men had some C rations," said Fitch. "That served to make the rest of us that much hungrier.

"At daylight we were awakened with the rumor that we were to have some breakfast. After two hours of milling around and counting and recounting, we started down the road again. This time we went about four kilometers and were taken off the road to wait for trucks or breakfast. Neither came. About noon we were back on the road. About 2:00 P.M. we arrived in Cabcaben and were herded into the school yard. We were very hot and thirsty. Stillman, Semmens and I slipped away and filled our canteens at the barrio pump. We were slightly beaten for our pains, but the water was worth it.

"About 3:00 P.M. a Jap 105 mm battalion opened fire on Corregidor. This battalion was about three to five hundred yards in the rear of the school yard in which at least a thousand of us were. Corregidor promptly returned the fire with 155s. Corregidor had no observation but they made a damned good guess. We decided to leave a lot quicker than our guards decided. We passed about two yards to the flank of the 105 Bn. I saw one of their guns blown from its pit by our fire. Capt. Welchel received a splinter through his thigh.

"At dark we arrived at Limao [about ten miles from their starting point]. Most of us had a much needed bath in the Bay. We found an artesian well and drank all the water we wanted. We held a conference and decided we had enough of marching in the sunlight. We decided to get up about 2:00 A.M. and march to Balanga where we had been told we would be fed.

"Without taking the Japs into our confidence, we formed for the march on schedule and started. The guards came along without protest. We arrived in Orion about 8:00 A.M. and were marched into some rice paddies and ordered to sit. There we stayed until mid-afternoon in the heat of a bright day of the dry season. We were not allowed to get water or move around. About 4:00 P.M. we resumed our march to Balanga, arriving just before dark. [They had traveled about twelve miles.] We were placed in some open fields, already overcrowded with American and Filipino prisoners. We learned they had not been fed and insofar as they knew there were no provisions at Balanga.

"I noticed an increase in the number of corpses along the road between Orion and Balanga. I noticed also that many of them had not been dead two days; they had been killed since the surrender. My friends at Balanga explained anyone who became exhausted and fell out of the march column was immediately shot or bayoneted by the guards.

"There were no sanitary facilities at Balanga. This did not concern most of us much as we had been three days without food and could never get enough water to spare for urine. There were two small spigots at Balanga and it was necessary to stand in line for several hours to get your canteen filled. We found there were a few small turnips in the ground. By digging for an hour with a sharp stick, I obtained one apiece for myself and my lieutenants. It is impossible to imagine how incomparably delicious they were.

"After not having any breakfast, we were formed in columns and put in open fields for another day of 'sun cure.' Late in the afternoon, we resumed our northward march. The marked increase in the number of dead along the road kept even the weakest in column. Some time during the night we arrived at Orani. We were marched into a barbed wire enclosure so crowded that it was very difficult to sit down. The ground was well covered with the feces of the dysentery patients that had already been there. We had reached a point where little things like that didn't bother us very much. And if we couldn't sit down, we could sleep standing up. I had developed a very bad bronchitis and it was now beginning to tell on me.

"The next morning I found a blanket that someone had abandoned. That made me a member of the upper class, owning valuable property. It did my morale a lot of good too. In addition, I had slipped out of our cage during the night and filled my canteen. About 9:00 A.M. we started marching north again. The troops were tired and we were going at a very sharp pace. Even the Americans began breaking down and falling out along the road. I helped Chaplain Duffy along until he quit trying. I then commended him to his maker and left him to the gentle mercies of the Japanese. While we were crossing the bridge at Colis Junction, old man Uddenburg jumped off the bridge and was shot in the water.

"I ran into a classmate of mine, Jimmy Vaughn, a signal corps major who was in poor shape. I helped him along and every now and then he'd stop and sit down, then we'd get him on his feet and move on. Finally, I couldn't get him up and a Jap came along and told me to move on. I tried to explain to him but he jabbed me in the butt with his bayonet. Then he shot Vaughn through the chest. I've been told that late that night Filipinos took him to one of their houses where he died a few days later. I saw two American soldiers bayoneted for crawling into the shade alongside of the road. The number of Filipino bodies along the road was shocking, even to us, who abhorred the sight of a Filipino soldier."

The route for everyone was the same, from Mariveles up the eastern shore of Bataan along Manila Bay towards central Luzon. Tom Gage, with those of his squadron whom he could locate, remembered passing the Cabcaben airbase on the southeastern tip of the peninsula, within four miles of Corregidor.

"We were held on the road before crossing the air strip. As time went on the jammed marchers backed up. It soon became obvious what was happening. We were crowded along the waterside of the road. On the inside, a Japanese truck convoy was moving down towards Mariveles. It was intended that the prisoners of war would act as a shield for the truck movement.

"It wasn't too long before we heard the first twelve-inch projectile coming in from Corregidor. It landed at the base of the hill and must have hit a supply dump as it resulted in large quantities of black smoke. Those twelve-inchers didn't whisper like the 155s. They rumble more like a freight train. We all broke to the side for cover and to lay down through the barrage. Several more rounds came in and then the guards started poking us up on the road. The trucks had all passed by. As we crossed the air strip we could see one direct hit on a field piece. Before all of our column cleared the strip another round came in and a few people at the tail end were wounded by shrapnel.

"From now on we were not allowed to choose our pace or to straggle. The guards became a little more menacing and pushy. In general the Japanese troops, being mainly front line soldiers as opposed to housekeeping forces, left us alone. We passed one artillery outfit sitting atop a stone wall. One individual was having a field day giving us the old Bronx cheer in true New Yorkese. Another time, a short, bowlegged fellow came hustling out and jerked my air corps field bag off my shoulder. For the next few miles I grinned and grinned as I thought of his surprise as he examined the contents of his prize. All he got was my tin helmet and the copy of Hemingway's *For Whom the Bell Tolls.*"

Although tens of thousands partook of the death march, the mass of humanity dispatched from Bataan was not one endless column. Instead, packs of a thousand to fifteen hundred men formed groups overseen by parties of guards that seldom exceeded twenty-five. Without any schedule or routine, the only consistent aspect was a merciless urging to move as quickly as possible.

John Olson, who survived the trip, recalled: "Shuffling along through powder thin dust that was often four to six inches deep, prisoners and guards soon had their sweat-soaked bodies covered with a thick coat of tan that gave a uniformity of appearance to both groups. Half strangled by the layers of dust that clogged their noses, the pitiful victims had trouble breathing. Some Japanese wore surgical-like face masks that strained out much of the air they breathed. The haze that hung over each group billowed up into the trees as the endless processions of Japanese trucks, tanks and artillery pieces passed en route to positions at the base of the peninsula.

"Sometimes, if a prisoner was indiscreet or careless enough to come close to one of the troop carriers, a few of the occupants thrust menacingly at him with their bayonets while emitting animal-like screams and jeers. Those who were targets of these attacks and did not move quickly enough to dodge were slashed or even severely wounded. These unfortunates were forced to tend to themselves as they continued to stagger forward.

"The Japanese guards would tolerate no stopping at any place other than the spots where they had been instructed to halt. Anyone who attempted to fall out of the march was quickly set upon with a club, rifle butt or a bayonet. Pushed or kicked to his feet, the sufferer would be thrust back into the ranks. In the beginning, some men screamed at their tormentors that they were sick, wounded or too exhausted to go on, and refused to move. The reaction was swift and decisive. A fierce jab with a bayonet into the chest or a bullet in the head was administered with dispatch and the body was pushed into a ditch or the bushes. This message quickly sank into the aching heads of the others. Keep going no matter how hard it is to put one foot in front of the other! He who cannot move will soon be unable to move forevermore!"

Harold Johnson remembered self-protective measures and even a slightly more benign approach. "Everyone had a different pace he followed during the march because there were plenty of opportunities to hide out. You didn't know what the result would be if you got caught. Some people were bayonetted. Other people were helped into calesas, the little cart pulled by a pony and sent on. It depended on the whim or mood of the guard. Some days we covered eight to ten kilometers; others we spent the entire day in the broiling sun. Some days I just hid out, rested and Scouts gave me a hand. There were stops at regular intervals where the Japanese tried to take care of us. There was always a water source, maybe one spigot with hundreds lined up.

"I had one advantage, the services of the Philippine Scouts. The Scouts were moving around relatively freely. They would search for their officers and say, 'You come see me in an hour and I'll have some rice for you.' You would find them an hour later with a gallon can, half filled with porridge, rice and they would give you a section of sugarcane so you could suck it."

As the accounts indicate, the principal assembly points en route were Lamao, Orion, Balanga and then Lubao, where they soon passed out of Bataan. For many, Lubao provided brief relief from the physical demands of the march, but few amenities. "I was dead tired," said Fitch of his arrival at the site. "I doubt if I could have gone another hour. I had been a prisoner five days, walked more than eighty-five miles and eaten one raw turnip. My worldly

wealth consisted of a blanket, a towel, a spare pair of socks
and a canteen, all except the canteen picked up along the
road."

On their first morning at Lubao, Fitch and his companions were given a half cup of "very dirty unsalted rice porridge. We stayed at Lubao several days, continuing to
receive the same luxurious rations. There was only one
small water spigot for three or four thousand men. It was
only with great difficulty that you could obtain one canteen of water a day. I saw one American soldier bayonetted
to death for trying to buck the water line. They took another across the road and shot him, though I could never
find out why. Many Americans and Filipinos died here. We
had no tools for digging so the dead were simply stacked in
one corner of the yard.

"One morning, two thousand were marched to San
Fernando [about ten miles north]. I went along. We spent
two days in San Fernando. Here again there were no sanitary facilities and only one small water spigot. The Japs
gave us three meals of 'lugao' [rice porridge] a day and
pointed out we should be very grateful as our own army
had fed us only twice a day. Two days later we were taken
by train to Capas, about twenty-five miles north, and we
marched from there to the partially completed Philippine
Army camp at O'Donnell. I was damn glad to arrive, little
knowing that the name O'Donnell would make the black
hole of Calcutta seem a Sunday school picnic."

The short train trips to Capas gave the hapless prisoners
no relief. John Olson says, "These tiny boxcars were similar to the World War I French 'Forty and Eight' [forty men
or eight horses]. But into each of them were forced one
hundred, not forty men. Too crowded to sit, much less lie,
they watched the doors slam shut. Then began three to
four hours of excruciating sweltering in this fetid sweat
box. Some collapsed, the weakest died. Even the Japanese
guards suffered. A few disregarded their orders and
cracked or even opened one of the doors while the train
was in motion. In so doing, they undoubtedly saved a

number of lives. Even so, when they finally stopped at the station in Capas, everyone who descended was wobbly and totally exhausted."

According to Olson, when he stumbled from the box-car, hordes of Filipinos materialized in the Capas train yards. While the Japanese rushed about shouting commands and perhaps counting—it was gibberish to the prisoners—the civilians eyed the gaunt, gasping, sweat-soaked human cargo. "A Filipino boy dashed over to one of the Americans and thrust a stalk of sugarcane into his hands and scuttled back behind his comrades. Others, encouraged by his success, emulated his action with bananas, sugarcane, rice wrapped in banana leaves, sugar cane candy and cups of water. A Japanese, suddenly aware of what was going on, uttered a strident command. Instantly, the guards turned on the crowd and by jabbing, shoving and shouting, forced them back. Sullenly, they withdrew but expressed their animosity by hurling the remains of the food over the heads of the guards to the expectant Americans."

The captives, clutching what items they could field, formed up for the last brutal leg of the Death March, the final six-kilometer hike under a broiling sun to O'Donnell. As Olson and his contingent of Americans, along with a large number of Filipino prisoners, trudged towards their destination, the locals furtively flashed the Vee for victory with their fingers, tossed more food and even stashed cans of water along the way. His group was the first to reach the camp on April 14, and as successive waves arrived at Capas the citizens continued to offer what succor they could. When guards kicked over cans of water set out for prisoner use, the people cunningly hid them in places that the marchers could discover.

The Death March along the Bataan peninsula to O'Donnell stretched 105 excruciating kilometers, or about 65 miles, and lasted about two weeks. The bulk of those consigned to the camp reached it between April 14 and 25. Exact numbers on deaths from disease, thirst, malnutrition or mistreatment at the hands of guards along the way do not exist. But hundreds of men undoubtedly perished. Even worse, the horrors of the Death March coupled with the woeful diet and miserable health conditions endured during the three-month siege of Bataan weakened the prisoners to the point where massive losses would follow in the confines of the hellhole at O'Donnell.

CHAPTER XIII

CORRIGEDOR FALLS

ALMOST IMMEDIATELY AFTER the Bataan garrison waved the white flag, Japanese artillery moved into positions where it could rain explosives upon the fortified islands still held by the defenders. The last bastion lay only three miles from the enemy guns. When the first battery shelled Corregidor, the heavyweights on the Rock retaliated. Tom Gage remarked on the accurate guesswork of the Corregidor gunners and Paul Bunker, in command of the big guns, noted that spotters had worked from the muzzle flashes of the enemy pieces. But Wainwright, apprised of the still heavy presence of friendlies in the target area, halted any counterbattery efforts until April 12, presumably when most of the lost Filipino-American forces had started the Death March. Even after that, maps showed the precise location of Hospital Number Two on the mainland, where about eight thousand sick and wounded remained. Wainwright's order proscribed attacks on the site although Japanese batteries ringed the installation.

Overhead, the air raids increased in tempo but the ever mounting fury of the artillery exacted the greatest toll on the defense. On April 13 Paul Bunker noted in his diary, "This was another day of artillery activity. The Japs plastered us with shells from morning to night." A few days later Bunker reported, "Six heavy bombers attacked Fort Drum and dropped bombs, but all were misses, for I distinctly felt them in our tunnel. This evening a flash came in, saying that Tokyo this morning was under a four-hour bombardment. It cheers us up to think that maybe Nippon is at last getting a touch of her own medicine." Indeed, the B-25s under Lt. Col. James Doolittle, taking off from a carrier, had raided the Japanese capital, striking a blow for morale, though damage was limited.

Albert Svihra, the Army legal officer, had been among those transferred from Bataan to Corregidor. He described a relatively secure existence that dissipated as the attacks intensified. "During March and April, although we were under intermittent artillery fire and bombardment from the air, we were able to take off a little time now and then to sit outside the east entrance of the tunnel [Malinta] under a tent fly with a number of wicker chairs to have a cigarette—no smoking being permitted inside the tunnel—and to discuss the news. At 12:30 P.M. each day our radio station, the Voice of Freedom, broadcast the news from the United States.

"About the only other pleasures of the tunnel were reading and an occasional bridge game. We were on reduced ration as in Bataan. If anything, we were on about one-third, instead of one-half. Our meals, prepared by Chinese boys, formerly employees of the Officers Club at Fort Mills, and served cafeteria fashion, consisted first [breakfast] of either a small portion of cooked raisins or cracked wheat, a piece of toast, two small pieces of bacon and all the coffee you wanted without sugar. For lunch a cup of soup, and either a piece of whole wheat bread or a biscuit, or a small meat pie. Supper, the only decent meal, consisted of rice or a small canned potato, stewed corn beef or corned beef hash, or occasionally fresh carabao or baked ham; one vegetable—corn, peas or sauerkraut—a piece of bread, a small portion of dessert, usually a fruit cobbler, custard cake or fruit, and a cup of coffee. Towards the end, the food particularly at luncheon increased somewhat but at no time did one leave the table satisfied. However little we got, still the meals were fairly well balanced and the deficiency diseases seldom appeared on Corregidor, although not uncommon at Bataan, where food was more scarce and less varied."

Despite his protestations of meagre fare, Svihra's description of meals tends to corroborate the image of life in the rear echelons held by the unfortunates fighting on Bataan. The presence of orderlies and mess boys rather than potential defenders on the Rock is also indicative of skewed priorities when choosing people for residence at the fortress.

Conditions rapidly worsened as Svihra observed. "Artillery fire and air bombing were increasing in intensity. Our outdoor toilets and shower baths, about one hundred feet [away] had been demolished. The shells and bombs shook the very tunnel itself, often landing just over or near the entrance, filling the tunnel with smoke, dust and the acrid fumes of picric acid, and making it so dark inside that despite lights, one could scarcely see ten feet, and causing apprehension that the entrance had been blocked. The power plant was off for days, and the tunnel lighted by an auxiliary diesel engine, which on occasions went out of commission, throwing everything into total darkness. Meals were often delayed and sleep often became impossible.

"One evening, there was quite a gathering of enlisted men at the west entrance to the tunnel, out to have a cigarette. It was a moonless but otherwise clear night. Suddenly there was heard the whining of a shell, then a burst, followed by a shower of stones from the top of Malinta Hill, just above the entrance. There was apparently a terrific rush for the entrance, in which several men were knocked down and trampled on. There followed another big shell which this time landed between the high, steep sides of the entrance, killing or injuring some fifty men. It was a grim sight to watch litter bearers carrying in armless, legless and even headless forms through the main tunnel to the hospital lateral."

Juanita Redmond, an Army nurse, dealt directly with the casualties of the attack mentioned by Svihra. "We worked all night, and I wish I could forget those endless harrowing hours. Hours of giving injections, anesthetizing, ripping off clothes, stitching gaping wounds, or amputations, sterilizing instruments, settling the treated patients in their beds, covering the wounded that we cannot save." The unfortunates, fourteen dead and seventy wounded, had disobeyed an injunction against such gatherings.

Whether directly exposed or seeking protection, the defenders could not escape the consequences of the continuous barrages. One explosion collapsed a cliff-side emplacement, entombing about fifty Filipino artillerymen. Direct hits on bunkers by huge cannons killed or maimed hundreds, and those not physically injured wilted from the constant stress. The Japanese made preparations for a final assault upon the fortress Corregidor.

On April 29, the Navy flew up a pair of PBYs from Darwin to pick up a cargo of officers and Army nurses. The two seaplanes, overloaded with about fifty people, skimmed off the water just before daybreak. One ship was totally wrecked during its landing at Mindanao and a submerged log tore a hole in the bottom of the other. The crew patched the latter sufficiently to take off for Australia but the passengers aboard the ruined PBY would eventually become prisoners.

The route to freedom through Mindanao began to close down. Hostile forces landed there and quickly occupied the western half of the island. The Visayan group fell into Japanese hands and the situation in the southern part of the archipelago seemed almost as desperate as that on Corregidor.

Few on the Rock could afford to even think about the fate of the men and women packed in the PBYs, for the date marked Emperor Hirohito's birthday, and to celebrate it the Japanese unleashed the heaviest bombardment yet seen. They continued to torment the occupants of Corregidor for the next six days. The puny remnants of the U.S. Pacific fleet soon sank to the bottom of the Bay as gunfire destroyed the minesweeper *Tanager,* gunboat *Mindanao* and tug *Pigeon.* Crews scuttled several other small vessels.

The defenders sensed the imminence of the final act as Japanese planes and artillery shifted their aim from the gun emplacements and installations on Corregidor to its beaches. Around 9:30 P.M. on May 5, searchlight units equipped with sound detection systems reported the sound of landing barges warming their motors. About two thousand Japanese soldiers clambered aboard the small craft for the quick run to their assigned stretches of the coast.

Unfortunately for the Japanese, the preparations for the assault went largely for naught. The coxswains operating the launches could not make out the landmarks by which they planned to steer. Strong currents conspired to carry them a thousand yards away from their planned touchdown points that would have located them close to Malinta Hill. When the first waves approached the shoreline, they met the fire of the well-dug-in 4th Marines and a bunch of GI and Philippine Army refugees from Bataan, coast artillery Scouts and even some Filipino messboys. Machine guns, rifles and a few pieces of artillery slaughtered the hapless enemy trapped in the flimsy barges.

A Japanese lieutenant who made a second landing attempt at 4:00 A.M. said, "The big guns of Bataan were supposed to cover us with direct fire on shore defenses. But our boat squadron was ten minutes late owing to unusually rough waves in the channel. The plan went awry.

"Before we got there, we were detected and became impotent targets of a merciless barrage at close range. American high-powered machine guns poured a stream of bullets on us from all directions. Rifle fire augmented that hail of death. Our men who were huddled in the center of the boat were all either killed or wounded. Those who clung to the edges of the ships' sides were hit by shells that pierced the steel plating. The boats leaked badly. In the mad dash to the shore many were drowned as they dropped into the water. Many were killed outright. One boat carried seventy-six men. Seven made it to shore. Air cover came with dawn."

One Japanese officer estimated that only eight hundred of the two thousand participants in this initial seaborne assault reached the beaches. Other reports indicate somewhat fewer casualties but still a significantly high number.

While the defenders staggered the invaders in this encounter, the Japanese troops established a beachhead. And once they penetrated the thin crust of resistance at the water's edge, the Nipponese were able to push forward. In support, Japanese batteries on Bataan raked the island and kept Wainwright desperately shifting units of his diminishing army. Japanese reinforcements numbering around six thousand started to arrive, bringing with them light artillery and ultimately a handful of tanks. Untrained American sailors and airmen equipped with rifles could not cope with the determined, well-schooled foe. Although the American-led forces fought hard for hours, even counterattacked and persuaded General Homma the issue was in doubt, the defensive perimeter continued to shrink.

By 10:00 A.M. on May 6, the Japanese were closing in on the Malinta Tunnel. Already between six and eight hundred defenders were dead; the thousand jammed into the laterals of the Malinta Tunnel would be massacred if the fighting continued.

Throughout the siege of the Philippines, Washington had issued a series of messages that falsely raised hopes of aid and contained admonitions not to yield. When Wainwright succeeded MacArthur, President Roosevelt directed him "to continue the fight as long as there remains any possibility of resistance."

Wainwright recognized the situation was hopeless. He radioed President Roosevelt: "With broken heart and head

bowed in sadness but not in shame I report . . . that today I must arrange for the surrender of the fortified islands
of Manila Bay." A similar message went to MacArthur.

Madeline Ullom remembered the cease-fire: "A corpsman stopped to gravely inform us he saw the white flag at
the tunnel entrance. We heard the time of a broadcast was
set. We gathered around Major Richardson's radio in the
dental clinic. A desolate, numb, unbelievable feeling engulfed one. We listened to the words we had pushed to the
backs of our minds. Tears came to our eyes. No one spoke.
We walked away as though we were in an unrealistic
situation.

"Col. Paul Bunker, Lt. Col. Dwight Edison and a bugler marched to the Topside parade grounds. Taps were
played while they stood at attention. The flag was lowered.
A white sheet was run up. Many had tears running down
their cheeks."

Giving up turned out to be considerably more complicated than running up a white flag or announcing a willingness to cease resistance. The Corregidor radio station,
starting at 10:30 A.M. and twice more during the next hour
and fifteen minutes, had broadcast a statement to the Japanese command that the defenders would end hostile action
at noon on May 6, lower the American flag and hoist the
white one. Upon complete cessation of Japanese shelling
and air raids, Wainwright would dispatch a pair of staff
officers to Bataan where they could meet the Japanese and
arrange a formal surrender.

The attackers continued to bombard the beleaguered on
the harbor forts and the ground forces pressed ever closer
to the Malinta Tunnel. Wainwright sent off three messages
just before noon. One went to Maj. Gen. William F. Sharp,
head of the Corps that covered the Visayan-Mindanao
troops, the southern island defenses. Wainwright advised
Sharp he was relinquishing his command of those forces
and Sharp now would report directly to MacArthur in Australia. By this means, Wainwright hoped to surrender only
the men on the Manila Bay islands.

The brief statement to President Roosevelt summarized the hopeless military situation and defended his decision: "There is a limit of human endurance and that limit has long since been passed. Without prospect of relief I feel it is my duty to my country and to my gallant troops to end this useless effusion of blood and human sacrifice."

MacArthur received a similar message in which Wainwright noted, "We have done our full duty to you and for our country. We are sad but unashamed . . . Goodbye, General, my regards to you and our comrades in Australia. May God strengthen your arm to insure ultimate success of the cause for which we have fought side by side."

Shortly before 1:00 P.M., with the enemy fire continuing, Wainwright chose Marine captain Golland L. Clark, Jr., to lead a truce party inviting the senior Japanese officer to meet the American commander at the Malinta Tunnel. Clark, accompanied by a bugler, flag bearer Lt. Alan S. Manning with a white piece of sheeting on a pole, and an interpreter set out from Malinta Tunnel. The group dodged mortar and shell fire while plodding seven hundred yards towards the enemy.

When the quartet passed the last defensive outpost, the bugler sounded his horn, while Manning vigorously waved his white flag. Intercepted first by a perplexed enemy private, the Americans passed through the hands of a corporal and ultimately to an officer who firmly rejected Wainwright's invitation, insisting the losers must come to him.

Having carefully taken his pistol from his holster and placed it on a desk, Wainwright with four from his staff drove in a Chevrolet sedan bearing a white flag to a rendezvous point. They were met first by a Lieutenant Uemura, who demanded that Wainwright surrender all the Filipino-American forces in the Philippines. The general, still hoping to salvage a resistance under Sharp in the southern part of the archipelago, was not about to discuss terms with a lieutenant. He demanded an audience with a higher authority. Col. Motto Nakayama from General Homma's staff appeared, and when Wainwright claimed his authority was limited to the harbor forts, the colonel angrily insisted in Japanese that any surrender would have to include all military units in the Philippines. After one of Nakayama's lieutenants translated the harangue, Wainwright countered, "I will deal only with General Homma and with no one of lesser rank."

Nakayama agreed to arrange a meeting with Homma at Cabcaben [Ceballo to the Japanese] on Bataan. Wainwright with one of his staff was led by Nakayama and his translator towards a dock. En route, a barrage of Japanese shells forced the group to halt. Wainwright yelled, "Why the hell don't you people stop shooting? I put up my white flag hours ago." Nakayama replied through his interpreter, "We have not accepted any surrender from you as yet."

After some delay, an armored tank barge anchored off shore; Wainwright and the others boarded it by means of a rubber raft and set off to meet Homma. From the Cabcaben dock the general and several of his officers were driven to a battered white house with a large porch. A second boat brought in more from Wainwright's staff. Sipping cold water, they waited for Homma. From where they sat the Americans could see explosions on Corregidor, a mix of enemy shells and demolition of supplies and weapons by their colleagues.

A bevy of Japanese reporters and cameramen gathered to record the glory of the moment. According to Kazumaro Uno, employed by the Press Bureau of the Imperial Japanese Army, there was considerable angry talk about why the enemy had not surrendered the previous night "to avoid the dreadful massacre [of the invaders] in the dark hours that preceded dawn. The Japanese should fight on until every single one of their dead had been paid back ten to one or at least in equal ratio."

Uno described the scene: "It was easy to tell which was the American commander-in-chief, for he was the eldest, tallest and most distinguished looking in the party despite the tired, haggard, frightened look on all their faces. Several of the Japanese staff officers had also arrived and the newsreel cameramen began taking long-distance shots. But General Wainwright turned away as soon as he was aware that he was the focus of all cameras.

"Colonel Katsuya [chief of Japanese Army information and Uno's boss] climbed the stairs, saluted Wainwright and said something. Wainwright and his staff stepped down from the veranda and lined up for photos. The journalists were appeased."

About 5:00 P.M. a Cadillac brought Homma to the house. Soldiers started to unload beer, orange juice and fresh fruit, presumably to cap off the negotiations. Uno noted that the guards looked envious. The Army Press Bureau reporter remarked that Homma understood English but chose to have a translator say, "Welcome to Ceballo. You must be very tired and weary."

Wainwright answered, "Thank you, General Homma. I have come to surrender my men unconditionally."

Homma then declared, "I accept the surrender of the entire Filipino-American forces in the Philippines."

The American protested, "I can only surrender my men on Corregidor and the other fortified islands in the vicinity."

"But you are the commander-in-chief. Even the latest Washington reports confirm your position, General Wainwright."

"I was recently relieved of command over American forces in the southern islands. General Sharp is now in command there. He comes directly under General MacArthur."

According to Uno, the statements by Wainwright produced an uproar as the Japanese commander conferred with his subordinates. Homma thumped his fist on the table. "At the time of General King's surrender on Bataan, I did not see him. Neither have I any reason to see you if you are only the commander of a unit of the American forces. I wish only to negotiate with my equal, the commander-in-chief of the American forces in the Philippines. I see no further necessity for my presence here."

The burly Homma, 5'10", 200 pounds, started to rise from his chair. Wainwright's aide de camp, Lt. Col. John Pugh, said Uno, cried "Wait!" Homma remained as Wainwright hastily conferred with his chief of staff, Gen. William Beebe, and realized that his host would not accept further piecemeal surrenders.

"I will assume command of the entire American forces in the Philippines, at the risk of serious reprimand by my government following the war," announced Wainwright.

But Homma's gorge seemed to overflow and he flatly rejected the change of heart. "You have denied your authority and your momentary decision may be regretted by you. I advise you to return to Corregidor and think this matter over. If you see fit to surrender, then surrender to the officer of the division on Corregidor. He in turn will bring you to me in Manila. I call this meeting over. Good day."

Uno said the Americans were "bewildered" by the abrupt departure of Homma. Indeed, the Wainwright people had to be stunned and appalled. Acting on the premise of an end to fighting, the garrison had already destroyed their weapons. The enemy could slaughter them with impunity.

The Americans debated alternatives and finally Pugh offered, "General Wainwright will surrender the entire American forces in the Philippines to General Homma unconditionally. We have given orders to our men to lay down their arms. Take us to General Homma and General Wainwright will dispatch me to Mindanao to instruct General Sharp to comply."

Because Homma left with his interpreter, Uno said he himself translated Pugh's English for Colonel Nakayama. The latter agreed to return to Corregidor with Wainwright, enable him to surrender to the local commander, get Homma to endorse the arrangement and find out what the Japanese commander wanted Wainwright to tell Sharp.

Exhausted, the gaunt Wainwright accepted the deal. Uno remarked, "I noticed soldiers reloading the iced beer on a truck, symbolic in itself of a sudden startling hitch in the proceedings."

For the trip back to Corregidor, the Japanese provided a speedboat capable of carrying the eight Americans who had comprised the surrender party. Mishaps continued to plague the venture. The craft grounded on a rock in shallow waters near the fortress. Everyone except Wainwright, because of his age and feeble physical condition, and Beebe, badly seasick, was ordered out to push. In hip-deep water the Americans struggled unsuccessfully to free the launch. The six able-bodied U.S. officers formed human sedan chairs to carry their two senior companions to shore. Beebe's crew stumbled and everyone pitched into the water.

On Corregidor, Al Svihra, aware of Wainwright's mission, prepared himself for the inevitable. He packed his musette bag with a first aid kit, toilet articles, some personal papers and group pictures of his wife and daughters, then awaited his future in a tunnel lateral. "Around 5:00 P.M., a Jap officer, accompanied by soldiers armed with tommy guns and flamethrowers, entered the tunnel. Instructions were to stand by in headquarters lateral, to unload all arms and stack them and have with us such articles of equipment and clothing as we could conveniently carry.

"We were ordered to move out of the lateral into the main tunnel, which by that time was a mass of humanity, empty tin cans, discarded arms and equipment, filth and trash. We tried in vain to make our way in a column of twos, through the mass of people to the west entrance. Even then we could hear enemy planes outside, bombing somewhere on the west side of the island. The enemy continued to shell this island with artillery fire."

Because of the danger outside, the Japanese permitted the inhabitants to remain inside the tunnel. When an officer started to inspect the area, he was followed by armed guards. "The latter stopped here and there along the way and plucked watches, rings, fountain pens from among the unfortunate lining the path through the tunnel," said Svihra.

The prisoners remained inside for a restless night, their discomfort alleviated by discovery of a food cache with crackers, canned sardines and some canned fruit. A few broke open their last bottles of whiskey, which they had hoped to use on a happier occasion. Japanese soldiers continued to loot what they could from the conquered.

By midnight of May 6, the Japanese had completed a document of submission and Wainwright signed it. The provisions specified by Homma required the American general to surrender all forces in the Philippines, including those in other areas, within four days. All commanders were to assemble their troops and report to the local Japanese authorities.

In the morning his captors pressed upon him the task of fulfillment of the terms. To do so, Wainwright had to rescind his directive to General Sharp and reassume command of the Visayan-Mindanao area. To ensure Sharp's compliance, Wainwright sent an emissary with a letter. Adding to Wainwright's humiliation, the victors ordered him to broadcast from Manila instructions to some smaller units still operating in northern Luzon. A pair of Americans also traveled to this area to personally contact the commanders. The bulk of these Luzon remnants refused to concede, however. They hid themselves in the mountains and became part of guerrilla movements.

Floyd "Sammy" Forte, the USMA graduate of 1934, had posted a last letter to a classmate in the United States explaining how he had occupied various defensive positions on Iloilo, Panay, Negros and Cebu, and now was on Mindanao. "I joined the Army to see the world and really got to see the Philippines. It broke my heart on losing Bataan. Many of my people have gone. [Forte originally served with the 45th Regiment, Philippine Scouts.] But I'm sure they gave the Japs hell while they could. My lieutenant, who took over my company, got the Congressional

Medal of Honor [Lt. Willibald C. Bianchi]. I was tickled pink to learn that and also my old company really did well.

"I honestly believe the enemy is of inferior quality," continued Forte, "but they got there 'fustest with the mostest,' and I might add bestest equipment. I'm sure the 'first team' will really mop up when you get put in.

"Jawn, old man, remember how we used to sit around drinking and bitching about the dead wood in the Army. I believe you'll have a chance to do something about it. For God's sake, get rid of it. We can't stand for incompetence or inefficiency in our army. We can't let sympathy for social friends or their wives prevent our kicking the unfits out of the Army.

"I believe you're going places in our army [the recipient of this letter would be KIA at Cherbourg in 1944] and expect you not just to make it good but make it absolutely efficient.

"Honestly, it's been wonderful knowing you and Helen. It's been a wonderful life. If there's no more, Sammy has no regrets. I only hope one thing above all and that is that I'll live up to our song 'Alma Mater.' I was thinking about that once when I was in a particularly tight spot. It's really remarkable how appropriate it is.

"Thank you for the grand times we've had together. Remember the swell parties and give my regards to all my friends. Lots of love and keep 'em flying."

Forte, assigned to a staff job with Corps Commander Maj. Gen. William F. Sharp, persuaded Sharp during the last days of organized resistance to let him take some hundred stragglers and go to the active front. A survivor from the Mindanao campaign said, "When we were in the hills after the surrender, we heard that Sammy just went berserk when things folded and he refused to pull back. He and his driver took a position and kept firing until they were overrun." Forte's body was never recovered and he was described as officially missing on May 7.

The largest segment of Filipino-American combat soldiers still under arms belonged to Sharp. Although the enemy had taken about half of Mindanao, most of Sharp's army remained intact. Even as Sharp had absorbed Wainwright's original message giving him independence from the Corregidor leadership, MacArthur, mindful of the imminent fall of the Rock, radioed Sharp, "Communicate all matters direct to me," thereby assuming command of Sharp's Visayan-Mindanao Force.

Upon hearing Wainwright's Manila broadcast in which he retrieved his authority over his Corps, Sharp relayed the gist of the statement to Melbourne and requested clarification. MacArthur quickly responded, "Orders emanating from General Wainwright have no validity. If possible separate your force into small elements and initiate guerrilla operations."

MacArthur advised George Marshall in Washington of the situation and stated, "I have informed him [Sharp] that Wainwright's orders since his surrender have no validity . . . I believe Wainwright has temporarily become unbalanced and his condition renders him susceptible to enemy use."

At his headquarters in Australia, MacArthur of course had not been privy to the details of the meeting between Homma and Wainwright. He could not have known that the Japanese held the entire ten thousand survivors on Corregidor as hostages against surrender in the southern islands. If Sharp failed to accede to Wainwright, the enemy might very well execute close to ten thousand soldiers, sailors and airmen. While neither Homma nor any of his staff ever issued a threat of this nature, Wainwright and his staff feared that, at the very least, the Japanese would resume firing on the now utterly defenseless residents of Corregidor.

Sharp reserved his decision until he met with the officer bearing a letter from Wainwright that set down reasons for him to capitulate. Once Sharp became convinced of the very real possibility that the enemy would resume its war against the defenseless garrison on the Rock, he felt obliged to follow Wainwright's lead. He ordered weapons stacked, the white flag flown. Sharp issued orders to subordinates for submission on other southern islands, but poor communications delayed receipt of the word. In some instances local commanders were unwilling to accept defeat. In a number of places units as large as battalions vanished into the interior for rebirth as guerrilla orgnizations. However, by June 9 the Japanese were satisfied that all organized outfits had yielded and told Wainwright, "Your high command ceases and you are now a prisoner of war."

CHAPTER XIV

PRISONERS OF WAR

ARMY NURSE MADELINE ULLOM remembered scenes shortly after Wainwright acceded to Homma's demands. "Miss Davison [the chief nurse] told ten of us to report near the hospital tunnel to have our picture taken with Colonel [Wibb] Cooper [top ranking medical officer]. The Japanese officer, who was in charge, told us he was a graduate of the University of Utah." [The officer may have been the journalist Kazamuro Uno, who held a degree from that school.] "He assured us in excellent English not to be afraid. He wanted a picture of us in a line with a Japanese armed guard at each end to show we were protected. The pictures would be forwarded to General MacArthur's headquarters.

"Retinues of high-ranking Japanese officers inspected Malinta Tunnel. The white sheet which covered the entrance to the nurses' lateral was once quickly jerked aside and the delegation of Japanese attempted to enter. The alert, stalwart Miss Davison demanded a courageous, 'Halt!' They did immediately. She informed them they could not enter without previous arrangements. Heat and humidity of the lateral was intense. Many nurses were ill with malaria, dengue, dysentery and skin conditions. Several nurses had elevated temperatures. Only a bottom sheet could be spared for the beds. Miss Davison strode to our commanding officer to report the incident. A brief time passed before a standard with a sign in Japanese was placed at the entrance. Thereafter, arrangements for inspections were made well in advance."

Al Svihra, during the first days in captivity on Corregidor, shared a large room with more than a dozen other officers. "Since we were given the freedom of the tunnel the first day, we were able to pick up a supply of canned goods cached in various parts of the tunnel. We had plenty of wet rations [cans of meat, vegetables, beans, hash], milk, coffee, some fruit and a few odd cans of various other foods. Jap sentries guarding the tunnel came in frequently to use the toilet and bath. Although they had evidently been instructed not to molest us, some were bold enough to stop on the way out to see how they could despoil us."

According to Svihra, the Americans played bridge, read old magazines or books, did laundry and prepared food. At the entrance to the tunnel lay the bodies of dead soldiers. As several days passed, bodies bloated, flies swarmed and terrible odors mixed with the foul stench of a broken latrine. The Japanese refused permission for burial parties.

On May 11, Svihra became one of the last to move to a beachfront installation of two balloon hangars and a work shed, the former home of the 92nd Coast Artillery. "There were already jammed into the area about ten thousand to twelve thousand officers and men. With the exception of a few hundred in each hangar, the men had hastily prepared shelters from the sun by spreading out shelter halves, blankets, pieces of canvas cloth, anything readily available, propping them up by means of poles. Most of the men were in dirty and tattered uniforms. It was no uncommon sight to see a soldier wearing an army cotton shirt, sailor trousers, Marine shoes and a Philippine Army fiber helmet.

"Sanitary conditions were deplorable. Men were using any place in the hills, forming a perimeter of the camp as a latrine. The Filipinos were even relieving themselves in the sea, the only place we had for bathing or washing our clothes. I was told that for the first two days or so, the Nips issued no food for the prisoners. Thereafter they issued limited supplies, not to exceed two meals a day and consisting mostly of rice, dry and wet rations, corned beef hash, flour and shortening.

"The only source of water at first was a shallow well located near one of the hangars. Later a pipe line which had been put out of commission was repaired and one spigot furnished an additional supply."

The captors organized the prisoners into groups of a thousand with a pair of American officers assigned as leaders. A further subdivision created units of a hundred with a captain and lieutenant in charge. The arrangement facilitated distribution of rations, but without cooking utensils or organized messes the inmates at the site ate poorly prepared meals and these only on an irregular basis. Dysentery, diarrhea and skin diseases inevitably spread. Svihra scrounged some sulfa tablets to cure his condition, but with medical facilities limited no general relief could be achieved until the tools to dig latrines, garbage and trash pits became available. The increase in the water supply and proscription on use of the sea as a toilet improved health conditions.

Svihra spent most of his twelve days in this camp seeking to avoid the sun and keeping his body and clothes as clean as possible. For two days he supervised work parties of enlisted men, including Marines, and came in closer contact with Japanese guards.

"One thing," said Svihra, "was their evident satisfaction in completing the Philippine campaign. Judging from their sign language, they had evidently been well fed with the idea of their superiority over American troops. They showed this in many ways. One was to point to the impressive size and strength of the Marines and then to indicate to us how small they were in comparison. They were strangely amused by the hairy arms of the Marines, comparing them with the absence of hair on their own. They reminded us of Hong Kong, Singapore, Java and hinted at the same dark fate for Australia and Honolulu. They also reminded us of the attack on Pearl Harbor, the bombing of Corregidor. Very pleased with themselves they were! We could only listen patiently."

Elmer Long, Jr., the Marine who swapped his horn for a rifle, barely survived the assault on Corregidor. "I was wounded by the shell fire, bombing and bayoneted by a Japanese. They held us at the 92nd. It was 120 degrees on a concrete slab, the aircraft taxi area. You could not sit on it in the middle of the day. After four days without food and one water tap we were loaded on ships. We went first to Bilibid Prison and then to Cabanatuan [a permanent camp in central Luzon].

"In September 1942 I was sent to Manila to work as a stevedore, unloading ships. The Japanese officer, a Captain Sagusa, said he had attended UCLA and knew that Americans knew how to work in order to eat. He promised, 'If you unload these ships, no Japanese will beat up anyone.' He was as good as his word.

"It was very hard work; the first day you think you're going to die unloading coal burning ships. But you had a chance to loot cargo and get food. Nobody died except for one man killed in an accident. There were about four hundred sailors and Marines on the detail and we lived on the second floor of a building across the street from Pier 7. I stayed there more than two years."

Unpleasant and as hazardous to the health as circumstances were for the captured on Corregidor, the situation for the Bataan prisoners was far more deadly. Their life under the victors had begun with the Death March. Those who did not perish en route had reached the destination of Camp O'Donnell weakened by malnutrition, dehydration and disease, and battered by maltreatment from their guards. The horrors multiplied in the camp, a site without facilities for the more than 50,000 residents (8,675 Americans, roughly 42,000 Filipinos), who had neither food, water or, perhaps most important, the sanitation vital for preservation of already weakened bodies. O'Donnell was a sun-baked, almost shadeless, water-poor, semi-desert. There was no mosquito control and malaria was rampant.

"O'Donnell, drenched in the glaring, blazing heat of a tropical sun, was certainly no place to be with a shortage of water," said John Olson. "For some fifteen days we did not have a drop of water for washing teeth, face, hands or mess kit. I licked my mess kit as clean as possible, wiped it with paper and set it in the sun to sterilize." Ultimately Olson compared the place to the infamous Confederate stockade at Andersonville during the Civil War, where thousands of Union soldiers died because of the conditions.

Of his arrival at O'Donnell, Tom Gage said, "I remember two things: Filipino soldiers digging graves, graves, graves, and Filipinos in the river, bathing, urinating and drinking. They died like flies."

Just about every arriving prisoner still on his feet lurched and tottered onto the grassless parade ground in front of what was the Japanese headquarters. Soldiers, wearing fresh clean white shirts, khaki shorts or breeches, and armed with large sticks, pummeled the arrivals into a formation for the first indignity, a shakedown that took away blankets, pencils, pens, watches, lighters, cigarettes, shelter halves—in short, just about every personal item the men had managed to retain during the Death March.

The camp commandant, Capt. Yoshio Tsuneyoshi, an overage caricature of a Japanese soldier, decked out in very baggy shorts, riding boots with spurs and a white sport shirt, whose printable nicknames included, "Baggy Pants," "Whistling Britches," "Little Napoleon" and "Little Hitler," then delivered what John Olson called his "God damn you!" tirade in his native language. Through his interpreter he iterated and reiterated four themes. His sole interest was in dead Americans and those that died. They who were alive were not prisoners of war and the Japanese did not care whether they lived or died. Only the generosity of the Japanese spared their lives. The penalty for attempted escape was death.

The rationale that denied official prisoner-of-war status was that some USAFFE units had not surrendered and would not do so until August. In addition, Japan had never signed the 1929 Geneva Agreement regarding the humane treatment of prisoners, although it had issued statements that so far as circumstances permitted it would act in accord with the Geneva provisions. In practice, however, the handling of prisoners throughout the war fell far short of the minimum requirements of the Convention.

Tsuneyoshi seemed to work himself into a frenzy as he harangued the, literally, captive audience. One observer described his performance as hysterical. "He was jumping up and down like a duck on a hot plate." The camp commandant fulminated that Japan and the Allies were opponents for eternity and his country would fight for a hundred years if necessary. He predicted victory, with the Imperial Army occupying the United States.

After listening to Tsuneyoshi, the men dispersed to sections of O'Donnell, formerly a camp under construction for training local troops. Segregated from the far more numerous Filipinos, the Americans subdivided themselves according to their military organizations. The largest group, from the Air Corps, occupied one area; coast artillerymen, Marines, civilians, tankers and infantrymen moved into other parts of the camp. All lived in either bamboo barracks or wooden shacks. Five buildings housed a hospital that, rather than curing the sick, was instead a place for men to die.

Mess halls with the rudiments of kitchens served tiny portions, providing the starving men with less than twenty percent of the daily amount of protein required to preserve muscles. Bugs and microbes feasted on the poorly prepared, contaminated fare, filling the hospital with their victims. With few people to attend the patients or cope with their problems, the wards themselves became hives of infection.

Initially, the Japanese did not distinguish between officers and enlisted men. All would receive the same treatment, and rank conferred no power. Tsuneyoshi refused to meet with General King, the senior American, or King's opposite number among the Filipinos. Instead he would see only their representatives, through whom he passed on his edicts and listened to requests and questions. Obdurate, harsh and prone to tantrums even in these sessions, Tsuneyoshi refused to allow implementation of many of the simplest means to improve conditions. The death toll climbed steeply after the first week of O'Donnell's use as a prison camp.

Tsuneyoshi had warned that anyone who tried to escape would be killed, a violation of the Geneva rules. At first glance conditions at O'Donnell seemed to invite breakout. Only a few strands of wire marked the boundaries and at night the thick grass could hide a figure from sentries posted on the handful of watchtowers. Beyond the enclosure lay a dense jungle, ideal for evading a search party. But the ordeal of Bataan, the Death March and the first days at O'Donnell sapped the mental and physical strength of even the most resolute of men. Men who could barely totter to a latrine could hardly imagine themselves able to endure the effort required for flight.

Olson, who kept what records he could of life at O'Donnell and who interviewed many survivors, says there were no genuine attempts to escape. However, the Japanese executed at least a dozen prisoners, almost entirely those discovered in possession of items believed removed from the bodies of their own comrades on Bataan.

The condition of most captives can be gleaned from Alva Fitch, who wheezed into O'Donnell with bronchitis. "I began after three or four days to recover but promptly came down with malaria. I had no money; quinine was very expensive and very rare. Nearly half the camp had malaria and hundreds were dying from it. My friends obtained a little quinine for me now and then. I had no appetite and continued to get weaker. The food was rice, camotes and mongo beans, occasionally a little flour and, about once a week, half an ounce of meat. The cooks were prisoners strong enough to do the work; they eventually learned to cook rice but always scorched the beans and flour gravy to the point where I couldn't eat them. I went down to ninety pounds.

"Henry Packard took charge of one of the messes and prepared a little special food for me. I am sure he saved my life. I [saw] men try to go from the barracks to the latrine who were too weak to walk and would fall down in the mud and rain, unable to rise. Their friends, officers or enlisted men, would sit in the barracks sheltered from the rain and look at them without moving to help them. I [saw] men, not one but fifty or more at a time, lying in their own feces too weak to move and no one to move them.

"Certain doctors and particularly the enlisted men obtained most of our small supply of medicine by simply taking it from the dispensary. This they sold at very high prices to those who could afford it. They, of course, robbed all corpses. Anyone who did anything for anyone else was a man of distinguished moral character. Harry saved my life as surely as if he had rescued me from drowning or carried me from the battlefield."

"Most days in camp were monotonously alike," said Sam Grashio. "We were awakened about 6:00 A.M. by the bugler, if we had not been already roused by the maniacal yelling of the Japanese taking early morning bayonet practice. Then we went to mess hall for breakfast. This always consisted of about half a mess kit of lugao, a soupy form of rice. Many men simply ate their meagre breakfast, then lay down again and slept most of the day, a habit that became increasingly prevalent as we grew weaker from the lack of food. The main activity of everyone in camp who was not dead or wishing himself dead was trying to get more food.

If someone was sick and about to die, others stayed close to him, less from compassion than from hope of getting his rice ration."

Because of the chance to pick up a bit more food on a work detail, Grashio said there was no shortage of volunteers. While at O'Donnell, Grashio took charge of a work detail of twenty enlisted men taken to a town fifteen miles away to load bags of rice onto a truck.

"I was specifically instructed to have nothing to do with Filipinos and to pass these orders on to the enlisted men, which I did. The starved and weakened men went to work wrestling the 158-pound bags of rice onto the truck. A Filipino boy of perhaps fifteen began to whistle 'God Bless America' to get my attention. I looked in his direction. He made the 'Vee for Victory' sign, pointedly dropped a bag in the street and walked away. Oscar Wilde once said he could resist anything except temptation. He must have been thinking about people like me.

"I ignored what I had told my own men, walked over to the bag, picked it up and was immediately observed by a Japanese guard who had also seen the Filipino boy. He ordered both of us to come to him. First he beat the boy unconscious with his fists and rifle butt. Then he took me to a nearby warehouse. Some five hundred fully outfitted Japanese were standing nearby. The guard motioned for five of them to break ranks and join him in taking me into the warehouse.

"Once inside the place, the five soldiers set upon me methodically. They slugged me, kicked me in the groin, knocked me down at least twice, blackened both my eyes, knocked out two teeth, spat on me and finished by laughing at me and mocking the American surrender at Bataan. The guard then took me back to the truck, which by now was loaded. I ached from head to foot, and burned with humiliation in the bargain because I had been beaten for something I had ordered my men not to do.

"Incredibly, the Japanese driver smiled at me and pointed to the back of the truck. There was the sack the

Filipino boy had tried to give me! Back at the camp the driver gave the sack to an enlisted man who eventually brought it to me. It was full of flat brown sugar cakes about the size of saucers. For a starving man it was a princely gift."

Gage recalled the routine at O'Donnell. "Sleeping was on the floors on hay or dead grass and leaves. Few had any spare clothes and blankets were almost nonexistent. Each day we would gather in groups, sit in the shade and trade rumors. Arthur Campbell and I both almost became outcasts because in the daily bull sessions we both contended that we were in for two, three or more years as POWs.

"I tried eating the leaves of a certain shrub as it was supposed to stop diarrhea. I also ate quite a bit of clean charcoal, supposedly another good remedy. At least mine eventually dried up. We were losing people daily from dysentery and malaria and despondency."

According to John Olson, many, many more of the incarcerated would have died of malnutrition or starvation but for truck drivers and work crews dispatched to chores outside the camp. Filipino civilians donated or sold food to the Americans on the work details. The transactions occurred when the attention of the guards was elsewhere or even with knowledge of more humane, merciful soldiers. In turn the prisoners carried items back to the camp, ingeniously hiding the contraband during routine shakedowns. Some of the fortunate shared their treasures gratis while others sold or bartered for profit.

Tom Gage joined a work party that took him by truck back to Bataan. "The truck quartermaster company treated us very generously. I can't think of a single mean thing they did. For supper the first night we had two buckets of steamed rice and either soup, meat or a vegetable. It was plenty." He and his companions seized an opportunity to buy mangos, canned applesauce, corned beef and other edibles from local people. At another site he was allowed to browse through discarded materials from a Coast Artillery unit, and managed to replace some tattered clothing.

"This was a good detail, light work and plenty of food. I made it a long way back to normal physical status—I've no doubt this probably saved my life."

For more than fifteen hundred Americans and an estimated twenty thousand Filipinos there was no help. They died, mainly during the first two months at O'Donnell. The numbers appalled the Japanese high command, if not Captain Tsuneyoshi. Starting in June an American exodus began to a new, somewhat less malignant installation at Cabanatuan. Also, with hostilities in Bataan and Corregidor ended, the Japanese dismantled Hospital Number One and shipped the medical personnel with their equipment to O'Donnell. In addition, the cessation of fighting brought release of the surviving Filipino soldiers into the civilian population. Although the hellhole of O'Donnell did not discharge its last inmate until January 1943, it no longer figured as an element in the fate of the erstwhile defenders.

The first weeks of imprisonment for those held on Corregidor had differed significantly from that of the men on Bataan. There was no Death March for them, but the time did come for them to join their colleagues in camps on Luzon. After almost two weeks the incarcerated on Corregidor, bearing backpacks made soggy from a downpour, hiked to one of the island docks. Fishing launches ferried them out to a pair of freighters converted into troop transports. The Americans anxiously observed the ships' courses, concerned the direction might carry them to Formosa or Japan. To their relief the vessels veered towards Manila.

The landing craft at the city disgorged the men in relatively shallow water, from knee to armpit depth. "It must have been a rather amusing spectacle for the Japs to see us kerplunking into the green polluted water of the Bay," remembered Svihra. "We waded some hundred yards into shore where we were promptly formed into groups of a hundred willy-nilly and then marched up the Boulevard. Our shoes were soaking wet, making it extremely uncomfortable to walk with the water oozing out of them each step. A few had taken off their shoes before debarking and carried them on their shoulders to keep them dry. When these reached shore, they attempted to change socks and put on their shoes. However, the Japs had other ideas. They compelled these people, with rifle butts as prods, to put on their shoes and without tying them to form with the nearest group.

"We marched up the Boulevard under supervision of mounted Jap guards, past the Polo Club and other familiar places. There were no cars on the Boulevard and no calesas and only an occasional Jap military lorry, some of which [U.S. trucks] were evidently captured in Bataan.

"As we approached the residences on the Boulevard we noticed a few people, Americans and Filipinos, gathered in groups. They were kept well back from the street by sentries and Manila police, evidently to prevent any communication with us. Occasionally someone in these groups (when the guards' backs were turned) would wave to a friend, relative, or perhaps a wife waved to her husband, for there were many American Manilans who had enlisted or were commissioned in the Army at the outbreak of war. They all looked pretty sad and we observed many tearful eyes.

"We were halted for a few minutes to permit us to obtain water from some GI cans which were very conspicuously advertised as an act of charity by the Japanese Women's Club of Manila. We had hardly taken off our packs when we were ordered to form a column again. We continued our march up the Boulevard. As we reached the High Commissioner's residence we noticed the Rising Sun flying from it. The same was true of the Elks Club.

"This was practically an uninterrupted march of about seven to eight kilometers, on a hot, sultry May day. As a result many were forced to drop out. Most were made to rejoin their groups by thumpings with a rifle butt. Colonel Rawlitzer, who had already discarded one of two suitcases he was carrying, fell out, but upon being forced to resume, had to abandon the other suitcase and then fortunately found someone to carry his musette bag."

To Svihra's shock, their destination was Bilibid Prison, a massive pile of stone and dungeonlike buildings that ordinarily housed convicted Filipino criminals. The erstwhile legal officer was pleasantly surprised by the better sanitation in the new digs and the three meals a day, although the food was limited. Prisoners supplemented their diet through what Svihra labeled "Jap soldier-racketeer sentries," who acted as intermediaries between the inmates and Filipino peddlers outside Bilibid. The guards let down baskets from their posts atop the walls; the vendors put in bananas, mangoes, molasses and the like. The prisoners passed up money, most which went into the pockets of the troops before it got to the sellers.

The Japanese, who had signaled a sense of respect for the privacy of the Army nurses captured on Corregidor, continued to deal benignly with the women. Nurse Josephine Nesbit described the move from Corregidor to the mainland: "During the trip to Manila the Jap officer in charge of the boat graciously offered tea and rice cookies to the officers and women. It was mid-afternoon by the time the boat docked and the passengers were unloaded. The officers and men were taken off first and most of them marched away. Incapacitated patients went in trucks. When the women assembled on the dock, the thirty-eight Filipinas were put in one group and the sixty-eight other women in a second group. All were counted several times before trucks arrived to take them away from the dock. The Filipinas went to Bilibid Military Prison.

"The American women were taken to Santa Tomas Internment Camp [site of a local university and known to inmates as STIC] where they were received excitedly by more than three thousand internees. While baggage was searched and the women were interviewed by the Japs, they were fed their evening meal, the most satisfying food they had had in months. The fresh pineapple was the first fresh fruit they had eaten since the war began.

"Rooms had been prepared for these women in the main building but at the last minute the Japs would not permit them to stop there. Santa Catalina Girls Dormitory, a building just outside the main university grounds, was taken over. They were driven to it in the camp truck."

The Army nurses lived at Santa Catalina for eight weeks, receiving three meals daily from the central kitchens at Santo Tomás. Along with the regular fare came gifts of fruit and nuts, as well as clothes, flowers, toilet articles and cosmetics from the internees. According to Nurse Nesbit, Mrs. Ida Hube, an elderly former nurse, born in Germany and therefore not an American citizen, visited the women at Santa Catalina. Shocked by their lean and hungry appearances, she became a one-woman guardian angel, bringing large amounts of food and other necessities.

When Santa Catalina was converted to a hospital, the nurses were transferred to Santo Tomás. There they employed their skills on behalf of the three thousand confined to Santo Tomás. Conditions within the confines of the university were better. Recalled Madeline Ullom, "Army nurses who married businessmen in Manila and acquaintances in the hospital and clinics often invited us to their shanty or patio space in the courtyard of the main building for a meal. The majority of the people who invited us to their shanties received food through the Package Line [a system that supplied the internees with supplies from outside until the Japanese sealed off the camp in February 1944]. The luncheons and suppers were delicious as well as generous. The kindness of the internees was unsurpassable and we were very grateful."

When several trunks of unclaimed clothing reached the camp, the nurses restored their wardrobe, sewing blouses and skirts from oversize men's shirts. "Sometimes when we were off duty," said Ullom, "we picked a beautiful big hibiscus which we wore in our hair. The hibiscus remained open all day and compensated for the lack of cosmetics, especially lipstick."

The Japanese permitted limited recreation. "We clomped to the ball park where we sat on the grass to watch and cheer our favorite team. After the game we joined a group who sat on the crowded plaza to listen to the announcements and music. Classical music was usually played on Sunday evening. Semi-classical, operas, western selections were favorites. Jazz was disapproved by the commandant. Don Bell [the news broadcaster who had been the first to tell many they were at war] was the announcer. On Saturday night, internees enjoyed the play, skit, quiz or program which Dave Harvey and his group presented."

A Jesuit conducted a course in anthropology; someone else lectured on landscape architecture; and lessons in Spanish drew wide enrollment. Hobbies, handcrafts and choral singing helped combat boredom. For a brief period a camp newspaper circulated, but it was discontinued because it consumed too much paper.

Mary Rose Harrington, the Navy nurse trapped in Manila at the end of December, spent nearly a year at Santo Tomas. "There were patrols in the buildings, hall monitors. You always bowed when you passed a guard and did not leave the quarters after nine at night. We had a few shot, a few beaten, but that didn't happen every day. Three young Brits went over the wall. They beat them and then shot 'em. It put fear into us.

"Everyone who worked did better than those who sat and waited for MacArthur to return. Many were depressed, sitting the war out. One supply officer went to the wall and jumped to his death."

As the population at Santo Tomas swelled the Japanese decided to shift some of their able bodied captives outside of Manila. They opened a camp at Los Banos, southeast of the city on Laguna de Bay, at what had been an agricultural division of the University of Manila. The first contingent erected some of the basic structures for the camp. Navy nurse Mary Rose Harrington volunteered for a berth at Los Banos. "In the country we did better in terms of food, growing much of what we ate. It didn't feel as confined, even with barbed wire around us."

Jean George joined the Santo Tomas population in June 1942. Until then she had remained free in Japanese-occupied Manila. "They thought Daddy could convince the Filipinos to give the Japs whatever they needed [vital war materials like oxygen and acetylene]. When that didn't happen they sent us into camp. My sister, her husband and a newborn son born December 19 during one of the bombing raids were already there.

"Each internee *had* to perform certain duties—room cleaning, bathroom duty, sanitation, vegetable detail, etc. I signed up for the vegetable detail—clean, cut, wash, put into a bushel-size wicker basket and with the help of another internee carry a full basket to the kitchen. I also cleaned cereal when it was available, served trays to hospital patients. I seemed to work from sunup to sundown.

"When we were interned, I heard a tale about a Jap who had tried to rape a woman, but when the Japs in charge learned about it the accused was severely reprimanded and sent out of the camp. There was never another incident.

"At first the Japs didn't pay much attention to us, but as our 'protectors' changed from civilians to Japanese military, many things changed. We were instructed to bow to them. We had to stand outside our rooms for roll calls and bow when they came by. Food rations were cut drastically. They commandeered supplies from the various gardens the internees had grown."

George heard from her soldier fiancé, lodged now at Cabanatuan. He requested quinine for his malaria. Warned to destroy any such messages immediately after reading, she remembers nothing else of the contents. Her father, through the underground market, arranged for medicinal tablets to help the sick man.

Betsy McCreary, the boarding school girl "captured" by soldiers in a taxicab, had been interned at Camp John Hay before the close of 1941. She remained separated from her family, who were confined to other places. Moved to another site in the mountains, Camp Holmes, she endured a waiting game, segregated at night with others of her sex and sleeping on a bunk bed in what had once been a Philippine Constabulary barracks.

"The men were guarded more closely and we had some guerrilla activity near us. Donald [another internee] would tell us that we had a new guard and describe him, warn us to keep out of his way as he was a real bastard who had slapped someone or yelled at another. One day he told us of a new young one who was really nice. He'd joined the boys in a pillow fight and he knew a bit of English.

"A couple of nights later, a soldier came in and we just knew he was the one who was okay. He stopped and made motions of writing on his hand. I gave him a large square piece of paper I'd found while on my job in outdoor sanitation and Colleen lent him a pencil. He sat on one of the lower bunks and started to draw Mt. Fuji. We *oh*-ed and *ah*-ed appreciatively. I noticed his rifle propped casually right in front of me. I caught Colleen's eye and we both smiled, recognizing that we both had a momentary impossible dream of glory. But we weren't Errol Flynn or John Wayne—just two school girls.

"The next night after curfew the soldier artist came by. Again he sat on the bunk and propped his rifle. Out of his wallet he took some pictures, one of his best friend killed in Bataan, another of his sister. Then he said, 'MacArthur no good. Run away. American soldiers no good.'

"We countered with, 'American soldiers come Baguio.' He repeated, 'American soldiers come Baguio' and then pointed an imaginary revolver at each of us. 'American soldiers come Baguio, *fosforo, fosforo*'—the Spanish-Filipino word for matches. We understood that if the town was retaken, we would be shot and the city burned.

"We were the enemy, he was the enemy. I was a noncombatant but that didn't make me neutral, neutered or Swiss. I was their enemy. Our nice, lethal soldier came by another night. We smiled, pointed to his drawing, but didn't socialize again."

As a bored adolescent, McCreary found a modicum of excitement by breaking curfew to sneak into the nearby mess hall kitchen but she avoided serious risks. Few considered escape although one could easily have crawled under the fence and disappeared into the thickly timbered mountains. The rugged terrain itself was a deterrent unless one could find friendly people.

In 1943 the Japanese permitted inter-camp mail, small slips of paper. Friends wrote McCreary that "Santo Tomas was fabulous. I would love it. There was a little restaurant and a store in camp where you could buy clothes. And they'd met these interesting guys who had worked for Pan-Am."

McCreary was reunited with her parents in 1943 at Santo Tomas. Her first impression of her new home was ecstatic. "Deck chairs, green lawns, flowering hibiscus bushes. It looks like a resort, a country club. There were people in clean, pressed clothes lounging about, listening to music coming from a public address system. I saw women wearing lipstick and, even more surprising, red nail polish.

"In Santo Tomas at that moment, if you had money and connections on the outside you could order little luxuries from a city still stocked with items the Japanese Army hadn't found essential for their war effort. Hot lunches came in for wealthy internees and they even sent their laundry out to be washed and sent back by former servants. All packages were inspected at the front gate by soldiers, but they seemed pretty lax to me."

But, as McCreary also noted, all of this changed within a few months. Conditions at Santo Tomas would worsen dramatically. Similarly, the state of health at camps for servicemen declined and death began to call with increasing frequency upon the men delivered from the charnel house of O'Donnell.

Less than a year after the swift strikes of the Japanese forces devoured huge areas of Southeast Asia and extended their control almost to the shores of Australia, the Allies had begun to strike back. Although MacArthur would not return to the Philippines for two years, the Japanese began to plan their defense of the archipelago and began to clamp down on their captives.

CHAPTER XV

FIRST STEPS TO RETURN

BECAUSE THE PACIFIC THEATER extended over such a huge area and depended so heavily upon control of the seas, the Joint Chiefs of Staff in Washington, D.C., split responsibility for operations. They named MacArthur Supreme Commander for the Southwest Pacific (he referred to himself as "Commander-in-Chief") and nominated Admiral Chester Nimitz as head of the Central Pacific Ocean zone.

MacArthur's area of responsibility included Australia, the Philippines, the Solomon Islands, New Guinea, the Bismark Archipelago (between the Solomons and New Guinea) and the Netherlands Indies (with the exception of Sumatra, which was reserved for the British). His resources were soldiers, airmen and some naval units. The forces under Nimitz included not only fleets of ships and submarines but also Marines. In some instances, Navy or Marine commanders controlled Army soldiers who expected to deal with the enemy installations in the island groups known as the Marshalls, Marianas, Carolines, Palaus. Later it would become Nimitz's responsibility to seize the volcanic outpost of Iwo Jima and the chain closest to the Japanese homeland, the Ryukyus.

If MacArthur ever subscribed to the notion of the Japanese as paper tigers, he no longer held that view. As the other top military brass and the political leadership absorbed the reality of the enemy conquests, they embarked on an intensive mobilization of resources. Volunteers, reserves and draftees—farm boys, factory hands, college kids, office workers, high school grads, executives, enrollees in government programs—flooded stateside installations often erecting their own buildings for housing and instruction.

Although the Allies agreed to make the European Theater, including North Africa, the first priority, neither MacArthur nor Nimitz could allow the enemy a free hand in the Pacific. But after MacArthur reached Melbourne in March 1942, he quickly understood he was Supreme Commander over a huge domain with very little resources for his stewardship. On hand in Australia he could count perhaps twenty-five thousand recently arrived U.S. troops, mostly command and service personnel. The few combat soldiers were still laboring to learn their trade and had been equipped with only minimal tools for the job. Nor could he count on immediate reinforcements from the States. Transforming millions of citizens into soldiers required time. He lacked tanks, artillery and planes, all of which were either being built or only existed on blueprints. The Navy could offer only minimal help. Japanese planes and vessels had inflicted heavy damage upon the small fleet of U.S. ships that had fled the Philippines. Much of the American seapower that was not rusting under the water at Pearl Harbor still sat in shipyards undergoing repairs. Escort duty for convoys to Britain, North Africa and the Soviet Union meant fewer men-of-war for Pacific operations. Nor could the Supreme Commander draw upon the local army. The bulk of Australia's soldiers were more than ten thousand miles away, desperately trying to prevent Germany's Gen. Erwin Rommel from ousting the Allies from North Africa.

Far from having the resources in manpower or ships to save his comrades in the Philippines or to begin his return, MacArthur faced the disastrous possibility of the Japanese blocking U.S. access to his new base. Nipponese troops and naval forces had swept away Allied resistance in Borneo and the Dutch East Indies, closing off northern approaches. Landings on New Guinea, Papua, New Britain and New Georgia Islands extended the Imperial reach. The Japanese marshalled tens of thousands for invasion of Australia.

According to MacArthur, the Australian chiefs of staff, dismayed by the relentless success of the enemy war machine, conceded the loss of a large part of Australia. They traced a line across the country where they would make their ultimate stand. "The concept was one of passive defense," said MacArthur. "I felt it would result only in eventual defeat. Even if so restrictive a scheme were tactically successful, its result would be to trap us indefinitely on an island continent ringed by conquered territories and hostile ocean, bereft of all hope of ever assuming the offensive."

MacArthur, the student of military history, the innovative strategist and devotee of offense, sounded his tocsin to a spellbound audience of journalists: "Attack! Attack! Attack!" He pored over his maps and astutely concluded he must advance the front line a thousand miles forward and prevent the enemy from exploiting strong footholds in New Guinea and its huge bastion of Rabaul on New Britain. Movement by sea of Allied forces to New Guinea, however, exposed the Navy to enemy bases in the Solomons, particularly to an airfield under construction on Guadalcanal.

The Solomons straddled the demarcation between the MacArthur and Nimitz empires. The debate over who would do what under which command was settled with MacArthur being placed in charge of the moves to reverse the foe's advance in New Guinea while Nimitz's people struck the first U.S. ground offensive blow of the war by landing the 1st Marine Division on Guadalcanal on August 7, 1942.

In both cases, the Allied forces were confronted by stiff

resistance. But some of the GIs exposed to combat in these campaigns would be on hand when MacArthur triumphantly stepped onto a Philippine beach.

The 32nd Division, a National Guard outfit from Michigan and other midwestern states, nicknamed the Red Arrow because of its shoulder-patch design, sailed from San Francisco in April 1942, during the dark period: Bataan had already fallen, Corregidor was on the verge. A comfortable few months savoring Australian hospitality ended abruptly with airlifts to New Guinea and deployment against the enemy in the mountains.

Roland Acheson, a sergeant with the 32nd, had joined the outfit in 1940 when it still pasted signs on trucks to denote them as tanks and trained with WW I artillery. Maneuevers in Louisiana and mountain training in Massachusetts occupied the GIs before the trip across the Pacific.

"Australia was in pretty tough shape then," says Acheson. "They were bombing places like Darwin and Townsville. They even shelled Sydney."

Within a few months, the 32nd was sent to the southwest coast of New Guinea. "They took the coveralls we had and dyed them, like camouflage. They were supposed to be weatherized but they didn't breathe, the hottest things I ever wore. We were then at Moresby, taken by Liberty Ship, and from there went by boat to a place called Kalamzoo, the kickoff point to go over the Owen Stanley Mountains.

"They issued us a bunch of junk, like one-cell flashlights. What in the world would you do with them? Third day on the trail, we throwed them away. We started over the trail with ordinary combat shoes. By third day, all the heels were gone. By this time the replacements the Japanese were going to send to Buna were going to Guadalcanal. And the 5th Air Force got lucky and sunk about four of their troop transports."

Acheson's laconic mention of the Owen Stanley range downplays the incredible marches of the oppposing forces. Covered by dense jungle, cut by steep gorges and swift running rivers, with peaks poking thirteen thousand feet towards the sky, the Owen Stanleys blocked the way between Buna, in Japanese hands, and the Allied base at Port Moresby.

The narrow track of the Kokota Trail through this primitive wilderness seemed the last route anyone could choose for movement of soldiers lugging seventy-pound packs and loaded with even the lightest of weapons. Nevertheless, both the Japanese and the Allies—Australians and Americans—climbed and hacked through the mud, rock and jungle, plagued by disease, parched with thirst, short on food, until they met in a series of battles. Unable to bring in reinforcements because of the dire need for them on Guadalcanal, the Japanese retreated against the dogged persistence of their foes and faced the loss of their base.

"Away we went to Buna," says Acheson. "They sent supplies in by barge. But dumb Americans like we are, we did our supply during the day. Japan-man would always barge at night. Their planes sunk about five of our barges. From then on everything was by air. We had no artillery until about the last week, and then only little twenty-five pounders.

"They was all dug in at Buna, pillboxes, redoubts. We had no artillery, no flamethrowers. [The Allied firepower was probably less than that deployed by the hapless defenders of Bataan.] Japan-man was very smart. Lot of their equipment was stuff they had captured from the British, Lewis or Vickers machine guns. They'd turn it right around and use it on you.

"We first hit the enemy November 22, 1942; it was my birthday and I was twenty-one. We had quite a few casualties on the following day and when they finally pulled our outfit out on New Year's Day, 1943, there was seven left from our company. I got shot up December 19 up near Terokina." Acheson suffered from malaria as well as wounds. He was evacuated by hospital ship to Australia.

The vanguard of soldiers involved in the recapture of

ground now controlled by the Japanese included a former National Guard regiment, the 132nd Infantry based in Chicago. Bob Manning, inducted during 1941 in the first U.S. peacetime draft, assumed he would wear a uniform for only a year. "Basic training was at Camp Croft, South Carolina, and was cursory at best. The cadre as well as the trainees were not very interested in what was going on."

Upon completion of this phase of his military career, Manning moved to the 132nd Regiment, an agreeable assignment since Manning grew up in Chicago. The unit participated in Texas-Louisiana maneuvers and late in 1941 was issued M-1 Garand rifles. Manning still expected to be released from service early in the next year.

But on January 22, 1942, while MacArthur was still hoping to keep the "cork in the bottle" by defending Bataan and Corregidor, the 132nd sailed from New York City, part of a convoy with twenty thousand troops bound for the Pacific. It was already obvious to anyone, except the beleaguered in the Philippines, that these troops would never relieve the garrisons under siege.

After a brief stopover in Australia, the bulk of the GIs arrived at their destination, New Caledonia, eight hundred miles east of Australia on the fringe of the Coral Sea. At this former outpost of the French Empire, the American presence forestalled Japanese occupation through an invasion or by invitation from France's Vichy government, now subservient to the Axis powers.

The 132nd and two other regiments, the 164th and 182nd, hastily erected defenses against a possible attack and settled in for housekeeping and training. This trio of units formed the only Army division activated overseas and the division also became the sole such organization to have a non-numbered designation. In deference to their home base the units formed the Americal Division.

As the stay on New Caledonia lengthened, widespread changes in command required an infusion of junior-grade officers. Rather than wait for recruits from the States, the

Americal established its own Officer Candidate School. Bob Manning attended the six-week course in Nouméa. "It was in no way up to the level of OCS at Fort Benning," says Manning. "But as far as I know the officers from this school performed well and none were relieved for incompetence."

After two months, at the time the Marines on Guadalcanal were desperately fending off repeated assaults by the reinforced Japanese, the 164th Infantry from the Americal Division on October 13, 1942, took up positions in the vicinity of the island's battered Henderson Field. A month later the 182nd Infantry joined the fray, and the last element of the Americal Division, the 132nd, followed to engage the enemy on Guadalcanal.

"The terrain was impassable," recalls Manning, "and the Japanese were not about to quit. The constant rains and the heavy vegetation were pressures we were not acclimated to but had to be endured. A platoon leader like myself was for all practical purposes a lead scout, and 'Follow me' was more than a slogan. I was fortunate in that I could order men into life-threatening situations without overly dwelling on the danger because of the 'follow me' method and I had been exposed to the action." Indeed, after the Japanese subjected a wire detail to withering fire, Manning led a counterattack and won a Bronze Star.

Manning's matter-of-fact tone hardly does justice to the ordeal. One member of the 132nd said, "For the Marines, and the Army infantry who fought there, the battle was a nightmare of almost constant bombardment from land, sea and air. It was a sheer hell. It was a vivid, continuous, never-relenting fight. It was fought in disease-ridden, insect-infected jungle, surrounded by shark-infested waters."

Cletus J. Schwab, a baseball pitcher in high school and later a semi-pro player—a talent he was to exploit with hand grenades—was drafted in January 1941 at Toledo, Ohio. At Camp Shelby, Mississippi, the cadre of the 148th Infantry, 37th Division started to mold Schwab into a soldier. However willing the flesh was, the equipment was pitiful. "Since there were not enough uniforms to go around," recalls Schwab, "some of the men were issued World War I uniforms. Rifles were scarce too. About every other soldier was issued a 1903 rifle. In the third month we were issued new uniforms and by this time most men had either a rifle or pistol. Marches increased to thirty or forty miles with fifty- to sixty-pound packs plus rifle and ammunition. Our training also included hand-to-hand fighting, throwing of hand grenades, use of gas masks and instruction on mine fields."

The work intensified after December 7, 1941, and Schwab moved up the noncom ladder to staff sergeant, second in command of a forty-two-man platoon. His salary rose to seventy-eight dollars a month as the division shipped out to the Fiji Islands in anticipation of a Japanese strike there. In December 1942, the 3rd Battalion of the 148th Regiment, with Schwab in charge of the L Company machine gun sections, dug itself in around Henderson Field to protect the base and root out snipers or infiltrators. During the day, enemy planes constantly raided the field. At night, Japanese ships lobbed shells at the Americans.

In July 1943 the 37th Division turned its attention from Guadalcanal to New Georgia Island and the enemy airbase at Munda. "The first day, to gain over a hundred yards we faced twenty-five machine guns, small and large mortars and 75 mm field pieces. During the night we dug foxholes while ships brought in more supplies. At daybreak, as the main Japanese force had retreated deeper into the jungle and hills during the night, tents and a field hospital were set up for our wounded, the worst taken aboard ships for treatment.

"As we moved northeast we met the 5th Marine Raider Battalion of about fifteen hundred men. Their mission was the same as ours and the 145th Regiment was moving in from the southeast. It took twenty-eight days to secure the island. When the battle started we had only ten days' rations. For eighteen days we lived on jungle plants, Japanese rice and fish."

Just when the campaign seemed over, the foe mounted a furious counterattack, punching at the ridge positions occupied by Schwab and his company. "There was a storm of rifle, machine gun and mortar fire coming from the direction of our company outpost. Snipers were moving in on us. They had filtered along the ridge during the dark of the night. We heard Japanese firing weapons from several new directions. They were all around us, trying to break through our barbed wire.

"We were only protected by jungle grass. The Japanese were firing from the cover of the jungle. One of my sergeants reported to me that six or seven of his men had been hit by machine guns and mortars and two were dead." Another company from Schwab's battalion hit the enemy from its flank and relieved the pressure.

"Six Japanese made *banzai* suicide charges with bayonets. They were all killed. We had stopped the attack and I estimate about eight hundred or nine hundred Japanese were killed or wounded. A patrol reported that forty or fifty of their dead were lying in the barbed wire fence.

"I had forty-two men in my unit when the battle for New Georgia started. At the end I had twenty; the rest were either dead or wounded. I was wounded in the back but remained with my platoon."

Sam LaMagna, son of an Enfield, Connecticut, pharmacist, enlisted in the state's National Guard after completing four years of high school, spending two years learning to be a machinist at a trade school, and studying electronics through correspondence courses. "I was assigned to F Company, 169th Infantry, 43rd Division. I was issued an old WW I helmet, wool wrap-around leggings, knickers and shirt, brogan shoes and a beat-up WW I Springfield .30-'03 rifle that was dragged through every trench in France. Every Tuesday an army truck would pick us up at the local bus station and drive us to the armory for a three-hour drill. We spent three weeks on maneuvers in upstate New York with the regular army. For 60 mm mortars we had stove pipes. For tanks a jeep with 'tank' written across it and for machine guns we had two by fours."

LaMagna and the others of the 169th marched through the streets of Hartford as the President federalized the division. Trains carried them to a raw stretch of Florida designated as Camp Blanding. They would eventually be turned into infantrymen and compose one-third of the 43rd Division's foot soldiers.

John Higgins of New Haven, Connecticut, actually began his military training as a member of the Depression-inspired federal program, the Civilian Conservation Corps. At age twenty in May 1940, Higgins enlisted in the 169th Infantry Regiment, 43rd Division National Guard. In the spring of 1941, according to Higgins, "At Camp Blanding, Florida, we received new clothing, M-1 rifles, new mortars and many new vehicles. [LaMagna believes he received his new gear only after Pearl Harbor.] Compared to our National Guard induction period, we were in excellent shape. Many officers and NCOs had attended all sorts of specialty training schools. Many noncoms were selected for Officer Candidate School.

"In late October 1941, about 125 senior NCOs over age twenty-eight were separated from service, returned to their home states and assigned to the Enlisted Reserve Corps. Still, in almost every case the officers at command level, regiment, battalion and company were National Guard officers on active duty. A captain commanding a rifle company, fifty-six years old, had a heart attack and died in the training area. Shortly after the start of 1942 [and with the United States now at war] the ones considered overage in their posts were reassigned out of the regiment to other non-infantry units."

In October 1942, as the Marines desperately strove to hang on to a small stretch of Guadalcanal real estate and the Americal Division formed on New Caledonia before embarking for Guadalcanal. Higgins and his associates shipped out to the southwest Pacific. On the eve of the departure Higgins, then a master sergeant, received a promotion to warrant officer, junior grade, the transition slot between his status as an enlisted man and a full commission as a lieutenant.

LaMagna, Higgins and the rest of the 43rd Division stopped for short stays at New Zealand and New Caledonia and then headed towards Guadalcanal. "We found out what war was all about on the way to Guadalcanal," says LaMagma. "About 7:00 P.M. I was watching the fluorescence among the waves when flares lit up the whole sky. A horn blew and general alarm sounded. We were told to get below deck. I ran and hid by a hatchway and watched our destroyers fan out. Then tracers ran up like huge fingers as if to grab something. I noticed Jap bombers flying overhead. The ship's machine guns and antiaircraft fire started when a lieutenant, junior grade, ran by me, stopped, came back and said, 'What the hell are you doing!' I told him I was watching the fireworks; boy was he pissed off. He didn't think it was funny and ordered me to get my ass down into the hold and stay there until the all clear. He slammed the hatch door behind me.

"In the hold it was dark except for a red light. Every near miss shook the ship like jelly. Everybody was quiet waiting for the worst. Then Norby yells out, 'Anybody want to buy a watch?' That broke the tension. The all clear sounded and we went above deck. The general alarm sounded again, only this time it was a Jap sub. We were to stay topside. Everyone had their own thoughts. 'Will the Jap torpedo hit under me?' 'Will we all be blown up?' 'I can't swim.' I could see the beautiful destroyers zigzagging around the convoy. Then the wonderful music to our ears, 'All clear.' Seven Jap bombers had attacked us. Seven Jap bombers were shot down."

The 43rd never encountered the enemy on Guadalcanal. Instead LaMagna, Higgins and their mates expected to attack about four hundred enemy troops at Pavuvu in the Russell Islands. The first amphibious landing almost killed

LaMagna. "We got off a destroyer into Higgins [no kin to John] boats. These don't have ramps. We had to climb over the sides. The water was rough, the boat bobbing up and down; I had a 60 mm mortar on my back. One foot was over the side when the other caught onto a rope or strap. With the mortar hanging on my head, a wave hit me and then the side of the boat. It went up and I went into the drink, mortar and all. My mouth filled with sand and sea water; the mortar was a mess. I dragged myself and the mortar to the beach. At that point I didn't give a damn about the war or the Japs."

However, as they had done previously at Guadalcanal, the enemy evacuated its men rather than attempt a futile defense. The wandering 43rd now set its gunsights on New Georgia Island, part of the Solomons. Higgins, serving as assistant to the 169th Infantry's S-4 (Supply), recalled his baptism in combat on New Georgia. "Our regimental trains area was attacked this first night by Jap infiltrators. About seven or eight of our personnel were killed and several others wounded. The Japs carried their wounded and KIAs away prior to dawn.

"[Later] we were cut off on the MSR [Main Supply Route] about three miles from the beach. My S-4, Captain Sawyer, some engineers and three or four of us tried to break through the road blocks. A Jap machine gun opened up on us, killing three GIs and wounding Captain Sawyer among others. Sergeant Mackie and myself pulled Sawyer into a ditch and gave him first aid, then carried him back to our regimental aid station. He was badly wounded but the doctor said he would live. He was killed by Japs the next day.

"I was in control of a seventy-five-native carrying party. While trying to evacuate some wounded along a side train we were again hit by the Japs, including snipers. My number one native guide was wounded along with others by snipers. Several days later we tried to recover air-dropped supplies well up the trail. Many of the parachutes landed in high jungle trees or in Jap areas. We recovered only one-third of the supplies. The weather was hot and rainy, trails were just deep mud, malaria was rampant along with jungle rot, dengue fever. We had only C and D rations."

Sam LaMagna hit Zanana Beach on the island, then proceeded up the notorious Munda Trail that led to the objective, an airfield. "The first couple of nights gave us a taste of what jungle warfare was all about. The Japs were experts. They were Imperial Marines, the elite armed forces of Japan who had fought in China for many years. Munda Trail was thick with trees, brush undergrowth, vines. Sound was more important than sight. You could hear someone before you could see him.

"After many casualties we learned to fight a Jap war. At night, stay in your hole until the surrounding area has been sprayed with machine gun and BARs. Sort of like spraying for mosquitoes. You can't see them but they're there. At first daylight, Jap snipers would shoot anyone walking around or into our foxholes. They tied themselves up in trees and it was a great morale booster to see Japs hanging after machine gun and BAR bursts.

"At night it was an individual war with everyone fighting for his life. The screams pierced the jungle night and sent chills up my spine. Art Delorge, Syl Bottone and Gildo Consolini stayed in different foxholes. Farmer Bederski and I shared one. At first break of dawn we'd peek over and wave as if to say, 'Hey, I'm okay.' One morning Syl and Gildo waved back but not Art. Farmer came back and notified us Art was killed by his foxhole buddy who thought Art was a Jap and panicked. Art was bayoneted. Later, Gildo was killed by a Jap at night. Every morning I'd hear who was killed or wounded. Company F had about thirty percent casualties and the men were getting jittery. Rumors went around that the Japs were yanking GIs out of their hole by the helmets and to keep helmets unbuckled. At night I could hear teeth chattering.

"One day, our platoon sergeant told me Joe was getting edgy, would I take him in my foxhole because he and I got along and maybe I could calm him down. We dug our night's foxhole and got ready for the night's nightmare. Joe was uneasy, restless. He kept looking for Japs. I told him to relax. I'd stay awake while he slept. Around midnight, Joe was muttering to himself and he said he heard Japs sneaking around. I listened and all I heard were land crabs scavenging for food. He seemed to calm down.

"About 1:00 A.M. I felt something on my left shoulder. I reached and found a grenade with the pin still in. When Joe put a second one on my shoulder I grabbed his hand and asked, what the #%*! was he doing! He said he was getting ready for Japs. I took away his other grenade and told him to sleep. An hour later he stood up in our hole shouting for the SOB Japs to come on, he's ready. I pulled him down; he kept raving. I had to quiet him or he'd alert the whole damn Jap army. I rapped him across the mouth with my .45 pistol, put the muzzle to his head and told him if he didn't shut up, I'd blow his #%*$ head off. Don't worry about Japs, worry about me, I said. He slumped down and was quiet the rest of the night.

"In the morning I explained to the platoon sergeant and suggested Joe be evacuated for the safety of others. The sergeant said he and another noncom would share a foxhole with Joe and the two of them should be able to control him.

"It was quiet until about midnight, when I heard pistol shots from the sergeants' foxhole. Then a voice: 'Shoot him! Shoot him or he'll kill us all!' Then two more shots. By now all the Japs knew our positions and sent in a barrage of artillery and mortar rounds. My first thought was Joe, and when shells started to explode all around me, I drew my knees up against my chest and prayed.

"A shell landed near my hole and felt like someone hit me across the head with a baseball bat. My hole caved in and I passed out. In the early morning, two guys dug me out. I was covered with dirt, my nose stuffed with mud and blood, a cut on my right shin and knee. I was dazed, glassy-eyed. I passed out on a litter and was sent to a hospital on Guadalcanal.

"I awoke on a cot next to the platoon sergeant. I asked him what happened and he said, 'Joe grabbed my .45, thought he saw Japs and started shooting. A bullet went through my knee into my chest.' The other sergeant had to shoot and kill Joe or they both would be dead.''

Because of his injuries, the medics tagged LaMagna for shipment back to the States. But after five weeks of begging to return to Fox Company, a doctor agreed to discharge him as fit for duty. He rejoined his outfit, now reduced to less than one-third its normal complement, for further action in the New Georgia area.

Leonard Glenn Hall, an Oklahoman by birth and a Texan from an early age, graduated from high school in 1940 and was among the first twenty-year-olds drafted from his county. At Camp Roberts, California, he learned the trade of rifleman. Schooled first in the Springfield '03, then the M-1 Garand, 60 mm mortars, BARs, bayonets and grenades, Hall recalls two valuable tactical lessons: a night infiltration action and an exercise that stressed scouting and patrolling.

Shipped from California to New Caledonia and a replacement depot, Hall had not handled a weapon during the three-month interval between completion of basic training and his appearance at the repple depple. Short hops on a destroyer and a landing craft brought him to the New Georgia mainland and a posting to Company F, 172nd Infantry Regiment, 43rd Division.

He and his companions picked up their weapons from a salvage pile, some hundred yards from the front. The best that Hall could find was a Springfield with rope sling replacing the standard leather one. There was only a single canteen available to each replacement. They dropped the burdensome gas masks.

On the following day, Hall and the other newcomers learned a valuable lesson. As they cautiously walked along a trail, a well-concealed machine gun opened up. They dropped in their tracks as bullets zipped about them. "No one had told the replacements that the first rule of survival was to get off the trail," says Hall. His trouser leg was stitched by the enemy fire and the calf of his leg burned by a grazing shot. Later, a veteran blasted them for their failure to form a defense when attacked.

A few days later, Hall and another replacement, Trinidad Borrego, acted as lead scouts. "Only the depleted condition of the company," says Hall, "could justify the two green soldiers being the advance men on an unknown, forbidding ridge. Both of us knew something was wrong when we reached a rusted barbed wire fence, but neither wanted to be considered a coward so we kept moving forward. Ten feet into the clearing past the fence were pillboxes.

"Suddenly, shots rang out and I saw smoke curling from the rifle pointing out of the nearest emplacement. Quickly raising the old bolt action '03 I placed a shot at the butt plate of the Japanese rifle without ever seeing the enemy. The rifle fell and a thrashing sound came from the enclosure."

From his vantage point, Hall could see more Japanese soldiers entering the pillboxes. He kept firing to provide cover for Borrego, who leaped to his feet and raced back to the safety of the jungle. The noise died out and Hall saw a Japanese helmet on a stick, an attempt to lure him into firing and showing his position. Hall held back awaiting genuine targets.

Tiny pebbles struck the ground around him and Hall, who says he was already resigned to his death, summoned the courage to glance backwards. He saw Borrego beckoning him to retreat. The 6'4" Hall sprinted to the rear, leaped the barbed wire fence and tumbled into a half-dug foxhole as machine gun bullets whizzed overhead. "Repeated attempts to capture this strong point in the days ahead," says Hall, "were disastrous. This ridge became the final resting place for many American soldiers."

Lae, a port on the northeast coast of New Guinea, anchored the Japanese positions on that portion of the island. MacArthur planned to have a column of Australian troops coming from the direction of Port Moresby strike from the east while another formation, covering much of the distance by air, would approach from the west through the Markham Valley. The strategy depended upon seizure of an unused airfield at Nadzab.

The final script called for the 503rd Parachute Infantry Regiment, overseas since the fall of 1942, to drop on Nadzab, surprising and overwhelming any defenders. "I was 1st Scout for the Third Squad, Third Platoon of Company G," says Rod Rodriguez. "Hugh Reeves was 2nd Scout. I would be the first to say that Reeves, 'a good ole boy,' knew his trade better than I. He was a superb woodsman. But we were both satisfied with this arrangement and operated well as a team."

As it did with so many young Americans, the war brought together this disparate pair. Reeves, son of a Cruger, Mississippi, farmer who went bankrupt, and Rodriguez, the offspring of an immigrant from Cuba, while of different ethnic backgrounds, had both endured the grim poverty of the Great Depression. A country boy at heart, not studious, Reeves preferred hunting over football and boxing. Rodriguez on the other hand says he had concluded that, "When I made up my mind to work hard I could earn good grades. Many times I felt I had to work harder than others, but I developed a philosophy of 'whatever it takes.' " He applied the same approach to sports, particularly prize fighting, his determination making up for lack of size and athletic talent.

Rodriguez signed up with the Florida National Guard in 1940 and shortly after the war began responded to a circular seeking volunteers for the newly formed parachute troops. "The challenge of testing myself in an elite unit—at the time there was only the original test platoon and two battalions that had just been formed—appealed to me. Also the jump pay of $50 a month seemed a princely sum when a private's monthly pay had just jumped from $21 to $31 a month. In truth, compared to the poverty I had known in Tampa, the Army seemed like a good deal. All my material needs were provided. There was ample food and from a scrawny kid of 120 pounds I had gone within three months to a lean 155 pounds."

His friend Reeves, however, entered the U.S. Army as part of the first contingent of draftees from Yazoo City. Friends had tried to convince him to enlist, but Reeves says, "I was working in an oil field four days a week and driving a cab five nights a week, making from $12 to $20 weekly."

He had been in uniform for ten months when the company commander announced the news of Pearl Harbor. Because the captain considered Reeves a "screwup"—Reeves had been involved in several confrontations with noncoms and engaged in some good ole boy behavior that annoyed his superiors—he was ticketed for military police duty in New York. A magazine clipping that asked for paratrooper volunteers alerted Reeves to an alternative: paratroop training.

In the tent city of the Fort Benning training center, which would become famous as the "frying pan," Reeves and Rodriguez met. They would live, train and then fight together.

Although they were among the early graduates of the paratroop school, a long interval followed between the Fort Benning frying pan and the southwestern Pacific fire fights. In Australia, says Reeves, "we learned how to survive in the jungle, how to make bread from bread trees. We learned that a man could survive indefinitely just from the milk from the green coconut, what trees and bushes to avoid, that most bright and colorful fish were poison, not to duck in the creeks and rivers if it could be avoided, and to boil your clothes whenever possible.

"About the third night we were in Australia, somebody produced a small portable radio and we were listening to Tokyo Rose, about the only station we could get. Suddenly she announced that the 503rd Parachute Combat Team had just been wiped out. A fleet of Japanese bombers had flown over Townsville [their encampment] and bombed us out of existence."

Their extinction notwithstanding, the 503rd readied for the Markham Valley drop. "It was a delicate operation involving the first major parachute jump in the Pacific War," said MacArthur. "I inspected them and found, as was only natural, a sense of nervousness among the ranks. I decided that it would be advisable for me to fly in with them. I did not want them to go through their first baptism of fire without such comfort as my presence might bring to them." He observed the action from a B-17.

"There were B-24 bombers above us, fighter planes above them and A-20s all around us," says Reeves. "As we approached our destination we could hear the B-24s with their machine guns chattering away, strafing the jungles below. Then came the order, 'Stand up, hook up and go!'

"I was in the sixth plane in our group, and when I went out the door I could see nothing but tree tops. My chute opened, made one pendulum swing and I felt myself crashing through limbs. All I could do was fold my arms to cover my face, keep my feet together, point my toes down and say a quick prayer that I would not hit a large limb, for just as I reached the outer edge of that one swing, I saw my chute collapse like a busted paper bag as it hit the top of the tree before I did.

"When I came to, there was a medic standing over me, pointing a tommy gun and saying, 'Lager.' Our answering password was 'Label' because the Japs had trouble with the ell sound. I looked up at my chute still hanging to a large vine with thousands of one-inch-long needles sticking out. My guardian angel had looked after me once more, for that tree was well over a hundred feet high and that would have been a free fall had that pine not been there to slow me down."

"The airfield was seized without opposition," says Rodriguez, "being manned by service personnel who fled on our arrival. However, I quickly became a jump casualty when I landed in a tall tree and drove a branch as sharp as a spear completely through my thigh, emerging in my groin area. Doctors later told me it had grazed the main artery flowing into my right leg and had it been cut I would have bled to death in seconds. For two days I was kept hopped up on dosages of morphine, until the airport was opened and I could be evacuated."

With Rodriguez out of action, his battalion and the 9th Australian Division headed towards Lae. His squad was at the point of the advance and the troops, thirsty, hot and tired, became reckless after frequent false alarms of enemy presence. Towards evening, the Japanese suddenly opened fire and within minutes three were dead. The Markham Valley operation was an unqualified success but the 503rd had now been bloodied.

From New Georgia, the 37th Division in November 1943 with Cletus Schwab would move on to Bougainville, the biggest of the Solomons. The outfit was part of a fifty-thousand-man invasion force that included the Americal Division. That organization, following the defeat of the Japanese on Guadalcanal, was sent to the Fiji Islands for rest, recuperation and refitting. According to Bob Manning, an epidemic of malaria delayed a scheduled attack on the island of Bougainville.

During the Bougainville campaign, Manning was promoted to captain and placed in charge of I Company. He added a cluster to his Bronze Star for leading an amphibious rescue of a cut-off patrol. One of his platoon leaders was Joseph Wapner, who would achieve fame later as the presiding magistrate on TV's "The People's Court."

"Bougainville was an entirely different situation from Guadalcanal. The mission was to protect the airfield by establishment of a perimeter. Constant pressure was maintained by combat patrols and recon to avoid surprise attacks."

While reconnaissance responsibilities often devolved upon ordinary riflemen, the Americal Division also deployed a special outfit, the 21st Cavalry Recon Troop. Bill

McLaughlin, a sixteen-year-old native of Boston's Dorchester section, had enlisted in the National Guard cavalry unit while it still relied on horses. "I had four years in the horse cavalry and was a good rider, jumper, machine gunner and horse trainer by 1940 when our unit was changed to artillery. I hated it, and was the last man in the regiment to change my yellow campaign hat cord for a red one [the colors signified type of army service]."

At the end of a ten-day leave over Christmas and New Year's (1941–42), McLaughlin received a transfer to a military police platoon for duty in New York City. "I raised such a storm that the CO told me if I could find a replacement, I could stay with the outfit. I had learned we were scheduled to go overseas and didn't want to miss it. I spent the whole night talking a brother sergeant into taking my place. Later, he became an officer and lived it up in the fleshpots of wartime America. When his letters came, I would bend over in the steaming jungle and say, 'Kick me.' "

In charge of a machine gun section for the artillery on Guadalcanal, McLaughlin reports that many of the GIs were issued the bulky, unreliable 1917 Lee Enfield rifles. "When we asked for machetes we were given Dutch cavalry sabers, basket hilted and leather sheathed."

After surviving Guadalcanal, McLaughlin sassed a green lieutenant during the respite on Fiji. Reduced to the rank of a private, he began a new career with the 21st Recon. "On Bougainville, we spent a year patrolling and holding our mile or so perimeter on Empress Augusta Bay while the Japanese had the rest of the island. We had nothing but what we'd brought with us. We put hobnails in our boots to save the leather, then got replacements from the Marine Corps. We were under the Marines for the first two years of the war. Food came partly from Australia, and mostly we scrounged, picking oysters off the rocks, shooting beef cattle on the sly. We had a man detailed as 'deer slayer' who killed one a day in the hills.

"In March 1944 they attacked and we had a grand fight

as they piled up some thousands of bodies on the wire, penetrating to within a half mile of the sea. Every man in the Army was fighting them that day and they buried them with bulldozers when it finally ended."

Within a week of their arrival on Bougainville in November 1943, the 37th Division had carved out a fifteen-mile-long, seven- or eight-mile-wide stretch to create a safe haven for supplies, a hospital, radio station and large air-field. Once the Americans secured their perimeters with open fields of fire and barbed wire, they assumed a defensive stance. "It became a waiting game now," recalls Cletus Schwab, a member of the 37th Division, "because we knew the Japanese forces would try to drive us into the ocean."

Six months elapsed before the enemy forged a five-thousand-soldier-strong sledge to hammer the entrenched Americans of the 37th and Americal Divisions. In a two-day battle, the attackers lost as many as four thousand and thenceforth could only mount small-scale operations. Slowly the Americans, working with Australian soldiers, Fiji Scouts and New Guinea "Police Boys," seized total control of Bougainville.

After the 169th Regiment of the 43rd Division had captured the Munda airfield on New Georgia and taken some satellite islands, it entered into a period of regrouping and retraining. John Higgins believes casualties from battle fatigue, like the unfortunate Joe described by Sam LaMagna, were one of the worst problems. "Most of these had to be evacuated out of the combat area for rest and rehabilitation. Many returned to active duty after a week or so in a quiet area."

Turnover in the division was high with unsatisfactory junior officers quietly transferred out and the commanding general relieved. Higgins was promoted to second lieutenant and assigned as the S-4 for the 3rd Battalion.

He recalled, "We moved to Aitape, New Guinea, and it could be possible that this was even worse than the Solomon Islands. Hot, muggy rain most every day, all the jungle diseases and the Japs still fighting tough. We as a regiment were in much better shape and considered ourselves combat veterans. We did much better in our combat role at Aitape.

"During the New Georgia campaign, the regiment received about five hundred replacements, most of whom had no infantry training. They came from the transportation corps, quartermasters, air forces, almost every MOS [Military Occupational Specialty] except the infantry. Some even had rank up to staff sergeant. As replacements they became basic privates and were slipped into various infantry units. Before leaving for New Guinea we received more replacements but most of these did undergo basic and advance infantry training in the States.

"Late in 1944, the 6th Australian Division assumed the entire 43rd Division's mission at Aitape. All of our planning was now devoted to the move on Luzon in the Philippines.

"We all knew Mr. Douglas MacArthur wasn't going back to the Philippines by himself," says Paul Austin, who served with the 24th Infantry Division. A native of Fort Worth, Texas, who had lived mostly on farms, Austin signed up with the National Guard when he was sixteen. "I was underage and had to fib a little on my application. But we did go to summer camp and in 1937 a person would do almost anything to get out of the cotton patch or cornfield for a couple of weeks. We found the money was very good at that time. To young boys a few bucks was worth quite a lot."

By 1940, as the world situation heated to a boil, Roosevelt federalized a dozen National Guard divisions. "Our federal service began November 25 [at the time Austin was part of the 36th Division]. We were supposed to stay for a year and we would be released. I really thought that Roosevelt was rattling a saber but it turned out it was the proper thing to do in the long run.

"On December 7, 1941, my brother and I were in a movie theater in Brownwood [Texas] watching *Sergeant*

York. All of a sudden the movie stopped and a voice on the loudspeaker told all the members of the 36th Division to report to Camp Bowie, which adjoined Brownwood, immediately. Most of our people were on weekend leaves or furloughs.

"By midnight it seemed like the entire division had assembled. Next day our regiment received orders to move to the West Coast. We spread up and down the coast, in Oregon and Washington. We guarded military planes at the Portland airbase, twenty-four hours a day. We were concerned about sabotage. We found what it meant to walk a guard post four hours in the middle of the night in about eight inches of ice and snow. Our feet would practically freeze."

In May 1942, while MacArthur glumly contemplated his pitifully weak legions from his Brisbane, Australia, headquarters, Austin entered Officer Candidate School Class '39 at Fort Benning, Georgia. Three months later, half the graduates reported to the East Coast while Austin and more than a hundred other freshly minted second lieutenants traveled to San Francisco, on their way to the Pacific Theater.

In Hawaii, Austin checked in with the 24th Division's 34th Infantry Regiment, and eventually was assigned to Easy Company's heavy weapons platoon. "The first day I took this platoon to a field area for training, the platoon sergeant halted the men when we got there. I stood in front and he introduced me to every man. He took me through each squad and section, then gave the men 'at ease' and walked with me under the shade of a tree.

"He was probably then in his early forties and he'd been in service for about twenty years. Here I am twenty-one, a brand-new ninety-day wonder and he said, 'Lieutenant, I know my job and I want to do my job. I hope you let me do my job. I can train these men and I know how to train them. But I would appreciate anything, any suggestion you might make pertaining to their training.'

"Looking at him, I could tell here's an old soldier who

knows what he's doing. I immediately said, 'Sergeant, I like your proposition. I like your attitude and the way you're going about things. Our command post will be under the shade of this tree. If you need me or want to talk to me, or any of the men want to, I'll be right here.'

"He got a big smile on his face and said, 'Thank you, sir.' He started teaching the men. They set up their machine guns and mortars and went through the dry-run firing. He did know his job and in the 34th Infantry, as in most of the rifle companies, the platoon sergeants were regular army. They had been in service for a number of years. The discipline was excellent. I had never before seen it carried out to such an extent as in our regiment. Everything was highly organized and well planned. Our training was very, very physically hard on everybody. That was exactly what we should have been doing, getting used to the tough times because that's what we had coming."

In July 1943, the regiment boarded a former German ocean liner seized back in WW I and sailed to Australia. The 24th Division built its own home, Camp Caves, on the east coast of the country. "Not since Fort Benning had we used live ammunition but here in Australia we used live mortar shells, live hand grenades and live ammunition. We went through every aspect of infantry operations, fire and movement, concealment, learning to set up night defenses. We trained to get ready for the Japs to strike against us from any direction, against their ability to infiltrate. We spent two weeks on a transport ship sitting off the harbor at Brisbane, running up and down the rope ladders. We'd make a landing every morning, every afternoon and two or three times a week at night."

After he transferred to Fox Company as exec, Austin and the division performed an exercise involving a company attack on enemy trenches and pillboxes containing machine guns. The military inspectors awarded passing grades; the 24th was deemed combat ready and directed to land on New Guinea in late April 1944 as part of a several-prong thrust. The 34th Regiment aimed at Hollandia, a center for three Japanese airfields on New Guinea.

Youngest of three brothers in the hamlet of Ahtanum (pop. 125), Washington, Hanford Rants grew up in a three-room house built by his father at a cost of less than five hundred dollars. A well furnished water, the Sears catalog provided toilet paper for the privy and kerosene lamps lit the dark until electricity flowed in 1933 when Rants turned ten. From fourteen on, Rants picked fruit, sprayed trees, dug out stumps, loaded and unloaded boxcars, plowed and fought forest fires to boost the family income.

A tall kid and an outstanding athlete in high school, Rants won an athletic scholarship to what is now Washington State University. After Pearl Harbor, many of his fellow collegians dropped out to enlist. "My parents pleaded with me to finish my freshman year because no family member had ever reached college."

By June 1942, the middle Rants son was on the battleship *New Mexico*, but the draft rejected the oldest boy as physically unfit. Han Rants asked to be called for voluntary conscription. "My choice was Navy but I was put in the Army. I was an angry nineteen-year-old and told them so, but I felt nothing but pride and joy in the infantry as basic training started. No matter how much the Navy and Air Corps softened the enemy, the infantry had to go in and mop up in hand-to-hand, man-to-man fighting."

Having completed a preliminary course of instruction in how to kill and survive, a thirteen-week cycle trimmed by seven days, Rants and thousands of other raw GIs sailed to Hawaii. There he received assignment to the 34th Infantry Regiment of the 24th Division as a member of the wire section.

After two months the entire division put to sea, bound for Australia and their home near Rockhampton. The division, says Rants, became known as "the ice cream soldiers" because of the huge amounts consumed. Australian beef was abundant, with steaks served frequently. Rants at 6'7" bulked up to more than 220 pounds. "Our stay in Australia had really been an enjoyable experience," says Rants (a feeling expressed by most Americans stationed there), "but I was now twenty years old and feeling more indestructible than ever. I was eager to move towards combat."

Crossing a swift-flowing stream that emptied into a huge lagoon, Rants demonstrated his sense of power by plunging into the water to help save the life of a fellow soldier in danger of drowning. The division commander pinned a Soldier's Medal on Rants but he had little time to savor the honor, for the 24th was now sent into combat at Hollandia.

"My greatest concern was that I would freeze or lose control when faced with extreme fear. Publicly, no one would discuss having fear. Some who boasted the most courage and told what they would do, turned into jelly as we started to climb over the side of the ship into landing barges. Others lost control of bowels and bladders as we hit the beach.

"Without really knowing Christ in a true sense, I considered myself a Christian and I prayed in my way that I would not show fear or be a coward when facing death. Some of the sailors told how in earlier campaigns the officers had to hold a gun on some of the Marines to get them to go over the side into the landing barges. I believe this helped our green outfit because we had to tell them to watch our smoke and generally smothered any sign of fear that might otherwise have been shown."

The 34th's Hollandia venture began, however, without any sign of resistance. Rants and other members of the 24th Division advanced about five miles along a road before nightfall, and then while the riflemen dug foxholes, wiremen like Rants set up the field telephone communication lines between battalions.

"The first night of combat for a green outfit is a nightmare for everyone within rifle range," says Rants. "Knowing that the enemy preferred to sneak in at night, we were all overly alert to any movement or noise. Although our training taught us to hold fire unless absolutely certain, thus not giving away our position, we threw hand grenades and fired rifles all night long. Dogs, monkeys, water buffalo, birds, snakes, land crabs and everything imaginable except the enemy were fired upon that night."

Bruce Price, a South Carolinian, enlisted in his home state's National Guard in September 1940 for a year of service. The regulations mandated a discharge upon completion of the term, and Price was a civilian at the time of Pearl Harbor. "In February 1942," recalls Price, "a girl on the local draft board told me I would be drafted in March. I reenlisted as it meant drawing thirty-one dollars a month instead of twenty-one dollars."

After repeating basic training, Price applied to OCS and graduated from the Fort Benning academy in December 1942. In Hawaii, Price became a platoon leader with 19th Infantry, 24th Division.

"There was no problem with the sense of responsibility for men under me and decisions that would mean life or death to them. Being an enlisted man for more than two years and an officer for two and a half helped me know how the enlisted men thought and I established a rapport with them. They knew I was subject to the same results of my decisions that they were and knew I would not act foolishly.

"I was not in the initial invasion at Tanahmerah Bay as I was in the hospital on Goodenough Island where we staged. I rejoined the regiment a week or so later. There was no heavy fighting as there was not much opposition. Most of our time was spent on patrols around Lake Sentani and the mountain trails leading towards Finchhaven. The Japs' 18th Army had been cut off by the Hollandia invasion and a lot of them tried to come up the trail thinking they still held Hollandia. Most of the ones we found were dead of starvation or killed by the natives because the Japs were raping their women."

Among those introduced to combat in Dutch New Guinea was a former refugee from Germany, Eric Diller.

With a Catholic father and Jewish mother, Diller fled Bavaria in 1936 to begin a somewhat unsettling life as a schoolboy in New York City. He endured taunts about his pronunciation and accent as he struggled to master English, a language he had only studied in a vocabulary book while aboard ship. "In six months I was fairly fluent, enough so I was selected for a school play to represent Abraham Lincoln. It was a proud moment and a great honor.

"Because of the prevailing anti-Semitic feeling that I encountered in Germany, I never told my friends about my mother's religion [Diller was raised as a Catholic]. I listened to many nasty comments made about Jews. Ironically, I was also the recipient of some nasty anti-German remarks since Nazi Germany was not very popular in the United States."

Denied an opportunity to enlist because his parents' attempts to obtain U.S. citizenship were delayed by investigations to which all German, Italian and Japanese aliens were subject, Diller nevertheless was drafted in June 1943. "When processed at the Camp Upton, New York, induction center, an 'Enemy Alien' stamp in bold letters was printed on the cover of my papers, causing some unfriendly glances." But he was eager to serve and managed to conceal from the medical examiners the limited use he had of his right hand because of a childhood injury. They disregarded a mild heart murmur.

Following basic training in Texas, Diller sailed to the South Pacific as an infantry replacement. Assigned as an ammunition bearer for a .30 caliber machine gun section in the heavy weapons unit, Company H of the 34th Infantry, Diller says, "Most GIs with the outfit had spent nineteen months protecting Waikiki Beach against an invasion which never came. Then they trained for seven months in Australia, preparing for jungle combat, all without seeing a single day of combat. They must have been waiting for me." The waiting ended as the battalion embarked for the Hollandia campaign.

As a corporal in the 1st Battalion of 339th Engineers, Joe Hoffrichter went ashore near Hollandia. A Pennsylvania draftee, Hoffrichter naturally gravitated to an engineering outfit; he drove a truck for a family business dealing in construction materials. The 339th spent some seventeen months engaged in engineering projects in Papua New Guinea (the southeastern part of the island, held by the Allies).

Hoffrichter recalled the scene during the invasion of the New Guinea beach overlooked by a site dubbed Pancake Hill. "An hour of shelling from our ships was followed by aerial bombardment. Going over the rail of the troop transport, we descended into LCVs [Landing Craft Vehicles]. About halfway down the rope ladder, a man froze. He had things tied up, at a standstill. The poor man was so frightened, he couldn't even speak. Two men were sent down to pry his locked fingers from the rope in spite of his pleas to stop. When his fingers were freed, he fell backward. He landed on the eighty-pound jungle pack he carried. While this cushioned his fall, his helmeted head hit the steel deck with such force the back of his helmet caved in. He lay unconscious.

"Resistance was relatively light. But [if the Japanese had had] a few artillery pieces, some mortars, and a few well-placed machine guns, we would still be trying to land and secure Pancake Hill."

Kansan Phil Hostetter was a youth so poor during the Great Depression that he declined to attend medical school when first accepted in order to earn money as a "bughouser"—an untrained psychiatric attendant in a state mental institution. The forty dollars a month plus living expenses enabled him to reapply to med school, and also to meet Helen, whom he married in his senior year. "After the ceremony we went straight to Kansas City, Missouri, and both got jobs with the Robinson Neurological Hospital. The hospital furnished us a bare room on the fifth floor and told us not to use the elevators. They were for patients."

Immediately after graduation in 1942, Hostetter qualified for a commission as a first lieutenant in the Army Medical Corps. He spent a year interning in Wichita before he reported to the Medical Field Service School at the Carlisle Barracks in Pennsylvania.

"Medical schools," says Hostetter, "had taught us very little about the actual practice of medicine in civilian surroundings and nothing in the military. Our teachers at Carlisle, talented and hardworking as they were, had no knowledge of combat conditions."

Assigned to the 407th Medical Collecting Company upon completion of the Carlisle course, Hostetter's duties mainly involved physical exams for men scheduled to go overseas. Just before the 407th itself embarked for the Pacific, the medics went through the standard infantryman infiltration course, climbing obstacles, crawling under barbed wire and enduring live machine gun fire at night. They also practiced climbing cargo nets.

In February 1944, the outfit docked at Milne Bay, New Guinea. They lived fairly comfortably in a tent city, gawked at the indigenous Micronesians, dined on Spam, dehydrated potatoes and eggs, listened to the Armed Forces radio and awaited the opportunity to treat casualties. While staging for the Hollandia invasion at Goodenough Island, personnel like Hostetter learned to use the .30 caliber carbine, an indication of the status of medics in the eyes of the enemy.

Behind the infantrymen of the 24th Division and the engineers attached to it, amphibious vehicles, "Ducks," brought Hostetter to the beach near Hollandia. "We stood around wondering what to do next. The first casualty we saw was a man crushed to death by a boulder. He was bathing at the water's edge when the boulder rolled down the cliff from high above where a soldier was building a road with a bulldozer. We sent a litter squad to get the body.

" 'Lay him on the grass,' I said. 'The Quartermaster

Department will take care of the body.' We were not responsible for the dead, only the disabled.

" 'I can't do it!' the boyish young soldier by the litter blurted out. This was his first encounter with real violence and his first sight of death. Two sergeants gently laid our dead comrade on the grass. They then took the litter to the beach to wash off the blood.

"Inland a little farther an enemy soldier lay on the ground. He was mortally wounded, unconscious and gasping for breath. I knew he would soon die. We felt no sense of exhilaration over the small victory. It was not small to him."

Hostetter and the others with him continued to see very few casualties. The concept of a unit to gather up wounded borne from frontline aid stations back to the regimental medical center seemed pointless. Detached to an evacuation hospital he began treating patients in two large tents. "All had a psychiatric condition. It was up to me to determine what their condition was, treat them if feasible and evacuate them to other hospitals if necessary.

"Those who had broken down under exceptional stress and exhaustion we called 'battle fatigue' cases. In a state of chronic anxiety, exhausted, they could not relax. They were so jumpy you could practically see daylight between them and their cots when a truck backfired. They had little appetite and when they did eat they were apt to have stomach cramps and perhaps vomit. Their sleep was fitful, marred by vivid nightmares of battle experiences and friends being mutilated. Some told of 'fugues' when they would become conscious after running for miles and not knowing where they were.

"Battle fatigue cases constantly asked when they could return to duty. They would hear reports of their units on the radio and feel required to return as quickly as possible. They felt obligated to help their buddies and guilty because they had failed when needed most.

"To help my patients rest I prescribed huge doses of the

sedatives nembutal and phenobarbital. The other doctors thought my doses excessive but I had seen these amounts used in mental hospitals for the severely disturbed and knew they were suitable. Before long, the other doctors agreed with me.

"We would assess their fitness for combat by estimating the severity of the stress that put them in the hospital. If it had been great, as often it was, they recovered in about two weeks and returned to their outfits. The Army had a wise policy of keeping the men as close as possible to the combat zone. They still had high motivation to return to duty. The farther away they got, the less they cared about recovery and the poorer they did."

The background and experiences of these earliest arrivals from the States in the South Pacific reflect the inconsistent pattern of troop deployment throughout the war. Intensively schooled infantrymen and combat veterans frequently fought side by side with poorly prepared replacements hastily recruited from non-combat outfits or drawn from the ranks of the most recently inducted. Huge manpower requirements in both Europe and the Pacific, errors in intelligence about enemy strength, underestimation of the enemy powers to resist and sudden reverses often forced hasty assignment of GIs regardless of their MOS or background. However, none of the American soldiers went into the field with as little background or instruction as the hapless members of the Philippine Army of 1941–42. Much of the armies that brought MacArthur back to the Philippines came to the task bloodied and full of respect for the enemy's ability to fight.

CHAPTER XVI

ON THE BRINK

THE GRAND STRATEGY of MacArthur, with which Nimitz concurred, was to secure first the bastion of Australia and then seemingly to leap from island to island to draw closer to Japan. To a staff member who questioned whether they had enough resources to conquer the many strongpoints still held by the enemy, MacArthur explained, "I . . . said, I did not intend to take them—I intended to envelop them, incapacitate them, apply the 'hit 'em where they ain't—let 'em die on the vine' philosophy. I explained that this was the very opposite of what is termed 'island hopping,' which is the gradual pushing back of the enemy by direct frontal pressure, with the consquent heavy casualties which would certainly be involved."

As operations progressed, the Allies indeed skipped some Japanese strongholds, places like Rabaul on New Britain and Truk Island. However, capture of a certain number of stepping-stones scattered through the Pacific remained necessary.

Hollandia turned out to be a somewhat hollow triumph. Planned as a heavy bomber base, the soil in the area was too soft to support the weight of the big planes without some time-consuming work by engineers. Three nearby islands, Wakde (actually named Insoemoar), Biak and Noemfoor, offered more hospitable turf. Furthermore, seizure of these outposts protected the Allies' New Guinea territory. The first venture on Wakde, May 15, by elements of the 41st Division seized an airfield, but further east on the island, Japanese veterans of fighting in China occupied a well-camouflaged and concealed web of caves, pillboxes and dugouts containing hidden artillery pieces. The advance bogged down and the 41st incurred severe losses. U.S. 6th Army commander Gen. Walter Kreuger summoned the 6th Division to replace the battered Americans on Wakde.

"We used to say that we were the most over-trained division in the Army," comments Arndt Mueller, K Company commander in the 6th Division's 63rd Regiment. A South Dakota State football star as blocking back and linebacker, Mueller with four years of ROTC earned a commission on graduation in June 1941 and immediately was called to the colors.

"We joined the 6th on the Fourth of July. They were completing a training cycle and preparing to go on Louisiana maneuvers. Then it was back to Fort Leonard Wood for another training cycle until after Pearl Harbor, more training, then Tennessee maneuvers with two armored divisions. Hey, we're headed for North Africa to kick Rommel's ass. Then we loaded out for the California desert— hey we're going to North Africa for sure. Then we load out for the Pacific—beach positions on Oahu, relieving the 27th Division.

"Our troops learned a lot manning beach defenses, even riflemen learned how to operate .30 caliber water-cooled machine guns, how to establish a security system that will not miss reporting enemy action and swift reaction by reserves, and jungle warfare training, indoctrination on the enemy, amphibious training and exercises."

The next port of call was Milne Bay, New Guinea, where the 6th hacked a tent camp in the jungle and drew another training cycle. Almost three years after Mueller checked in with the division as a new lieutenant, the 6th went into action. For all of the preparation and schooling, actual combat taught new lessons.

"During training," says Mueller, "we practiced all of the classic forms of maneuver at company level—envelopment, double envelopment, penetration, infiltration. It all seemed so neat. But when transferred to the battlefield real practical problems reared their heads.

"First, when maneuvering with platoons, they were supposed to be kept within no more than one and one-half effective-small-arms-range of each other. A platoon by itself can be easily isolated, defeated and maybe even completely destroyed. During our first attack I tried to outflank the enemy with the reserve platoon; they were stopped dead in their tracks. But being within supporting distance also greatly increases the possibility of friendly fire casualties. Unless the enemy target is an outpost unsupported by nearby troops, maneuvering by platoons is tricky business. If done, it had better be well thought out.

"We learned that in the jungle quick response by a high volume of marching fire was a valuable method to overcome the enemy. We also found that battle drill [a formation that places key elements in certain positions] was essential in facilitating a rifle company to meet sudden tactical emergencies.

"The preferred method of assault was to move the rifle company as closely as possible to the target under supporting fires [artillery, mortars, even tactical air], then lift those fires and jump the enemy with all of the company fire power deployed.

"I was too busy to worry about casualties the first time we came under fire. It wasn't that I had no qualms about men being killed and wounded; my responsibility as a commander was to direct and manage the battle, and the battlefield is a harsh and unforgiving taskmaster.

"Our resources during the first battle were not entirely adequate and the deficiencies continued during the entire war. The best asset of the rifle company was the M-1 rifle.

It beat anything the Japs had. An experienced rifleman could trigger it rapidly, almost like automatic fire. But in the jungle we found a critical need for rapid firing individual weapons. Artillery and mortars were of limited use because the shells burst high up in the jungle canopy. The automatic weapon of choice in a rifle company was the BAR. We loaded up on BARs when we could. It was very light [about fifteen pounds], very accurate. It did not climb during firing [a problem with submachine guns]. But it only had a twenty-round magazine. A thirty- or forty-round magazine could easily have been developed except for the institutional arteriosclerosis of the Ordnance Corps. The light machine gun was anything but light. It overheated easily. Our heroic light machine gunners did a great job of firing this misnomer.

"Their light machine gun was superior to ours. Their heavy machine gun did not have the sustained rate of fire of ours. We did not have anything like their so-called knee mortar which was more like a grenade thrower with a projectile slightly larger than a grenade. Their 81 mm and 150 mm mortars were comparable to ours. Our artillery was vastly superior. They did not have the capability to mass their artillery firing like we did. But they massed their mortar fires."

U.S. ordnance, with its plusses and minuses, superior manpower and support, and the inability of the Japanese to reinforce or supply their garrison, enabled the 6th Division to grab a large chunk of Wakde, although some defenders held a piece to the end of the war.

The 34th Regiment of the 24th Division, largely limited to a reserve role in operations on New Guinea, received orders to join the 41st Division, which invaded the island of Biak in the western shadow of New Guinea on May 27. Biak offered the closest opening to Mindanao.

According to Paul Austin of the 24th Division, intelligence figured between four and five thousand Japanese held Biak, but the number instead proved to be about eleven thousand. Supply dumps, communications equipment and troops occupied deep caves surrounded by nests of pillboxes and other fortifications. "Our regiment," says Austin, "was thrown in to reinforce a beachhead that in some places was so thin it was held only by patrols, and to take two airfields. The 41st had already captured one."

Having achieved the objective, Austin's F Company pushed forward until it reached an area where a brother unit, E Company, appeared to be pinned down by heavy enemy fire. "The battalion commander had us turn left, take part of another ridge which put us in the rear of the enemy position. We looked down and saw a Japanese bivouac with a lot of Japanese troops either eating, sleeping or resting while in support of the rest of their combat team then doing all the firing. About sixty-five M-1s and BARs opened up at one time. F Company destroyed this bivouac and everyone in it." The Americans then prepared to pull back, anticipating a division artillery barrage.

But Austin now heard that one of his squads had gone to reconnoiter and a group of Japanese had popped up out of the ground and killed all seven men. The platoon leader insisted he had checked to make sure they were all dead. But as company commander, Austin was reluctant to abandon the casualties.

"There was something telling me I must not leave, that there might be a wounded man out there whom we did not want to leave behind. I said I can't leave and the platoon leader said, 'Paul, they're all dead. If we go out there and hunt somebody we don't know is even out there, we're going to get shot too. There'll be eleven more of us laying out there.' He made so much sense. He was a good officer, knew his job and what he was doing. But I couldn't bring myself to say let's get out of here.

"I said, 'You fellows get down on your bellies, cover me. I am going out there and see if there is someone still alive.' I crawled out; it was as if something took charge of my brain and body and sent me in a certain direction. I crawled past one of our dead boys, looked at him, then went on a straight line. A few moments and yards later I saw a pair of combat boots sticking up in the grass. I inched up and looked into the face of an F Company rifleman and he blinked his eyes. He was still alive. I swung him around, put my hands under his armpits and dragged him a foot or two at a time until I got him back to our lines. The boys put together a makeshift litter with ponchos and saplings and eight or nine of us proceeded to carry him out of there. Jap snipers fired at us, hollered and laughed at us. Every time they did, we'd fire back.

"But they agitated us, laughing. I learned later from the man I rescued, that they came out and ran a bayonet through the bellies of each one of our men lying on the ground to make sure they were dead. Thirty years later I spoke with the survivor and he told me that while he was laying there he thought, 'I am twenty-seven years old and I have never said a prayer in my life. I knew I was going to die in a few minutes. All they had to do was find me and they would kill me. In my mind I said, Oh God, send somebody to save me.'

"I asked him how long was it before I got there and he said only a few minutes. I always marveled that here was a man laying in a jungle on an island where ninety percent of the people in the world don't know where it is, about to be killed and something got a hold of me and told me to go out and get him. He and I agreed, many years later, that an angel suddenly appeared to direct me to answer his prayers. God decided to answer that prayer and used me, my body. That's one of two such instances from the war that stuck in my mind.

"The smell of death and war was all over that place. At one particular road junction a tank battle took place. The Japs had attacked the 41st Division with eight or ten tanks, small ones that inflicted some heavy casualties. Our Shermans moved in from the beachhead and knocked out all but one of the tanks, which turned and fled. There were bodies blown apart; human parts laying about the area.

"Some places were just engulfed with the smell of death. The decaying human body puts out a fierce odor that permeates the area. We could not dig much to bury them on Biak because the island was largely coral and rock. The only thing we could do was find a little sump hole in the coral, pour gasoline on the bodies and burn them to ashes. It eliminated the big blue blowflies and a lot of the stench. The flies contaminated the food and dysentery hit our company heavily. It got me so badly I passed out. I finally made my way to an aid station and came out of it in a few days.

"Biak, being our first actual combat experience, cost us six dead, and four or five wounded. It was pretty traumatic to most of us. I began to ask myself what did I do wrong that caused these men to get killed. One of them was a medic assigned to our company who volunteered to go on the patrol. I realized that the platoon leader who had ordered the reconnaissance had every right to do this; he had a responsibility to cover his flank. He was trying to gain information which he needed to know. I never reproached him."

On Biak, Eric Diller, the "enemy alien" in the midst of the 24th Division, confronted war. "As we moved forward to relieve a company engaged in a firefight, the walking wounded were moving slowly to the rear. I came to realize that the enemy were shooting to kill. I saw men in bloody bandages, with each step the bandages becoming a deeper shade of red since the crude first aid administered was not enough to stem the flow of blood. Others were carried on stretchers by four men struggling through ankle-deep, muddy terrain. As we got closer to the sound of gunfire, I noticed two covered bodies with their GI boots sticking out from under a poncho."

The final objective in this round was Noemfoor, some sixty miles west of Biak. The Allied air arm dumped more than eight thousand tons of bombs on the island to soften any hostile reception for the 158th Regimental Combat Team, already battered when it encountered stiff resistance on Wakde. On July 4, 1944, flights of C-47s left Hollandia carrying members of the 503rd PIR for a drop on the

Noemfoor Kamiri airfield. Halfway there, one of the engines on the plane carrying Hugh Reeves and Rod Rodriguez cut out. The pilot decided to abort the mission and land at Port Moresby.

"That turned out to be a chilling experience," says Rodriguez. "The plane was losing altitude and we still had to cross the Owen Stanley Mountains, the spine of New Guinea. To prevent loss of altitude, all bundles with our combat gear and anything else that could be jettisoned was thrown out the cargo door. As we crossed the mountains, it appeared to me we could almost touch the peaks. Dropping the platoon itself into the wilds of New Guinea was considered another option but fortunately we made it back. Several days later we flew to Biak and by landing craft rejoined Company G on Noemfoor."

In fact, Reeves and Rodriguez lucked out with their trip aboard the crippled airplane. Their fellow 503rd troopers, leaping from less than four hundred feet, smashed into a hard coral field strewn with wreckage and surrounded by unforgiving trees. The jumpers sustained almost ten percent casualties, far more than the enemy would inflict with weapons.

Back with the company, Rodriguez pushed into the jungle in search of the enemy. "Lieutenant Phelan had designated the 3rd Squad as the lead element and as 1st Scout I would be point man. I put on my webbing, which carried a first aid kit, trench knife, canteen and three extra drums of .45 caliber ammunition. I also carried four fragmentation grenades and a Thompson submachine gun which was ideal for close-in jungle fighting.

"Even before we were far into the march, I seemed to have a sense that today was going to be the real thing. We were now running into unmistakable signs of enemy presence. There were items of discarded clothing and equipment along the trail. In other places the tall grass that grew along the trail was bent, suggesting that troops had recently lain there.

"We were moving slowly and cautiously. Suddenly,

about a hundred yards ahead I saw something that froze me. At a bend ahead and on the trail were a man's legs. I observed for a while and concluded it was a dead Japanese soldier, but then the legs moved. I approached cautiously forward with Reeves about seventy paces behind and the platoon following. As I came closer, I understood the reason the legs moved. It was a dead Japanese soldier with a deep wound on his thigh and an angry dog was feeding on this leg, jerking it when he stripped the flesh.

"We continued the march. For all my bluster I frequently wondered how I would react when the moment came and I had to kill a man. Although I would not describe myself as religious, I wrestled with this thought as did others. Our jumping chaplain, Father Powell, tried to alleviate these concerns by reminding us of the righteousness of our cause.

"About two hours after we had passed the dead Japanese we were approaching a clearing. On the other side I saw Japanese soldiers laying on the ground. At first I thought it may be a repeat of what I had seen earlier. I continued to move cautiously forward, followed by Hugh Reeves, Phelan and the platoon. As I did, I pointed my Thompson directly at them. I could not believe they could be so careless as to sleep alongside a trail without posting lookouts.

"I was now no more than twenty steps from them and my trigger finger seemed frozen. Was I going to squeeze the trigger? The spell was finally broken when a distant gunshot suddenly awakened one of the young soldiers. He sat up quickly, ramrod straight and stared at me with huge, startled eyes. For moments, which seemed an eternity, we looked at one another. Reeves and Phelan were still far enough back that they could not see all that was happening. Then he lunged for his rifle and shouted some words. I began firing and when I had emptied my first drum, I took cover on the other side of the trail, reloaded and continued to fire.

"By this time, they were firing back and lobbing

grenades at us. Reeves and Phelan ran up to learn what was going on and we heard the Japanese withdrawing. The platoon was brought up and we moved forward. There were five dead Japanese and the rest had departed. But now we were pretty confident of the approximate location of their main elements.

"The next day we came back up the trail in force with the rest of the battalion and several days later the Japanese were trapped in this remote part of Noemfoor. Before the final attack, we laid in a heavy barrage of artillery which destroyed many of their troops and then we overran their last position. They fought with their usual tenacity. I guess there must have been several hundred in this last stand.

"As a footnote, when we searched the bodies of the five that fell in the firefight, we found pieces of human flesh in their pockets. The next day, one of our patrols recovered the bodies of two of our troopers who had been killed and found a very professional job of butchering where the most edible portions had been removed: calf, arm muscles, buttocks and body organs.

"I was in the patrol that a few days later took photographers from MacArthur's headquarters to the site to obtain evidence. Not a word appeared in the media. We were told the reason for the silence was that the story would have a negative effect on home-front morale."

With the subjugation of these sites, forces began to mass for the onslaught on the Philipines. They were drawn from an enormous arena. The 7th Infantry Division, a regular Army organization, fresh from maneuvers in the California desert, sailed to the Aleutian Islands off Alaska, where in a useless exercise the Japanese had moved troops into Attu and Kiska.

Inappropriately outfitted, poorly prepared and ill-served by a command shaken by the schism between the overall Navy and Army leadership, the GIs in May 1943 absorbed a drubbing in their first encounters on Attu even though they outnumbered the defenders. Brute strength then reduced the enemy garrison to a final futile *banzai* charge in which many, out of ammunition, wielded only bayonets. The Imperial Army, recognizing its inability to resupply or reinforce its men on Kiska, managed to remove everyone without U.S. awareness. When an American armada of two hundred ships and thirty-five thousand soldiers came to Kiska they discovered it enemy-free.

Refitted and rested in Hawaii, the 7th Division then gave an excellent account of itself at Kwajalein in the Marshall Islands, albeit under a naval command. A succession of sea battles—Coral Sea, Bismark Sea and Midway—trimmed Japanese freedom on the ocean as superior planes and a vast number of new carriers to bring them to the fight endowed the United States with dominance over the water and its islands. Having lost its power for offense long before, the Imperial Navy rocked back on its heels.

After the Marshalls, Nimitz, undoubtedly with the blessing of MacArthur, set his sights on the Marianas, a chain with three resonant names from military history—Saipan, Tinian and Guam. Air bases, particularly on Saipan, would put the Philippines and Japan itself within bomber range. The 2nd and 4th Marine Divisions, together with the Army's 27th Division, attacked Saipan. Underestimation of enemy strength, differences in approaches to combat by the two different service branches and perhaps some weaknesses in leadership made Saipan far bloodier than expected.

A second joint venture, on Guam, this time consisting of the 3rd Marine Division and the Army's 77th Infantry Division, pursued the honor of taking back the first U.S. territory seized by the Japanese. The 77th, composed of several regiments that had been part of the American Expeditionary Force in 1917, opened for business in March 1942, less than two weeks before Bataan surrendered. Heavily populated in the beginning by draftees from New York and New England, many of whom had already spent as much as eighteen months in uniform, the 77th trained an additional two more years before its initial combat mission at Guam.

Tech Sergeant Henry Lopez, drafted in 1940 when he was already twenty-six, landed on the beach at Guam with Company C of the 307th Regiment. He said, "The first night spent on Guam was a rather quiet one, with the exception of the occasional distant crack of rifles and machine guns, and bursting shells." Lopez, like Paul Austin, was appalled by his first experience with maggot-infested enemy war dead, "bloated, blackened bodies blown up like gruesome balloons. This disgusting sight, as well as the stench, made many men sick and caused them to throw up their recently eaten rations."

Within a few days, C Company engaged the enemy. "I am not ashamed to say that when I first came under fire," says Lopez, "I was scared to death on Guam, as well as all through the war. The only way I could cope with it was to think of the platoon, keep busy and not let anyone know my feelings."

Buck Creel, who came from a family with a long tradition of military service, traveled the OCS route to become executive officer with G Company of the 306th Infantry, a unit of the 77th. The outfit reached the beach on the second day, and according to Creel, "the first night was a disaster, much panic and indiscriminate firing of individual weapons. No enemy were to be seen—just shadows and strange noises in the jungle." A soldier in Creel's headquarter's company group stuck his head up and his own foxhole mate put a fatal bullet through his head.

During his first firefight, the carbine customarily issued to officers jammed. "I got rid of it," says Creel, "and started carrying an M-1. I found that the additional firepower gave me more confidence when leading the platoon on many combat patrols."

Unlike Saipan, the Marines and Army troops on Guam developed a confidence in one another as both organizations performed in highly effective fashion. They had overrun the island by August 8, 1944, eliminating the garrison defending Guam in less than three weeks. Since the Japanese used the island as a warehouse for other areas, the

The U.S. Navy base at Cavite burned after Japanese bombers struck the site on the south shore of Manila Bay a few days after the raids upon Pearl Harbor. (*U.S. Naval Institute*)

John D. Bulkeley advanced to lieutenant commander in 1942 after his PT boat carried the MacArthur party from the island fortress of Corregidor to a point where they could be flown to Australia. (*U.S. Naval Institute*)

Saburo Sakai, a pilot in a Zero, and an ace of the Imperial Japanese Navy who scored 64 victories during WWII, shot a big hole in Sam Grashio's left wing during a dogfight over Clark Field, Dec. 18, 1941. The pair held a reunion in 1991. *(Sam Grashio)*

Japanese tanks paraded down the stately boulevards of the city as the Japanese occupied Manila. *(National Archives)*

Beleaguered Americans on Bataan exploited the thick jungle for cover. *(U.S. Naval Institute)*

Wearing WWI–style steel helmets, the defenders manned an anti-tank position on Bataan. *(National Archives)*

In the Malinta Tunnel on Corregidor, a glum MacArthur and his chief of staff, Richard Sutherland, directed operations to stave off the enemy. *(National Archives)*

Left: Defeated Americans left the tunnel of Corregidor in May 1942 under the guns of the victorious Japanese. *(National Archives)*

Below: Captives, carrying those no longer able to walk, trudged along the infamous Death March to Camp O'Donnell after the surrender of Bataan. *(National Archives)*

Members of the 6th Ranger Battalion headed for the shoreline at Dinagat Island off the coast of Leyte after a pre-landing bombardment. *(National Archives)*

Rangers moved through Dinagat Island in the Leyte Gulf without encountering any Japanese. *(National Archives)*

Two regiments of the 24th Division invaded Leyte at Red Beach on A-Day, October 20, 1944, meeting considerable opposition in some sectors. *(National Archives)*

MacArthur waded ashore with Sutherland (right of MacArthur) within a few hours after Red Beach was secured. He repeated the episode at White Beach, captured by the 1st Cavalry Division. *(National Archives)*

Near Tacloban on Leyte, a mine blew up under a tank. A medic treated one of the wounded. *(National Archives)*

Soldiers acted as stevedores unloading supplies from LSTs in the surf at Leyte. *(National Archives)*

A torpedo seriously damaged the cruiser *Honolulu* during the invasion of Leyte. *(National Archives)*

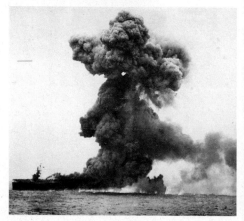

Smoke billowed from the carrier *St. Lo*, a victim of a *kamikaze* during the October 24–26 sea and air combat in Leyte Gulf. *(U.S. Naval Institute)*

Mortally wounded by a *kamikaze* during the Battle of Leyte Gulf, the aircraft carrier *Princeton* burns fiercely. *(U.S. Naval Institute)*

Adm. William F. Halsey commanded the 3rd Fleet, not account-able to MacArthur. During the Battle of Leyte Gulf, Halsey left the 7th Fleet under Adm. Kincaid vulnerable, as he pursued the bait of a Japanese force to the north. *(U.S. Naval Institute)*

The *Suwannee* reeled from two *kamikaze*s' blows that killed 257 crewmen. The ship, after repairs, returned to duty and its aircrews attacked the enemy around Okinawa and Borneo before the war ended. *(U.S. Naval Institute)*

Half battleship, half aircraft carrier, the Japanese *Ise* was one of the targets that seduced Halsey into steaming away from the Leyte Gulf. *(U.S. Naval Institute)*

Shore batteries sank the LSM 20 off Leyte. *(U.S. Naval Institute)*

The Japanese carrier *Zuiho* burned and then sank after U.S. Navy carrier-borne planes from Halsey's 3rd Fleet ravaged her. *(U.S. Naval Institute)*

At Hill 311 on Leyte, a Sherman tank supported GIs from the 1st Battalion, 34th Infantry Regiment. *(National Archives)*

Barefoot Filipinos toted supplies along tortuous trails for American soldiers in northern Leyte. *(National Archives)*

Litter bearers on Leyte bore a wounded soldier across a shallow stream. *(National Archives)*

Right: A radio operator from the 77th Division sent messages as the outfit occupied Ormoc. *(National Archives)*

Below: An amphibious tractor known as a Buffalo crawled through the mud of Leyte with supplies. *(National Archives)*

The battleships *Pennsylvania* and *Colorado* steamed into the Lingayen Gulf to blast any beach defenses at the initial Luzon landing site. *(National Archives)*

A large patrol trekked towards Damortis during the first days of the Luzon campaign. *(National Archives)*

Troopers from the 7th Regiment of the 1st Cavalry Division slogged through one of Leyte's many swamps. *(National Archives)*

Crews from the 129th Infantry of the 37th Division set up their 4.2 mortars on the outskirts of Manila. *(National Archives)*

A field artillery piece fired a night mission. *(National Archives)*

The 804th Medical Evacuation Squadron flew out wounded from a field near Legaspi, south of Manila. *(National Archives)*

Men from K Company, 172nd Infantry Regiment, 43rd Division, used a flame-thrower on an enemy position some thirty miles east of Manila. *(National Archives)*

Armor from B Company, 716th Tank Battalion, carried foot soldiers from the 132nd Infantry Regiment, American Division, along a street on Cebu. *(National Archives)*

victors dined and wined on the spoils. "The Japanese canned food we found, such as salmon," says Lopez, "was very tasty, and their powdered milk was excellent. Their cigarettes were no good, but their sake, ah, now there was the best thing we acquired, and what a hangover it left you."

With the Marianas now bagged, MacArthur was in position to carry out the plans, formulated as early as March 1944, to liberate the Philippines. The original script called for establishment of a beachhead at Mindanao, the southernmost outpost of the archipelago, in mid-November.

The uninterrupted string of Allied successes testifies to the soundness of the strategy, the logistical effort, the training, and the might produced in American factories. But however gratifying the pace to its sponsors, it was woefully insufficient to meet the dire needs of the military captives in the Philippines.

Transfer from the hellish grounds of O'Donnell stretched the misery, but prolongation of the ordeal would only slow the mortality rate during the first months in the new camp. The Japanese had placed almost all of the Americans captured during the spring of 1942 in the compound at Cabanatuan. The surviving U.S. servicemen numbered from seven to twelve thousand—the numbers changed as the captors dispatched able-bodied POWs to work in slave labor camps. The occupiers freed the former Philippine soldiers.

A former U.S. Department of Agriculture station and then a site for Philippine Army draftees, the Cabanatuan camp featured an eight-foot-high barbed wire girdle while guards manned machine guns in a series of wooden towers along the perimeter. The barracks were in wretched condition when the inmates moved in: roofs leaked, plumbing facilities and electricity did not exist, the water supply was inadequate and no provision had been made for the treatment of the sick and injured.

Death stalked everyone, sometimes striking with stunning savagery. Four who attempted an escape were captured, beaten with fists and clubs, forced to dig their own graves, and while their fellow inmates watched, executed by a firing squad.

The Cabantuan administration organized its prisoners into cohorts of ten, with the members responsible for each other. If one sought to flee, the other nine faced execution. Sgt. William Delich, a Corregidor soldier, reported an occasion in which twenty GIs died after individuals from two groups broke out of Cabantuan. If a bullet, bayonet or beating did not kill, disease and malnutrition played handmaidens to a less violent death.

Deaths in the first months at Cabanatuan equaled those at O'Donnell. The victims succumbed to a variety of ailments stemming from the lack of food which began on Bataan, the rigors of the Death March, the abuses inflicted by cruel guards and the filthy, bacteria-laden environment. Irvin Alexander says, "On July 4, 1942, I observed an orderly from a Nip kitchen across the road from our area carry a garbage bucket to our enclosure fence and dump it inside. There was an immediate rush of half naked, half starved American prisoners, who fought over scraps of garbage like dogs fighting over the supper scraps outside the kitchen door."

Malaria exacted a heavy toll because the Americans had no more quinine and the Japanese did not pass any on until the late autumn of 1942. Dysentery ravaged the inmates. Poor sanitation and the absence of sulfa drugs sparked an epidemic of the disease. Beriberi and pellagra, caused by the food shortage, generated ugly, even grotesque physical symptoms and crippled or killed many. Since the Japanese Army pioneered in sanitation at the turn of the century, they could not plead ignorance of the minimum conditions necessary to protect their prisoners. Nor, says Sam Grashio, did it appear they lacked medicines. "When a diphtheria epidemic broke out among the prisoners in Cabanatuan, Japanese authorities immediately took preventive measures to protect their own troops. Even more significant, prisoners who were fortunate to have considerable money were able to buy medicines on the black market."

Nor can the starvation diet foisted upon the prisoners be excused on the basis of wartime shortages. Grashio saw soldiers casually feeding vegetables that could have saved Americans to livestock. Even when the conquerors allowed the conquered to cultivate some small plots of ground, they restricted what the growers could harvest for their own meals.

The struggle for life in the Japanese prison camps followed a pattern. When the captives first reached an installation, the place was bereft of the barest essentials. Supply and distribution of vital essentials like food, water and shelter fell beneath the level of what was needed for survival. With time, the Japanese administrators established some order, the captives developed means to improve their conditions, and life-saving supplements trickled or flowed in. According to Irvin Alexander, the residents improved the drainage and ditching and patched some roofs as their hosts grudgingly supplied materials. The Americans engineered a primitive water purification system, below what doctors considered healthy but better than none. They built latrines, covered them as best they could to ward off the incessant, disease-carrying flies. Not until 1943 would the Japanese consent to a prisoner-built septic system to handle sewage. The opening of a hospital enabled the transfer of thirty or forty sick men each day, beds becoming available because without medicine the hospital death rate almost equaled the number of newly arrived ill.

After the fall of Corregidor, the Japanese initiated labor projects for their captives. Men in good enough health to perform hard labor built airfields, worked as stevedores—Marine Elmer Long, for one—in Manila, and in construction. The benefits of the assignment were often better food and an opportunity to surreptitiously obtain items from the Filipinos, through purchase, barter or even by donation.

The population at Cabanatuan thinned out a bit.

Clifford Bluemel, in a diary he kept of his period as a POW, noted for May 10–April 11, 1942: "All generals and colonels sent to Philippine Army camp at Tarlac. Each put thirty-two pesos in mess to buy extras, improve mess. Got meat twice a week. Living conditions pretty good, given bunks, sheets, pillow and blanket.

"About August 1 told we would go to Taiwan. Left Tarlac by train. Bought food en route to Manila. At Manila given bread by Japs. Manila a sad looking town under Jap domination. Aboard *Nagara Maru*. August 14: At Takao, Formosa. No sub attack en route." Because the Japanese never identified the transports as holding prisoners, the threat of a torpedo from a U.S. submarine or bomb from an American plane menaced all such voyages.

"Transferred to *Otara Maru*, kept in stuffy hold during trip, ventilation poor. Acquired a severe headache. Food on boats better than received anywhere."

His final destination, after a three-kilometer march when the ship docked, was Karenko, Formosa. When he flopped down at the new site, an American doctor diagnosed him as a beriberi patient. From somewhere the physician procured pills that slowly restored Bluemel's health, although it would be six months before he was inclined to report further on his experiences.

Other American captives of lesser rank sailed to sites on Formosa and Manchuria to work for their Japanese masters. Although the Geneva Convention expressly forbade use of slave labor, the Japanese proposed to pay a minimum sum to each captive, part of which was deducted for a postal savings account that helped finance the war effort against the forces seeking to liberate the incarcerated.

Coast Artillery commander Col. Paul Bunker, staggering from weakness and unable to eat, had been loaded on a truck with two others after Corregidor surrendered. They had been driven to a makeshift small hospital run by captured U.S. Navy medical personnel in what had been a school in Manila. Bunker, who had lost forty-four pounds, remained there slowly recuperating.

"The Japs expect us to live on about a pound of straight rice a day and nothing else," wrote Bunker in his journal. "What a hell of a prospect. This noon, however, we got a cup full of alleged soup. We all contributed pesos to start a store . . . Today our alleged store opened but it was slow, tedious work to pass up the line and get waited on. And the prices! Here is my order: 3 duck eggs 24 cents; 2 corned beef, small, $1.80; 3 evaporated milk $2.80, 1 bean soup 65 cents, 1 catsup 70 cents."

Supplements from the "store" were available only occasionally and Bunker continued to note the shortage of anything other than a modest amount of rice. He struggled against the tedium of the daily routine. "My only amusement is to endure almost continuous defeat by all comers at cribbage [a fellow prisoner made the board] and to continue compiling the list of my property destroyed by enemy action.' I find this especially difficult as regards my books . . . I have Barrow's *History of the Philippines* but it is boring. What a lot of work I could do on my OPUS [*sic*] on the Bunker genealogy if—and to think of my forty years of work in that subject destroyed." (He ultimately concluded his lost property was valued at almost nine thousand dollars.)

He groused about a roommate and then remarked, "Bitterness and contempt of MacArthur seems to be universal among officers in this camp—also contempt for his staff. We try hard to be optimistic and think that our tour of this dog's life will be a short one but, if Mac's staff is now blundering as it did at Corregidor, then our prospects (and those of the United States and England in the Far East) are dismal indeed. And every day is so precious to me; I haven't so many of them left, at my age, and I begrudge every one that continues my separation from Landon [his wife]. I wonder if she ever received those handkerchiefs that I sent her last December?"

Although the Japanese overlords chose some senior American officers to transmit orders, arrange for work parties and supervise the preparation and distribution of food, they continued to deliberately make little distinction in treatment of inmates. In fact, according to Grashio, they beat up officers in front of enlisted men and assigned high rankers to demeaning tasks or labor that put them hip deep in slime. Without an effective hierarchy to establish order, the drive to survive induced an every-man-for-himself style of behavior.

Bunker said that on June 20, 1942, he and seven other colonels moved to a different building. "It seems filled with civilian employees, including old Negro John, the Corregidor barber, and Mr. Cook, PI Revenue and Customs Agent . . . enlisted men of the Army and Navy; officers of the Army and Navy including mustangs and many Navy Warrant and Petty Officers. The atmosphere is nauseating; it reeks of hoggishness and selfishness. You can't put a thing down anywhere and take your eyes off it for five minutes without it being stolen. Today I left half of my soap box and a half used cake of soap, plus a dirty old face towel, in the shower, and in ten minutes, it was gone."

In August 1942, Bunker left the Philippines for the camp at Karenko, Formosa. "Lined up in the sun, we stripped while the Jap G-2 inspectors frisked us and our clothes for papers, cutlery, lighters, matches. They did not take money. Our boss lieutenant made us salute, in unison, the colonel in charge of all prison camps, a sourpuss who barked and yelled at everybody. Then the major (with many campaign ribbons) in charge of this camp made a long speech in Japanese mostly telling us that the United States and England are licked, our Navy sunk and no planes left."

Bunker was pleasantly surprised by his first experiences at Karenko. His dormitory was neat and clean, and a bedding roll had been issued for each of the twenty-eight men with whom he would share the quarters. There were even cupboards to store items, although the prisoners possessed almost nothing. "We were given bath privileges at the laundry tubs and how everybody did enjoy it! It was like a flock of birds fluttering and chirping about."

Bunker jotted down a momentous occasion on December 8, 1942. "First anniversary of the start of this war; I have been a prisoner seven months, two days ago. Turned out at 9:30 for the ceremony of listening to the reading of the Emperor's 'Rescript.' They omitted the Jap version and a consensus of our officers declares that the Japs at this ceremony were lots less cocky than at the same ceremony two or three months ago, i.e. they realize the United States is now coming back." By this date, the Marines and the Americal Division had inflicted the first serious defeat upon the Imperial forces.

While the Americans may have reveled in the uneasiness they detected in their captors, their own situation worsened. Bunker, although not well, had volunteered to work on a farm with other prisoners. But with the food rations again trimmed, the sixty-two-year-old artilleryman developed some ominous symptoms.

On February 19, 1943, he reported, "was running to the *benjo* [latrine] all night long. This morning, felt rotten, so went to hospital. Had fever. Nearly passed out in getting there. I evidently have flu, and there seems to be lots of it in camp."

Two days later, after noting a sentry's assault upon half a dozen officers for laxity in saluting, Bunker wrote: "I broke down and opened my last can of corned beef as a desperate remedy for threatened starvation. I can hardly walk without staggering and am weak as a cat. I put one tablespoon of the meat in my bowl of soup and another in my rice and in that way it should last about six meals."

In the final week of February he described his decline. "Another done day—no work in the A.M. but yes in P.M. I am now siker [*sic*—at this point he began to mispell words] than hell. My left foot and ankle are almost bursting thru skin which in turn is so painful to touch as to be useless. My right torso, lungs and ribs are so painful as to immobilize me. I can't move without incurring devastating and wide flung plains [*sic*] . . . Even my hands look like bags of suet. But the worst is my appalling weakness. I can't heave my legs into bed, nor hardly turn over. Every position is painful. Have practically cut out smoking—it's easy when painful results are so prompt.

". . . Got milk and egg this morning! What a treat! But I squandered it all, at once. My hands and feet now terribly swollen. Spent feverish night with much coughing I fell [*sic*] so filled with phlegm and water that I have no leeway between suffocation if I stop panting to cough a bit. The night sure is a nightmare! It creeps along." He made this final entry on March 1.

Philip Fry, who relished a brief moment of triumph as the 57th Infantry repulsed a Japanese attack on Bataan, but then suffered a small stroke that cost him command of the regiment, was at Karenko. In his unmailed letters written for his wife, Fry reported, "March 14, 1943: Colonel Bunker much worse. Most of the time he is in a coma. None of us is strong enough to withstand even a minor illness. Our food and treatment still holding its own, and building up a little may tip the scales in my favor. The sun is out and morale much better. I love you.

"March 15, 1943: It is a pretty day. The Nipponese OD [officer of the day] announced a pig was to be killed. I couldn't believe my ears. It sounded like a change of policy. Colonel Vance had been slugged by a sentry and this guard has been relieved. March 16, 1943: Colonel Bunker died tonight. We feel pretty blue. He should have gotten back, with half a chance. Colonel Bunker's funeral was today. An autopsy was performed."

The coast artillery commander had succumbed to starvation and infection with Jonathan Wainwright at his bedside. When he hauled down the American flag on Corregidor, Bunker burned it, but not before cutting out a small piece that he sewed beneath a shoulder patch on his khaki shirt. In the prison hospital, Bunker told a friend, Col. Delbert Ausmus, about the piece of the flag. Bunker gave Ausmus half of it, urging him to give it to the Secretary of War if he died. Ausmus recovered Bunker's portion from the dead man's garments and preserved the two pieces. Upon his liberation in November 1945, he carried out Bunker's wishes.

On March 19, Fry noted: "Just finished the first dish from the individual garden, a salad of raw carrots and radishes with the tops of okra greens for dressing and partly fermented rice. Not bad." On March 21, he exulted, "A red letter day. Pretty good food, news that the Red Cross has arrived and the congestion may be relieved with the transfer of about a hundred to a camp nearby. Morale sky high with word that mail may have come with the Red Cross. It gives you hope, so worth fighting for."

Although top brass like Bluemel, Bunker and Fry ended up on Formosa, Al Svihra, a temporary resident at Bilibid Prison, was sent by train from Manila to the camp at Cabanatuan. As the Japanese did to the unfortunates consigned to freight cars on the last lap to O'Donnell, the guards initially wedged about a hundred men into each boxcar. "We were so close to each other that most could not even squat, but were forced to stand," recalled Svihra. But on this occasion, the soldiers removed men and stuffed them into some empties at the rear of the train.

During the trip, a guard who spoke English served as a middleman between the prisoners and Filipinos who gathered on the tracks at stops with trays of bananas, mangoes, candy and other foods. The soldier gathered money from those who had it, gave the vendors a small sum, pocketed the surplus and then handed out the fruit to everyone regardless of whether they contributed.

At Cabanatuan, Svihra worked on a farm and in December 1942 noted his first payment of 640 pesos from the Japanese for four months of work. "Received in actual cash only 30. It is understood that the balance of 610 returned to the Japanese government to be placed in postal savings."

Like so many others in his situation, the former legal officer coped with periodic bouts of infections. Dosed with the available medicines, he recovered, even managing to stave off an attack of appendicitis. Red Cross packages and some sent from the States brought cans of corned beef, Spam, jam, chocolate bars, raisins, laundry soap, cigarettes, shoe laces and even athletic equipment. The camp headquarters appropriated the recreational materials: "We want to borrow these."

On August 31, 1943, Svihra, whose intent was to present the account to his wife, wrote, "Our anniversary, dear. Do you recall fifteen years ago? Little did we think about war in those days. When I think of the food I had to get along on these past two years it makes me ill to remember how fussy I was about food at home."

Through clandestine radios and from Filipinos, the inhabitants picked up tidbits of news and rumor. "New Guinea in the hands of Allies." "Rommel surrenders [false]." "President Roosevelt and Wallace received Democratic nomination unopposed." [Truman actually replaced Wallace on the ticket at the 1943 convention.] "Wilkie and Dewey fighting it out for Republican nomination."

Interspersed with Svihra's notes on details of camp life and reminiscences are grimmer entries: "Private Connally missing from farm detail . . . Private Connally's body reviewed by group commanders at morgue in horribly mutilated condition." "Lt. Cols. Biggs and Breitung, with a Lieutenant Gilbert of the Navy, attempted escape; were caught by Am. [American] perimeter guard and turned over to Japs. Can't understand actions of B and B trying to escape. B and B tied to guard house at Main Gate to Camp since about midnight. All practically naked, exhausted from going over. This A.M. about 9:00 taken in direction of Camp 3, followed by armed guards and Jap details with shovels. A tragic affair."

At Cabanatuan, Irvin Alexander observed amazing improvisational talents. "Labels from tin cans were carefully saved and utilized for scratch paper, of which the Nips had very little. We saw a man obtaining his own thread by unraveling a sock to make a creditable repair job on his diliapidated articles of clothing. Two men who could repair false teeth were discovered and from then on led a busy and lucrative life. When there was no material for filling teeth, filings from silver coins were used to good advantage.

"Probably the most ingenious of all the articles constructed in camp was a one-tube radio receiver which brought in broadcasts from San Francisco, nearly seven thousand miles away. The set was built by Lieutenant Hutchinson out of salvage materials except for the tube which was smuggled in. He cut the bottom off a regulation army canteen and built his set small enough to fit into the canteen. Moved to a barracks which had not been furnished with electricity, he solved that problem by building a battery from scraps of copper and zinc using the acid stolen from the battery of a Nip truck and zinc buttons cut from trouser flies."

The tiny radio, smuggled copies of Japanese newspapers and Filipino digests of U.S. broadcasts, kept the inhabitants of Cabanatuan reasonably well informed on the progress of the war. The authorities allowed the inmates to amuse themselves with weekly dramatic productions after headquarters approved the scripts. The prisoners chortled over a sketch with a very slow-moving, thick-witted character topped by the punch line, "He is slower than the second coming of MacArthur."

The Japanese showed movies once or twice a month, mostly ancient films made in America. They also ran propaganda pictures. Alexander said he recognized one on Pearl Harbor as obviously a mock-up for filming. However, one on the Malayan campaign that appeared genuine provided insight into Japanese military discipline.

"One scene of a heavy artillery piece going into action [showed] the big gun being moved into position by a large number of Japanese soldiers pulling tow ropes. Two soldiers, who appeared to be completely worn out, dropped in their tracks before the gun had reached the desired position. An officer, overcome with fury at the soldiers shirking duty, rushed to them, drawing his sword.

Apparently, he ordered them to continue dragging the rope but, when they did not move fast enough to suit him, he beheaded them one after another with two mighty blows of his sword. That picture helped us understand why the Nip soldier was so much afraid of his officers."

In October 1942, the Japanese offered volunteers from Cabanatuan an opportunity to work at a different locale. When his squadron leader Ed Dyess signed up, Sam Grashio again followed him. Altogether the enemy recruited about a thousand men who figured almost anywhere was preferrable to Cabanatuan.

Aboard a filthy old ship, Grashio nervously noted the absence of any markings to identify the human cargo to U.S. subs. He knew that the scores of gasoline barrels on board would guarantee an instant huge explosion if a torpedo hit. He recalls a much improved diet, only partially due to the generosity of the crew. The prisoners chivied an opening into the hold and stole much of the extra food. Some unfortunates gorged their shrunken stomachs and soon endured the consequences, but even with diarrhea as a constant presence, the fresh sea air revived spirits and health.

The new home on Mindanao was a former penal colony near Davao. The prisoners—there were already a thousand in residence—worked an extensive tract of farmland, timber, rubber plantations and other agricultural enterprises.

"Overall," says Grashio, "the regular work was good for us. It gave the stronger men something to do and so kept up their morale. Many outside jobs also provided opportunities to pilfer food and thereby maintain strength and health. Nonetheless, some tasks were tough. Planting rice was the worst. Not only was there no chance to steal extra food, when one was hip deep in the mud in a rice paddy but the work itself was unhealthy and fatiguing."

Even though they lived in an area of abundance, the prisoners ate poorly, as the Japanese for the most part kept them on limited rations. Red Cross relief packages helped and opportunities to buy from Filipinos or to cop something while on a labor detail sustained the inmates for a while. Some of the guards proved as sadistic as those on the Death March, capriciously gunning down a man for a minor infraction and administering beatings with fists and rifle butts for perceived acts of discourtesy. A few of the soldiers behaved kindly and even socialized in a limited way with their charges. The Americans were allowed to form a band, put on a Christmas variety show and even played a baseball game with their captors, who won 14–10.

As Grashio, Dyess and some associates labored at various jobs, they started to consider escape. Working outside the enclosure gave them an opportunity to reconnoiter. Furthermore, the guards regarded the thick jungle and swamp as impenetrable and believed no one could get away except by use of a well-watched single road.

Grashio, with a job in the kitchen, began to smuggle food out the gate and cache it in the jungle. The conspirators accumulated medical supplies, matches, bolos, field glasses, a sextant, a hammer, file, pliers, watches and compasses, which they hid beyond the gate. It was a well-rounded group, carefully recruited by the initial instigators, Dyess and three Marine officers. The party included a Naval Academy grad, Lt. Comdr. Melvin McCoy, approached because he could provide navigational and boating skills for a sail to safety; a pair of enlisted men with reputations for their ability to scrounge; and the two Filipinos who as residents of Mindanao could serve as guides. Both of them were in the penal colony for murders.

"On April 4, 1943, ten of us and two Filipino convicts walked out of Davao into an uncharted jungle," says Grashio. They plunged into a miasma of gloom. Vegetation was so thick the sun's rays rarely penetrated to touch the ground. Leeches, slithering rats, raucous monkeys, wandering crocodiles, sharp thorns, vines that dripped a skin-itching poison, mud, slime, streams—all bedeviled them. A wall of swamp-grown sword grass seven to ten feet tall nearly did the party in. Bedding down for the night, they heard the disquieting sounds of rifle fire, machine gun chatter and even the whomp of mortars.

"We followed a single trail," recalls Grashio, "a short distance to a railroad track. Scattered about were expended .25 caliber cartridges, Japanese rations, Japanese G-strings [the soldier's underwear], other bloody clothing, Japanese cigarette butts and numerous footprints pointing in all directions. It seemed obvious now that the gunfire we had heard the night before had come from a skirmish between Japanese and Filipino guerrillas."

A day later they saw in the distance a pair of figures with rifles, but the two disappeared before Dyess could approach them. Further on they met a Filipino and one of the guides explained who they were and their wish to meet the guerrillas. The man told them to wait. "Suddenly, we were surrounded by several dozen ominous-looking characters brandishing a variety of weapons. They were led by a tall husky man, much larger than most Filipinos, who carried a .45 revolver at his waist and a Browning automatic rifle in his hand. This was our introduction to the guerrillas of the Philippines."

The irregulars took the escapees to the beach town of Medina, the headquarters for the American guerrilla operations in the southern Philippines. A former mining engineer recalled to service at the start of the war, Col. Wendell Fertig (given the title of "General" for status) was nominally in command. While he maintained contact with Australia through radio and submarine contacts, Fertig governed a very loosely knit organization. Focusing his efforts on intelligence gathering and occasional acts of sabotage, he avoided open conflict with a much better armed adversary. Some guerrilla bands operated quite independently, making their own strategic and tactical decisions. Others acted like common brigands, in pursuit of strictly personal gain. Without any accepted military hierarchy or genuine civil government, the guerrilla movement, while performing valuable services, was wracked with schisms fueled by personality clashes, individual ambitions and ethnic division.

Grashio and a number of his companions became part of Fertig's staff, seeking to bring order to the chaos of operations. But in the summer of 1943, three men from his group, his squadron head Ed Dyess, the Navy's Lt. Comdr. Melvin McCoy and West Pointer Steve Mellnik, a refugee from Corregidor, rendezvoused with a U.S. submarine forty miles off shore and made their way to Australia. Dyess provided MacArthur and his staff with an eyewitness account of the Death March from Bataan and the horrors of O'Donnell. Concerned that public disclosure of the atrocities might bring reprisals upon those still incarcerated, the policy makers hid the story for months and newspapers did not report the grim details until early 1944.

Grashio accepted an assignment to procure supplies useful to the guerrillas. He circulated through parts of Mindanao and visited some adjacent islands, wheedling, cajoling, even mildly threatening merchants and others who could supply useful commodities. He issued a receipt that promised payment after the war. The guerrillas controlled enough of the area for Grashio to be able to warn of imprisonment or reprisals if an individual refused to sell.

Grashio became increasingly fearful of capture by Japanese patrols. He endured several terrifying trips on tiny sailboats in raging seas, narrowly missed being shot down by sentries who thought him part of an enemy force, passed among Moro tribesmen with a reputation for belief that killing a Christian guaranteed them a place in heaven. Eventually, the submarine *Bowfin* bore Grashio to Australia in the fall of 1943.

While the captives struggled to stay alive, expired because of disease or abuse, or in a few instances escaped, the march towards liberation approached its climax and everyone involved seemed to know what was coming. Bruce Price, the 24th Division platoon leader, remembers, "While we were staging and training in Hollandia for the next invasion, we were not told where it would be. However, we were given sections of maps that showed our objectives. The only clue we had was some of the towns had Spanish names. We were informed by Tokyo Rose on our company shortwave radio, "To the butchers of Hollandia, we are waiting for you on Leyte and promise you will get our revenge."

CHAPTER XVII

RED BEACH

THROUGHOUT THE CAMPAIGNS that involved the Solomons, Marshalls, Marianas and the New Guinea locale, MacArthur and Nimitz cooperated without serious disagreement about objectives while occasionally squabbling over allocation of resources. But as enemy-controlled areas shrank, Army and Navy top brass debated whether some former targets might be bypassed. Instead of invading the Philippines, some policy makers, including Chief of Naval Operations Ernest J. King, suggested the Japanese forces in the archipelago be left to wither on the vine while combined operations plucked Formosa or even struck directly at the home islands. Not so innocently, the options of Formosa and the home islands fell within the purview of the naval authorities; the Philippines lay in MacArthur's fief.

MacArthur lobbied strongly for occupation of the Philippines. "The Philippine Islands had constituted the main objective of my planning from the time of my departure from Corregidor," he said later. "As the Allies advanced westward along New Guinea and across the Central Pacific, a wide divergence of opinion developed among international planners and military strategists as to the methods of defeating Japan, but I never changed my basic plan of a steady advance along the New Guinea-Philippines axis, from Port Moresby to Manila."

He advised the Joint Chiefs that bypassing the Philippines would be a military mistake and would entail tremendous loss of prestige in the Far East. General Marshall responded that MacArthur should not allow his personal feelings about the Philippines nor his concern for politics in the area interfere with the top priority, winning the war. He remarked that "bypassing" was not synonymous with "abandonment."

Closer to the scene than Admiral King or General Marshall, Navy leaders like Adm. William Halsey, head of the 3rd Fleet, recognized that without some base in the Philippines, moves against Formosa or Japan itself would be highly risky.

Nevertheless, with the war approaching its third anniversary, the Joint Chiefs in the summer of 1944 searched for a plan to accelerate the pace. Without committing themselves to taking back Luzon, the Navy agreed that for a start it would be necessary to capture southern and central Philippine areas. Mindanao, vulnerable since the conquest of Wakde, Biak and Noemfoor, seemed ripe for the opening thrust, and then Leyte, strategically sited in the middle of the islands. A tentative schedule was set with November 1 as the date for landings on Mindanao.

During the first two weeks of September, carriers from Halsey's fleet launched a series of preparatory strikes on Mindanao and the central islands. Halsey now reported to Nimitz that his pilots had destroyed the Japanese fuel supplies, sunk almost all visible vessels and encountered few aircraft. Most significantly, a downed flier rescued by Filipinos brought back the startling intelligence that there were no Japanese soldiers on Leyte. Halsey recommended that the combined forces attack Leyte instead of Mindanao.

Even as Halsey radioed his findings, the Navy carried out landings in the Palaus, due east of Mindanao and Leyte. For all of the naval talk about the virtues of skipping over a possible objective, no better argument for such a policy exists than their attack on Peleliu, one of this island group. A strategically worthless piece of real estate, Peleliu ground up Americans and Japanese for three months, costing the United States more than a thousand dead and five thousand wounded, while the defenders fed the slaughterhouse about fifteen thousand. The Americans occupied other undefended Palaus and one of them, Ulithi, became a major supply port and depot.

Although MacArthur's staff correctly pointed out that the Filipino report of no enemy troops on Leyte was dead wrong, the Joint Chiefs, MacArthur and Nimitz concurred on an invasion of Leyte rather than Mindanao and scheduled amphibious operations to open October 20.

Tokyo Rose had bragged that the Japanese Army was ready for the Americans at Leyte and, indeed, Imperial General Headquarters thought the enemy had now left itself vulnerable to a decisive blow. In fact, it was the Japanese who, basing their strategy on woefully inaccurate information, would place themselves in direst jeopardy. While Gen. Tomoyuki Yamashita, from his headquarters on Luzon in command of all Philippine forces, opposed a confrontation with the Americans on Leyte, the Imperial High Command rejected his advice.

To reduce the capacity of the Nipponese to interfere with operations around Leyte, a component of the U.S. Navy's Fast Carrier Force, Task Force 38, steamed into the China Sea and hammered the Formosa airfields and installations. Planes on the island engaged the carrier-based Americans in a furious, three-day affair.

The attackers wrecked more than five hundred aircraft based on what is now Taiwan, sank about forty cargo vessels and blasted ammunition dumps, hangars, barracks, maintenance shops and manufacturing sites. The naval air arm also rampaged across Luzon, targeting fields and fortifications around Manila. Simultaneously with these raids, the U.S. Army's Far Eastern Air Forces, taking off from Morotai, Biak, New Guinea and other locales, pummeled enemy airdromes in the Philippines—Mindanao, Negros, Cebu—and laid waste to installations in the occupied Netherlands East Indies.

During the Formosa engagement, the defenders crippled the cruisers *Houston* and *Canberra*. A bomb bounced off the carrier *Franklin* and a flaming enemy bomber skidded across that ship's flight deck. Antiaircraft and dogfights cost the Americans seventy-six planes. While casualties among personnel aboard the three vessels saddened shipmates, the disabled cruisers reduced Task Force 38's power only minimally; the *Franklin* remained fully serviceable.

However, the Japanese Navy enthusiastically accepted extravagantly false claims of success from their fliers and issued a communique triumphantly listing eleven carriers, two battleships, three cruisers, one destroyer or light cruiser sunk, another eight carriers, two battleships and as many as fifteen other ships severely damaged or set afire. The Emperor issued a special rescript to commemorate the great victory while civilians and military plunged into a mass celebration of the fictitious triumph.

Just as optimistic projections misled the Americans responsible for the defense of the Philippines, the roseate view victimized the Imperial High Command. It had eagerly sought a moment when it could swing the combined, full weight of the Army, Navy and Air Forces against the now staggering Americans. Even though Admiral Halsey radioed Admiral Nimitz on October 19 that he was "now retiring towards the enemy following the salvage of all the 3rd Fleet ships recently reported sunk by radio Tokyo," the Japanese persisted in the belief that they had won a great victory.

U.S. intelligence, not fooled by erroneous information that indicated no occupying army on Leyte, estimated a garrison of twenty thousand one month before the scheduled invasion. But with more than four hundred thousand Japanese stationed throughout the archipelago, no one doubted that sizeable reinforcements could be rushed to areas under siege.

The battle order started with the 1st Cavalry, 7th, 96th and 24th Infantry Divisions, plus the 77th and 32nd as reserves. With the auxiliaries and service personnel, a total of more than two hundred thousand men headed for Leyte. Because the nearest strips for fighter cover lay five hundred miles off, the major burden for air support lay with the Navy through its carriers. Also ready to contribute, however, were Army Air Corps bombers that would hit Japanese installations and be ready to blast ships carrying reinforcements for the island defenders.

The opening salvos from the U.S. fleet crashed down upon Leyte two days before A-Day (with D-Day now so firmly associated with the Normandy invasion, the planners had abandoned the tradition that dated to WW I and started to use other designations to mark events). Planes from carriers concentrated upon neutralizing enemy airfields while the 6th Ranger Battalion eliminated installations on four tiny islands in Leyte Gulf. In the armada of seven hundred ships, MacArthur himself sailed on the cruiser *Nashville*. On the eve of the landings he said, "I went back to my cabin and read again those passages from the Bible from which I have always gained inspiration and hope." He makes no reference to which particular words lifted his spirits.

At 0600 on A-Day, battleships along an eighteen-mile line from San Jose down to Dulag, on the northeast coast of Leyte, shelled the beach defenses. From two miles offshore, MacArthur witnessed the start of the action. "I could clearly see sandstrips with the pounding surf beating down upon the shore and in the morning sunlight, the jungle-clad hills rising behind the town. Landings are explosive once the shooting begins, and now thousands of guns were throwing their shells with a roar that was incessant and deafening. Rocket vapor trails crisscrossed the sky, and black, ugly pillars of smoke began to rise. High overhead, swarms of airplanes darted into the maelstrom. And across what would ordinarily have been a glinting, untroubled blue sea, the black dots of the landing craft churned towards the beaches."

As his F Company from the 34th Regiment, 24th Division approached Leyte, Paul Austin, the company commander, says, "We were awakened about 4:00 A.M., had the usual pre-landing breakfast, steak and eggs. This was the only time we ever got that kind of food.

"The 24th Division landed on Red Beach with the 34th on the right and the 19th Regiment to the left. The 1st Cavalry Division landed three or four miles north of us in the vicinity of Tacloban and near the Leyte commercial airfield. Their objective was that airfield and Tacloban, the capital city.

"Our objective was a series of low lying hills about one mile off the beach. My company landed about 10:05, in the second wave. As we came out the boats, we ran across some shallow water and hit the sand. The first wave was still lying there. I asked what company is this and was informed K Company. I said, 'You're supposed to be about fifty yards in. What's the holdup?'

"They told me there were snipers and a machine gun that pinned them down. Shells were falling all over the place. I looked out to sea and saw a landing boat take a direct hit, probably an artillery shell. That boat literally disappeared, nothing left except a few pieces of scrap and steel helmets. The entire boatload, maybe twenty-five soldiers lost along with the coxswain. Other boats were on fire, two LSTs and LCIs.

"Rifle fire was coming in pretty heavy. Our Captain Wye from regimental headquarters was killed a minute after he set foot on the beach. Another company commander from the 1st Battalion was killed very near Col. Red Newman [Aubrey, regimental CO]. I looked back and couldn't see anybody moving forward. Snipers, machine guns, mortars, artillery had everyone pinned down on the beach sand. The beach was covered with palm limbs, fronds; the bombardment had stripped the coconut trees by the thousands. It was pretty hard to walk because of the heavy layers of limbs while the trunks of the coconut trees stuck up in the air like telephone poles. Very few had any branches."

As a telephone lineman with the 2nd Battalion's Headquarters Company, Han Rants recalls a seven-day voyage to the shores of Leyte. "It was a time of great anxiety among the troops. There was much meditating, cardplaying, talking through the night. We liked going anywhere by ship because we felt the Navy food was really something compared to what we got in base camp or wherever we happened to be. While down in the hold our thinking all the time was that a torpedo hit would come right into the hold. That doesn't give you any real peace of mind.

"During the cardplaying, few of the fellows really had any money and they would play on the basis of IOUs. As that gambling went on, there was a fellow from Gardena, California, Pfc. Harold Moon, who won lots of money. He was a real rascal as far as a garrison soldier was concerned. He would have been in the stockade all the time because he wasn't a real spit-and-polish soldier. Within the first day of our trip from Hollandia, Moon showed up with a set of Navy fatigues, their blue work clothes. On occasion, he would slip on that outfit and could go through off-limits areas to get ice water or whatever he needed. He even showed up with a first lieutenant's bar for his Army fatigue hat. Moon was quite a poker player and he won big. I think he had around twelve hundred dollars in cash on him as we hit the beach at Leyte.

"The tension builds in any beachhead convoy and the nearer the island, the more tension. The day and night before a landing are wide awake times with more knife sharpening and gun cleaning. Some of the tommy gunners file or cut plus or ex marks on the cartridge heads. If properly done, this causes the slug to split four ways when it hits the body so that a large hole and much damage results.

"Many GIs stand at the rail all night, some weeping,

some meditating, some cursing but all weighing their chances of getting through another campaign. It gets to be pretty emotional. Some buddies sit quietly after having lived together day and night, never more than an arm's length away. You know the other guy's family; you know his sweetheart; you know everything about everyone. I remember so vividly the last few nights with fellows saying, 'If I don't make it, will you do this for me.'

"Between 5:00 A.M. and 6:00 A.M. the landing barges went over the side by crane and cargo nets rolled down the side of the ship into them. Soon after 6:00 the troop units were called to the deck in the order they will be landing. Rifle companies are called first. About fifteen men go over the side next to each other and down the net just like a ladder. As the first row of heads clears the deck on the way down, the next fifteen go over the edge. It is critical to grab only the vertical ropes because the guy above will step on hands stopped on horizontal ropes. If a man's hand is stepped on, his yank usually pulls the foot of the stepper out so that he falls, taking all those below him twenty to thirty feet into the steel-bottomed boat.

"When the people are loaded in the landing craft (LCVP) they go away from the ships and circle until everyone is loaded. As we got into our circling position, our planes had gone in to do some bombing of the beach and our battleships who were out deep behind us were throwing shells over our heads. The beach seemed to be one big explosion. We got to feeling confident that there couldn't be anything alive in there with all of this. The LCIs were going in closer and firing with heavy machine guns. They also had some multiple-launch rockets fired at close range. The destroyers in shallower waters would blast away with five-inch guns.

"Just before 10:00 A.M. we were circling in those boats with people getting really sick in them. They pop around the ocean like corks and the smoke from the motors is somewhat like following a city bus, just breathing in the fumes, a horrible smell that you breathe continuously. After riding around a length of time, many of the troops would just as soon die if they could reach the beach.

"Right at 10:00 A.M. the shelling stopped and all of these boats spread out and started in. It was deathly quiet as there was no firing while we're going in because they don't want to take a chance on shells falling short, hitting us. As we got about two hundred yards from the beach, enemy shells started coming out. Mortars sometimes hit a barge but usually missed. They turned artillery and antiaircraft guns on us. Everybody was scared. The Navy men driving these barges were up on raised platforms like sitting ducks. They stood up high with a very small shield and wanted to dump us and get out. They smacked the beach and really yelled at us to get out. Sometimes, some of them started back before the last guy got out of the barge. They had to go back and get another load and come in later.

"We were supposed to be the fourth or fifth wave but we got there second or third. As our barge hit the beach and the door flopped open, we jumped out, scared as can be. There is no pain or hurt as bad as being scared to death, and scared to death we were.

"There was no combat group in front of us, no troops to gain some ground and make a place for us to set up a headquarters. As wiremen we had no rifles but our switchboard and rolls of wire for telephone communications. Our weapons were .45s, meant to defend ourselves at close range.

"We tried to hang at the beach but as we came off that landing barge, within ten feet of us was a fellow that had been cut in half by an artillery shell. There was no bottom half of him and he was stretched out, guts pouring from the bottom half, which was half in the water, and half out.

"Everybody just stopped, looked at some of the dead people hit in the first wave and then looked at each other. We knew we couldn't run back into the water because there was no place to go there. People seemed stunned. The Navy had to stop shelling but the landing barges had .50 caliber machine guns firing over our heads.

"About this time, Colonel Newman, a big redheaded man and a real tough guy with a lot of guts, jumped up on the beach twenty or thirty feet from me and said, 'Get the hell off the beach! Get up and get moving! Follow me!' It was just enough to get everybody awake. GIs started moving, crawling, jumping, running combat-style. You run a little, roll over and try to take cover before moving again.

"We thought we would get some sort of position before they saw us but they apparently knew we were coming because they had managed to build some pillboxes. They had coconut logs covered with dirt and machine guns shooting from narrow slits in these mounds of dirt and logs. The only way you can get people out of these places is to be close enough with a flamethrower or get in closer under the machine gun fire and toss a grenade in.

"A hero came forth but we knew he had come to this battle to die. He was a big Hawaiian captain, one of the most popular officers. Before we left Hollandia he had received word his wife just had a baby although he'd been away for twelve months. This really shook him and we knew he was going to fight with everything he had, even if he got killed in the process. Word passed that he was really ripping and had knocked out three pillboxes. With real luck, he was jumping, running, dodging and crawling under machine gun fire to get hand grenades in the fortresses. At about the fifth one they got him, laced him with fire and he was hit ten times through the chest. He was the one who really broke the spell enough for our people to start moving in."

Austin's memory of the morning action is slightly different. "For all of that heavy bombardment, the enemy fire was very heavy. I heard someone—I'm pretty sure an officer from K Company—yell 'Let's go!' [Newman was about 150 yards away from Austin] and K Company jumped up and ran into the jungle off the beach. I let them move about fifty yards ahead and then shouted for F Company to move. Our two platoons on the beach started forward.

"My instructions were to follow the 3rd Battalion, K Company as it turned out, to a certain point and then we would pass through them to take up the attack. F Company would lead under the theory that by the time we covered three hundred yards, the 3rd Battalion would have suffered so many casualties, the second wave would have to take over the advance. Luckily it didn't turn out that bad, although K Company had taken some casualties. I had my men get on their bellies and crawl, trying to make harder targets for the snipers. I kept them on their bellies for at least seventy-five yards.

"A light tank came roaring down the beach and he turned into our area and drove the tank right up to the 3rd Battalion line to our front. Colonel Postelwaite, the Battalion CO, walked up behind the tank, took the telephone in his hand and talked to the gunner and driver. He started directing fire from that tank. They put a 75 mm shell into everything that even looked like it might contain a Jap or a machine gun. He'd fire at two or three targets, then move the tank forward twenty or thirty yards and repeat the process. I knew he destroyed two log pillboxes with shells right into the apertures of them. Colonel Postelwaite moved his front line right up to the edge of a big rice paddy full of water. I saw him talking to the tank and then the gun swung around, to line up on a building across the rice paddy. It put a shell into a small building a few yards away from a house and blew it to pieces. I could see chickens and chicken feathers flying."

At this point the 3rd Battalion directed Austin to pass through, out into the rice paddy. "At the deepest point, the middle, the water struck me just about chest high. I was terrified that I was about to step into a hole and go straight under and drown. Loaded down like we were with all that equipment, there was no way in the world you could swim out of there.

"We got through the beach landing and across this rice paddy without a single casualty. We were lucky that the Japs didn't come up and catch us out in the middle of that paddy. Later, I realized they had already fallen back in retreat in the face of all that firepower coming towards them."

On the trip to Leyte, Bruce Price relished a moment of sweet revenge. "I was assigned as mess officer for the troops on our troopship. All I knew about the kitchen was through experinces gained in a lot of long, hard KP duty while I was an enlisted man. Of course we ate separately from the ship's crew.

"The first day out, a soldier walked up and reported that he was assigned as our mess sergeant for the trip. I knew him; he had been mess sergeant at Camp Walters, Texas, while I was in basic training there. He must have been a direct descendant of the Marquis de Sade. He was so mean and his position gave him absolute power over us kids. He was like a lot of others who were given power and weren't qualified. They made up for this defect by being cruel.

"I told him I was glad to see him, although he did not recognize me. I had lost some weight and was a yellow pea-green color from taking atabrine pills to ward off malaria. I refreshed his memory. I told him I would be in the ship's mess officers' quarters during the trip, playing gin rummy, drinking gin and smoking cigars. And if I had any complaints about our mess I was going to have him transferred to my rifle platoon where he would be a first scout and everyone knows they have a short life span. I got wonderful compliments on the mess this trip."

As his outfit started to clamber down the nets to their landing craft, Price remembers the loudspeaker on the ship playing a hit song, "Lady Be Good." "We prayed that Leyte would be good to us as well. Going down the nets you had to be alert for men freezing on the nets, hands could just not let go. It was an involuntary reaction usually caused by looking down forty or fifty feet and seeing the little landing craft bouncing up and down with men who were already kneeling with their rifles resting on the bottom of the boat, muzzles pointed up, and ready to catch a falling body. To get the men moving down, their hands had to be stomped on until they turned loose and descended.

"The front ramp dropped and we charged off the craft in waist-deep water, thankful that a Jap machine gun was not spitting bullets into our open ramp [The 1st Battalion of the 19th Regiment assaulted the section of Red Beach south of the 34th Infantry.] My confidence in the effect of firepower, of tons of steel hurled on the beach, was shattered when a billy goat walked out of the trees amid sniper and machine gun fire. Miss Rose had been right. They were waiting for us on Leyte. The beach was not wide and we ran across it to the edge of the coconut plantation.

"Just before we entered the trees a huge tank carrier pulled up right beside us on the beach. There were three manned gun emplacements on the bow. I heard a big explosion, glanced back at the LST and the three gun positions had been swept clean; a mortar barrage wiped the guns and men off the ship.

"That gave my platoon the incentive to get off the beach. We entered the plantation shooting at snipers. We came to an antitank ditch about twenty feet deep and twenty yards across, freshly dug. We had pushed ahead of the others and could see a quarter of a mile in each direction along this ditch. I could just imagine Jap machine guns zeroed in, waiting on soldiers trying to cross the ditch. But we had to get past it.

"Meanwhile, snipers were still shooting. I had learned that the best way to prevent being hit by snipers was to keep moving. During training, I used to put men in trees to act as snipers and then send the rest through the jungle while the snipers tried to get them in their rifle sights. By rotating the role of snipers the men all found it was almost impossible for them to be caught in the rifle sights if they kept moving.

"We went through the tank trap and out in record time

without a mishap. In a part of the plantation that was soft and mushy after being trampled by water buffalo, I gathered my squad leaders in a big circle to go over our next objective. Just as I finished my instructions we heard a slop-sucking sound and there right in the middle of our group was a Jap mortar shell, the size of our 81 mms with about half of it sticking out of the mud. I don't know if it was a dud or if the mud was so soft it did not push the detonator button on the front. Our atabrine-yellow-colored faces turned an albino white as we looked at it. We could all have been killed if it had exploded. I confess I wet my pants. Fortunately, we were right on the edge of a rice paddy that we had to cross. I stepped in up to my waist and hoped no one noticed my pants before.

"We went through two or three more, ducking under the black, stinking water to avoid bullets. Reaching the road from Tacloban to Palo we scurried across and scrambled up the side of our objective, Hill 522. We were the first to get to the top. Hill 522 was shaped like a two-tined fork with a space between the tines, a vale maybe twenty feet deep and forty feet wide. On top of the first tine or prong was a trench that had just been vacated by the Japs who retreated to the second one where their mortars had caused so much death during the landings."

Price sent a runner back with a map overlay directing fire on the area occupied by the enemy. The requested barrage fell, uncomfortably close but on target, then lifted. Price ordered a charge, hoping to get to the foe before they recovered from the concussive effects of the explosions. Since they had retreated to a tunnel it was unlikely any had been killed or wounded.

"When you get up and say, 'Follow me!' and give a rebel yell like you imagine your great-grandfather gave during a charge in the War between the States, you fight a terrible temptation to look back and see if they are coming behind you. You depend upon your training and the confidence you gave your men in the past. As I led my thirty

men across that vale, I could not look back. If they weren't
coming, I was dead from the fire from the Jap trenches.

"I thought my luck that had been good so far had run
out. As we came to the top of the second prong of Hill
522, we were met by six-foot Jap marines from their
northern islands coming out of their trenches where they
kept the mortars. However, aided by the pounding from
the shells, the vibrations in their tunnel, the noise and the
rebel yell that my men copied—a sound of bravado and
fear—and the fact that the Japs in their tunnel could not
see us climbing up the side of the hill, they still thought
the fighting was at the foot of the prong. They were kind
of stunned and we finished them off in hand-to-hand
fighting. Then we turned their mortars around and fired
what rounds were left into the flat land behind the hill
where we could see enemy troops.

"Taking this position with its battery of mortars saved a
lot of lives and equipment. The Japs had range cards
marked with the positions of logs anchored in the Bay and
on the beach. When a landing craft came near a log they
simply dropped a shell in a mortar set on that log. The
shells that wiped out the guns on the LST came from these
mortars and so did the one that hit the mud and did not
explode. Maj. Gen. F.A. Irving, division commander, said,
'If Hill 522 had not been occupied when it was, we might
have suffered a thousand casualties in the assault.' Occupation of the height actually cost the 1st Battalion fourteen
killed, and ninety-five wounded."

"I first learned I was going to Leyte," says Joe Hoffrichter, "when I was accused of being one day AWOL on
my return from my furlough." While he had been away,
his engineer regiment had reorganized and shifted its location from Hollandia. As a consequence the innocent Hoffrichter got to the new encampment a day late. "My stripes
were taken away and I found myself in the 24th Infantry
Division."

As an outsider and buck private, Hoffrichter worked the

worst details his first weeks with the 24th. After a bone-wearying period loading sandbags in the sweltering heat, a sergeant took him to a supply tent. "He emerged holding a flamethrower which he threw at me. 'This is a flame-thrower,' I protested.

" 'Right, and it's all yours,' the sergeant replied. I said, 'Sergeant, I just got into the infantry. I don't know the first thing about a flamethrower.' Starting with almost a whisper and progressively getting louder and louder he repeated, 'I know you don't know anything about a flamethrower, but by the time we hit the beach in the Philippines, you're going to be the best damn flame-thrower operator in the entire Army.'

"For two years I was a model soldier and in less than two weeks I was accused of being AWOL. Stripped of my stripes and dignity, I found myself in the infantry with no infantry training and now discovered I was expected to operate a flamethrower in the coming invasion."

Hoffrichter underwent a two-day crash course in the operation and care of his new weapon. He was assigned to an LST that carried M-8s, self-propelled artillery pieces that resembled tanks. At a briefing he and others in the unit saw maps of the area they would hit. Hoffrichter and four riflemen were assigned to support an M-8 bent on destruction of enemy bunkers. "If fire from the M-8 failed to silence a bunker," says Hoffrichter, "I was to move forward under protective fire. I was to find an opening in the bunker and at close range hit the opening with several bursts from the flamethrower.

"After the briefing I felt as though I had been hit in the stomach with a sledgehammer. I kept thinking how inexperienced I was and why I had been chosen to wield such an awesome weapon. It made no sense but that was not unusual in the Army. You didn't need a PhD from MIT to operate a flamethrower. Privates, especially replacements, were considered expendable, referred to as 'cannon fodder.'

"The medics drilled us constantly to keep our distance

from Filipino females. They were capable of carrying all the venereal diseases we knew from training films. Also, tuberculosis was prevalent and highly infectious. There was a litany of dos and don'ts if wounded. One that stuck in my mind was, 'In the event of a belly-wound, stick your finger in it to stem the flow of blood and keep your guts from spilling out.' "

On October 19, after a final rundown on the specific missions, Hoffrichter noticed that all the joking had ceased. Few slept, and as a newcomer Hoffrichter was excluded from small groups who spoke quietly to one another. The novice flamethrower operator says he spent the night thinking of his "beautiful young wife, parents, kid brothers and sisters and a role model from high school, a football coach." At the Mass conducted by a chaplain, Hoffrichter prayed not so much that he be spared but that God grant him the strength and courage to face what lay ahead. He could not stomach the steak and eggs and munched on a piece of roll with his coffee.

Scheduled for the third wave, Hoffrichter and his group donned their gear at 9:30 A.M. "A fellow by the name of Johnny Lomko helped me get into the harness of my flamethrower. As he did, he said, 'There you lucky bastard. No Jap will dare get close to you.' Indeed I was the lucky bastard . . . Johnny would die shortly after we landed.

"At 10:30 or thereabouts, the twelve LSTs headed for shore at full speed and soon attracted Japanese artillery fire. Before reaching shore, four had been hit and one was burning. The one I was on came to a grinding halt long before reaching the beach. We had hit a sandbar. Engines were reversed and the commander of the ship swung the rear of it back and forth for what seemed an eternity. We became a sitting target. Japanese artillery shells kept falling to the left and to the right, closer and closer. Suddenly they also started dropping to the front and back of the ship as they tried to zero in on us. I had never experienced such a feeling of despair and hopelessness.

"We all took cover under vehicles on deck. Some men

fought for places of safety. Others prayed, out loud. I did so inwardly, as I lay with the upper part of my body under a truck, my feet beneath a jeep. The rest of me was exposed. Fortunately, a destroyer saw we were in serious trouble. They shot a line to our LST and in no time we were freed and headed out into the Bay. Our second run was successful and we poured onto the beach."

Like the others, Hoffrichter was astonished to find the troops from the earlier waves still burrowing into the sand of the beach. The words, orders and leadership of Newman galvanized the men around Hoffrichter. "A fellow dug into the sand not far from me, looked at me, got up, moved forward and said, 'Give 'em hell, Buddy!' "

A tank trap temporarily blocked passage for the M-8 with Hoffrichter but a bulldozer from the 3rd Engineers filled the obstacle. "The bunkers were well concealed, hard to see. But the concentration of firepower coming from them gave us an idea of where they were located. The first three were silenced by fire from the 75 mm cannon of the M-8. The fourth, despite countless 75 mm shells, was not completely silenced.

"Lt. Francis Wai ordered me to move in with my flame-thrower. Once we moved off the beach, things were happening so fast the adrenaline kicked in and helped ease my initial fears. Now it went into high gear. I was so focused on what I was supposed to do I didn't have time to think as I moved under protective fire towards the bunker.

"I reached the dirt and log emplacement miraculously without drawing fire. Two machine guns were still firing. I could not find an opening to use the flamethrower although the shells from the M-8 had caused part of the bunker to cave in. As I leaned forward against the logs of the bunker, about four feet in front of me, I suddenly began to see dirt between the logs start crumbling. A few seconds later I saw the shaft of a sabre push through, creating the opening I needed.

"As soon as the sabre was drawn back inside, I placed

the nozzle in the hole and shot three bursts into the bunker. The screams I heard were of intense agony. The machine guns were silenced and the stench of burning flesh drifted through the openings where the guns were. I vomited on the spot. Four more times on A-Day I used the flamethrower and I vomited each time. After the third time there was nothing left to bring up. The last two bunkers left me with nothing but the dry heaves."

By mid-afternoon, the team with Hoffrichter had accounted for sixteen bunkers. As he, Lieutenant Wai and the other riflemen took cover in shell craters, a barrage from an unseen dugout blasted their M-8. Wai ordered Hoffrichter to see if the M-8's .50 caliber machine gun atop it could be salvaged.

Reluctantly, Hoffrichter shed his flamethrower, climbed up on the disabled vehicle and inspected the .50 caliber. "I saw an armor-piercing shell had hit the barrel, splitting it with a gaping hole. Through all the noise of gunfire, I heard someone shout, 'Put your hand through it!' Reacting to the order I stuck four fingers from my left hand through the hole in the barrel. At the same instant I glanced down to where the order came from. Down on his knees, pointing a big press camera at the disabled tank, was a man, armed only with the camera. I jumped off and said, 'Who the hell are you? You're going to get your head blown off. Where's your gun?'

"He turned and started to run at full speed towards the safety of the beach. As he did, he shouted back at me, 'Watch for your picture. I'm with *Yank* magazine.' Sure enough, the picture appeared in the December 1944 issue of *Yank* [a publication produced by GIs]."

Paul Austin, Hanford Rants, Bruce Price and Joe Hoffrichter, all veterans of previous campaigns, had come under fire before Leyte. But for replacements like Charles Card, Red Beach baptized them in the terror and blood of combat. Assigned to the 1st Platoon of Company B in the 34th Infantry, Card would perform the gamut of infantry duties—rifleman, BAR ammo bearer and operator, scout, messenger. He even worked with light machine guns and mortars.

"It was impossible," says Card, an erstwhile trumpet-playing college student, "for the seventeen-week basic infantry course to integrate the value of teamwork and the training in New Guinea, to make a combat-effective soldier. At Red Beach I was absolutely scared silly. I wore spectacles which constantly steamed over due to my nervous reaction. I hugged the ground, prayed to God and needed guidance and insistence from the squad leader to move, fire and advance.

"I saw my first dead GI, head completely severed, veins, cords, breathing tube hanging out his neckline. Really got scared then but apparently some degree of reactionary training in weapon use and tactics, which may have been programmed into me, occurred. Survival became the primary motivator. While others may have controlled or directed themselves from a platform of bravery, hatred of the enemy or tactical expertise, my situation focused on personal survival, not only in my baptism of fire but in every firefight thereafter."

"At Red Beach," said MacArthur, "our troops secured a landing and began moving inland. I decided to go in with the third assault wave." Actually, the moment chosen to carry out his promise to return happened about four hours after the third wave reached the shore. The general's account of the trip on his barge notes: "The coxswain dropped the ramp about fifty yards from shore, and we waded in."

In his biography of MacArthur, William Manchester reports that the wet landing was unexpected. The vessel with the Supreme Commander and his party ran aground. "MacArthur had counted on tying up to a pier and stepping majestically ashore, immaculate and dry. Most of the docks had been destroyed in the naval bombardment, however, and while a few were still intact, . . . the beachmaster had no time to show them where they were.

Like all beachmasters, he was as autonomous as the captain of a ship. When he growled, 'Let 'em walk,' they had no choice."

In the famous photograph of the event, as MacArthur strides through the shallow water, he wears a grim scowl on his face. Manchester attributes the look to a "wrathful glare" at the offending beachmaster, rather than a stare of steely determination.

Red Beach at that moment was only shakily secured. Japanese snipers occasionally harassed the invaders. Fire from automatic and small arms weapons ripped through nearby groves as GIs pressed forward. American planes from carriers passed overhead and naval vessels hammered at distant targets. Those responsible for MacArthur's safety sweated out his tour as he inspected the 24th Division command post, kicked over a couple of enemy corpses, drafted a brief message to President Roosevelt and then stepped to the microphone hooked up to a mobile communications truck.

A sudden, heavy shower of rain did not deter MacArthur from his announcement. "People of the Philippines: I have returned. By the grace of Almighty God, our forces stand again on Philippine soil—soil consecrated in the blood of our two peoples . . . The hour of your redemption is here . . . I now call upon your supreme effort that the enemy may know, from the temper of an aroused people within, that he has a force there to contend with no less violent than is the force committed from without . . .

"Rally to me. Let the indomitable spirit of Bataan and Corregidor lead on . . ."

Han Rants held a ringside seat for the appearance of the general and had his own interpretation of the event. "It had been quiet on the beach perhaps an hour or so when some ceremony or commotion seemed to be coming from out on the water. About three landing barges were coming in, and from the flags we could see it had to be MacArthur. We really didn't have a lot of love for MacArthur because as a general he wanted to win wars fast. He wanted to push as many people as fast as he could to get it done, so he had spoken out against rotation of troops so old ones would get a leave home. He wanted to keep the veterans until the war was won.

"We had only about twelve hundred yards of beach but here came the landing barge with the tide right for a good, flat dry landing. I have an idea it was kind of staged too, as it stopped a little short, the gate flopped down and MacArthur with fifty aides of his, officers of various levels, waded about knee deep through the water. Cameras were grinding to film the triumphant return. Later, after the war was over, we saw the very same picture with the caption in *Collier's* magazine reading 'MacArthur leads the troops ashore.' It was quite some time later than H hour and it just hadn't been safe any sooner.

"I happened to be hanging in a coconut tree close enough to hear the speech loud and clear. He mentioned that three years ago he told the people of the Philippines that he would return and now, 'I have returned.'

"While seeming to be a kind of grandstand thing for a show, it really took some kind of courage for a man of that level to be there. [The Japanese commander, Gen. Tomoyuki Yamashita, later said had he known MacArthur was there he would have sent a suicide squad to assassinate him.] As much as we disliked the guy from the standpoint of his wanting to use veteran troops to win wars, we knew there was no one who knew the Philippine Islands better, and we knew that had we landed somewhere else, we probably would have had a lot more people killed than we did."

Other members of the 24th Division voiced similar sentiments. "We were still pinned down, no more than two hundred yards from the beach," says Eric Diller with H Company, the heavy weapons unit, "when I saw General MacArthur wade ashore, wet to his hips, corn pipe in his mouth, where he proclaimed, 'I have returned.' Most of us hunkered down on the beach would have appreciated it more had he said, 'We have returned.' " (In the photograph of the scene there is no sign of the corncob pipe.)

At his Collecting Company station on Red Beach, Phil Hostetter learned from wandering GIs of the imminent arrival of MacArthur. Hostetter elected to remain at his post for orders. A second report confirmed the general's appearance and that he wet his trousers to the knees. Casualties grabbed Hostetter's attention and he administered plasma to an infantryman with a compound fracture of his arm from a bayonet fight.

"After a while, someone asked," recalls Hostetter, " 'Do you know who was just here? General MacArthur and some admiral! They watched you for quite a while.' No one told me we had visitors so the general watched me but I was too busy to see him. We thought the presence of our highest officers on the beach at that time was foolhardy. We did not understand the significance our Filipino allies saw in his coming. The general said he would return and he did.

"The next day some guerrilla soldiers came to the beach. One said, 'I am delighted to see you here but where is General MacArthur?'

" 'He was here yesterday, we all saw him,' I replied, lying a little.

" 'Oh, I cannot believe it,' he answered with great joy. 'This means you are here to stay. It is no commando raid.' The general understood very well the Oriental regard for personal leadership."

Before he returned to the *Nashville,* MacArthur examined some corpses of the enemy and drew further satisfaction on seeing they belonged to the 16th Division, the lead unit for General Homma's Bataan campaign.

As darkness enveloped them, the 2nd Battalion of the 24th, wary of the Japanese propensity for night assaults, prepared for the possibility. "Colonel Newman," says Paul Austin, "ordered G Company to set up a roadblock a quarter of a mile down the road towards Pawing [a Leyte village]. Approximately thirty men dug in astride the highway. I felt in my bones we'd be attacked that night. They had boasted they would throw us back into the ocean if we landed there.

"About 1:00 A.M. rifle and machine gun fire erupted down at the roadblock position. That woke everyone up. Almost immediately a Japanese mortar shell hit the roof of a building right near our foxhole. I became pretty frightened and worried about our situation as the gunfire got hotter and hotter down the road. Presently my two machine guns, set up to support each other with crossfire, opened up."

Han Rants in the communications section of headquarters company for the battalion says, "Telephone lines were kept open so those men out on points to spot trouble could kind of whisper, 'We've got people coming in.' On this particular night, Private Moon, the guy who won all the money on the ship, was holding one of the point positions with a couple of buddies. He called in and said, 'This is the big one, they're really coming and they seem to be all around.' They used a rice paddy and not only had machine guns but mortars mounted on rafts in the water. They could move the raft quickly, and they'd fire a burst then move real quickly so when we returned fire, it wasn't there.

"They came near Moon's point and he would kill three or four of them who tried to take it. The enemy determined they would try to take that point before anything else. It was kind of fortunate they did since it bought us a whole lot of time until daylight came. The Japanese started to maneuver to get the three guys in that hole and finally killed two of them. Moon was there alone but well supplied with a tommy gun and clip after clip of ammunition plus grenades.

"We could hear exchanges; some of the Japanese spoke English and would yell at him. He knew he should be quiet so they couldn't really zero in on him but he really meant business and called them all the names in the world.

He kept yelling 'Come and get me! If you want me, come and get me!' As he fought on, Moon called back coordinates of some enemy positions and GI mortars blasted these targets."

Joe Hoffrichter, having completed his assignment in support of the M-8, located his unit, Company F under Paul Austin. Hoffrichter shared a foxhole with Troy Stoneburner who awakened him from a sound sleep as gunfire shattered the silence in the G Company sector.

"It went on for hours," says Hoffrichter. "Suddenly the firing stopped. We could hear clearly an American GI cussing and taunting the Japanese to come and get him. There would be a short burst of fire, then more cussing at the Japanese. At one point Troy said it looked like the fellow doing the cussing was out of his foxhole, firing bursts from an automatic gun. 'No way,' I said. Soon Troy poked me and told me to look towards the beach between two clumps of trees. I located the spot and silhouetted against the open background, a man was standing, firing a gun in rapid bursts. We were both convinced this was the nut doing all the cussing and shouting.

"About 4:00 A.M. a major shootout took place in G Company's area and then it grew silent. Early the next morning, we learned that they had repulsed a night attack and that a kid named Pvt. Harold Moon had killed countless Japanese within a few feet of his foxhole before he was overrun and killed. [Remnants of Moon's platoon broke the enemy line with a fixed bayonet charge.]

"As we moved up the road at daybreak, I saw a lot of dead Japanese and one dead American soldier. Before they covered his body with a poncho, I saw his face. It was the same kid who winked at me on the beach and said, 'Give 'em hell, Buddy' and it was Pvt. Harold Moon!

"Moon had fought by himself at the roadblock for an hour or hour and a half," says Austin. "He took all the ammunition his buddies had left lying around and with his Thompson machine gun and a box of grenades he had fought those Japs until they finally gathered in a large group, knocked him down and killed him. That morning there were fifty-five Jap bodies all lying in front of his foxhole. Across the entire front of our battalion, we estimated some six hundred to seven hundred Jap bodies. Part of them were from an air strike called in from a carrier. We marked the ends of our lines with red panels and the pilots coming over the area after daylight could see the area. Their bombs fell right in the midst of the Japanese soldiers. I saw one bomb go off and two or three bodies flying in the air, mixed with debris, mud and water."

Harold Moon was awarded a posthumous Congressional Medal of Honor.

CHAPTER XVIII

WHITE, ORANGE, BLUE, VIOLET, AND YELLOW

ON A-DAY, after the customary pounding of the shore defenses from the air and sea, the 1st Cavalry Division including amphibian tanks raced towards White Beach, a two-thousand-yard-long strand of coral sand that began almost a mile north of Red Beach. Rifleman Sal DeGaetano, newly acquired by B Troop, 12th Cavalry Regiment, rode the first wave ashore. Originally a member of a coast artillery unit in January 1941, DeGaetano shifted to an antiaircraft outfit where his talent for "messing up" cost him his noncom stripes and bought him a trip to New Guinea and the 1st Cavalry as a rifleman with B Troop. His regiment struck in the center, with the 7th Cavalry on their right flank and the 5th on their left.

"As we neared Leyte," says DeGaetano, "the Navy was all around us. As the first wave formed, I looked at some of my buddies to see if they were as nervous as I was. I was fascinated by the big smoke rings the big guns made as they pounded the beach, and then walked the bombardment inland while we prepared to land. I was amazed at the little resistance we encountered that first day. But in spite of that, in my foxhole that night, my buddy Ray York and I were shaking like leafs with apprehension until we fired at some noise and then settled down."

Indeed, compared to what the 24th Division endured,

the passage to White Beach and immediately beyond proved relatively easy. The pounding administered by aircraft and ships-of-the-line drove the defenders to abandon most of their fortifications. The 12th's most difficult task during the first day seemed to be crossing a deep swamp. By nightfall, the division had achieved its objectives with minimal casualties.

The 24th and 1st Cavalry Divisions, grouped as the X Corps, formed the right flank for the assault, with the 1st Cavalry responsible for the northernmost zone. Some fourteen miles south of the edge of the 24th's Red Beach, the six-hundred-ship convoy bearing the XXIV Corps, composed of the 96th and 7th Divisions, zeroed in on a series of beaches designated as Orange, Blue, Violet and Yellow.

Unlike the other divisions, the 96th came to Leyte unbloodied. Its GIs were also a mix of extremes in education and background. Bob Jackson, a platoon leader in the 382nd Regiment, recalls its composition while training the newly activated organization in the States: "Many of the noncoms were not draftees or even early volunteers, but men who, in the severe Depression of the late thirties, found a home in the Army. While not highly sophisticated, they had learned 'the Army.' We draftee officers [he graduated from OCS] were a different lot. Most of us were recent college graduates."

The need for replacements for outfits already overseas drained the 96th of some of its people. To fill the gaps in the 96th, large numbers of men from the recently closed down Army Specialized Training Program [ASTP], an operation that sent GIs to college, entered the 96th's ranks.

"It was a sad situation," says Jackson. "They had no military training to speak of. A barracks was set aside and we were charged with making soldiers of these men. They were very bright—they must have had very high IQs because they'd been accepted at prestigious universities—but they knew nothing about soldiering. We were given about six weeks to bring them up to speed. Discipline was the greatest problem. They were not used to the restraints on their individuality that the Army required. Most turned out to be superior soldiers in combat."

Dick Thom, a lawyer in civilian life and older than most at his level, was a regimental staff officer. He too fretted over the infusion of these raw newcomers. "They turned out to be smart kids, quick to learn, good riflemen, good shooters, solid killers and thoroughly reliable."

For the former ASTP soldiers, infantry life inflicted culture shock. Norman Fiedler, a New York City youth drafted in 1943, completed basic training at Fort Benning before attending Chicago University to study engineering. "When the ASTP program closed down, the transition was immense. At Chicago University maids cleaned our rooms, made our beds, and we ate first class at the university's fine dining rooms. With the 96th, we were put to work digging foxholes, running the infiltration course with machine guns firing over us while we crawled like a snake. The training before Leyte was very comprehensive. We were taken out two miles in the Pacific on rubber rafts at 2:00 A.M. and left to our own devices to get back to shore. We climbed mountains and on numerous field trips had to return to camp in the dead of night by means of a compass."

George Brooks, one of the former college boys who served previously in the Air Corps, had no weapons instruction, unlike Fiedler who had completed a basic course at Benning. "We'd been assured that if the [ASTP] program was terminated we would be returned to the service branch from which we came. When we were told we were all going to the infantry we were disappointed and more than a little bitter. The basic infantry training I received in the 96th amounted to a total of three weeks. We had rifle training, threw grenades, crawled under machine gun fire, got in foxholes while they ran over us with a tank and had close order drill. Altogether I would say it was inadequate but the subsequent amphibious instruction was very good.

"The noncoms who trained us were very civil and very helpful. But when we completed our basic and were assigned to various companies, it wasn't long before some of the enlisted men showed their resentment. Many of them had very little education and were wary of college boys."

Marvin Margoshes traveled the same route as Brooks, from the Air Corps to college and then the 96th. "We spent more time singing than firing rifles," he says of his Air Corps duty. "My education"—he had graduated from one of New York City's best high schools and spent a year at the University of Mississippi through the ASTP—"set me apart from most of my unit, Company C of the 382nd Infantry. They [the older 96th GIs] had little education. Our master sergeant couldn't read. It wasn't that we disliked each other or looked down on them but we had little in common in our backgrounds and interests."

Washed out of flight training because of hayfever, Bob Seiler attended Bradley Polytechnic courtesy of the ASTP before coming to the 96th. "They overtrained us in some things, such as rubber boat training. We used LCVPs and LCIs and amtracs [amphibious tractors] in both our landings [Leyte and later Okinawa]. As far as my reception in the division, I think they felt we were a bunch of smart guys and they were going to show us. I'm sure we received the best basic training anyone ever had. I was honored to be a rifleman; in fact I was lucky enough to carry extra ammunition for our BAR man. The rule book called for a Pfc. stripe for the job but being from ASTP it was overlooked."

The preliminaries off Orange 1 and 2 and Blue 1 and 2 featured a barrage led by the battleship *Tennessee*, a survivor at Pearl Harbor, along with the big guns on three cruisers and a destroyer. Within thirty-nine minutes, the ships methodically painted the area with 2,720 rounds of high explosives. In addition, Navy carrier planes swept over the sector unloading more bombs and strafing targets of opportunity. As the amphibious tanks and landing craft rendezvoused for the final swing to the beaches, LCIs

added a barrage of rockets and mortars to the rodomontade.

Elmer Polcyn, a tech sergeant with Company K of the
382nd wrote, "As we were sweeping in towards the beach,
a line of LCI rocket ships pulled up in front of us and fired
rockets at the beach. All we could see of the beach was
smoke and flames. Our landing craft was about twenty
yards from shore when a Jap mortar dropped three shells
right alongside our tractor. And then we were on Leyte,
the Philippine Islands.

"I was the first one to get off our landing craft. I took
only a few steps when a bullet knocked a coconut to my
feet. The tree had been hit during our shelling and the
coconut had been even with my head. A few inches closer
and I would not have gone further. One of the boys in my
landing spied a Jap tied up in a tree and cut him in two
with a .50 caliber machine gun mounted on the tractor.

"We quickly moved inland so that the troops in other
waves would have room. The objective of the platoon was
a hill four hundred yards from the beach and we could not
stop until we took it. We kept moving, stopping only to
shoot at the Japs who were in our path. We did not have
time to stop and find out where all of them were. That was
a job for the troops behind us.

"We reached the base of the hill and started up, which
was made difficult by our shelling. After a hard climb we
reorganized. Things were in a state of confusion. Men
were missing; some were injured and sent back to the
beach. At last things started to straighten out. Missing men
joined us on the hill and I found out the first man killed in
the second platoon was Mark Grant, an old Army man
who volunteered for the infantry. It was hard to realize
that he was gone. He had walked in front of a pillbox and
was shot between the eyes. We were getting used to seeing
men fall and die."

"I was one of the lucky ones to go in on the first wave at
Leyte," says Bob Seiler. "The night before my platoon

sergeant made a racquet, similar to one for tennis, using a piece of cardboard. Because I was the tallest in the platoon, I was to stand up and bat away any hand grenades that the Japs might try to throw into our amtrac. Because of this, I got to see everything.

"It was like a hundred Fourth of Julys, all at once. The rockets were the most impressive. They looked awesome. How anything could live through that was hard to believe. Our driver was very good. There was a tank trap in front of us but he managed to get just one track across and even though we were at about a thirty-degree angle we made it over.

"I remember seeing my first Jap almost immediately and because at first there was a lot of confusion, I thought he was one of ours and didn't shoot. His uniform was just about the same color and I didn't want to shoot one of our own."

George Brooks recalls the tense early moments. "There was very little conversation while we were loading into the amtracs and then heading for shore. On the way in, one of the guys sitting opposite me on the other side of the amtrac was very nervous, as we all were, and fiddling with the safety on his rifle. He had the rifle butt down on the deck with the barrel up alongside his cheek. All of a sudden we heard a loud bang and when we looked at this guy, his eyes were bulging way out with a startled expression on his face. There was a black powder mark up the side of his face and a hole through his helmet. Nobody laughed.

"The amtracs were supposed to carry us on shore for a hundred yards or more, but when we got to the beach there were coconut logs driven into the sand at the water's edge like pilings. There were three or four logs cabled together and spaced so closely an amtrac could not get between. So we stepped out into the water from the rear of the amtrac and raced across the beach as fast as possible. It was 10:00 A.M. when we hit the beach and ninety-eight degrees Fahrenheit. I found one of our guys passed out from heat exhaustion. His canteen was empty. I called a medic over and went inland. That very first day our battalion commander flipped his lid and had to be taken back.

"We continued inland through a swamp, waist high or more. Of course one thinks of snakes in this environment but I didn't see any. Late in the afternoon, we got orders to dig in."

Don Dencker, an ASTP refugee who felt himself readily accepted within the ranks of Company L of the 382nd, says, "We were as ready psychologically as any outfit could be for combat after so long on ships. I spent fifty days on LST 745. Physically, however, we were not in such good shape to be exposed to the very high humidity and temperature on Leyte.

"I initially didn't have much fear as I was so excited. Later fear sank in but almost everyone managed to live with it. As an assault company we reached Blue Beach 1 about 10:00 A.M. and Companies L and K took Hill 120, six hundred yards inland, in forty-two minutes. We had twenty battle casualties on the landing day, including five or six when the Navy shelled Hill 120 a few minutes after we took it from the Japs.

"The immediate reaction when coming under fire for the first time is self-preservation," says Norman Fiedler. "The ingrained training received through basic training caused one to immediately react as a combat man—hit the ground, seek protection behind rocks, trees, etc., and move forward. Some men lagged behind but no one stayed behind, the noncoms incessantly urging, 'move forward, move ahead.'"

Norman Fiedler's outfit apparently bumped into a more determined band of defenders. "Our company was pinned down just beyond the beach, in what appeared to be rice fields. We dug foxholes by nightfall but because of the water table, they filled up with water. Because we could not leave the foxholes, we remained in water up to our necks all night. In the morning, our entire bodies were wrinkled from being soaked."

A Company 382nd Regiment weapons platoon leader

Bob Jackson remembers his battalion as the middle one of three that came in abreast. "Though we were in the first wave, we all became mixed together on the beach and no one seemed to know what was going on. I surely didn't and went into a sort of numbness. I was able to gather up most of the platoon along with a platoon from B Company and get the mortars and machine guns aimed inland. We didn't know whether we were under fire or not but there were a great deal of weapons banging away at something. It was noisy as hell.

"Soon, my runner found the other elements of our company and we joined it. That night we set up a fear-filled perimeter under the shattered coconut trees near the beach. It was to be the first of a long series of wet foxholes."

Elmer Polcyn's 3rd Battalion made contact with the 2nd Battalion on the right flank and GIs from the 7th Division to the left. "At four in the afternoon we all jumped off in attack. Tanks had come up in the meantime but as we hit swamps they could not go along. We sure did hate to leave them behind with their 75 mm guns, ideal for knocking out pillboxes. We moved for about ninety minutes and then were ordered to stop and dig in for the night. It was about six when we started to dig and saw our first Philippine rain. It started out as a light shower and then kept up all through the night.

"We had expected a Jap counterattack and made plans to deal with it if it came. Just before daylight we heard a lot of screaming and yelling of *banzai*. The counterattack had come but it was to our left in the 7th Division's sector. Part of it hit our battalion, striking L Company. It was greeted with well-placed machine guns and automatic weapons. The Japs came in riding horses, two to three men on a horse and on foot." The assault was repulsed with few of the well-entrenched Americans hurt.

"Of course no one slept that first night," says George Brooks. "Off our left flank we heard a lot of shooting and noise. We heard that Japs had made a *banzai* charge in the

7th Division area. One of our guys, whom I knew very well, got out of his foxhole and crawled towards the company CP. Someone shot him in the head. We had been told over and over not to get out of our foxholes at night. They thought he may have heard something on the radio and was trying to crawl over and tell the company commander."

Marvin Margoshes says, "My unit went in at H plus 1 and it was a quiet landing. As soon as we got ashore, I dived head-first into a shell hole. When I picked myself up I saw that I had fallen on a scorpion and luckily crushed it. We had been shown maps of the landing area with two roads parallel to the shore and were told to regroup between the roads. There was nothing that we recognized as roads so we went inland about two hundred yards and decided to stop. I sat down with my back against a tree, lit a cigarette and looked around. Back towards the beach there were soldiers crouched in shell holes pointing their guns in my direction. I saw nobody when I looked inland. I realized we were ahead of the front and didn't know it. That's how green we were."

Official accounts speak of light resistance and limited losses but says Seiler, "When word came that Private Grant was killed, I think this sobered all of us in a hurry. I don't feel we had a lot of enemy fire at the beach but I now know there were more people hurt than I realized."

A-Day called for the 32nd, 184th and 17th Regiments of the 7th Division to penetrate the one mile of coastline denoted as Violet 1 and 2 and Yellow 1 and 2. A swamp separated the Yellows. The strategists earmarked Dulag, a barrio beside Highway 1, and its airfield as the principal objectives. The 32nd at Violet 1 and 2 encountered fierce opposition from well-emplaced defenders who temporarily held up an advance spearheaded by tanks. Intensive fire eventually silenced the foe. Elsewhere the GIs pressed ahead with a minimum of interference. By nightfall, the invaders held Dulag, occupied the turf at the edge of the air strip and straddled Highway 1.

There was now a broad enough beachhead from which to fan out and a shoreline to accommodate an influx of troops and supplies. On October 21, General Yamashita activated *Sho Ichi Go*, Victory Operation Number One. Acting in cooperation with the brother services, Yamashita, as head of the 14th Area Army designated to defend the Philippines, announced a major effort to eliminate the invaders. During the afternoon of that day, however, Yamashita's nemesis, Douglas MacArthur, paid a second visit to Leyte, splashing through shallow water to observe the 1st Cavalry at work. His annoyance over the first day's wet steps to the beach had vanished once the dramatic photographs of the event appeared.

Neither the broadsides issued by the Japanese authorities nor the sonorities of MacArthur meant a spent cartridge to the GIs now struggling inland. The 7th Cavalry Regiment [descendant of the ill-fated outfit commanded by George Armstrong Custer] battled its way into the island capital of Tacloban. The Japanese, embedded in the fifteen-hundred-foot hills that overlooked the town, hiding in buildings and sniping from foxholes, fought tenaciously. It took tanks, artillery, mortars and dismounted cavalrymen to roust the foe. The citizens of Tacloban showered the GIs with gifts of eggs and fruit and vigorously waved the Star Spangled Banner.

All along its front, the 1st Cavalry expanded the American controlled territory. Squadrons from the 8th Regiment drove northward near the shoreline to combine efforts with men from the 7th Cavalry ferried up the coast. Together they secured approaches from across the San Juanico Strait, which lies between Leyte and neighboring Samar where a large garrison of enemy soldiers might seek to reinforce their comrades on Leyte.

These initial 1st Cavalry operations surpassed the projected achievements and were carried out with reasonably small losses. Some of the 24th Division infantrymen to the south struggled against large numbers of determined defenders and unfriendly terrain. After his first night on

Leyte, Paul Austin, F Company commander in the 34th Regiment, had left the safety of his foxhole for a quick look down the road to where Harold Moon took his stand when an enemy machine gun sent him scrambling back to safety.

"I got behind a tree trunk and he just kept pouring bullets into it. I waited until he gave up and then dashed for the foxhole. When I got in there I looked at Cuffney [a replacement lieutenant sharing the space with Austin] and realized there was something wrong with him. 'I'm hit,' he said, 'in my hip here.' He pulled his trousers down and below his hip joint I could see the point of a bullet sticking out of his skin. It seemed to have come all the way through his thigh and ended up on the other side.

" 'We'll get a medic, Cuff, and get you out of here as soon as we can,' I told him. He lay there, not saying anything and he wasn't bleeding. He'd evidently been struck by a ricochet; plenty of them had come off the trees and ground. Medics came and took him away. I laughed as he was leaving and said, 'It's been good knowing you, Cuff.' And he was gone, having been with F Company only a month and after his first night on Leyte. Other fellows went all the way through the war without ever being hit."

Early in the afternoon, Austin and his men headed for their next objective, Hill 331. "We had sent patrols in there and the report was there were no Japs to be found on the ridge. The only way you could get access was by two trails up the side. We had about ten men get to the top when a large force of Japs, maybe an understrength battalion, suddenly came charging over the other side of the ridge. They had timed their attack perfectly. Our men opened up on them but the going was so steep and slow that before we could get enough firepower the Japs were close enough to throw hand grenades and set up a machine gun. There was nothing we could do but pull off that ridge.

"I told the men to fall back, bring the wounded and their weapons. There was a little panic in one of the squads. They kind of ran off and left everybody but by and large the company made a controlled withdrawal under fire. We finally got out of range and dug in for the night. We had four men killed that day, another four or five wounded. Colonel [James] Pearsall [the battalion commander] came over and said, 'Paul, take that hill in the morning and hold it. This time you're going to have artillery fire and you're also going to have an air strike before you go up there.'

"I felt real bad about having to withdraw from that ridge. I felt we had failed. I felt it was my fault. I relied solely on the report of the patrol that reconnoitered the area. With all of our recon ability and intelligence gathering, we should have known how large a force was on the backside. Then we could have saturated the area with artillery and mortar shells, everything we could have thrown at them."

The next morning, following the artillery barrage and the Navy air support, F Company climbed to the summit without a single casualty and settled into position. For the next few days Hill 331 became F Company's home while enemy snipers picked away at them, hitting a machine gun section sergeant between the eyes and wounding several others.

"One of the first details, after the first night on Leyte," says Han Rants, "was to go out and get Moon. One of the lieutenants headed that detail and the guys all knew Moon had twelve hundred bucks on him. The lieutenant took charge of the money and as far as we know, he sent it back to the family. Moon had been shot many times, and they had cut him up with a saber or knives, even after they killed him, out of extreme anger at the number he had killed. Even in their hurry to try and take us, they took time to take out some frustration on him."

Rants says he observed on Leyte the results of GIs' experiences with the enemy. "From our very first contact with Japanese soldiers in New Guinea we saw and felt them violate the very rules of war and of humane treatment of civilians and soldiers. The great majority of enemy soldiers we faced were worse than uncivilized savages or wild beasts seeking to kill. A savage or an animal has some sense of self-preservation or desire to stay alive.

"To the Japanese soldiers we faced, honor and life-ever-after came only from being killed in battle for their god-like emperor. They said they would be forever disgraced and disowned if they returned home without victory. A badly-wounded savage or animal would allow assistance. A wounded Japanese soldier would fake death to sneak a chance to use a grenade or shoot someone before killing himself. We learned quickly that we must go out after each battle and make sure all bodies left were really dead. The best way was to put one more bullet through the head if not sure or to kick them in the testicles.

"Their barbaric torture of civilians and my buddies triggered an anger and hatred in me that resulted in my doing things that are unacceptable in the civilized world. Each of us had to cope with their butchery in our own way but for me vengeance was the answer. It took many years for me to share some of the deeds that I regret so deeply and some will go to my grave with me except for dear war buddies who respected my fighting ability. Absolutely no one can make judgment on a combat soldier's behavior until he/she has lived like a hunted animal in a hole for a year or more.

"Some of us were gold-tooth collectors, and it was helpful to be in the wire section with a good pair of pliers to collect the gold. From the minute when you knew you were going to be killed yourself to the time that it had gone the other way, the GIs were out picking up what they could find." That first morning when his outfit had narrowly escaped annihilation, Rants recalled, "We were all so close to being wiped out. Not much longer than ten seconds later the cleanup that happens in war, which is barbaric but releases anger, began. The live enemy were gone and our guys jumped up, ran out and started picking up sabers, guns, watches, rings, whatever souvenirs were available."

According to Joe Hoffrichter, the only time he heard a policy on Japanese prisoners articulated it involved a desire for intelligence. That required a live prisoner. "Rarely did they surrender," says Hoffrichter. The greatest honor they believed they could attain was to die: first for their Emperor, as they were imbued with the belief that he was Divinity; second, for the honor of their country.

"I think most GIs saw a high degree of bravery and courage in the way the Japanese fought but it was difficult to determine what degree of their courage could be attributed to religion as opposed to patriotism. In view of their mistreatment of our POWs captured at Bataan and Corregidor, the slave labor they brought from Korea and that to their own soldiers, it was often hard to see the Japanese soldiers as humans. Their legendary brutality was impossible to comprehend. The one word that best describes how I viewed them at the time is 'fanatics.' "

"I thought the Japs were good soldiers. I never had the good luck to run up against one who was not," says former platoon leader Bruce Price, with the 19th Infantry Regiment. "We were told that if we took prisoners, we would have to feed them out of our rations, which were not too plentiful in combat. I did not consider them to be inferior humans. They could kill me as well as I could kill them. Headquarters also said, 'If we want prisoners, we will send out units to get them.' "

His B Company atop Hill 522 investigated a tunnel at the end of the trench formerly occupied by Japanese marines. He discovered that the passageway had been engineered with a series of angles that reduced the effectiveness of grenades thrown into it. The defenders had excavated down the slope towards the river and the village of Palo. Price placed a pair of sentries at the mouth of the tunnel and during the night they killed a number of enemy who tried to sneak into the GI positions. For a tense forty-eight hours, he and his associates remained cut off from the main body of the regiment while the enemy jabbed at them and at Palo, now in the hands of Americans.

"On the third and fourth day, after the space between the beach, the hill and Palo was secured, the top of Hill 522 looked like a porcupine. It bristled with antenna from our artillery and naval gun forward observers calling for fire on targets in front of us. With six-inch naval guns firing over our heads I had a moment of concern. If they fired while the ship was rolling down towards the beach they could completely blow away the top of our hill. Then I remembered the automatic gyro control on the guns and ships."

On the extreme left flank of the American forces, the 7th Division fended off tank counterattacks and a *banzai* charge at the apex of its junction with elements from the 96th Division. Both outfits slogged forward, overcoming sporadic to stiff resistance with the terrain among the most formidable of foes.

"The mosquitoes and other animals were awful," says Bob Jackson, the heavy weapons platoon leader for Company A of the 382nd Infantry, 96th Division. "This swampy country was home to leeches and we had all been frightened by the medicos about the liver fluke for which this animal was the host. Our feet were a mess because we dared not take off our boots; we might not get them on again. Most of us had developed fungus—about which the medicos had warned us—but we were unable to take the correct precautions of changing socks. I took off my boots about the fourth day and was shocked at the huge ring-worm-type lesions all over my feet and up my legs. The carefully husbanded foot powder was about as useful as an invocation to the gods."

"Leyte is kind of a soggy place in some areas," remarks George Brooks, a rifleman with the 96th Division's 382nd Regiment. "The water table is very close to the surface. The jungle is very thick with undergrowth so we couldn't see very far either in front or in back of us. Some amphibious tanks came up in our rear, firing their machine guns like crazy. We feared they would overrun us because we couldn't see them and they couldn't see us. Someone must have got in touch with them because finally the shooting stopped."

Bob Seiler, the rifleman and a supplementary ammo bearer for the BAR man with Company K of the 382nd Regiment, recalls, "On the second or third day we woke up to find most of our rifles were rusted and we had trouble freeing them. We changed to Jap oil and never had that problem again. The BAR ammo clips stood up very well in the terrible conditions but they were awfully heavy to carry and hurt like hell when you had to jump for cover.

"Supplies of food and water were nonexistent the first few days because nothing could move through the swamp we were passing through. Water was always in short supply. We got it about once a day but it was always close to a hundred degrees every day and water didn't last long enough. One day we passed through some very high co-gon grass and I passed out because there was no air to breathe. When I came to, my old buddy Horowitz was using his water to revive me. And water was scarce. I used my Halazone tablets [for water purification] every day. We would shoot holes in coconuts and drink the juice. Chewing on a piece of sugarcane helped.

"It seemed like it rained every night, and one night we had a typhoon. That time you had to bail out your foxhole to keep from drowning. I cut some banana leaves to cover myself, thinking I would stay a little dryer, but nothing helped. You just took for granted you were going to be wet all night. Some nights it felt rather cold and your teeth would chatter. I would think maybe I'll catch pneumonia and get sent back but I couldn't even catch a cold.

"At first we went without food for days. The first thing we got came from a small observation plane dropping something like dog biscuits and salt tablets. We had to take atabrine tablets [anti-malarial drug] every day and we were all yellow and had dysentery.

"Looking back, I think the Japs were more afraid of me than I of them. Either that, or their plans were just to slow us down. Very few times did they stand up and fight. Once or twice we had *banzai* attacks but they lasted only a short time. We were asked to try and get some prisoners but we all felt the only good Japs were dead Japs. I was always fearful that the wounded or dead were booby-trapped and would rather put another round in them to be sure. Because I was cautious about booby traps, I never picked up any souvenirs. Also, because I was on the line every day, what would I do with them? We carried as little as possible, even throwing away our knives and forks, just keeping our spoons."

In the late afternoon of their third day on Leyte, the 382nd Regiment squooshed through several swamps and encountered enemy positions around dusk. Mortar shells crumped among the GIs. Shrapnel struck a pair of sergeants in their arms and after first aid they hiked back for additional medical treatment. George Brooks remembers the sudden outburst of explosions. "We hit the ground, but my buddy Frank Brown and I got hit anyway. It must have been a tree burst because the shrapnel came down on us from above. It tore a piece out of my helmet and carried it into my left shoulder. Frank was hit in the thigh of his leg and it made quite a large hole. Our medic, Vaughn Luebee, took care of Frank and I found another medic to patch up my shoulder and back.

"The noise from the explosion was so loud I couldn't hear for a while but that cleared up shortly. They took us back to the aid station where we waited for transportation to the beach since we were several miles inland. Finally a guy came with a Weasel, like an amphibious Jeep. Frank and another guy were put on stretchers in the back and two of us who could walk sat in the front with the driver. It was a pitch black night but the driver found his way. We got to the beach, boarded a LCVP which took us out to the hospital ship. There were some terribly wounded guys in that LCVP. One individual lay on a stretcher with part of his scalp blown away. You could see gray matter oozing out. Another man was in a straightjacket. He was writhing, trying to get loose, foaming at the mouth.

"On board ship the medics worked on me to get the shrapnel out of my shoulder and back. The doctor pulled one large piece of metal out and dropped it on the table. He said I could use it as a watch fob. It looked like a piece of my helmet that had been carried into the wound. Some shrapnel went in so deep, he couldn't get it out. I still have pieces in me, some buried in the bones of my shoulder joint.

"Afterwards I went up and located Frank Brown. He was very concerned about losing his leg. He said they had given him seven pints of plasma, and the doctor who operated on him gave him a transfusion from his own arm while doing the surgery. I looked up the doctor to find out if they had to remove the leg and he told me no. I went back and told Frank to ease his mind. Then I sat down and wrote V-mail letters to his wife and one to my parents. They received them before they got the telegrams from the Army and were grateful for that.

"Frank was later sent back to the States because his wound included some serious nerve damage. We [on the hospital ship] only stayed at Leyte about another day and then had to hoist anchor and move out. The Jap fleet was closing in."

"About the fourth day after the landing," says Bob Jackson, "in the morning we were shaking ourselves out of another night in watery slit trenches and we retained the fear of being cut off. While I brushed my teeth—isn't it wonderful how we hang on to civilization—one of my light machine gunners arose from his slit trench and shook himself like a dog. His fatigues were as wet and stuck to him as if he'd jumped into a swimming pool.

"His mistake had been to dig in where there was a spring and he was unable to move under the night discipline of the perimeter defense. We were kidding him when we heard airplanes and saw two P-38s banking over our heads; what a gorgeous sight! Literally, a cheer went up.

We knew that we had air cover and that the airstrip at Tacloban was secure. Further, it implied that being cut off was no longer a danger."

The possibility of being cut off, which Bob Jackson now believed was over, actually was now approaching a climax. But like Jackson, even the top brass did not realize it. The area seized by the invaders of White Beach, its flank protected by the 24th Division on Red Beach to the south, enabled MacArthur to disembark from his floating command center on the *Nashville* and set up headquarters in Tacloban. The Navy was delighted to be relieved of the Supreme Commander's presence, for his departure freed up the *Nashville,* at a moment when every ship was needed.

CHAPTER XIX

THE BATTLE OF LEYTE GULF

ATOP HILL 331, Paul Austin says, "We could turn around and see the entire Leyte Gulf, the San Pedro Beach, all of the shoreline practically from the Tacloban airfield way down to Hill 522 [held by the 19th Regiment] near Palo. We could see all the ships in the armada that brought us there, all the supply ships, sitting out there, hundreds of them.

"On the morning of the third day, we were standing up eating breakfast. I heard a noise overhead and looked up. There were nine Japanese Betty bombers coming directly over us and headed straight for the bay and all of our ships. They were at a pretty low altitude and we could see the rising sun on their wings. Just as I thought they're going to bomb our fleet and there is no way they can be stopped, I heard what sounded like a giant string of firecrackers going off. It came from way up in the air, above the bombers. All of a sudden, each one of those Bettys began to smoke, began to burn. As they glided on towards the beach, one by one they turned belly up, plunged into the ground within the beachhead. Some hit the highways, one went into a long glide after which he guided that plane right into the side of a Liberty ship and exploded."

What Austin and his comrades observed was the overture to the full-scale involvement of the Japanese air and sea forces in Yamashita's proclaimed *Sho Ichi Go,* the victory operation. The focus of the action around Leyte shifted from the efforts by GIs to widen their patch of the island, to Leyte Gulf and the imminent titanic battle involving the opposing navies, land-based Japanese aircraft and the limited U.S. Army Air resources in the area.

On October 24, operating from bases on Luzon, the defenders mounted massive air raids directed at the American Leyte cantonment on land and at sea. As an estimated 150 to 200, mostly twin-engined bombers approached, antiaircraft gunners peppered the skies while U.S. combat air patrols from the carriers at sea and some ground-based Army fighters fell upon the slower-moving, poorly protected foe.

Among the huge armada of American ships participating in the Leyte venture was the *Suwannee,* one of four escort aircraft carriers (CVE) converted from fleet oilers. With a combat history dating back to the landings in North Africa in 1942 and a Pacific presence that eventually included a dozen island campaigns, the *Suwannee* served as home for Air Group 60, equipped with both torpedo/bombers and Grumman Hellcat fighters.

Roy (Tex) Garner, who flew one of the latter, came aboard the *Suwannee* after an incident while assigned to the *Hornet.* "They had issued me a .45 automatic with a box of shells. Even though the first time I picked up the .45 I shot four rounds, hit four bull's-eyes and qualified, I wasn't comfortable with it. I knew I'd have to practice up if I was ever going to defend myself with it. At the crack of dawn on the island of Hawaii, I went out the Bachelor Officers Quarters, walked out to the trees and saw a bunch of coconuts. I wanted to see if I could hit them. I began to fire at them at about 5:00 A.M. I got about half a clip out and I was surrounded by Marines. I was taken to the commandant. I told him I'm here to fight a war; they gave me a pistol and I wanted to see if I could hit anything with it. That didn't go over very well and he released me to my air group CO. I knew I wasn't going to do well in that group because they had a surplus of pilots. I thought it would be wise to move on and got to the *Suwannee*.

"*Suwannee* was much smaller than the *Hornet* and we took mostly catapult shots off it, maybe ninety-nine percent were cat shots because of the extreme loads we carried and the very low wind condition over the deck. But it was an excellent ship. We started supporting the troops, first for me was Tarawa, then Eniwetok, Kwajalein, Guam. Ground personnel were highly appreciated. They respected our efforts because we bore right in there. We would come in and work an island over for about a week before a landing, become familiar with the terrain, know how to lay our ordnance in to do the most good, destroy as much of the gun emplacements as we could, and then keep the air clean of planes.

"With the Wildcat [earlier Grumman Navy fighter] we were out-airplaned and we knew it real bad. We could not dogfight with the Zero which was top dog in the South Pacific at that time. It had tremendous range for nine hundred horses, good speed and a lot of maneuverability. They sacrificed self-sealing gas tanks. Their planes exploded more easily and the pilots didn't carry parachutes when we first started. I saw only one during the entire time I was in the Navy. They sacrificed armor plating for the pilots and armor protection for the engines. We had all that in the Wildcat but the added weight meant we could not turn with the Zero's sharpness but we could get him in a dive. Then the Hellcat came and it was fantastic. We knew we could go against the Zero. We were not fighting from an underdog position as in the past.

"The Japanese pilots, as far as I am concerned, when we first saw them were very good. They were seasoned, had been in China. As the war went along, those men were thinned out and the quality of Japanese pilots deteriorated fast. By the same token, ours were getting stronger all the time. Every carrier and air group had some fantastic people in it. But our being together for thirteen months was an opportunity for camaraderie most carrier pilots never get."

On October 24, Garner, who had knocked down his first enemy, a twin engine "Lilly," a month before the *Suwannee* came to Leyte, flew in a four-plane pre-dawn patrol. He recalls, "We had been on station about four hours and were ready to return to the *Suwannee*. A radio reported, 'Tally Ho. Eight bombers at ten o'clock heading towards Leyte.' I swept the sky and spotted a formation of Lilly bombers [fast, twin-engine aircraft]. I Tally Ho'd them. We dropped our empty belly tanks and climbed to intercept them.

"Lip Singleton and I set up one line of the formation while Edgar Barber and Ralph Kalal set up on the other wing of the Vee. We all rolled in at the same time. It was perfectly coordinated and four Lillies were knocked down on the first pass. Each pilot had a bull's-eye.

"After that run we whipped the Hellcats around for another target and for an instant all four fighters had the same bomber and fired at him—so long Lilly. All four scrambled for another bomber. Lip burned one, Kal exploded one and the last bomber pushed over, hellbent for our landing ships. I called on my Hellcat to give her all, closing very slowly. I was trying to get to him before he got to the fleet because there was no way he would miss 'em. I began to realize some of our AA were trying for him too. I either had to break off or go for him into our ships' AA.

"I bore in firing all six .50 caliber guns. He began to smoke. I noticed the bomb bay doors open. There was no way he should have done that because that slowed him down enough for me to catch him. I closed to within four feet. I thought I'd ram him. I came across from his left engine, left wing spar, cockpit, right spar, right engine. On the sweep back as I crossed the cockpit area, I saw like an accordion door open and the pilot appeared. The six guns cut him in half. The plane exploded with the bombs still on board.

"I knew I was in a tight spot with all those ships still firing and if I pulled up I was a dead man. I pushed over, leveled off at about eighteen inches off the water and went zigging through the ships like a scared rabbit, hunkered down behind the armor plating and praying. I was amazed when I reached the other side, wringing wet but still alive, with eighteen holes and nothing serious."

For the Japanese air arm, the first day of the Battle of Leyte Gulf was catastrophic. Sixty-six planes were definitely shot down with eighteen probable kills. Three U.S. aircraft crash-landed—two on the Tacloban strip and one in the water. The ability of Imperial High Command to threaten the U.S. fleet from the air was seriously impaired.

Notwithstanding this weakness, elements of the Japanese Navy hastened towards the area, threatening to sever the lifelines of those ashore on Leyte and to open up easy access for tens of thousands of defensive reinforcements from elsewhere in the islands. Short on seaborne aircraft, the Imperial Navy mustered seven battleships, including two that were bigger, faster and mounted larger guns than anything in the U.S. Navy arsenal, and thirteen heavy cruisers as well as destroyers. If the massive firepower of these ships could be brought to bear upon the Americans, the Japanese believed they could destroy a significant amount of the enemy's surface sea strength.

The grand strategy devised by the Imperial Navy called for its forces to be divided into three fleets. Vice Adm. Jisaburo Ozawa, head of the Northern Force, commanded a convoy dominated by a pair of old carriers half-converted for aircraft operations, several legitimate carriers for whom few planes or pilots were available, and a batch of cruisers and destroyers. The Ozawa group, approaching from the north, would be a decoy to lure the strongest of the U.S. forces, Adm. William Halsey's 3rd Fleet, most notable for its mighty carriers and concentration on air operations.

Meanwhile, Vice Adm. Takeo Kurita, in charge of the First Striking Force, guided the principal armada towards Leyte Gulf. Most of the battleships and heavy cruisers sailed under Kurita's banner. Passage to Leyte began after fueling operations in North Borneo. Kurita's ships, divided into sections, followed a circuitous route to avoid submarines, threading through the Philippine waters of the Subuyan Sea to enter the San Bernardino Strait and then Leyte Gulf.

A smaller complement of ships designated as the Southern Force sailed under the flag of Vice Adm. Shoji Nishimura. The van of this group included two battleships, a heavy cruiser and destroyers. Another aggregation under Vice Adm. Kiyohide Shima, comprised of three cruisers and nine destroyers, trailed Nishimura, departing from Formosa to add its weight to the offensive planned for Leyte Gulf.

There would be one further weapon hurled at the Americans, the *kamikaze*. By the autumn of 1944, the Japanese admirals charged with waging the naval air war against the onrushing Allies, recognized what Tex Garner had noticed: they were no longer a match for their adversaries in either pilots or planes. Desperate to reverse the tide or at least inflict severe enough losses to cause a standoff—or obtain better surrender terms—Vice Adm. Takajiro Onishi of the 1st Air Fleet called for volunteers to act as suicide pilots. By crashing their bomb-laden planes into ships they could do far more certain damage than through conventional raids. The first *kamikaze* corps had entered a training phase October 19, a few days prior to the start of the great victory operation.

As A-Day unfolded, the American admirals, for their part, did not expect an onslaught in the vicinity of Leyte. Once again the divisions of command created possibly serious consequences. The Leyte campaign involved the 7th and 3rd Fleets, two separate organizations. Vice Adm. Thomas Kincaid headed the 7th Fleet, the organization responsible for landing and supporting the invasion force, and he reported to MacArthur. Flotillas of troop and supply ships, dozens of destroyers, a handful of battleships, escort carriers like Garner's *Suwannee* and support vessels comprised the 7th Fleet.

The 3rd Fleet of Bull Halsey, air-oriented, consisted of

the Fast Carrier Force under Vice Adm. Marc Mitscher to which was assigned most of the Navy's big carriers, plus some cruisers, destroyer screens and support ships. Halsey came under the command of Admiral Nimitz and felt little obligation towards the 7th Fleet. "Its mission was defensive," said Halsey. "It had bombarded the beaches, convoyed the transports to the landing area, and stood by to guard them while they unloaded and then retired.

"My mission was offensive. When I received orders to cover the Leyte landings my mission did not change. It was still offensive. The tasks assigned my force were to gain air supremacy over the Philippines, to protect the landings and to maintain unremitting pressure against Japan . . . Finally, should opportunity for destruction of a major portion of the enemy fleet offer, such destruction would become the primary task of my forces."

Indeed, Adm. Raymond Spruance had been severely criticized for hanging about the Marianas to protect invading Marines rather than aggressively pursuing enemy naval forces. After the success of the Leyte landings, Halsey was confident that he had some breathing time and he sent a portion of his fleet back to Ulithi for provisioning and rearming.

Submarines attached to both fleets prowled the sea lanes searching for any enemy naval reaction to the invasion. At the helm of the *Darter* was Comdr. David McClintock, at one time a young submarine officer aboard the *Plunger* headed from the States to Pearl Harbor on December 7, 1941. "On the ninth," said McClintock, "we entered Pearl. We had heard a San Francisco broadcast reporting a battleship sunk. That's all we knew. Many of the crew had big bets that it was all a drill.

"The *Plunger* stood up the channel [at Pearl] first. The channel was choked with fuel oil. The *Nevada*, partially sunk, came into view just short of the turn near Ford Island. The division commander said, 'Well, guess they had to get one.' Next the ruins of Ford Island hangar were sighted. Then around the turn—no one said anything for at least a minute gazing with awe at the sunken battleships. Then from the division commander, 'The whole damn battle line! They got the whole damn battle line!' The *Arizona* was still smoldering. We could hardly believe our eyes."

Following a series of voyages aboard subs, McClintock assumed the con of the *Darter* for her final two patrols. On October 10, 1944, *Darter* and *Dace*, under Comdr. Bladen Clagget, formed a two-ship wolfpack with McClintock in charge. Alerted to the invasion on October 20, the pair roamed the Balabac Strait, the shortest route for the Japanese fleet from Singapore to Leyte. Some radar signals indicated possible enemy ships but these had vanished from the screens after several hours of pursuit.

A few minutes into October 23, after a rendezvous to communicate with *Dace* by megaphone, McClintock received word from his conning tower, "Radar contact— thirty thousand yards—contact doubtful—probably rain." McClintock said, "*The Jap Fleet* was what flashed through my mind. Almost immediately the radar operator stated the contact was ships. *Dace* was given the range and bearing by megaphone. The partner sub replied, 'Let's go get them.' By twenty minutes after midnight both *Darter* and *Dace* were chasing the contact at full power. The ships were in Palawan Passage, headed north.

"It was now apparent that we had not a convoy, but a large task force, which we assumed was headed for Leyte to interfere with our landing. Three contact reports were sent—the final one estimating that the force included at least eleven heavy ships. I decided we should not attack before dawn, considering it vital to see and identify the force.

"The left flank column, nearest us, consisted of five heavy ships, the last gave by far the largest radar pip. Probably a battleship. There may have been more ships in this column but at the long range at which we were tracking and the probably close formation this is all that showed up on the radar screen. I picked this column for *Darter*'s target, hoping for a crack at what we thought was a battleship. *Dace*, trailing us very closely, was assigned to the starboard column. We planned a periscope attack at dawn.

"At about 0430 all hands were called for coffee before the expected attack. At about ten minutes before five we manned battle stations and ten minutes after five we reversed course, headed down the throat of the column. It was getting faintly light in the east. There wasn't a cloud in the sky. In twenty minutes we wanted to shoot.

"The first periscope look showed a huge gray shape. It was the whole column seen bows on. A look to the southeast where the light was better showed battleships, cruisers and destroyers. The gray ships kept getting larger. We would pass on almost parallel courses. At 5:25 the first ships in the column could be identified as heavy cruisers, with huge bow waves. There were sighs of disappointment through the conning tower that the targets weren't all battleships. A beautiful sight, anyway. We could imagine the Japs at general quarters, watertight doors closed, officers in white pacing the bridge. I hoped the lead ship would be the flag ship. At 5:27 the range to the leading cruiser was under three thousand yards. All tubes were ready.

"Then the column zigged west to give a perfect torpedo range of just under a thousand yards. Their profiles could be seen clearly—*Atago* [class] cruisers. I had the 'scope up for what seemed like several minutes, watching. The leading cruiser looked huge now. She had a bone in her teeth. The forward slant of her bridge seemed to accentuate her speed. [It was] the *Atago* [with Admiral Kurita aboard], my favorite target on the attack teacher. Estimating the angles on the bow off her flat bridge face was easy; I had done that many times before on models."

The range dropped further and McClintock called out instructions with a final, "FIRE ONE!" He unloosed five more forward fish as a searchlight on the cruiser flickered signals. "Did she see our torpedoes," wondered McClintock. "She was going by now. No, she wasn't zigging!

" 'Shift targets to second cruiser . . . bearing mark . . . Give me a range, give me a range,' yelled the torpedo officer." Finally accommodated with the requisite data, the stern torpedoes left the *Darter*. As they did, the sub rocked from heavy explosions.

"Depth charges!" exclaimed the exec officer. "Depth charges, hell . . . torpedoes!" McClintock responded. Another officer, jumping up and down with each explosion, shouted, "Christ, we're hitting 'em, we're hitting 'em!"

Recalled McClintock, "After the tenth torpedo was on its way, I swung the periscope back to the first target which had been hit with five of the bow torpedoes. She was belching flame from the base of the forward turret to the stern; the dense black smoke of burning oil covered her from forward turret to stern. She was still plowing ahead, but she was also going down by the bow. Number one turret was cutting the water. She was finished."

McClintock knew for certain he had sunk one vessel and probably another. The crew of *Darter* had little time to exult as the enemy destroyers attacked with depth charges. But deep below the surface, the sub escaped damage. The *Atago* went down within eighteen minutes, carrying 360 of the crew to their deaths. A Japanese destroyer plucked survivors, including Admiral Kurita, from the water.

Lt. Comdr. R. C. Benitez, the executive officer aboard *Dace*, remembered the moments leading up to the attack upon the huge enemy fleet. "It was David and Goliath once more, for against that force we could muster only two submarines. The odds were not exactly even but we were more than willing to take the chance. None of us would have traded places with any other man in the Submarine Force. As the night approached its end, however, tension heightened. The jokes became fewer and fewer as the conversation gradually died out. Each man was busy with his own thoughts as the ship crept closer and closer to its attack position. At 0500 the word was passed to man battle stations. It was a useless command. During the night, the men had slowly gravitated to their stations and in a matter of seconds each man was reported at his appointed place.

"A faint glow to the east heralded the approach of dawn as the radar man at 0510 reported the *Darter* disappearing from the radar scope. She had submerged. We continued northward, feeling alone and naked."

Under the surface now, Benitez's sub stalked its target even as its companion fired its torpedoes. According to Benitez, Clagget, the *Dace* commander, watched the results through the periscope and reported, "It looks like the Fourth of July out there. One is burning. The Japs are milling and firing all over the place. What a show! What a show!"

Within minutes, Clagget selected his prey, picking out the biggest ship in the line, another heavy cruiser. *Dace* sent off six missiles from its forward tubes and four found the mark.

"The offensive phase was over," said Benitez. "Now it was time to start running and we wasted no time in doing so. On our way down, a crackling noise that started very faintly but which rapidly reached staggering proportions soon enveloped us. It was akin to the noise made by cellophane when it is crumpled. Those of us experienced in submarine warfare knew that a ship was breaking up, but the noise was so loud, so gruesome that we came to believe that it was not the Jap but the *Dace* that was doomed."

A quick check discovered the sub intact but then a new fear developed, that the enemy vessel's wreckage would drop upon the *Dace*. But as the noise subsided, that worry vanished only to be replaced by a genuine menace. A string of depth charges announced the presence of Japanese destroyers. "They were going off all around us," said Benitez, "and they were close. The boat was being rocked considerably. Light bulbs were being shattered; locker doors were flying open; wrenches were falling from the manifolds. The Japs were very mad—and we were scared."

Like *Darter, Dace* also escaped. The pair discovered the cruiser wounded by *Darter* limping away and laid plans to finish her off at night when the destroyers shepherding the stricken ship would be less of a threat. Approaching midnight, and racing along at seventeen knots to get into position, McClintock figured he could administer the *coup de grace* within an hour.

Suddenly, in the early hours of October 24, the hunter turned victim. "We hit a shoal," said McClintock. "The officer of the deck and myself were on the bridge, and he and I thought we were gone. I thought we had been torpedoed. I watched the stern go under water, as far as the engine room hatch. We seemed to be going down quite rapidly. Then the stern rode on up, and after several seconds we came to rest high and dry.

"The navigator came running to the bridge. I said, 'We are aground.' He disappeared into the conning tower apparently to check the chart. Very shortly thereafter he was back up on the bridge. 'Captain, it can't be that we are aground. The nearest land is nineteen miles away.' "

Maps notwithstanding, *Darter* was hung up on a reef. With high tide approaching in an hour and a half, the crew frantically sought to lighten the sub. The gunner's mates jettisoned all ammunition except for a few rounds to stave off a destroyer observed on radar. They dumped commissary provisions, fuel oil and fresh water, then attempted to free the boat. But *Darter* remained firmly stuck. The tops of the screws churned air, not water.

Aware of a Japanese airfield less than a hundred miles away, McClintock decided he would have to abandon ship before dawn. He requested *Dace* to cease efforts to finish the stricken cruiser and to retrieve his crew. Waiting for rescue, the sailors began to destroy machinery, radios, radar and other gear, set fire to publications and documents. McClintock pondered what souvenir suited him and settled for an ashtray with *Darter* engraved on it.

With only two six-man rubber life boats available, Benitez on the *Dace* said the transfer of men began at 0200 and took until 0439 before the captain of the *Darter*, the last man to leave the ship, appeared at the side of *Dace*. Before he boarded the life raft, McClintock checked a demolition time clock in the control room of his doomed vessel. From *Dace*, he heard a series of five small explosions, none of which seemed to have fractured the *Darter* hull. *Dace* expended its last four torpedoes attempting to sink *Darter*, but every one of them hit the reef rather than the grounded sub. The sister vessel's gun crew fired twenty-one rounds at *Darter* with its deck gun, but to no avail. When a lookout reported an enemy plane approaching, *Dace* dropped below the surface and headed away from the scene.

To McClintock, the finish of the adventure must have seemed ignominious. Nevertheless, the two-sub wolfpack deprived Admiral Kurita of three major ships-of-the-line and also provided the 7th and 3rd Fleets with vital intelligence on the deployment of enemy naval forces.

Halsey immediately recalled the units steaming towards Ulithi and dispatched search teams to locate the armada discovered by the submarines. On the morning of October 24, planes combing the area west of Luzon and Leyte spied the Japanese flotilla bearing down on the Tablas Strait on a presumed course for the Leyte vicinity. The 3rd Fleet commander directed three of his fast carrier groups into attack positions.

Limited as their resources were, the Japanese threw the first punches even as Halsey's subordinates maneuvered their carriers. From Luzon, enemy bombers and torpedo planes went after Task Group 3, which included the big carriers *Essex* and *Lexington* and two lighter ones, *Princeton* and *Langley*.

Hellcats from these four carriers met the enemy and downed most of them. One pilot, Comdr. David McCampbell of the *Essex*, alone knocked down nine, an all-time record for carrier-based fighters. However, in another attack, a lone bomber, hidden by cloud cover, suddenly emerged in perfect position to plant a 550-pounder on the *Princeton*'s flight deck. The bomb crashed through the thin skin of the deck before exploding deep in the ship's innards. The blast ignited gasoline stores, then set off a series of torpedoes on planes sitting in the hangar deck. Damage-control crews on the *Princeton* and from other ships that lent assistance fought valiantly to squelch the inferno. Further detonations from the ship's own munitions not only doomed the *Princeton* but wrought heavy casualties aboard the *Birmingham*, a cruiser trying to serve as a tugboat. A useless hulk, the *Princeton* stubbornly refused to sink. American torpedoes finally scuttled the ship.

Although the *Princeton* succumbed, the 3rd Fleet now exacted some revenge. On October 23, before *Darter* and *Dace* discovered the Japanese ships, the task groups under Halsey had refueled and held gunnery practice. Lt. Bill Anderson, Jr., a torpedo/bomber pilot, was pulling one of the targets. "Suddenly," remembers Anderson, "all three task groups made a 180-degree turn. Their wakes became white streaks; the battleships moved out front at flank speed. They were heading somewhere in a hurry. We all got orders to return to our ships."

In Anderson's case that was the *Cabot*, a light carrier with Air Group 29, a composite unit that included nine torpedo/bombers and twenty-one fighters. Anderson, a native of Westerly, Rhode Island, was a fortunate youth in the Great Depression because his electrician father and his mother both found work at the local power company. He had studied chemical engineering for two years at the state university when a naval aviation recruiting team came to the school in June 1941. "They put on a good show," says Anderson, "promised us wings of gold and furthermore if you did your four years of service you would get the large sum of five hundred dollars for each year in the Navy when you went back to college."

He was already undergoing flight training in Florida at the time of Pearl Harbor. With those seductive wings pinned on, Anderson first faced an enemy when posted off the coast of North Africa as a pilot based on the *Santee*, a converted oiler from the same class as Tex Garner's *Suwannee*. "There was very little resistance by the French in North Africa," says Anderson, "we had not much to do."

For two full years the *Santee,* with Anderson as one of its fliers, worked antisubmarine warfare. "Each torpedo/bomber was accompanied by a fighter which was expected to deal with a gun crew on a submarine if one surfaced. We carried depth charges. But we never saw a submarine on the surface nor attacked one underwater."

From ASW duty, Anderson went to Hyannis on Cape Cod for intensive schooling in torpedoes. "We dropped them daily, learning the right speed and altitude, how to drop them hot, straight and normal. A freighter grounded in Cape Cod Bay acted as the target and we used cement replicas of torpedoes; cameras showed how we did."

Air Group 29 replaced Air Group 31 on the *Cabot* during the first week of October 1944. Anderson had been in the air off Formosa, but Leyte Gulf would be his first chance to strike a serious blow at the enemy. "There were five of us from the torpedo squadron who took off the next morning [October 24]. Our commander was Irvin McPherson, an experienced pilot who occasionally did odd things. For example, he always flew wearing leather bedroom slippers because he said if was shot down in the water and he had to swim for it, he did not want to be burdened with flying boots." Also on the mission was exec John Williams, and two of Anderson's good friends, Howard Skidmore and John Ballantine.

"Somehow we became separated from McPherson and Williams and we never saw them when we reached the Japanese fleet or on the way back. Williams was shot down and rescued but he never rejoined the squadron. The three of us came over the Japanese fleet at about fifteen thousand feet. We circled them looking for a target and we started down. Our Hyannis training kicked in. I automatically adjusted speed and altitude. The ideal was at about 270 knots and an altitude between 150 and 300 feet. The only way you could get that kind of speed in a TBM was through a steep dive at full power and when you leveled off you might be at about 315 mph. You would rapidly slow down but if you could pick up your aiming point and drop the torpedo from 300 feet up, chances were for a good torpedo entrance. It was a fairly restricted envelope in which to work. You also had to have wings level, not nose up or down, when you released or else the torpedo might not have the proper attitude when it hit the water.

"The torpedoes were armed through two wires. One wire ignited a mixture of alcohol and water to provide the steam that drove the torpedo. The other was for a fuse in the nose which activated the exploder. It needed a run of five hundred feet to fully arm the torpedo."

At Leyte Gulf, Anderson picked out a battleship and started his attack. "There were bursts of antiaircraft fire all around but not close enough to rattle anything in the aircraft. We lost sight of our other planes. The Japanese fleet started evasive maneuvers and it was necessary for me to pass over the battleship and pick up a cruiser target on the other side. They were shooting at us with their major caliber weapons. A sixteen-inch shell is not a proper weapon against aircraft; the chances of being hit are like those of being struck by a lightning bolt. They did throw up geysers of water and you'd turn so as not to be hit with falling water. The water would be full of color (from the exploding shell); the Japanese did this in order to tell how close they came.

"We got in pretty close, straight and low, opened the bomb bay doors and picked off the torpedo. Any torpedo pilot who says he saw where it went after he dropped it is probably dreaming because after you fire it you're so busy making a hard turn to get out of there you can't stop to look over your shoulder. My gunner, Richard Hanlon, said he saw it drop and head for the cruiser before he lost sight of it. The radioman, Joe Haggerty, said he saw it hit the cruiser. I was credited with having hit the cruiser and got a Navy Cross but I'd be hard-pressed to swear to the fact."

Anderson and the others from Air Group 29 were part of wave after wave of Hellcats, Helldivers and Avengers from Task Group 38.2 who sortied across Leyte and against a fleet bereft of air cover. Shot and shell from every gun on the Japanese ships, including the main batteries of the mighty battleships, ripped the air but managed to down just eighteen of the several hundred aircraft buzzing about the targets.

Howard Skidmore, one of the other torpedo plane pilots, made a run on the lead battleship. He dropped his "fish" and then flew through a rodomontade of flying metal. A direct hit on one side of the plane carved a hole large enough to make visible the ocean below; a path marked by tracer bullets intercepted him as he rose into the sky. In the crackle of voices over the radio, Skidmore heard someone report a TBM afire. Because he did not smell smoke, Skidmore assumed it was someone else's problem. (Forty years later he learned from his gunner, Don Hambidge, that it was his ship.) At the moment, however, Hambidge told the pilot that their radioman, Danny McCarthy, was wounded. A shell from one of the battleships had sprayed him with fragments. Under these circumstances, Skidmore received priority to land on the *Cabot*. Almost blinded by leaking oil on his windshield, Skidmore barely managed to set down without smashing into a catwalk.

Like Anderson, Skidmore could not be sure which ship, if any, his torpedo reached. But on the afternoon of October 24, *Musashi*, one of the two biggest dreadnoughts, reeled under a crushing nineteen torpedoes and seventeen bomb blasts. When she finally rolled over and sank, *Musashi* carried more than 1,000 of the 2,300-man crew to watery graves. The attackers also scratched another cruiser and inflicted minor damage on three other battlewagons.

Still powerful with his galaxy of battleships, cruisers and destroyers, Admiral Kurita temporarily halted his voyage towards Leyte in hopes that forays of land-based aircraft might drive off the American carriers or protect his fleet from the deadly stings of the American planes. Unfortunately, there were no planes available to support Kurita. Urged on by his superior who assured "divine guidance," Kurita's fleet again steamed towards the San Bernardino Strait. His plan was to swing his massive firepower around the northern tip of Samar and then into Leyte Gulf to confront the less heavily gunned U.S. 7th Fleet. The hours wasted while Kurita's fleet dallied eliminated any hope the Center and Southern Forces could rendezvous at the appointed hour in Leyte Gulf, to form a kind of nutcracker enveloping the 7th Fleet. Admiral Nishimura, in command of the Southern Forces, also wavered momentarily after air strikes against him, but shook off the minor destruction and plowed on.

Meanwhile, Admiral Ozawa to the north artfully coaxed Halsey to chase him. He issued radio messages, hoping American intelligence would intercept them. He wandered around the Pacific Ocean off Luzon, dangling his ships out in the open to tempt a prying spyplane. He even mounted a seventy-six-plane strike on a group of 3rd Fleet ships. In his hare and hounds game, Ozawa took his carriers away from the area and the Japanese aircraft headed for friendly fields on northern Leyte. Desperate to lure the Americans, Ozawa directed his pair of ships that were half-battleship and half-carrier, the *Ise* and the *Hyuga*, to run south and find the hostile fleet. U.S. planes scouring the area finally spotted the pair around 4:00 P.M. on October 24. Other searchers located the main carriers an hour later; the fish lunged for the hook.

Halsey was an eager candidate for the bait. He knew the enemy retained a formidable number of aircraft carriers and he salivated for an opportunity to attack them. Although Halsey always insisted the 7th Fleet possessed ample weapons to handle an enemy fleet like Kurita's, he seemingly took steps to ensure that if the 3rd Fleet left the area, adequate reinforcements for the 7th Fleet would be on hand if needed. He had created Task Force 34, replete with battleships and cruisers, for such a purpose. But it was a paper organization and not specifically charged with responsibility for guarding the San Bernardino Strait. Activation required an order from Halsey.

Critical intelligence errors added to Halsey's misperception. The aviators returning from their missions against Kurita's Center Force exaggerated their successes. Halsey claimed he was told, "At least four and probably five battleships torpedoed and bombed, one probably sunk; a minimum of three heavy cruisers torpedoed and others bombed; one light cruiser sunk, one destroyer probably sunk and four damaged . . . Reports indicated beyond doubt that the Center Force had been badly mauled with all of its battleships and most of its heavy cruisers tremendously reduced in fighting power and life." The first information from returning pilots advised that Kurita's fleet was moving west, away from Leyte Gulf.

Halsey's information on Ozawa's armada was also faulty. The pilots who flew over the *Ise* and the *Hyuga* mistakenly identified them as full-scale battleships, not realizing that the ships had sacrificed four of their twelve big guns when outfitted to serve as half-battleship and half-carrier. Instead of a fleet with a quartet of dangerous battleships, Ozawa packed much less weight.

The evidence, however, persuaded Halsey to sprint after the retreating Ozawa. Task Force 34 remained a figment so far as the Gulf of Leyte was concerned, for all of its vessels sped north, where the 3rd Fleet planned to blaze away with all its big guns in conjunction with the carrier-launched bombers and torpedo planes. Even after intelligence advised that, contrary to early reports, the Central Force of the Japanese was now heading towards Leyte rather than retreating, the 3rd Fleet command refused to release Task Force 34 to guard the San Bernardino Strait. Actually, even if Halsey had left the task force behind, the rest of the 3rd Fleet still easily overmatched Ozawa's seventeen vessels. Halsey later argued he had not activated Task Force 34 to block the San Bernardino Strait entrance into the Gulf because he considered Kincaid's 7th Fleet strong enough to deal with any interlopers.

Aware of Admiral Nishimura's Southern Force, divided into two sections and picking its way through the archipelago via Mindoro and then towards the Surigao Strait between southern Leyte and Mindanao, but ignorant of the gaping hole of the San Bernardino Strait in their Leyte Gulf line, the 7th Fleet strategists plotted a devastating reception for Nishimura's forces.

Kincaid ordered Vice Adm. Jesse Oldendorf to deploy the U.S. ships in preparation for a night engagement. Oldendorf had six battleships, four heavy cruisers, four light ones and almost thirty destroyers at his disposal. Included in the mix were a pair of Australian Navy ships. Oldendorf's forces far outnumbered and outgunned anything that Admiral Nishimura could bring to bear. The grand assortment of ships-of-the-line formed a stately procession, steaming back and forth across the Surigao Strait mouth, a scant twelve miles in width.

At the southern end of the Strait, where the enemy would enter, Oldendorf stationed a flotilla of forty-five PT boats that would detect the arrival of the enemy and then harass them with torpedo runs. In the absence of night-flying, radar-equipped planes, the PTs became the Navy eyes when darkness fell.

As a gunnery officer, James L. Holloway III was aboard the *Bennion,* a destroyer attached to the left flank of the American screen. "At sunset, we had set Condition One, and we could overhear on the TBS [Talk Between Ships, a voice radio] the tactical commands and reports among our own ships as we waited tensely for the enemy during this dark and squally evening. By midnight we began to think that the Japanese would disappoint us and a general relaxing was perceptible.

"Suddenly, at about 0200 over the TBS [official accounts place the contact with the enemy fleet several hours earlier] we heard the PT boats, reconnoitering in the southern strait, excitedly call out, 'I've got a big one in sight!' then a pause and 'My God, there are two more big ones, and maybe another.' Suddenly the TBS became alive

as the 'Martinis'—that was the call sign for the PT boats—
got ready for their torpedo attacks."

In the hit and run melees that lit up the Strait with
gunfire, searchlights (from the Japanese ships) and exploding shells, the PTs unloosed thirty-four fish. Only one
struck home, wounding the cruiser *Abukuma*. Nishimura
kept coming while the gun crews under Oldendorf readied
their weapons.

Blessed with ample warning, the Americans fretted only
over a shortage of the proper ammunition. Because the
original mission called for shore bombardment, the magazines were stocked mainly with high-explosive shells rather
than armor-piercing projectiles required for damage
against the thick plate on enemy battlewagons and cruisers.
To increase effectiveness, the tacticians decided that the
main battle line, with its fourteen- and sixteen-inch guns,
would hold their fire until they closed within seventeen
thousand to twenty thousand yards, a trade-off that put
them within easy range of hostile batteries. Also on the
scarce side were torpedoes for the destroyers.

Gunnery officer Holloway thought that the Japanese
might retreat after the Martinis' attack, but soon the enemy force showed up on his ship's radar, advancing at
twenty-five-knot speed. As the Japanese ships emerged
from the Strait, the American destroyers responded by
charging towards them, pouring out black smoke as they
cut through the water at thirty knots.

"From my battle station [in the fire control director] I
had a view of the whole scene from the panorama of the
two fleets to a close-up of the Japanese ships through the
high-powered lenses of the MK 37 director. As our destroyers started the run to the south, we were immediately
taken under fire. It was an eerie experience to be rushing
through the dark towards the enemy at a relative speed of
fifty knots, not firing our guns or hearing the enemy fall of
shot around us. The awesome evidence of the Japanese
gunfire were the towering columns of water from the
splashes of their fourteen- and sixteen-inch shells, some

close enough to wet our weather decks. Star shells hung overhead and the gun flashes from the Japanese battle line illuminated the horizon ahead.

"Oldendorf's battleships and cruisers opened up with their main batteries, and it was a comforting sight. Directly over our heads stretched a procession of tracers from our battle line converging on the head of the Japanese column. I recall being surprised at the apparent slowness of the projectiles. They almost hung in the sky, taking fifteen to twenty seconds in their trajectory before reaching their target. It was a spectacular display. Through the director optics I could clearly see the bursting explosions of our battleships' and cruisers' shells as they hit the Japanese ships, which were now enveloped in flames.

"Our column was headed directly for the lead battleship, the *Yamashiro,* so the division had to turn in a corpen movement for a clear shot, each destroyer launching successively as it executed the turn. As *Bennion* was the second ship in the last element, at a fifty-knot relative speed, our firing point closed rapidly with the Japanese battle line. We started launching our five torpedoes at a range of about seven thousand yards. At this distance, the silhouette of the *Yamashiro* completely filled the viewing glass of the rangefinder optics. [I thought] that looks exactly like a Japanese battleship with its pagoda foremast and then realized that it *was* a Japanese battleship."

In his account of the action, Oldendorf noted, "When our destroyers attacked, they attacked fairly close together and the enemy radar evidently was not very discriminatory as to bearing, so that the two destroyers appeared as one blip on the enemy screen. They fired at the center of the blip which made their shells fall exactly between the attacking destroyers so that none of the destroyers in this attack were hit."

When the tin cans had closed the distance to seventeen thousand yards, Admiral Oldendorf ordered his biggest ships to open fire. He said, "It seemed as if every ship on the flank forces and the battle line opened at once, and there was a semi-circle of fire which landed squarely on one point, the leading battleship. Explosions and fires were immediately noticed.

"The semi-circle of fire evidently so confused the Japanese that they did not seem to know what target to shoot at. I remembered seeing one or two salvos start in the direction of my flagship [the heavy cruiser *Louisville*], but in the excitement of the occasion I forgot to look to see where they landed."

Aboard the *Bennion,* Holloway observed the turmoil. "As we retired to the north in formation at thirty knots, still making max black smoke, explosions erupted close off our port beam. It was one of our destroyers, the *A.W. Grant,* being hit by large-caliber shells. The scene of the action was becoming confused and Oldendorf ordered his battle line to cease fire for concern of hitting our retiring destroyers in the melee."

In fact, Oldendorf noted that after some of his destroyers launched their torpedoes and came under heavy fire from the enemy, the Americans quickly fled directly up the Surigao Strait. Some of the U.S. fleet mistook these friendlies for the foe. "The *Grant* was hit by some of our own six-inch shells from the light cruisers, as well as by shells from the Japanese ships."

With his smaller ships racing out of harm's way, Oldendorf brought his five cruisers to bear upon some battered burning Japanese ships. Salvos dispatched a pair of destroyers.

About 4:30 A.M., as dawn approached, Oldendorf directed the units that included the *Bennion* to retrace their path south and engage any surviving Japanese ships. "In the pale, pre-dawn twilight," says Holloway, "the scene in Surigao Strait was appalling. I counted eight distinct fires, and the oily surface of the gulf was littered with debris and groups of Japanese sailors who were clinging to bits of wreckage and calling out to us as we raced past.

"*Bennion* did not pause to pick up survivors, as we had sighted the Japanese destroyer *Asaguma,* badly damaged, on fire and limping south. *Asaguma* was still afloat, and if she still had torpedoes aboard, she constituted a definite threat to our ships. With orders to destroy the Japanese ship, we changed course to close the *Asaguma* and opened fire with five-inch salvos at about ten thousand yards. We shifted to rapid, continuous fire at six thousand and she blew apart and slipped beneath the waves as we passed close aboard."

As the *Bennion* came about to rejoin its formation, a Zeke, a Japanese Navy version of the Zero, popped out of the clouds. An AA battery shell exploded within a few feet of the plane and it blew up in a flaming spectacular. "Aboard *Bennion*," remembers Holloway, "the crew was dog-tired, but spirits were elated. As we listened to the reports come in from the TBS and witnessed the hundreds of survivors clinging to the smoking wreckage of the Japanese fleet, we all sensed that a great victory had been won." The final tally for the Battle of Surigao Strait: two Japanese battleships and three destroyers sunk; a cruiser and a destroyer badly damaged but able to escape. The American losses were thirty-nine killed, 119 wounded, mostly on the *A.W. Grant,* which had been struck by its sister ships.

The celebration on the *Bennion* and the other vessels in Oldendorf's command halted abruptly. According to Holloway, "Suddenly—and the transformation of spirits was dramatic—elation turned to real alarm when over the TBS we heard that the TAFFY groups [the light and escort carriers left behind to protect other entrances of Leyte Gulf] were under attack at close range by Japanese battleships and cruisers. We couldn't believe it. We thought all of the capital ships of the Japanese reaction force had been destroyed in the night battle in Surigao Strait."

CHAPTER XX

THE *KAMIKAZES*

WHEN ADMIRAL KINCAID sent Oldendorf to block the Surigao Strait in an anticipated night action, he kept sixteen escort carriers—"baby flattops" or "jeep" carriers—steaming back and forth across Leyte Gulf to the north off Samar. These slower, smaller ships, accompanied by a screen of nine destroyers and twelve destroyer escorts, were organized as Task Group 77.4 and divided into Taffy 1, 2 and 3.

On the morning of October 25, the Taffies began to catapult their planes for antisubmarine searches and combat air patrols. A few minutes before 7:00 A.M. lookouts aboard the ships noticed antiaircraft shells in the distance and radios picked up Japanese voices over the interfighter net. But no enemy ships were believed within 100 to 150 miles to account for it.

Suddenly, one of the antisubmarine patrol pilots reported sighting four Japanese battleships, eight cruisers and a flock of destroyers. An unbelieving Rear Adm. Thomas L. Sprague, chief honcho for Taffy 1, demanded a check on the identification, believing the airman had spotted part of Task Force 38 from Halsey's 3rd Fleet. The answer came promptly from a source close to home. Not only did the lookouts on Sprague's ships see the unique, pagoda-shaped superstructure of Japanese battleships poking up over the horizon, but brightly colored splashes signaled hostile shells.

Without Task Force 34 on the scene, no one had watched the San Bernardino Strait, and Admiral Kurita, with the Center Force intact, passed into the waters off Samar without detection. Kurita packed a tremendous potential wallop in his battlewagons, but he had no carriers to provide air cover. The Taffies could muster several hundred planes but their surface weapons in the destroyer screen amounted to popguns compared to the huge batteries pointed at them from Kurita's battleships and cruisers. The lineups presented a near classic encounter between an armada of seagoing behemoths and the lighter, aircraft-dominated U.S. forces.

The unexpected appearance of the Japanese so close at hand exposed Task Force 77.4 to disaster. The Center Force had an opportunity to blast the carriers and their screens before they could assume any defensive posture. Apparently, the Japanese believed they might face battleships and full-size carriers. Admiral Kurita, still fearful of another series of air attacks and an eyewitness to the ineffectiveness of his AA gunnery, erred tactically, ordering a general attack instead of directing his ships into position for more effective, coordinated firing.

About twenty miles separated Taffy 3 from Taffy 2 to the southeast, with Taffy 1 as much as a hundred miles off. The Center Force began the action of Samar blasting away at Taffy 3, commanded by Rear Adm. Clifton "Ziggy" Sprague—no kin to the CO of Taffy 1. Caught in the sights of enemy cruisers and battleships, Ziggy Sprague circled his wagons, the six carriers operating around a diameter of twenty-five hundred yards while the destroyer screen steamed in parallel, six thousand yards from the center. All ships ran at flank speed, made smoke to hide themselves while the carriers emptied their flight decks faster than ever before. Nature smiled faintly upon the

Americans, adding a rain squall to further obliterate them as visible targets, and poorly functioning Japanese radar hampered the enemy gunnery.

Temporarily shrouded, Sprague signaled his three destroyers to counterattack the big enemy ships—boys sent to perform men's jobs. The *Johnston* ran a gauntlet through the heavier vessels of the foe and scored a few hits from her main battery on the cruiser *Kumano,* and then let fly all ten of her torpedoes at the *Kumano.* At least one, perhaps more, exploded on target and eliminated the cruiser from further combat.

But inevitably the Japanese gunners pinpointed the destroyer. A fusillade of shells ripped into the *Johnston.* Huge holes opened up in the deck; one explosion knocked off pieces of the radar on the mast; the falling debris killed three officers. Many died below deck as projectiles pierced the thin hull and then blew up. Still, the destroyer doggedly persevered.

Others from the Taffy 3 screen, destroyers *Hoel* and *Heermann,* plus the "Little Wolves"—destroyer escorts— charged at their oversize foe. They dashed through the roiling, explosion-riven water, threw their much smaller size shells at their antagonists and launched torpedoes, with little if any success. The Japanese registered hits upon the little boys.

Abandon ship had sounded for the *Hoel* and a DE, the *Roberts,* when the *Johnston* engaged in its finale, an exchange with the light cruiser *Yahagi* and a destroyer. The *Johnston* scored a number of hits before a firing squad of enemy ships surrounded it and hammered away until it went dead in the water, then rolled over on its way to the bottom.

Taffy 3's screen inflicted little material damage upon its much larger adversaries but the torpedoes and five-inch guns required the Center Force to take evasive action and deal with the interlopers. Although the disarray would buy time for the planes of Taffy 2 to enter the fray, four heavy Japanese cruisers stalked Taffy 3's six carriers. As his ships desperately attempted to steam away from the ever closer shell splashes, Ziggy Sprague advised them to use their puny, single deck gun: "Open fire with the pea-shooters when range is clear."

The long-range weapons of the attackers began to find their marks. Some of the armor-piercing shells tore through the thin skins of the converted oilers and passed out the opposite sides of the ships. But multiple hits killed, wounded and damaged. Crews immersed in as much as five feet of seawater plugged holes, repaired engines, sealed ruptured pipes while helmsmen hand wrestled with controls designed for mechanical rather than manual operation.

The first casualty among the carriers was the *Gambier Bay*. The Japanese cruisers narrowed the gap to the American vessel and at ten thousand yards put a shell into her that ignited fires. *Gambier Bay*, slowed by her wounds, staggered as the enemy gunners peppered her. The carrier capsized and sank.

A sister ship, the *White Plains*, insists its "pea shooter" vanquished its chief tormentor, the heavy cruiser *Chokai*. The five-inch 38 gun on the fantail claimed six hits upon the *Chokai* that knocked out both the forward turret and her engines. Whatever the *White Plains* achieved, a flight of torpedo bombers executed the *Chokai* with fatal blows amidships. It blew up and sank within five minutes.

In support of Taffy 3, Taffy 2 mounted three strikes that included both fighters and torpedo bombers. They started their raids about ninety minutes after Kurita's Center Force hove into view. The planes from the two Taffies, using torpedoes, bombs and incessant strafing, rattled the commander of the enemy fleet. Fighter planes, including some which had expended their ammunition, dove on the enemy vessels repeatedly, forcing them to use up their shells and bedeviling the crews.

Taffy 1, which included the *Suwannee*, also scrambled planes to meet Admiral Nishimura's group in the Surigao Strait. Tex Garner says, "They were shooting at us before we even got to them. They shot at us in every color there was. The whole sky was just full of different color bursts. [As they did in surface gunnery, the Japanese employed color as a means of zeroing in on targets.] I said to myself, 'There's no way you're going to get through that kind of barrage.' But we did. We went in and hurt 'em as much as we could. I took my four planes in and I got my four out. We had holes in us, but we were still flying." The furious action and the extended flight time from the carriers to the combat area drove some of the American pilots to land on the Tacloban air strip, secured only five days before.

Well out of range of the Japanese ships, Taffy 1 staved off land-based Japanese air raids. The task group received the dubious honor of enduring the first successful *kamikaze* attacks. In the days preceding the Leyte Gulf sea battles, rumors of special pilots committed to crashing their bomb-laden planes into American ships circulated among American sailors. One alleged source was a deciphered Japanese message to a pilot that read: "It is absolutely out of the question for you to return alive. Your mission involves certain death . . ."

About twenty minutes or so before 8:00 A.M., on October 25, spotters among the Taffy 1 ships saw four enemy planes breaking out of the clouds about ten thousand feet up. Gunner's Mate 3/c John B. Mitchell, son of a WW I wounded vet, and a shipyard worker before he enlisted in 1943 at age eighteen, had already been under fire when his ship, the escort carrier *Santee*, performed antisubmarine patrol in the North Atlantic, supported the invasion of North Africa and participated in some of the New Guinea area campaigns. Mitchell captained gun mount five. The 40 mms were not loaded because, according to Mitchell, "on several invasion landings men got kind of jumpy and there were occasions when guns were fired by accident, error or stupidity. I was wearing the combat headphone set and it was reported that we had some bogeys in the area. Almost immediately the gunnery officer, Lieutenant Commander Mills, yelled that a bogey was diving in on us, dead astern.

"I ordered my 'pointer and trainer' to bear on the target. Both used gunsights. One man had responsibility for the horizontal and the other for the vertical position of the gun. It took a great deal of practice for the two of them to act in unison. We did have a Mark 14 Sight and there were fire control men who could automatically fire our guns, but you always needed a pointer and trainer in case the electrical system failed.

"I ordered the crew to load and cock both guns. Before we were able to bear on the target, the bogey was in a dive and strafing the stern deck. I watched it come in all the way. I could not believe that the plane was not coming out of its dive. I was screaming, 'Pull out, you bastard! Pull out!'

"It came in so fast and with such surprise we didn't get off a single round. The plane used our aft elevator as a target and crashed just a few feet forward and to port of the elevator."

Another of the *Santee* crew, Walter Butler, saw one of the aviation painter men hanging over the side of the bridge in a boatswain's chair painting Japanese flags on the side of the bridge. "When the Jap crashed, he couldn't get out of the way. A piece of shrapnel, shaped like a dinner plate, struck him in the head and was embedded in his skull. It didn't kill him, but I don't see how he made it. During this time, Allen, who was the ship's painter, had gone below to get more paint. As he was walking across the hangar deck, the suicide hit. When it crashed through and exploded, shrapnel cut both of his legs off."

Aviation mechanic Donald Krops, after a night of work, was on his way below to hit the sack when General Quarters sounded. "I was on my way up to my battle station when the suicide plane struck. I thought one of our planes had crashed. When I got to the top of the ladder on the hangar deck, looked back and saw all that fire and smoke, I knew the Japs had hit us.

"I put on my Mae West life preserver and stood by my station just off the forward end of the flight deck. On the hangar deck I saw those depth charges on fire. They looked like fire crackers burning, spewing fire upward. I saw some of the guys rushing back and forth with carts, wheeling the bombs to the starboard side and throwing them overboard."

Some seven minutes after having had the dubious honor of being the first ship to be hit by a *kamikaze,* the *Santee* took a blow from a more conventional enemy as Japanese submarine I-56 executed a successful torpedo run. "It hit directly below my gun mount," remembers Mitchell. "The first sensation I had was that of the deck suddenly being pulled out from under my feet. I don't know how high in the air I went but I was told later that I was tossed above the gun mount.

"When I came down I thought I had been pitched overboard and immediately started to swim. I was attached to the mount by my combat phone and for some reason my helmet was still on my head and there I was, flailing my arms, thinking I had gone into the drink and all I was doing was swimming back to the spot in my gun tub where I normally would be. The gun tub was filled with wet debris and several dead bodies."

The spotters on the ships in the area had seen three of the original four planes dive towards the carriers. Gunners had thrown up a wall of metal but, as Mitchell saw, one aircraft penetrated the curtain of fire and, blazing away with machine guns until the final moment, crashed onto the forward deck of the *Santee.*

A Zero making for the *Sangamon* exploded in midair when a five-incher from *Suwannee* struck home. A third *kamikaze* dropped into the water after concentrated AA fire shattered its controls or else killed the pilot.

Suddenly, from four thousand feet up, the last of the quartet of *kamikazes* dropped almost straight down. It seemed as if every weapon in Taffy 1 was shooting at the Zero [some say it was a Judy, a navy dive-bomber], which trailed a thin stream of smoke, as if afire. The concentration upon him notwithstanding, the pilot held his course and drilled into the *Suwannee* flight deck to explode into pieces, the Zero's nose penetrating three decks below, just shy of reaching the aviation fuel stores. In the flight deck, the suicide plane carved an impression of its front silhouette, a round hole for the engine and slits from the wings.

Second Class Petty Officer Erich Kitzmann, a native of Detroit and the son of immigrant parents from Germany, bossed crews that prepared planes for operations. When the "Flight Quarters" signal was blown at 0300 October 25 during blackout conditions, Kitzmann and hands worked in the dark getting the TBFs topside.

Hours later, Kitzmann and half of his plane handlers were at breakfast eating beans, the standard Wednesday fare, when General Quarters sounded. He tossed aside his mess tray, carelessly slung his life jacket over one shoulder and strapped his helmet under his chin. He checked his hangar deck for fire hazards and saw to it that auxiliary fuel tanks were removed from aircraft there and jettisoned. Then he headed forward to a hatch where he could look out.

"I could see the *Santee* burning and listing to port," Kitzmann recalls. "A Japanese Zero was coming in from the starboard at mast level and strafing us. I drew back behind a stanchion to get out of the line of fire when I heard this crash, which was the *kamikaze* hitting the flight deck. I never heard the bomb go off."

Kitzmann next remembers finding himself in the sea. "I saw my helmet turning over and over under the clear blue water of the Mindanao Trench as I surfaced. I discovered that my dungarees were no longer on my body except my belt and shorts, no shoes or socks. Yet my life jacket was still on my shoulder. Trying to gain my composure, I looked around and saw smoke billowing from the stern of the *Suwannee*. It was a big blur as I was bleeding from my eyes and began struggling to put my other arm into my life jacket. My face felt like someone had hit me with a baseball bat.

"I regained my senses; it became apparent I was not

alone. Mournful cries of help and despair were all around. A body came up near me without a head and it did not shock me at the time. It did make me aware of my situation. As my ankle began to pain, I was afraid to look down to see if my foot was still with me. Survival is an instinct that moved me. As I realized I was going to make it, panic and fear left me.

"The next thing I remember is the bow of the *Bull* [a destroyer escort] plowing through the water and her Skeeter [as they call the commander of a destroyer] calling on her speaker horns, 'Rendezvous in the rafts we are going to drop and we'll pick you up later.' I don't know how many men in the water understood the message but I did. I began to swim for the rafts and when I reached one I discovered it had flipped upside down in the water. It was no small thing as I dove under it to reach the paddles and began paddling around to find shipmates.

"I don't recall how long it took but I picked up Frank Yeomans and H. O. Olson, aviation machinist mates, third class. Olson was holding up Yeomans as I pulled them onto the raft. Yeomans was hit hard by the blast and did not become coherent until later that night aboard the *Bull*. I picked up two black men who were burned badly. Their skin was hanging from their bodies. One had lost half of one leg and the other had a hole in his neck. I put my belt around the man who had his leg half gone to stop the bleeding. I administered morphine to both men.

"To get the morphine I had to dive under the raft to bring up the five-inch shell can that contained medical supplies. I could not open the can and asked Yeomans for a knife. I'll never know how I was able to open that container with a Navy jackknife. About that time the man with a hole in his throat asked for water. The water keg I brought up from the bottom of the raft had no cup so I opened the spigot and let the water run into his mouth. It came right out his throat.

"Later in the afternoon, it seemed like years, the *Bull* returned and sent out her whale boat to pick up our survivors. As I climbed the cargo net of the *Bull*, the little pains began to ache. But I was alive and that was all that mattered at the time.

"In the wardroom of the *Bull*, a pharmacist mate told me I was bleeding from my shoulder, ankle and groin. I told him to take care of the man laying on the table whose ankle was blown away. The pharmacist mate offered me a glass that contained some liquid medicine. After I drank it I walked out on the afterdeck to identify the bodies of some of my shipmates. Sneed, from Redding, California, was lying there without a mark on his body. Anglin was still alive with a hole through his stomach, begging me to put a .45 to his head and end his pain. At this point, the world seemed to spin and I dropped to the deck, out cold."

While other vessels plucked men like Kitzmann from the sea and tended to their injuries, Phil Phillips, one of the three flight surgeons on the *Suwannee*, narrowly missed injury or death himself. The precocious child of a Methodist Evangelist father and a mother who managed some real estate holdings in Arkansas, Phillips was born in 1915, graduated from high school at fifteen and signed enlistment papers for the service while still in college. "The speech that Hitler made one night before he took over Austria convinced me that war was obviously coming and I sure as hell did not want to be in the Army when I got out of school." To support himself while studying medicine, Phillips worked as a night clerk in a Little Rock hotel for three years and then in his final year treated psychiatric patients in a hospital, as had the 24th Division medic Phil Hostetter.

Phil Phillips had donned his Navy uniform immediately after graduation from medical school. "I had no particular instruction about handling the sick before we went to sea. There was no specific educational process to prepare except to familiarize ourselves with the ship and the potentials for dealing with sick people. The medical department on the *Suwannee* was adequate in a rustic sort of way. It had an eight-bed sick bay and a little room for holding sick call. We had about ten first-rate hospital corpsmen; most had training ashore but some didn't and they were eager learners." The medical team included three doctors and a dentist.

"Well before Leyte Gulf, during an inactive stretch," says Phillips, "one pilot requested a circumcision. I didn't see why not; we weren't doing anything active at the time. It turned out all right and now other guys wanted it." Among those who volunteered for the procedure was Tex Garner. After the surgeon performed the operation on Garner, the Texan said he'd like to try to do it. "He did one," says Phillips, "and he did a good job. But one was all he wanted to try and altogether we did close to a dozen. They all said they were just keeping the surgeon's hand in. If they ever needed surgery the doc would be sharp after trimming all these boys."

Phillips remembers standing in the parachute loft when the *kamikaze* struck with a five-hundred-pound bomb and a load of gasoline. "The stretcher bearer assigned to my battle station was wounded. The explosion was so horribly loud and the sheet of metal on the inside surface of the parachute loft where I stood was riddled with shell fragments. There were so many dead and wounded on the hangar deck that I scrambled out of the parachute loft and headed for the hangar deck to do what I could.

"Going by the main sick bay, I could see that our little ward had quickly overflowed with patients. Stretchers lay in the passageway and on the deck of the operating room. Others were being carried into the pharmacy and the clerical office. Quickly the wardroom became an emergency aid station.

"The hangar deck was still filled with smoke. Through the eerie light streaming in from the hole in the flight deck it was easy to see that here lay our worst casualties. Mangled bodies and portions of bodies lay about the deck, where they had been blown from the explosion. Steel decks were slippery with blood. Men followed with stretchers and one by one we gathered the wounded from their ghastly surroundings, applied temporary dressings and sent them to the wardroom.

"In the wardroom were six to eight long tables on which we could put patients that needed immediate care. It was a helluva bad day and we lost fifty-five dead that morning and more than that were wounded.

"Most of the men were doing their best under the difficult circumstances. Through the night gun crews stayed at their guns while scores of volunteers assisted the doctors and hospital corpsmen in caring for the wounded. But one senior person hid himself in an ensign's room with a bottle, trying to intoxicate himself."

Tex Garner, aloft in his Hellcat on October 25, heard over his radio that the *Suwannee* had been crashed amidships by a *kamikaze* and was afire. As he considered his options, a message informed him repairs were in progress and he should return. Over the stricken vessel, Garner saw sailors fixing the hole in the flight deck as sparks flew from the welding torches.

"I finally received a 'Prep Charlie'—Prepare to Land—by blinker light," recalls Garner. "Ninety minutes after being *kamikazied*, I get a Charlie. I can't believe it but I come out of the circle and head up the starboard side with the hook down. As I approached the carrier I notice the five-inch gun tracking me. Funny time for practice, but after all, they've been under attack. Frog LaFargue [another pilot] was talking to the gun crew. 'It's a Hellcat, it's Tex.' I dropped my landing gear and flaps all in one motion. This is like slamming on the brakes due to increased drag. All of a sudden that five-inch gun exploded, BAM! right in my face. I broke off and began a radio chew out. I couldn't believe that the gun crew that shot down a plane five hundred feet off the *Santee* could miss me so close!

"After landing, as the plane strolled down the deck, the hook couldn't find any arresting cables. We used to have thirteen of them. I found only the first three. I don't know whether I wet my britches or it was sweat but my flight suit was messed up. I felt like it was permissible."

The day was momentous for another *Suwannee* Hellcat pilot, Jack Smith. An Iowa native, supported by his widowed mother and subsequently a stepfather during the Great Depression, Smith already held a private pilot's license when he enlisted in 1942. Assigned to Air Group 60 as a replacement pilot in December 1943, Smith was assigned to the *Suwannee,* then berthed at San Diego. After intensive practice in field carrier landings, commonly known as "bounce drill," and night exercises, Smith qualified as a F6F Hellcat pilot.

As a "new boy" Smith flew mostly combat air patrol when the *Suwannee* supported the conquest of the Marshall Islands. He gained practical experience in the basic two-plane section tactic that consisted of a leader and a wingman. Because the single-seat fighters had no guns aft, the arrangement provided mutual protection against an attack. By the time *Suwannee* and Taffy 1 took up station in Leyte Gulf, Smith was a veteran of a number of campaigns.

In the pre-dawn hours of October 25, Smith and three others formed a division—a pair of sections—assigned to combat air patrol over southern Leyte. As he prepared for takeoff, Smith discovered a malfunction in his aircraft. He switched to another ship, displacing the standby pilot. When a second member of the division also found a defect in his Hellcat, only three planes were launched.

"We were scheduled to patrol at twenty thousand feet, back and forth, from Surigao Strait to Ormoc Bay. We arrived as dawn was breaking and reported to the control station. He had no radar contacts, so we took up the patrol. We continued to bore a hole in the air, plodding back and forth, and were held on station beyond the scheduled time, without being told why our relief would be late. All we knew was that our fuel supply was being diminished." Smith and his associates remained unaware that all aircraft in the vicinity had engaged in the desperate struggle to contain the Center Force of Kurita.

At one point the Hellcat patrol had noticed a flight of four FM2 Wildcats, friendly aircraft. Subsequently, Smith spotted a quartet of planes but now he says, "I was surprised to spot a fifth aircraft gently S-turning about five hundred feet below and almost directly under the other flight. It was a Zeke! I called a 'Tally ho' on the radio, dropped my belly tank and charged my guns. Monty and Dew must have seen the Zeke at about the same time, because we all initiated a dive together."

Smith was puzzled why the four other fighters did not also respond to the target. "I glanced over to see what the other flight was doing and was dumbfounded to notice that instead of a flight of four FM2s, we were preparing to dive under a flight of four Zekes. We had taken the sucker bait. I immediately altered course to get a shot at the higher group. When the Japs saw what was happening, their formation broke apart like a clay pigeon impacted by shotgun pellets.

"We each picked a Zeke to follow. My target descended in a diving right-hand turn. A Zeke at high speed rolls relatively easily from right to left but has a tough time rolling left to right. The root of this roll behavior is that the Zeke was designed without an aileron trim tab.

"In this right-hand diving turn, G-forces were too high for accurate firing. Furthermore, as we rapidly descended into warmer air, the cold cockpit canopy condensed moisture, obscuring my vision. I turned on the defroster but until it warmed sufficiently, I had to rub the windows vigorously and often to keep from being completely blind."

When his Zeke reached the limit of his descent, he leveled off and headed over the water. "I got off a good burst. I could see the tracers and incendiaries hitting him but I didn't strike anything vital," remembers Smith. "We were both flying at full throttle, but the F6F is faster than the Zeke so I was getting closer all the time.

"At the instant I pressed the trigger to fire the next burst, he dumped both his landing gear and flaps. It was like slamming on the brakes. To miss ramming him I had to execute a steep chandelle [an abrupt climbing turn] to the left and immediately follow this with a diving turn also to the left to come back to my original heading astern of the Jap plane. The diving turn brought my speed back to near what it had been and the maneuver amounted to a 360-degree turn at a steeply inclined angle.

"Since the Jap had slowed significantly by his maneuver, he was now reaccelerating but I rapidly overtook him. He again tried the same move, but I was ready for him and put a burst into his right wing root where the gas tank was located. The incendiaries ignited the gasoline and he blew apart. It was a strange feeling to fly through the debris of an exploding airplane. The pieces rained down onto the water and by the time I had completed another 360-degree turn there was no longer any evidence that there had ever been another aircraft in the vicinity."

Smith learned his companions each downed a Zeke. "We regretted that two got away but I felt that I had lost my 'virginity' and done for the first time what a fighter pilot is supposed to do." Of more immediate concern was low fuel. Smith elected to set down in the soft, sandy loam at Tacloban where several of the heavy American planes nosed over during the roll-out. Smith had plenty of company at Tacloban; he counted a hundred planes, mostly from Taffy 3, either in the holding pattern or already on the ground. He touched down without incident.

The Air Group 60 pilots at Tacloban downed some food, then scrounged fuel and ammunition for their planes. A Navy ground controller organized patrols. Smith and company made routine sweeps of the area before a late afternoon return to the patched-up *Suwannee*. "Debris on the hangar deck was still scattered about," says Smith, "and the stench of burnt flesh there was nauseating."

Because of a misunderstood radio transmission, the flight commanders on the carrier had believed Smith had crashed in Ormoc Bay and left him off the next day's flight schedule. When he came aboard with his aircraft he was added to the list but not assigned to a mission until the afternoon.

"Shortly before noon, those of us scheduled for the early afternoon launch got into our flight gear, proceeded by the galley to get lunch and again went to the ready room to eat. The stewards had outdone themselves; in an attempt to boost morale, they had prepared fried chicken."

Several fliers forced to spend the night at Tacloban had returned in the morning. Their aircraft along with several others, some of which were already fueled and armed with bombs and napalm, sat on the flight deck. A few TBMs, having finished their morning's work, were being taken aboard and one was in the process of taxiing to the forward elevator.

"Then the sound of antiaircraft fire came unexpectedly from the carrier's guns," remembers Smith. "A fraction of a second later, the squawk box was sounding the bugle for General Quarters but the words 'General Quarters! General Quarters! All hands man your battle stations' were not yet completed when there was a tremendous explosion. It was the sort of thing that you don't really hear but rather feel as your chest heaves in and out from the differential pressure passing by. We were stunned and surprised, but my most vivid memory is of pieces of fried chicken flying through the air as people bolted from their seats to proceed to battle stations. Everyone streamed from the ready room and up to the flight deck.

"A second, less violent explosion was heard by the time we gained the passageway. Upon reaching the flight deck we found that beyond the forward elevator it was completely obscured by smoke."

The *kamikaze* had evaded radar discovery by disguising itself as a friendly. It trailed close enough to Air Group 60 planes, *Suwannee*-bound, to be mistaken for one of them. The suicide crashed the carrier atop the taxiing TBM, annihilating the plane and killing all three crew members.

The blast wrecked the elevator and gasoline leaking from the aircraft spread fires on the deck. The second explosion probably resulted from the rupture of the compressed air tank of the ship's catapult.

Many ship's crew engaged in handling planes and ordnance died outright. Others received terrible burns, some fatal. Smith heard sporadic antiaircraft fire mixed with rounds from .50 caliber machine guns cooking off in burning airplanes. "The bridge had been severely damaged," says Smith. "Several there had been killed, including the air officer and the navigator. Others, including the captain [W.D. Johnson], were wounded. Some personnel on the bridge were either blown or jumped over the side. Though bleeding badly from shrapnel wounds, the captain remained on the deck and encouraged those involved in fighting the fires."

On the edge of exhaustion after a pre-dawn mission, Tex Garner had grabbed a bunk ordinarily used by a flier who'd gone into the water. Jolted from a sound sleep, he pitched in with first aid after the *kamikaze* struck. Making his way forward, Garner found Captain Johnson sitting on the deck with his back braced against a bulkhead, and injected him with morphine. "Captain Johnson had a butt full of shrapnel," recalls Garner, "and didn't even say *ouch* as I stuck him. He told them to go fight the fire, save the ship. He would be okay." The fighter pilot continued his search for others to succor. He worked his way to his own quarters, next to the catapult, and found his roommate dead.

Hunting for survivors, Garner turned up Leve Steber, a steward's mate with a deep head wound. "I picked him up and was surprised to hear him ask for a drink. I could see two inches into his head. There were plenty of broken fresh water lines. I looked for something to put it in. A full bottle of Canadian Club floated by. I opened it, took a good slug, poured the rest out, filled it with water for Steber. He died later."

Men with serious burns accosted Garner, who would

ask who they were. " 'Tex, don't you recognize me?' They were black with burns," says Garner. "I'd tell them the light was bad and smoke was in my eyes."

Bill Dacus, an assistant to the navigator of the *Suwannee,* regarded the Navy as a kind of family business. His father had done a tour before WW II, having enlisted at sixteen; his mother had been a Navy nurse; and a brother also was a Navy sailor. When WW II erupted his father returned to service and Dacus even held a brief reunion with him in 1943 at a small island in the Pacific.

Dacus had begun as a deckhand but once assigned to quartermaster duties demonstrated such aptitude that he climbed to the exalted title of chief quartermaster. Dacus recalls that after the initial explosion on October 26, "A group of us were laying on the passageway deck in front of the Chief's quarters, when someone wanted to get up and run into the hangar deck. Other sailors laying there told him to stay down. He kept getting up, wanting to run to the hangar deck where the explosion occurred. I finally said in a very authoritative voice, 'Get down and stay down!' He did and it was then we heard a second explosion, from the catapult.

"It was a good thing the man hadn't moved because that explosion killed everyone in the hangar deck. The blast went through all passageways fore and aft. They actually had to scrape a sailor off a passageway bulkhead.

"Shortly after, Chief Shipfitter William Brooks came up the passageway with a hose on his shoulders. He told me to grab a hose on the bulkhead nearby. I did and followed him up the passageway to the hangar deck. As we went, we both looked out a porthole. We saw our sister ships quite a distance from us and a lot of sailors in the water with 40 mm shell containers [for flotation] spotting the ocean. I asked him if we should jump out. Brooks, who was a very chubby guy, said very emphatically, 'I don't know about you but I'll never make it.' I just followed him up the stairs with the hose."

As Dacus struggled to connect his hose to a valve,

another explosion rocked the ship, knocking Brooks unconscious for a few seconds. When he regained his wits, Brooks crawled under the planes on the hangar deck and opened valves from a sprinkler system. The heavy spray prevented the fire from spreading to the gassed planes. Dacus managed to keep his poise and, following Brooks's lead, started washing the high-octane gas on the hangar deck into the elevator well, as if cleaning the sidewalk.

Flight surgeon Phil Phillips, not having eaten for thirty hours, had been in the squadron ready room, tucking away a meal of chicken, mashed potatoes and peas. "I was eating when an ensign stuck his head through the door and said, 'Doc, they're getting ready to land two or three planes that had to land on another carrier yesterday. Can I sit up on your observer seat on the aft end of the island while they bring them aboard?'

"I said, 'Sure, I'm not going anyplace. I'm starved.' He went to this seat they had arranged for me on the aft end of the island, right where the planes catch the restraining wires on the deck. Five or ten minutes later the second *kamikaze* hit the forward elevator. The ensign was hurt badly, which would have happened to me if I had skipped lunch and gone to watch the planes land."

The conflagration heated the metal in some areas until it was too hot to touch, forcing some sailors to abandon ship. But with everyone, including the flight personnel, tending the fire lines the *Suwannee* remained afloat, although she was down in the water four to six feet at the bow.

Unable to function and with at least half the thousand of her complement killed or wounded, the *Suwannee* received orders to transfer her most seriously injured to hospital ships, bury her dead and steam for the Palaus to repair the damage. Bill Dacus recalled dealing with dead shipmates. "They brought up Robert Wilding, a good friend of mine, on a stretcher. I tried to tell him something of encouragement. One of the stretcher bearers told me he was dead. A sailor came up to us and said we should come with him to the forward, starboard 40 mm gun turret. There he pointed to three bodies in the fetus position, hugging one another and burned so badly that we could not recognize who they were.

"Harry Martin, a parachute rigger, had been told to put dead sailors into body bags for burial at sea. However, he had only one bag so he made them from parachute cloth. The burial service went on twenty-four hours a day for a couple of days."

Jack Smith witnessed the ceremonies aboard the *Suwannee.* "The corpse was wrapped in canvas or heavy cloth with six bricks between the legs to provide weight for rapid sinking. Placed on a plank, the body was taken to the side of the deck and draped with a flag. During the service, that plank was raised with a portion extending over the side. After the padre, Chaplain Walsh, said his words, the inboard end of the plank was raised and the corpse slid down, under the flag and into the sea."

Santee sailed to Hawaii under its own power. Walter Butler remembered a band that greeted them in the harbor and a flotilla of welcoming vessels. "The captain had the crew at quarters, standing at attention on the flight deck. All the walking wounded were standing there, all bandaged up. I remember the aviation painter standing there, all bandaged up, with a hunk of metal still embedded in his head. Doctors at the Naval Hospital in Pearl Harbor removed it. Some of us were looking down when we saw Allen, who lost both legs. He looked up, folded both hands together, giving us the signal, 'Keep up the good work.' "

John Mitchell mourned eleven dead shipmates, including several close friends, and spoke for most survivors of the first *kamikazes.* "My personal reaction was first one of fright, then of astonishment that someone would desperately fly a plane and deliberately hit a ship."

Both *Santee* and *Suwannee* lived to fight other campaigns, but as they limped from the scene, the survival of Taffy 3 and perhaps Taffy 2 remained doubtful in spite of the massive air effort. A number of vessels had been lost, including the carrier *St. Lo*. Oldendorf, hearing of the surprise appearance of a massive enemy force off Samar, considered hastening to reinforce Task Group 77.4. His staff wanted the group to stay together and meet the enemy at a site of its own choice, particularly since it was running low on ammunition and would be at a disadvantage in a running exchange. Also, Oldendorf would not be able to reach the battle site for three hours. Initially, Oldendorf received word from Kincaid to stand-by some miles north of the locale of the Surigao shootout. That move doomed any possibility of rescuing the hundreds of Japanese sailors clinging to wreckage from their sunken ships.

When word of the Japanese thrust was received by Halsey, he replied that he was already involved with the enemy but would order a carrier group under Adm. John McCain to come to the aid of the Taffies. Unfortunately, the carriers commanded by McCain were well over three hundred miles from the scene. It would be noon before their planes could come to the rescue.

Greatly concerned, Nimitz radioed Halsey a coded question: "Where is Task Force 34?" The yeoman assigned to transmit the query thought he detected a note of emphasis in Nimitz's voice. He added a repeat of the first two words, "Where is." And when actually sent, padding was inserted on both ends of the question to mislead eavesdropping Japanese. As a consequence, the complete transmission read: "TURKEY TROTS TO WATER RR FROM CINCPAC ACTION COM THIRD FLEET INFO COMINCH CTF SEVENTY-SEVEN X WHERE IS RPT WHERE IS TASK FORCE THIRTY FOUR RR THE WORLD WONDERS."

The communications people on Halsey's flagship, *New Jersey*, recognized the "TURKEY TROTS TO WATER" as intended to fool the enemy and deleted that from what was handed to Halsey. Unfortunately, the staff believed the final three words purposely included, and an irate Halsey read, "Where is, Repeat, Where is, Task Force 34, The World Wonders." He interpreted the final phrase as a rocket from Nimitz. Months would pass before he accepted an explanation for what he regarded as a deliberate insult.

The postmortem investigation into what happened also became an argument about language. The dispatch from Halsey on October 24 that described a "Battle Plan" named the specific ships which "will be formed as Task Force 34." The seabag lawyers now debated whether a "Battle Plan" can be extrapolated to indicate a battle or operation order. Critics of Halsey insisted "will be formed" meant this would now happen rather than indicating the creation of TF 34 was a conditional future.

In his own review, MacArthur refused to criticize any individual. Instead he reiterated his disapproval of divided commands. "The near disaster can be placed squarely at the door of Washington. In the naval action, two key American commanders were independent of each other, one under me, and the other under Admiral Nimitz, five thousand miles away, both operating in the same waters and in the same battle." It was a problem throughout the war and somewhat akin to MacArthur's attempts to retain control after he left Corregidor.

The issue, however, became moot due to timidity by the aggressors. Although the total losses for the Japanese off Samar added up to just three cruisers with some minor damage to other vessels, Kurita became convinced of imminent defeat by superior forces. He withdrew, although had he persisted, his outfit could have thoroughly whipped the Taffies. To cap the farrago of mistakes, Halsey now dispatched Task Force 34 to block off Kurita's escape but it was far too late. If given orders when Kincaid first requested help, the battleships of TG 34 could have been in position to demolish Kurita's Center Force.

To the north Halsey, despite the distractions regarding the plight of the 7th Fleet, fell upon what he believed were the main elements of the Japanese Navy still afloat. Admiral Ozawa now reaped the bitter rewards of his scheme. With a paltry dozen or so planes for a combat air patrol from his carriers, the Japanese admiral's seventeen ships depended upon antiaircraft fire to defend themselves. The torpedo-bombers and fighter-bombers from the *Essex, Lexington, San Jacinto, Intrepid, Langley, Belleau Wood* and *Franklin* overwhelmed the enemy. When the sixth and final air strike of the day—a total of 527 sorties were flown—landed on the flight decks, the U.S. airmen had wiped out four carriers and a destroyer. American cruisers and submarines disposed of two more destroyers and a cruiser.

The toll exacted by the 3rd Fleet meant the end of Japanese carrier-based warfare. But on Luzon and other Philippine territory large numbers of enemy planes operated from a number of bases. Marauders from these sites continued to menace American ground and sea-going forces.

CHAPTER XXI

LEYTE SECURED

WITH THEIR SUPPLY and reinforcement lifelines now protected, the Americans drove deeper into Leyte. The 7th and 96th Divisions focused on the town of Dagami, headquarters for Japanese units sealing off access to the island's western coast. The ultimate prize beyond Dagami was the port of Ormoc through which the Imperial Army could still funnel troops from Luzon and elsewhere.

During their initial days in the Philippines, Norman Fiedler's G Company of the 382nd Regiment endured considerable physical discomfort but relatively minor casualties. That changed as they approached Dagami. "The first man in my outfit to get killed," says Fiedler, "was someone that I had become friendly with in my squad. As we were moving up an embankment from a stream to attack Dagami, machine gun fire was directed at us and we were all able to scramble back down except Shapson. He was hit in the legs and unable to move about thirty feet from the embankment where we were pinned down. Several of us attempted at different times to get up there and retrieve Shapson. However, the enemy fire was constant.

"Shapson was continuously moaning, groaning, crying, but we couldn't help him. We threw a rope to him but he couldn't attach himself to the other end. Then his moaning and groaning stopped. After we surrounded the enemy machine gunners, we moved forward and found he died of his wounds."

"When we dug in a few nights after the landing," recalls Marvin Margoshes, "I shared a foxhole that blocked a path with heavy growth. Late at night we heard something coming down the trail, so we opened up with rifles and grenades. It took a lot of both before the noise stopped. It seemed like we had beaten off a Japanese patrol. But when dawn came we saw a very dead carabao in the path. A day or so later, we were headed towards a road on the other side of a swamp. Two Japanese soldiers came into view, carrying a machine gun on a tripod which they started to set up on the road. They were quickly killed by rifle fire. If they had done the smart thing, they would have come along the far side of the road and set up the gun there to shoot just over the embankment. We had no cover, so they could have done a lot of damage. It was my first experience with the Japanese soldiers' blind obedience to orders. In this case I suppose they were told to go on the road and not behind it.

"That night we had our first *banzai* attack. It was so rainy and dark that I literally couldn't see my hand in front of my face. I tried that experiment. We were all shooting blindly but it worked. I don't think we suffered a single casualty and there were several Japanese dead on the road where we had a 37 mm gun loaded with shells like over-sized shotgun ammunition.

"We moved down the road and ran into some opposition. Someone hit a Japanese machine gunner with a bazooka and literally blew him into little pieces. We were told to pull back about a hundred yards to give the artillery a chance to work. I sat down off the road, by a stream. A round landed on the other side of the stream. I was still green enough to assume it was one of ours so I didn't take shelter. The next round wounded me, shrapnel in the hip, and instantly killed another soldier who was sitting not much more than a yard away. I was taken to the beach and after initial treatment put on an LST for New Guinea.

When I saw myself in a mirror on the ship, I thought it was another person. The invasion made at the start of the rainy season had turned the dirt roads to mud and we got ammunition but very little food. I estimated that I lost twenty pounds in only ten days."

Elmer Polcyn, a tech sergeant with Company K of the 382nd Regiment, led a platoon-size patrol overnight towards the enemy positions near Dagami. After bedding down in a small deserted town, Polcyn says a Filipino reported enemy about two hundred yards away. The sergeant led his men single file across a deep marshy bog with the local man as a guide.

"We had just crossed the swamp and gone about twenty-five yards when the Filipino opened fire at a banana grove ten yards to our front. Barnett, Luchtel and I were right in front when Barnett started to fire his submachine gun. He only got off a few rounds when the Japs started to shoot, one short burst hitting Barnett and Arndt, who had come up behind him. Luchtel and I threw all our grenades and opened fire with our rifles. The platoon was still crossing the swamp and Sergeant Oeder brought them up and built up a firing line. Sergeant Ray and the aid man were giving first aid to Barnett and Arndt. Barnett, who had won a DSC in Alaska, was shot through the left lung. Arndt, celebrating his nineteenth birthday, was shot in the stomach.

"We stopped firing and heard the Japs moaning. Luchtel, Polhill, Reinert and I went into the grove as the rest of the platoon covered us. We found several wounded Japs whom we shot or bayonetted. We had killed fourteen enlisted men and one officer, captured two light machine guns, two of our own automatic rifles, pistols and about a dozen of their rifles. I picked up a pair of Jap flags as souvenirs.

"We started to move our wounded buddies after we made litters from bamboo. This was rough going as we had to cross the swamp and the sun was very low. We took turns carrying the litters about a mile when we got relief.

The medics gave the wounded men blood plasma and loaded them in Jeeps."

A day later, Polcyn and his unit entered Dagami along with men from the 7th Division. "This was Sunday morning and we saw Filipinos going to church. They all smiled and put up their fingers in the Vee for Victory." Another week passed and Polcyn took another patrol forward after a general advance behind tanks halted because of a typhoonlike downpour and the uncertain location of the enemy. "I had gone about seventy-five yards when I noticed two men standing under a tree about fifteen yards in front of me. Because it was raining so hard, I couldn't see far and called out to them. When they didn't answer and started to move behind the tree, I realized they were Japs and fired, killing both. As I fired, all hell broke loose. I realized it was a trap where they tried to draw in the battalion. A kid standing next to me was hit in the chest and fell. The rest of the patrol hit the ground and started firing as we saw Japs all around us. In back of us, when the company started to come to our aid, they were fired upon by Japs who emerged from concealed holes. The patrol was surrounded and in a very poor position. The medic came up to the wounded boy but he had died instantly.

"The company soon cleaned up the Japs to our rear and the patrol began to withdraw. The medic and I were the last to move. As I started, I was hit in the left shoulder by a Jap machine gun. As soon as I was wounded, I went to the ground and crawled behind a banana tree. It was not good protection but pretty fair concealment. The medic came up and gave me first aid but every time he tried to dress my injury we were fired upon. Finally, he stopped the bleeding and I headed for the aid station. I went about seventy-five yards but because of loss of blood wasn't strong enough to go any farther. Someone brought up a litter and they carried me about a thousand yards to the aid station. We were under sniper fire all the way."

Polcyn's wound was serious enough to require evacuation all the way to a hospital in Hawaii. In less than four weeks on Leyte, his second platoon of thirty-eight GIs counted six dead and fifteen wounded.

To the north, the 24th Division, whose mission was to grab the beaches at Carigara and forestall the landing of enemy reinforcements, also started to encounter stiffening resistance. The outfit's 34th Infantry Regiment approached a critical natural barrier, the Mainit River [to the Americans it amounted to little more than a creek]. Col. Aubrey "Red" Newman, the 34th's commander, saw his lead unit stopped cold at the Mainit River bridge. Twice the 1st Battalion tried to advance to the banks of the stream but were repulsed by intense rifle fire.

As Newman considered his options, a former Filipino guerrilla, Vicente Sydiongco, offered a solution. Sydiongco's background and experiences were typical of many of the local irregulars. A native of Leyte and son of a former government official, Sydiongco was a first-year college student when called to active duty from the Philippine Army reserve the day after Christmas 1941. "Our military unit never faced the Japanese in a military confrontation," says Sydiongco, "except in two instances when we fired at unidentified planes before the surrender and disbandment of our company in May 1942. I became a member of the Leyte guerrilla forces sometime in October of that year.

"Our initial guerrilla unit was organized by a retired Philippine Scout. There were two such units operating in the area, made up of men with previous military experiences, ones who had arms and ammunition and commissions in the defunct Philippine Army and U.S. Army, college students, high school kids and close relatives of those already guerrilla leaders. Twice a week we would hold close order drill but never practiced extended order for use in combat.

"Our outfit got its food from civilian donations. Not until the early part of 1944 did we receive very limited arms and ammunition from the Southwest Pacific Area Command, shipped in by submarine. In fact, I know of only one such shipment for the Leyte guerrilla command.

In northern Leyte, the guerrilla units maintained peace and order in their respective sectors of operation. In our area we didn't experience any organized group who robbed or plundered other people. There was one instance of piracy but the couple who did it were liquidated by their own men who later joined our organization."

Sydiongco became friendly with Dr. Phil Hostetter and when asked how he sensed the imminence of the Americans, answered, "We thought the war would last perhaps two years longer than it did. Then the children started bringing in sticks of chewing gum with the message the Americans would soon be returning and not to give up hope. The messages had been dropped from planes. Americans knew the children could not resist a stick of gum, and would bring in the message."

According to Sydiongco, the Japanese clustered in the urban areas during the occupation of Leyte, leaving the rural sectors largely unpatrolled. Anyone leaving a town or city was observed closely and interrogated for possibly aiding guerrillas. "I was almost the victim of a Japanese agent, a Filipino," says Sydiongco, "but I intercepted a letter addressed to the commander of the Japanese garrison in the nearest town. The message stated I was a guerrilla, described the unit I was assigned to and the gun issued to me. Fortunately, the agent was picked up by another guerrilla unit and nothing further was heard about him or the matter."

His organization had worked with the American invaders near Tacloban, creating a diversion, drawing off enemy troops and setting up an ambush for any trucks carrying reinforcements. Now, serving as a scout who could supply information about the terrain, Sydiongco informed Red Newman of a lightly defined footpath that led to a ford for the river. Newman, convinced his foe might not be aware of the crossing because of the speed of the GI advance, immediately ordered the 2nd Battalion to exploit the opening.

"Colonel Pearsall, the battalion commander," recalls

Austin, "said, 'Paul, you lead off. Cross that creek and head for the bridge.' I gathered my platoon leaders and sergeants and we squatted on the ground while I started to tell them our orders and what we were expected to do. Red Newman stomped his foot, turned around and very angrily asked Colonel Pearsall what it was going to take to get this man to move. I heard him and that made me upset. When Pearsall said, 'Paul, move out,' I demanded, 'Am I not going to be allowed time to tell my leaders?' He said, 'No, just get going.'

"Disgustedly, I told the men to hit the trail, go down to the river and get on the other side. I didn't even have time to line up the platoons or give any instructions except to follow the guide. It was very disorganized, squads and platoons mixed up. I felt sure some would make the wrong turn, go off the right trail. We had been taught since Day One, 'Don't make any fast moves; always have a plan and pass it on to subordinates.' When I walked down the trail, I looked forward and saw no one and when I looked back I didn't see a person either. I was alone on the trail in some high kunai grass. I said to myself, 'This is going to be suicide. I'll be dead in the next fifteen minutes.' We got to the river and to my surprise the trail didn't have any forks in it. Two platoons had already crossed the river. We started down a gravel road leading down to the bridge."

As his F Company advanced on the bridge, a Japanese soldier came running along, oblivious to the approaching Americans. A volley of shots and he disappeared. But Austin knew the sound must have been heard by the main body of troops guarding the bridge. "I waved my arms and said let's move. Most of the boys had fixed their bayonets. I told myself I'm not going to take a stroll down this road and let them shoot me down like a dog. They were going to have to kill me while I was running at 'em. I started, at a fast trot, and yelled to everybody, 'C'mon, let's go!'

"The guys all started to run. We saw blue smoke coming out of the ground right in front of us. There were three mortar pits, with two men on each gun hitting the

1st Battalion. We ran up on 'em so fast that they didn't know we were coming. One of our sergeants charged the first one and dropped hand grenades in. He and I eliminated the crew in the second one and then the sergeant and another soldier eliminated the third.

"I got back up on the road, ran and trotted about five hundred yards. About halfway to the bridge a mortar shell hit the road some twenty feet in front of me. The concussion spun me around but not even a piece of gravel and no shrapnel struck me. One of my platoons on the right ran into some machine gun fire and had one wounded and two killed. But the men kept charging, with bayonets, and killed the machine gun crew."

Among those involved in the assault was Joe Hoffrichter, the displaced engineer, now a rifleman. "When the command to fix bayonets came, I scarcely remembered how to do it. The last time had been two years earlier in basic training. We moved slowly at first. When we could see the Japanese we began to run towards them, yelling over and over 'Lo-oraine . . . Lo-oraine' with an emphasis on the two Os. Why Lo-oraine and whether it was meant to scare the Japanese or get our adrenaline going I don't know. But I was never so frightened in my life. The nearest I had ever come to hand-to-hand combat was in the movies.

"I ran as fast as I could and tripped over some vines. I fell flat on my stomach, gun in both hands extended before me. I hit so hard my helmet was jolted forward, covering my eyes and caused a cut on the bridge of my nose. As I pushed my helmet back and got up, six feet to my right were three Japanese in a foxhole. One was trying to load his rifle, one looked like he was hit and the third came out of his foxhole and at me with only his bayonet in hand.

"I grabbed the end of my rifle at the muzzle end and swung at him with all my might, hitting him squarely in his ribs. I heard bones break and a loud guttural sound. The force of my blow knocked him back into the foxhole. The one with the gun was still trying to load. Without thought or hesitation I shot from the hip, killing them all. I put another clip into my M-1 and continued to run, shooting from the hip at random."

Says Austin, "We killed forty-two Japs and we got there so fast that the Japs didn't have time to blow the bridge, which was rigged with mortar and artillery shells for demolition."

Some time later Newman spoke to Austin and, according to the latter, the regimental commander said, "I knew you were upset when you left. But you didn't know we were under extreme pressure to get to Carigara and take the beaches there. It wouldn't have taken but a minute to tell you what the urgency was but I chose not to because I was afraid that before you could get to the river, the Japanese would cover it." In fact, Newman used the incident as the basis for an article in *Army* expounding on the critical importance of time and timing in combat.

A few days later, however, Newman chose the wrong time to be in a particular place. The regiment, capitalizing on the Mainit River bridge capture, raced towards Carigara. Well-dug-in enemy troops, concealed beneath shacks that lined the highway from Jaro to Carigara, withstood artillery barrages and even held up a tank-led advance. Newman came to the head of the American column and led another assault. The GIs, respecting him, followed and the enemy responded with a fusillade from rifles, mortars and artillery.

A shellburst cut down the colonel with a severe stomach wound. He insisted on remaining at the scene to direct mortars, but as soon as possible he was put on a poncho and dragged to safety and medical aid. The infantrymen regretted his loss. "This was a time when everybody had a bit of depression and disappointment," says former wireman Han Rants. "Our real gutsy colonel got shot up pretty bad, although he did live through it. He had to be evacuated to the town of Jaro, a very small place really. It became a center for treatment of injuries. I remember a young man from Iowa who came back with a really pulverized elbow. In spite of the pain he was saying, 'So long suckers, I'm going home now.' We knew he would lose that arm and he did. The medical jeeps were really busy, bringing in four at a time as it was a bloody mess in this area.

"We found some friendly Filipinos who were trying to do a job for us. Someone had rumored that they'd get so much a head if they brought in Japanese heads. That's exactly what they did, no other part of the body, just a head hanging from a stick. I remember two fellows coming in like you'd picture an old deer hunt, with the deer upside down on a stick across their shoulders. Only these men had a stick about six feet long with four or five Japanese heads hanging by their hair from the stick."

As Rants indicated, the 24th Division was already bleeding badly if not hemorrhaging from the constant battles with the enemy. The Japanese had succeeded in shifting thousands of soldiers from Luzon and Panay to Leyte through Ormoc and now prepared to mount vigorous counterattacks. The weary, depleted ranks of the Americans, drenched in torrential rains spawned by a typhoon, struggled through a morass of high grass, steep hills and thickly wooded pockets. A series of battles for a group of strategic outcroppings known as Breakneck Ridge, Corkscrew Ridge and Kilay Ridge ensued.

The 1st Battalion of the 34th Infantry outflanked the enemy, coming by sea from behind their lines to attack positions on Kilay Ridge. Charles Card, a diffident and bespectacled replacement consigned to B Company, says that every one of his days and nights in combat was a "terrifying experience." He was particularly impressed by his battalion commander, Col. Jock Clifford. "I witnessed him relieve a struggling noncom by transferring the man's backpack, an 81 mm mortar baseplate, to his own back as we made an almost vertical climb up towards Kilay Ridge." Clifford, an aggressive commander, was equally demanding when dealing with the rear echelons. During the siege at Kilay, he messaged headquarters, "Either you give us artillery or I'm going to pull my men off the Ridge and leave the Japs looking down your throats." The requested artillery barrage followed swiftly.

"We were behind the lines without supply for the first few weeks," says Card, "and depended solely on airdrops of food, ammo and medical supplies. At times the C-47s would use parachute drops but mostly they pushed the cartons out of the door and hoped to hit our ridge positions. They rarely did and we would have to move out of our places to recover the supplies, in both chute and carton drops. The Japs naturally were attracted to the drop area and firefights were the rule when recovering supplies. The cartons were always broken and we gathered the stuff in our ponchos. The Japs sometimes got to the supplies before we could. The C-47s would be subjected to Jap rifle and machine gun fire on almost every run and there were few double runs to assure accurate drops."

Recognizing that outfits like the 24th were becoming less effective, the 6th Army chief Gen. Walter Krueger drew upon his reserves, the 32nd and 77th Infantry Divisions, as well as a pair of organizations already on Leyte, the 11th Airborne Division and the 112th Cavalry Regimental Combat Team.

The first of these to go into action was the 32nd, the Red Arrow Division. It coordinated with and then relieved elements of the 24th Division in the vicinity of Ormoc. Charles Evans, drafted during his final year at Oklahoma Military Academy, learned the essentials of heavy weapons at Camp Walters, Texas, before he was assigned to the 32nd Division as a replacement while his outfit, the 3rd Battalion of the 128th Infantry, was engaged at Aistape.

"We had a tough time there," says Evans. "I was wounded, shrapnel in my left hand from an exploding grenade thrown at us." But his war quieted down as he traveled to an outpost about twenty-five miles from Hollandia where the Americans set up a defense in the event the enemy sought to recapture Hollandia. "We saw nothing, did nothing and then were relieved to return to Hollandia and work at stevedoring chores. There were no docks, just barges from ships. We knew something big was coming because we unloaded a lot of aviation gas, bombs, small arms ammo, food. One day a shipload of beer arrived. It was the first we had seen. The beer was hot but good, and each of us got a case a month.

"Then they loaded us on ships to sail for Leyte. We were told we would be in reserve, stay on the ships and not land. It was good news, even though we were bombed several times while en route. When we got to Leyte, we saw a hospital ship in the distance, well lit, its crosses brightly illuminated. We watched the Japs bomb that ship. Another reason we didn't like them. They didn't believe in anything.

"We thought we would sit it out but then we were ordered onto shore to relieve the 24th Division. We went up a highway towards Carigara Valley and the town of Limone. The rains came, every day, all day. The roads were nothing but mudholes. We spent an awful lot of time trying to get our vehicles with supplies moving up to the front. My foxhole was on the side of a slope. The rain would run down the side, fill up the foxhole while I bailed like mad. But once you got wet you stayed wet. Your skin began to pucker up. The mud was worse than the enemy, because they weren't doing anything anyway.

"We sat there overlooking Limone, which turned out to be one or two buildings. We never did get there but instead went along the sides of the valley towards a mountain top. It was essential to take that peak because it was a strong point. Our first assault was repulsed and we had to retreat clear back to where we staged from. After a couple of days they decided to make a night attack. We headed back to the same hilltop. We got up within almost a hundred yards of the top. The 1st Battalion was on one side, the 3rd on the other. Only about a hundred yards separated us and we couldn't use our mortars or artillery for fear of hitting the other battalion.

"We had many men wounded and needed medics and

blood. They requested volunteers to go through Jap lines and back to battalion headquarters to lead up litter bearers and medical supplies. I volunteered, not because I was a hero but I felt the outfit would get clobbered that night and probably wiped out.

"We started down, quietly, slow and easy, passed through the Japanese lines. Suddenly all hell broke loose as someone started shooting at us. The sergeant whispered he thought it was our own men. He said he'd yell to them we're Americans and if there was more firing, we'd all just roll down the hill. On no account should we stand up. After a slight pause he shouted, 'Don't shoot, we're Yanks.'

"They said, 'Oh my God, is that the 3rd Battalion? We're litter bearers trying to come up by ourselves.' We stayed there for the night. When daylight came we went back up but things remained the same. The Japs were still there and wouldn't allow us to take the mountain. We tried for four days and finally the 1st Cav relieved us. We pulled out and the 1st Cav next day just walked in, nobody was there. The Japs had retreated during the night. I got a Bronze Star for my part in this episode."

Whayland Greene was also a replacement in the 32nd's 128th Infantry, a member of the 1st Battalion's C Company. His basic training sergeant had regarded him as something of a Sad Sack—"Greene, you won't last thirty minutes in combat." Greene had incurred his mentor's ire after the sergeant lectured forcibly about the techniques for killing a man in hand-to-hand combat. The recruit innocently inquired, "Sergeant, I have this killing down pretty pat. What I want to know is, when do we get to the class where you learn how to keep from getting killed. That is what I am interested in." The instructor repeated his description of murderous techniques and declared, "It is all part of the same class. You kill to keep from getting killed."

Unlike Evans, Greene had spent little time under fire until Leyte. "When we started towards the front lines it was raining real hard. You could hear the machine gun fire and rifle fire and also artillery. But not being used to combat I could not tell if it was our guns or Jap guns firing. We kept going and soon we looked beside the trail and there we could see three dead American soldiers. I remember how young they looked. They were the first American soldiers I had seen killed by enemy fire and I thought to myself that this is getting real serious now.

"Before we started to dig our holes for the night, I looked up and saw someone moving out in the woods some distance from us. I asked the sergeant what that man was doing way out there alone. He said, 'That's a Jap.' He got me and another guy to aim at him but told us to hold our fire because the Jap had not seen us and was still coming closer. We let him keep coming and I thought, 'I sure hope the sergeant is going to be the one to shoot him.' and sure enough when the Jap walked out from behind a big tree, the sergeant shot one time and the Jap was dead before he hit the ground. I think this is the only one I hesitated to shoot."

Greene slept little that night. A patrol from his company went off early in the morning and Greene recalls, "In a short time you could hear rifle fire and by this time you could tell that all of the rifles were not ours. There was a difference in the sound." Soon, Greene's squad headed out on a trail. "We had started back when the Japs opened up on us. We all hit the ground immediately. I fell into a mud hole that had a little hump of dirt in front and I was real thankful for that hump of wet dirt. They were firing at us real fast and we were firing back. We could not see them but could hear them talking real good. I saw one hand that was making the motion to come on. I shot as fast as I could in that direction and I must have hit him because they were bunching up and talking like they were more excited. Black Out's gun jammed on him and he had to pull back. That left Spence, Beege and Hale in front of us. We noticed that they had quit firing and thought that all must have been killed.

"One Jap got close enough to throw three hand grenades at James Bryant, Smitty and myself but they did not quite reach us. I thought then that it's time for someone to give ground. I knew that the Japs would not, and frankly, I was too scared to get up and run. I looked to my left and to my surprise there was a Jap between Bryant and me. We had both been concentrating so much on the ones we could hear talking, we neglected the area to our left. I saw him about the same time he saw me. I was ready to fire just a second or two before he could get ready. I shot and killed him. It scared me real bad, but I did not realize how much until later that afternoon. We pulled back to a place we were to dig in for the night. Beegie and Hale said Spence had been killed but they were able to get off the hill. After we had dug in, every time I tried to close my eyes I could see that Jap on his hands and knees. It was not because I felt sorry for him, but because it scared me so much. Sergeant Sullivan had told us that, whatever we did, not to shoot one and then feel sorry for him because it would run us crazy. He had seen young guys in New Guinea go crazy from this. I could see that Jap when I closed my eyes, day or night, for almost two weeks." During his first twenty-four hours under intense combat, Whayland Greene had learned to distinguish friendly from enemy fire and to overcome his buck fever.

Another newcomer to the 32nd, Max Papazian, also saw no combat while with Company F of the 126th Regimental Combat Team in New Guinea. He had participated in the seizure of a radar station on Morotai in the Dutch East Indies but again the enemy offered little or no resistance. "The 126th was kept in reserve temporarily while the rest of the 32nd Division moved inland on Leyte," notes Papazian. "A few days before we were to head up from our base, we had a Thanksgiving dinner with all the trimmings. While we were eating by our foxholes, the Japanese started shelling us with a large railroad cannon that had been hidden in the mountains. When this happened, my turkey went in one direction while I went in the other diving into my foxhole. As I listened to the bombardment, I prayed to God for protection and that no one get hurt, and the shelling stop. After a short time it did, and later we heard there had not been any casualties. God answered my prayers!"

Papazian ascended into the mountainous area with his comrades, coming upon numerous cave systems that required flamethrowers to seal off. "After about a week we were positioned to start an assault. Our platoon had dug a foxhole large enough to hold about six to eight men. We were all tired, hungry and wet. I prayed to God to get me out of there, no matter how He did it, just as long as I could walk out on my own.

"The next morning, December 15, we began to move up the hill to engage the enemy who had tanks setting on the crest of the hill. The battle started in full force. As I was crawling forward, I looked up and spotted a Japanese hand grenade sizzling about six to eight feet in front of me. I shouted, 'Oh God!' and started to turn to avoid the direct blast. The grenade exploded, causing my helmet to blow off my head and knocking my M-1 rifle out of my hands. My right hand and arm had been hit with flying shrapnel fragments in addition to flecks of metal on my neck, causing what seemed to be a lot of bleeding. I made my way downhill, found a medic who cleaned me up as best he could and bandaged my visible wounds. I continued on to an area in the rear for transportation to a field hospital. Some of my buddies were not so fortunate. As I was walking back to the rear, I began to calm down and suddenly realized that God had heard and answered my prayer of the night before again!"

Although the two U.S. fleets had vanquished Japanese seapower, enemy pilots using fields on Formosa and other islands of the archipelago had continued to plague the invaders. Upon returning from its mission against Admiral Ozawa's northern fleet in October, the *Cabot* now ravaged the enemy airstrips. On November 19, Bill Anderson, a torpedo bomber pilot from the *Cabot*, was in a flight that attacked the West Lippa air station. "The idea was to crater the strip and do as much damage as possible," says Anderson. "The Japanese gunners around an airfield were generally much less accurate than those on a ship who pretty much knew where you were going to hit them. But as we went into our dive, my gunner reported that my wingman and roommate, John Ballantine, had lost a wing. As I passed over the field I saw his smashed plane on the runway. Nobody could have gotten out alive."

Anderson says there was nothing he could do except to strengthen his resolve to attack the enemy. Some measure of revenge came during an assault upon the former U.S. base of Clark Field. "I was the flight leader," says Anderson. "The visibility and weather were reasonably good and we could see the Jap fighters taxiing to take off. We went into our bomb run to crater their runways and prevent takeoffs. My gunner told me he saw one fighter veer off, then ground loop. Another one ran right into a crater and crashed. It was as good as shooting them down."

Carrying out these missions in Philippine waters exposed the *Cabot* to marauders. On November 25, a group of *kamikazes* swooped down upon 3rd Fleet Group 2's quartet of carriers. Air cover disposed of a pair but shortly before one in the afternoon the survivors began to score. A portion of a wing fell on the deck of the *Hancock;* a second Zeke slammed into the *Intrepid* and then a third plane rammed the *Cabot*.

On the bridge of the *Cabot* was Gene Masucci. Pearl Harbor, according to Masucci, was a good excuse for him to drop out of high school at age sixteen, forge the date on his baptismal certificate and enlist in the Navy. With only twenty-three days of boot camp, he shipped out on the seaplane tender *Albemarle* for duty in the Atlantic and Caribbean Oceans. Because of his small size—5'5" and 117 pounds—Masucci switched from heavy-duty assignments like handling ammunition to a quartermaster berth.

"Combat fear started with me onboard the *Mable* in the North Atlantic and Caribbean in 1942. German U-boats were sinking ships all over the ocean and at all the choke points on the Atlantic coast. We steamed without sounding gear or depth charges on board and often without destroyer escorts. While we had many alerts and scares, a torpedo attack never materialized.

"On board the *Cabot* when radar picked up bogeys, you knew our CAP and the ship's guns would soon go into action. Being a carrier and a small makeshift one, we knew we were a priority for the Japanese. You always felt fear. Your main worry was were you going to survive a combat action. What kind of a hit could the ship take? Would it be a bomb, a torpedo or a *kamikaze*? Could we get our aircraft airborne in time? Could we recover our aircraft safely?

"When our ship's guns started firing, the enemy was very close. The noise, smoke and smell of the guns really got the adrenaline flowing. Gun Control, above the navigation bridge, was an open platform with Gunnery Officer Lt. Frank Zimanski giving orders to 'Guard your sector! Guard your sector!' He was afraid a gunner in one sector would look elsewhere to see what was happening and permit an enemy plane to sneak in and clobber us.

"Once the guns started firing it was difficult to stop them because of the excitement and the need of the gunners to work off all those hours of tension and apprehension. Below, often in sealed-off dark compartments, other crew members stood by in engine rooms, damage-control parties or stretcher parties and could only wonder what was happening topside. The air intakes of the ship's ventilating system would pull in the acrid smoke of the gunfire and stimulate these men's overworked imaginations. High-speed engine vibrations and rapid turns with the ship listing seemingly on her beam's end caused items on shelves and in cabinets to crash all over the deck. At these moments, all hands wondered if she could right herself and recover. We all knew she was top-heavy and fragile. Even the captain had expressed concern that she might capsize.

"Being a CVL [light carrrier] we were much smaller and probably a little less conspicuous compared to the CVs who were the main objects of any 'K' attack. You could actually see enemy pilots bypass several ships and head for the larger carriers. Often they were killed in the attempt. The 'Ks' were awesome in their death dive. They would burst into a fireball if hit or disappear in smoke and flame when they struck a ship. Invariably when they hit a carrier, planes and AV gas [fuel] and sometimes the ordnance on board were involved and the conflagration was something to behold. A prayer of thanks almost subconsciously offered that it wasn't us would come from every man aboard the ships that were spared." But on November 25, the *Cabot* was not spared.

Masucci recalls the task group running at high speed during the attack of November 25. "Suddenly the gunnery control officer shouted over the sound phone, 'Commence firing! Commence firing!' I looked up and coming at us in a moderate dive was a single-engine airplane. Our guns were firing like hell and all the tracers were merging on the rapidly closing airplane. He seemed headed right for me on the bridge. I heard Captain Michael order, 'Hard right rudder' to Ole Langsted, who was on the wheel. As we had only one gun on the stern, the captain wanted more of our battery to concentrate on the oncoming airplane. At this moment there was a TBM on our catapult, revving up to be launched. The enemy was hit by our guns and burst into flame but kept coming towards me. I hit the deck, covered up and felt this enormous hot fireball scorch my back and just miss the bridge. It crossed over the flight deck and crashed forward on the catwalk and gun tubs right alongside the catapult."

"Just as I had taxied onto the catapult and was hooking up for the shot," remembered pilot Howard Skidmore, "the task force commander ordered all carriers to cease launching. By the sound of the 40 mm and 20 mm, I knew the enemy planes were close. I positioned myself in front of my armor plate, lowered my seat and adjusted my gear to give me as much protection as possible. The next thing I knew I was sitting in a flaming furnace. I ordered my crew out and climbed onto the starboard side of the flight deck.

"The *kamikaze* had crashed just ahead of us on the port side of the TBF [his torpedo bomber]. The bomb had exploded and the plane was burning. I ran aft through heavy smoke to a catwalk and ducked onto an ammo storage room when I heard the gunners open up again. Another Jap plane was shot down, close to the *Cabot*. It crashed into the port side amidship at the waterline, with much damage and loss to the gun crews. My helmet was charred on top, some hair singed, and all my fingers on the left hand had blistered from the heat while I was in the cockpit. I was very lucky; thirty-five of our shipmates were killed by the two *kamikazes*."

Frank Zimanski, the gunnery officer mentioned by Gene Masucci, was the son of Polish immigrants. Zimanski says, "When I was eleven years old and my family moved to Brooklyn, I plucked a book from the public library shelf with the title, *The U.S. Naval Academy*. Upon reading it, I firmly resolved to enter the Academy. Since my folks were illiterate in English, I alone initiated correspondence with the Academy, and conducted an inquiry within all the boroughs of New York to determine which high school would prepare a candidate best for the entrance examinations."

Zimanski, armed with his diploma from Stuyvesant High School, a forty-minute daily subway ride from his home, was not able to obtain an appointment to Annapolis from his congressman. "My only recourse was to join the enlisted ranks and I was lucky enough to be one of just twenty-five in the entire New York/New England area chosen in June 1932. After completing a year of service, including nine months of sea duty, I was assigned to the Naval Academy prep school." There he heard the instructors, all from the 1925 Annapolis class, emphatically and unanimously insist war with Japan was inevitable.

After earning his commission as an ensign, Zimanski served on several ships before assignment to the *Cabot*. "The *kamikaze* attack was well coordinated. The first *kam* approached about a mile from astern and our stern guns promptly took it under fire. We must have hit the pilot or controls or both since the plane was unable to make the slight change of course necessary to hit the bridge, its target. Instead, it struck the propeller on Skidmore's plane as it revved up. It pitched into the adjacent gun tubs where it and its five-hundred-pound bomb exploded, killing so many of our crew.

"As the plane approached, it was at my eye level and about twenty feet from where I stood above the bridge. I peered directly into its cockpit when suddenly came the explosion. We all ducked as fire and debris struck us, fortunately doing me and others on the bridge no harm. I anticipated the second *kam* approach slightly above the water and from almost dead ahead. Since the first *kam* destroyed our port forward battery, only our 40 mm mount on the forecastle was able to bear. The crew's performance was heroic, shooting the plane down only seconds before it would have reached our bridge."

Bill Anderson missed the scene on the *Cabot*, having taken off shortly before the strike upon his ship. On November 25 he actually flew a pair of missions against Japanese airfields.

Following the *kamikaze* attacks, *Cabot* was withdrawn from combat duty in Leyte Gulf and sent to Ulithi for repairs and replacements. The carrier mourned thirty-five victims, most of whom were blown overboard; an additional seriously injured seventeen were transferred to a hospital ship.

The western approaches to Leyte, via the Camotes Sea that led to Ormoc Bay, offered entry to the island by reinforcements. Pilots of carriers like the *Cabot* and land-based fighter bombers from the now liberated eastern portion of Leyte struck at this backdoor opening, but only surface ships could slam it shut with night and day patrols. American destroyers and PT boats roamed the Camotes Sea searching for the enemy. When aircraft sighted a "Tokyo Express" run steaming in the direction of Ormoc, the destroyers *Allen M. Sumner, Moale* and *Cooper* sailed from Leyte Gulf on December 2 to intercept them.

Detroit-born George Berlinger, drafted after graduation from high school in the spring of 1943, says, "My father and two uncles were in France in the Army during WW I and told me stories of mud and all the dirty things that happened to them. My Uncle Roy was in the Navy during that war and told me a sailor has a clean bunk to sleep in and three square meals each day. At the induction center they asked what service I wanted and I said Navy."

Sent to gunnery school, Berlinger had never seen salt water when assigned to DD 695, the *Cooper*. A newly built vessel with a fresh bunch of hands, the *Cooper* underwent a series of exercises and drills to qualify for fleet duty. The ship took up station in Leyte Gulf a few days after the great sea battles with Admiral Kurita's fleets.

As the December 2 mission began, Berlinger recalls the *Cooper* using radar to make its way through the fog. Approaching Ormoc Bay, Japanese aircraft detected their approach and the bogeys showed up with increasing frequency. "The *Cooper* took three under fire, the second or third salvo causing a plane to burst into flames and crash into the water about four hundred yards ahead. Our fantail 20 mm guns [his station] were never fired."

Another gunner's mate on DD 695 was Al Masulis. He too watched the plane make its run on the destroyer and estimated that it had closed within two hundred yards before it splashed. "I glanced at the *Moale* to see if she were tracking the same target but it seemed as if her guns were tracking and firing at a target off her port bow. Suddenly a shadow seemed to cross her bow and a large column flame shot up from the face of turret two, a bright, angry flame which leaped to a height of a hundred feet and was whipped back over its stern as if the ship were entirely in flames. We gave her up for lost but the flames were active only a few minutes, the damage-control party had the fire under control in a very short time. Control advised us that a *kamikaze* had crashed the *Moale* but had only wiped off a wing on turret two and then gone over the side. The front of the turret was sprayed with gasoline which had ignited."

The tiny American flotilla continued to duel with the enemy aircraft, knocking down three or four [some accounts say nine] plus the suicide that tumbled across the *Moale*. On the *Cooper*, the mess staff brought around hot soup, crackers and coffee shortly after eleven. The moon rose over the nearby mountains and lit up the sea. Under a scattering of fleecy clouds, just before midnight, the destroyers entered Ormoc Bay. Gun crews readied themselves.

"At 2400," says Masulis, "Schade, the gun captain of mount 44, called out, 'Surface craft bearing zero five-oh, range 15,300 yards, all guns stand by.' I climbed on top of a barrel box with binoculars and noticed a large Jap destroyer anchored along the beach, perfectly silhouetted by the moon. Our little group was zigzagging, steaming at thirty-four knots, the *Sumner* leading, the *Moale* in the center and the *Cooper* behind.

"At 0001 Schade repeated, 'Salvo fire, commence firing.' All six of our 38s blasted out flame and burning cork with a deep, shaking roar, then there was silence. I watched six specks of light converge on the target and the Nip destroyer was silhouetted by a big splash as the projectiles hit the water and exploded. I yelled, 'Over!' to our gun crew to let them know that our salvo had missed and was beyond the target. The second salvo was short, for when the splash occurred I could not see the target for an instant and I called out 'Short!'

"The third salvo sped on its way but when the tracers winked out, there was no splash and I realized that we were on the target and I called, 'Hit!' The guns cut loose with rapid salvo fire and there were very few splashes, indicating practically all shells were on the target. After nine or ten salvos, I wondered how much more of a battering it could take. There was a big flash of flame from the target and a Nip can folded up and joined Old Man Jones's locker. I then noticed red, winking lights along the shoreline and from the Nip convoy along the beach and I realized that they were returning our fire."

The details supplied by Berlinger differ slightly. "About two minutes after midnight, contact was made with surface ships and a minute later we commenced firing. Our first salvo fell short about two hundred yards but the second struck the Jap ship right between the two forward guns. The Jap ship was a large destroyer carrying troops. [It was] hit repeatedly from stem to stern which threw many of the troops topside into great confusion. After eight minutes of firing, the Jap destroyer was thoroughly wrecked and sinking.

"Cease fire was ordered to train the guns on a second target and in a minute we were firing on a Jap ship of destroyer escort size. The first salvo hit the target, followed by several more hits. Firing ceased in order to clear the *Moale* as the Jap ships were passing astern. The *Cooper* came to the right momentarily, gunners on the fantail could see the two blazing ships who were only a few hundred yards away. Just before reaching the formation course, our ship was hit by a terrific concussion. We had taken a torpedo on our starboard side amidship. The explosion was almost drowned out by the shudder of the ship as she took her death blow. The main effect of the explosion was below decks and topside, midship. Almost every man near the explosion was killed instantly.

"When we were hit, the stern seemed to drop like an elevator with a shudder. Then the ship rolled over to starboard. Before the ship rolled, I saw debris flying through the air and I dropped to my knees. As the ship rolled, I went under water. My phones were still on me when I came to the surface. My line had been cut by one of the men on the gun crews. His leg was caught in my phone wire. I was below water until he cut me loose and I owe my life to that radioman striker.

"When I looked at the ship again, the bow and stern were about fifty feet apart. The bow was sticking out of the water at an almost vertical position. The numbers 695 could be seen without any trouble in the moonlight on the stern. The depth charge racks and rudders could be seen sticking high up out of the water. I looked at my watch. It was about 0015. The *Cooper* went down fighting. One of the five-inch guns had fired a last salvo which ricocheted off the water. I turned for a final look at our gallant ship and she was already out of sight on her way to a watery grave." The *Cooper* sank less than a minute after the torpedo from the Japanese destroyer *Take* exploded.

"I felt myself flying through the air, end over end," recalled Masulis, "but I could not feel my legs. I was sure I had been blown in two. I hit the water and went down, down, down. I felt around my waist and was surprised to find my body intact. I ran my hands down each leg and was further surprised to find them both still with me. It puzzled me because I couldn't feel my hands on my legs. I reached down again and after much fumbling around I untied both shoelaces, pulled off my shoes and pinched each foot as hard as I could but I felt nothing. There was no response in either leg when I tried to kick them."

The blast had broken Masulis's back but he was fortunate: one-half of the crew had died as the destroyer blew apart. At that he nearly drowned as the rudder of the sinking fantail snagged his jacket and pulled him below the surface. He had started to inhale water, cough and sputter when the shattered hunk of ship popped above water and threw him clear. He heard voices and one inquired, "Anybody find a raft?" Somebody behind Masulis answered, "We've got a couple of rafts over here. Everyone swim this way." When Masulis had swum what seemed to him a massive distance, helpful hands lifted his broken body—his left elbow was also smashed—onto the raft.

"The entire scene was a Buck Rogers [the 1940s sci-fi comic strip] spectacle," says Berlinger, "with guns firing from the ships on both sides, two Jap ships burning, shore batteries firing at our ships from the shore, Jap boats in the vicinity and Jap submarines lurking below the surface of the water. Bombs were dropped from planes overhead and the tracers from 40 mm guns formed an arching glow to the various targets. The light of a full moon was diffused just enough to illuminate the ships in an eerie setting as a white haze of steam rose slowly from the water, marking the resting places of the Jap ships.

"In the water it was a terrifying sight. We could see our own ships leaving the bay with their guns blazing, the shells lobbing over our heads with an indescribable shine or whistle. *Sumner* and *Moale* were outlined beautifully. Their black and gray camouflage made them look almost unreal, like toys. The five-inch guns looked like six eyes on each ship. The Japs continued to fire long after they had departed. A Japanese float plane roared over at low altitude and strafed the water with machine gun fire that was frightening, but looked beautiful in red, orange, green and yellow tracer colors.

"I joined three men in the oil-filled water. We grouped together and decided to strike out away from where the *Cooper* went down. The water was filled with survivors, hollering for help and in pain. Whistles and flashlights that were standard on lifejackets blared and flashed, letting the Japs know just where we were. We sighted a ten-man raft and swam to it. It was very crowded and a wounded man whose leg was broken occupied most of it. Donald Fish, a seaman first class, sighted another raft with only a few men on it a hundred feet or so away. Fish and I swam to it and in a short time there were nine of us on the raft."

The group saw a small island, identified as Polar in the Camotes group, some miles off and one of the men, a navigation officer, recalled that on the maps it was listed as abandoned by the enemy. They headed for the tiny piece of land, hampered by broken paddles and a dragging piece of the raft. They pushed, pulled and jockeyed their way towards the island the rest of the night while anxiously fearing the appearance of strafing enemy planes at daylight. "About 0800 we heard the drone of aircraft. Our hearts were gladdened when four beautiful P-38 Lightning fighters came over. They circled above us as air cover for about an hour and then were relieved by four P-47 Thunderbolt fighters."

When the raft floated within half a mile of the island, outrigger canoes ventured out from the beach. "The paddlers kept a good distance," says Berlinger. "They carried Filipinos who thought we were Japs; we were well tanned and had brush haircuts." Several of the survivors waved their hands wildly and the Filipinos swiftly headed for them. "We told them we were Americans and they were overjoyed to see us. They said they had watched the 'great battle' that night. We were so exhausted from pushing and pulling the raft that the natives carried us ashore in their dugouts. The people were Roman Catholics. They even had crosses tattooed on their arms. They were very happy to see a holy medal hanging around the neck of one of the boys."

On his raft, Masulis endured an equally scary night. With his companions he saw the two sister destroyers pass within a few hundred yards, firing and running from Ormoc Bay. "The boys cursed the two ships for not stopping for us, even though we knew it would have been suicide for them. At dawn a thick fog settled down with a drizzle. Someone spotted two masts appearing above the fog and bearing down on us. Our hopes took an upswing; perhaps they were rescue craft. We watched as two subs passed about three hundred yards from us, their bows and conning towers showing intermittently through the banks of fog. Then we saw the Rising Sun flapping dismally from the tallest mast. We knew the remnants of the Jap force was leaving the Bay. All the boys slid from the rafts and submerged as far as possible. I felt as big and conspicuous as an elephant as I laid across that raft.

"A Jap freighter, small destroyer and a large one sailed by. They passed within a hundred yards of us. We could distinctly hear commands being shouted, the murmur of the blowers, could see men spread out all over the deck like cordwood, sailors walking around among them and gun crews at their stations, all searching the skies. But none of them looked at the water."

Company showed up as a pair of rubber boats loaded

with survivors—including the sunken vessel's captain, Comdr. Mell A. Peterson—met the raft party. The newcomers, however, shoved off in an effort to find a deserted stretch of beach and meet U.S. Army troops. Masulis drifted in and out of consciousness, dimly aware of a plane that appeared to take a run at those in the rubber boats and others trying to swim to shore. He begged for morphine as shock wore off and agony replaced it. But there were no medical kits on the raft. He saw the Lightnings and Thunderbolts come overhead for protection but in his semi-delirium counted many more planes than Berlinger observed. "Occasionally," recalls Masulis, "one of them would come down very low, landing flaps and wheels down to slow the plane as much as possible. As they sailed by the pilot would wave or give us the 'thumbs up' sign. They were certainly morale boosters."

Coming out of a sleep period, Masulis suddenly discovered a canoe with Filipinos bobbing at the side of the raft. The natives transported the Americans to land where a group of sailors from the *Cooper* carried the injured man to a village. George Berlinger, already there, welcomed him, and throughout the remainder of the afternoon survivors from the sunken ship, aided by the island residents, made their way to the safety of the beach.

The locals dispatched a dugout to an area of Leyte to advise the American forces of the survivors. A pair of "Black Cats," the Navy's PBY 5 Catalina patrol bombers, set down on the water near a pier and loaded up with the Americans. One ship, stuffed with fifty-six survivors and overloaded by three thousand pounds, set a record with its cargo of humans. To take off the plane taxied two miles. Altogether, the aircraft brought 104 men to safety. Of the original 359 in the *Cooper* crew, 168 were saved.

Radar specialist Russ Catardi, a twenty-four-year-old former sheet-metal worker aboard the *Moale*, escaped injury when the suicide plane glanced off, but years later he spoke for many. "If the Japs could fly that night, where were our planes? They sent us up there with nothing but our balls and when, considering the number of men that were lost that night, we got our asses kicked." Who won this encounter in Ormoc Bay might be debated, but efforts to deter potential reinforcements through this opening influenced future operations.

Meanwhile, the Manila-based Japanese commander of the area, Gen. Tomoyuki Yamashita, perceived the burgeoning air support from land-based planes on Leyte as a threat both to his troops and the homeland lifelines. He directed his subordinates to seize or destroy the major sites on Leyte. The missions called for coordinated efforts by ground and air units.

On the basis of coded enemy messages that had been intercepted, captured documents and interrogations of the few prisoners, U.S. intelligence knew that something was afoot but the precise nature was unknown. The notion of such an assault seemed far-fetched to the Americans. Patrols discovered no signs of movement along the trails and no one believed the enemy capable of an airborne assault. However, as a precaution, positions about the airfields were strengthened and an alert mounted.

The 11th Airborne Division had arrived on the island to relieve elements of the 7th Division and now guarded the area around Burauen, which included several air strips. The opening gambit of the Japanese occurred on November 27 as three enemy air transports glided over Leyte Gulf about 3:00 A.M. with no lights. One of them crash-landed twenty-five yards offshore. GIs from a nearby amphibious tractor outfit investigated and exchanged shots and grenades with the enemy. They killed two but more than a dozen escaped into a swamp. However, the Americans found many demolition bundles in the wrecked airplane. The attack had been thwarted but there was little doubt that suicide missions against the airfields were a reality.

What the Japanese dubbed *Operation Wa* involved a double strike—ground troops from the 16th Division combined with parachutists. The foot soldiers totaled only five hundred as they began their trek towards the Buri airstrip. An unhappy bunch, sustained largely by coconuts and bananas, so short of men they abandoned any wounded along the way, they bumped into a buzz saw of U.S. artillery that reduced their number to only three hundred. Nevertheless, aided by a Filipino guide, the infiltrators slipped into the airfield environs, falling upon GIs still asleep. A number of Americans died before the rear-echelon soldiers, bolstered by the quick dispatch of infantrymen from the 96th Division, prevented the first intruders from gaining a solid foothold.

The second half of *Wa*, airborne drops at airfields including nearby San Pablo and Buri, had been scheduled to occur simultaneously with the abortive attack by the infantry but the paratroop mission was postponed until dusk. Using fighters and bombers to soften up the drop zone, the ambitious operation involved more than 450 well-drilled jumpers.

When the aircraft roared over the Burauen complex, antiaircraft fire greeted them and shot down as many as eighteen of the fifty-one planes. Nevertheless, chutists dropped from the transports, sixty floating down near Buri and between 250 and 300 at San Pablo. Someone had coached them in a few American phrases—they were heard to shout, "Hello, where are your machine guns?"—words unlikely to fool the GIs. However, at San Pablo the defenders consisted of only a small detachment of airborne engineers, signalmen, artillerymen and service troops. Confused by the sudden presence of the enemy, the soldiers fired wildly and without effect.

The parachutists blew gasoline dumps, demolished buildings, torched liaison planes and captured some weapons. Gen. Joseph Swing, a West Pointer and at forty-eight a bit older than his contemporaries heading up American paratroop units [Matthew Ridgway, James Gavin and Maxwell Taylor, all in Europe], led the 11th Airborne. He had set up a command post at San Pablo. At daylight, Swing himself organized his handful of engineers, cooks, clerks, artillerymen and a few regular troopers into defensive positions while reinforcements from the 11th's own 187th Glider Infantry and the 38th Infantry Division rushed to the scene.

Linking up with survivors from the 16th Infantry Division who had concealed themselves on the outskirts of the Buri field, the Japanese chutists seized total control of the strip. Elements from the 149th Infantry Regiment, a component of the 38th Division which reached Leyte from a base in New Guinea, checked in with General Swing for a counterattack against the enemy at Buri.

Milt Pearce, a Rhode Island native and a white collar worker bored with his job until the draft snatched him up in September 1941, says he fought a running battle with the Army to avoid being shunted into a clerical position. "It wasn't my idea of soldiering. I wanted to be in the field." Armed with a commission from the infantry OCS he was assigned as a machine gun platoon leader in the 149th's 1st Battalion.

En route to Leyte, Pearce had seen a *kamikaze* shot down. "The plane we downed was piloted by a youth and we could see the tracers going into him before his machine disintegrated at mast height above the ship on our port. I often think of that 'boy,' admire his guts and am a little depressed at the memory. Then I remind myself of the death and destruction he would have created had he gone on and plowed into that ship as he intended. The troop ship on our starboard was hit a moment later by another *kamikaze* and immediately the entire boat seemed engulfed in smoke and fire. Another weapons company, men whom I knew, was aboard that ship in one compartment. Their losses in dead, burned and wounded were horrendous.

"Our battalion's toughest fight with the most casualties took place on the Buri airstrip," recalls Pearce. "The resistance comprised mostly Jap paratroopers who apparently had a plentiful supply of sake. Many of them dressed in

American uniforms and some used our weapons which made their identities uncertain and caused us a lot of trouble.

"The fighting went on for three or four days, much of it in a pouring rain and with no food part of the time. There were no heroes in my platoon. All of them just did their jobs as they had been trained to do. They behaved magnificently under the worst conditions. I saw a leading rifle platoon, under fire for the first time, suddenly turn towards the rear and run back through the bushes. I grabbed one of the men by the arm, told him to hold it right there. 'You beat it out of here now, you're only going to have to come back again, and that'll be even more dangerous.' The men listened, got low in the bushes and built up a line. They held steady. A few minutes later, they proceeded forward, maybe a little more carefully than before. But they kept moving.

"That's where the first officer was killed, a lieutenant who one night had confided to me how much he and his wife loved each other. We had dug in near the airstrip when we began receiving fire from behind us. His captain ordered him to send a squad to take the gun out. He started to send a squad leader who began to object, the only time I ever saw such an instance. The lieutenant said, 'Oh, hell, I'll go myself!'

"I heard the burst of automatic fire. A few minutes later the squad came back through my position. I asked what had happened. 'The lieutenant stood up and swung his arm to point to where we should attack. As he did, the Japs opened up on him.' I believe we had about two hundred killed and wounded out of probably seven hundred or eight hundred actually fighting."

The initial success of the assault on the Burauen complex melted as more battalions of U.S. infantrymen arrived to counterattack. When a stream of bullets ripped through the walls of the building housing Gen. Ennis Whitehead, commander of the 5th Air Force, the furious officer demanded an explanation. One of his staff telephoned the nearest 11th Airborne CP to protest the "promiscuous firing." Informed that the Japanese were guilty, the airman insisted the weapons were U.S. .50 caliber machine guns. "That's right . . . and the Japs are doing the shooting," reported the paratrooper on the other end of the line. The enemy in his last spasm had employed the arms seized from American stores. When the Air Corps man complained, "The bullets are coming right through the general's quarters," the answer was, "Tell the general to get down on the floor [in some versions, "tell the goddamn general to get his goddamned ass down"]. Incidentally, that yelling you hear is a *banzai* raid on our mess hall."

Wa proved to be another of those desperate, suicidal operations that temporarily disconcerted the U.S. forces, but ultimately the enemy forces were eliminated with no serious disruption of the Leyte campaign.

While the 24th and 32nd Divisions coped with the forces defending the highlands, the 7th and 96th Divisions fought towards the western coast, and the 11th Airborne parried thrusts at the air support. The 77th Infantry Division, bloodied on Guam in the capture of the Marianas, had started to come ashore on Thanksgiving Day, November 23, to perform behind-the-lines support. Two weeks later, the Statue of Liberty Division carried out a brilliant maneuver typical of MacArthur throughout his career. "I had long recognized the decisive advantage by severing the enemy's supply lines at Ormoc," said the general, a belief amply demonstrated in the efforts by the likes of the ill-fated *Cooper* and the other two destroyers. "Heretofore, the lack of fighter cover to ensure the safety of the convoy, and the fact that supporting naval forces did not have sufficient landing craft and resupply shipping to maintain amphibious operations had prevented the mounting of any sizable seaborne assault. These conditions were now remedied, and I decided that the time had arrived when the enemy's 'back door' to Leyte could be slammed shut by a strike on the west coast. Accordingly, orders were issued for the newly arrived 77th Division to land in the Ormoc area in conjunction with a coordinated drive from the front."

On the morning of December 7, a day whose significance could not have escaped MacArthur's notice, GIs from the 77th splashed through the surf behind the usual naval bombardment and a generous amount of air cover supplied now by elements of the Army's 5th Air Force supplemented by Marine aircraft operating from Leyte airfields.

Henry Lopez, a sergeant with Company C of the 307th Regiment, says, "The air over Ormoc was dominated by the Japanese air force, so consequently Japanese Zeros were very active during the landings. Several enemy aircraft dove at the landing crafts headed for shore. American planes intercepted the enemy and a dog fight ensued. The Japanese on shore had been taken completely by surprise, and only slight resistance was encountered."

The troops quickly overcame that opposition and moved inland. Meanwhile, the American fliers discovered a number of enemy transports on their way with reinforcements and supplies. In a devastating attack, the airmen sank a major portion of the convoy, wiping out as many as four thousand soldiers.

The end run so surprised the enemy that during the first night ashore an enemy landing ship, its skipper unaware of what had happened, attempted to land on a beach near where the Americans had dug their foxholes. As the hapless Japanese soldiers scrambled through the water, a sustained and withering storm of fire slaughtered more than seven hundred—the entire contingent except for one man who hid himself in the crow's nest of the vessel.

The enemy regrouped to offer stiff opposition as the Americans pushed towards Ormoc. In spite of the havoc wreaked by the 5th Air Force and its Marine cohorts, the Japanese continued to strike at the infantrymen. After two enemy planes attacked his battalion, Lopez notes, "The men, nervous from enemy aerial attacks, fired at three low-flying American Corsairs, mistaking them for Zeros." The recognition factor also bedeviled the GIs in the 306th Regiment. A very youthful executive officer for Company G of the 306th Infantry, Buck Creel, remembers, "A beautiful flight of aircraft, two Vees of four each flew over our battle area. We all shouted, 'They are ours. Don't shoot.' They disappeared into a cloud overhead and came screaming down on us from it. It seemed like they came from eight different directions. They bombed and strafed the hell out of us, waggled their wings and flew off. Only as they attacked us had we noticed the Rising Sun on the wings. From then on we fired at everything that flew over us unless it was an L-4 [liaison artillery spotter], a P-38 [fighter twin tail boom] or a C-47 [troop transport]. The entire 77th Division was guilty of this. The situation got so bad that the commanding general, I believe, of the 5th Air Force sent a message to the CO of the 77th Division, to wit, 'If you desire continued air support from this Air Force, you will cease fire immediately on all friendly aircraft. We were receiving too much and too accurate antiaircraft fire from your command.' I remember the response of the troops when learning their antiaircraft fire was 'too accurate'—pride. But we were all a little more careful after that."

The 306th and 307th regiments squeezed the foe in a pincers maneuver and by the morning of December 9, GIs entered the streets of Ormoc, ablaze with the inferno of white phosphorus shells, burning buildings and exploding ammo dumps. Street by street, house by house, the Americans eliminated holdouts until an elated 77th Division commander, Gen. Andrew Bruce, advised his corps commander, Gen. John R. Hodge, "Have rolled two sevens in Ormoc. Come seven come eleven."

Whatever enemy listeners may have made of this craps table language, Bruce was inviting the two nearest counterparts to his outfit, the 7th Division and the 11th Airborne, for a linkup on the western coast of Leyte.

Genes nominated William "Buzz" Miley for the 11th Airborne. "My father was a West Point graduate, Class of 1918, and it was an old army family, father to son from way back. I graduated from high school in Columbus, Georgia. My father, then a major stationed at Fort Benning, organized and trained the first parachute troops. He commanded the first unit, the 501st Parachute Battalion and then the 503rd Parachute Regiment. He was deputy commanding general of the 82nd Airborne and then commanding general of the 17th Airborne which fought in Europe.

"I guess I was destined to get into the parachute troops since I hung around the early training areas. I lived jumping out of planes at home, envied my father and all the young troopers of the 501st Battalion. I was in prep school in Washington, D.C., at the time of Pearl Harbor and when I finished school figured the United States couldn't win the war without me. I volunteered and signed the papers June 25, 1942."

After basic training, OCS and jump school, 2nd Lt. Buzz Miley filled the slot of platoon leader for G Company of the 3rd Battalion in the 511th Regiment, the paratrooper component of the 11th Airborne Division. "My first combat action was on Leyte, in the mountains. My platoon was leading and my scouts reported tents and shelters of a bivouac area ahead. We spread out and walked into a small Japanese camp. Most were sleeping. We killed all in the camp, approximately twenty-five, and I didn't feel much excitement since I was the leader and pushing everyone forward, yelling, 'keep shooting' since no Japanese were surrendering. No Americans were wounded."

One of Swing's platoon leaders, Eli Bernheim, Jr., whose grandfather had served in the French Army and whose father had been an officer in WW I and was on active duty again, volunteered on December 8, 1941. "The psychological exam asked one question, 'Did I like boys or girls?' After four years of ROTC at the University of Pittsburgh, Bernheim was a natural for OCS. Although initially schooled in armor, Bernheim fled the confined space of tanks for the open spaces of paratroop training.

"I had never experienced the sense of purpose or morale that I did in the airborne. Being Jewish I experienced minor anti-Semitic slurs from one individual but in the paratroops we were all in the same boat. Of course there were no blacks in any of the parachute units I was in. Blacks were then considered second-class citizens. I was raised in affluent but desegregated society, although when I attended the University of Pittsburgh I was amazed that the only blacks allowed on athletic teams were in track.

"Paratroopers usually grabbed anything that was not tied down. In New Guinea they assigned us to unload a ship. We became known as Ali Baba Swing and his eight thousand thieves. We stole vehicles, generators and BARs from other units because we had none in our T/O [Table of Organization]. The BAR was not authorized for paratroop units but we acquired many of them by moonlight requisitions. After we lost two machine gun cradles carried by a carabao that went over a cliff on Leyte, I as a second lieutenant forged the signature of a colonel to requisition replacements at an ordnance depot.

"The supply system for the 11th Airborne failed during the Leyte campaign. My battalion received an average of one-third K ration for a thirty-day period, no rations at all for a five-day period. From intuition I lugged a carton of twenty-five Hershey tropical chocolate bars into the jungle and they kept my platoon going. We never had enough fragmentation grenades. We used a lot of white phosphorus ones. Our battalion had to carry a lot of color smoke grenades and flares that were rarely used.

"My baptism of fire on Leyte came when I walked through a Jap fire lane cut low in the jungle. I looked down, heard a crack of passing fire and saw tracers. I was amazed at first and then scared bad. There were no front lines there. We had a great relationship with the Filipino people. They were deliriously happy at our arrival. The guerrilla units attached to our battalion did well except they had a tendency to sleep on the perimeter. Gen. Joe Swing was an inspiration and was everywhere in combat. I personally witnessed him exposed to much danger."

Swing, the 11th Airborne chief, wrote to a former mentor, his father-in-law retired Gen. Peyton March, about his organization's work. "It appears that we are a 'secret weapon' although we have been in the line since November 20. You notice that no mention has been made of our activities in the daily communiques. Nevertheless, we've killed over two thousand Japs and have moved through the mountains to the west coast.

"Two of my regiments equipped with light packs, no pup tents, no ponchos, no extra clothing or footgear have been fighting through mountain trails for twenty-five days. We ran smack into the Jap 26th Division, a fresh division landed south of Ormoc. We have knocked them back twelve miles as the crow flies, and about twice as far as by mountain trail. They are now pinched between ourselves and the 7th Division. From now on it's a process of extermination and they fight like cornered rats.

"Casualties on our side are not light because when disorganized, the individual Jap hides in a hole, up a tree, in debris around deserted barrios. There is always the danger of a lucky shot. On the whole they are lousy shots and must be within almost fifteen paces to hit the bull's-eye. Had one sniping at me the other morning from a coconut tree. Couldn't locate him until some of the men shouted he was in a tree not ten yards from me. I ran forward and stood at the base of the tree while the men riddled the so-and-so over my head.

"Fortunately, many of our wounds are from the .25 caliber [rifle] and incapacitate for ten days or two weeks only. Most damage is from hand grenades. Many Japs have thrown away all arms but knives or bayonets and hand grenades. Then garbed in Filipino clothes or oddments from our own uniforms, they endeavor to infiltrate at night close enough to toss a couple of grenades. If caught they do not hesitate to use the grenades on themselves."

To support his forces in the hills, Swing arranged a drop of a battery of mountain-geared artillery pieces. Supply for the entire operation relied upon artillery liaison planes and as many as 188 officers and men, including two surgical teams, parachuted into the isolated sectors. Boasted Swing, "The two teams have established two small hospitals and performed miracles, operated for belly wounds and head wounds. The men are receiving the same care they would receive in a general hospital. Have even found time to drop them ice cream (we purchased an ice cream machine in Australia) and persuaded the troop carrier to fly it right over base camp on the beach.

"It's a queer war but I get a kick out of beating the Japs at their own game—the so-called tactics of ambush infiltration to the rear, surrounding small units, etc."

Swing's account makes the campaign through the hills sound like little more than a rugged walk in the woods, but Buzz Miley and G Company spent ten desperate days. "Company G got the mission to attack west down the trail to seize and hold the next high ground, later known as Hacksaw Ridge. The trail there had a steep drop-off on each side so we were restricted on movements. As we approached the top of the ridge, the Japs pinned the 3rd Platoon Scouts down. Someone radioed they were pinned down by at least two flanking MGs and had casualties. I was told to move the 2nd Platoon in, hold there so the 3rd Platoon could move back. We found three dead in a clearing on the ridge, the platoon leader and two Scouts. There were also two Jap bodies."

When one of Miley's scouts reported the enemy coming on, the company commander directed a pullback into a perimeter defense. The troopers were forced to leave their dead at the scene, gathering up only dog tags and weapons. Cut off, and stuck in this position for several days, Miley and company awaited instructions. Told to move to another area, the platoon followed a stream bed, "but very slowly," says Miley. "Hunger was catching up with us. We could hear the Japs talking above us. Our lead scouts made contact and Pfc. Matt Pike was shot through the shoulder and came tumbling down the hill. Since we were all very weak, Wheeler [his CO] pulled us back. We went looking for a clearing to put out our recognition panels in hopes of getting a ration resupply and batteries for the radios.

"Starvation Hill was a small cleared area on a slope. We saw at least two airdrops by C-47 to the 3rd Battalion. The only food we had was rice taken off Japs blundering into our perimeter, and plenty of camotes, which seemed to have been partially a crop in the cleared area and which we dug up and cooked. We displayed two panels, one the company identification and the other a 'rations required.' An L-5 [small observation plane] flew over near us, up high, but obviously at first thought we were Japs since we were hit with white phosphorus the second day. We thought they were marking rounds and dug deeper but no artillery followed. We did have two casualties from burns. By this time we were all very weak and were cooking everything we could dig up including the insides of palm and banana trees which made a pretty good mush or soup. There was never any problem with water since a fast-rushing stream was at the bottom of the hill."

Several patrols composed of volunteers infiltrated through the enemy lines in search of rescuers. The bulk of the troopers remained and, notes Miley, "Back on Starvation Hill we received an airdrop of two cases of C rations [canned food] in a free drop. The rations hit, split, broke, burst and scattered chow all over the terrain. We ended up scraping food off bushes and the ground but not enough to do anyone any good.

"On the tenth day, a GI scout was challenged coming up the hill; he damn near got shot. A small patrol was behind him and they said that if we could follow them out to an adjacent hill, a unit was there to carry us to the coast if necessary. We moved to their perimeter and each of us was issued one heavy can of C ration which was too much for our bellies. We got sick real quick. The next day we were escorted to the beach and told to take it easy until the 511th came out of the mountains."

Sal DeGaetano, as a rifleman with B Troop of the 12th Cavalry Regiment, remembers a Starvation Ridge reserved for him and his associates. "When we hit opposition on the last ridge before Ormoc Valley, we dug in for what we thought would be a short stay. A typhoon—wind, rain and mud—took its toll. My feet are still discolored fifty years later from the ulcers that covered my legs as I stood in foxholes with water. Our rations gave out and I ate crackers I had thrown away and were soggy from rain and mud. I picked them up by putting my mess kit knife underneath and then licking the cracker off. They tried to airdrop ten-in-one rations but they dropped on both sides of us, down into the valley. The following day, one fell about ten yards down the slope. I retrieved it but my movement resulted in a barrage of mortar fire, wounding one man. At that point I really didn't care whether I lived or died. I was hungry, filthy and exhausted."

Occupation of Ormoc reversed the flow of combat for the Nipponese and the Americans. Now it was the Japanese who struck at shipping in and around Ormoc Bay. Kenneth Coleman, a nineteen-year-old from Newburg, Pennsylvania, was the youngest of three brothers in the service. The oldest, Harper, had already splashed ashore on Utah Beach as a member of the 4th Infantry Division on D-Day, June 6, as a member of the Normandy invasion army. The middle brother, Arthur, crewed on an amphibious tractor preparing for his role in the liberation of the Philippines. Ken Coleman, after attending signal school, was assigned to the LSM 151, a landing ship designed to make quick runs to beachheads delivering vehicles, supplies, fuel and ammunition.

"We would load from Leyte beaches in the early afternoon," says Coleman, "and would proceed to Ormoc in the early afternoon. The quickest and easiest way to get to Ormoc was through a narrow channel between Leyte and some islands. Most of the air attacks came around 1700 hours as the convoys passed through here." On December 11, one day after the 77th Division entered Ormoc, Coleman's LSM in a grouping that included the destroyer *Reid* entered the danger zone in late afternoon. Ten Jills, Japanese Navy torpedo bombers, attacked.

"The *Reid* was protecting us on our starboard side," recalls Coleman. "Immediately, as the alert came in, she went to flank speed to get between us and the Jap planes, approaching from head on. As I raced to the signal deck, I saw three planes heading for the *Reid*. When I reached the main bridge deck, up one short flight of steps, I saw two planes in flames go into the water and the third hitting the destroyer's aft gun turrets. There was a tremendous explosion and within two minutes she went under. I remember seeing the last man get off, stepping into the water as she went down.

"We were directly behind the *Reid* when she sank. Her torpedoes and depth charges were set to explode at a certain depth and there was a huge blast. Because of our landing ship design we drafted only five or six feet at the bow. The underwater explosion lifted it a short distance out of the water and then it fell back, causing severe vibrations. Water lines and steam lines ruptured but luckily no lines to the engines were affected. But our compasses and steering control were broken, making it necessary to follow the other ships in the line with manual steering."

Handicapped in its ability to maneuver, LSM 151 plowed on, forced to cut a swath through the sailors from the *Reid* struggling in the water. "We may have killed or injured some of them," notes Coleman. Perhaps half of the destroyer's crew were rescued.

"Any ship caught on the beach at sunrise would be subject to air attack and artillery [from the hills behind the front lines]," says Coleman. "A few days after our invasion at Ormoc, Jap resupply barges attempted to land on the beaches at the same time and place as we were there. It was most confusing. We couldn't fire at them because our guns were for antiaircraft only and had guards that prevented surface firing. There was a squadron of PT boats and I think they saved the day. The enemy barges, however, delayed our offloading and we were late getting off the beach. Our captain said the tide would start to go out and we would be at the mercy of Jap artillery in the hills. He directed that five thousand gallons of our diesel fuel be pumped into the sea to lighten the ship. He walked to the front, measuring the water depth and to see how the tide was moving. We came off very easily but at least three of the others did not. The artillery fire started. The LSM 38 was stuck and their captain was the best friend of ours. Our captain said I cannot let him set there. We went back and towed him off. The other two LSMs were destroyed."

Buck Creel of the 77th Division, like Han Rants, was also startled by the ferocity of some guerrillas. "We often had Filipinos claiming to be guerrillas want to join our unit for rations and arms, usually telling us, 'Me very fine Filipino guerrilla, killed many Japanese with bolo.' We would give them a mission, feed them and send them off, usually never to be seen again. While at the Libungao Road junction, three men professing to be guerrillas came into our position with the typical song and dance. Through our Tagalog interpreter they told us they knew where five armed Japanese were located. We fed them, gave them the job of destroying the five Japanese and told them we wanted definite proof, not some rusty old Japanese rifles one could pick up anywhere. They disappeared and I figured that was the end of it.

"About dusk of the following day, the trio came trotting back into the defensive perimeter. 'Captain-san, we did what you asked. Can we now join your unit?' I noticed one guerrilla had a rice straw bag over his shoulder. Upon a nod from the head honcho, he shook it out and five Japanese heads tumbled out at my feet. They also had five sets of weapons and equipment along with some papers, which we sent back to the intelligence officer. Needless to say, our newfound 'Scouts' were welcomed into G

Company and spent the rest of the campaign as an integral part of our unit."

According to General Swing, his paratroopers, operating strictly as foot soldiers, brought a fresh style to the combat. He wrote to Peyton March, "I really believe this is the first time the Japs have run against American troops that never stop coming. It has been the custom in this so-called jungle warfare for troops to start 'holing up' an hour or more before sundown and form their so-called perimeter from which they never venture forth until after cooking individual breakfast at daylight, taking an hour or an hour and a half. As a result the Japs bivouac at their ease, have scouts watch the formation of the perimeter and then heckle our troops all night. We changed that, made our troops keep going until dark, then dig in so the Japs don't know where we are located and finally got them to the point where they would start out just before the crack of dawn *without breakfast.*

"As a result, we've killed about twice as many Japs in proportion to our own casualties as has any other division. The last day, the twenty-second [December], when we busted down out of the hills to where the 7th Division was *sitting* on the beach, the dawn attack caught three hundred Japanese sleeping *outside* their foxholes and we slaughtered them with bayonet, knife and hand grenade. From then on it was a field day as we had four bns in column, as fast as one showed the least sign of tiring, sent the next one thru and by noon we had gone four thousand yards, took a break for breakfast and at 2:30 we were on the beach at the 7th Division bivouac. Counted approximately 750 dead Japs and didn't go down the cliffs where many of them rolled off."

Al Ullman, who was the son of an immigrant from Russia and a native of Brooklyn raised in South Carolina, volunteered for the paratroopers "out of patriotism. I saw a cause. In my nineteen-year-old perception, our freedom conceivably was at stake." As a medical aid man, Ullman entered the mountain campaign and his diary speaks of "three miserable weeks, eating K rations and living from day to day. Three times the Japs pulled *banzais* and three times we repelled their advances. But each time it cost us blood. To see the fanatical yellow bastards trying desperately to climb up into our area screaming and tossing grenades right and left is a sight not to be forgotten. I prayed plenty." Ullman also notes that the medics on Leyte learned to discard their Red Cross insignia and carry weapons; the enemy did not grant dispensations to medical personnel.

Pvt. Norman Fiedler with the 96th Division also recalls the experience from a less sanguine perspective than General Swing. "Leyte was a hellhole. Terrible rain, jungle conditions, heat and insects made living conditions at times unbearable. I had alternately been assigned as first or second scout for my platoon and would be the first one observed by the enemy. That was one of the functions of a scout. At times I visualized myself as the American Indian with ear to the ground, sensing vibrations and the slightest movement up ahead. I was wounded twice on Leyte. The medics were wonderful. In complete disregard of their own safety, they immediately attended to my wounds, saw that I was taken to the rear . . . On the first occasion, standing around just before dark, our position was hit by enemy incendiary shells, one of which blasted my right temple, right trigger finger and back, causing severe burns. I was sent to the rear and the wounds healed, except for my trigger finger. I went back to the front with a bandage on that finger. Another wound was sustained while filing through the jungle. A bullet grazed my right arm and penetrated the neck of the lieutenant who was following me."

Fiedler, like many of the GIs, sensed the growing desperation of the enemy in the mounting frequency of *banzai* attacks. "They were frequently telegraphed by a band of enemy running towards the perimeter with guns and swords waving in the air, hollering obscenities and what they believed to be insults such as 'Babe Ruth eats shit.' Most occurred in the early evening or at night. We would light up the sky with flares, lighting the area like daytime. These *banzai* charges were really suicide missions. Having been involved in numerous ones, I don't recall any one of our men having been injured. We had our perimeter in the shape of a square with heavy machine guns placed at each corner and it was slaughter."

The Americans expanded their Philippine fief as the new year approached. Elements of the 1st Cavalry completed their conquest of the small garrison manning Samar to the east of Leyte. Men from the Americal Division endured a long boat trip from Bougainville to speed up the conquest. Among these newcomers was Dick Cohen, a Philadelphia native, who in 1938 had chosen the National Guard as a relief from the tedium of high school. "During peacetime maneuvers in 1941, we used a rented dump truck as a tank, a wood tube propped up on a stick as a mortar."

Conditions changed rapidly with the advent of war and Cohen ascended the noncom ladder, then attended OCS. He came to the 164th Regiment of the Americal as a replacement officer on Bougainville. By then combat was winding down, although he participated in patrols. "On Leyte, it was supposed to be a mop-up but these were major operations, although we did not take a lot of casualties."

The official U.S. Army history of the Leyte campaign omits the Americal participation. Nevertheless, in addition to the 164th Regiment, the 132nd (with Bob Manning, who earned his commission at a six-week course overseas) and the 21st Recon Troops (with the erstwhile cavalry fan, Bill McLaughlin) also pursued the enemy on Leyte.

On December 15, Americans had stormed ashore on Mindoro to begin the process of sealing off the southern islands of the archipelago from Luzon. An unheralded event at the time, it would soon develop as a critical move. Meanwhile, GIs pushed northwest from Ormoc to occupy the peninsula closest to Luzon. The 24th Division, replaced in the line by the 32nd, undertook the job of eliminating a company-size group of soldiers put ashore on the northern shore. The 32nd itself engaged the foe over a series of steep, craggy hills, drawing supplies mostly from air drops.

On Christmas Day, General Yamashita notified his commander on Leyte that he had written off the island, and the troops still there would have to sustain and support themselves with no further aid from outside. On the same day, MacArthur, declaring that all organized resistance had ended, announced the close of the Leyte campaign. For thousands of GIs on the island, however, particularly men of the Americal Division, the killing and the dying continued even as the Supreme Commander prepared for the invasion of Luzon.

CHAPTER XXII

S-DAY,
THE LINGAYEN GULF INVASION

EVEN WITH THE SUCCESS of the campaign against Leyte, a few diehards like Admiral King clamored for bypassing further Philippine campaigns, but MacArthur, now backed even by the likes of Halsey and Nimitz, refused to consider any other objective than full liberation of the archipelago. In preparation for the invasion of Luzon he said, "I needed one last stepping-stone before a main attack could be launched. The island of Mindoro was selected. It was located just south of Luzon in a central position towards the coast. Its possession would enable me to return to my strategy of never leaping ahead of my own air cover." Although having Mindoro (in area about half the size of New Jersey) under U.S. control would halve the air distance to Manila for planes then based at the Leyte airfields, the shorter flying time was only part of its attractiveness. The nearly continuous downpours on Leyte and enemy air raids slowed construction of strips capable of handling heavy bombers and the number of fighters appropriate for air cover. Seizure of existing Mindoro installations would deprive the enemy of useful bases and create valuable ones for American planes.

The move on Mindoro began on December 12, two weeks before Leyte was declared secure, as several convoys

sailed from Leyte Gulf to the western approaches of the
target. The Japanese responded with furious air raids from
Philippine airbases and from other sites. The *kamikazes*
scored some deadly blows but they were insufficient to
interrupt the overall operation. As the transports, freighters and landing craft crowded into the Mindoro anchorage
on December 15, enemy planes bore in on the ships. Russ
Catardi, the signal man on the destroyer *Moale,* which only
a few days earlier had been engaged at Ormoc Bay, remembers: "One of the landing craft, number 738, was hit
by a bomb and started to sink. We went alongside and
rescued about seventy soldiers. Just as we were pulling
away 738 exploded, killing a few of our crew and wounding many more."

Although those at sea reeled under such punishment,
the GIs from the 24th Division's 19th Infantry Regiment
and from the 503rd Parachute Regimental Combat Team,
serving as foot soldiers, landed virtually unopposed on the
beaches. Subsequently the 21st Infantry also arrived. The
small enemy garrison on the island, numbering about a
thousand augmented by perhaps two hundred survivors of
naval encounters who took refuge there, was hardly a
match for the twelve thousand U.S. combat troops delegated to conquer them. By the end of the first day the
beachhead extended seven miles inland and engineers frantically commenced work on two airstrips.

William "Woody" Braswell, a member of the Florida
National Guard in 1938, came to B Company, 19th Infantry, as a replacement platoon sergeant at the end of the
Leyte campaign after prolonged service in noncombat operations. "The first enemy action I saw, other than the
tracers in the sky when the paratroopers hit the airstrips at
Leyte, was in the convoy on the way to Mindoro. A Jap
suicide plane hit the cruiser *Nashville* [the vessel from
which MacArthur had earlier watched the Leyte landings].
At Mindoro I saw a number of *kamikazes.* One of them
blew up a cargo ship loaded with ammunition. It caused a

tidal wave on the beach. The sand was rolling under us like one of those California earthquakers I experienced back at Fort Ord."

While on Leyte, Phil Hostetter, chafing over his assignment to a medical collecting company that struck him as providing a minimal contribution to the war effort, had achieved his dubious ambition, a transfer to the 19th Infantry's 1st Battalion as its surgeon. In a beach encampment on Leyte, where the troops prepared to board ships for their next engagement, Mindoro, he heard Tokyo Rose, "Hello darlings. How are my big, brave soldiers today? Enjoy yourselves now. Tomorrow you die. Right now you are all packed up to move. We know all about you and your convoy. You will all drown."

While Hostetter admits he was disconcerted by the broadcaster's seeming knowledge, he was shocked further when a GI put the muzzle of his M-1 under his chin and pulled the trigger. "Potentially suicidal men were supposed to be reported but none of his associates had reported anything. He was not dead because he had to tilt his head to reach the trigger and the bullet went through his jaw."

For once, it appeared the Allied intelligence had successfully gulled Tokyo Rose's sources. Hostetter's outfit stayed put for ten days. And when they did sail to Mindoro, the woman broadcasting as Tokyo Rose never mentioned their departure.

On the beach at Mindoro, Hostetter saw the *kamikaze* mentioned by Braswell career into a ship. "A second later, the ship loaded with explosives blew up in a single, colossal blast. I stepped behind a tree to avoid the shock wave and watched our aid station tent jump back six inches as a single unit. The explosion, which produced a mushroom cloud, raised a wave of water twenty feet high that completely covered all our emplacements and the men manning them. Happily none of our men were injured but everyone on the ship was killed."

Repairs and preparation of the airfields proceeded so

rapidly that within five days the first 5th Air Force fighters took up residence at one field and a week later a second base opened for full operations. The defenders on Mindoro offered scattered resistance, falling back into the mountainous, largely uninhabited areas well north of the U.S. encampments. In the first two weeks on Mindoro, the U.S. ground troops incurred just sixteen dead, four missing and seventy-one wounded while the enemy losses added up to about 170 KIA and another fifteen taken prisoner.

For the U.S. Navy and Army Air Corps, however, the period between the operation against Mindoro and the invasion of Luzon brought very heavy losses. In addition to the initial damage air raids wreaked upon the Mindoro-bound convoys, a vicious typhoon ravaged the 3rd Fleet of Bull Halsey on December 17, sinking three destroyers, damaging twenty-eight ships and wrecking two hundred planes. There was a loss of 790 lives.

On December 26 a small group of Japanese warships sifted through the air defense screen to come within range of the Mindoro beachhead and airfield areas. "We were in our foxholes, dugouts and barbed wire emplacements," says Woody Braswell, "when the Japs started firing a string of parachute flares lighting up the beach for miles. I thought it was our Navy doing this until I saw salvos of Naval gunfire landing out in the sea." The attackers were driven off before the shelling could inflict any permanent damage onshore but the bombardment temporarily prevented American planes from setting down on Mindoro. Low on fuel and bucking bad weather, a number crashed while seeking refuge on Leyte. Meanwhile the departing enemy ships absorbed some serious lumps from Allied air forces.

Towards the end of the month, suicide planes and conventional bombers struck at Allied transports, sinking three Liberty ships and forcing another trio to run aground rather than founder. They damaged a destroyer, some PT boats and other craft, and in a night assault blasted fighters and bombers on the ground. Unfortunately for the Japanese, every *kamikaze* foray ended with the loss of a plane and pilot, regardless of whether they crashed into a ship. They could not sustain the intensive effort against the Americans around Mindoro.

With the airfields secured, the foot soldiers advanced into the hills to deal with the shrinking number of enemy. Guerrillas cut down many. Woody Braswell was bemused by genuine pygmies, Mangyans ["Mang Yangs" in Braswell's pronunciation], a tribe that used bows, arrows and spears. "They were small people who filed their teeth and chewed beetle nut that caused their lips to be very red. They were almost naked and had long black hair they used to make their bow strings. I saw them put poison on the tips of their arrows." Braswell attempted to teach them American Indian lore. He took one of their arrows, split some bamboo to make fins which he attached to the back end of an arrow and then coaxed a pygmy to shoot his own arrow and then Braswell's. "His arrow visibly wobbled through the air," says Braswell. "As they say, mine went straight as an arrow. I said through an interpreter that my arrow was better. He shook his head, no. I could imagine what religion missionaries had to go through."

The string of Allied victories and the growing blockade of ships bound to and from the Philippines had a harsh effect on military prisoners still in Japanese hands. As their holdings shrank and the entire southern half of the archipelago was put in jeopardy, the occupying authorities dispatched some captives to the home islands or the Asian mainland. Tom Gage, the erstwhile pursuit squadron clerk, for example, left the Philippines in 1943 for an odyssey that carried him to several camps in Japan before a final destination on Kyushu.

The Japanese also closed up outlying camps and transferred the inmates to Luzon. Among those sent from an installation at Davao to the Cabanatuan camp was Calvin Graef, a former first sergeant in a coast artillery battery who had been captured on Bataan and who survived the

Death March. To Graef, the increasingly frequent flights of U.S. planes over the Philippines augured well for liberation. But he and his mates were also aware that, contrary to the Geneva Convention rules, prisoners were being sent to Japan, Formosa and Manchuria as labor details. Chosen for one of these work crews in early October 1944, Graef in the company of eighteen hundred others traveled from Cabanatuan for a brief stopover at Bilibid Prison, and then boarded the *Arisan Maru*, a freighter headed for Japan.

"When we first saw the ship, we figured it would be just fine," says Graef. "It was in the five to ten ton vicinity which is extremely small for such a large detail of men. I thought it would be impossible to keep the group even in two holds of the ship and that a lot of people would have to be out on deck. But we sure weren't.

"All 1,815 of us were put into one small area so tight there wasn't sufficient room for everyone to even sit down. We worked it out, alternating with half sitting at one time while the other half stood. On the second or third day, the commanding officer of the group got permission to put maybe five hundred of our personnel in a forward coal hold. That gave all of the people left a place to at least sit. There was no way you could lay down. People died while sitting and you didn't even know they were dead. The trip lasted from the tenth of October until only the twenty-fourth but in that two weeks, there were very few dead that the Japs would even let us bury." With the hatch covers off, a small amount of light penetrated the darkness of the hold but the temperatures, according to Graef, stayed above a hundred degrees.

"The majority of the men had amoebic dysentery, a very contagious form of intestinal parasite. It eats away your insides, and you pass blood and mucus. What kills you is you just bleed to death inside. Our guards were very young, nineteen or twenty, and extremely mean. They would take our buckets that we brought to the top of the stairs and one of them thought it was the funniest thing to take those buckets and dump them back into the hold."

Like many others, Graef had learned during the long years of confinement that kitchen duty offered benefits—perhaps a chance to add scrapings of burnt rice at the bottom of the cauldrons to one's meal, an opportunity to scavenge in the garbage cans and usually extra gulps of water. For those confined to the hold, supplements devolved from the dead. "If a man next to you died, you could send his canteen cup up for water and his mess kit for a ration of rice. That way you had your water and food and his."

On October 24, as the ship wallowed in a sea buffeted by the remnants of a typhoon, Graef was on deck, cooking rice for the prisoners. "Around 4:00 P.M. the Japanese started running from one end of the ship to another. Looking around, we could see torpedoes. The first missed the forward part of the ship; the second passed by the rear end, but the third landed right in the middle. One of the guards with a machine gun opened up on our detail, telling us in no uncertain terms to get down into the hold. Most of us just dove back into it. Right after that the guards put the hatch covers back on, locked down tight.

"We knew we were definitely hit. But there was no way we could get out that I could think of. The torpedo hit, I believe, in one of the holds with prisoners. They acted like cotton, took up the shock waves, took up the noise. The torpedo hit probably killed hundreds. There were mostly little bits of people over everybody in the main hold.

"Finally we were able to get the hatch covers off and found out that the Japanese officers had taken a lifeboat and gone to a destroyer maybe two miles off. They left the balance of the crew, civilians, women and children and all of the Japanese guards." Graef reports that the prisoners took revenge for the cruel treatment they had received, murdering the guards. Then they raided the food and water stores.

The *Arisan Maru* broke in two and those prisoners not killed by the torpedo blast abandoned the vessel before it sank after several hours. A few clutched life jackets while others clung to bits of floating wreckage. Graef, an excellent swimmer, kept himself afloat without aids. "A lot of people from the ship had gone to the destroyer thinking they would be picked up. The Japanese on that destroyer had long, sharpened bamboo poles they used to spear fish and as the men came close to the destroyers, that's what was used on them."

Graef avoided the warship. In the morning he and four others clambered into an empty lifeboat. A passing freighter rescued them. Of the 1,815 prisoners on the *Arisan Maru* only the five in the lifeboat and perhaps four others survived. Among those lost was Al Svihra, the former legal officer and West Point graduate.

Harold Johnson, the USMA alumnus who served with the Philippine Scouts, had barely survived his first weeks of incarceration. "I became sick and in one twenty-four-hour period I made thirty-six trips to the slit trench. There were a lot of times when you wondered whether God up there in the sky was going to pull you through. God was close and real in these hours. Finally I was moved into the hospital. At that time people just didn't come out of the hospital except when they were hauled out, placed in a stack to be carried away and buried." Johnston, however, eventually tottered out on his own legs.

At the Cabanatuan camp, Johnson held jobs like adjutant for personnel and then commissary officer dealing with purchases from local vendors who came to the camp. He wrote notes for the sellers to carry, asking permission for them to procure items for the prisoners. Otherwise, guerrillas would stop them. He also lent a hand in the thirteen-hundred-acre garden that helped feed the prisoners. The men worked the plots without farm implements, using only their hands and a few meagre tools.

"I played a lot of poker," says Johnson. "I once wrote a check for $1,098 to one man. I didn't regret it at all because I figured if I came out of there broke but I came out alive, I was ahead of the game."

In mid-December, Johnson, after being crammed into a

forty and eight for the trip to Manila, boarded the *Oryoko Maru,* another ship bound for Japan. A total of 1,619 prisoners were loaded onto the *Oryoko Maru,* including Irvin Alexander, who recalled, "We had seen some Nips in uniform going aboard earlier but were surprised to see that the top deck was crowded with civilians, men, women and children. One very nice and intelligent-looking Japanese woman stood by the rail at the head of the gangplank holding her two-year-old daughter. For the half hour that I saw her, she could not keep her eyes, friendly ones, off the prisoners. I heard her tell her daughter to say, 'Hello, Americans.' "

The prisoners were crowded into a tiny, almost airless, dark compartment. When movement down a ladder halted, the human gridlock infuriated the guards, who pounded the men still on deck with rifle butts. Once below Alexander, like Graef, could barely sit, much less stretch out. "Those of us who had our backs to the wall could squat down, provided we allowed the men in front of us to sit on our knees."

To his surprise, his hosts provided more rice and water for supper than they had been given at any single meal in the preceding year. The ship, part of a convoy, crept out the mouth of Manila Bay and picked up speed. However, it was the day of the Mindoro invasion and American aircraft pounced on the Japanese vessels. "At first we heard a few rounds of antiaircraft fire from some of the more distant ships which was called a practice drill by Mr. Wada, the Nip interpreter, who was looking down the hatch into our hold at the time. The heavy increase in gunfire, interspersed with numerous bomb explosions, gave us all the information we needed to know that, contrary to Mr. Wada, we were in the midst of a powerful attack. The gun mounted just outside the hatch almost directly over our heads joined in the heavy fire. If there were any lingering doubts, they were completely dispelled by the first dive bomber's attack on the *Oryoko.* The bomber came in, its engine roaring at full throttle and all of its .50 caliber machine guns firing.

The gun overhead was shooting as fast as it could but the plane did not falter. It passed over us with a roar that was followed almost at once by the heavy explosions of bombs. They hit close alongside the ship, giving us a considerable jolt.

"We underwent similar attacks all day until late afternoon. The *Oryoko* was hit by several light bombs. She did not appear to be badly damaged but slowed down. We hoped we were near the beach because we knew we might need to abandon ship. We had learned from the Dutch survivors of a sunken ship who joined us at Cabanatuan that the percentage of prisoners saved from a ship might not be very great. The end of the bombing in late afternoon brought us a twelve-hour respite.

"Mr. Wada came to the top of the hatch to order six of our doctors topside to give first aid treatment to the Nip wounded. The doctors returned after an hour or so and reported they had been seriously handicapped by an almost total lack of facilities and medical supplies. They had treated some two hundred Japanese, many of them women and children. They estimated they dealt with not more than half of the wounded and there were approximately a hundred bodies stacked in two large rooms, bringing the total killed and wounded to around five hundred. They also said the *Oryoko* was better off than most of the other ships in the convoy for they could see fires from ten to twenty burning ships close around us."

Alexander stayed aboard the battered steamship for a second night. "Several men who had been talking incoherently for some time grew weaker and weaker until their voices could no longer be heard. A few made strange noises which we concluded were death rattles. A dozen men, who seemed to have gone mad, tried to walk over the heads of the crouching men to the ladder that led to the top deck. Most of them were thrown back but one man who fought like a demon was beaten to death."

On the following morning, Alexander abandoned the stricken vessel for one of the numerous survivor-bearing rafts in the water and helped paddle it to shore. Many men from the steamer attempted to swim and some drowned. Harold Johnson was one of those able to stroke his way to safety. After a spate of grim days penned up in a makeshift camp, a stifling sixteen-hour train ride and a hike to another beach, the captives climbed into landing barges just vacated by arriving troops. Ferried out to a freighter on December 30, the Americans were gratified by the simple pleasures of ample room to lie down and life-saving doses of fresh air. On January 9, Alexander peered out on the ship-thick harbor of Takao, Formosa. As he downed a portion of rice, he heard the ominous sound of antiaircraft fire.

Bomb bursts rocked the ship. "After the attack was over, I walked around as best I could through the debris. The entire hold was filled with dead and severely wounded, some so badly mutilated they were unrecognizable. I encountered two ghouls who were searching the bodies for jewelry and other valuables. Hoppy, who was with me, spoke harshly to one whom he knew as a soldier who had been a member of his command. The man snarled wickedly, telling Hoppy to shut his lousy mouth and went on with his revolting activity. The following day Hoppy and I could not escape a feeling of satisfaction when the rude despoiler sickened and died in a few hours."

On his third ship now, Alexander, along with a bare four hundred from his original sixteen hundred, reached Moji, Japan. From there he was taken by train to the industrial city of Fukuoka where, reduced to ninety pounds, he bedded down in a work camp. Overall conditions were terrible but the food issued in camp and the help tendered by his companions and some compassionate Dutch prisoners sustained him.

The series of raids upon the ships carrying Alexander to Formosa and Japan presaged the last chapter in MacArthur's campaign to liberate the Philippines. According to the Supreme Commander, with Mindoro now in his pocket, "I now faced my final and decisive objective, the recapture of Luzon. It was a difficult and dangerous problem, for the Japanese ground forces greatly outnumbered my own." This appraisal was made in retrospect but in December at the time of the Luzon invasion Maj. Gen. Charles Willougby, his intelligence chief, estimated the total Luzon defenders at 152,500 troops of all categories, which would have been fewer than what MacArthur had at his disposal. However, Yamashita actually controlled nearly 275,000, including naval combat and service units as well as what was left of the air force. The original assault force put together from General Kreuger's 6th Army and Gen. Robert Eichelberger's 8th Army added up to roughly 191,000 with about 131,000 classified as combat troops. But as S-Day approached more units were added and, together with the known guerrillas—rated as equivalent of perhaps an infantry division—MacArthur would field about 230,000 on the ground. The United States committed more men to this campaign than to those in North Africa, Italy or Southern France. Only central Europe involved a greater number of troops.

Numerical measurements of the two ground armies not only ignores matters of firepower, armor and supply resources—far superior on the American side—but also the contributions made by air and sea forces. Although the U.S. admirals and generals feared a deluge of bombs and *kamikaze* attacks from aircraft on Luzon and Formosa, the Japanese High Command regarded additional planes for defense of the Philippines a waste and refused to replace the badly depleted stock in the archipelago. The invaders would not face any strong threats from the air. Similarly, the Imperial Navy, its carriers destroyed, could no longer confront the Americans. To survive to fight for the home islands the Japanese Navy withdrew from the area. To minimize any interference from the air and enemy ships, the bombers from the 3rd Fleet paid a call upon the Luzon airstrips and blew up some largely disabled equipment. They then turned their attention to Formosa and the surrounding waters.

The plan created by MacArthur called for landings in the Lingayen Gulf, on the west central side of Luzon, as the initial objective. It was the natural place for the expeditionary force because the Gulf cuts diagonally into the side of the island to provide direct access to the heart of Luzon, the central plains and the Manila Bay region. It had been the principal avenue for the Japanese in 1941 and any other site would have almost instantly confronted a marching army with mountains, narrow trails, swift rivers, deep gorges and easily defensible natural barriers.

After several postponements because of severe weather, airbase construction and the need to assemble adequate shipping, convoys from as far off as New Guinea, harassed by air attacks and an occasional foray of an enemy ship, converged on the rendezvous area in Lingayen Gulf for S-Day, January 9. At 0700 the boom of Navy guns signaled the overture. By 0900, the first amphibious vehicles were churning towards the nine miles of beautiful, firm sand on the Gulf's southern shore. Units from the 37th and 40th Divisions spearheaded the assault upon the right flank; 6th Division infantrymen struck in the center and on the left flank regiments of the 43rd Division sped to the beach.

Arthur Coleman, the middle of the three brothers from Newburg, Pennsylvania, served as gunner on an amtrac with the 37th Division. "We had 120 of these which weighed sixteen tons and were powered with a nine-cylinder, Wright Cyclone engine. A large cargo box in the rear was equipped with a ramp which when lowered gave access to a Jeep, cannon, cargo or thirty fully equipped infantrymen. There were two .50 caliber machine guns mounted forward of the cargo box above the engine and two .30 caliber guns, one on each side. A crew of three manned the amtrac. Tracks with grousers—double cups—propelled it on water at five miles per hour and fifteen mph on land. Drawbacks were few except the grousers would break off the tracks when operated on concrete roads."

Coleman and his amtrac sailed to S-Day on an LST.

"Dawn on the ninth found us off the beaches of Lingayen Gulf. Bow doors opened, the ramp went down and we drove off into the water, fully loaded with 37th troops. As we emerged onto the beach I saw a dud sixteen-inch shell [from an American warship] directly in our path. I quickly pointed it out to the driver and he narrowly avoided it. I quite likely saved us from disaster.

"I was apprehensive as were most all the way in but I think after so many months of training and waiting they were glad to start fighting. There was no return fire. The entire beachhead was virtually unopposed. Jubilant Filipinos greeted us, carrying American and Philippine flags."

When the Selective Service Act took effect in 1940, Stanley Frankel, a graduate of Northwestern University with 20/400 eyesight and an uncle as chairman of the Dayton, Ohio, draft board, expected to remain a civilian. Instead, his Uncle Max proudly congratulated him for having been chosen and the examining doctor assured Frankel that the Army could always find a job for a near-blind recruit. Indeed, he carved a niche in the clerical staff on the nascent 37th Infantry Division. Even when war came and the outfit headed for the Fiji Islands early in 1942, Frankel's military skills focused on how to pay troops and type intelligence reports. He never had to bother with hikes, calisthenics or weapons.

In Fiji, a colonel of intelligence suggested Frankel attend a local Jungle Warfare Officers Candidate School and after certification as a ninety-day wonder, Frankel would return to Division headquarters. Frankel performed at the near bottom of his class in weaponry, agility and foxhole digging but his instructors believed as he did that those areas were irrelevant in view of his destiny. However, on his graduation the acute shortage of platoon leaders marked him for combat duty. His protests and his lack of proficiency during training notwithstanding, Frankel entered upon the life of a combat soldier and acquitted himself well enough in several campaigns to become a regimental staff officer.

With the 37th scheduled for S-Day, Frankel with his associates sailed from Bougainville for three weeks until they reached the final assembly area. A last briefing based on intelligence from friendly Filipinos indicated the Japanese 58th Independent Mixed Brigade, "the gang involved in the Rape of Nanking," says Frankel, manned the positions destined for the 148th Infantry Regiment. His colonel encouraged him, "Frankel, you will have the honor of commanding that part of our regiment which will have the hardest time."

"I thought to myself this was one honor I could do without, and I also made certain I carried a GI shovel with me so that the minute I hit the beach, I could start digging a foxhole to protect myself against enemy fire."

He almost aborted his role when he slipped while climbing down the net from the transport to the assault boat but a supply sergeant caught him. "We started sailing towards land, but were advised that the Navy had another half hour of shelling before we would go in, so the assault boat circled. The water was rough; I have a queasy stomach; in about ten minutes I was seasick. Shells were whistling overhead and we thought that some of those shells were incoming from Japanese emplacements near the beaches.

"Seasickness is one of the worst maladies I've ever had and I got up from my squatting position in front, leaned my head over the side and threw up. The company commander in the boat screamed at me. 'Frankel, get your goddamn head down or it's going to be knocked off.'

"Finally we went in; the front section of the boat cranked down, and we charged the beach. The shelling was still intense and I figured it was both ours and theirs, so as I hit dry land I pulled out my shovel and began digging like hell. I was almost underground, frantically throwing the wet sand all around the hole. Suddenly, I heard a strange noise as the bombardment quieted. This was the sound of human voices yelling, 'Veectorie!' I looked up and to my astonishment I recognized the friendly faces of a dozen Filipinos, who were then swarming all around us. 'Where are the Japanese?' I asked. 'All gone . . . two days ago . . . running to Manila.' Our intelligence as usual was flawed; there was no opposition to our landing and the only casualties I noted were a few dead horses, goats and sheep."

On the right flank of the 37th, units from the 40th Division raced for their objectives. In the second wave was S. Sgt. Paul Gerrish, a farm son of itinerant parents, who changed schools twenty-five times by the eighth grade as the family drifted around the western United States. As an eighteen-year-old in 1934, Gerrish entered the Civilian Conservation Corps, then hunted for farm and construction jobs until drafted in 1941. Trained as a radio operator, Gerrish expected assignment with an infantry regiment in the 40th Division but instead he became a "shotgun volunteer" for the newly formed 40th Division Cavalry Reconnaissance Troop. He was eventually named communications chief for the outfit.

The Troop consisted of three recon platoons plus a command-service-supply unit. The platoons broke into three teams, each of which included an M-8, a six-wheel armored car equipped with a 37 mm cannon and a .30 caliber machine gun in its turret. A crew of four manned the vehicle. Completing a team were a pair of three-man Jeeps. One carried a mortar and a .30 machine gun, the other two of the latter. Those platoons numbered thirty men apiece. The command-service-supply unit of about fifty men included the Company's brass, who rode in four M-8s, communications specialists like Gerrish and other assorted soldiers. All qualified as combat troops. Additional vehicles included some seldom used halftracks that mounted .50 caliber machine guns.

The 40th Division staged at New Britain for the long voyage to Lingayen Gulf. "Daylight came on January 9, 1945," recalls Gerrish, "and we were getting nearer the big guns we had been hearing for hours. As H-hour approached all types of landing craft were lowered from the ships and filled with men and equipment. The barges would keep returning to pick up successive waves. Due to the attrition on landing barges, each wave would be smaller than the one before. My thoughts were with our first platoon going in with the first wave in those awkward amphibious tanks." Temporarily staffed with men from the Recon Troop, the amphibious tanks employed a six-man crew and had the same weaponry as an M-8.

"It seemed like ages before someone announced over the PA system, 'The first wave is on the beach and advancing against light opposition. Second wave prepare to debark.' An LST came to the side of our ship and our vehicles were loaded on it. We had more than forty vehicles on the LST with just three of us to drive them off. The LST would not stay on the beach long enough for us to drive all off so we were hoping that some of the rest of the troop would be in the area. It was noon and we ate dinner with the LST crew, boiled potatoes, tomatoes and bread as the LST crews had just about the lowest ration priority in the Navy and as low as that of the combat units in the Army which was just about rock bottom.

"We were in luck as the LST beached where the men of our second and third platoons could see us and they dashed over to help unload. Soon there was a driver in each rig with men to spare. Captain Robinson and I rode off in the turret of our M-8 which was our usual positions. We found a small grove of palms that would help conceal us and set up a temporary CP.

"It was 4:00 P.M. when the first platoon came back to the CP with the amphibious tanks which they were calling paper tanks and creeping coffins. They had stopped a tank-led Japanese charge with one gunner, Gene Brunstetter, knocking out five Japanese tanks with five shots. Gene said, 'I knew I couldn't take a chance of them getting off a shot with one of their 57s.' The 7.7 Japanese rifle and machine gun bullets fired at close range could penetrate the thin armor on the sides of the amphibs. Several of the men were wounded and one young machine gunner was killed.

"We got all hands to help unload the amphibs. We put the radios back into the first platoon's vehicles. We removed all rations and ammunition and then ran the tanks under some trees where we left them parked. We never heard what happened to the amphibs. They may have been junked, given to the guerrillas, used for training or even rejuvenated for one more operation. Slow, awkward, they had played their part."

The 6th Infantry Division, veterans of New Guinea, left their camp on that island for an assault in the center of the invasion line. Among them was 6th Division intelligence specialist Min Hara, a Nisei born on Terminal Island in Los Angeles harbor, who had traveled further than most to reach the Philippines. Although Hara's father had come to California before the turn of the century, the law denied him both U.S. citizenship and Social Security. Both parents returned to Japan and Min Hara accompanied them. "It was a hellish ten months of misery. I couldn't speak or read their language and there was a shortage of good food due to heavy export to troops invading China and Manchuria. The principal of the local school made fun of us Nisei since we wouldn't conform to their way of thinking."

He came back to the United States to finish high school. "In the spring of 1942, hundreds of FBI agents raided our hometown. They entered our homes without any search warrant and turned everything we owned upside-down." Worse followed. "A Marine corporal came knocking at our door, pointing an automatic .45 and saying, 'You people of Japanese ancestry have forty-eight hours to get off this island.' " For a few days the Terminal Island Nisei stayed in San Pedro, then at a Los Angeles hostel before being loaded onto train coaches, with curtains drawn to prevent them from seeing the countryside, and hauled to an Arizona detention camp. "The humiliation of being rounded up and herded into a railhead just because we looked like the enemy was indescribable. Why only us Japanese-Americans and not the Germans and

Italians who were also in a war against the United States of America?"

In November 1942, after six months of incarceration, Hara volunteered to attend intelligence school at Camp Savage, Minnesota, for a twenty-six-week intensive course in the Japanese language. Caucasian graduates of the program routinely received commissions, although their command of Japanese was often rudimentary while the much more literate Nisei could not advance above the rank of noncom. Completion of the initial instruction, however, qualified Hara for basic infantry training and then more translation practice until he headed overseas as part of a ten-man language team.

At Milne Bay the detachment broke into two-man units attached to each regiment of the 6th Division with four of their original number assigned to division headquarters. Hara interrogated his first prisoners, remnants of the Japanese air force captured at Hollandia who were all but dead of starvation. Subsequently he moved to a forward sector where there was bitter fighting. "Taking prisoners was out of the question. Besides, they fought till the last man." When Hara finally got a crack at the trickle of captives, he noted "they were shell-shocked or badly wounded."

Understanding the language, Hara obtained insights beyond the ken of the ordinary GI. "I was able to pick out each and every Japanese that practiced cannibalism by just looking at their eyes. Upon interrogation their only comment was, 'It's a matter of survival.' " Hara asked combat veterans if it were true that dying soldiers shouted, *"Tenno heika banzai"*—Long live the Emperor! "Maybe one soldier in ten thousand," they told him. Another interjected, "One in twenty thousand is too high." They told Hara, "All they ever heard was the *'Oka San'*—mother—on their dying lips. Most of them being veterans of North China campaigns were apologetic for being captured, but like any human, some didn't give a damn."

On S-Day, Hara marveled at the first sights. "It was my first massive naval bombardment at close range and I was amazed to see our warships move sideways each time they laid down a salvo from all their guns. The whole Gulf was full of floating brass shells which reminded me of timberland cut down with nothing but tree stumps. I saw a few Japanese aircraft trying to bomb our ships without any success. They started to crash-dive—*kamikaze*—our ships. Due to some snafu by our high command, our fighter air cover did not show up in time. Thousands of antiaircraft fire turned the morning dawn into night by smoke cover. Our overdue fighters arrived but we had to tell them to get away before some of our ack ack took care of them.

"We landed two to three miles west of our assigned beach. The ground was pockmarked by our naval bombardment with holes large enough for a house to fall in. We hiked eastward to our assigned area and established our new CP. Within an hour I interviewed my first prisoner, dressed in civilian white shirt and khaki pants. He was wounded with bullet holes clean through his thigh, arm and shoulder. I was called back a month later to Army headquarters as a witness for a general court-martial a month later for this prisoner. The court sentenced him to be hanged as a spy."

The sector chosen for the 43rd Division, at the extreme left flank of the invasion force, presented a foreboding aspect. Three tiers of ridges overlooked the trio of beaches, offering defenders prime natural locations to dig in while supported by protected artillery and mortars. Leonard Hall of Company F, 172nd Regiment, drew the assignment of the left outer edge. "The highlight took place the night before the Luzon landing. Troops were trying to relax on deck in total darkness when the sailor on watch shouted, 'Look over this way. Something is really going on ahead of us!' Everyone came to their feet and watched first a flurry of tracer fire, orange-red in color, closely followed by a burst of green colored tracers. Several such volleys followed, and then came a reverberating boom like thunder and a large area of illumination. Then there was complete silence. It was broken by the ship's loudspeaker as an

excited voice announced, 'For the benefit of all personnel . . . one of our cruisers spotted a Japanese destroyer
trying to infiltrate our convoy. You will be happy to know
that the explosion that you just heard was the destroyer!'
Cheers rocked the boat.

"I was assigned to man one of the .30 caliber machine
guns on an amphibious tank. We watched with great interest the strafing runs of our fighters along the landing
beach. None of us had ever seen a rocket launching LCI
and when it released a rack of rockets over our tank we hit
the deck. It was embarrassing to climb back to my gunner's position.

"We reached the beach without opposition and gawked
at the huge fragments of naval shells. Someone remarked
that it seemed impossible for a pissant to have survived
such a barrage but some two hundred yards inland we
encountered scores of Filipinos. A few had wounds but
most had tunneled into the reverse slopes of hills and
stream beds and were not physically hurt. We secured three
small hills, our first-day objective."

Assembled in Aitape, the 43rd absorbed hundreds of
replacements, many of whom, according to the 169th
Regiment's John Higgins, "came from every branch of the
service except the infantry and it became a real problem
to integrate them into our units." Whatever their background, most of the newcomers went to the rifle companies, and the veterans had only about a month to teach the
skills of a foot soldier. After a Christmas dinner ashore, the
3rd Battalion with Higgins and his associates embarked
from Aitape on a U.S. Army transport ship, *Sea Witch,* a
step down from what Navy vessels offered. "Quarters were
poor, food was the pits and the TC personnel treated us
poorly."

But on January 9, after twelve days at sea, H-hour saw
Higgins, as part of the second wave, on a landing craft
circling the battleship *California.* "Just before we moved
out towards the beach area, the *California* fired all nine of

her fourteen-inch guns and kept firing overhead. Most of us could not hear for a long while after.

"We landed left of San Fabian a little after 0930 and followed the first wave inland. There was very little small arms fire but some artillery and mortar rounds incoming. The biggest problem was getting around the shell holes from the USN fourteen-inch and sixteen-inch guns. Some holes were thirty to forty feet across and ten to fifteen feet deep."

"The terrain just inland from the beach rose a little—small farms, a few bamboo shacks. Some Filipinos greeted us. It was not until later in the afternoon that we saw our first Jap soldiers. As we moved into the 3rd Battalion area west of the Bued River, two Jap soldiers jumped out of their hiding places and ran to the east. We were all startled, then started to fire at them. I could see rounds hitting the pack on one Jap; the other went down KIA. The one hit in the back turned and shot back, hitting one of our sergeants in the arm and shattered his carbine. The Jap dropped and was dead when we got to him. We dug in for the night on a low hill."

Among the replacements in the 169th's ranks was Missourian Arden J. Kurtz, assigned to the 60 mm mortar section of F Company's heavy weapons platoon. A night student at St. Louis University who finished classes at 10:00 P.M. and then worked the late shift at a steel plant, Kurtz held a draft deferment. "In the middle of 1943, I decided I did not want any more deferments. The war hysteria was pretty high at that time and a lot of people, they might not say it to your face, but everybody was saying, 'Why aren't you in the service?' That's how much the propaganda had been pushed."

While at Aitape, technically still a combat zone, his outfit taught him the perimeter guard setup with machine guns, "so you'd have a clear field of fire in case somebody decided they wanted to visit us. The ships we trained on had runways down each side. We would run down these onto the beach and into the jungle to simulate an attack. I learned water discipline in a hurry. The group in my platoon were the most unselfish group of people I have ever been associated with. In an unassuming way, they tried to educate me in the ways of combat so that I would have a better chance of living through the coming campaign. Colonel [Harry] Sellers was our battalion commander and he worked our butts off to get us in shape for the coming campaign and believe me he did get us in shape. He also gave us plenty of time to play, and we played volleyball and softball.

"At Lingayen Gulf, we were to be the first wave. We started in, in a zigzag pattern. When we were getting close to the beach, Jap artillery opened up on us. We could see the spouts of water as the shells exploded and we were heading right for them. One shell exploded close enough to spray water on us. The reality of war came home to me. Those guys were shooting at me and trying to kill me.

"We hit the beach without too much opposition, mostly small artillery fire. It still scared hell out of you. I followed the guy in front of me into a big shell hole. The sand kept giving way. It's funny now but at the time I didn't think so. We moved inland without too much opposition and bivouacked that night."

An upstate New York farm boy, Curtis James Banker attended a one-room schoolhouse through the eighth grade and after his second year of high school worked as an agricultural laborer. "I hated school and I was very small in stature so all the children picked on me. I learned to fight and got the nickname of 'Iron Man.'" He enlisted in the field artillery shortly after his eighteenth birthday in 1942. Following extensive training on the 155 mm "Long Tom" and schooling in infantry tactics, Banker traveled overseas to the 103rd Infantry of the 43rd Division. Assigned to Cannon Company, Banker drew a post with a gun crew on an M-7, a self-propelled 105 mm howitzer installed in the chassis of an M-3 tank.

"I came under fire the first day landing at San Fabian.

On the second day our first casualties were two of my best friends. Cpl. Alvin Isaacson was killed trying to get a fellow crewman off an amphibious tank that was burning from a direct hit. He could have saved himself if he had stayed undercover. In these first days, our engagements were mostly from large artillery caves dug in the mountains to the north."

On S-Day, a beachhead four miles in depth and about twenty in length resulted from Yamashita's decision not to offer opposition at the water's edge. The absence of the foe allowed MacArthur to return to the Philippines for a third time. "As was getting to be a habit with me," he said, "I picked a boat that took too much draft to reach the beach, and I had to wade in." According to Admiral Kincaid, however, MacArthur himself directed the script for this second encore performance. In preparation for the his arrival, Seabees created a little pier but as the coxswain steered for it the general "said no, he wouldn't land there. So they bypassed the pier. He jumped out in the water and waded ashore." The Filipinos in attendance cheered loudly as what had once been a spontaneous act became a ritual. MacArthur then set up his headquarters at Dagupan, the first town captured by the 37th Division.

Coleman thought that the enemy had fled to better defensive terrain after looking down from nearby mountain tops and seeing the huge armada. Actually, although MacArthur attempted to decoy Yamashita into thinking the attack would start elsewhere, the Japanese commander expected an opening gambit through the Lingayen Gulf. Even with the enormous number of soldiers he controlled, Yamashita never intended to defend the beachhead. Instead he split his command in three. The Shobu Group, under his direct supervision, would defend the northern half of Luzon, which included a mountainous region as well as the fertile Cagayan Valley. The Manila area, the southern territory and southeastern finger of the island came under purview of the Shimbu Group, headed by Lt. Gen. Shizuo Yokoyama. Aware of the problems that

MacArthur encountered when he retreated into Bataan with far too many people for maneuver and supply, Yamashita detailed just thirty thousand of the Kembu Group, led by Maj. Gen. Rikichi Tsukada, to resist there.

Manila lay only about 130 miles from the American beachheads but for the internees at Santo Tomas the hope of liberation was tempered by the rapidly deteriorating conditions. The blockade of the Philippines mounted by the U.S. Navy, the almost daily destruction that dropped from the skies and the increasing boldness of guerrilla forces created genuine shortages of food and supplies. The wretched conditions endured by American servicemen confined at Cabanatuan and Bilibid now enveloped the civilian internees. Betsy McCreary, the schoolgirl from Iloilo, had watched the almost carnival air of STIC seep away and noted a decline in prisoner-guard relations when the facility was taken over by the Japanese military police. "They further isolated the camp, strung it up tighter with rules and regulations. There was a general sobering, a sense of standing still and waiting, waiting. We were finally reduced to about seven hundred calories per day which is maybe okay for a week's crash diet but not for any length of time. I saw some eating out of garbage cans. I saw one man eating hibiscus leaves and one evening a grizzled older man asked if I was not going to eat part of a camote—a native yam—that was rotten and I'd spit out. He didn't mind and he took it. The pigeons disappeared from the roof and I also heard that all stray cats had disappeared.

"When we experienced shortages to the extent that lunch had to be eliminated and we only had a thin rice gruel for breakfast and rice and a watery vegetable stew for dinner, a recipe-writing craze began. Women started exchanging recipes, reciting recipes. The camp doctors said it was a form of insanity preceding starvation." (The men in the prisoner-of-war camps in Europe and Asia replicated the phenomenon by creating elaborate menus of the first meals they would eat after achieving freedom.)

Army nurse Madeline Ullom recalls, "Internees who

worked in a garden near the fence heard a radio broadcast from the outside which stated our forces landed at Lingayen. Navy bombers attacked sporadically during the day. Early in the morning residents of Shantytown found four-page leaflets with pictures of General MacArthur and 'MacArthur has returned. General MacArthur keeps his pledges.'

"Unauthorized traffic in STIC was forbidden. We felt when we walked to and from duty we were running a gauntlet. If anyone went to the hospital to visit a patient, a pass was necessary. The Japanese guards were also carrying hand grenades besides the rifles. They patrolled all the time. The effects of starvation and malnutrition took its toll. The medical staff requested special consideration for some internees during roll call. Many were falling and fainting. Certificates were issued to those who could not attend. Many were allowed to bring a folding chair to sit in except during the time the Japanese were at that room's formation. This was an extensive concession, but Lieutenant Abiko [considered the cruelest of the camp authorities] canceled the procedure. An internee had to be in bed to receive a pass. The death rate increased greatly. Beriberi was a predominant cause. About thirty men were reported dying in the gymnasium. The hospitals were without empty beds. Many were ill in their rooms.

"The Santo Tomas stare appeared. Internees who had engaged in friendly conversation now passed to the stage in which they walked beside each other without speaking or stood and stared at each other. They seemed to mentally appraise the washboard ribs of the men, the dull eyes, the hollow cheeks, the wrinkles in the skin and wonder how long so-and-so would last."

Life at the Los Banos camp was slightly better, according to navy nurse Mary Rose Harrington. "There were guerrillas all around who could slip in and out of camp, bring us information and food." Because it was away from a big city, in an agricultural area, there was more food available. The area was free of malaria and while some of the guards behaved badly, others respected the medical personnel.

At Santo Tomas, Los Banos and the military prison camps of Cabanatuan and Bilibid, the internees and captives impatiently waited for the invaders to reach them.

CHAPTER XXIII

THE MANILA PLAIN

ONCE THE AMERICANS held a substantial beachhead, the strategy for the immediate future was obvious. While widening and strengthening the flanks, the U.S. 6th Army would forge southeast towards Manila in a more or less straight line, hewing to a pathway with the least natural barriers. To protect the extreme ends of the front, additional GIs from the 63rd and 158th Regimental Combat Teams and the 13th Armored Group, which included tank battalions such as the 754th, disembarked. The 6th Ranger Battalion assumed responsibility for perimeter defense of the entire operation's headquarters at Dagupan and the 25th Infantry Division settled in as a ready reserve.

The 754th Tank Battalion, like most of the armor in the Pacific Theaters, operated without a permanent "parent" and instead worked with a number of different infantry divisions. Thomas Howard, the child of parents who reared their family during the Depression by dint of the Works Progress Administration, entered the Army via the draft. As a member of Company A in the 754th, Howard first encountered the enemy on Bougainville. On December 15, with their five tanks on an LSM, Howard's platoon departed on a five-thousand-mile voyage to Luzon.

In Lingayen Gulf, while awaiting orders for his vessel to approach the shore, Howard watched the landing craft churn for the beaches and marveled at the duels involving the fleet, its air cover and Japanese aircraft. Heavy surf combined with an inexperienced crew kept the tankers at sea until the early hours of January 12. For the first week or so, Howard and his mates relaxed behind the lines, cleaning their guns, performing maintenance on their tanks and socializing with civilians. He noted, "Talked to some Filipino girls. They are really nice. Now I found where they get the girls for the Dorothy Lamour pictures. One thing is you have no privacy. You can't wash or take a shower without them standing there watching you. We talked with the men and women. They are hurting for clothes, wanted undershirts and shorts. They beg you blind or pester you for work. The women want to wash your clothes and the men want to clean the tanks and guns, carry gas, oil or water. Of course they want to be paid. They can't understand why we have no money.

"We went for a walk after dinner and saw some sights. The houses are all made of grass and bamboo. They are built on stilts, have ladders for porch steps. The carabaos, pigs and chickens all sleep under the house at night. The houses are beautiful inside. They polish the bamboo until it shines. Partitions are woven of grasses into intricate designs. They are always clean, although sometimes smell from the closeness of the animals. The Filipinos constantly wash themselves and keep clean.

"Food must have been very scarce or recently nonexistent. Little kids beg for food with an old number ten can with wire handles. You can hardly eat your meal without kids sticking their pails in your face. You can't help but feel sorry for them, even going without part of your food yourself."

On January 15, Howard was assigned to telephone outpost duty and reported to the site where he sat and waited for instructions. "While sitting there, a convoy of Jeeps came up. It was General MacArthur and his staff. Saw him up close. He was wearing his five-star cluster. He and his staff met with General Kreuger and his staff at the cross-

road. It must have been some meeting. MacArthur was
yelling and pointing and carrying on. Everyone was scurry-
ing around as if they didn't know what direction to take.
After their confab, I received orders to relay to the company for it to move out and get to San Carlos as soon as
possible and remain in reserve position with the 37th
Division."

MacArthur's impatience wiped out the lassitude that
seemed to pervade the first days of the campaign. However, progress depended upon the speed of the soldiers on
foot because there was an absence of trucks to transport
them and supplies, the latter rapidly piling up on the
beach. At the town of San Carlos, the bivouac area for
Tom Howard's tank outfit and a truck and supply depot,
the Americans repaired the railroad that led to Manila.
Transportation specialists scrounged a few freight cars and
in place of a locomotive, engineers rigged a Jeep with
grooved wheels to fit on the rails. The first trainload of
supplies rumbled behind the advancing 37th Division
soldiers who, less than two weeks after landing, now entered the rubble of Tarlac halfway to Manila.

MacArthur insisted "there was no fixed timetable. I
hoped to proceed as rapidly as possible, especially as time
was an element connected with the release of our prisoners. I have always felt, however, that to endeavor to formu-
late in advance details of a campaign is hazardous, as it
tends to warp the judgment of a commander when faced
with unexpected conditions brought about by the uncer-
tainties of enemy reaction or enemy initiative. I therefore
never attempted to fix dates for anything but the start of
operations. The rate of progress in this operation was fast
and more than fulfilled all hopes and expectations."

MacArthur's concern for the prisoners was genuine. He
undoubtedly felt some guilt for having left his army to the
mercy of the enemy in 1942, but even more compelling
were the reports of the cruelty and atrocious conditions
from escapees like Sam Grashio and intelligence sources.
MacArthur noted that "the latest information was most

alarming. With every step that our soldiers took towards Santo Tomas University, Bilibid, Cabanatuan and Los Banos, where these prisoners were held, the Japanese soldiers guarding them had become more sadistic.''

Spurred by the Supreme Commander, the pace quickened. Tanker Tom Howard remarked: "Made all-day advance of twenty-five miles. Saw spots where we were the first Americans through. Advanced ahead of infantry into town of Paniqui but found the town burned and the Japs killed or chased away. We are moving so fast that the rear-echelon troops are not always able to follow up in our footsteps and occupy the positions. The Army is trying to organize the guerrilla force of Filipinos and get them armed to fill the gaps. The dirty, the ragged and the ones already armed with old Enfield rifles, Winchesters and machetes, they're the ones doing the fighting not the showing.''

While the XIV Corps of Krueger's 6th Army—the 37th and 40th Divisions—was driving south on the right flank of the American line, the 37th and its attached 754th Tank Battalion focused on Clark Field as the gateway to Manila. Meanwhile, on the extreme end, the 40th Division expanded the beachhead along Luzon's west coast.

Paul Gerrish of the 40th Cavalry Recon Troop, attached to the 185th Regiment, recalled the progress through Port Sual and to a road junction at Alaminos. On the eve of the operation, remembers Gerrish, "Father Herbst, division chaplain, joined us and circulated among the men with his cheerful words. 'You don't have a thing to worry about as I always bring good luck. I've been on a number of long-range missions and have never had to bury a man. I'm sure we will all return.'

"As we approached Labrador, the men who had been on patrol showed us the Japanese they had met. They were still sprawled where they had fallen and already were partially eaten by dogs. A Filipino told us, 'We'll bury them later. They won't hurt the dogs.' Progress was slow as we were often stopped by Filipinos who wanted to give us information about the Japanese and tell us about their hardships during the occupation. There were stories of tongues being cut out, water treatment, hanging by thumbs and beheadings. 'They took our rice, they took our chickens, they took our cows and they took our wives.' "

Near Aliminos, guerrillas advised the troop of the presence of the enemy. While a foot patrol reconnoitered the town, a message from division intelligence asked for prisoners. The patrol reported the Japanese oblivious to the Americans on the scene. The GIs with their M-8s, Jeeps and guerrillas slipped into Aliminos. Gerrish, in an M-8 with the troop commander, Capt. John Scott Robinson, says he saw two of their men near the city hall, headquarters for the Japanese unit. "I asked the captain, 'Sir, are Nunes and Lowe supposed to be over there near the city hall?' The captain answered, 'What in hell do those crazy kids think they are going to do?' He didn't have long to wonder as each of them picked a window and tossed a grenade through it. Rifle fire followed quickly and when the platoons heard the shooting, they thought they had missed a signal and dashed pell-mell towards the action. I saw two prone Japanese about fifty feet in front of our M-8 and started to lay a high-explosive shell between them when the captain shouted, 'Don't shoot, those are guerrillas.'

"As I started to train the turret guns on another target, the two Japanese got up and ran to join their fleeing comrades. The captain emptied his carbine at them. Some Japanese elected to stand and fight. They took cover behind trees and hedges and started shooting. With our patrols closing in from three directions, they could not keep out of sight and were like sitting ducks. Seeing their situation, more of them followed their departing comrades. Our men were handicapped by being in one another's lines of fire. We had to let a lot go for fear of hitting our own men. We were further handicapped by not being able to tell the Filipino guerrillas, many of them dressed in Japanese clothes, from the enemy. In future battles we would insist the guerrillas stay behind the M-8s to avoid that problem.

"The fight lasted about twenty minutes with all of the Japanese who hadn't fled being dead. We came through without a man scratched." Captain Robinson asked for the Filipinos to bury the corpses and again the people agreed, "but only after the dogs fed themselves." The Troop failed to bag any prisoners but at least Chaplain Herbst's prediction proved accurate.

The invaders from the I Corps, the 6th and 43rd Infantry Divisions, meanwhile set their sights on several major highways, starting with a stretch of Route 3 between the towns of Damortis and Rosario. That road intersected Route 11 opening access both to Manila southeast, and into the heart of Yamashita's Shobu Army girding for its stand in northern Luzon. The newly arrived 158th RCT in front of Damortis challenged a strongly entrenched defense. The 172nd Regiment of the 43rd Division, after three days of relative quiet, had jumped off on January 12, with a mission to seize control of high ground overlooking Route 3. In that engagement, the unit absorbed its first casualties of the Luzon campaign.

With the F Company machine gun squad, Len Hall dug in. "During the night," recalled Hall, "the Japanese had charged, screaming into the company lines, and been repulsed. In the dark hours before dawn they changed their tactics and began infiltrating the company positions. Catching two soldiers asleep in their slit trench, the infiltrators bayonetted them both and seriously wounded others." In succeeding days, the losses mounted in small but saddening increments.

To the right of Hall's outfit, the 169th Regiment also started to bleed. The 3rd Battalion S-4, John Higgins, speaks first of increasing incoming artillery and mortars. "To secure rations, ammo and water I returned to the beach, confiscated two Alligators (tracked personnel carriers) and loaded them. While crossing the Bued River, a wide but fairly shallow stream, we came under mortar attacks and Cpl. Henry Aregeau and I were blown off the Alligators into the water. The tracked vehicles kept moving while we then came under MG fire from the Japs in the hills. My battalion commander, Lt. Col. Arthur W. Ballard, said he thought he was going to lose his S-4. The next day, while on recon, Ballard was shot in the head when a Jap machine gun opened up. He died about an hour later. During our movement into positions for an attack on Hill 355, our battalion surgeon, Capt. Tom Hill, lost his right hand while we were under a mortar attack. This really bothered me as I had served with him in New Zealand, New Guinea and now Luzon. He was a fine doctor and friend.

"I was contacted by a Filipino from the local area. He was looking for arms to kill Japs. Said he had twelve to fifteen men who wanted to join us. After having the battalion intelligence check him out, we gave him the arms they needed and assigned patrol missions. A couple of days later, one of his men came in and said they had twenty to twenty-five Japs holed up about five miles from us and wanted help to take them. I set up a patrol of about twenty and we headed out. We found the area and I took command of the Filipinos. We laid down a base of fire and sent three enlisted men and a sergeant to drop grenades. As soon as this was done, I ordered a charge. When we secured the area, we had killed nineteen Japs and captured one badly wounded man. I turned over the wounded man to the Battalion S-2 and medics. Had to watch the Filipinos as well as some of my own men who wanted to kill the prisoner. But we got him back."

Higgins's experience was not unique. Other officers found it necessary to issue direct orders to preserve the life of captives. Leonard Hall says, "I am aware of only one instruction given about enemy prisoners. We were told not to shoot wounded as they would sometimes talk. I did admire the fighting ability of the Japanese but one event caused me to lose respect for them as human beings. We discovered the bodies of two young Filipino women and two young Filipino boys. They had been bayonetted through the stomach with hands tied behind their backs. The young women were pregnant and the boys appeared to be under ten years of age. The war became much more personal after that."

The assault unit for Hill 355, the regiment's F Company, included mortar man Arden Kurtz, staggering forward with a load of seventy-five to ninety pounds in the intense heat of the day. "In the attack," says Kurtz, "our platoon leader got killed and the machine gun section lost about half their people. The company commander and the executive officer got hit. Since the machine gun section got hit so hard, they transferred me to it from the mortar section.

"We headed for the Sison road junction and started to receive some fire. Colonel Sellers was setting up our perimeter. In my mind, I can see the guy saying, 'Dig your machine gun in there.' He was standing in the middle of the road and he didn't bat an eye at the incoming fire. You drew strength from the guy. You say to yourself, 'If he can handle it, I can handle it.' He was a West Point man and he lived up to the tradition.

"After it got dark we could hear them coming. If anything moved at night you shot it. I saw a couple of them in the moonlight in the field in front of us. My machine gun sergeant grabbed my carbine and without looking, stuck it over his head and got off a couple of rounds. He didn't even know what the hell he was shooting at. Suddenly all hell broke loose. My gunner got hit so we moved him to my hole and I took his place. The shooting went on almost all night—rifle fire, mortars, artillery. Half the mortar section that I had been in got killed that night. They called in our artillery to try to ring our perimeter close as possible to try and give us some help. Some of the people were crying and screaming for God to help them. Seemed to me it was a little late to be screaming to God for help. The time to pray was before the shooting started and try to be as decent a guy as you could.

"After it got daylight, those of us who were left got orders to pull out with our wounded. We were still receiving fire. To get to the road, there were some spots where we had to walk on dead men. There were so many of them. I remember one American in this ditch with a bayonet rifle sticking out of his chest and three dead Japs right around him.

"Colonel Sellers got killed that night. The Catholic chaplain who said mass on the hood of his Jeep the morning after we landed was killed. I was told they tried to stop him from going with us but he came anyhow. He was the only chaplain I saw during the entire war. The Presidential Unit Citation we got said there were over 150 enlisted men and eight officers killed in this action and we got credit for killing over nine hundred Japs. Our platoon sergeant was the highest-ranked man left in our company. All the other noncoms had been killed or hit."

Len Hall with F Company of the 172nd climbed Hill 1500, a section of a ridgeline near Route 3, to replace Filipino irregulars. The guerrillas had relieved the Americans who had actually pushed the Japanese out. To reach the crest, Hall says, the men pulled themselves up hand over hand through stretches marked by an almost ninety-degree rise. The officer at the top who greeted them groused about the previous night with the irregulars as a "real bitch. The damn fools talked and smoked all night long. One man was killed and several were wounded. I would have felt safer on a hill full of Japs."

Forewarned, F Company dug in, spacing the machine guns, disposing of a stinking enemy corpse by shoving it over a precipice, hunkering down as field pieces from a nearby four-thousand-foot peak whistled rounds overhead. The four-man crew of which Hall was a member dug two positions, piled sandbags in front of the weapon. One foxhole served Meredith and Savage, the senior crewmen. Willard Mitchell and Hall occupied a slit trench just below the muzzle of the gun. Hall could not lie down because the water in the trench was too deep. Instead, when it was his turn to rest, he dozed on an ammunition box. At night, he carefully placed a large number of grenades on the trench parapet where they would be readily available.

One particular night, a hard, cold rain accompanied by lightning and loud claps of thunder pelted them. The noise and darkness offered the best possible conditions for infiltrators. Hall was dozing while Mitchell stood guard. Hall awoke abruptly, as his companion grabbed his knee and shouted, "My God, look out front!" A flash of lightning illuminated a trio of enemy soldiers only three feet away. A burst of machine gun fire wiped out all three, as either Meredith or Savage triggered the weapon. The muzzle blast revealed all three enemy down.

Hall recovered quickly and instantly reached for his grenades, then hurled them in the direction of a possible attack. As he turned to grab some more, he saw a sparking object falling into his trench. He started to launch himself from the hole while yelling "Jump!" to Mitchell. Whether it was a grenade or a mortar round, Hall never got out of the trench before the missile exploded. It threw him into the air, but because he had already extended himself, he absorbed most of the blast on the lower portions of his body. Hall slid down a hill and called for a medic who, working in the dark, applied a pressure bandage to the obvious wound, a large gouge in the rear of Hall's left thigh. The tearing metal lost some of its malignity when it ripped into the Bible that Hall kept in his pocket, thereby saving him from a worse injury or even death.

The machine gunner tried to advise some nearby riflemen where he thought the attack came from; then he lost consciousness from loss of blood and shock. He was carried out on a litter and evacuated through a series of hospitals until finally bedded down in the States. His slit trench buddy, Mitchell, had also tried to escape the incoming explosive and been seriously wounded.

The 6th Infantry Division, operating immediately to the right of the 43rd, maintained a static line during the first few days as its neighbors battled towards the desired high-

ways. General Krueger, the Army commander, delayed the
6th because he feared a vulnerable gap might open between the two divisions if they advanced too swiftly. Once
he divined the nature of the Japanese concentrations, however, Kreuger directed the 6th Division to anchor the left
flank and he inserted his ready reserve, the 25th Division,
between the 6th and 43rd. Subsequently, the left flank of
the American forces would welcome a further infusion of
troops, from the 1st Cavalry Division.

The 44th Tank Battalion, another "bastard" with no
"parent" organization, sprang from the 12th Armored Division ranks in 1943. Lt. Col. Tom Ross assumed command. Once overseas, the companies of the 44th often
operated on separate islands while affiliated with different
larger groups. Together, the four companies comprising
the 44th (three equipped with Sherman medium tanks and
one with M-5 Cadillac light tanks) had fought on Wakde,
Biak, New Guinea, Morotai and Leyte. The 44th debarked
over a three-day period on the Lingayen beachhead. On
S-Day, C Company, the first on shore, trundled off to
serve under the 6th Division.

Don "Moe" Mercier, a Wisconsin graduate of the CCC
program, served as the gunner in the lead tank of C Company's first platoon. The mission of the 6th Division
brought Mercier and his fellow tankers into the Cabaruan
Hills, a grim collection of ridges infested with a strongly
entrenched enemy. "We made good time on the concrete
highways," says Mercier, "but the mountainous fighting
was much slower. You would never know when you'd run
into antitank guns. Their 37 mm armor-piercing shells
could set a tank on fire. Mortar fire often forced the tankers to button-up, which made it harder to spot the enemy.
Going up a steep hill left the periscopes useless." For three
weeks, C Company tanks were engaged in the Cabaruan
area against infantry, artillery and enemy tanks. Every single Sherman received at least one hit and three burned out
and were blown up.

For the 25th Division, the going quickly proved equally

tough. After his Czech-born family lost its farm for the second time in 1936 due to crop failures, the 25th Division's Emil Matula, who did not speak English until he entered school at age eight, enlisted in the Army because one of his friends had volunteered. "I found Army life to be every day like a Sunday on the farm," says Matula, who was then twenty, "and I thought it would be the home to retire from. I was in a machine gun company and we had .30 caliber Brownings which were pulled by a mule with a sulky as ammo carrier. There were no ratings available and most of the men served at least three years as a buck private at $21 a month. After three years I reenlisted and, assigned to the 35th Regiment, went to Hawaii. I could not believe December 7 that I was standing in the quadrangle under an earthquake alarm and being strafed by Japanese planes. Our company kept its cool and when the second wave of Jap planes came, all our machine guns were in action."

The regiment, as part of the 25th Division, guarded Hawaiian installations and trained there until it sailed to Guadalcanal and began a long tour of the Pacific battle-fields. On Guadalcanal, Matula worked with woefully obsolete weaponry—WW I machine guns, ancient mortars and old ammunition that produced many short rounds and casualties among their own troops. However, the members of what was known as the "Tropic Lightning" Division, because of its shoulder patch design, developed an attitude towards the enemy. "The experiences we had on Guadalcanal, New Georgia, Vella Lavella was that when a Jap was giving up, he waited for a group of GIs, then let a grenade from his armpit or G-string explode. I ordered my troops if they weren't stripped naked, shoot them first, and then question them later."

By the time the 35th Regiment stepped onto the Lingayen shore January 11, Matula held the post of first sergeant for D Company, a heavy weapons unit. While in reserve the GIs of the division labored as longshoremen, but unlike at Guadalcanal they employed mechanized equipment to offload the latest in ordnance.

Leaving the beach duty behind, the 35th entered the lists January 17, sending out patrols to probe the defensive lines. Within a week, the regiment with its brother outfit the 27th approached a major objective, Umingan, a vital point on a secondary road leading to the town of San Jose. Control of the junction and the surrounding area would choke off the avenues by which Yamashita's southern Shimbu Group could maintain contact with his Shobu Army on northern Luzon.

The well-entrenched Japanese garrison at Umingan presented a formidable obstacle to further progress. The American strategists plotted an enveloping move in which the two regiments circled the town, cutting off the defenders from the outside. A *banzai* charge, aimed at breaking out, tangled with barbed wire at a U.S. roadblock. Gunners cut down fifteen Japanese whose bodies were found hanging on the wire. The Americans, initially bogged down by a determined enemy, finally overwhelmed the Japanese troops at Umingan and started down Highway 5 towards the next two objectives, the villages of Lupao and San Jose.

The 27th Regiment incurred the brunt of casualties at Umingan, but the 35th suffered when its frontal and flank attacks on Lupao stalled as enemy artillery, mortars and small arms ravaged the ranks trying to cross dry rice paddies that offered no cover. Emil Matula of D Company remembers a February 2 attack against positions that were bolstered by two pieces of artillery, a pair of dug-in tanks, machine guns and supporting riflemen. Almost all of his unit's officers, and a number of noncoms and enlisted men, were wounded or killed. With the company commander at battalion headquarters to direct operations, Matula delegated a subordinate to handle his first sergeant duties while he assumed command of a pair of machine gun platoons. The fighting there raged for six days as the

Americans brought on tanks, M-7 self-propelled howitzers and more men.

In a third-person account, Matula wrote, "The night of February 7–8 saw the death throes of the Japanese garrison at Lupao. At 0100 the Japs decided to make a run for it. Company A knocked out one tank with seven hits from a bazooka, and damaged another. At the same time, eight Japanese tanks loaded with troops broke through the road blocks of Company D and B. Company D bagged two with bazookas fired by Sergeant Ciecioka, Sergeant Sanders and First Sergeant Matula. Company B bagged another one and damaged two others. The other three managed to slip away into the foothills of the Caraballo Mountains. The rest of the tanks in town were found abandoned and their crews eliminated.

"After the Japanese tanks were knocked out, there were many Japanese soldiers that were trapped in the tanks all night. Finally at about 0700 many of the soldiers got out of their foxholes and went to hunt for gold teeth, Japanese swords and weapons. As the scavengers were going over the bodies of the dead, one of the Company D soldiers kicked the helmet off one that appeared dead, hoping to find a flag. As the helmet came off, the Jap came up with a bolo knife. The soldier was lucky that I was standing close enough to knock the knife out of his hand with my rifle butt. As I did this, the Jap began to run. I shot him because he did not stop when I called him.

"After this incident and the events of the day, I sat down in my foxhole and started to clean my carbine and pistol. Suddenly my mouth started feeling like it was full of gravel. I walked over to the 1st Battalion aid station so that I could have the dentist check my tooth which had shattered in my mouth. Was I surprised when the dentist told me I had been shot through the left side of my face with a sniper's bullet, which had hit my tooth! The bullet deflected and lodged in my upper jaw bone and sinus. I was sent to the field hospital where the doctors performed surgery and removed the bullet. My face swelled up and I had to spend twenty days in the hospital. Even though I begged the doctor to let me go back to duty, I was stuck for the twenty days."

The Japanese in the vicinity of San Jose, the 6th Infantry Division's objective, presented a defense in depth, with a series of isolated strongpoints. Tanks and artillery buttressed the enemy infantrymen but instead of deploying the armor for mobile operations, the Nipponese dug in the tanks as pillboxes. They recognized that the lightly skinned tanks were highly vulnerable to U.S. weapons and armor as well as aircraft. But the arrangement limited options and enabled the American attackers to execute flanking maneuvers with less difficulty than if the tanks were mobile. Such a weakness notwithstanding, advances were measured in yards as the defenders held off the U.S. 6th Division in fierce and deadly combat.

During the first weeks of the Luzon fighting, a number of Army commanders seemed reluctant to utilize tactical air support. Gen. Edwin Patrick, CO of the 6th Division, was particularly adamant in his refusal to accept such aid. A Marine air liaison officer said of Patrick, "He was scared of airplanes; that is scared of their accuracy and lack of ground control." Undoubtedly, an incident a few days earlier in which a strafing Army B-25 killed two and wounded twenty-five men from the 6th Division colored Patrick's outlook.

Early in February, Patrick visited with Gen. Verne Mudge, his opposite number with the 1st Cavalry, as the latter dealt with a stubborn enemy force holed up behind a ridge. From their near impregnable positions, the defenders poured out heavy machine gun fire and dropped mortar rounds on anyone who ventured towards the ridge line. Mudge summoned an air strike to aid his troops. A fascinated Patrick listened as the Marine bombers flew over the scene while their ground control officer instructed them to dump their ordnance on the back side of the hill, precluding any injury to the GIs.

The two division commanders watched white phosphorous bombs mark the target zone. Shortly after, the first bomb erupted just below the crest on the Japanese side. Seven dive bombers roared in behind, expertly blasting the enemy positions while the cavalrymen cheered as if at a football game. After the planes flew off, a patrol carefully picked its way up the ridge and reached the summit without any opposition. On the other side lay the wreckage of eight machine guns and fifteen mortar emplacements amid about three hundred dead enemy soldiers. The troopers also secured another eleven unmanned heavy machine guns. The scene converted Patrick to an enthusiastic user of air support.

Carlie Berryhill was a farmer's son who left school after the sixth grade to work. A veteran of New Guinea combat and a member of I Company of the 63rd Infantry in the 6th Division, he recalls a small Filipino boy about fourteen years old who approached him as the outfit was about to attack. "He asked if he could help carry some ammunition. I told him he should go home and he said the Japs had killed his father and most of his family. He wanted to stay with me and help fight. I received permission for him to be with my unit, got him some clothing and gave him a carbine rifle. His name was Terso Gilman and he turned out to be a very good soldier who was still with I Company when the war ended."

Berryhill's unit needed anyone capable of handling a weapon as the company hemorrhaged from the intensive action. "At the time we were attacking San Jose. One morning at sunrise, we had to cross a level rice paddy for about five hundred yards. By ten o'clock that morning we had 137 men either killed or wounded out of my company of 189. Out in the open field, we had no place to hide, or take cover. That was the most we ever lost in a single day."

As an intelligence expert and interrogator, Min Hara stuck close to the 6th Division forward echelons. In the fierce exchanges around the town of Munoz, the Americans gradually outflanked the enemy. "During the battle of Munoz," Hara recalls, "our forces wiped out a regiment of the Japanese 2nd Armored Division, destroying fifty-seven medium and light tanks. There was an urgent call from the front, asking us AJAs [Americans of Japanese ancestry] to volunteer. They claimed they had the CO surrounded in a huge bunker so they wanted to take him alive. The dugout was large enough to hold fifteen–twenty men. I crawled about twenty-five yards to the entrance, but our infantrymen kept lobbing smoke grenades so not one enemy soldier was alive by the time I had a chance to call out.

"Then our infantry advanced beyond this bunker and fanned out two–three yards apart and the next thing I heard was 'Fix bayonets!' What a spine-tingling order! I was supposed to entice a Japanese colonel to surrender and suddenly, I'm involved in a bayonet fight. As we were advancing on the town with fixed bayonets, I noticed the farmers had their corn stalks stacked up in a pyramid shape like our founding fathers in the New England states. Japanese soldiers were behind every stack waiting for us to engage them in hand-to-hand combat. Due to our abundance of ammo, we shot them instead of getting into such dangerous maneuvers. A GI alongside me shot a charging Japanese soldier who started to go down, clutching his stomach. The GI immediately dropped his rifle and drew his knife from belt and rushed towards him. I thought he was going to stab him, but no, he grabbed the man by the collar and started to cut off his rank insignia. Our infantry colonel was shouting, 'No, boys, it's too dangerous!' But this GI was still nonchalantly cutting away as I passed him. I wondered to myself, how souvenir hungry can a guy get, risking his life for a mere trophy."

Moe Mercier, on board a Sherman tank as a gunner in the 44th Tank Battalion, remembers that on February 5 "we were hit in the sprocket by a 37 mm shell. We destroyed the antitank gun but now could only back up. We were towed into camp. That night the tank was parked on the perimeter facing Munoz where the Japs were trapped. After dark we heard some rumbling. It sounded like a convoy coming. They stopped about three hundred yards away. We could hear them making repairs on equipment and hollering, 'We are Americans.' I manned a .30 caliber machine gun in the assistant driver's position and scanned the darkened highway. As the Jap column advanced, the first tank was destroyed with one round from one of our tanks. After that, all hell broke loose. I suddenly realized my face could be reflecting the moonlight and I was a perfect target. I jumped to the ground. Immediately after I hit the ground there was an explosion above me. The next morning I checked and sure enough there was a large hole in the hatch. My head would have been blown off had I not moved.

"Company C suffered one man killed, eleven men wounded, two tanks damaged. The Japanese had 245 men killed and lost ten medium tanks, one light tank and four other vehicles. I gave several wounded men morphine and helped them to safety while others were fighting off the Japs—some even hand to hand. As we had done all through the war, we had set up our own perimeter because the infantry and artillerymen thought tanks drew mortar fire. We were happy to be alone as many of the others were too trigger happy." The shootout between armor in the Munoz–San Jose area was one of the hottest tank-to-tank fights of the Pacific.

The pressure on Yamashita's forces increased with a second beachhead. At the time of the Lingayen Gulf expedition, the Army command had plotted a strike by the XI Corps well to the north of Lingayen Gulf at Vigan. The official U.S. Army history of the campaign states that after witnessing the intensity of enemy air attacks against the convoys around S-Day, MacArthur concluded the second site lay too close to enemy planes based on Formosa. Now, with the invasion force streaming towards Manila, MacArthur chose a coastal site much farther south, in the Zambales region, about twenty-five miles northwest of Bataan. By swiftly cutting off access to the peninsula, the Supreme Commander could prevent the enemy from using

Bataan, Corregidor and the Kembu Group as threats to Manila, whose fall he expected imminently.

In his version of events, MacArthur asserts that strategic considerations were reinforced by the need to react to decisions by Washington. One of these decisions removed seventy of his transport ships for the task of bearing supplies to the Soviet Union. MacArthur commented, "Shortly after the transports were taken from me, I was instructed to return most of the Pacific fleet to Admiral Nimitz to be used in the attack on Okinawa. These ships comprised much of the naval forces I was using. As a result, my supply base at Lingayen would be defended only by a portion of the 7th Fleet . . ." MacArthur claimed that this second landing would enable him to open a new supply route if the Japanese battered the Lingayen operations from Formosa.

The Lingayen Gulf entry to Luzon, however, was not seriously threatened after the first weeks of the invasion. On the other hand, well-placed officials in the Navy continued to doubt the wisdom of the massive effort in the archipelago, preferring to hit the enemy much closer to home, and not coincidentally, in a region that lay under Admiral Nimitz's command rather than MacArthur's. They focused on the coming invasions of Iwo Jima and then Okinawa as far more important than the liberation of the Philippines.

The new landings were an instant success. Filipino guerrillas in small craft sailed out to the American convoy and informed the Navy there would be no need for any pre-invasion barrage. There were no Japanese in the area. Elements of the 24th and 38th Infantry Divisions debarked without incident. Guerrillas under Capt. Ramón Magsaysay, a future president of the Republic, had already overrun the nearby San Marcelino airstrip, and a recon troop that dashed to the north shore of Subic Bay met no enemy. The entire XI Corps counted only a single casualty, an unlucky soldier gored by carabao.

Once the invaders trudged inland, however, the enemy greeted them with artillery rounds. Ernest Chaplin, raised by a widowed mother and then a sister when she died, was one of nine brothers from Charleston, South Carolina, who served in some branch of the military during the war. While overseas, Chaplin held reunions with three of his brothers, one in New Guinea, and two on Luzon. As a graduate of the Civilian Military Training Corps program, Chaplin, upon receipt of his draft notice in 1941, completed courses that made him eligible for a direct commission. As a second lieutenant in the field artillery he trained at Fort Bragg and then became a battery officer for the 150th FA Battalion, part of the 38th Division. He held the post of forward observer and in that capacity either spotted targets from an L-4 Piper Cub single-engine plane, dumped leaflets from the air or occupied an up-front post where he could instruct gunners on targets and direct their aim.

"At Subic Bay," says Chaplin, "we drew artillery fire when we placed our guns and dug in. I saw one disaster when one of our L-4s was hit dead center over our position by a friendly artillery unit firing 155 mm Long Toms from behind us. The L-4 belonged to our battalion and my close buddy, the pilot, was blown to pieces along with the observer. Flying these missions, you had only a .45 caliber pistol, carried field glasses and no parachute."

Forward observers like Chaplin frequently teetered on a very thin line. "I brought in some artillery rounds too close to an infantry unit on a hill—no casualties, thank God—and the infantry regimental CO who happened to be on the hill called my battalion CO and said the forward observer was going to kill all our men. My CO came to the area later in the day and saw the situation and he accepted my explanation. In a different action, our shells had fallen on an infantry group when another forward observer was firing at a target where I could see both the gun position and the target. I called down to the guns and told the major at the firing direction center what I saw. Back came the answer that all checked out okay at the guns, and he told the FO to continue the fire mission. When he did, another round fell on the soldiers. I called again, telling them of the short round. The fire mission was called off. Years later a gun sergeant told me he was in that battery and noticed one gun tube lower than the others. But I caught hell when I came back to the battalion position and was told, 'You could get us all sent to Leavenworth!' "

Despite such mishaps, the Americans rapidly seized Olongapo, the Subic Bay port, and sealed all passageways into Bataan. Unlike 1942 no more troops could retreat into that peninsula's mountainous jungles for a last-ditch defense.

MacArthur committed further resources. Two days after the Zambales landings, the 11th Airborne and another regiment of the 24th Division surfaced at Nasugbu on the Luzon coastline southwest of Corregidor. The maneuver put in motion the envelopment of Manila and eventual isolation of the Shimbu Army on the southern half of the island.

Meanwhile, American forces heading towards Manila from Lingayen Gulf had to deal with concentrations of enemy strength at two former U.S. Army installations, Clark Field and Fort Stotsenburg. U.S. intelligence estimated about four thousand defenders around Clark Field, a base greatly enlarged by the Japanese to spread over a fifteen-mile-long complex of air strips. In fact, the Kembu Group responsible for this area totaled thirty thousand troops. Although about eighty-five hundred were well-schooled combat troops, the rest were a motley assortment of navy men, construction engineers, service troops, and grounded air crews. Still, arrayed from Clark back down into Bataan and embedded in high ground that overlooked the Manila plain, the Kembu Group presented a serious barrier. On the other hand, the XI Corps's 24th and 38th Divisions had taken up positions near the neck of Bataan, ensuring that no reinforcements would rescue the defenders around Clark Field.

The opening round saw the 40th Cavalry Recon Troop on the outskirts of Bamban, on the Manila rail line a few miles from the heart of Clark and Stotsensburg. On the left flank of the 40th ranged the 620th Tank Destroyer Recon and the 37th Division's Cavalry Recon, which employed light tanks instead of the 40th's M-8s. Paul Gerrish from the 40th says, "It dawned on us that the three lightly armored reconnaissance units were the armor that would try to take Clark Field from the stubborn Japanese defenders." Typically, the soldiers at ground level received little or no information on the grand scheme of the attack and knew nothing of how much of whom had been committed.

The three lightly gunned outfits advanced only to come under intensive artillery and small arms fire on the outskirts of Bamban. Obedient to orders, they retreated and then approached from a different angle while an infantry regiment assumed responsibility for Bamban. Driven back several times, the 40th ultimately traveled a distance east, away from the foothills of the Zambala Mountains where the strongest natural defenses stood. "The next time we turned south," says Gerrish, "we captured the Bamban airstrip after a brief skirmish. Japanese were still at the far end of the strip as a Piper Cub came in for a landing and under fire. The pilot jumped out, gave it a quick look and dashed over, saying, 'Look out for those Japanese. They are firing live ammunition.' "

By late afternoon, Gerrish's recon outfit had fought running fights with the defenders and it was time to bed down for the night. Headed for safety, the 3rd platoon suddenly informed the troop commander of a large force of enemy about to charge. The commander, Captain Robinson, ordered all vehicles to reverse course at full speed. "As we turned south and raced away from our own lines," says Gerrish, "the first platoon ran off into a grass covered swamp. There they were up to their hubs in mud, all three armored cars and six Jeeps. Many commanders would have abandoned that platoon. Others would have taken the men out on the remaining vehicles. But we had Captain Robinson who could reconnoiter the badlands of hell. We needed those men and we needed the equipment. Picking up the microphone, Robinson shouted into the troop radio, 'Back third platoon and fight the Japanese off. Second platoon pull the first out!'

"Winch lines were run out on the double. Those were brave men running winch lines through a hail of bullets. Soon one M-8 and two Jeeps were back on the dry runway. Even as they were being pulled out of the mud, men were pulling their winch lines towards the still stuck vehicles. Soon the entire platoon was back on solid ground.

"We dashed south again, firing at any Japanese luckless enough to get in our way. For several miles we raced south, running a gauntlet of Japanese. When the situation had cooled down we turned east, away from the Zambales Mountains, bristling with gun barrels as big as telephone poles and swarming with Japanese troops. Later we turned north to get back to our own lines. After dark we came to a large sandbar by a river. Captain Robinson decided we would hole up there because if we continued on we might come under fire from our own infantry.

"The vehicles were circled in the middle of the sandbar so that the Japanese would have to attack across an open space and we knew they were usually reluctant for such an assault. When the motors stopped and it was quiet enough to hear, we were hailed across the river by a good American voice. 'What outfit is that? We would have fired but we heard your American profanity.' We were across the river from one of the 37th Division's infantry regiments that had moved up that day. We enjoyed a good night's sleep."

Originally the American commander believed his forces should be able to overrun the defenses in one or two days. But the enemy stubbornly refused to concede ground, tenaciously contesting almost yard by yard and holding on for a week. However, the resources and the manpower of the combined efforts of the 40th and 37th Divisions slowly crushed the Kembu units, inflicting twenty-five hundred casualties as against 710 of their own.

From the beginning MacArthur's staff had counted on the guerrilla forces as a significant factor, the equivalent of a division of infantry. Submarines regularly deposited meteorologists, demolition experts and radio operators at remote sites where they could work with guerrillas, and the same system delivered to the indigenous fighters weapons, ammunition, batteries for radios, medical supplies, and other vital items. Initially, the irregulars fed back information, ambushed work parties and committed sabotage. They were not expected to fight pitched battles, but the presence of GIs on Luzon changed the situation.

The former engineer, Col. Wendel Fertig, loosely governed the many different bands operating through the southern islands, but the Southwest Pacific Headquarters felt that effective coordination with U.S. troops on Luzon required closer contact. Jay Vanderpool, a former artillery officer, had volunteered to go behind enemy lines in northern Luzon and liaison with the guerrillas. From the submarine *Cero,* Vanderpool and his team of specialists climbed into canoes for a trip to a guerrilla camp, bringing with them much needed supplies. To make his way through the bush, Vanderpool hired mountain people, Dimagats, whom he described as about five feet tall, dark skinned, wiry, agile and strong. The chief accompanied the American on the trek and the headman's daughter honored Vanderpool by toting his burden.

At a small village he stayed overnight in a Catholic church. When a Japanese patrol approached during the day, the guides scattered while Vanderpool hid in the belfry. The nuns prevented the foe from further investigation with a show of modesty. On the outskirts of Manila, Vanderpool was perplexed about how to get through the city, which was teeming with enemy soldiers, to meet his next contact. He finally located a nervous taxicab driver who agreed to drive him through the nighttime curfew to the outskirts of the city.

"I met with guerrillas. One leader was from the U.S. Naval Academy and another from the USMA. Other military schools were also represented. There were ten or twelve different [guerrilla] outfits which would as soon fight one another as they would the Japs. We started getting revenue returns when we began swapping for pilots who had been shot down. They were real good trading material. The Navy and Air Corps wanted their people back. We suggested that while picking pilots up they could bring in a load of this or that so they packed a PBY or sub with a bunch of goodies. We salvaged and traded for twenty-two pilots in December 1944 alone.

"I was trying to put over to the guerrillas one of the things Steve Mellnik [an escapee from the Philippines who while in Australia became an intelligence specialist focusing on the guerrillas] taught me in a briefing. He said, 'Remember Warsaw. Don't go charging into taking the Japanese Army on by yourselves because if you're wiped out, you're no good to anyone. Wait until the Americans get here and coordinate your work with that of an American ground officer.' "

One of the more difficult situations involved the fierce Hukbalahap tribe. "They were very anti-Japanese. It was my theory they might be an enemy after this war but at the time we were fighting the same enemy. I informed Luis Taruc, leader of the Hukbalahaps, that I would supply them with ammunition and medical supplies but I would not give them new weapons. They wanted more, but what I offered was better than nothing. After the war the Filipinos did have to fight the Huks but they had some good men."

Once the American troops launched the drive towards Manila, Vanderpool switched from the job of liaison to command of guerrilla forces. One of the battalions under his leadership was all Huk and Vanderpool praised them as

"outstanding." He led them as they protected the right
flank of the 11th Airborne when it beached on the west
coast. Homegrown units began to become involved in direct tactical operations rather than through *sub rosa* missions.

Although the ranks of effective combat soldiers swelled,
the now slowing tempo of the American advance aroused
anxiety among those concerned about the welfare of the
captives. About thirty miles beyond the U.S. lines lay the
compound at Cabanatuan with an estimated five hundred
enfeebled prisoners. There was growing fear that the enemy might slaughter them all rather than permit liberation.
At 6th Army headquarters, intelligence experts, guerrilla
commanders and leaders from the Rangers (the U.S. version of the British commandos) and the Alamo Scouts (an
elite unit created in New Guinea to infiltrate to the rear of
Japanese positions) conferred about a way to rescue those
held at Cabanatuan.

Lt. Col. Henry Mucci, the commander of the 6th
Ranger Battalion, Maj. Bob Lapham, an American-born
guerrilla leader, and veterans of the Alamo Scouts developed a plan for night marches through enemy territory
with 107 Rangers backed by 160 Filipinos. The men,
wearing soft caps, carrying only weapons, K rations and
some packs of cigarettes and candy for the prisoners,
slipped past the front lines on the evening of January 28.
The guerrillas accurately detailed the locations of Japanese
soldiers and cautioned the local residents to muzzle dogs
and to pen up other livestock that might signal the movements. The area people eagerly cooperated; recent atrocities against civilians in retaliation for guerrilla operations
brought hatred and a thirst for vengeance. When the raid-
ers neared the camp, a patrol insinuated itself close enough
to return with precise information on the layout of the
camp, the number and positions of the guards, and the
location of the prisoners. After everyone was thoroughly
briefed, the attack was set for the night of January 30.

Sorties by U.S. warplanes captured the attention of sentries who kept their eyes on the skies.

At 7:45 in the evening, a first shot, aimed at a guardpost, rang out to signal the assault. The attack completely surprised the defenders as accurate fire and grenades killed the sentinels. Across a nearby stream, a contingent of eight hundred enemy soldiers, awakened by the sounds of battle, rushed to aid their comrades. But the guerrillas were prepared. Charges placed under a bridge blew the span and when the Japanese troops, supported by tanks, tried to wade across, machine guns, antitank rockets, grenades and other small arms turned the water bloody, discouraging further efforts. Inside the camp, the Rangers swiftly eliminated the befuddled officers and men. Within fifteen minutes, hardly a Japanese soldier in the camp remained alive.

Teams of guerrillas and soldiers feverishly fashioned litters out of field jackets, rifles and other gear to carry more than two hundred emaciated, weakened prisoners. Another three hundred were able to walk out on their own power. A column of Japanese trucks with reinforcements approached but lurking Army night fighter planes blasted the convoy into flame and wreckage, discouraging further advances towards Cabanatuan. Beyond the camp limits, across a wide but fordable stream, the raiding party loaded the liberated men into a previously stashed collection of oxcarts. Rangers and guerrillas manhandled the wagons through the deep mud of the roads back towards the U.S. front. At noon on January 31 came the first contact with friendly troops. During the three days since the adventure began, the U.S. forces had advanced nearly twenty miles. The Rangers lost two men who died of wounds but had rescued 511. An emotional MacArthur congratulated Mucci before visiting the freed men at a hospital.

The Cabanatuan expedition coincided with the siege of Manila by U.S. forces. Yamashita, like MacArthur three years earlier, considered Manila doomed as enemy forces approached from all sides. He stationed only a small garrison there to maintain order, protect the movement of supplies for as long as possible, and destroy bridges over the Pasig and Marikina Rivers to delay the Allied forces. However, demonstrating that divisions in command were not exclusively a U.S. problem, the Japanese Navy brought in a substantial number of men as part of the Manila Naval Defense Force and placed them under Rear Adm. Sanji Iwabuchi. That decision would turn Manila into a bloody battleground and cost Yamashita his life.

The 1st Cavalry and the 37th Division plunged towards the city. The former's top hand, General Mudge, created two motorized squadrons or Flying Columns. The 44th Tank Battalion spearheaded one Flying Column. Even as the 44th rumbled to the outskirts of Manila, its men mourned the loss of their commander, Lt. Col. Tom Ross, gunned down by Japanese rifle fire while in his Peep (armored forces name for a Jeep). Undeterred and aware that the 37th Division was hammering at the gates of the city, the 1st Cavalry brass determined to enter Manila first. The Flying Columns accelerated their pace and, with the permission of the corps commander, took the honors.

John Hencke, a former New Yorker and a crewman for a B Company tank, remembers the final dash for the city. "At Guimba, just above Cabanatuan, we had set up a bivouac camp and put up tents for one or two days. All the kids in our unit—I was twenty-eight—stared at the women who went bare-chested while doing our laundry. We left our duffel bags, any papers that might identify us, like letters, and started forward. We came to the place where Colonel Ross was killed while reconnoitering a bridge, passed Cabanatuan, saw some of the Rangers who freed the prisoners coming up the road. We paused occasionally to fire into pillboxes around the camp and one of the Filipino soldiers who hitchhiked from Leyte with us, went into the camp. He said there were mounds of dead Japs and brought back sake.

"We lost a couple of hours looking for bridges, most of

them were blown up. We had to dismount everyone so the tanks could ease across a trestle with about half an inch clearance on either side. We went through a village where the Filipinos greeted us, gave us eggs. A group of guerrillas showed up. They were ferocious looking. A village photographer with a camera that might have been fifty years old set up and took our pictures with them. We crossed another deep ravine on a very narrow, rickety bridge. I guided the tank across; a lot of creaking and groaning from the wood.

"Then we hit a smooth highway. There was a car burning in the middle of it and our driver hit it with the side of the tank, clearing the way for Jeeps and trucks. Everybody was buttoned up; there were supposed to be a lot of Japs around. We heard that ten thousand of them had just gone up that same road towards Baguio where they made their stand. The next thing I can remember is the ringing of bells, church bells out across the fields. Filipinos out there started running towards the road, waving their arms. It was a very pleasant sight to see. We were on the outskirts of Manila." Actual honors for first into the city belongs to "Yankee," a Sherman tank from the 44th Battalion's B Company.

"We were now about three or four miles from the internment camp at Santo Tomas," says Hencke. "People kept coming up to us to barter. They were starving and didn't have much, jewelry, rings, clothing. We had no food to give and we continued on. We were running out of gas when three trucks from our service company caught up with us. They had come down the same road as us with only a .50 caliber machine gun to protect them and had to use it three times. One of the men had stayed at the gun, firing at Japs, and he received a Bronze Star.

"We reached a large, open boulevard. It was like a parade without tickertape, the people yelling, hollering, climbing up on the tanks. They were everywhere. Then some Jap snipers fired a few shots and everybody disappeared. We fired back into the upper stories and rooftops of buildings to discourage anyone pointing a gun at us and continued down the boulevard. We crossed trolley tracks and the radio aerial on the tank touched the overhead lines, sparking. The radio caught fire and we were left without a radio. The captain pulled over, waved to the other tanks to take their antennae down.

"We came to the internment camp [Santo Tomas]. It was already dark. I stayed in the tank while the driver [Alfonso], Trujillo, and Captain [Jesse] Walters walked to an entrance on the side. As they approached a pillbox—made of a pile of sandbags—a Jap poked his head up and I believe he tried to fire at them. Trujillo had his carbine and later he told me he had killed two soldiers.

"But before he got back I spotted something from behind the fence come arching in the night sky, like a fire cracker. It may have been a stick of dynamite but I yelled 'Grenade!' Trujillo heard me because he just ran to the tank and dived in while the captain looked for protection elsewhere. There was an explosion. Within a minute or two, Trujillo got the order to go through the gate. We weren't prepared yet; my turret was open, my machine gun still out on the mount. But we didn't think about that. As we began pushing through the gate, I sensed something coming at me. It was a span of concrete over the gate and I just managed to get one side of the turret hatch down. I didn't have time for the machine gun or the other half of the hatch. I managed to get my head and my arm down, though. The concrete cracked the hatch catch, snapped the machine gun off the swivel. I was yelling to Trujillo to stop but because our radio was out, he couldn't hear me.

"Inside, I popped my head up, opening up one side of the hatch. Somebody yelled, 'Give us a light down here.' I reached down and turned on our searchlight. What I saw in the circle of light sent chills through me. There was a man about six feet tall, dressed all in white, a flowing robe and a white beard that hung halfway to his navel. In his hand was a staff. I thought I was seeing Saint Peter but after a few seconds I learned he was one of the monks who had come down to guide us and show us where the Japs were. We went up the road towards the buildings, very slowly, my searchlight sweeping the grounds, looking for a pillbox or anything like it.

"When we got to within ten or fifteen feet of the first building I saw a doorway that had a bamboo screen covering part of it. Beneath it I saw some feet. I yelled, 'We're Americans! Come on out!' A boy and girl, teenagers, scared to death, came out. Once they saw who we were it didn't take them long to be happy. People started coming from everywhere. Before I knew it, one of the interned crawled onto the tank. He asked if we had any food and we got some stuff from ration boxes like bean soup, canned bacon strips, pork and egg yolk, none of it too good unless you were hungry.

"We moved the tank further, to the education building. I shined my light on the doorway and there was a Jap officer, standing there, hands on his hips, guns on his belt, just looking at us. He stared at me maybe a minute, seemed like an eternity, then walked back into the building. We didn't fire because we knew there were internees all over the place. Eventually we did receive an order to fire and we raked the first story, where the Japs were supposed to be. When the bullets came through the windows and doorway, the Japs went upstairs among the internees— they had maybe two hundred to three hundred of them. Nobody fired up there and we stopped shooting because we weren't doing any good.

"We kept the searchlight shining over the building, spotted a young fellow in one of the windows. He drew my attention to another window and when I shone my light there, I saw a Jap with his gun pointed down. I handed the searchlight to [Peter] Dillon, told him where to put it while I reached for my tommy gun. The light was shot out of Dillon's hand. There was a blackout and in the dark everybody scattered. Dillon was hurt but I didn't know how bad. I got him down onto the ground and tried to find a medic. Nobody seemed to know where there was one. I asked an internee did they have a hospital or a doctor. He told me where to go, a little dispensary.

"I brought Dillon there and he was bleeding quite badly. The glass from the searchlight had been shattered into a thousand pieces. He had a pack of cigarettes in his pocket which took the brunt of the blast and stopped most of the glass. I left him there, went back to the tank but nobody was around. I crawled back into the tank, got up in my gunner's seat with my tommy gun and waited there all night in the darkness. I was less than fifty feet from the entrance and I knew there were Japs inside. I got scared when I thought about the tank being empty but nothing happened.

"The next morning, I stuck my head out at daylight and people were still looking out the windows. One fellow yelled I'd better keep my head down but there was no more firing at the moment. Meanwhile people would drop ropes down the side of the building and we'd tie canteens of water to them. Trujillo ran over from behind the building and crawled into the tank while I protected him with my guns from the turret. We backed up and pulled around to a side of the building. The Japs fired every so often at internees or soldiers in exposed places. Two days later, an agreement was made for them not to surrender. They could leave, take their handguns and rifles but no machine guns or grenades. At daybreak, with American soldiers lined up on both sides, the Japs all came down, to be escorted out through the gate, taken five or six blocks, told there are the front lines, you're on your own."

Inside STIC, hope sprouted shortly after the start of the new year. Recalls Betsy McCreary, "The commandant's office started burning their papers. From somewhere we heard there was a task force sighted on the way to Lingayen Gulf. On February 3 a lone plane flew over the camp and the pilot dropped a pair of goggles with a note that read, 'Roll out the barrel.' We knew the last line to the stanza was ' 'Cause the gang's all here.' But I wasn't counting on it."

Blackout conditions and a 6:00 P.M. curfew confined McCreary and others inside. On this particular evening, as the lights went out, she left the library for a few moments via the arcaded walkway of the patio. "It was dark, but not pitch black and I heard a small, piping voice say, 'Daddy, the Yanks are coming.' I grumbled to myself, 'Ye Gods, now even five-year-olds are starting to spread rumors.' But there was a certain tension in the air, and something going on in the plaza. There were moving searchlights.

"I heard shots and a loud voice say, 'Yeah, hey!' A woman yelled out one of the windows, 'That's an American and that's a tank.' Suddenly, the whole sky was lit up by a green rocket and then a beautiful red one that slowly fizzled out. I raced down the stairs, ran into Margaret Morris, who pointed out that internees were going outside. We should go too but I held back. We were under curfew and all I could see was the silhouette of a man with a gun. She urged me on and right in the middle of the plaza, surrounded by four or five internees, was an American soldier holding a rifle. He was huge. Really only about 5'10" but compared to the more recent uniformed men in our lives, he seemed gigantic. I was just incredulous to see him. I couldn't believe he was real. I put the palm of my hand on his sleeve and I felt the sweat that had come through. He was real. He handed out cigarettes and I took one.

"Then towards one side we heard this chant coming from a large circle of internees. I broke into it and saw our hated Lieutenant Abico sprawled on his back. There was blood all over his shirt and the muscles or tendons of his neck were moving. He was dying; internees who formerly might have been bank managers or ladylike hostesses had turned into savages, spitting on him, kicking him, swaying and chanting, 'Abico's dead. Abico's dead.' Not one of our finer moments but it was cut short by a loud American voice shouting, 'All civilians inside. All civilians inside.'

"I went back to my room. Most of the occupants in the building hadn't stirred. Probably only about ten minutes had passed but it seemed much longer. I couldn't understand why they were too frightened to leave the room and refused to believe we actually had American troops on the plaza. I assured them the troops were really here. 'I touched one of them and he was real. Look at this —an American cigarette. The blue letters on it say Camel.' The cigarette passed among three or four and convinced them.

"Then I heard machine guns. They were shooting into the education building next door where the Japanese were. [This is the site where Hencke's tank exchanged fire with the enemy.] A woman screeched from one of our windows, 'Stop it. Stop it. My husband and son are in there.' Shortly thereafter I heard an order for a cease-fire. By now the lobby was crowded with as many soldiers as internees. The astonishing news was that we, the internees of Santo Tomas, had been the objective. We had not been an adjunct to a battle, but the target, the goal, the prize."

McCreary watched her former captors depart under the agreement that spared them and the internees of the education building. "It was a very tense moment. There were no demonstrations from the internees. The Japanese were armed and could have fired at us or the American soldiers flanking them on both sides.

Jean Stark says she became aware the Japanese were losing the war from broadcasts over an illegal radio in the camp. The internees making comments over the loudspeaker dropped hints with puns like "Better Leyte than never" or played the song "Pennies from Heaven." "Every time the Japanese lost a battle they cut our ration. Towards the end we were getting about one cup of rice water twice a day. When we were liberated it was bedlam. What a WONDERFUL! sight it was to see all those tanks and troops. To we scrawny internees our liberators looked like giants. We didn't stop to think of whether or not we might be endangering the men or ourselves. Several days after the garrison bargained for their freedom, the Japs started shelling Santo Tomas. I was halfway down the hall when a shell hit the room I had just left. One of my friends lost an eye and another had her nose blown off."

The liberation of the camp, freeing between thirty-five hundred and four thousand people, was the first victory in Manila but before long the embattled naval defense force of Admiral Iwabuchi forced the American and Filipino liberators into a block-by-block, house-by-house, month-long struggle. During this period, the Japanese fiercely resisted the GIs while unleashing a brutal campaign of rape, torture, and butchery against thousands of civilians.

CHAPTER XXIV

THE BATTLE FOR MANILA

THE FLYING COLUMNS that penetrated the Manila outskirts struck from the northeast. At first the overall plan envisioned a move by the 11th Airborne to a place where the parachutists and glidermen would block any attempt to relieve the Manila garrison from the south. Subsequently, Gen. Robert Eichelberger, now in charge of the U.S. 8th Army, received permission from MacArthur to change the mission and attack Manila from the south, penetrating what was known as the Genko Line.

With two glider-infantry teams ashore from a seaborne operation that placed them a scant forty-five miles from Manila, the script had decreed an airborne operation by paratroopers on Tagatay Ridge, heights that overlooked the strongest fortifications of the defenders. Building upon the former U.S. installations of Nichols Field and Fort McKinley over a three-year period, the Japanese had constructed reinforced concrete pillboxes dominating the avenues into the city. In the passage of time, nature had contributed vegetation to aid the skillful camouflage efforts of the Japanese.

The glider infantrymen progressed swiftly towards Manila until they bumped up against an enemy dug in along the slopes of the mountains between them and the city. Medic Al Ullman scribbled in his diary for February 2,

"Tired of marching, slept on the ground last night. Expect trouble soon. At noon it happened. Jap artillery opened up, everyone dived for ditches but some were not so lucky. At least ten killed and no wounded. Assisted major in performing an amputation in a ditch with a trench knife, artillery landing around us. A miserable day. That night was on guard, boy was I scared."

After some debate about the risks of an airborne drop on Tagatay, 6th Army commander Kreuger signed off. General Swing's paratroopers crowded aboard C-47s on Leyte on the morning of February 3, the same day the first Americans burst into Manila from the northeast. With only forty-eight transports available, the troop carriers flew a dangerous three-shift operation, one in which the last two shifts could meet deadly antiaircraft fire from an alerted enemy.

Buzz Miley, as leader of the 2nd Platoon in Company G, says, "We were in the first echelon. I will always remember the beautiful sight of Lake Taal as we approached from the south, made a wide circle around the lake and dropped on an east-to-west pass. Even though later reports stated we jumped early, I don't believe my stick did since we landed just north of the Manila Extension Hotel, about 200–330 yards from the highway. We landed without incident, assembled and started moving south to the highway. We smelled a terrific stench and discovered a dead Filipino next to a small fire. His feet had been burned off. We naturally assumed that the Japanese had done it but none were sighted until that afternoon."

Although Miley describes an uneventful drop, others were significantly wide of the mark as so often seems to have happened with airborne maneuvers. As the first seventeen aircraft dropped men right over the target, the lead ship of the second section dumped out its equipment bundles. Figuring this was their cue, jumpmasters standing in the doors of the trailing planes signaled go. The parachutes of 540 troopers blossomed and the jumpers touched down four to five miles away from the drop zone on Tagatay

Ridge. After the planes returned to Leyte and loaded up again they repeated the mistake as the jumpmasters, peering down, spotted the hundreds of discarded chutes of those who had missed the target and ordered their own sticks out. Purely by luck, and unknown to the descending paratroopers, the Japanese had not posted any troops on Tagatay Ridge. Luckily, the mistakes had no serious consequences for the small number of Americans who landed there. And on February 4, the final batch of troopers dropped in the proper place.

The men of the 11th Airborne forging towards Tagatay Ridge on the ground joined their comrades who came by air. The troopers and glidermen attacked the foremost enemy emplacements. Hard fighting followed as the outfit forced a crossing over the Paranaque River. A grim notation in Ullman's diary reports, "Today we had nineteen wounded men to be evacuated. By now a man's guts are no new sight to me. Today the first of my buddies died from his wounds. I kept saying my prayers."

As the airborne GIs slogged towards Manila, the 1st Cavalry began the job of evicting the defenders. "We beat the 37th into Manila," recalls Sal DeGaetano, "but only after crawling across bombed out bridges and past dead civilians. We came into a courtyard and spotted some Japs across Malate Circle at a gas station and house. We crossed the opposite side of the street to the station where the Japs had disappeared. I heard voices from a basement window, level with the ground. I recognized the language and tossed a grenade, at the same time as one came out. I had dropped to the ground and when I heard my grenade go off, I raised up and got bits of shrapnel in my wrist, head and shoulder. Luckily, I had raised my hand or I might have been hit in the left eye."

Medics evacuated DeGaetano to a hospital at New Bilibid Prison in Quezon City. While he recuperated there, he wrote to his mother, "I take a walk every day and talk to some American civilians the Japs held captives for so long a time. Some of them were damn near starved to death before we came. Personally, I'd rather be fighting Japs than be under them for three years." Referring to his wound, he added, "A Purple Heart Medal isn't anything that thousands of other GIs haven't got but you can be proud of mine when I send it home."

From southwest of Manila, the 38th Division, with the 34th Regiment of the 24th Division attached to it, expected to cut across top of the Bataan peninsula and meet the troops driving down from Lingayen Gulf on the highway between Clark Field and the city. Paul Austin, promoted from company commander to executive officer of the 34th's 2nd Battalion, endured a miserable march of nineteen miles in the heat before his outfit reached the now deserted village of Olongapo. From there the GIs traveled east along a road known as Zig Zag Pass. It was a mountainous area and all the terrain sloped down towards the south. The noses of the ridges went down to the road which zigged and zagged around each one.

"We were in reserve when the 38th made contact with the Japanese," says Austin. "They had had two and a half years to prepare their defenses along Zig Zag Pass and done their work very well. Back on the highway, three or four miles behind the 38th, we saw those two-and-a-half-ton trucks haul men out of there, bodies piled in the back like cordwood. They had the road under observation and as our troops moved into a certain area, all they had to do was go to their reference table, put the gun to a certain setting, fire half a dozen rounds and literally blow men to pieces. It was that accurate.

"We moved up closer on February 3. We hiked in under a 90 mm mortar barrage. I came walking down the road and as the shells got closer and closer, I grabbed the base of a tree trunk and flung my body over the edge of a deep dropoff. I hung my body over that gully, while clinging to that tree. I was scared. There is nothing more terrifying than those mortar shells. You cannot hear them coming.

You have no warning. Before you hear anything at all, it has already exploded, thrown or torn your body. I managed to get back up and we moved on.

"The 38th was pulled back for reorganization and rest. They had suffered tremendous casualties. We continued up the road. We had a couple of tanks with us, artillery firing coming over constantly. We drove 'em back probably a quarter of a mile. The next day we made maybe half a mile. On February 6, we ran into several mortar barrages that literally destroyed the 2nd Battalion. F Company walked into a forty-round barrage and they came out with just twelve men. A sergeant came to me crying, tears running down his face. He was devastated. All his friends were gone. It was a family thing and it tears at a man's guts when the family he's been living with, trying to survive with, the men he loved and respected and that loved him, and they're all gone."

Joe Hoffrichter, the onetime engineer reassigned to F Company, had developed a blister from ill-fitting shoes and the extended marches to Zig Zag. "We had two Sherman tanks that led our convoy of a few vehicles and a truck with ammunition and other supplies followed. I asked the driver if it would be okay to ride on the back of the truck until we got up through the Pass. He said 'Hop on,' and I did.

"Slowly the tanks and truck crawled forward. About three-fourths of the way to the summit, we came to a wide curve and relatively straight piece of exposed road. Suddenly, to the right and above us, all hell seemed to come alive. I saw the first tank get hit and begin to burn. Almost immediately, the tank in front of my truck was struck a glancing blow that spun it to the right. An antitank gun trained on the rear of that tank missed its target and hit the left front of our truck, blowing it and everyone in it over the side into a ravine in the dense jungle.

"As I flew into the air, I saw a shoe flying by. What's my shoe doing there, I wondered! In a split second it was over. I have no recollection of where or how I landed. After seeing the shoe, my mind went blank. When I opened my eyes, it was dark and I was laying on a cot. I had no idea where I was, how I got there, what time it was, nor for that matter, what day it was. I next became conscious that I was in great pain. My legs were numb and my back hurt so badly I could hardly breathe.

"To my left I saw what looked like a huge person, laying completely still. To my right was a man on a cot, leaning on his elbow and looking at me. In a thick southern accent, he whispered, 'How ya all doin'? I heard ya moanin'.

" 'I hurt,' I replied. 'Where in the heck am I?'

" 'Youse in a a hospital in Olongapo.'

"About that time someone walked between our beds and turned on a flashlight. I thought I had died and gone to heaven. A foot away was the face of a beautiful woman. She said, 'Hi, I see you are awake. I'm Lieutenant Powell.' She told me I was brought in late that afternoon. They had dug some shrapnel from my back which was severely damaged. She gave me a shot of morphine and I drifted off to sleep.

"When I awakened I saw I was in a room with thirty wounded men. The fellow next to me with the southern accent was a black man from South Carolina. He was a cook and was burned on the legs when a field stove blew up. After watching them administer my first injections of morphine with three needles, he would often say, 'Man, how in hell can ya take those long-ass needles.' He couldn't understand that I looked forward to them to manage the pain. The big fellow to my right had a severe wound in his stomach. He was in bad shape and had gone into shock. Brought in with me, he died three days later.

"Later, I learned the truck had exploded. The transmission was found two hundred yards above the road where the Japanese had a bunker and a network of trenches and caves. The driver and a man riding shotgun in the cab were never found."

Wireman Han Rants of the 2nd Battalion's Headquarters Company had laid in telephone lines to each of the companies. Around 4:00 P.M. he heard the sound of heavy blasts in the E Company sector. Notified communications were out, Rants led a wire section to repair the telephone system. "Each of the shells that had come in had been a direct hit, as if someone had been looking at the men and dropped the shells right on them. The shock was seeing a body lodged up a small tree. There were bodies blown in all directions. They had thirty-four killed and many wounded. We established a new line, got the wounded and the bodies of the dead back to Headquarters Company for the move back to regiment.

"We were just settled, the time probably about 5:00 P.M., still daylight. We heard five more thunderous explosions like those that had hit E Company. These were in the direction of F and G Companies. We just assumed they had been hit horribly with the same big mortars. It was such a sickening sound. Again we took off to be sure the line was in place. We took some able-bodied soldiers, plus medics because we knew there would be casualties again. The sight was almost the same as seeing E Company. There were many guys blown apart, badly wounded with lots of need for medics and many, many dead. We repeated the same operation we had with E Company but just could not get all the dead because it was getting late at night."

Rants barely escaped injury as artillery tried to support the GIs against an unseen enemy. A shell clipped the top of a nearby tree and showered his position with big pieces of red-hot shrapnel. One chunk ripped into the rear end of the colonel with him. Snipers, at least one of whom boosted his firepower by using an American M-1, peppered the medics who carried out the wounded officer. Meanwhile, Rants and another lineman scampered between bursts from the sharpshooters to repair the broken wires.

On the following morning, the huge mortars zeroed in on the headquarters company position. "I was perched on a field telephone, sitting just off the ground, eating some breakfast after the days of heavy, heavy work and fighting. Even in the fear, hunger came through. As I sat there, these shells exploded and I was blown some six feet into a hole." The carnage was fearsome, wiping out close associates, exposing Rants to gruesome sights of dismembered dead comrades. One man could only be identified by a ring and watch still around the remnant of an arm.

"I will always remember the sight of our battalion physician, Captain Cameron, just racing about with his medics. He hadn't been hit, and the medics would run from victim to victim hitting them with shots of morphine. We noticed that Lombardo, one of our guys that always kind of lost it in a thing like this, went into shock and was wandering around dangerously. We had to tackle him, and hold him down. Someone would sit by him for a few minutes and he always came out of that shock within fifteen or twenty minutes. Rodney went into shock in his own way, froze in a position with a silly half-smile on his face. He was like a lump. We had to have someone lead him as we were going to move to a new position."

Austin spent an anguished night in a foxhole with Major Snavely, his CO, and in the morning greeted a handful of men on the road. "There was an artillery observation team sitting there, two or three medical jeeps with aid men eating their breakfast, C rations. I squatted down talking with the sergeant of the observation team when I got a funny feeling. Something was going on in my gut, maybe diarrhea. It got very intense, a feeling I had to move and which I couldn't resist. I walked back up to my foxhole, put on my steel helmet, wondering why I was doing it. At that instant, three 90 mm mortar shells hit in the area. One struck dead center of the forward observation team. Another landed in the road and destroyed the Jeeps with the medics. The third exploded in the foxhole with the battalion sergeant major and killed him. That was it. They fired just these three rounds. I went back down the road and all of the men I had been talking to were blown to pieces.

Body parts lay all around the rations; the medics had shrapnel wounds that tore their bodies up. One man was blown in two and I saw a boot with a leg still in it.

"About that time, Major Snavely and the battalion surgeon, Dr. Cameron, showed up and told me to take every man I could find and go down into a gully. Just as we got everybody under cover, the regimental CO, Colonel [William] Jenna, rode up in a Jeep. He stopped and immediately wanted to know what we were doing, standing there when we were supposed to be moving up the road in an attack. He said to me, 'Captain, get those men out of that ditch and up on the road and start moving.' I said, 'Yes, sir.' I was in a battlefield situation in the face of the enemy and my colonel had given me an order and the only thing I could do is obey.

"Dr. Cameron asked if he could speak with Colonel Jenna and when given permission told him the situation of the 2nd Battalion. He said he knew where all the units were, and their approximate strength, and in effect told the colonel, 'You don't have a 2nd Battalion anymore.' Colonel Jenna said, 'I didn't know this. I'll have trucks up here in an hour and you're going back to a rest area.' We went back to our holes and sure enough trucks came and carried us back twenty miles to a bivouac area on a stream with shade trees. I spent several miserable days there as I thought about our friends and what had happened to them."

"On the first night just out of Zig Zag Pass," says Rants, "I made a decision that has made my entire life a series of blessings in God's service. I had believed I was a Christian because I believed in God and lived the kind of life I thought He would want me to live. An occasional trip to church perhaps three or four times a year was a way of confirming my support. I was very grateful to God for the physical gifts I had, but I really thought that I was the one who performed the deeds and God simply said, 'Well done.' This night I realized that I was not in control at all and that I had been accepting credit and compliments for achievements which He was responsible for. The fact that I had been blown through the air and received only a small wound was one more in a series of miracles, a blessing, if you will, which I finally realized God was providing. He gave me direction in the kinds of things I did, had me in the right place at the right time. As I prayed and talked with God, I asked forgiveness for feeling that I had done so much and I surrendered all credit to His glory. I told him that whatever amount of days or nights I had left in my life would all be dedicated to His service."

The official figures reported 325 battle casualties for the 34th Infantry and twenty-five psychoneurosis cases in less than a week, nearly half as many as were lost during seventy-eight days of combat on Leyte. Austin insists the total was closer to twelve hundred at Zig Zag but he may have included the losses to the 38th Division in his count.

The results at Zig Zag brought the dismissal of the 38th Division commander as well as assorted regimental and staff officers for a "lack of aggressiveness." Austin, from his perspective responds, "From General MacArthur on down, every one of our leaders knew that place was fortified but they sent us in there, men with rifles and grenades and they chewed us to pieces. We had no air support, did not bomb the area before we went in, didn't napalm it, nothing to soften it up for the infantry. Later they fired the entire load of 105 ammo from a Liberty Ship into the Japanese on Zig Zag Pass. They marked it off in sections and gave a section to each gun, literally blowing the area to bits. Finally, when the boys with rifles got up there, they could pretty much walk through with no problem." In addition to the heavy artillery dumped on the defenders, planes from the airfield on Luzon repeatedly bombed the area.

While the GIs waged a deadly contest for the route from the west coast, the 37th Division, on the right flank, beaten into Manila by the 1st Cavalry with its more mechanized troops, nibbled at the edges of the city on February 4. Stanley Frankel, the would-be clerk transformed into a line lieutenant who had graduated to command of head-quarters company for the 2nd Battalion of the 148th Infantry, recalls a brief interlude for the 2nd Battalion in Balintawak while they waited for engineers to throw a bridge across the Tuliahan River. A scout investigating a cluster of buildings discovered a warehouse with huge vats. From faucets and holes in the tubs poured a thick brown liquid with a yeasty odor. It was ice cold to the touch and the soldier scooped a handful up and poured it on his sweating head. A few drops rolled down and dripped onto his tongue. It was beer, refrigerated beer. Within a few minutes the troops crowded in, swilling, filling canteens, ration cans, all but bathing in the mash.

According to Frankel, it was a mild brew and produced only a pleasant buzz rather than falling-down stupors. Indulged by their battalion commander, the 538 GIs—the remainder of an original unit of more than eight hundred—slaked their thirsts and awaited orders to move out. Meanwhile, 37th Division commander, Maj. Gen. Robert Beightler, accompanied by corps commander Lt. Gen. Oscar Griswold had hastened forward to learn why the advance had stalled. Informed that another hour of work was necessary before the engineers completed the span, the pair then demanded to know where the infantrymen were. "A frightened platoon leader," says Frankel, "explained that the soldiers were gathered in an assembly area shaded from the sun so they could get the maximum of rest. Griswold and Beightler moved to the assembly area and were immediately impressed by the enthusiasm, the singing, and the laughing voices within the walls. Griswold commended Beightler on the high esprit of the men after the long march down the plains, and Beightler (who knew his men) expressed his thanks and got awfully suspicious. When the two generals entered the gates of the brewery, a beer-happy GI with a helmet full of beer in one hand and his rifle in the other stumbled onto the four-stars. He immediately straightened up, dropped his precious weapon to the ground, shifted the beer gingerly from the right to the left hand, came up with a snappy salute and followed it up with a low bow.

"The generals demanded to see the officers in charge, but the officers, grade captain and above, had discreetly gone on inspection tours. A second lieutenant was summoned and he told the generals about the two-hour break, the ice cold beer, the long march and the happy men. And by God, general, what would you do? Griswold *hrmph*ed and Beightler *hrmph*ed and they stomped out of the gate, telling the second lieutenant: 'We can't sanction this sort of thing but as long as we know nothing about it, Old Man Kreuger can't burn us. Just be sure those men are in condition to fight when the bridge goes across.' "

The GIs moved out at the appointed hour, their canteens and bellies full of beer. They crossed the bridge, walked cautiously down Rizal Avenue towards Bonifaico Monument, with nary an incident other than outbursts from cheering throngs. By nightfall, the beery battalion settled in a few miles from Bilibid Prison where Americans had been imprisoned since 1942. On the following day, an advance element of the 148th approached Bilibid, bearing in mind an intelligence report that said the Japanese planned to blow up an ammunition dump in the prison when the GIs came on the scene.

As members of F Company approached Bilibid, an enemy machine gun sprayed the boulevard and snipers let fly. The soldiers, lounging on the curbs along with the Manilans who were showering them with greetings and offerings, scattered. Company commander Sidney Goodkin dispatched a platoon to bypass the sources of resistance. When they did not return after an hour, a patrol went in search. Cautiously moving forward, the ten-man group, led by Sgt. Rayford Anderson, attained a vantage point from where they saw a pair of Japanese sentries lolling about the main entrance of Bilibid. Anderson gave the word and a fusillade of bullets cut down both guards. The commotion aroused hostile but ineffectual bursts from a nearby machine gunner.

Rather than confront that automatic weapon, Anderson chose to reconnoiter the rear of the building. A member of the patrol shot off the lock from a side entrance and broke into a storage area. Prowling the building they came upon boarded-up windows. When Anderson pried the slats off he peered out into the prison courtyard and saw about fifty people huddled together. The Americans realized these were Caucasians and probably prisoners. They called out to them, urged them to open a locked iron gate. To the inmates, the unfamiliar silhouettes of the American helmets and their rifles, gear that postdated their knowledge, generated the suspicion the armed men were Japanese assigned to murder them. The crowd refused to budge. Not even a few verses of "God Bless America" sufficed to convince them. Sergeant Smith tossed some Philip Morris cigarettes to the frightened prisoners and that did the trick just as the Camels did for Betsy McCreary. In short order, the entire battalion, including the formerly lost platoon, occupied Bilibid and the surrounding streets, liberating twelve hundred people of whom several hundred were military men. Many were in the hospital on the verge of death from injuries, disease and malnutrition.

Gunner Tom Howard of the 754th Tank Battalion's Company A had checked in with the 37th Infantry Division. Says Howard, "Had briefing on the section of the city that is ours. Had to familiarize ourselves with the city streets and names of principal intersections and landmarks, such as statues and buildings so that when we enter the city proper we can get around without getting lost.

"With the dark came the plague from the city. From burned-out homes, those caught in the middle of cross-fires, the homeless, the helpless having nothing except what they carried. Men begging for food or the opportunity to work for food; the little children foraging in the garbage pits with their tin cups for scraps of food; the girls peddling their flesh for a bite to eat. We wondered whether there were any Japanese filtering in or through, using the crowd to escape or to wreak havoc on us. We had to trust that the Filipinos would recognize any Japs and report their presence."

After so much anticipation of trouble, Howard and the other tankers rolled into the city streets on the heels of the infantrymen and entered upon a spontaneous Mardi Gras parade rather than a war. "The Filipinos came from their homes, their shops, appearing from everywhere to greet us, waving and yelling. Some Filipinos invited us into their homes and really set up the drinks. One elderly Filipino man brought out an old bottle of Three Feathers whisky that he had hidden during the Japanese occupation. He said he had saved it for just this occasion. We gladly helped him drink it. Some played the piano for us and others cleared the floor for dancing. To hell with the war. Forgot about eating lunch. Snake [the company commander] came looking for us and even he is dancing."

Boozer 3-4 [the code designation for the third tank in 4th Platoon of Company A] resumed its wanderings through the celebratory streets. "We met a lot of Spanish people and also some Swiss but the hell with them, we're looking for Japs to kill." They discovered none, only fires started in the Chinatown neighborhood, but the tank had to mount piles of burning rubble to reach the assembly point. Howard had another grand time that evening, partying with the residents and chatting with one of the girls. "She finally invited me back into the house to sleep on the floor instead of the sidewalk. So ashamed, I have no seat or knees in my pants and haven't washed in I don't know how long."

The 754th's tanks rambled deeper into the city, trying to draw a reaction from Japanese soldiers that would reveal their locations. But fierce blazes consuming Manila kept both sides from contact. Boozer 3-4 stopped at Bilibid Prison, now liberated, and then at Santo Tomas before it entered the downtown section. With the rear of the tank backed into the entrance of the Commonwealth Life Insurance Building, the crew overlooked the strategic Jones Bridge over the Pasig River and received orders to hold the

span whatever the cost. "We had to button up inside the
tank because of sniper fire. Getting dark and that means
the strictest of guard. Anything that moves will be shot.
Have pulled a grenade out and taken the pin from the
grenade and am holding the grenade in my hand where it
will be handy and also keep me awake because if I fall
asleep and release the pressure on the grenade it will
explode."

Across the Pasig, entrenched along on its banks in fortified emplacements, some fifteen thousand Japanese
soldiers and sailors prepared to battle the Americans. To
confound their attackers, the defenders detonated preset
charges that ignited everything flammable. The fires from
the Japanese side leaped the Pasig, raking Manila with a
huge, uncontrolled blaze. In a series of small intense actions, the GIs from the 37th coped with the intense heat,
ever-prevalent snipers and pillboxes that dominated approaches to the river. Bob Viale, a replacement officer with
the 148th who was regarded by his colleagues as naively
concerned with detail and obsessed with the welfare of his
K Company platoon, took his troops on a mission to eliminate enemy positions on the Pasig. When a scout reported
the location of three emplacements across a causeway over
a small stream, Viale formed a three-man assault team,
consisting of a squad leader, a BAR man and himself. To
conceal them from the enemy, Viale directed a rifle grena-
dier to lob several smoke grenades to the far end of the
causeway.

Invisible in the cloud, Viale and the two others raced
over the span. After noting the locations of the objectives,
he instructed the BAR man to keep the occupants of the
most distant dugout distracted with a stream of bullets
into its aperture. While the squad leader spattered a second
emplacement with his M-1, Viale pursued the nearest target. The officer stuffed his shirt with smoke and fragmentation grenades, dragged his carbine in one hand and
crawled towards a machine gun nest about twenty-five
yards away. The occupants saw him and creased his butt

with one round but he escaped further injury by tossing a pair of smoke grenades at them.

The enemy fired blindly in what they figured was his direction, but Viale zigzagged out of the line of fire, jumped up and reached the top of the roofless dugout. From one-yard range, he killed three soldiers with his carbine and then returned to his subordinates. Accompanied by the squad leader and hidden once again by the cloud from a smoke grenade, Viale attacked the second objective. The two men, using covering fire and leapfrogging one another, dispatched a two–machine gun, four-man operation. Viale summoned a bazooka man for the last of the obstacles. Three direct hits smashed the walls of the position, killing six and destroying two more weapons.

The platoon now faced the danger of incineration as a wind-whipped inferno threatened to encircle them. Viale guided them through the maze of streets only to come upon an intersection with a pair of pillboxes, located at the corners of buildings, impervious to ground-level assault by infantrymen. The intrepid lieutenant combed the nearby structures for a vantage point from which they might drop grenades onto the fortified positions. The troops crowded into a house with a ladder to an upper story. Viale climbed up and saw a window that overlooked the pillboxes. From the upper rungs on the ladder he pulled the pin of a grenade. At that moment a bullet from somewhere struck his arm, causing him to drop the explosive down among his troops. Within five seconds it would go off. Viale jumped from his perch, grabbed the grenade and frantically sought somewhere to hurl it. According to those on the scene he could not see how to get rid of the grenade and jammed it into the pit of his stomach while doubling over.

No one else was hurt when the grenade exploded. He died within thirty seconds muttering, "Damn fool." Viale was one of four men from the 148th Regiment who earned a Medal of Honor.

Tom Howard's 2nd Platoon reported in to the 145th Infantry Regiment on February 9 and led infantrymen towards their objective. Howard noted, "The tank commander reported an antitank gun and directed his gunner's fire upon it. The weapon was completely destroyed. Platoon credit for the engagement was 12 dead and instrumental in killing 113 of the enemy." Subsequently, while protecting the Quezon Bridge, Howard halted a charge by the enemy with rounds of 75 mm cannister.

"The state of seige had settled down into a condition where bodies of civilians and Japanese were still strewn over the streets, in gutters, on lawns and in the middle of the pavement. Attempts to remove them were met with sniper fire, so instead of removal, when dusk came, the bodies were covered with quick-lime to hasten their deterioration and to stifle the smell. Upon entering any of the buildings on sniper patrols, the halls, corridors and rooms had scattered Japanese bodies which it was impossible to get rid of. To keep from being tricked by a sniper pretending to be dead, we pulled all the bodies to the walls and sat them up leaning against the wall. We proceeded to shoot each one in the forehead regardless of whether they were already dead. In this way, we could immediately tell upon entering a room or a hall if any bluff was being pulled. Anything that lay in the middle of the floor was shot again, then placed against the wall. It was a grotesque, gruesome picture to see these row-by-row bodies along the walls. These were the day-by-day necessities to survive one day more."

From the buildings overlooking the Pasig River environs, the tankers provided an observation post for U.S. artillery while holding their own fire so as to avoid detection. "We had to watch while the Japanese soldiers dragged out nuns in their habits and tied them to the flagpole and proceeded to whip them. We had to endure the sight of a group of Japanese soldiers drag Filipino women out into the open and rape them. It was hard to hold fire and observe the events. There was no way to describe the emotion of hate of the Japanese and the anguish of not being able to help the women, but orders were orders and we had to comply."

From the southwest, platoon leader Eli Bernheim of the 11th Airborne contrasts the catch-as-catch-can confrontations in Leyte where front lines hardly existed to the fight for Nichols Field. "We had the classic coordinated attack on Nichols Field, airborne artillery, 75 mm pack howitzers against Japanese five-inch naval guns in concrete pillboxes and many 20 mms. It was very, very difficult. My battalion took friendly fire from marine dive bombers. A five-hundred-pound bomb hit a platoon CP." The struggle for the airbase lasted four bloody days.

Art Coleman, a gunner with the 672nd Amphibious Tractor Battalion, had circled east around Manila to assist in crossing the Pasig. "En route, we crossed the Wack Wack Golf course, doing extensive damage to the fairways and greens. Other members of our battalion liberated the San Miguel brewery. General MacArthur came by and was stopped while an enemy machine gun was taken out. A soldier invited him in for a beer. He drank it and remarked that it was very good. Our buddies there did not forget us and sent two milk cans of beer to our position at the Santa Ana Racetrack. I peered over the racetrack wall and saw thousands of bombs and shells stacked and strewn about from attacks by our planes.

"We ferried troops across the river under intense enemy fire. This was the first time that I prayed and meant it. An engineer battalion started a pontoon bridge across. They would get shelled every time they tried, being blown off into the water, then crawling back to work. Finally, the engineers gave up on the bridge which broke loose and came to rest along the river bank, a total wreck. Even so, two Japanese dressed as natives came along in a canoe while I watched them. I turned away just as they rammed the ruins of the bridge detonating a tremendous charge. Pieces of metal from the bridge showered us, one hitting our vehicle just inches from my head. The fire was coming from Fort McKinley up the river and it continued until the 11th Airborne captured the place after horrendous fighting on the Genko Line. Manuel Perez, a paratrooper who knocked out about ten pillboxes blocking the way to McKinley, won the Medal of Honor in this battle. He was killed later by a sniper bullet, just as a message came to get him off the line."

Joe Swing, commander of the 11th Airborne, scrawled a letter to Peyton March: "We have been having a real scrap for the past ten days. All the Jap's defenses were organized south of the Pasig, and with the exception of the Walled City [Intramuros] which is still uncracked, the heaviest pillboxes and armament was found in our sector. Finally got some tank destroyers and tank support to augment my little 75 howitzers and in the past couple of days have knocked them out of Fort McKinley to the north of Laguna de Bay. The 1st Cav will be given the credit for capturing Ft. McKinley as it was in their zone. However, the defenses all faced my way. I had to go take it or sit here and be pummeled by the naval guard which I might say were a little disconcerting." After the war, Swing recapitulated his experiences for General Eichelberger's memoirs and insisted that his 188th Glider Infantry actually overran the post, killing 961 enemy and occupying the premises.

In his correspondence with March, Swing added, "Right now have got a bunch of Japs, about two hundred, left, neatly surrounded about two miles south of McKinley. There were about six hundred to start with. We're killing them off with artillery and TD fire night and day. There's no particular hurry and I'm just going to 'waste' ammunition until they are exterminated. General MacArthur came down in a Jeep yesterday to see what we had been doing. Think he was a little surprised at the opposition we had encountered at Nichols Field [Al Ullman indicated that battle was his worst experience as a medic]. Said I had done a fine and grand job." Since landing on the Luzon coast, the division had incurred more than nine hundred casualties. However, who did what where drew little attention from those at ground level. Now that the 1st Cavalry was on the scene in force, Swing's 11th Airborne returned to its original mission, which was to focus on the south.

The Shimbu Group, and an army under Gen. Shizuo Yokoyama, within whose purview Manila came, entertained the notion of a counterattack against what its intelligence faultily described as a limited U.S. presence in the city. At the very least, Yokoyama believed he could open an escape route for Admiral Iwabuchi's men. Yamashita, however, angry that Iwabuchi had been permitted to attempt a defense, needlessly sacrificing people, vetoed any plans for an offensive. He ordered that his subordinate only attempt to extricate the naval soldiers from the city. Yokoyama's efforts were disastrous. The 1st Cavalry, aided by devastating artillery, slaughtered the Japanese seeking to open a route out of Manila.

At the same time, the paratroopers of the 503rd Regimental Combat Team prepared for another daring adventure, the capture of Corregidor. The blueprints specified a combined airborne-amphibious operation, assigning a battalion from the 24th Division's 34th Regiment to assault the tiny island's beaches. Intelligence figured that the Japanese garrison numbered only 850 and with two thousand GIs dropping from the sky and another one thousand coming from the sea, the prospects of overwhelming the enemy seemed excellent.

But U.S. intelligence was flawed and the battle plans overlooked serious problems. Instead of 850 defenders, Corregidor bristled with about five thousand. Because the highest portion of the island, Topside at five hundred feet above sea level, afforded the defenders the most devastating opportunities to repel water-borne invaders and anyone landing on the lower ground, the 6th Army planners chose the small areas of the old parade field and golf course on Topside as the drop zones. The restricted size of these zones, the tricky winds, the steep cliffs alongside, the tangle of shell holes and wreckage from the 1942 Japanese attack, and the coarse vegetation combined to create hazardous conditions. A shortage of troop carrier planes and the tiny area in which the chutists were to land dictated a series of flights, which meant those who arrived first would have to hold off defenders intent on repelling further airborne deliveries.

In the American's favor was the conviction of the defenders that no one would be so foolhardy as to attempt an assault by air. Furthermore, the Japanese underwent a furious aerial bombardment prior to the scheduled drops. Meanwhile, on Mindoro, the paratroopers loaded onto their C-47s at dawn on February 16.

Rod Rodriguez, as a member of G Company in the 503rd, recalls the drop. "The 3rd Battalion was scheduled to jump at 8:40 A.M. That was H minus two, two hours before the main assault by sea, and we were to secure the golf course and parade ground for the subsequent jump of the 2nd Battalion. Our mission then was to provide fire support for the infantry assaulting Black Beach, destroy the Japanese positions dug into the cliffs of Topside and methodically move down the island eliminating the Japanese garrison.

"On the flight over I was a bit tense. I was concerned that the men seated on the other side of the plane and facing me might note my apprehension. I nonchalantly rose and walked to the plane's door, which was removed, to look around. What I saw raised my spirits. There was an impressive array of U.S. power all around us. Above the C-47s were protective flights of P-38s and flying below us were flights of P-47s. In the sea below, the LCIs carrying the 34th Infantry to the beach were already under way. They were being escorted by cruisers and destroyers. It was an inspiring sight.

"We jumped at about four hundred feet. I believe this was one of the lowest-level combat jumps made by U.S. parachute troops in World War II. The purpose was to minimize descent time, during which we would be a floating target. Since it takes about 175 feet for the parachute to open, it meant the average trooper had about 225 feet of float time, not very long. The flip side is that any delay in opening may be fatal, and since one has very little time to stabilize the parachute once it opens, jump injuries can also mount. I was just a little over the treetops that lined the golf course when my parachute blossomed. I came crashing down on the edge of the course. The other guys from the platoon landed around me. I quickly slipped out of the harness, ran to the assembly area and we established a perimeter around the golf course.

"The enemy was caught by surprise and our battalion encountered only sporadic opposition on the jump. It would be different for the second battalion when it jumped two hours later. From our perimeter I could see a number of troopers hit in midair by rifle fire and ack-ack weapons. Others were hit as they landed and for the most part were men who missed the drop zone and came down in the cliffs outside the perimeter.

"A fortunate break occured when the Japanese commander [Naval] Capt. Akira Itagaki, was killed by our troops minutes after the landing. With an armed escort he had left his command post on Topside to inspect positions in the cliffs below and observe the amphibious operations. Suddenly, paratroopers who had missed the drop zone landed in his midst. Several of them were killed but Itagaki and virtually all of his armed escort were destroyed in the ensuing firefight." Rodriguez and the others Topside settled in for the night, setting up machine guns to help cover the amphibious assault, fortifying their positions, organizing fire lanes and patrols, and "tending to the wounded and injured. Although combat losses had been low, about twenty-five percent of the first jumpers had been hurt crashing into ruins of buildings, trees and the ground itself.

"About 4:00 A.M." says Rodriguez, "the man on guard in our three-man foxhole nudged us awake and pointed to the road. There were, perhaps thirty yards from our position, troops moving towards Bottomside. We were pretty sure that they were Japanese, since our troops did not generally move at night. They were not moving directly at us, so to avoid giving away our position, we held our fire. At that moment a flare was fired and illuminated the night sky. It was indeed a Japanese platoon marching towards the beach. Carrying satchels of TNT they raced towards the beach and were met by withering gunfire. Several saw the folly of attempting to penetrate the beach and turned back in our direction. We held our fire until they were almost on us and then riddled them. Four died in front of our position and altogether about thirty Japanese were killed in this rather senseless suicidal attack."

Meanwhile, the first four waves of landing craft had beached their men without opposition. The barrage by naval vessels, the bombs dropped from the air and the landing of the parachutists stunned the defenders who stayed undercover until the fifth wave made for the shore. By the time the Japanese recovered their wits, the GIs of the 34th Infantry had achieved their initial objectives. Bill Hartman, a staff sergeant in charge of the 3rd Platoon of Cannon Company, started for Corregidor with three M-7 105 mm self-propelled howitzers. On the way from Subic Bay to Mariveles where the outfit was to embark he lost one M-7 because of engine trouble. "During the landing on Corregidor, we lost another M-7 to a mine which tore a track off and flipped it onto its right side. Luckily, everyone was able to walk away from it. At the end of the first day the only operable vehicles on our beach were one Jeep and my M-7.

"On the morning of February 17, my platoon leader told me the paratroopers need blood plasma, medical supplies and water Topside. He asked if I would send two men in the M-7 to do the job. I said I would go and Mike Nolan the driver of the M-7 volunteered. We were told that the road was probably mined and that we didn't control all of it as yet. We dismantled the breech block of the howitzer so that if the Japs captured it, they couldn't use it. We also left the .50 caliber machine gun on the beach for the same reason.

"We loaded the medicine, plasma and as much water as we could and with two gutsy paratroopers, who had missed the drop zone, checking for mines ahead of us, we started out. A lieutenant and another paratrooper climbed onto the back deck. As soon as we rounded the hill north of the beach, we came under intense machine gun fire. The paratroopers out front, not being stupid, sought shelter behind the M-7. As we proceeded, the machine gun fire was tearing rotating bands off the 105 mm shells which on this model of the M-7 protruded above the armor plate and slightly wounded the lieutenant in the face.

"The situation was pretty scary. We took a turn to the south and were out of the hail of fire. The lieutenant and the other man got off and our two front men resumed their road check. Mike the driver had a carbine, I had an M-1, the two out front each had a carbine and we had a box of grenades. Turning towards Middleside Barracks, we saw a bombed bridge. It was a little askew and narrow but I decided to chance it. It groaned but held the twenty-five tons, with the tracks hanging over both sides about four to six inches. We came to a point where we saw two five-hundred-pound parachute bombs lying in the road. They hadn't landed on their noses so they were probably live. We edged slowly around them, about six to eight inches to spare.

"Around a hairpin curve we came to our destination, the temporary hospital in bombed-out barracks. We unloaded and were told by the officer in charge he needed more of the same plus all the clean water we could haul. We loaded two badly wounded men on stretchers and headed back down the road. This time it's just Mike and me. We came around the bombs, over the bridge to where we got our first heavy fire on the way up. Nothing! No fire! We unloaded the wounded at the beach and they were sent out to an LST serving as a hospital ship.

"I talked to my platoon leader as we loaded up again. This time we had a tank trailer of water hooked on the rear. Again we passed around the corner and into a hail of machine gun fire. I spotted where it was coming from. We crossed the bridge, over a thirty-foot drop, and we meet some paratroopers. I told them where the machine guns were and they told me there had been Japs at Middleside when we went up. Evidently, the Japs hadn't wanted to take on our 105 howitzer and so they hadn't fired at us. We got to Topside and unloaded again.

"The next morning, we took two more stretcher cases and had an easy trip to the beach. No fire at all. We unloaded our wounded and started the motor. It ran for about thirty seconds, then locked up. A broken oil line and we'd thrown a rod. I was glad it happened here, and not up on the hill under fire. Mike counted two hundred bullet marks from the front end of the M-7 over about three feet and gave up counting."

"For several days," says Rodriguez, "we were mainly busy eliminating enemy positions along the cliffs of Topside. They consisted of bunkers, underground tunnels and caves. Usually a small team would move forward to the target after softening up by artillery or other heavy weapons. The machine guns, BARs or mortars would lay down fire while the squad approached the mouth of the fortification. Once you were close enough, the flamethrower or phosphorous grenade did the rest of the job. The Japanese frequently would come rushing out in flames. In other cases we had air observers attached to our unit who would radio in map coordinates. Once the target had been identified, pilots would dive and drop a napalm bomb with pinpint precision into the mouth of the bunker or tunnel. The sight of those soldiers running out of their bunkers, engulfed in flames, is a vivid memory." Much of the fighting on Corregidor was of this kind, advancing bunker by bunker and cave by cave to eliminate a stubborn enemy.

The amphibious troops of the 34th Infantry also had quick success on the first day, seizing Black Beach and then

Malinta Hill, three hundred feet high. The infantrymen of the 34th Regiment, as Rodriguez notes, managed to climb Malinta Hill above the web of tunnels occupied by the Japanese defenders. From their positions, the GIs could now shoot at anyone who poked so much as a head out of the caves. *Banzai* charges emptied the underground bunkers of desperate Japanese and an orgy of killing ensued.

The climax of the battle for Corregidor occurred about ten days after the paratroopers descended upon the Rock. An arsenal, cached under Monkey Point, detonated in an enormous blast, caused either by an act of suicide or a U.S.-fired tank shell. "Most of the 1st Battalion," says Rodriguez, "was on top of the hill and the explosion caused many deaths and injuries. We must have been fifteen hundred yards behind the 1st and yet we had huge rocks and boulders raining down on us. Fortunately, we had enough time to reach cover." The explosion tore apart the bodies of men from both sides, buried some under rock slides and threw a medium tank fifty yards in the air. At least two hundred Japanese died instantly while U.S. casualties were about fifty killed and 150 wounded.

When MacArthur set foot on Corregidor, nine days short of three years since he boarded Bulkeley's PT boat, more than forty-five hundred Japanese were counted as dead with perhaps another five hundred either sealed in demolished caves or drowned while attempting to swim for their lives. Only twenty prisoners were taken. The American casualty count added up to more than a thousand.

During the battle for Corregidor, another airborne-led foray attempted to save the remaining captives on Luzon—the 2,147 people, including Navy nurse Mary Rose Harrington, held at Los Banos near Laguna de Bay. For this expedition, the 6th Army marshaled elements from the 188th Glider Infantry, paratroopers of the 511th PR, guerrillas, the vehicles of the 672nd Amphibious Tractor Battalion and supporting tank and tank destroyer outfits. According to a letter from Swing to Peyton March, the internment camp lay about thirty miles down the coast of Laguna de Bay from his southernmost outpost. "All bridges were out so if I went after them by land, the devils would have plenty of time either to massacre the group or remove them farther into the hills. Besides, half the prisoners were so weak they couldn't walk ten miles to safety. The Japs would have murdered them with artillery.

"I infiltrated my reconnaissance platoon into the hills just short of the camp. They spotted the position of every sentry with the help of guerrilla guides. Picked out a jump field in the rice paddies, just five hundred yards from the camp. I put a battalion in amphibious tractors to hit the Los Banos garrison at daybreak from the Laguna itself."

Amtrac gunner Art Coleman recalls, "After a couple of weeks at the race track, we got word to make contact with the 11th Airborne. We were told we were going to liberate those held at Los Banos and could expect one-third casualties. Two-thirds of the prisoners might be lost. Going through the city, we saw bodies everywhere, mostly natives but also combatants from both sides. The sports stadium was overflowing with dead.

"At 2:00 A.M. February 23, loaded with two companies of troopers plus artillerymen, Jeeps and guns, we set off across Laguna de Bay towards Los Banos on the southeast shore. We were told paratroopers would jump at dawn. At first light we had eyes glued straight up as we neared the lake shore. Suddenly, at treetop height, nine C-47s rounded a hill and 120 paratroopers poured out and in split seconds were on the ground. We could not believe it, dropping from planes so low. Some troopers later said they couldn't either. We crawled ashore and unloaded our troopers who went into the jungle and set up a defense of the area. We proceeded to the camp."

Swing described the action: "The camp has a morning roll call at 7:00 A.M. Timed everything to hit at that hour. There wasn't a hitch—the Recon Platoon murdered every sentry as the roll call gong was ringing, barged into camp and kept the main barracks under fire until the parachute company came in and exterminated them. [Some on the scene say the garrison was on the ballfield in loincloths partaking of morning calisthenics.] The amtracs hit the beach at 7:00, grabbed a small beachhead and kept right on inland two miles to camp while a 75 battery kept the Banos garrison quiet. Another battalion attacked south from Calamba and drew all reserves in that direction. We loaded the people in the amtracs and shuttled back to my lines. At 5:00 P.M., 2,134 evacuees removed, we had withdrawn from the beachhead to the bridgehead at Calamba. Three evacuees slightly wounded; my own casualties, two KIA, three WIA and not a d— Jap got away.''

Coleman reached the camp right after the shooting. "The wire was down as I got there and people started to come up to us. One man saw my cigarette which I was hiding and said, 'Don't throw away that butt.' I gave him all my remaining few. One lady said, 'Oh, there is Peter Miles. He went over the wall the other night.' Peter, Ben Edwards, and Freddy Zervoulakos did escape and bring extremely valuable information to the 11th AB planners before they returned with us in the amtracs.''

Navy nurse Mary Rose Harrington, one of those incarcerated at Los Banos, says, "We had word in advance that they would try to liberate the camp. We weren't given any details but we had people who regularly went through the wire and contacted the guerrillas. Of course they always made roll call in the morning. Peter Miles had been in and out a number of times and he was gone a couple of days.

"I was outside hanging up bandages when I felt these vibrations on the ground from the amtracs coming towards us. Then when I looked up I saw the planes and something came out of one. I thought it was a bundle of supplies—the man had his body doubled up—and thought it's going to land outside the camp. But once the paratroopers started to land, the guerrillas and the men on the ground attacked the pillboxes. It was all over very quickly.''

Both the newly freed and GIs like Coleman wondered

why the barracks began burning—Mary Rose Harrington and others thought tracers might have ignited the structures. Later they learned that the captives seemed under the impression that the Americans would remain on the scene and they expected to celebrate. But the camp lay twenty-five miles inside enemy territory containing as many as ten thousand Japanese troops. The task force leader ordered the buildings torched to convince the civilian internees it was time for a hasty departure.

On the whole, those at Los Banos were not as physically debilitated as the internees at STIC. "There was less competition for food out there," explains Harrington. "We probably ate a little better. Still, towards the end, they sent about a hundred old men to us. Some of them undoubtedly needed help or had to be carried to the vehicles."

With between thirty or forty people on the amtrac, Coleman's crew headed for Laguna de Bay. "A Filipino boy pointed to a sheet metal–covered building, mouthing, 'Japs in there.' Every available machine gun opened up, turning the place into a junk heap. No one approached to see the results. We entered the water, having been instructed to stay away from the shore on the return. The 1st Platoon wanting more action, went close in with all those people on board and promptly the enemy opened up. They turned away and the bullets struck the tailgates which could withstand the fire better. No one was injured. On reaching the safe shore, the freed people boarded trucks and ambulances. We immediately returned to Los Banos and brought out the paratroopers. As we entered the water, mortar and artillery fire descended on us but not one round found its target. The commander of the task force, Maj. Henry Burgess, later told me he could hear the Jap officers giving commands as we withdrew. The operation took less than one day."

"Old Doug," wrote Swing, "sent a wire, saying it was 'magnificent' and old Walter K. [Kreuger] made a sour face and said he was pleased. You see, we don't really belong to his army. We were just taken over from the Eight and there's just a wee bit of jealousy on somebody's part."

Within Manila, however, the trapped defenders refused to quit. A considerable number holed up inside Intramuros, what had been an old walled Spanish city that backed up on the bay. Great stone blocks piled as high as twenty-five feet and as much as forty feet thick at the bottom surrounded the mostly stone structures. Units from the 1st Cavalry and 37th Divisions with supporting outfits assaulted Intramuros and large government buildings in the environs.

The 754th Tank Battalion brought its armor and 75 mm guns to bear upon the targets, blasting away at the downtown edifices. On February 15, Tom Howard's 2nd Platoon had rumbled out of Company A's command post, located in the yard of Bilibid Prison. As Howard's tank crossed a pontoon bridge over the Pasig River, a lone enemy plane flew over Bilibid and dropped a bomb. "It landed about five feet from the command tank, killing company commander Coy 'Snake' Rogers and three of his crew: driver Earl Bartling, gunner Fred Kassman and bow gunner Russell Cattamelata. Nine men were wounded. Since the CP had been carefully selected to hide the tanks, a spy, an enemy observer or a collaborator must have reported our whereabouts and pinpointed our exact location.

"Garbled communication had been received all morning concerning the events at the CP. It was unbelievable. We couldn't comprehend what happened. Here we were at the front, on the firing line, and those in relative safety were gone. It was definite that 'Snake' was among the dead, as his arm had been found and the tattoo 'Panama' easily discernible. We felt like our head had been cut off or that we had lost a parent. We were like orphans waiting for word on what would happen next or who would assume control."

In the middle two weeks of February, Howard's A

Company listed twenty battle casualties, including six dead. Other medical problems, such as malaria, amoebic dysentery, hepatitis and routine cuts and bruises while operating the tanks, depleted ranks further. "We had started with seventeen tanks at the time of the landing but now we had eleven that would run, but only enough men to man eight, using the cooks, mechanics and administrators. We would recruit infantrymen to fill positions of machine gunner or loader for the 75 mm cannon. Although we could never get a volunteer to come back a second time, we were able to get men on direct orders from the infantry officers."

In a moment of tranquility, Howard and his mates pondered the question, "Why them, not us?" They reminisced about the past and mourned their losses—"proud, arrogant, stately, yet one of us, 'Snake' Rogers; Fred Kassman, our prized basketball player when we were on Bougainville; Theriot, with his blond hair, handsome features and a body he was always developing by exercise and weights. We who were left were a motley-looking crew, unwashed, unshaven, clothes in tatters. I existed as the rest did by stripping dead Japs of their jackets and pants and stockings. We were tired, absolutely weary. I remember I sat and cried for no apparent reason, uncontrollably, unashamed, and not cold, but spent and exhausted. I had forgotten when I had last eaten a hot meal, instead of picking on a cold can of C ration, had a full night's sleep, had taken a crap—must have been constipated since the attack of dysentery."

On February 21, their tanks serviced, restocked with ammunition, food, water, and first aid kits, Company A in support of the infantry zeroed in on the Manila Hotel. MacArthur was close enough to the site to watch as the Japanese inside supposedly set fire to his pre-war penthouse suite. Howard writes, "We were told to zero in on the hotel and then hold fire until the word was given. Each of the five tanks selected a partition between two windows and sat tight. Lt. William Dougherty, on the ground outside his tank, was to give the command to fire. We had never rehearsed a command *not* to fire. When 'Junior' gave us the sign, we opened fire and the building came tumbling down. We continued to rotate our turrets so that the 75 mm cannon would pour shells into the interior with the shells exploding inside and the shrapnel tearing the Japanese to pieces. Unknown to us, the order given was supposed to mean *not* to fire since MacArthur wanted to keep the hotel as best as possible. MacArthur chewed 'Junior' out for not having controlled his tanks. To a little second lieutenant this meant nothing, particularly at a time like this. We laughed about it over and over, to think that the building was more important than soldier's lives.

"MacArthur wrote, 'Every landing was a fight. Of the penthouse nothing was left but ashes. It had evidently been the command post of the rearguard action. We left its colonel dead on the smoldering threshold.' "

Impatient with any delay in the liberation of the city, MacArthur virtually trod on the heels of the combat soldier. Platoon sergeant Cletus J. Schwab of the 37th Division participated in the block-by-block fighting. "We were pushing the Japanese towards Manila Bay this day and about to be attacked on our right flank when one of my sergeants hollered to me that General MacArthur and his escort were coming up the street we were fighting in. I hurried back to stop them. I reported to the general my name, rank and reason for stopping him. He wanted to know how long the Japanese could hold out. About that time all hell broke loose. It was about half an hour before the general and his staff could retreat to safety." About a week later, Schwab received a battlefield promotion to second lieutenant and a transfer to another company.

To better support the foot soldiers and reduce turnaround time, the maintenance and ordnance details moved closer to the tanks at the front. Armor with flamethrowers trundled forward spouting napalm that adhered to the stone and concrete sides of buildings, even flowing around corners. But the 75s could not seriously dent the walls of

Intramuros. The heaviest-caliber artillery, 155 mm and 240 mm guns, methodically blasted breaches in the walls of Intramuros and the stalwart government buildings. Still, infantrymen aided by tanks underwent the ordeal of a room-by-room struggle against an enemy resigned to death in battle. Iwabuchi's men held thousands of Filipinos as hostages inside. Many died from the shelling or were murdered by the defenders. The attack halted temporarily when the GIs who ran through the shattered walls discovered three thousand civilians who took sanctuary in the churches within Intramuros. The refugees, mainly women and children—most males had been executed—were escorted out before the Americans resumed firing. About a thousand Japanese died in the warrens of Intramuros.

The last stages of the battle of Manila centered around a complex of government buildings constructed along the lines of those of the United States in Washington, D.C. Massive piles of thick concrete, they slowly collapsed from an onslaught of heavy artillery bombardment. Late on March 3, a month after the siege began, the corps commander, General Griswold, advised 6th Army chief, General Kreuger, that organized resistance in the Manila area had ceased. In and around the city, the Americans had killed about sixteen thousand enemy while casualties for the GIs totaled 1,000 KIA and 5,500 wounded. One estimate claimed 100,000 Filipino civilians lost their lives. Manila itself was wrecked, without power, water, or sewage systems. Few buildings escaped damage if not total destruction. With much of the housing demolished, those residents who survived occupied condemned hulks of structures or simply camped outdoors. Men and children begged the troops for food, women peddled their bodies for something to eat. Giant holes and heaps of debris rendered many streets nearly impassable. Little more than chunks of concrete remained of landmarks like the four-hundred-year-old Intramuros. The price of liberation was high and would continue to climb.

CHAPTER XXV

BEYOND MANILA

WITH THE CONCLUSION of the Manila campaign, the three Japanese armies were effectively isolated. Although they could no longer support one another or exchange men and equipment, they fought on, determined to exact as much of a blood penalty as they could before succumbing to the superior forces arrayed against them.

As the last pockets of Japanese resistance in Manila vanished, the grievously hurt city echoed with the tramp of GI boots and the growing noise of motors. A natural hub, Manila played host to the liberating army. Aside from vice born out of desperation, Forward Observer Ernest Chaplin described a distillery and a brewery as major attractions. "When they opened up to sell booze, the lines of GIs would be several blocks long. Inside, the Filipinos would be barefoot in the shallow vats filling bottles and GI cans which we took back to our units for resale. When the brewery opened, we drove down from our Clark Field position and filled water trailers with hot, no-foam beer."

R & R, however, was extended to few as the U.S. commanders hammered at the retreating enemy without pause. The U.S. 6th and 43rd Divisions and units from the 2nd Cavalry Brigade pursued the enemy soldiers concentrated to the east and northeast of Manila. Again, despite the prevalence of guerrillas able to sift through the

CRISIS IN THE PACIFIC

countryside, intelligence underestimated the number of those dug in along terrain that favored a defensive stance.

As the commander of the 3rd Battalion, Maj. Arndt Mueller grappled with the enemy forces along the Shimbu Line in the mountainous area east of Manila. On the maps, "Hill 400" and "Hill Z" denoted the critical territory assigned to his outfit. Mueller surveyed the terrain from an observation plane, compiled data on the phases of the moon and its hours of illumination and then plotted a night attack. "The battalion, contrary to most units in the Pacific War," says Mueller, "had experience on at least three occasions in night operations on Luzon. The troops to carry out a night attack under the given circumstances possessed confidence born of experience to accomplish the mission."

The script entailed recognition procedures among the GIs to prevent confusion about who was the enemy, a carefully outlined schedule of mortar and artillery fire that would both harass and distract the enemy, and a display of flares for specific fire support missions. A wire team would accompany the command group to create telephone communications; radio silence could only be broken in a grave emergency and then by employing a brevity code to signify tactical contingencies.

Mueller commandeered as much tracer ammunition as he could for aid in directing effective fire during the dark. "We also had a standing operating procedure that on a deep operation such as this, the riflemen of units in reserve carried mortar ammunition which they dropped by platoon or company piles when they went into action. You'd be surprised how much three hundred men can carry, expecially if it might mean their lives!

"Another item of special attention covered individual equipment. No letters, diaries or items showing unit identification. No mess kits which were always a source of rattles. Canteens and canteen cups muffled. Any shiny helmets dulled—mud usually. Face blackened provided we could find the material. In those days camouflage grease sticks were not an item of issue. Grenades carefully secured to prevent sounds and accidental detonation. We probably issued a day's ration with the precaution they might have to make it last for two days. Usually we included one emergency ration, a large, highly concentrated chocolate type bar. Personal items were limited to a change of underwear and socks, a poncho, an olive-drab towel usually draped around the neck, shaving equipment, soap, toothbrush and dentifrice."

Although some initial actions that set the plan in motion failed to meet Mueller's expectations, the troops moved out as daylight faded into a darkness pierced only by bright moon. "The ghostly, silent movement of those soldiers sent chills up my back. How confident they were! How calm they appeared to be! But I knew every nerve fiber in their bodies was tingling, supercharged with anticipation, alert for enemy action. Before we departed, a good friend of mine, Dwight Dickson, the regimental operations staff officer, saw us off and gave me a chew of tobacco for luck. I did not smoke or use any form of tobacco at the time but the shot of nicotine in my unadjusted system charged up my tired body which had not had very much sleep in the preceding thirty-six hours."

A brief firefight broke out on one flank and the troops started to turn towards the direction of the shooting and away from the path to the objective. But because Mueller with the command group was right behind the infantrymen, he was able to get them back on track. As the columns pushed ahead, leaving behind the cries of Japanese wounded—no Americans had been hit—the radio operator informed Mueller of a code transmission that called for him to plug into the telephone line. "Bad news! The column had been broken because one of the connecting files had fallen asleep during the engagement with the Japanese outpost. Some soldiers are very adaptable to the situation. Evidently the connecting file was one who could fall asleep easily." Mueller impatiently waited for the stragglers to catch up and then the advance continued.

"The moon still shone brightly. Nervously, the formation crept forward. But the discipline held. No soldiers saw ghosts; none fired at phantoms. When troops are advancing in darkness across unfamiliar terrain in the presence of suspected enemy forces, it is not uncommon for them to begin firing at imaginary figures. Even veterans are sometimes subject to an attack of nerves. The unforeseen, however, suddenly halted progress. The brush at the foot of Hill 400 was a tangle of undergrowth, as much as ten feet high and full of long thorns. Passage required time-consuming labor."

At this point, Mueller's battalion was deployed so that I and K Companies were in the vanguard with L bringing up the rear. Suddenly a group of Japanese soldiers marched along a road from the north. Machine guns from I Company scattered them. Mueller had hardly digested the news when K Company saw more enemy swarming up the slope between them and Company L. Mueller could only speculate that these defenders came from well-concealed caves in the bush or from a dry stream bed. Because of concern for the whereabouts of L Company, Mueller ordered K Company to keep its fire below the crest of the slope. As the GIs poured devastating fire on the enemy coming up the hill, a number of Japanese soldiers gained the top and stood upright for a few moments. Suddenly, the hitherto invisible L Company soldiers opened up. "A storm of fire swept the Japanese from the crest. They had approached within hand grenade range and suffered a barrage of fragmentation and white phosphorus grenades for their pains. Several unfortunates came running off the hill in flames. The K Company troops cheered when they saw the results. The action had been short, furious, and now over, we had no casualties yet reported."

But the defenders now knew of the threat from Mueller's forces. "Our time to suffer had come. A thunderstorm of mortar fire pelted K Company. I sought refuge between two K Company soldiers snuggled up against the bank of the dry stream we occupied. After what seemed like an eternity, the firing ceased. I lay quietly for a few minutes to make sure that the firing definitely had ceased. One of the oldest mortarmen tricks was to suspend firing for a few minutes to deceive their targets into believing that the firing had terminated and then blasting off again hoping to catch targets in a vulnerable posture.

"Convinced that the mortar fire had terminated, I gingerly got to my feet. Cries of 'Medic' and the groans of the wounded dominated the air. I paused, listening intently for any more sounds of mortar 'thumps' signaling the discharge of shells from their tubes. Then I spoke to my two K Company comrades who were still embracing Mother Earth, advising them I thought the fire had ended. I got no response. I noticed that both were bloodied. I turned them over and checked their pulses; both dead. My God! Both dead, one on each side of me. I was shocked and unnerved."

From his command post, now shifted to another small hill, Mueller noticed that short rounds from his supporting mortar fire beat down the thorny underbrush that blocked his infantrymen. He arranged for a walking bombardment of the obstacle and a corridor up Hill 400 opened. Driven to cover by a barrage directed at the command post by the Japanese, Mueller never saw his men scale the heights of Hill 400 and establish a strong defensive position.

The enemy responded, infantrymen attacking, backed by intensive artillery and mortar fire. Mueller credits the American 81 mm mortarmen for preventing the enemy overrunning the GIs atop Hill 400. "Their actions were without a doubt one of the most heroic and dedicated unit actions I observed during the war. They suffered severely for their self-sacrificing devotion to duty. Among the casualties was their platoon leader, Lt. J.H. Childs. I saw him as he was carried to our location. Ugly steel shards of a 150 mm shell had penetrated his body. When the shelling ceased, the evacuation of wounded began after dark. I remember saying to my comrades there was no doubt in my mind that Childs's wounds were fatal. But he survived, although he spent the rest of his life in a wheelchair."

Mueller also observed the opposite end of the courage-cowardice spectrum. A captain in command of a support-ing 4.2 mm mortar company pulled out with his men and weapons as soon as the enemy shelling allowed. Outraged, Mueller described to his regimental commander what had happened and wanted to proffer charges against the of-fending officer. He learned that because the officer was not attached to Mueller's outfit but officially only designated as support, he had the prerogative to locate where he saw fit.

A day later when the same captain reported in for an-other support mission, Mueller borrowed a carbine and led the captain forward to orient him about coming opera-tions. "Be sure your weapon is locked and loaded because there might be some Japs lurking around," Mueller ad-vised the mortar commander, and then escorted him through the GI positions.

They headed out for some five hundred yards and then reached a point where Mueller suggested they crawl under a hut on stilts to conceal themselves while they looked over the terrain around them. "I turned to him and asked, 'Why did you run out on us during the shelling?'

" 'I talked to the Lord and told Him that I was going to pull out to save my troops from that awful shelling. I asked him to give me a sign if that was the wrong thing to do.'

" 'What was his answer?'

" 'When I ask him to give me a sign He always answers very soon. I waited for some time and then asked Him again for a sign if I was doing the wrong thing. But there was no sign, so I knew that it was the right thing to do.'

" 'Well,' " replied Mueller, " 'I also talked to the Lord. I said to Him, "Lord, what shall I do to that officer who ran out on us when we needed him so urgently?" And the Lord answered, "Take him out and show him the prom-ised land." I knew what the Lord meant. He meant for me to take you here and show you the land where we have never set foot. And that is the land between here and Hill Z over there, including the hill itself. Where do you think our front line is?'

" 'Aren't we on our front line?' " he asked.

" 'Do you see any sign of our troops? We left our front line when we passed through those machine gunners back there. This here is Jap country. Do you know what we are going to do if the Japs attack us? We are going to fight to the death, you and I, if we have to. And you are not going to turn around and run. Do I make myself clear?'

" 'Yes sir,' stammered the captain, visibly disturbed."

Mueller completed his lesson with an explanation of what he expected the captain to do on his next mission, but on return to the American lines Mueller related his conversation to the regimental commander. He told him he did not want "this nutty officer and his unreliable outfit in support." Mueller never heard from or saw the officer again.

According to Mueller, the crest of Hill 400 resembled a moonscape. "The entire top was dug up. Since the force had been reduced to about sixty fighters [the Japanese had all but abandoned efforts to reclaim the position] there are plenty of empty foxholes, all very deep because of deadly 150 mm mortar fire and some direct fire 77s from Hill Z. A very wide field of barbed wire and mines surrounded the entire position. 'We're wired in like a prison camp,' said one inhabitant. There were both light and water-cooled heavy machine guns, a couple of 60 mm mortars. Ammunition of all types was stockpiled in great quantities in the extra foxholes.

"The stench of decaying flesh was unbearable, quite like that of hundreds of bodies on Lone Tree Hill, our first battle in New Guinea. There were innumerable bodies tangled in the barbed wire barrier, the result of numerous attempts by the Japanese to retake the hill. There were probably more bodies at the bottom of the hill. Our enemy was not known to spend much time and effort to recover their dead. Eating a meal out of canned rations became a real problem because of the voracious appetite of the flies [attracted to the decomposing dead]. Because of these extremely harsh conditions, we frequently rotated troops on the hill. Morale remained surprisingly high. Soldiers seemed to regard it as a badge of honor to have served on 'Hell's Hill.' "

Grit and courage notwithstanding, Mueller also dealt with breakdowns from the stress of combat. Subsequent to the action on Hill 400, Mueller investigated a company bogged down in an attack on the town of San Isidro. At the battlefield he noticed a young enlisted man casually leaning against the bank of a ditch and then saw a lieutenant who led a platoon. "I knew him well because he was one of our old-timers who had trained with us in the States and served in all campaigns up to this point. The lieutenant did not seem to be aware of my presence. He was bent over praying a rosary. I watched him for a while because I did not want to disturb him during his prayers and maybe it would do some good. But there seemed to be no end to his prayers.

"I looked questioningly at the young soldier. He shrugged, threw up his hands and said, 'That's the way it always is. That's why we never get anything done!' " Mueller questioned the officer and, unhappy with his vague responses, sought out the company commander.

"I instructed him to execute a left hook through the wooded area to strike San Isidro from the north. After some detail, I asked if he had any questions. The captain turned to the first sergeant: 'You heard the battalion commander; do you have any questions?' When the first sergeant replied in the negative, the captain said, 'See to it that the instructions are carried out.'

"This was most unusual; company commanders ordinarily issued orders personally to platoon leaders. I left the captain to track down the first sergeant and his party. 'How long has this been going on?' I asked.

"Someone replied, 'For some time. The captain is not well.'

"I had noticed that the captain's hand was trembling and his arm twitching. He jammed his hand into his pocket and tried to keep his arm rigid. He was also one of our old-timers, in training, stateside maneuvers, New Guinea and the battles on Luzon. I dreaded the duty I had to perform—I hated it; but the battlefield is a harsh taskmaster, unrelenting, unforgiving. Infantry soldiers deserve the best leadership; their lives and bodies are daily on the line when they are in combat. What matters is what you do today—not what you did in the past.

"With deep regret I had to order both those old-timers, the captain and the lieutenant, to battalion headquarters, leaving the company in charge of the senior officer present. Despite the personnel changes, the company drove the Japanese intruders out of San Isidro the same day."

John Higgins, with the 3rd Battalion of the 43rd's 169th Regiment, recalls, "During the later part of February, we received about eight hundred enlisted and some officer replacements. Most had their basic training and had a few days to become adjusted to their new assignments and know their commanders. In early March, we moved to Bambam to relieve the 40th Infantry Division. This was a regimental combat team relieving an entire division. Each battalion took over an area formerly held by a regiment. The terrain was very rough with thousands of Jap soldiers. We came under the control of the 38th Infantry Division.

"It was very tough fighting; the Japs had to be dug out of caves and pillboxes. While leading a supply column with about a hundred Filipino carrying personnel [we paid them two pesos per day in silver only, no paper money accepted] and about fifteen of my enlisted men, I was notified of a Jap position down a draw. Taking five or six men we checked it out. There was a hot firefight that ended with four Japs killed, two machine guns and four rifles captured. None of my men were hurt. I received my second Bronze Star for this action."

Subsequently the 169th traveled to the Ipo Dam area, which featured limestone palisades several hundred feet high that were honeycombed with caves harboring Japanese soldiers. "More replacements came in at about 2100 hours," remembers Higgins. "Each of the rifle companies sent a guide down to the CP area to pick up its replacements, with about twelve–fifteen for each company. The next morning we had to move out two or three of the replacements through medical channels since they were killed that night during a Jap attack. At a staff meeting that afternoon I strongly recommended that any time replacements came up in the dark, they remain at the battalion CP site until daylight to enable them to at least see the sergeants and officers in their new unit. Also they would get some idea of what was happening. The CO agreed and it became SOP."

Curtis Banker, the gun crew member of Cannon Company in the 103rd Regiment, rode out a number of engagements in his M-7, self-propelled 105 mm piece. "Some of the time we did direct fire into caves and at night there were fire missions for harassment or to help stop *banzai* attacks. The terrain to the north, around the summer capital [Baguio], was very mountainous and easily defended. The weather there was better than New Guinea and we could get some fresh food on Luzon. I had jungle rot, malaria and yellow jaundice. The first thirty-eight days of combat on Luzon cost the 103rd Regiment 172 killed in action, 1 missing and 551 wounded.

"I had been wounded near San Fabian; two of my fingers were severed near the first joint and sewed back on. Combat fatigue was diagnosed by the doctor after I was recuperating from yellow jaundice. I was transferred from a Manila field hospital to a unit on Leyte by air. I requested to be returned to my unit which was advancing on Ipo Dam. Instead, I was sent to a replacement company in Manila. I threatened to go AWOL and they allowed me to rejoin my company. I traveled by train and then many miles on foot. I was not that fatigued before I went to the hospital but I sure was afterwards."

Arden Kurtz, the mortarman posted to a machine gun

crew after losses near the Clark Field shootouts, recalls his company was picked for reconnaissance as the division approached the Ipo Dam area. "We went across this flat area and about five hundred yards ahead of us are some cliffs. They're looking right down our throats and boy they started to pour it on us. Boy, everybody tried to get their whole body into that helmet. I had some shrapnel bounce off my helmet. They had the whole company pinned down. We couldn't move.

"They called in an air strike for us and there must have been thirty or forty planes. They'd come in real low, right over our heads. Boy were they noisy. The planes hit them with rockets, napalm, bombs, machine guns and really softened them up. Just before the planes left, we started moving up. When our regiment got through the cliffs to the other side, we stopped and dug in to consolidate our position."

Carlie Berryhill with the 6th Division says, "My Regiment, the 63rd Infantry, had 112 days of continuous combat without a break. We wore our clothes sometimes for a month or longer without a change. It rained so much they never had much time to dry on your body. I remember a couple of times when I removed my socks they would just tear off in pieces."

Tom Howard's tank platoon from the 754th Tank Battalion, attached to the 103rd Infantry Regiment, maneuvered to positions for firing at caves carved into the mountains. "The caves are all on the reverse side of the mountains," notes Howard. "You can move up, but when you pass, they open on you from your rear. The tank turrets must be traversed 180 degrees to face the rear. You have to be extremely careful when you fire back towards your own lines. Maybe there is method to their madness. Once you get in, you have to fight your way out."

Ordinarily, the tankers lived a bit more comfortably than the foot sloggers. The armor sometimes set up its perimeter at a barrio, enabling the crews to commandeer a few houses where they could maintain good observation and sleep indoors. Even when out in the field, the kitchens could advance and set up shop in the center of a circle of tanks. Occasionally, Howard and the others were granted passes to visit Manila.

"We learned to live off the land," says Howard. "We fixed fish by drying, we boiled then dried sugarcane syrup that we had squeezed and made sugar bar candy. We boiled and dried peanuts from wild plants. We gathered sweet potatoes—camotes—and fixed them by cooking them into a paste, then drying it. Our mixtures could later be diluted in hot water and prepared like soup. By using bows and arrows, we killed wild chickens and cockatoo birds for meat." Obliging Filipinos even taught the Americans how to capture monkeys, turning them into useful pets. "We fed them the fruit from trees and berries from plants first. If they were poisonous the monkey would not eat them."

The Japanese slowly fell back into northern Luzon and the summer capital of Baguio in the mountains. Among those pressing the shrinking forces of Yamashita's Shobu Group were the 25th, 32nd, 37th, and 1st Cavalry Divisions. Emil Matula, the First Sergeant of D Company for the 25th Division's 35th Infantry Regiment, had remained in a field hospital for twenty days because of the sniper's bullet that penetrated his upper jawbone and sinus area. "Those were the worst days I experienced during the entire war," says Matula. "My weapons were taken away from me and when it became dark, the guards around the hospital became trigger happy. I was afraid the Japs would come in while we lay there without a weapon."

Finally discharged from the hospital and sent back to duty, Matula returned to his company where he learned he had been awarded a field commission and transferred to Company G in the 2nd Battalion as a platoon leader. The I Corps command expected 25th in tandem with the 32nd to carve a wide swatch up the middle of Luzon, exploiting the two-lane gravel road known as Route 5. Matula's 35th Regiment, blessed by exceptionally heavy air, artillery and mortar support, and confronted at first by poorly organized Japanese defenders—a rarity—stepped out faster than the 27th and 161st Regiments. But by the end of March, all three encountered ever stiffening resistance.

While fighting towards the final redoubts of the Yamashita Shobu Group, Matula directed his platoon as it captured one of the endless hills and killed twenty of the enemy. "We received orders from Battalion to turn over the defense of the hill. During the night, the Japs ran the platoon of guerrillas off, capturing a machine gun from them and using it against the 2nd Battalion CP. My platoon had to take the hill back. We turned the defense over to the same guerrillas after killing another twenty Japs and recapturing our own equipment. That night the same thing happened again and I lost my platoon sergeant to a sniper. After that I refused to allow the guerrillas on the hill again."

Others held the irregulars in much higher regard. In the southern half of Luzon, the 11th Airborne counted on the guerrillas to supplement their limited numbers. The 11th's Joe Swing wrote to his mentor, "Have the 158th Regimental Combat Team attached to me but no replacements of my own—the stuffy army staff doesn't like airborne and won't do anything about getting me any. I'm really in somewhat of a fix with my front extending completely across the peninsula some thirty-five miles and my rear fifty miles back on the outskirts of Manila and General Kreuger coming down about every other day telling me not to stick my neck out—when it's been sticking out a mile ever since I landed. The only thing that keeps my lines open and allows me to spread so thin is the fact that I have organized five thousand guerrillas and have them attached to all the infantry, artillery and engineer units. Even have a picked company at headquarters. They call themselves GSOG (General Swing's Own Guerrillas)—the PQOG are President Quezon's own but mine are really tops. Let them wear the 11th AB shoulder patch over their left breasts. They are proud as punch and really fight. Put artillery forward observers with them, give them all the captured Jap machine guns and mortars and they keep on pushing and making the Japs like it.

"Cleaned up Teruate yesterday using mostly guerrillas and captured twenty-five Q boats. They are a two-man suicide job, carrying two depth bombs. They sneak up alongside a large boat at night, blow up themselves and the boat and usually sink the cargo craft."

Swing paid grudging tribute to the Supreme Commander. "Heard today on the radio that MacArthur will not go any further north and that Nimitz . . . will take over. If it's true it's too bad. He's the most clever military man we've got and is *lucky* to boot. It makes me sick when I read about the casualties on Iwo Jima. It can be done more scientifically. There is no doubt in any of our minds but what this 'Howlin Smith' [the Marine general] is actually howling mad. We laugh at the fruitless method of the Jap in his *banzai* attack and yet allow that fanatic to barge in using up men as though they were a dime a dozen and apparently boasting about it."

Swing also groused about the lack of appreciation in either official or press reports of the 11th Airborne's contributions. He concluded, "Wrote the [public relations officer] at GHQ saying that the only mention we had from *Time* was 'notable work at Corregidor' on which island no member of the division had ever set foot. Suggested he inform the *Time* representative if he couldn't get the record straight just to skip completely any mention of the division."

Swing was not the only one who was concerned about public relations. At the top of the heap stood MacArthur. His chief of staff, Richard Sutherland, told historian Louis Morton after World War II ended: "General MacArthur is an egomaniac. All decisions he made were always based on their effect on one man, General MacArthur, and his position in history. He personally checked all publicity reports and wrote some himself. His dispatches were replete with references to the deity but he has no more religion than a

goat." Sutherland indicated to Morton that MacArthur refused to permit any accounts of his actions which were in
the slightest degree unfavorable or critical of his command.

What was printed or reported about the achievements
of units depended in considerable measure on the importance attached to this aspect by a commander. Arndt
Mueller says, "The decision was made at 6th Division
headquarters that reporters would receive no special treatment, that they would have to live under the same conditions as the officers and men. Quite fortuitously I observed
how the 38th Division treated the war correspondents.
They set up a large tent, could have been a hospital tent. It
was equipped *not* with the standard, uncomfortable Army
cots, but with hospital beds and mattresses, pillows and
linen. There was a well-stocked bar, electric lighting, supplied by a generator. There was also a comfortable latrine
and showers available." The difference in accommoda-
tions, Mueller believes, resulted in the 38th Division rather
than the 6th Division getting credit for cracking the
Shimbu Line.

While the Japanese opposition to Swing's forces were as
dedicated as those in the north, they were fewer in number
and could not exploit the landscape as well as those directly
under Yamashita. The route towards Baguio for the 32nd
Division lay through the Villa Verde Trail, and Whayland
Greene, serving as a platoon runner, carried a radio for the
platoon leader. "Lieutenant Hamerker, who'd been with
us on Leyte, a quiet, easygoing man who carried a Bible
but never tried to push it or his religion on anyone, had
been killed on Leyte. His replacement, Lieutenant Coolie,
was twenty-five and Sergeant Sullivan was about thirty.
They got to be good friends and used to joke with each
other lots. Lieutenant Coolie would say, 'Let's go get
them, Sullivan.' He'd keep this up until the sergeant would
say, 'Hell, Lieutenant, I'll go anywhere you go and I'll go
first.'

"It came time for Lieutenant Coolie to take our platoon
and try to take a hill. We were all real nervous and I re-

member asking the Lieutenant if he was ready to go get them. He said, 'Greene, I am not any more ready to go get them than you are.' I said, 'If that's the case let's don't go get them.' He said, 'I wish it could be like that.' We started up the hill and began drawing fire from a machine gun, rifles and hand grenades. Our men that were up the hill a little ways, James M. Valentine and another fellow, pinned down the machine gun, firing across the hole and kept them from throwing grenades from there. The Japs started shelling us with a large mortar from another hill. One shell hit real close to us and killed Lieutenant Coolie. A piece of shrapnel had gone through Valentine's helmet. Another piece hit James Bryant in the wrist. Joe Weaver got hit real bad with something. The breath was knocked out of me and the 536 radio had been destroyed. I had just gotten in contact with the company commander and handed the radio to Lieutenant Coolie. The Lieutenant was dead in just a few seconds. After I got my breath back the Sergeant asked how bad it was. At first I told him that it was real bad but found out it was just a little piece of shrapnel in my leg and the rest was only concussion. The Sergeant said for us to pull back before we all got killed. We all started down and when we did the machine gun raised up and helped us move faster. We got almost back with the wounded and something hit a man named Camarino in the head and killed him. When things settled down again, I thought what a price to pay for a small hill in these islands. In two days I think we had lost eight men killed and about twelve wounded on that hill.

"It wasn't long after this that Sergeant Johnson came to me and said, 'Greene, I am going to make you and Valentine squad leaders.' I told him I was still a platoon runner and had never even been an assistant squad leader. He said, 'As of now, you and Valentine are squad leaders.' I was a Pfc. A squad leader was supposed to be a staff sergeant. I took over the squad and we got some new men and we had to start fighting before I even learned all of their names. This was real bad for us. We were moving down a valley and one of the new guys came right up over a Jap in his hole. Sergeant Sullivan said, 'Shoot him, that's what you were sent over here for.' He said, 'I can't.' The Sergeant shot the Jap."

On the Villa Verde Trail, Bob Teeples, an acting platoon leader while still first sergeant of Company L, 128th Regiment of the 32nd Division, was a former member of the Alamo Scouts where he won a Silver Star. Teeples led a reconnaissance patrol. "I sent out the two scouts and I followed behind them. In turn, behind me came the BAR man, his assistant, the other members of the patrol and a corporal known as Jim Snyder. As we moved out, the wetness of the red clay from the foxholes made our uniforms glisten against the green foilage, like walking bull's-eyes.

"We had barely started onto the plateau we were supposed to reconnoiter when we came to a mound of fresh dug earth. It was still smoldering and I warned the scouts to keep a sharp lookout as the Japs had undoubtedly just buried one of the victims of our artillery barrage. As the BAR man's assistant climbed onto the plateau, a shot rang out and he fell back over the edge. Almost immediately another shot and the BAR man grabbed his throat and ran forward towards me. As he ran, he began to cry, fell down on his knees, onto his face and lay still. By this time the two scouts and I were flat on the ground as a Japanese machine gun had opened up on us from the high ground to our left. I crawled to the BAR man and felt for his pulse but he was gone. I thought back to a couple of nights before when he had proudly showed me a picture of his wife and their one-year-old son. Now another machine gun started to fire on us from a position on our right flank and the twigs and branches were snapping all around us. The sound of the bullets over my head reminded me of a group of wires being rattled together. The Japs started to drop occasional mortar rounds. I realized we would have to withdraw.

"I motioned for my scouts to come back, and I tried to keep firing towards the Jap position to keep the scouts covered as they made their way back past me and over the edge of the plateau. A bullet ricochetted off the helmet of the first scout but otherwise they made it back safely. I tried to drag the BAR man's body towards the edge of the plateau but his ammunition harness kept catching in the brush. I managed to drag him back almost to the edge, when all of a sudden it felt like someone hit me in the head with a sledgehammer. The first thing I saw when I regained consciousness was a light flashing on and off. As my mind became more clear, I realized I was in a tent, apparently the rear aid station. The light turned out to be a small bulb swinging back and forth as the wind shook the tent.

"I must have been unconscious all day because it was now dark. I felt my head and there was a bandage wrapped around it over my ears. I looked around the tent and I could see a couple of men lying on cots. About that time a surprisingly clean-looking Corporal Snyder came in and said something to a tired-looking medical captain. The captain came over, and with a pair of surgical scissors cut the bandages from my head. 'Jim,' I said, 'there must be a dance tonight. You look like you are ready to go get your girlfriend.' 'Better 'n that,' Jim said. 'While our platoon was drawing all the enemy fire, another platoon with an artillery observer spotted the Japs from the flank and after calling in an artillery strike on the Jap positions, they cleaned them out. You had been knocked out by a mortar round just before you got to the edge of the plateau. A couple of medics dragged you to safety. The best news though is that our division has been relieved and we are on our way to the rest area.'

"After Jim left, I put my head back on the cot, thanked God for bringing me safely through another day and prayed that my folks back home were all well." When Teeples reached the rest camp, he pinned on a set of gold bars after appointment as a second lieutenant.

Max Papazarian, as a member of the 126th Infantry, briefly left the combat scene for a two-week tour in Manila.

"Company F was assigned to be a personal security guard for Gen. Douglas MacArthur and his staff. It was deemed an honor for us. However, it was all spit and polish for those of us who had been through so much, making it a burden to have our uniforms clean and boots polished all the time. But we ate well and were able to feel better during this period which lasted about two weeks after which we moved back into the fighting.

"One evening we began to settle in on a razor-backed ridge and dug our foxholes. I dug mine deep enough so that I could just see out. We were really deep in hostile territory and we weren't about to expose ourselves any more than we had to. We were supplied with as much ammunition and grenades as we wanted to see us through the night. There was no moon out that night and it was pitch black, so dark that you couldn't see your hand in front of your face. It made the situation that much more critical and tense. It was to be the most fearful night for me. We had to be alert to any possible enemy activity. To communicate with one another, we had string going from foxhole to foxhole and to let our next buddy know it was his turn to stand guard. It was complete silence. Up the trail about a hundred yards from me were the light machine gun crews' installations.

"During the night we would hear enemy soldiers rustling through the underbrush. Upon hearing the sounds, I would pull the pin on a hand grenade and lob it over the hill and let it roll down the side. I don't know if the exploding grenades got anyone or not but we were extra cautious. In spite of all the steps, some enemy soldiers managed to overrun one of the machine gun positions and put a saber through one man. He might have fallen asleep while on guard duty. I can still hear him calling, 'Sully, help me!' Security troops and the backup machine gun crews opened fire and sprayed the area. At dawn we found our dead buddy and numerous dead Japanese soldiers. I still have a problem in a completely dark room with closed doors after all these years."

By the time the 32nd Division finally cleared the Villa
Verde Trail, over a nearly four-week period, it counted almost three thousand combat killed and wounded with an
additional six thousand men withdrawn from the lines because of sickness or psychoneurotic problems.

In December 1944, while in New Guinea, Sgt. Sam
LaMagna was chosen for rotation back to the States with a
twenty-one-day furlough. After a joyous reunion with his
family and friends in Connecticut, LaMagna boarded a
train for the trip back to the war. Along the way, a succession of misadventures that began with a beery session at a
bar during a layover in Chicago broke LaMagna back to
private before he finally docked at Manila in April. "It was
a mess," says LaMagna. "The Japs had blown up all the
bridges that crossed the Pasig River. Ships were sunk in the
harbor with masts sticking out of the water. MPs kept personnel, Filipinos and Americans out of the danger zones."

After LaMagna checked in, he hitched a ride on a truck
going in the direction of his battalion currently operating
with the 112th Cavalry near Hot Corner, an intersection
in the vicinity of Ipo Dam. "The driver told me to hop in
the back, handed me his rifle and said, 'Watch out for Jap
snipers.'" At the Company F position, LaMagna says,
"Johnny Petrone was cleaning his weapon. I sat on top of
his foxhole and said, 'Hi, you dirty ole man! How's business?'

"He looked up and said, 'What the hell are you doing
here? You better get your ass in here before it gets shot off.
We're supposed to be secured but you never know when
those bastards show up.' I looked around to see if I could
find any of my buddies. Most were new to me. Then the
important questions: Where's Henry? Where's Farmer? Is
Tietjen still here? He said Henry was still with us. Farmer
was wounded and evacuated. Tietjen was killed by Jap artillery. I felt bad. I would have liked to have seen him and
patched things up."

Paired off with one of the replacements, Mike Borowy,
LaMagna found his new foxhole companion congenial.

"We had a new company commander, a new platoon leader to replace Tietjen and whose name I didn't recall. Turnover was so high, you didn't even get to know their first names.

"Towards the end of April we formed a line along the edge of a road, expecting a *banzai* attack to keep us from reaching Ipo Dam. Around midnight, I heard small arms fire and then machine gun fire down the hill from where we were at. I expected Japs to come charging up at us. I reached over and touched Mike. He acknowledged. Then searchlight beams came on. Glory be! What a sight! The whole area lit up like an Xmas tree. No Japs could sneak up on us. Instead they were ambushed by our rifles, mortars and machine gun fire. What was left of them turned tail and fled. Those that tried coming up the hill went back down, the hard way."

Sam LaMagna, having resumed his career as a foot soldier, staggered along while beset by malaria episodes and regular bouts of diarrhea. He was cheered by the efforts of a local guerrilla commander, Col. Marcus Agustin, who commanded tens of thousands and who, supposedly after listening to an American general, remarked, "I don't need anyone to tell me how to fight Japs." It was the Marcus Agustin brigades that seized the northern end of the Ipo Dam before the Japanese could detonate the hundreds of pounds of TNT planted there. But gnawing at LaMagna was the memory that from his original company at Camp Blanding, Florida, only nine men were still on their feet.

Introduction of replacements to the combat area varied according to which outfit a newcomer was assigned. As John Higgins indicated, those posted to his regiment were plugged into line companies almost immediately. On the other hand, Edwin Hanson, who had enlisted in an Army Reserve program that provided the same college education offered by the ASTP, reached Manila, via Bougainville, around the third week of February. The discomfited Hanson learned there that, although trained as an engineer, he would be an infantryman in F Company, 148th Regiment of the 37th Division. Still, as he bedded down in the city, he says he was told that he was fortunate. "In fact, we were lucky according to one of the fellows in the building where we spent the night. The replacements assigned that morning to the 129th had been taken to their outfits immediately and several already had been wounded in the fighting." He was also better off than another replacement, drawn from the field artillery, who needed lessons on how to dismantle an M-1 for cleaning. On February 23, a truck dropped Hanson off at the locale of F Company of the 148th, where the regiment had been drawn off the lines for a rest.

Hanson pulled guard duty, but no KP, prowled around the city, wrote letters, bought souvenirs and apparently was taught nothing about what lay ahead. Not until mid-April did he approach the combat zone, as the 148th advanced on Baguio. Hanson saw his first dead enemy, a pair of soldiers flushed from cover, a bit farther up the trail. He also endured a baptism of Philippine combat weather, a persistent rain that drenched him and mucked up the path. "We slipped, crawled and slid up that almost vertical embankment that was all mud and no handholds. When I reached the top, I was mud from head to foot, my rifle was clogged and I hoped it would rain long enough to wash me off. I have yet to see anything wetter than the rains in the mountains of northern Luzon."

When darkness enveloped his unit, Hansen dined on a cold C ration. "I had dug a hasty hole with Manning and Lampkins, which wasn't long enough to lie down in and too shallow to get much cover. Manning and Lampkins were both small but we found out that size had little to do with one's comfort. By lying down we exposed our faces and lower legs and boots to the rain and it soon crept up and soaked the clothes that had partially dried out. It wasn't long before we were too cold to do anything including sleep."

Hanson's outfit stayed atop that hill for four days, with a view of the Baguio Road winding through the mountains affording glimpses of American tanks grinding ahead of the infantry, with occasional pauses for what appeared to be a skirmish. "The first warning of any Japs in the area came the first day. Manning was on guard behind a bush and he saw someone with a netted helmet poke his head up not fifteen feet away. Killer was the only one in the platoon with a netted helmet, so Manning called to him by name. Whereupon the head vanished, followed by a great crashing in the underbrush as if he were trying to escape. Suddenly Manning realized it must have been a Jap but by that time he was gone. Needless to say, Killer immediately tore the net off his helmet.

"The next morning about noon, around the time I was setting down at our hole to eat lunch, Lampkins gave a *'Psst*—Swede' plus a few beckoning gestures. I made a grab for my helmet and rifle, but by the time I was ready, he'd already let go a blast with his BAR, killed one Jap and chased another around the bend in the trail with bullets. They had both come along completely nonchalant, without a care in the world with their rifles at sling arms." Later, the F Company GIs located a nearby cave with abandoned Japanese supplies.

As Company F pressed on, the defenders nibbled at their ranks from well-concealed positions. Hanson's platoon leader was among those hit and the continuing gunfire prevented litter bearers from promptly evacuating the wounded. The lieutenant, a field-commissioned officer who previously served with another unit, died. "Anywhere in the hills, if you were wounded bad enough for a stretcher, your chances were not too good, because it meant a torturing ride for hours up and down hills, jouncing sliding, being dropped and just generally mishandled in spite of four well-meaning bearers.

"Mountain Filips were soon recruited for stretcher bearers and supply hauling. The mountain men and women were the strongest, hardiest people I had ever seen. A small, undernourished woman could carry a case of C rations up a mountain, never bat an eyelash and dance along having a good time while I'd have to tell them to slow down, my heavy rifle was making me tired. And not one trip, but as many as time would permit each day."

Moving up farther, Company F attempted to assault a knob atop a ridge line. The Japanese, from their burrows, responded. "All hell broke loose," says Hanson, "grenades, rifle shots and even the *brrp* of a Nambu. Frankie said, 'Oh.' I asked him if he was hit, he said yes, and turned to get out. I kept on crawling and grenades were exploding—mostly behind me—and men were shouting. Then all of a sudden it was quiet. I looked around to see why and saw a man disappearing down the gulley with another right behind him. And then nobody else. Good Lord, was I being left here on this accursed hill?

"I immediately crawled back down to where I could stand up and prepared to dash down to the gully. My attention was drawn to a thrashing in the weeds next to me. It was Moore, moaning and groaning, trying to move. His chest and arms were bloody but he was conscious enough to want to get out. I tried to get him to walk and he couldn't. I tried to pick him up and I couldn't. I told him the only way out was for me to drag him. I dropped my rifle and helmet and took hold of his feet, started pulling him down the gully bottom. After about twenty yards I stopped, ripped open his jacket and tried to stop the slow bleeding with bandages. Then I started dragging again. I was sure the Japs would swarm down any minute.

"About halfway down I was fagged out, so I stopped, rolled him behind a log, gave him my last grenade, and told him to throw it if the Japs came—I was going for help. He was too weak to do anything even if he had to. I dashed down the gully a ways, whispered F Company a couple of times and then finally got a response. Whoever it was said the rest had gone down the gully to the bottom and I continued my half-running, half-flying trip. About another fifty yards from where I left Moore I met Renfrew. I told him my troubles and he said he'd get Bill, so I turned and scrambled back towards Moore and the Japs, without any weapon at all.

"I got back to Moore, who was worse, waited an eternity for Renfrew and Bill, and almost called them cowards when they poked their rifles, followed by their heads, over the nearest drop. I was getting irrational. We carried, dragged and lifted Moore down the remainder of the gully. About halfway down, Bill set him down, looked him over and said to wait a minute, he wouldn't last long. When I heard that I almost fell over. He'd been conscious when we'd started; he'd even helped me get him over the worst of the drops; he couldn't die. He was hit in the lungs, though, and didn't last long. We carried him down to the bottom, up a hill and over to the company. I sat down and tried to rest.

"Maunu was dead and eighteen out of the first platoon were injured. Some bad, some just a scratch, but hit and out of commission. Bob Fritter had it in his hand. Boyd had shrapnel in his upper arm, pretty bad. Frankie had a flesh wound. Bris had a grenade go off right next to his head and knock him half silly without scratching him. There were about a dozen of us left in the first platoon." In a day or so, a patrol reported the knob now deserted. Hanson and the other GIs explored the positions without incident. For his effort to save a fallen comrade, Hanson earned a Bronze Star.

By the end of April, neither the Kembu Group in Bataan nor the Shimbu Group in the southeastern portion of Luzon offered organized resistance. Iwo Jima, the tiny volcanic outcropping seized by Marines at extremely high cost, served as an emergency airbase for B-29s bombing Tokyo from either Saipan or the Philippines. Three of the U.S. divisions that subdued the Japanese on Leyte were now locked in a brutal struggle on Okinawa, only 350 miles from southern Japan. And as Yamashita's Shobu Group, increasingly short of food as well as war materiel, continued to retreat north, MacArthur staged the final acts for liberation of the entire archipelago.

CHAPTER XXVI

THE OTHER ISLANDS
AND THE END

ASIDE FROM THE FORCES directly under Yamashita, almost all of the surviving 102,000 Japanese troops in the central and southern Philippines occupied four islands: Negros, Cebu, Panay, and Mindanao, with a small detachment on Palawan. The combat-effective men, exclusive of service, navy, and air force personnel, numbered about 35,000 scattered over the four sites. Whatever the makeup, the defenders could expect no help from the beleaguered Yamashita or from home and faced declining amounts of ammunition, artillery, and eventually food. The generals understood they could not expect to defeat the Americans. Their sole duty was to delay and inflict losses that might allow a peace with honor.

The campaign beyond Luzon opened at the end of February with the 186th Regimental Combat Team from the 41st Division clearing out an area on Palawan. Lying between the South China Sea and the Sulu Sea, Palawan seemed ideal for airbases that could support assaults both on the southernmost Philippines and the former Dutch East Indies. Unfortunately, the soil composition and compaction defied the best efforts of engineers and delayed immediate exploitation of Palawan.

Mindanao, the second biggest and most southern of the Philippines, was the next card drawn from MacArthur's strategic deck. Under Col. Wendell Fertig, the Mindanao guerrillas operated with increasing boldness and even controlled an airstrip at Dipolog for supply operations on the north coast of the Zamboanga Peninsula, a 145-mile-long neck of land on the western end of Mindanao. Two days before an amphibious assault, Marine fighter bombers, protected by guerrillas and troops from the 24th Division, began operations at the Dipolog site.

Fertig assured General Eichelberger and the 8th Army that landings near Zamboanga City would be unopposed. Underwater demolition teams, engineers and guerrillas sanitized the beaches of mines and marked out zones without interference but, taking no chances, a pre-invasion bombardment pounded the sparse enemy artillery positions inland. When the troops of the 41st Division stepped onto the Zamboanga shores some met little or no fire while others quickly took casualties.

Richard Feddersen, a native of Ottuma, Iowa, having graduated from the state university as an honors student in the ROTC program, commanded Company G of the 162nd Infantry Regiment. "On March 10," says Feddersen, "the barge grounded on a bar. We waded in hip deep. With the lead squad, I struck inland. A machine gun felled Staff Sergeant DiLaura with a shot through the leg. In a crater with me, he ignored the medic working on his leg and pointed out the machine gun. A squad flanked and silenced it. By the road I nearly tripped on a dead GI, a machine gun bullet through the head. Another man was also wounded."

On the following day, a 41st supply dump blew up as enemy artillery pinpointed its location. With the aid of binoculars, the GIs located a forward observer tied to a tree. From a distance of two hundred yards, Feddersen himself, using an M-1, dispatched the lookout. Battalion headquarters requested a prisoner for interrogation and Feddersen saw an apparently unarmed soldier camouflaged in a cornfield. A patrol endeavored to snare him but when the man detected its presence he ran. A machine gun fired at the fleeing figure who blew up. "He had," says Fedder-sen, "lashed a mine to himself for a suicide rush. Company G vowed to take no prisoners."

Dr. Alexander J. Pasterak, supported by parents who operated "Mom and Pop" grocery stores, attended Western Reserve University Medical School. Pasterak accepted a first lieutenant's commission as a medical officer upon completion of his studies. "I realized that with the world falling apart, I no doubt would be called up in event of war. After my internship at Harper Hospital in Detroit, in 1939, I had some general hospital work in Akron and two tours of army maneuvers. In August of 1941, I went on active duty at Fort Knox, Kentucky. I had no special train-ing." Pasterak shipped to New Guinea in 1942 as a mem-ber of the 10th Evacuation Hospital Unit.

"I was made a sacrificial lamb by conniving com-manders of the 10th and the 162nd Regiment which trans-ferred me to the 162nd as a battalion surgeon in exchange for a medical corps lieutenant who wanted out of the in-fantry because he was fearful he'd be killed in combat. He didn't want to be shot at. I learned about these fears later. I first came under fire in the final phases of the Buna-Gona, New Guinea, campaigns. The battalion surgeon was at high risk. He was at the front lines, the worst spot for a doctor. Directly ahead is the enemy. In combat the aid medic usually is the first to treat casualties—emergency first aid, control pain, control hemorrhage, bandage, splint if a fracture is probable and arrange evacuation by litter bearers if possible to the aid station. Additional emergency therapy is given at the aid station. I lost two aid men killed in action and my staff sergeant and aid station clerk were killed by friendly fire." Pasterak himself was awarded a Purple Heart for a non-disabling shrapnel wound to his knee. He also received a Bronze Star.

"A battalion surgeon's duties did not involve combat tactics, of course, unless exposed to close fighting—*banzai* attacks or deep penetration of the perimeter areas. I was armed with a carbine which fortunately I never had to use."

Some two weeks later, the 162nd engaged in a decisive action at Mt. Capisan, high ground on which the enemy occupied well-prepared positions. The rout of the Japanese signaled the end of effective resistance on the peninsula and the 41st Division's soldiers pursued the retreating foe. Within a single month, the original eighty-nine hundred Zamboanga defenders were reduced by nearly four thousand, almost all dead. Subsequently, the Zamboanga command assigned Feddersen to direct a school for guerrilla officers on the island.

To conquer the eastern part of Mindanao, occupied by a mélange of fifty-five thousand soldiers and armed civilians loyal to the Imperial Empire, the 24th and the 31st Division in the third week of April landed on beaches a hundred miles from the main objective, Davao, a port across the waist of the island. The Japanese apparently expected the approach to be from the Davao side and the bulk of their defenses were oriented in that direction. The Americans, aided by guerrilla intelligence and operations that ensured an absence of hostile forces, moved rapidly in the first weeks.

Han Rants, the 34th Infantry wire section chief who says his terrifying experiences during the battle for Zig Zag Pass converted him into a devout Christian, left Mindoro for Mindanao after a period of R & R. "We had been warned there were Moslem tribes—Moros—there, and there were Huks who actually held communist-type beliefs and they hated any outsider, not just the Japanese. Fortunately for us, we found that they hated the Japanese much more."

The march to Davao took Rants and his buddies through the interior, largely uncharted section of the island. "We had seen in *National Geographic* magazine tribes that had been untouched by civilization and lived the way they had in the past. The natives were stripped to the waist, both men and women. They wore very little clothing and hunted with spears along a small river. As we saw these tribes we prayed they would be friendly. We never had any interference from them.

"As we crossed the center of the island and got on the Davao side, still some fifty miles away from the city, resistance got heavier and heavier. Where they had blown bridges, they would set up machine guns across streams or rivers so that as we crossed they could pick us off in the water. As we came to these streams it took a long time to send out scouts and patrols, get the area cleared, so we could ford the stream and keep on going."

Even though it must have been obvious that Imperial Japan had been defeated, a few local people still cast their lot against the Americans. Rants reports that some Filipino traders approached the battalion and said they could lead the GIs to an enemy encampment. "My good buddy from L Company, David Flaherty, had been wounded in each campaign we had and he was one of the best line sergeants in the battalion. Flaherty was picked to lead some fifty-four men who went with these Filipinos since we felt we could trust them. But when Flaherty came out, he was one of only five left alive. Those Filipinos had led them to an area the Japanese had laced with crossfire from higher positions. Flaherty was awarded the Distinguished Service Cross because of extremely heroic action he took trying to save the group. He became a nervous wreck for life. He was in college with me some years after the war and he just couldn't stay in class. He dropped out and I lost track of him."

The strategy and tactics of the Japanese failed to halt the advances but succeeded in drawing considerable blood. A number of men who had been with Rants from the beginning went down with serious wounds as his battalion struggled towards Davao. "One of the things that was very upsetting was that we had visitors who were being punished. We were racially segregated in World War II and there weren't any blacks in the fighting units. [Actually, there were already a handful of all-black combat outfits including one infantry division, and at the time of the incidents described by Rants a decision had been made to increase the numbers considerably.] They were assigned to port details, truck driving, things like that. Once in a while we would have two black guys brought in from the rear and left with us overnight or for a couple of nights. We were told these were people who had been stealing supplies like the cigarette ration and other items and selling them to other outfits or to Filipinos. We were told they were being punished by having to spend two or three nights at the front.

"It was very frightening for them, and of course this didn't make it with us. We were wild-eyed angry because if this was a punishment, why were we there every day and having to go through years of it." [The illogic of the arrangement exposes the absurdity of a system that in its zeal to deny African-American equality worked in this instance to the extreme detriment of the whites. Rants is probably correct when he says the tactics worsened racial feelings. Integration in the military, which began right before the Korean War, became complete during the Vietnam conflict where the draft system sent a disproportionate number of poorer, less well-educated Americans into combat. As a consequence, blacks served there in combat beyond their proportion in the general population.]

David Mann, one of eight hundred replacements, most of whom had only just completed basic training and met their companies while on the ships headed for the invasion of Luzon with the 24th Division, held a newly minted OCS commission as he became a platoon leader for G Company of the 34th Infantry. "I was a very green second lieutenant," says Mann, "awestruck that I would have to lead these veterans in battle." And his initial engagement was the disaster at Zig Zag Pass. "I received a Bronze Star there," notes Mann, "for following orders to organize a small covering force as F and G Companies withdrew.

"At Zig Zag, in three days the Regiment lost 61 killed

and 258 wounded to which should be added at least 25 cases of severe psychoneurosis or shell shock. On the other hand, Mindanao was a long drawn-out campaign of seventy-five days. On May 14 I noticed my platoon was almost at full strength of forty men. This number soon dwindled until the last week in the month it was down to two squads of ten men each. The other rifle platoon was the same size. These forty men in the two platoons were the only ones in the company who wanted to fight. All the rest made sick call, one way or another."

Battalion surgeon Phil Hostetter accompanied the 19th Regiment to Mindanao and his duties covered a wide spectrum from teaching first aid, sanitation, and psychology to treating horribly wounded men. "We received fifteen recruits fresh from the States in the medical detachment. I decided to have a class in giving blood plasma. None of the men had ever done it." Hostetter divided them into pairs but while he would not require them to use a needle on one another, he suggested they learn by doing. "I heard, 'By God, no one is going to stick me.' I said, 'This is the way to do it as I put a rubber band around the arm of one fellow. I inserted a hypodermic needle and drew back a little blood. Now you do it to me.' The venopuncture had not fazed him, but I thought he might go into shock with that order. He may have imagined what would happen if I lost an arm or even if he messed it up. I did not expect him to be good the first time, but he did a fine job. Everyone in the group then performed the exercise with success and felt confident."

Back on the trails with the troops, Hostetter became briefly pinned down in an exchange of gunfire. When it subsided, one soldier could only drag himself on his elbows. "My legs won't work," he cried out to Hostetter. The doctor recalls telling the man, "I am going to fix your legs and you will be all right." Hostetter flexed one thigh against the GI's body and then the other. Then he declared, "Now you can walk." The soldier stood up and walked back, his hysterical paralysis cured.

An epidemic of diarrhea, "the worst I had encountered," according to Hostetter, devastated the battalion. In spite of his efforts to treat the troops with Sulfaguanidine tablets, they continued to weaken. "At the same time the battalion commander told me he had located some enemies but was not able to clear them out because he didn't have enough men. Everyone knew the only honorable way a soldier could be relieved of duty was through the medical department, me in this area. I knew almost every man was affected by the epidemic, yet we were required to keep fighting. Men kept coming to me in their weakened condition believing they could never make another patrol, and I had to send them out anyway. I decided a man whose temperature was less than 101 degrees would stay on duty.

"I sent the regimental surgeon a message saying the battalion was in very bad health because of gastroenteritis, and could not carry out its mission for long. He spoke to the regimental commander and the battalion was immediately replaced by another. With no excessive demands on their strength, the men recovered within a few days."

Men rarely died of the GIs, as the disease was known, but around Hostetter, even at this late date in the war, the maiming and killing continued unabated. " 'Medic!' someone shouted. I ran over to where a soldier writhed on the ground. His abdominal wall was blown away, exposing the loops of intestines. He must have been hit by a grenade or land mine." As Hostetter approached him, the injured man, "functionally decerebrated or unable to think" from extreme shock, tore at his own insides. "We put him on a litter. Someone restrained his hands while I wrapped a large towel from our medical supplies around the abdomen. I cut perforations in the ends of the towel with the pocketknife I always carried, and laced it tightly together with a roll of bandages. This served to hold in the intestines, prevent further loss of fluid and restore blood pressure. We gave him a syrette of morphine, started blood plasma and moved him towards the nearest hospital. He may have lived. I never knew because I hardly ever heard what happened to such patients." At other times, Hostetter saw his patients die before they could be evacuated or in other instances the explosions and gunfire snuffed out the lives before he could even start treatment. And his medical unit was not immune from injury as several close associates, seeking to succor the wounded, lost their own lives.

The fight to control the eastern area of Mindanao introduced replacement Marvin O. Reichman to war. As a boy in Chicago, Reichman grew up in the home of his grandparents. Reichman had enlisted at seventeen in September 1944 and shortly after his next birthday towards the end of November, he reported for active duty. "I was inducted at Fort Sheridan, Illinois," says Reichman, "and I was quite surprised to see German POWs serving our food, walking all over our post. The day before I got there six of them had been killed in a truck accident. I was surprised to see a German funeral procession for them conducted on Patton Road with all the POWs in the procession."

Reichman trained at Camp Hood and almost immediately upon completion of his seventeen weeks of basic training boarded a ship for Leyte. On the way over he learned the war in Europe had ended. Within a few weeks, an LCI brought him to Mindanao where he was absorbed by K Company of the 24th Division's 21st Infantry Regiment. "I was told what to expect by the platoon sergeant and most of all we were told not to run away in the face of the enemy. My role was that of a scout and rifleman, to precede the squad and try to draw fire from the enemy. They were smart and usually would let me go by and then hit the unit.

"I came under fire a day or two after I arrived. I saw my first casualties, ten to fifteen American soldiers in a two-and-a-half-ton truck. They were dead and I was amazed that their combat boots were so new. They hadn't even any wear on them. We crossed a river and came upon Japanese casualties and destroyed equipment. From that day on we were constantly under fire.

"Every night we dug in wagon train style. We usually put out trip wires with grenades. There was usually an attack every night and it was scary. One night they came and threw themselves on the trip wires. Quite a few were killed that way and we killed the rest of them with rifles and machine guns. On another night I heard some rustling out in front. I fired four rounds. Later I learned I had killed a carabao. But I also fired four rounds at a shadow going into a hole next to me. I didn't know who I shot at because during the night we were not allowed out of our foxholes. The next morning I found I had saved a man's life. A Japanese soldier was attempting to finish off a wounded man in that hole.

"We didn't take prisoners. The regimental headquarters finally said that if one were taken, the man who got him would receive a Bronze Star. That's how desperate they were for prisoners to interrogate. One day on guard duty during the rain, I was eating. Suddenly, someone came up behind me, put his hand on my forehead and his bolo against my neck. He was a guerrilla and said if I were a Jap I would be dead. He really taught me a lesson."

In climate, disease, and the squalor of its living conditions, Mindanao was the same as Leyte, Luzon, and the rest of the islands. "It rained constantly," says Reichman. "We developed jungle rot, because of the dampness, usually in the groin. I contracted malaria. Our food was primarily K rations. We did not get any hot meals."

Combat conditions and the behavior of the enemy also did not vary from that experienced in the other campaigns on the archipelago. "We were always exhausted, primarily from stress," notes Reichman. "As far as the big picture was concerned, we never knew anything about it. We didn't know where we were most of the time. We were told to advance from one point to another. You had to have your eyes darting about all the time because the Japanese were excellent in hiding themselves. We were in Kunai grass most of the time. It grew as high as ten feet and you could not see the enemy. Once I was off the road and I literally bumped into a Jap soldier coming in my direction. We both were startled. He jumped backwards, armed a grenade and threw it at me. It bounced off my chest and rolled away. I got out of there before the grenade went off. Some men from my squad and I killed him."

Friendly fire still stalked the troops. "We had tactical support from the air, Marines dropping napalm. In several cases they dropped it on us. I hate to say this but one came in too low and crashed. Everybody cheered. It was impossible for them to determine where we were because the lines changed constantly.

"On June 17 we were preparing to attack a Japanese position. We had fixed bayonets which we hardly ever did in combat. The forward observer apparently called in the wrong grids. The first shell should have been smoke. For some reason it wasn't, but VT [a timed fuse], which went off about twenty feet overhead, rained down shrapnel. Four or five of them came in before anybody could call back to stop the artillery. Every man in my squad was killed except myself and our sergeant. He pulled me out of the line of fire and bandaged my wound."

Evacuated to a hospital, Reichman quickly wrote a Dear Mom letter. "Before you pass out cold on the floor—either before or after you receive this letter, you'll receive a medal from me. It's the Purple Heart, but don't get excited. A piece of shrapnel went clear through my left leg. It's a nice clean wound. In a couple of weeks I'll be up and around again."

At the hospital on Leyte, an officer had come to his ward and read the citation that went along with the Purple Heart. Reichman recalls saying to the officer, " 'I don't think I deserve this medal because I was wounded by our own artillery.' His comment was 'Shut your fucking mouth and accept the decoration.' " Reichman also received a Bronze Star.

Two weeks after Reichman went down, Eichelberger

declared the eastern Mindanao operation ended. Nevertheless, armed Japanese continued to sporadically attack elements from the 24th, 31st, 40th, and 41st Divisions.

The 40th Division, exhausted from its Zambales Mountains labors on the left flank of the Lingayen Gulf invasion, had streamed back for a breather. "When we were relieved," says Paul Gerrish of the 40th Cavalry Recon, "none of us had been in a rest camp. We didn't know what to expect." On March 18, the 40th Recon went in with the first wave against a lightly defended beach at Tigbauan, Panay [the island where internee Betsy McCreary spent much of her youth].

The official estimates of the enemy strength on Panay reported only 2,750 Japanese defenders. Meanwhile, there were 22,500 guerrillas on the island, half of them armed, operating from the mountains. Many of these irregulars belonged to the Philippine Army of 1941–42 who refused to surrender and faded into the wilds where they lived off the land until the return of the Americans. While the 185th Infantry Regiment, supported by thousands of guerrillas, marched on the main city of Iloilo, Gerrish and the 40th Recon Troop headed out to seize the Santa Barbara Airport.

Near the town of Pavia, all of the platoons started receiving fire and the unit with Gerrish was surrounded. Division headquarters refused to believe any significant number of enemy could be involved since the infantry near Iloilo had seemingly trapped the bulk of the defenders. "I couldn't help wonder," says Gerrish, "if we weren't destined to join such immortals as the Spartans at Thermopolae, the Texans at the Alamo and General Custer's cavalry at the Little Big Horn, as the few who died fighting against impossible odds."

The troop commander summoned his 3rd Platoon to break through. "We heard the sound of heavy firing coming from the other side of the village," says Gerrish. "The 3rd Platoon drove right through the heaviest concentration of Japanese with all guns blazing. Some of the Jeep drivers managed to fire their tommy guns while steering their Jeep with one hand. Johnny Stapleton had more gas in his Jeep than the others and made several passes through the Nip positions and stopped only when he had expended all his ammunition."

The outfit broke out, learning that instead of being penned up in Iloilo as Division staff insisted, the bulk of the Japanese had passed through the U.S. lines the previous night and escaped towards the mountains, which may well have accounted for the amount of enemy that exchanged gunfire with the Recon Troop. Gerrish insists that his company-size organization faced at least eight hundred if not more. The fight for Panay, however, was over quickly as the invaders were content to allow the surviving Japanese to hide out in the mountains.

Simultaneously with the invasions of the other islands, the Americal Division struck at Cebu. For once the defenders could count on near equality of numbers. The understrength Americal, reinforced by roughly 8,500 guerrillas, would confront a garrison of about 14,500 Japanese. A second, unwelcome surprise for the invaders lay in the shallows in front of the undefended beaches. Extensive minefields transformed a smooth arrival into near chaos as two-thirds of the first wave of landing craft set off mines. Incoming traffic stalled behind the wrecked boats and a pile-up jammed the beaches. Had the enemy exploited the situation, the division would have suffered heavy losses. But wary of what U.S. seapower and aircraft could do to shore installations, the Japanese had retreated well inland.

Bob Manning, who won his commission while with the Americal Division's 132nd Regiment on New Caledonia, recalls a relatively easy beginning at Cebu. "Resistance was not intense although the beaches were heavily mined. Incoming artillery was sporadic. The main enemy force had pulled back to the center of the island and dug in for a long engagement."

John Cowee, a platoon leader and then company commander with the 132nd Regiment, had been a volunteer officer candidate immediately after Pearl Harbor. Hailing from Sheboygan, Wisconsin, Cowee's involvement in a war materials business might have qualified him for an exemption from service had he applied for one. Having spent roughly a year as an instructor at Fort Benning after he secured his commission, Cowee served briefly on Bougainville and New Guinea before his Leyte tour of duty.

"While the men in my company may not have 'loved' me, I believe they respected me. I never had any insubordination, desertion or instances of cowardice. I could never crawl off, walk off, eat or go to relieve myself without at least several of them going with me, weapons at the ready. When I would move to the front, they would say, 'Here's Rugged,' which seemed to be their private way of describing or identifying me.

"The terrain in the Philippines was rugged and hostile itself. It varied from thick, heavy undergrowth to almost barren hill and mountain sides that once were volcanic. Tactical fire support, both ground and air, were really quite good. Dive bombers were able to fly in towards the mountains, pull up sharply after releasing bombs that were aimed at Japanese artillery withdrawn on tracks back into caves. Those were not destroyable by normal bombing or the usually artillery trajectories. Ultimately the remaining ones were silenced by flamethrowers, grenades and individual combat."

On April 19, Cowee and a rifle squad advanced in search of machine gun positions to support a full-scale attack by his company. An enemy counterattack cut him and the squad off from the rest of the outfit. The official citation awarding Cowee a Bronze Star reads: "He made a personal reconnaissance under intense enemy rifle and machine gun fire to determine a route to safety. One of the men in the squad was seriously wounded and could be moved only at the risk of his life. Lieutenant Cowee sent the squad to safety along the route he previously found and he alone stayed with the wounded man until the man died. Several times a group of enemy came within a few feet of Lieutenant Cowee searching for him. After dark, Lieutenant Cowee was moving to a more secure position when he came upon an enemy machine gun and killed the gunner. All through the night, Lieutenant Cowee stayed in that area and took notes on the number, disposition, weapons and direction of movement of the enemy. The next day he returned to his company. The information he gathered was valuable to the battalion when the company at a later date pursued the enemy."

After Panay and while the GIs pursued the remnants of the defenders on Cebu, the 8th Army designated Negros Island for assault. A considerably large enemy force occupied Negros—as many as fifteen thousand with four thousand rated as combat effective. The 40th Division and the 503rd Parachute Regiment, staging at Mindoro, were committed to the operation. "We received another large infusion of replacements fresh from jump school in the States," says Rod Rodriguez. "They were in awe of the veterans and perhaps horrified with the human skulls that some displayed in front of our tents as mementos of Corregidor. Above all, I felt sorry for them because they never had the opportunity for bonding together as we did during those weeks in the 'frying pan' area at Fort Benning."

The paratroopers expected to go in by air but the drop was aborted and they traveled to Negros by boat, arriving shortly after the 40th Division put its first men ashore on March 29. Neither outfit encountered any opposition during the landings. The local commander, Gen. Takeshi Kono, withdrew his forces into the mountains, conceding the coastal plain to the invaders.

Hugh Reeves, the 503rd Scout and close buddy of Rodriguez, recalls a night that began with him finishing off his foxhole and starting to apply mosquito repellant. Someone called out to him that a Japanese soldier had just come over the hill and now squatted behind a bush only thirty feet away. "As it was almost dark, we did not fire our weapons," says Reeves, "unless absolutely necessary because it would give away our exact position. We still had the five-second grenades and I jerked the pin out and made a perfect toss. You could follow the course of the grenade by the trail of sparks from the burning fuse, but just before the sparks got to the ground, they arced right back over the exact route I had pitched. I knew he had caught my grenade and returned it. All I could do was get as low in the foxhole as possible. The grenade went off, just as it touched the ground. I got some dents in my helmet and gravel all down my back. I was stone deaf with one heck of a headache for the next ten hours.

"I jerked the pin out of another grenade, held it almost three seconds, and tossed it. Evidently it went off just as he reached to catch it. They said he called 'Medic' all night long but I couldn't hear. The next morning Keith went out, finished him off, came back and offered me his saber. I said, 'no soap.' As a scout I wanted nothing that might hamper my movements or make a noise. Neither did I care for souvenirs."

The paratroopers slowly pushed into the mountains, working with tanks at first and meeting stalwart defenses. But after a firefight where one of the tanks ran afoul of a minefield, the Japanese retreated. "The minefield had given General Kono and his men time to slip away. We continued on up to the top of this mountain; Rodriguez and I were trying to find out where they went to. We discovered a rope tied to a bush on the east and steep side of the mountain. When we climbed down the rope we saw some twenty or more cave openings on the face of the cliff. We picked out one of the larger ones and climbed in. We found bunk beds, two high on either side of the cave. I lifted up the mattress on the first and there were some Japanese coins. Rod and I continued back into the winding cave for maybe 150 feet. There were candles placed at intervals. We went through several large rooms. One had all sorts of hardware supplies. Another had what I estimated to be 150-pound bombs they were cutting open to make explosives." The two scouts arranged for a demolition team to bring primer cord and a fuse that blew off the mountain top.

Replacements continued to trickle in. "One I remember in particular," says Rodriguez, "was so eager. He said he had a hard time getting the Army to take him because of his job, a young wife and a small kid. Then the morning we started up Hill 99 he came to me with his wallet in hand and said, 'Rebel, I have a strong premonition I am going to get killed soon.' This gave me a sickening feeling because he was the fifth man to come to me like that and all had died soon after. I tried to convince him it wasn't so since he had not even seen any combat yet. And as a forward scout, I was much more apt to get hit than he was, but that I had bought me a round-trip ticket before I left home. Besides, only the chaplain could send or handle his personal stuff. I wondered why these men came to me with those premonitions—as a scout my life was rated at about eight seconds once enemy gunfire opened up.

"About halfway up the mountain, the officer in charge asked me to drop back and relieve the man carrying a case of grenades. I always traveled as light as possible and was stronger than most. About six hundred yards up the trail the officer, anticipating an ambush, had us swing off while going through some lantana grass. A Nip appeared in front with a white flag, then suddenly fell forward with a machine gun on his back—an old trick. His man behind him opened up at about a hundred yards, killing my new recruit instantly. The officer called back to me, but by the time I got there, the Nips had disappeared. I had two more men come to me with the same feeling. All were killed within two weeks of their declarations."

Reeves stayed on that hill for more than two weeks and during that period three different men were killed in his foxhole. "The first man, I was asleep and he fell on top of me during his turn to watch. I was never able to locate the sniper. The next replacement must have just stood up. I heard the rifle report after the bullet struck. I located that sniper in a tree branch about five hundred yards off. When

I shot, he dropped his rifle and swung head down for the rest of the day. He had tied a rope around his waist. The last man killed in that foxhole was my BAR gunner. He was stationed in the foxhole to my right and asked to jump over and talk. What I didn't know was that sometime during the night some Nips had come about midway down a clean slope, three hundred yards directly in front of me. When my BAR man was squatting on his heels facing me, the bullet went completely through his helmet." Reeves spied what he believed were helmets that looked like rocks amid some weeds. He instructed the machine guns to line up on the weeds. "I took my machete and sliced a Vee in my parapet, took Kentucky windage to the right of the weed and squeezed off a round. One Nip raised up, pitched forward on his face. Two more jumped up and ran for the woods. They never made it."

In northern Luzon, Yamashita still had fifty thousand troops at his disposal. But they occupied an ever shrinking area of mountainous jungle, and malnutrition stalked them as fiercely as it had the defenders three years before on Bataan. Cletus Schwab, rising in the ranks of the 37th Division with a battlefield commission earned during the fighting in Manila, recovered from shrapnel in the legs and became an acting company commander. He pursued the foe almost to Aparri, the northern site of the earliest landings by the Japanese in 1941.

Although men continued to bleed and die in the increasingly isolated engagements, the war against Japan for the seagoing Americans had shifted away from the Philippines. The huge American naval forces once gathered around the archipelago now plied waters much closer to Japan. The *Cabot*, with pilots like Bill Anderson who had participated in the Leyte Gulf battles, sailed in the armada destined for Okinawa. Anderson and his torpedo/bomber compadres helped sink the *Yamato*, the huge dreadnought that once menaced the 7th Fleet. Repaired in record time after being struck by the suicide planes, the *Suwannee*, with a new air group that replaced pilots like Tex Garner and Jack Smith, also fought in the Okinawa area. While navigator Bill Dacus remained on the *Suwannee*, Erich Kitzmann, the aircraft handler blown overboard by the *kamikaze* explosion and picked up by another ship, accepted an honorable discharge for "psychoneurosis," due to the stress of his experience. The destroyer *Moale*, with radarman Russ Catardi on board, fired in support of the Iwo Jima landing and acted as one of the picket ships threatened by *kamikazes* off Okinawa. After his injuries when the *Cooper* sank off Ormoc underneath him, George Berlinger was discharged in May 1945. The more seriously injured Al Masulis underwent operations and extended hospitalization.

On Luzon and the other islands, combat on land petered out. It had become a war of attrition with the last chapter the scheduled invasion of Japan itself. There were no large battles like those that occurred during the early days of the Luzon invasion and within Manila. Instead, small groups of men participated in deadly exchanges with defenders who were being forced ever deeper into the mountains, bereft of overall command and control, increasingly short of ammunition and food. After victory in Europe, the American forces could expect an influx of reinforcements. By June 1945 thousands of soldiers had begun redeployment from Germany to duty in the Pacific. Because of the availability of these resources, the Army had also begun to ship back some of the veterans like Emil Matula who left for home in June. Paul Austin, after a forty-five-day furlough, opted to transfer to a training unit in the States. Malaria and other fevers forced evacuation of John Higgins of the 169th and Dick Cohen from the Americal Division. Strictly by chance, a depressed Joe Hoffrichter, on his way back to the job of a combat infantryman, enountered an officer from his former behind-the-lines engineer battalion and happily accepted an opportunity to transfer back. Many old-timers like Hans Rants, however, were still expected to participate in the invasion of Japan.

As American adolescents achieved their eighteenth birthday, another source of reinforcement refilled the ranks. When the youths reported for military duty, most of the able-bodied, upon completion of their basic training, went to the Pacific as fresh troops for the final assault upon the Imperial Empire. The surrender by Emperor Hirohito on August 15 after the detonation of two atomic bombs brought a brief period of uncertainty before the surviving Japanese officers in the Philippines, the one area with ongoing combat, accepted their nation's defeat. But because the bulk of the more than one hundred thousand enemy troops spread through the Philippines were hiding out in inaccessible areas, the roundup and disarmament of them posed some problems.

Donald Dill, one of the new recruits to the 32nd Division, joined the 126th Infantry Regiment as a radio operator. "My only combat experience was a very distant machine gun and brief, but not brief enough for my tastes, mortar attack," says Dill. Even at the late date at which he arrived in the Philippines, Dill had been appalled by the sight of a truck loaded with dead American soldiers, covered with tarpaulins, their muddy boots sticking out from underneath, mute testimony that the fighting continued.

Unlike most of the Japanese military leaders, Yamashita, with some fifty thousand soldiers under his command and nominally still resisting at the time of the capitulation, saw no reason to commit suicide. Dill witnessed the defeated general being escorted from his mountain hideout by GIs. "However," says Dill, "his army did not follow and our commanders assumed that his troops were too sick or burdened with so many wounded men that they were afraid of the long trip down to the surrender point, a small town name Kyangan.

"I volunteered as radio operator to accompany one of several patrols sent to bring medicine into the mountains to get these men out. A three-day march through the most exotic wild jungles anyone might imagine brought us to the Yamashita headquarters, which was under the com-

mand of General Ishi, the chief surgeon I believe. The staff
sergeant who led our patrol had such bitter memories of
the fighting with the Japanese that he refused to talk with
the general. It seemed like a silly waste to me to have
hauled all those medical supplies such a long way and then
refuse to even discuss our mission. In any event, I took the
bull by the horns and said I would meet the general and
explain our mission in the sergeant's stead.

"General Ishi was a small, portly and dignified man with
shiny boots and a spangled chest, who must have been
amused or perhaps even offended at having to deal with a
lowly corporal. However, he bowed formally and we sat
down beneath a small palm-roofed ramada and discussed
the situation through his interpreter for all the world like
big-time diplomats.

"I explained that our officers were afraid that many of
his men were wounded or sick and might be reluctant to
make the long trek to Kyangan and we had brought medical supplies to aid them. The general, through an interpreter, a colonel who spoke excellent English, said that
although he appreciated our long journey with medical
supplies, it was food that was the problem. His soldiers
were fearful they were too weak from short rations to make
the long and dangerous trip back and many would die
before reaching Kyangan. I promised the general I would
pass this on to our officers via the radio. A small plane
visited us, usually twice a day for messages, and I relayed
the information to the pilot. We received a reply on the
plane's next trip telling me to inform the general that at
10:00 A.M. the following day, food rations would be
dropped in the area. On the next day, it looked like the
war all over again as cargo planes filled the sky and ration
cases came raining down like hailstones—no parachutes.

"Our patrol left several days later for our march back.
When next we saw Kyangan, which had been virtually
empty when we left, it was now lined with tents, stretching
from mountainside to mountainside, filled with surrendered Japanese. At this point I realized I was ill cast as a

warrior and instead felt proud that these men had peace-ably surrendered and not perished in the mountains of Luzon. Our officers were in apparently such great haste to bring Yamashita to justice and make an example of him, that no one bothered to ask him why his men had not followed him."

On this note, with its stark and ironic contrast to what had happened to the American defenders taken prisoner during the first six months of the war, the struggle between the opposing armies ended.

CHAPTER XXVII

MOPPING UP

WHILE TENS OF THOUSANDS of GIs from the Philippine campaign debarked at Japanese ports to perform occupation duty, the prisoners seized by the Japanese and transported to the Asian mainland awaited repatriation. Clifford Bluemel, one of the first captives taken from the Philippines, recorded the events of his final days at Karenko, Manchuria. On August 15, he noted the death of a colonel from tuberculosis and then wrote: "All factory workers were sent in about 11:00 A.M. PWs from outlying camps commenced moving in. Something has happened. Much excitement in camp. Some say the war is over. Won a small bet that we would be PWs today."

On the following day, Bluemel and his companions watched parachutes descend several miles away. "Impossible to tell if Jap, American or Russian. About 3:30 P.M. five or six men in flying suits arrived in the compound. They were taken to headquarters. Officer who saw them cannot determine if they are Russians or Americans." On August 17, Bluemel recorded, "word of an Armistice between Japan, the United States, Britain . . . we are still PWs and the Japs would retain control and protect us." Bluemel learned that the parachutists themselves narrowly escaped execution. Japanese soldiers stripped the airborne visitors, stood them against a wall and were about to shoot them until a Nisei interpreter persuaded the troops to obtain an audience with a higher-up.

Soviet Army troops actually liberated Bluemel and his fellow prisoners. "One wore gold shoulder straps," said Bluemel. "He addressed the crowd through an American sergeant who acted as interpreter [a member of the parachute team]. He said 'The Russian Red Army congratulates the American Army on its victory and from this minute you're free.' Such yelling and cheering!"

A ceremony followed with the POWs lined up and the camp garrison in formation. "The Jap enlisted men laid their rifles on the ground, also their belts, bayonets and cartridge boxes. The officers laid their sabers and pistols on the ground. Colonel Matsuyido gave the command, *'Sa Keri,'* and all made a prolonged bow to the emperor. The Russian [Bluemel apparently believed that label applied to all Soviet citizens] officer who made the freeing speech then announced through the interpreter that the arms of the Jap guards were being turned over to the American guards. He then gave General Parker a Jap pistol. The American guards then picked up the Jap rifle belts, bayonets and cartridge boxes. They were formed by General Beebe and counted off. The Russian then announced the Japs would be paraded past the Americans. It was now dark. The Japs faced to the right and with American enlisted men armed with Jap rifles, the prisoners were marched past their former prisoners."

Harold Johnson, who had survived the sinking of the *Oryoku Maru,* was in a camp at Inchon, Korea, at the time of the surrender. "On August 17," said Johnson, "the Japanese informed us the war was over and stopped guarding the camp. I was called to Japanese headquarters and handed a large stack of Korean money. As POWs, officers received the same pay as a Japanese officer of equal rank. I was short one hundred thousand *kwan* but that money went into their postal savings [and helped finance the Japanese war effort]." On August 22, a B-29 dropped food and supplies. A parachute team arrived two weeks later and on September 7, 7th Division troops came to arrange repatriation of the captives. John Olson, who volunteered for a labor party in 1943, was freed at a navy base on the west coast of Japan. He collected fifteen hundred yen, about a hundred dollars at the time.

While the last of the captives headed for home and MacArthur turned his attention to the task of an occupation that would transform Imperial Japan into a Western-style democracy, the Allies, as they had in Europe, conducted war crimes trials. Investigations uncovered documents that suggested a policy of murder. One paper instructed, "When killing Filipinos, assemble them together in one place as far as possible, saving ammunition and labor." The war crimes prosecutor introduced a statement from the commander of the 16th Imperial Japanese Army Division, Lt. Gen. Sasumu Morioka, that encouraged the killing of prisoners taken on the battlefield, including even those who submitted prior to the battle. The same authorities also cautioned that the actions should be handled with some circumspection "so as not to excite public feeling."

A number of diaries written by Japanese soldiers described mass murders, shootings, bayonettings, and burnings of victims. The prosecution provided evidence of 131,028 murders of Filipinos and Americans committed during the Japanese occupation. In most instances, those who tortured, raped, and killed escaped trial because they died in the futile defense of their occupation. Held accountable were both General Homma, the conqueror of Bataan, and General Yamashita, the ultimate defender against the liberation forces. No one could pinpoint actual deeds by either of the officers. The issue was whether a superior should be held respnsible for the crimes of subordinates.

Homma, relieved of his command in June 1942 because of dissatisfaction with the length of time he required to conquer Bataan, was still in charge at the time of the Death March. There was evidence that Homma had admonished his staff to see that all prisoners were to be treated "in a friendly spirit." However, he apparently made no attempt to see that his instructions were carried out. Nor, when it was learned that the number taken captive far exceeded the estimates, did Homma inquire whether there were adequate resources for handling them. The tribunal sentenced him to death along with a general and colonel on his staff.

The judges meted out a life sentence to Yoshio Tsuneyoshi, the O'Donnell camp commander known as "Baggy Pants," an implacable hater of Caucasians, and the man the captives viewed as most directly responsible for the wretched conditions. John Olson, a survivor of the Death March and O'Donnell, believes Homma, preoccupied with his military efforts against Corregidor, deserved a better fate, particularly in light of the mercy extended to Tsuneyoshi.

Conviction brought a hanging sentence to Yamashita, who in his role as the "the Tiger of Malaya" bore the blame for the brutal treatment of prisoners taken there as well as for the incidents in the Philippines. As in the case of Homma, there was little evidence to show he directed the campaign of terror waged against Filipinos during his three years of suzerainty or that he condoned the maltreatment of the prisoners. The atrocities, largely committed by the Japanese Naval Defense Force during the siege of Manila, were beyond his control. Admiral Iwabuchi, who commanded those Japanese guilty of the offenses, was killed during the battle for the city. When interrogated, Yamashita explained that he realized Manila was ill suited for defensive purposes and, had he been able to extricate all of his men in time, he would have declared it an open city as MacArthur had done.

But Yamashita was in charge for a sufficient period of time to be aware of the miserable conditions in the prison and internment camps, and of the reign of terror instituted and ostensibly aimed at guerrillas. If the principle that a commander is personally responsible for the acts of those beneath him—the other side of the defensive coin, "I was only following orders"—then the sentence upon him met the test of the times. Two members of the U.S. Supreme Court criticized the verdict. Justice Frank Murphy, a former prosecutor himself, commented, "The spirit of revenge and retribution, masked in formal legal procedure for the purposes of dealing with a fallen enemy commander, can do more lasting harm than all of the atrocities giving rise to that spirit." His colleague, Wiley Rutledge, called the tribunal "no trial in the tradition of the common law and the Constitution." The ultimate decision whether to execute Yamashita lay with President Harry Truman, who refused to commute his sentence.

During the war, the Japanese had specifically denied any obligation to follow the strictures of the Geneva Convention. That stance opened the way for much of the abuse, which was further fostered by the disdain for a foe who did not follow a replica of their own *Bushido* code that honored death as a warrior rather than surrender. Arndt Mueller, the 6th Division battalion commander, remarks, "The difference between the national psychology of the West versus East (represented by the Japanese) was dramatically demonstrated by the suicidal *banzai* charges and by the individual suicides when we overran a position. In Europe the enemy surrendered, sometimes in large units, when the situation appeared hopeless. Not so the Japanese. No unit ever surrendered to us—not even when they were completely out of ammunition. It was not unusual for Japanese commanders to leave small suicidal units behind when and if they withdrew." Westerners did surrender in Asia as well as in Europe. There was no disgrace attached to a commander or his troops if they did so when the situation became hopeless, as was the case with Bataan and Corregidor. Wainwright received a Medal of Honor after the war.

In light of their beliefs it is possible to explain the contempt exhibited by the Japanese conquerors towards those military forces who capitulated. However, the warrior code calls for mercy to the conquered, which would certainly require attention to the needs of military prisoners in terms of food, sanitation, and basic medical care. Furthermore, the physical abuse and killings meted out during the Death March were hardly compatible with the concept of mercy. Deaths of prisoners in the hands of the Japanese ran almost ten times higher than it did for those who were captives of the Germans. What happened to U.S. and Filipino military people after the collapse of the Bataan defense and the fall of Corregidor was at best outrageous indifference and at worst extreme cruelty.

That the Japanese took no prisoners after the Allies began to roll back their advance island by island is understandable if not excusable. A garrison in the Solomons, New Guinea or the Marianas, cut off from the homeland, could argue it had no means to accommodate prisoners whose care and feeding would tie up manpower and seriously interfere with the ability to defend an area. Indeed, some Americans involved in the Normandy D-Day landings recall unwritten instructions not to take prisoners during the critical first three days because doing so could jeopardize operations. However, this condition was not a factor in the Japanese conquest of the Philippines during 1941–42.

As any number of GIs have testified in this book, the American forces also rarely took prisoners. Although U.S. higher-ups in search of intelligence—not for reasons of mercy—constantly urged the taking of prisoners, they were foiled by the unwillingness of the soldiers. The foremost reason given was an inability to trust the surrender as genuine. In too many instances, the enemy pretended to give up only to strike a final blow. The widespread use of the ruse indicates it was taught to the enemy soldiers.

Certainly, some Japanese who tried to surrender were killed for revenge spurred by the loss of close friends and the evidence of atrocities. The denigration of the enemy as "little yellow bastards" from the top brass down just made the killing easier. The savagery visited upon those trudging towards internment or suffering within the confines of a prison camp during the period of Japanese victories, however, was a different matter. And when the tide turned and they were able to do so, American officers exercised some control over men who would have murdered their prisoners.

Bushido principles hardly account for the widespread rape, torture and murder of civilians, particularly since Imperial Japan propagandized that it would free Asia from the oppressive colonialism of the West. In addition, the conduct of the Japanese soldiers towards the peoples whose land they occupied defies the notion of *Bushido*, which stresses self-discipline. U.S. soldiers frequently commented on the discipline exhibited by their opposite numbers. They followed orders without much question, far more so than their American adversaries. Yet the slaughter of innocents and the vicious assaults upon soldiers and civilians indicates an absence of self-discipline. It is not far-fetched to speculate that the often brutal treatment of Japanese soldiers by their own superiors bred an anger and frustration that engulfed the helpless prisoners and local people. Whatever the source of the behavior, the upper echelons showed little inclination to suppress it.

To the Japanese, Americans had then, as now, a reputation for lawlessness and violence. But when the Japanese surrendered in large numbers, there was no question about the Americans providing adequate food, shelter, and sanitation. Nor did U.S. authorities permit abuse of either prisoners or the civilian population during the occupation of Japan.

The discipline of the Japanese soldier was both an asset and a failing in battle. Arndt Mueller believes, "Their tactics were governed by their concept of dedication to the Emperor. In one captured document they apologetically asserted that the reason for failure to execute the plan of operation successfully was because of lack of dedication to the Emperor and they must persist in order to vindicate their spiritual shortcoming. This attitude on the part of their officer corps was of great advantage to us because of the predictability of their actions." The American GI, less amenable to authority, sometimes flouting the rules, was far more able to function on his own, to improvise when the situation changed or the intelligence proved faulty. Men would refuse to move out if they realized the orders meant suicide and they voiced their opposition, as occurred at Zig Zag Pass.

Unconditional victory in the Pacific ended any possibility of nasty inquiries into why the Philippines fell during the first six months of the war. Court-martials flogged Admiral Husband E. Kimmel and General Walter Short, the two commanders at Pearl Harbor, for nonfeasance but nothing similar was even suggested for those in charge in the Philippines. It was easy enough to finger Kimmel and Short on the simple grounds they failed to maintain a proper alert. Their "crime" was a sin of omission connected to a single event.

The matter of MacArthur was much more complicated. The six months in which the twenty thousand Americans and their Filipino associates under MacArthur's command fought off the invaders gave the general an opportunity to refurbish his name. He was restored as a hero by the time he left Corregidor for Australia. Any suggestion that he was of lesser stuff might have besmirched the men trapped in the Philippines.

MacArthur was guilty of poor judgment in thinking that he could create an army sufficient to deter the forces of Japan. He compounded his error by flip-flopping on the defensive strategy. That in turn added to the logistical collapse. But any attempt to condemn MacArthur would have inevitably raised questions about the prime movers in Washington, D.C. Congress had refused to provide the barest amounts to fund an adequate Philippine force. Nor did the administration of Franklin Roosevelt forcefully argue the case. A full-scale investigation would have embarrassed many more than MacArthur.

Whatever MacArthur's failings before the invasion of the Philippines he waged a winning war that liberated the archipelago as well as the other islands occupied by the Japanese in the southwestern Pacific. Where possible, he stuck to the old baseball philosophy expressed to Clare Luce, "Hit 'em where they ain't," to minimize casualties. His decision to attack the Philippines undoubtedly was influenced by a sense of debt to the indigenous people there and the prisoners, but strategically it made good sense. The alternative to this campaign, advocated by Admiral King, would have bypassed the archipelago for targets closer to Japan. Even with the Philippines absorbing huge amounts of the enemy's resources as a result of MacArthur's operations, the subsequent assaults upon Iwo Jima and Okinawa commanded by Nimitz produced horrendous losses. Furthermore, Operation Iceberg, the invasion of Okinawa, was staged largely from the Philippines. Without the facilities there, the assault on the Ryukyus could have been even more costly. On the other hand, there seems no point to the invasions of Mindanao, Cebu, Negros and the other southern islands except for a desire to replant the flag and relieve the local population of the Japanese presence. The campaigns there liberated relatively few and, although enemy losses were far greater, the American troops in the Visayans area suffered significant casualties.

Aside from his generalship, MacArthur deftly manipulated people important to the war effort. To his chief of staff he remarked, "I have to fight the War Department, the Navy, the Prime Minister of Australia, the newspapers and all you have to do is fight the war." Sutherland noted, "Nobody could have handled Quezon the way he did." Although the Australian Prime Minister John Curtin chafed over his perception of the British attitude towards defense of his land, MacArthur won him over. While the Down Under politician addressed him with the respectful title of "General," MacArthur responded with the informal "John," thus asserting his superiority through the simple weapon of nomenclature. Walter Kreuger, "a detail man" according to Sutherland, said of his superior, "He can see farther on the horizon than any man I know."

Nevertheless, Navy people have denigrated Mac-

Arthur's abilities as a commander, perhaps in reaction to his adroit exploitation of publicity. Almost to a man they sneer at his belief that the Philippines were defensible. John Bulkeley, the PT skipper who brought the general out of Corregidor, is one of the rare Navy men to support MacArthur. Of MacArthur's detractors, he says, "They don't see the big picture. The most important thing I did in the war was bringing MacArthur and his staff out. That turned the tide of the war." Curiously, Bulkeley agrees with MacArthur's critics that the Philippines could not have been saved.

The verdict on their leader from the troops in his army is mixed. Joe Hoffrichter claims he realized as early as his days on Hollandia "what a brilliant commander General MacArthur was." Han Rants grudgingly voiced approval. "We had disliked him with passion because we felt that he should rotate the troops and send home some of the old-timers who had seen so much combat time. We disliked him because we thought he had no feeling for the troops. In reality, looking back, he wanted the best possible team he could put on the field for combat. His skill and ingenuity here [referring to the fight for Mindanao] made us almost like him." Tales of MacArthur's riches and land holdings in the Philippines circulated among the servicemen, but no one has ever shown that he had anything material to gain either in the defense or the liberation.

It was, of course, the soldier on the line who fought the war under MacArthur. In the fifty years since WW II, analysts and scholars have attempted to analyze and understand the behavior of the combat soldier. One well-publicized account by an official army historian, S. L. A. Marshall, claimed that only a small percentage of infantrymen actually fired their weapons. That startling announcement proved to be based upon a skewed, even fictitious survey. The interviews with the sources for this book indicate that only a desire to avoid giving away a position kept fingers off triggers.

More recently, *On Killing: The Psychological Cost of*

Learning to Kill in War and Society, by Lt. Col. David Grossman, explores the willingness of men to take the lives of the enemy. The author suggests that with each succeeding war GIs shoot more and show less compunction about killing. Leaving aside the greater firepower of the current M-16 rifle compared with WW II's M-1, the experiences of the soldiers in the Philippines hardly squares with such a thesis. Although no one has been able to separate out the number of dead due to artillery, air strikes, flamethrowers or mortars, it seems clear that of the roughly three hundred thousand Japanese soldiers killed in the Philippines a substantial total died from individual soldiers firing rifles or machine guns with deadly intent. The small number of prisoners taken, even when due allowance is made for those relatively few willing to yield, is further evidence of a willingness to kill. Although some like Whayland Greene and Joe Hoffrichter, to name a pair, initially expressed queasiness, the experience of enemy fire and the deaths of fellow GIs swiftly snuffed out regard for the Sixth Commandment. It should also be noted that an overwhelming percentage of those questioned supported the use of the atomic bombs. Whether nuclear devastation was necessary to end the war is not the issue; rather that because of their own experiences, these Americans approved the use of a weapon of mass destruction.

Some commanded, some provided leadership, some followed, some faltered, some overcame their fear and others succumbed to it. But in the main the defense and then the liberation of the Philippines, as demonstrated by the voices of this book, confirms that American soldiers accepted what the nation demanded, no matter what ethnic strains, economic or social strata, education or religious background they came from or how dirty, hungry, exhausted, disease-ridden, and wracked with the stress of battle they were.

ROLL CALL

Adair, Charles. Naval officer assigned to command staff of U.S. Asiatic Fleet, 1941. He retired as a Rear Admiral and is deceased.

Alexander, Irvin. Quartermaster officer transferred to 71st Division, Philippine Army in 1942, and held prisoner until 1945. Alexander returned to active duty only to be forced into retirement after an automobile accident. He is deceased.

Austin, Paul. Captain and battalion staff officer with the 24th Division. Austin worked as a manager for the telephone company until retirement. "I was sick to my stomach, of all those who'd been killed or got wounded. But that's the infantry story. You take the mud, the pain, do without food, do without water and you keep fighting." He now lives in Fort Worth.

Banker, Curtis. Crewman on a self-propelled gun for the 43rd Division. Banker, after a brief period as a civilian, reenlisted in 1947, drove a tank in the Korean War and served at a variety of military posts until he retired in 1963. He lives in upper New York State.

Benitez, R.C. Executive officer on the *Dace*, part of a two-sub wolfpack that discovered enemy ships headed for Leyte Gulf. He retired as a rear admiral.

Bernheim, Eli, Jr. Paratroop officer with the 11th

Airborne. Bernheim remained in the Army, did a combat tour in Korea and had stateside duty during the
Vietnam War. He retired as a colonel and, after a career
in business, now lives in Florida.

Berlinger, George. Gunnery crewman on the destroyer
Cooper sunk off Ormoc in 1944. Berlinger was recalled
from the reserves while a college student and served a
twenty-one-month tour on a destroyer during the Korean War. Subsequently, he went into business and now
lives in Michigan.

Berryhill, Carlie. Infantryman with the 6th Division. Berryhill made the Army his life's work, serving in Vietnam
and retiring in 1973 as a sergeant major. He then held a
civil service job for ten years before settling down in
Texas.

Bluemel, Clifford. Commander of the 31st Philippine Division in 1941, he continued his military career until
retirement as a major general. In 1947 he wrote to Gen.
Robert Eichelberger, "In my opinion, they [the Japa-
nese] are a race which is a detriment to the peace of the
world. They would rather lie than tell the truth when
the truth would benefit them more. It will take at least
three generations for the war idea which has been so
thoroughly and completely permeated by the Japanese
nation [*sic*] to be forgotten." He is deceased.

Braswell, Woody. Replacement noncom with the 24th
Division. Braswell, wounded by a grenade on Mindanao, heard about the A-bomb while in a Georgia hospital. He worked at a Navy base for twenty-five years after
the U.S. Post Office rejected him because of a disability.
He makes his home in Jacksonville, Florida.

Brooks, George. A rifleman with the 96th Division.
Brooks, on recovering from his Leyte wound, participated in the invasion of Okinawa. After the war he
earned a degree in engineering. He lives in Kalamazoo,
Michigan.

Bulkeley, John D. Head of the PT squadron based in
Manila that carried the MacArthur party to Mindanao

in 1942 where they boarded B-17s for the flight to Australia. He later served in Europe, commanding a flotilla of PTs and trawlers prowling the English Channel on the eve of D-Day, then served aboard the cruiser *Houston* in the Pacific. Bulkeley's active duty with the Navy, including special missions, added up to sixty-four years before he retired as a vice admiral to his home in Maryland.

Bunker, Paul. MacArthur's classmate at West Point, and a Corregidor coast artillery commander who in 1943 succumbed to disease and malnutrition in a Japanese prison camp.

Card, Charles. Infantry replacement with the 24th Division. Card took advantage of the GI Bill to attend Ohio University and was employed by various companies in both production and in human resources. He resides in Houston.

Catardi, Russ. Gunnery crewman on the *Moale* during the battle of Ormoc in 1944. As a civilian he was employed by a manufacturer and now lives in Glenside, Pennsylvania.

Chaplin, Ernest. Forward observer for the 150th Field Artillery Battalion. Chaplin became the superintendent of a paper pulp plant and now lives in North Carolina.

Cohen, Dick. Infantry officer with the Americal Division. Cohen later participated in the Korean War, was wounded and on recovery learned that one-third of his battalion had been captured. He brought home a Silver Star, Bronze Star and Purple Heart and, after attending General Staff College, served in Germany. With two small children and a wife to support, Cohen quit the military after twelve years of active duty and took over the family retail flower business. He then worked for the Pennsylvania state government as a rehabilitation counselor dealing with the handicapped. He lives in Upper Darby, Pennsylvania.

Coleman, Art. Amtrac gunner. After the war he took a job with the Letterkenny Army depot at Chambersburg,

Pennsylvania, and retired as a production controller in 1979. His home is in Shippensburg, Pennsylvania.

Coleman, Ken. Signalman on an LSM. He lives in Newburg, Pennsylvania.

Cowee, John. Platoon leader and company commander with the Americal Division. After the war he completed work for advanced degrees, including a PhD at the University of Wisconsin. He then taught and administered in the education field. Cowee, among the few to oppose the use of the A-bombs, retired to Aurora, Colorado.

Creel, Buck. Executive officer with an infantry company in the 96th Division, he was involved in the Okinawa campaign. Creel stayed in the Army and went to Korea and Vietnam before retiring as a colonel. He lives in Arlington, Virginia.

Dacus, Bill. Navigation specialist on the carrier *Suwannee*. He completed studies in liberal arts at Morgan Park Junior College in Chicago and put in a career with a paper manufacturing company before retiring to Pine City, Minnesota.

DeGaetano, Sal. Rifleman with the 1st Cavalry Division. DeGaetano worked for the Post Office for twenty-five years, then full-time as a bartender until 1993 when emphysema forced him off the job. He lives in Brooklyn, New York.

Dennison, Robert Lee. Navy officer assigned in 1941 to liaison with MacArthur and his staff, he was evacuated on a submarine in 1942. He retired as an admiral and is deceased.

Dill, Donald. Replacement with the 32nd Division. He resides in St. Louis, Missouri.

Diller, Eric. Infantryman with the 24th Division. Prior to his official discharge he was finally granted American citizenship. After advanced education in engineering, he became involved in NASA programs. When the aerospace industry fell into decline, Diller entered real estate sales and management. He resides in Redondo Beach, California.

Feddersen, Richard. Company commander with the 41st Division. Federsen maintained contact with former Filipino guerrillas he trained to become officers. Their letters after the war bitterly complain of a peace in which former collaborators prosper while those who fought the occupation received no benefits and were shut out of the economic recovery. Upon discharge, Feddersen operated an automobile dealership and farm in Iowa. He lives in North Liberty, Iowa.

Fiedler, Norman. Rifleman, 96th Division. After leaving the service he became an attorney and lives in Greenburgh, New York.

Fitch, Alva. Artillery officer with the Philippine Army in 1941. Fitch, after liberation, rose to the rank of lieutenant general and is deceased.

Frankel, Stanley. Staff officer with the 37th Division. Frankel entered public relations after the end of the war. His home is in Scarsdale, New York.

Fry, Philip. Infantry commander, 57th Philippine Scouts. Despite the cardiovascular disease that felled him on Bataan, he survived incarceration. He is deceased.

Gage, Tom. Air Corps clerk who arrived in the Philippines shortly before Pearl Harbor as a member of the 34th Pursuit Squadron. He survived the Death March, Camp O'Donnell and was in a camp 100 miles from Hiroshima. "The black smoke from Hiroshima came over our camp for three days." Gage has collected much information about Air Corps POWs and publishes an occasional newsletter on their experiences. He resides in Tulsa, Oklahoma.

Garner, Tex. Hellcat pilot on the *Suwannee*. Garner retains his license to fly and has been in business in Texas, making his home in Crockett.

George, Jean. The daughter of an Australian-born businessman, she was interned in June 1942 at Santo Tomas. Her fiancé, an American Army officer with the 31st Infantry, died in captivity and she subsequently married a fellow internee, Howard Stark. A widow since

1972, she lives in Bremerton, Washington, and maintains membership in the American Ex-POWs Association as well as the 1st Cavalry, 44th Tank and 31st Infantry Associations.

Gerrish, Paul. Communications specialist, 40th Cavalry Recon. After the war he was employed at a naval shipyard and then at federal power installations in the Paciifc northwest before retirement. He lives in Olympia, Washington.

Graef, Calvin. Air Corps ground crewman captured on Bataan. He survived the Death March and the sinking of his prisoner-of-war ship. Graef resides in Arizona.

Grashio, Sam. Pilot of a P-40 and captured on Bataan, he escaped from Mindanao and remained in service until he retired as a colonel.

Greene, Whayland. Rifleman with 32nd Division. After the war he operated a service station and used-car lot before retiring to grow tomatoes, which he does not sell but gives away. "It is my way of returning something to the town that gave me so much." He lives in Belcher, Louisiana.

Hall, Leonard. Rifleman, 43rd Division. He used the GI Bill to get a BS degree in both education and social sciences. At his own expense Hall obtained a master's degree in administration and supervision. He taught and worked as an administrator for thirty-one years.

Hansen, Ed. Rifleman, 37th Division. He earned a degree in engineering and worked for an agricultural machinery manufacturer for thirty-five years. Hansen defends the use of atomic bombs on Japan and is "very concerned about organized Japanese and American campaigns to rewrite history." He lives in Peoria, Illinois.

Hara, Min. Intelligence specialist, 6th Division. He reenlisted for one year with the Army of Occupation in Tokyo. "It has been forty-three years since that day [forced evacuation of Nisei in California to internment camp] and we still haven't had our day in court for our injust confinement." Hara resides in New York City.

Harrington, Mary Rose. Navy nurse captured in late December 1941 and liberated at the Los Banos camp. While interned she met Thomas Page Nelson, a U.S. Treasury official working in the Philippines, and they married after they returned to the States. They had four children after she resigned from the Navy. She lives in Virginia.

Hencke, John. Gunner with the 44th Tank Battalion. Hencke became a photographer and settled down in Highlands, Texas.

Higgins, John. Battalion staff officer, 43rd Division. Higgins retired from the Connecticut National Guard in January 1976 with the grade of colonel. He lives in Avon, Connecticut.

Hoffrichter, Joe. Rifleman, 24th Division. After rejoining his old engineer organization, he contracted hepatitis, nearly died from a misdiagnosis at a hospital and occupied a sickbed for three months. He returned to the family construction business and now lives in Port Charlotte, Florida.

Hostetter, Philip. Battalion surgeon, 24th Division. Hostetter retired from family practice in 1992 and lives in Manhattan, Kansas.

Howard, Tom. Crewman with 754th Tank Battalion. Howard went into industrial management and now lives in St. Charles, Missouri.

Kitzmann, Erich. Crewman on carrier *Suwannee*. He received a medical discharge in May 1945, six months after the *kamikaze* explosion blew him into the sea. Kitzmann worked in aircraft maintenance for more than thirty-three years before retiring to Sedona, Arizona.

Kurtz, Arden. Mortarman and machine gunner for the 43rd Division. Kurtz attended night school at Washington University in St. Louis for instruction in mechanical design. His home is in Brentwood, Missouri.

LaMagna, Sam. Infantryman, 43rd Division. LaMagna worked for a carpet company, an armory and finally at a post office in California. He retired to Ocala, Florida.

McClintock, D.H. Commander of the *Darter,* one of the two submarines that first made contact with the Japanese fleet steaming towards the Gulf of Leyte in 1944. He retired as a captain.

McCreary, Betsy. An American schoolgirl living in the Philippines, she was liberated from the Santo Tomas Internment Camp in 1945. After working in publishing for many years she retired in 1995 and lives in New York City.

McLaughlin, Bill. Recon trooper with the Americal Division. He graduated from Harvard with the help of the GI Bill, worked as a salesman and then set himself up as a broker in the paper business. He resides in Marston Mills, Massachusetts.

Mack, William. Destroyer officer stationed at Cavite in 1941. Mack later sailed to Java and then Australia on the *John Ford.* He retired as a vice admiral.

Mann, David. Platoon leader replacement with the 24th Division. He later served in Korea upon recall from the reserves. Mann worked in business and industry before switching to development at private colleges in Virginia, where he now lives.

Manning, Robert. Company commander, Americal Division. Manning went into business in the Chicago area. He lives in Flossmor, Illinois.

Margoshes, Marvin. Rifleman, 96th Division. Margoshes, with a PhD in physical chemistry, did research at Harvard Medical School, the National Bureau of Standards and two instrument companies, becoming president of a national scientific society. He lives in Tarrytown, New York.

Masucci, Gene. Quartermaster on the carrier *Cabot.* He finished high school, taught auto mechanics in the New York City schools, attended New York University and Hofstra for advanced degrees. "The mentality of the 'Ks' [*kamikazes*] and the suicidal events by both soldiers and civilians on many islands invaded by our Marines conjured up a vision of the Japanese as a maniacal race from whom victory would be achieved only at a very high price in human life. That thought alone justified the use of the bomb in my mind and fifty years later I still believe that this is so." Masucci retired as a director of school programs in occupational and technical education in a Long Island, New York, school district and now lives in Copiague Harbor, New York.

Matula, Emil. Platoon leader, 25th Division. Matula worked in sales for a soft drink company and a tea company. He retired in 1980 and lives in San Antonio, Texas.

Mercier, Don "Moe." Gunner, 44th Tank Battalion. He went to college on the GI Bill, taking a degree in accounting. "The atomic bombs gave us hope the Japanese invasion might not have to take place. We knew the Japs would all fight to the end. I was very upset with the Smithsonian Museum's Enola Gay display that presented the Americans as the aggressor and the Japanese as the victims. Thankfully, they did correct it." After thirty-one years of work he retired to live in Eau Claire, Wisconsin.

Miley, William "Buzz." Platoon leader and company commander in the 11th Airborne. Miley continued as a paratrooper with tours in Korea and Vietnam and was promoted to major and then lieutenant colonel. He was in the Army for thirty-one years before retirement and makes his home in Starkville, Mississippi.

Mitchell, John. Gun crewman on the carrier *Santee*. He followed his demobilization with "seven years of total unrest, a lot of drinking. I was suffering from combat fatigue, I suspect. I was too proud to turn myself into a VA hospital and I did it [came out of his funk] by myself." He studied thermodynamics at Pratt Institute and went into the air-conditioning business, moving eventually to California to become a manufacturers' representative. He lives in San Clemente, California.

Mueller, Arndt. Battalion commander, 6th Division. He continued his military career, attending the Command

and General Staff College as a student and then became a faculty member. After assignments to outfits like the 1st Infantry Division and the 101st Airborne, he closed out his military career as head of the ROTC program at the University of Miami. While there he obtained a law degree and became a member of the Florida Bar. His home is in Naples, Florida.

Murray, S.S. Commander of a submarine division as part of the Asiatic Fleet in 1941. Murray and a covey of subs sneaked beneath the enemy blockade to safety on New Year's Eve. He retired as an admiral and is deceased.

Olson, John. Staff officer with the 57th Philippine Scouts. Upon his liberation in 1945, elected to remain on the staff of the 8th Army to assist in the repatriation of prisoners. He retired as a colonel and then consulted for management and engineering firms. He also has done extensive research to produce books on the Scouts, the Death March and Camp O'Donnell, and a semifictional, semi-autobiographical novel about the war in the Philippines and the guerrilla movement. He lives in Houston, Texas.

Papazarian, Max. Infantry replacement, 32nd Division. He served as a member of the military police for several months during the occupation of Japan before being demobilized. He now lives in Fort Wayne, Indiana.

Pasternak, Alexander. Battalion surgeon, 41st Division. He hung out his shingle for general practice in 1946 after marrying his dentist, a female pioneer in a male-dominated field. His home is in Cleveland, Ohio.

Pearce, Milton. Platoon leader, 38th Division. He was a reporter for the Fall River *Herald* [Massachusetts] and later switched to photography. "No one in my barracks at Camp Wheeler had ever heard of Pearl Harbor. Following the attack, when I was on KP, some of us were sure we could send a couple of battleships over and blow 'that little island of Japan completely out of the water.' An old Army colonel warned us that Japan had been preparing for this for a long time, was well equipped with a tough army and this was going to be a long, hard war. None of us believed him." Pearce resides in Tiverton, Rhode Island.

Phillips, Philip B. Flight surgeon on the *Suwannee*. He was a doctor for twenty-two years in the Navy and then another thirty years in private practice. He makes his home in Pensacola, Florida.

Price, Bruce, Sr. Platoon leader, 24th Division. He became a salesman and credits his OCS training with helping him in his career. He retired to live in Anderson, South Carolina.

Rants, Han. Wireman, 24th Division. Rants returned to the Philippines for ceremonies marking the thirty-fifth anniversary of the Leyte invasion. "A group of Australians arrived and a group of about ten Japanese veterans also. I believe some of our Yanks and Aussies found it more difficult to accept and love the Japanese guests than the very people who suffered most at their hands." With an education degree from Washington State University, Rants taught in high school and then became a principal. He resides in Downey, California.

Reeves, Hugh. Paratrooper, 503rd Parachute Regiment. He worked in oil fields and then in sales. He makes his home in Yazoo City, Mississippi.

Reichman, Marvin. Replacement, 24th Division. Reichman was on occupation duty in Japan until October 1946. "I enjoyed being with the Japanese people. I learned to speak the language." Reichman was in the insurance business and he now lives in Chicago, Illinois.

Rodriguez, Rod. Paratrooper, 503rd Parachute Regiment. He persuaded the admissions office at the University of Georgia to enroll him in October 1945 even though the semester had started a month before. He completed the four-year degree program in three years, entered a master's program at Georgetown and did doctoral work at American University. "The war changed my life. I was no longer the smart-ass kid with a chip on his shoulder. I had considered staying in the service but wanted to understand much of what had happened." As a Senior Economist he specialized in Latin American affairs for the Department of Commerce, and then was a Senior Fellow at a think tank based in Washington, D.C. He lives in Arlington, Virginia.

Schwab, Cletus. Platoon leader, 37th Division. He now makes his home in New Bavaria, Ohio.

Seiler, Bob. Rifleman, 96th Division. He used a prewar course in watchmaking to enter a field in which he was employed for the next forty-four years. Seiler lives in Portland, Oregon.

Smith, Jack. Hellcat pilot on *Suwannee*. He remained in the Naval Reserve and was on the faculty of Iowa State University. He lives in Ames, Iowa.

Swing, Joe. Commanding general, 11th Airborne. Swing was appointed Commissioner of Immigration after he retired from the Army. He is deceased.

Sydiongco, Vicente. Guerrilla section leader. Sydiongco kept in touch with his U.S. comrades and eventually settled in Las Vegas, Nevada.

Teeples, Robert. Platoon leader, 32nd Division. He remained in the reserves and worked for a telephone company, then held the post of Director of Parks and Recreation in Black River Falls, Wisconsin, where he continues to live.

Ullman, Al. Medic, 11th Airborne. He followed a business career and was involved in local politics. He lives in Savannah, Georgia.

Ullom, Madeline. Army nurse interned at Santo Tomas. She continued to serve as a nurse until retirement as a lieutenant colonel and now lives in Tucson, Arizona.

Ward, Norvell. Junior officer aboard the submarine *Seadragon* in 1941, had narrowly missed injury or death during the bombing of Cavite and was still aboard as the sub made its way to the Dutch colony of Surabaya for repairs. Ward continued in the Navy and retired as a rear admiral.

Zimanski, Frank. Gunnery officer, *Cabot*. He held a variety of assignments in the Navy and served a tour of duty off Korea as a destroyer skipper. Zimanksi retired as a captain and his home is in Coronado, California.

BIBLIOGRAPHY

Alexander, Irvin. *Memoirs of Internment in the Philippines, 1942–1945* (West Point: U.S. Military Academy Library).

Belote, James H. and Wiliam M. *Corregidor: The Saga of a Fortress* (New York: Harper and Row, 1967).

Benitez, Lt. Com. R.C. *Battle Stations Submerged* (*U.S. Naval Proceedings,* January 1948).

Black, Robert W. *Rangers in World War II* (New York: Ivy Books, 1992).

Bluemel, Clifford. *Private Papers* (West Point: U.S. Military Academy Library).

Breuer, William. *The Great Raid on Cabanatuan* (New York: John Wiley & Sons, 1994).

Bunker, Paul Delmont. *The Bunker Diary* (West Point: U.S. Military Academy Library).

Cannon, M. Hamlin. *Leyte: Return to the Philippines, U.S. Army in World War II War in the Pacific* (Washington, D.C.: Center of Military History, U.S. Army, 1954).

Dacus, W.E. and E. Kitzmann. *As We Lived It—USS Suwannee (CVE-27)* (USS *Suwannee* and Its Air Groups 27, 60 & 40 Reunion Association, 1992).

Edmonds, Walter D. *They Fought with What They Had* (Washington, D.C.: Center for Air Force History, 1951).

Grashio, Samuel C. and Bernard Norling. *Return to Freedom* (Spokane, WA: University Press, 1982).

Halsey, Fleet Adm. William F. *The Battle for Leyte Gulf* (*U.S. Naval Institute Proceedings*, May 1952).

Hammel, Eric. *Munda Trail* (New York: Orion Books, 1989).

Hanson, Edwin. *Memoirs* (Unpublished manuscript).

Holloway, Adm. James L., III. *Historical Perspective: The Battle of Surigao Straits* (*Naval Engineer's Journal*, September 1994).

Hostetter, Dr. Philip H. *Doctor and Soldier in the South Pacific* (Unpublished manuscript).

Howard, Thomas. *All to This End: The Road to and Through the Philippines* (Unpublished manuscript).

Hudson, J. Ed. *The History of the USS Cabot (CVL–28)* (Hickory, NC, 1988).

Hall, Leonard G. *Brother of the Fox: Company F, 172nd Infantry* (Orange, TX, 1985).

Inoguchi, Rikihei, Tadashi Nakajima, and Robert Pineau. *The Divine Wind* (New York: Ballantine, 1958).

Ind, Allison. *Bataan: The Judgment Seat* (New York: Macmillan, 1944).

LaMagna, Sam. *Silent Victory: Fox Company, 169th Regimental Combat Team, 43rd Infantry Division* (Unpublished manuscript).

Lopez, Henry. *From Jackson to Japan* (New York, 1977).

MacArthur, Douglas. *Reminiscences* (New York: McGraw-Hill, 1964).

McClintock, Commander D.H. *Narrative* (Washington, D.C.: Typescript, U.S. Naval Historical Center, 1945).

McCreary, Betsy. *Interview Conducted by Rita Cumming Knox* (New York, 1992).

Manchester, William. *American Caesar* (Boston: Little, Brown, 1978).

Morison, Samuel Eliot. *History of United States Naval Operations in World War II. Vol 3, The Rising Sun in the Pacific* (Boston: Little, Brown, 1961).

Morison, Samuel Eliot. *History of United States Naval Op-*

erations in World War II. Vol 12, Leyte (Boston: Little, Brown, 1958).

Morison, Samuel Eliot. *History of United States Naval Operations in World War II. Vol 13, The Liberation of the Philippines: Luzon, Mindanao, the Visayas* (Boston: Little, Brown, 1959).

Morton, Louis. *The Fall of the Philippines, U.S. Army in World War II War in the Pacific* (Washington, D.C.: Center of Military History, U.S. Army, 1953).

Mueller, Arndt. *Hill 400: The Destiny and the Agony* (Monograph).

Oldendorf, Vice Admiral Jesse B. *Battle of Surigao Strait* (Washingon, D.C.: Typescript account, U.S. Naval Historical Center).

Olson, John E., assisted by Anders, Frank O. *Anywhere-Anytime: The History of the Fifty-Seventh Infantry (PS)* (Houston: John Olson, 1991).

Olson, John E. *O'Donnell: Andersonville of the Pacific* (Houston: John Olson, 1985).

Rants, Hanford. *My Memories of WW II* (Unpublished manuscript).

Reeves, Hugh. *World War II as I Remember* (Unpublished manuscript).

Smith, Cdr. John F. USNR (Ret.) *Hellcats over the Philippine Deep* (Manhattan, KS: Sunflower University Press, 1995).

Smith, Robert Ross. *Triumph in the Philippines, U.S. Army in World War II War in the Pacific* (Washington, D.C.: Center of Military History, U.S. Army, 1963).

Spector, Ronald. *Eagle Against the Sun: The American War with Japan* (New York: Free Press, 1985).

Svihra, Albert. *Transcripts of Letters to his Family and Diary* (West Point: U.S. Military Academy Library).

Ullom, Madeline. *Memoir* (Washington, D.C., Unpublished manuscript, U.S. Army Center for Military History).

Valtin, Jan. *Children of Yesterday* (Nashville: The Battery Press, 1988).

Van der Vat, Dan. *The Pacific Campaign* (New York: Simon & Schuster, 1991).

White, W.L. *They Knew They Were Expendable* (New York: Harcourt Brace and Company, 1942).

INDEX